D0212723

WOMEN AND MUSIC IN AMERICA SINCE 1900

WOMEN AND MUSIC IN AMERICA SINCE 1900

An Encyclopedia

Volume 2, L–Z

Edited by Kristine H. Burns

An Oryx Book

GREENWOOD PRESS
Westport, Connecticut • London

Library of Congress Cataloging-in-Publication Data

Women and music in America since 1900 : an encyclopedia / edited by Kristine H. Burns
p. cm.
Includes bibliographical references and index.
ISBN 1–57356–267–X (alk. paper)—ISBN 1–57356–308–0 (vol. 1)—ISBN 1–57356–309–9 (vol. 2)
1. Women musicians—United States—History—20th century—Encyclopedias. 2. Music—United States—20th century—Encyclopedias. I. Burns, Kristine Helen.
ML82 .W625 2002
780'.82'0973—dc21 2001054570

British Library Cataloguing in Publication Data is available.

Library of Congress Catalog Card Number: 2001054570
ISBN: 1–57356–267–X (set)
1–57356–308–0 (vol. 1)
1–57356–309–9 (vol. 2)

First published in 2002

Greenwood Press, 88 Post Road West, Westport, CT 06881
An imprint of Greenwood Publishing Group, Inc.
www.greenwood.com

Printed in the United States of America

The paper used in this book complies with the Permanent Paper Standard issued by the National Information Standards Organization (Z39.48–1984).

10 9 8 7 6 5 4 3 2 1

Contents

Preface

The major role that women have played and continue to play in the musical culture of the United States is indisputable. Although this role has been described in many books and articles, no single reference book to date has been published that thoroughly covers the subject. Herein lies the major difference between this encyclopedia and other reference books on music or on women and music. Some works, for example, limit coverage of women to only classical musicians. Other publications may be strictly biographical or may cover one type of musician, such as composers or songwriters. *Women and Music in America since 1900* represents the first major effort to describe the role of women in all forms of music in the twentieth century in the United States; it includes entries on gender issues, education, genres, honors and awards, organizations, individuals, and professions.

The field of music is quite vast, and women have been very active in it for a long time. This encyclopedia encompasses a wide range of women and issues. Although this two-volume project represents many people and genres, it simply cannot cover every individual and every issue involved in the field. An exhaustive encyclopedia of women and music would occupy many more pages.

DEFINING TERMS

For the purposes of this encyclopedia, the term "American" is applied to someone who meets the following criteria. First, the person must have been born in the United States, resided in the United States, or made most of her contributions in the United States. Although there are many women involved in music who were born outside of the United States, those who have had a significant career while living in the U.S. are included here. For example, although Lotte Lehmann was born in Germany, she performed extensively and influenced generations of opera performers throughout the United States.

The second criterion for inclusion in this project is that the individual must have been born in or lived primarily during the twentieth century. For example, although the field of hymnody dominated American Protestantism in the nineteenth century, the women composers associated with this music (Fanny J. Crosby, Clara H. Scott, Phoebe Palmer

Knapp, and others) lived into the twentieth century. Theirs are still some of the most widely heard songs and hymns in the world.

Third, an individual must have made major contributions as a musician, composer, scholar, activist, or the like that have advanced the role of women in music. For example, her compositions have won many awards, she was the first woman editor of an important periodical, she was the first woman conductor of a major orchestra, or her band was the most successful rock group, female or otherwise, of the 1980s.

THE ADVISORY AND EDITORIAL BOARD

The Advisory and Editorial Board members who oversaw the development of this book represent a highly knowledgeable group of individuals, all of whom have blazed new paths in the field of women in music. The Advisory Board was composed of three individuals—Harriet Hair, Pauline Oliveros, and Judith Tick. Harriet Hair is an internationally known music educator whose primary area of research is children's musical responses; her service in professional music organizations is widely known. In addition to serving as a role model for an entire generation of musicians—both men and women—Pauline Oliveros iconizes the quintessential spirit of an American composer. An internationally renowned musicologist, Judith Tick is one of the foremost scholars of women in music.

The associate editors included Judith A. Coe, Stephen M. Fry, Suzanne L. Gertig, Deborah Hayes, Cristina Magaldi, Patricia O'Toole, and Sally Reid. Among her many activities, Judith A. Coe serves as co-chair of the College Music Society Committee on Women, Music, and Gender, and she also serves on the Board of Directors of the International Alliance for Women in Music. Stephen M. Fry is a noted researcher of women in jazz and for many years organized the Pauline Alderman Award for excellence in women in music research. In addition to performing as a professional harpist and working as a music librarian, Suzanne L. Gertig is one of the leading Sophia Corri Dussek scholars. Highly respected musicologist Deborah Hayes has not only published many essays and articles on various topics on women in music, but she has also authored the book *Peggy Glanville-Hicks: A Bio-Bibliography* (Greenwood). Additionally, Hayes serves on the Board of Directors of the International Alliance for Women in Music. Cristina Magaldi is an important scholar specializing in Latin American music and music of the Americas. She has contributed entries to *The New Grove Music Dictionary of Women Composers* and *The New Grove Dictionary of Music and Musicians*, and she served as editor of the music section for the publication *Handbook of Latin American Studies*. Patricia O'Toole is a scholar whose work involving issues in qualitative methodologies and gender inequities produced through standard choral practices is well known. Her groundbreaking research is found in numerous books and articles. Composer Sally Reid is the past president of the International Alliance for Women in Music, one of the most important women in music organizations in the world. Her extraordinary leadership has led this organization to increased membership and higher visibility.

TOPICS

Members of the Advisory and Editorial Board suggested topics for inclusion in this publication. The Advisory Board was ultimately responsible for final analysis of the encyclopedia: who would be included and why, what topics were relevant, and how the material should be organized. The wisdom of the board's advice has ultimately provided a comprehensive approach to the topic of twentieth-century American women in music.

The *headword* list of topics includes individuals from all areas of music (rock, pop, classical, jazz, etc.) as well as all types of musicians (performers, composers, researchers, etc.). Associate editors were responsible for writing a *foundation entry* in their area of expertise. The foundation entries include topics such as gender issues, women in music technology, women in rock and popular music, and many more. These foundation entries present a broad historical overview of a particular area and provide the reader with background on a wide range of women musicians. The vast majority of text is devoted to these longer entries.

As each music-related area was shaped by the insight of the specific associate editor, the headword list was further refined, and experts from all areas of music were asked to serve as contributing authors for the project. These contributing authors wrote the entries, drawing from both primary and secondary sources, including books, articles, correspondence, and interviews.

The nearly 200 contributing authors, associate editors, and advisors come from a wide variety of musical backgrounds and experiences. These women and men include academics, professional musicians, and independent authors, musicians, and critics.

ORGANIZATION

This encyclopedia is organized alphabetically. However, several broad topic areas serve as the foundation for all other entries. These topics include associations, blues, classical music, country and folk music, education, experimental music, gender issues, gospel, honors and awards, jazz, multicultural musics, music technology, and rock and popular music.

Although many musicians defy strict categorization, every attempt has been made to include women active in both mainstream and non-mainstream areas of music. Significance of contributions, rather than popularity, has determined who or what appears in individual entries and longer histories. For example, although computer and electronic music have always had a small audience, exponents such as Laurie Spiegel and Pauline Oliveros have served as very important role models for many young women in the field. And although relatively few women to date perform as rap and hip hop artists, Queen Latifah continues to influence the next generation of women artists by performing alongside men in concert and on television. In short, women who are universally regarded as the best, most important in their field, whether it is rap or systematic musicology, have been included in these volumes.

Although there are certainly a large number of individual entries, this project does not provide "Top 10" lists of the most popular women in each category. Rather, the vast majority of prose is dedicated to longer histories to categorize a particular genre of music or trend in history. These comprehensive entries are better able to cut across disciplines, including performance, academia, sociology, and education. Occasionally an issue is so broad that it requires coverage in several places. Discrimination is such an issue because of its relevance in nearly every arena.

Entries for various honors and awards have been included for the most important women-only and mixed-gender awards and honors in various fields. Each such entry describes the award or honor and lists the women winners. Organizations, associations, publishers, and institutions include those groups primarily dedicated to women and music. Additionally, important women's subcommittees within other organizations are covered, as are associations in which women have been historically underrepresented. Entries discuss the history, development, nature, purpose, success, and influence of the particular group, in addition to size of membership, important individuals, and other issues. Topics in education and gender studies include not only specific women educators and researchers but also methods of addressing women's issues both in and out of the classroom.

Finally, each entry concludes with "For Further Reading," a short list of reference materials that will enhance and supplement the information presented. The second volume concludes with a comprehensive bibliography for the entire encyclopedia.

Kristine H. Burns
Editor-in-Chief
May 2000

Acknowledgments

Hundreds of contributors from across the world have come together to assist with the research for this project, thus providing valuable information that has never before been published. The countless hours spent with personal interviews, telephone calls, and correspondence have provided the most detailed account of women musicians in the United States to date. Of special note are the contributions from the International Alliance for Women in Music. Without the personal assistance and support of its nearly 800 members, this project would not have been completed.

Additionally, the encyclopedia certainly could not have been accomplished without the assistance of many spouses, siblings, parents, and children of the musicians listed herein. I would especially like to thank Colby Leider, my husband. Without his many hours of extra housework and child care, this project most certainly would not have been completed.

My greatest debt of gratitude is owed to Henry Rasof, senior acquisitions editor at Oryx Press, and to my Advisory Board. Henry assisted with every step in the process of developing this encyclopedia. Without his input and advice, the project would never have been completed. His knowledge and insight into musical issues were refreshing and very much appreciated. The Advisory Board—Harriet Hair, Pauline Oliveros, and Judith Tick—provided invaluable input as to whom and what should be included in the scope of this encyclopedia. They also assisted with identifying individual authors and researchers. The associate editors—Judith A. Coe, Stephen M. Fry, Suzanne L. Gertig, Deborah Hayes, Cristina Magaldi, Patricia O'Toole, and Sally Reid—worked countless hours adjusting the list of entries, procuring authors, editing, polishing the individual entries, and, as experts in their individual areas, writing entries of their own. Their effort has now been rewarded as this publication reaches fruition.

Introduction: Historical Overview

Much legislation has affected, for better or worse, the ability of women to achieve absolute equality. Women as a group have been affected by key twentieth-century legislation, including the Nineteenth Amendment and the Equal Pay Act. In 1920, the Nineteenth Amendment was ratified. This law guarantees women the right to vote by stating that "The right of citizens of the U.S. to vote shall not be denied or abridged by the U.S. or by any State on account of sex." In 1963, President Kennedy signed the Equal Pay Act, which states that men and women should receive equal pay for equal work.

Although women have had many legal successes, many indiscretions still exist in the enforcement of these laws. For instance, Congress established the Age Discrimination Act over 30 years ago, yet there are still a number of women who are reticent to divulge their actual ages for fear of age discrimination by employers. Therefore, when requested, birth year information has been omitted for certain individuals listed within these pages. All other birth and death information has been provided whenever possible.

Although women have achieved many professional successes in music, they have fought fiercely for equality. In 1907, Frances Elliott Clark became the first woman president of the Music Supervisors National Conference (later called the Music Educators National Conference). Other education groups were formed in the twentieth century to help facilitate women music educators. For example, in 1903, Eva Vescelius created the first journal of music therapy. In 1946, the service sorority Tau Beta Sigma was chartered to serve the needs of the growing number of women band musicians throughout the United States, and the Women Band Directors National Association was formed in Chicago, IL, in 1969. Finally, in 1984, the National Association of Jazz Educators Women's Caucus held its first meeting in Columbus, OH.

To reach the growing number of women composers in the United States, the Society of American Women Composers was founded in 1924 with Amy Marcy Cheney Beach as president. In 1930, Ruth Crawford Seeger became the first woman to win the prestigious Guggenheim Fellowship in music composition. During her time in Europe she composed her String Quartet (1931), one of the most significant string quartets written in the twentieth century. In 1975, Nancy Van de Vate established the International League of Women Composers, an organization that helped unite women composers through performances, recording projects, and mentorship. Other groups such as the American Women Composers and the International Congress for Women in Music soon followed. However, it was not until 1995 that these three important groups united to form a single coalition: the International Alliance for Women in Music.

Women composers and educators made great strides during the twentieth century, and so did performers and conductors. In 1936, Marian Anderson became the first African American singer to perform at the White House. Although the Daughters of the American Revolution refused to allow her to perform at a 1939 Constitution Hall concert because of her race, Anderson demonstrated her amazing range and vitality when Eleanor Roosevelt invited her, instead, to perform on the steps of the Lincoln Memorial on Easter Sunday. In 1938, Antonia Brico became the first woman to conduct the New York Philharmonic Symphony Orchestra.

Contemporary popular musicians have often found favor with the American public; however, respect and equality have been hard won. In 1959, Berry Gordy Jr. established Motown and immediately signed Mable John, Claudette Robinson, and Mary Wells among the first acts. One year after the Rock and Roll Hall of Fame was established, Aretha Franklin became the first woman inducted in 1987. Lilith Fair was founded in 1996 to assist women performers and singer-songwriters by providing performance venues all over the United States. Although it lasted only three years, Lilith Fair had a huge impact on numerous musicians and audiences.

In 1940, Carl Seashore wrote in "Why No Great Women Composers?" (*Music Educators Journal* 25/5, March 1940) that "Married women have not produced great compositions, but they have produced great composers." In 1999, Donald R. Vroon, editor of the *American Record Guide* (May–June 1999), stated that "no outstanding composer was a woman. . . . All the great composers were white males, and no amount of research will change that. . . . Nothing we have uncovered in the rush to find 'women composers' has affected that in the least." The views are clearly uninformed: not only have there been numerous outstanding women composers, but there have also been remarkable women performers, educators, and researchers. The present encyclopedia is testament to this fact. Over the years, countless articles and books have been written to dispute both statements, and more will certainly be written.

These two volumes present over 400 entries that address significant women composers, performers, researchers, singer-songwriters, computer programmers, radio DJs, electronica artists, and many, many others. There should be no question that women have contributed, and will continue to contribute, significantly to the field of music. The only question remaining is to what extent women will become even more involved in the music roles of the more traditionally male-dominated areas such as higher education and administration, audio production, music management, and computer music.

Twentieth-century American women

have possessed the indomitable pioneering spirit that defined the development of the country. Indeed, women have flourished and prospered in the face of adversity and discrimination. This publication is dedicated to those women musicians who came before us and those who will follow.

Chronology

1902 Gertrude "Ma" Rainey begins stage career and sets the pace for all blues women.

1903 Eva Vescelius creates the first journal of music therapy.

1904 The Musicians Union ends its exclusion of women when it joins with the American Federation of Labor.

1907 Barbara Duncan, perhaps the first woman music librarian, begins her career at the Boston Public Library.

Frances Elliott Clark becomes the founding chairperson of the Music Supervisors National Conference (later the Music Educators National Conference).

1915 Federation of Music Clubs establishes Young Artist Auditions.

1919 Margaret Anderton institutes the first college course work in music therapy (Columbia University).

1920 The Nineteenth Amendment is ratified. It guarantees women the right to vote by stating that "The right of citizens of the U.S. to vote shall not be denied or abridged by the U.S. or by any State on account of sex."

1924 The Society of American Women Composers is founded, with Amy Marcy Cheney Beach as its president.

1926 New York's first major choral concert is conducted by a woman, Margarete Dessoff.

1930 Ruth Crawford Seeger becomes the first woman to win the prestigious Guggenheim Fellowship.

1938 Antonia Brico becomes the first woman to conduct the New York Philharmonic Symphony Orchestra.

1939 Marian Anderson performs on the steps of the Lincoln Memorial on Easter Sunday. The concert is arranged by Eleanor Roosevelt to protest the refusal of the Daughters of the American Revolution to allow Anderson to perform in Constitution Hall because of her race.

American Music Center is established to build "a national community for new American music."

1940 In his essay "Why No Great Women Composers?" psychologist Carl Seashore states that "Married women have not produced great compositions, but they have produced great composers."

1943 Federation of Music Clubs establishes the Young Composers Contest.

1946 Tau Beta Sigma is chartered to serve the needs of the growing number of women band musicians throughout the United States.

1955 The first woman cantor in the United States, Betty Robbins, officiates at a worship service.

1956 Bebe Barron and her husband, Louis, create the score for *Forbidden Planet*, the first film score comprised entirely of electronic sounds.

1957 The Grammy Award is established to recognize excellence in the recording industry.

The Chicago Symphony Chorus is founded by Margaret Hillis.

1959 Berry Gordy Jr. establishes Motown and signs Mable John, Claudette Robinson, and Mary Wells.

1963 President John F. Kennedy signs the Equal Pay Act, which states that men and women should receive equal pay for equal work.

The Foundation for Contemporary Performance Arts, Inc., is founded.

1964 Title VII of the Civil Rights Act of 1964, as amended, prohibits discrimination in employment on the basis of sex, race, color, national origin, or religion.

1965 The Voting Rights Act is established to ensure that anyone over the age of 21 can legally register to vote, no matter what their ethnicity.

1966 The National Endowment for the Arts Composers Assistance Program is established to aid composers by providing funds for copying and completing scores and parts for orchestral presentation, as well as commissioning and preparing works for performances. The organization is later renamed the Composer/Librettist Fellowship, and still later the Composers Program.

1967 The Age Discrimination in Employment Act is established "To prohibit age discrimination in employment."

1969 The Women Band Directors National Association is formed in Chicago.

Barbara Kolb becomes the first woman recipient of the American Rome Prize for Musical Composition.

1970 Mother Maybelle Addington Carter and Sara Dougherty Carter Bayes, members of the Carter Family, become the first women elected to the Country Music Hall of Fame.

1972 The Equal Employment Opportunity Act of 1972 expands the Civil Rights Act of 1964 to include academic employment.

1973 Olivia Records, the first women's record label, is founded in Washington, DC, by Linda Tillery and Mary Watkins.

Patsy Cline becomes the first woman solo artist to be elected to the Country Music Hall of Fame.

1975 Ellen Taaffe Zwilich becomes the first woman to receive a doctorate in composition from the Juilliard School.

Nancy Van de Vate establishes the International League of Women Composers.

1976 Tommie Ewert Carl founds the American Women Composers, Inc. (AWC), "for the express purpose of alleviating the gross inequities that women composers have experienced in all areas of the music world."

1977 The U.S. Army commissions the first two women to serve as bandmasters: Nancy Bodenhammer and Ginny Allen.

1978 The Kennedy Center Honors is established to recognize excellence and life achievement in the performing arts. Marian Anderson is the first woman musician to be honored in its inaugural year.

Jeannie Pool establishes the National Congress on Women in Music.

1980 The Equal Employment Opportunity Commission recognizes sexual harassment as a form of sex discrimination and thus a violation of Title VII of the Civil Rights Act of 1964.

1982 American Women Composers, Midwest, Inc., is formed.

1983 Ellen Taaffe Zwilich becomes the first woman to win the Pulitzer Prize in music.

The Rock and Roll Hall of Fame is established in Cleveland, OH.

The Massachusetts Chapter of American Women Composers is formed.

1984 The National Association of Jazz Educators Women's Caucus holds its first meeting in Columbus, OH.

Gladys Stone Wright becomes the first woman to be elected to membership in the prestigious American Bandmasters Association.

New York Women Composers, Inc., is founded.

1986 First inductions into the Rock and Roll Hall of Fame are made; however, no women are honored until 1987.

The Pauline Alderman Prize is established to honor the authors of published and unpublished books and articles about women in music. Nancy B. Reich becomes the first woman to be honored for her book *Clara Schumann: The Artist and the Woman*.

Los Angeles Women in Music is founded to increase awareness of women's contributions to the business and art of music.

The Maud Powell Foundation is established to educate the public about the life and art of violinist Maud Powell.

1987 Aretha Franklin becomes the first woman to be inducted into the Rock and Roll Hall of Fame.

1990 Susan Slaughter founds the International Women's Brass Conference.

Joan Tower becomes the first woman to win the Grawemeyer Award for Music Composition for her orchestral composition *Silver Ladders*.

1991 The U.S. Navy appoints its first woman bandmaster, Lorelei Conrad.

Seeking to be placed in the same pay group as her male colleagues in the Munich Philharmonic, Abbie Conant goes to trial and wins. Although the decision is appealed, Conant wins again in 1993.

1993 Catherine Masters and Marcia Shein establish the Women in Music Business Association.

The Center for Women in Music is formed at New York University.

1995 The Audio Engineering Society Women in Audio: Project 2000 is created to increase the opportunities for women in the audio industry over the next five years.

The International Alliance for Women in Music is established.

1996 Lilith Fair is founded.

1997 Women Musicians' Alliance is established to serve the central Florida region by promoting independent women creators and performers of contemporary music.

1998 The National Women Conductors Initiative is established.

1999 Mary Simoni becomes the first woman to be elected president of the International Computer Music Association.

Cosette René Collier becomes chair of the Audio Engineering Society, Women in Audio Committee.

2000 Eunice Boardman is honored with the Illinois Music Educators Association's President's Award.

Barbra Streisand is awarded the Cecil B. DeMille Award, the highest honor for contribution to the field of entertainment bestowed by the Hollywood Foreign Press Association.

After nearly 40 years of performing, Cher receives her first Grammy Award, winning for her dance hit "Believe."

Guide to Related Topics

BROAD TOPIC CATEGORIES

Education

Children's Choirs
Choral Education
Dalcroze Eurhythmics
Early Childhood Music Educators
Gender and Feminist Research in Music Education
General Music
Instrumental Education
Jazz Education
Kodály Method
Music Education
Music Educators National Conference
Music Learning Theory
Orff Approach
Piano Pedagogy
Researchers in Music Education
String Education

Gender Issues

Aptitude
Bifocal History
Canon
Chilly Climate
Compensatory History
Constructivism
Cultural Appropriation
Discrimination
Equality
Essentialism
Exceptional Woman
Female Inferiority, Theories of
Feminist Music Criticism
Feminist Music History
Feminist Music Theory
Feminist Musicology
Gender and Curricula
Gender and Repertoire
Gender Coding
Gender in Music Analysis
Gender Issues
Gendered Aspects of Music Theory
Historiography
Internet Resources
Journals
Lesbian Music
Male Gaze
Multifocal History
Patronage
Professionalism
Pseudonyms
Separate Spheres—Sexual Aesthetics
Social Darwinism
Women-Identified Music

Women's Sphere
Women's Voice
Womyn's Music

Genres and Movements

African American Musicians
Asian American Music
Bands, Pop Rock
Barbershop Quartet
Bluegrass
Blues
Church Music
Classical Music
Country Music
Disco
Electronic Dance Music
Experimental Music
Film Composers
Folk Music
Garage Rock and Heavy Metal Bands
Gospel Music
Hymnody
Improvisation
Indie-Rock
Industry, Rock Music
Jazz
Jewish Musicians
Latin American Musicians
Motown
Multicultural Musics
Multimedia
Music Technology
Musical Theater
Native American Musicians
New Age Music
Performance Art
Rap
Rock and Popular Music Genres
Ska
Sound Design
Underground

Honors and Awards

Academy Awards
American Rome Prize in Musical Composition
Country Music Hall of Fame
Foundation for Contemporary Performance Arts, Inc.
Fulbright Fellowship Program
Grammy Award
Grawemeyer Award for Music Composition
Guggenheim Award
MacArthur Fellows Program
National Endowment for the Arts Composers Program
Prizes, Composer and Performer
Publication Awards
Pulitzer Prize
Rock and Roll Hall of Fame
Tony Awards

Musicians

Allyson, June
Amacher, Maryanne
Amos, Tori
Anderson, Laurie
Anderson, Marian
Andrews Sisters
Anonymous 4
Baez, Joan
Bailey, Pearl
The Bangles
Barkin, Elaine R.
Barron, Bebe
Battle, Kathleen
Bauer, Marion
Beach, Amy Marcy Cheney
Beardslee, Bethany
Bentley, Alys E.
Berberian, Cathy
Bianchi, Louise Wadley
Bish, Diane Joyce
Black, Shirley Temple

Bley, Carla
Boardman, Eunice
Boswell Sisters
Boyer-Alexander, René
Brown, Ruth
Bryant, Clora
Bryn-Julson, Phyllis
Caldwell, Sarah
Carabo-Cone, Madeleine
Carlos, Wendy
Carpenter, Karen
Carpenter, Mary-Chapin
Carr, Vikki
Carter, Betty
Carter, Mother Maybelle Addington
Cash, June Carter
Casterton, Elizabeth
Channing, Carol
Chapman, Tracy
Chen Yi
Cher
Clark, Frances Elliott
Clark, Frances Oman
Clarke, Rebecca
Cline, Patsy
Clooney, Rosemary
Cole, Natalie
Collins, Judy
Comden, Betty
Conant, Abbie
Cooper, Adrienne
Covell, Rebekah Crouch
Crane, Julia Ettie
Crawford Seeger, Ruth
Crider, Paula Ann
Crow, Sheryl
Cruz, Celia
D'Cückoo
Day, Doris
Dearie, Blossom
DeGaetani, Jan
Deutsch, Diana
Diemer, Emma Lou
DiFranco, Ani
Dudziak, Urszula
Durbin, Deanna
Eder, Linda
Estefan, Gloria
Etheridge, Melissa
Falletta, JoAnn
Fine, Vivian
Fitzgerald, Ella
Fluxus
Franklin, Aretha
Fullman, Ellen
Galás, Diamanda
Ganz, Isabelle
García, Adelina
Garland, Judy
Gideon, Miriam
Glanville-Hicks, Peggy
Glenn, Mabelle
The Go-Go's
Goetze, Mary
González, Celina
Gore, Lesley
Grant, Amy
Grigsby, Beverly Pinsky
Guillot, Olga
Haasmann, Frauke Petersen
Hackley, Emma Azalia Smith
Hair, Harriet Inez
Handy, D. Antoinette
Harry, Deborah (Debbie)
Hayes, Pamela Tellejohn
Hill, Emily
Hill, Lauryn
Hillis, Margaret
Hoffman, Mary E.
Holiday, Billie
Hood, Marguerite Vivian
Hoover, Katherine
Horne, Lena
Horne, Marilyn

Purim, Flora
Queen Latifah
Rainey, Gertrude "Ma"
Raitt, Bonnie
Ran, Shulamit
Rao, Doreen
Reynolds, Debbie
Richter, Marga
Rimes, LeAnn
Ritchie, Jean
Rockmore, Clara
Rodríguez, Albita
Ronstadt, Linda Maria
Ross, Diana
Rowe, Ellen H.
Sager, Carole Bayer
Sainte-Marie, Buffy
Salt-N-Pepa
Scaletti, Carla
Schonthal, Ruth
Selena
Sembrich-Kochanska, Marcella
Semegen, Daria
Shenandoah, Joanne
Shields, Alice Ferree
The Shirelles
Shocked, Michelle
Sills, Beverly
Simone, Nina
Slick, Grace
Smith, Bessie
Smith, Kate
Smith, Patti
Sobrino, Laura Garciacano
Spiegel, Laurie
Staple Singers
Streisand, Barbra
The Supremes
Suzuki, Pat
Svigals, Alicia
Swift, Katharine (Kay)
Talma, Louise Juliette
Tharpe, Sister Rosetta
Thome, Diane
Thorton, Willie Mae "Big Mama"
Tick, Judith
Tillis, Pam
Tower, Joan
Tripp, Ruth
Tucker, Sophie
Tucker, Tanya
Turner, Tina
Ulali
Vaughan, Sarah
Vega, Suzanne
Vincent, Rhonda
Walker, Shirley
Warwick, Dionne
Washington, Dinah
Waters, Ethel
Wells, Kitty
Williams, Mary Lou
Wilson, Anne and Nancy
Wilson, Nancy
Wynette, Tammy
Young, Phyllis
Zaimont, Judith Lang
Zwilich, Ellen Taaffe

Organizations, Associations, and Agencies

American Composers Forum
American Music Center
American Women Composers, Inc.
American Women Composers, Massachusetts Chapter
American Women Composers, Midwest, Inc
Center for Women in Music
Committees
Conferences and Festivals
Country Music Association
Ensembles, Jazz
Fraternities and Sororities, Professional
Grand Ole Opry

Indiana Home Economics Club Choruses
International Alliance for Women in Music
International Congress on Women in Music
International League of Women Composers
International Women's Brass Conference
Libraries and Archives
Lilith Fair
Los Angeles Women in Music
Maud Powell Society for Music and Education
Meet the Composer
National Federation of Music Clubs
New York Women Composers, Inc.
Organizations, Music Education
Organizations, Performer
Organizations, Professional Audio
Organizations, Regional Arts
Organizations, Research
Performance Ensembles, Classical
Performing and Mechanical Rights Organizations
Publishers, Women's Music
Sweet Adelines
Tau Beta Sigma
Women Band Directors International
Women in Music Business Association
Women Musicians' Alliance
Women's Philharmonic

Professions

Arranger
Audio Production
Composer
Conductor, Choral
Conductor, Instrumental and Opera
Copyist
DJ, Club
Ethnomusicology
Librettist
Military Music
Music Critic
Music Librarian
Music Management
Music Programmer/Host
Music Psychology
Music Theorist
Music Therapy
Musicologist
Performer, Brass
Performer, Choral and Vocal Ensemble
Performer, Keyboard
Performer, Live Electronics
Performer, Percussion
Performer, String
Performer, Vocal
Performer, Woodwind
Production Manager
Singer-Songwriter
Software Designer/Programmer
Songwriter
Sound Installation Artist

INDIVIDUALS ACCORDING TO GENRE AND PROFESSION

Alternative

Chapman, Tracy
Crow, Sheryl
D'Cückoo
DiFranco, Ani
Indigo Girls
Merchant, Natalie

Classical

Anderson, Marian
Anonymous 4
Barkin, Elaine R.
Battle, Kathleen
Bauer, Marion
Beach, Amy Marcy Cheney
Beardslee, Bethany
Berberian, Cathy
Bish, Diane Joyce
Bryn-Julson, Phyllis
Caldwell, Sarah
Chen Yi

Clarke, Rebecca
Conant, Abbie
Crawford Seeger, Ruth
DeGaetani, Jan
Diemer, Emma Lou
Falletta, JoAnn
Fine, Vivian
Ganz, Isabelle
Gideon, Miriam
Glanville-Hicks, Peggy
Grigsby, Beverly Pinsky
Hillis, Margaret
Hoover, Katherine
Horne, Marilyn
Kolb, Barbara
Lam, Bun Ching
Larsen, Libby
LeBaron, Anne
Lehmann, Lotte
León, Tania
Moore, Undine Smith
Musgrave, Thea
Norman, Jessye
Parker, Alice
Perry, Julia
Price, Leontyne
Ptaszynska, Marta
Ran, Shulamit
Richter, Marga
Rockmore, Clara
Schonthal, Ruth
Sills, Beverly
Talma, Louise Juliette
Thome, Diane
Tower, Joan
Zaimont, Judith Lang
Zwilich, Ellen Taaffe

Conductors

Caldwell, Sarah
Crider, Paula Ann
Falletta, JoAnn
Hillis, Margaret
León, Tania
Parker, Alice

Country

Carpenter, Mary-Chapin
Carter, Mother Maybelle Addington
Cash, June Carter
Cline, Patsy
The Judds
Lee, Brenda
Lynn, Loretta
Maddox, Rose
Mandrell, Barbara
McEntire, Reba
Parton, Dolly
Rimes, LeAnn
Tillis, Pam
Tucker, Tanya
Wells, Kitty
Wynette, Tammy

Educators, Patrons

Bentley, Alys E.
Bianchi, Louise Wadley
Boardman, Eunice
Boyer-Alexander, René
Carabo-Cone, Madeleine
Casterton, Elizabeth
Clark, Frances Elliott
Clark, Frances Oman
Covell, Rebekah Crouch
Crane, Julia Ettie
Crider, Paula Ann
Glenn, Mabelle
Goetze, Mary
Haasmann, Frauke Petersen
Hackley, Emma Azalia Smith
Hair, Harriet Inez
Hayes, Pamela Tellejohn
Hoffman, Mary E.

Hood, Marguerite Vivian
Inskeep, Alice C.
Jarjisian, Catherine
Jorgensen, Estelle Ruth
Kemp, Helen Hubbert
Lamb, Roberta
Larimer, Frances Hiatt
Lawler, Vanett
Liston, Melba Doretta
Low, Henrietta G. Baker
McElwee (Gonzales), Ileane
Monsour, Sally A.
Pitts, Lilla Belle
Rao, Doreen
Rowe, Ellen H.
Tripp, Ruth
Williams, Mary Lou
Young, Phyllis

Music Technology

Barron, Bebe
Carlos, Wendy
Grigsby, Beverly Pinsky
Hutchinson, Brenda
Klein, Judith (Judy) Ann
Knowles, Alison
McLean, Priscilla
Payne, Maggi
Rockmore, Clara
Scaletti, Carla
Semegen, Daria
Shields, Alice Ferree
Spiegel, Laurie

Experimental Music

Amacher, Maryanne
Anderson, Laurie
Berberian, Cathy
Fluxus
Fullman, Ellen
Galás, Diamanda
La Barbara, Joan
Lam, Bun Ching
Lockwood, Annea
Monk, Meredith
Moorman, Charlotte
Oliveros, Pauline
Ono, Yoko
Phillips, Liz

Folk, Bluegrass

Baez, Joan
Collins, Judy
Krauss, Alison
Lewis, Laurie
Mitchell, Joni
Ritchie, Jean
Sainte-Marie, Buffy
Vincent, Rhonda

Jazz, Blues, Motown, and Soul

Bailey, Pearl
Bley, Carla
Boswell Sisters
Brown, Ruth
Carr, Vikki
Carter, Betty
Clooney, Rosemary
Cole, Natalie
Fitzgerald, Ella
Franklin, Aretha
Holiday, Billie
Horne, Lena
Jackson, Janet
Joplin, Janis Lyn
Kaye, Carol
Kitt, Eartha
Knight, Gladys
LaBelle, Patti
Lee, Peggy
Liston, Melba Doretta
McPartland, Marian

McRae, Carmen
Rainey, Gertrude "Ma"
Raitt, Bonnie
Ross, Diana
The Shirelles
Simone, Nina
Smith, Bessie
The Supremes
Thornton, Willie Mae "Big Mama"
Vaughan, Sarah
Washington, Dinah
Waters, Ethel
Williams, Mary Lou
Wilson, Nancy

Multicultural Musics

Chen Yi
Cooper, Adrienne
Cruz, Celia
Dudziak, Urszula
Estefan, Gloria
Ganz, Isabelle
Gideon, Miriam
González, Celina
Guillot, Olga
La Lupe
Lam, Bun Ching
Little Coyote, Bertha
Masoaka, Miya
Mendoza, Lydia
Miranda, Carmen
Miyamoto, Nobuko Joanne
Montaner, Rita
Ptaszynska, Marta
Purim, Flora
Ran, Shulamit
Rodríguez, Albita
Ronstadt, Linda Maria
Sainte-Marie, Buffy
Selena
Sembrich-Kochanska, Marcella
Shenandoah, Joanne
Sobrino, Laura Garciacano
Suzuki, Pat
Svigals, Alicia
Tucker, Sophie
Ulali

Musical Theater and Film

Allyson, June
Barron, Bebe
Black, Shirley Temple
Carlos, Wendy
Channing, Carol
Comden, Betty
Durbin, Deanna
Eder, Linda
Garland, Judy
Jones, Shirley
LuPone, Patti
MacDonald, Jeanette
Martin, Mary Virginia
Merman, Ethel
Miranda, Carmen
Peters, Bernadette
Powell, Jane
Reynolds, Debbie
Suzuki, Pat
Swift, Katherine (Kay)
Tucker, Sophie
Walker, Shirley

Rap

Hill, Lauryn
Queen Latifah
Salt-N-Pepa

Researchers

Barkin, Elaine R.
Deutsch, Diana
Handy, D. Antoinette
Krumhansl, Carol L.
Lamb, Roberta

Tick, Judith
Zaimont, Judith Lang

Rock, Pop, and Punk

Amos, Tori
Andews Sisters
The Bangles
Carpenter, Karen
Cher
Day, Doris
Estefan, Gloria
Etheridge, Melissa
The Go-Go's
Gore, Lesley
Harry, Deborah (Debbie)
King, Carole
Lauper, Cyndi
Madonna
Midler, Bette
Minnelli, Liza
Nicks, Stephanie "Stevie"
Nyro, Laura
Phranc
Ronstadt, Linda Maria
Sager, Carol Bayer
Shocked, Michelle
Slick, Grace
Smith, Kate
Smith, Patti
Streisand, Barbra
Turner, Tina
Vega, Suzanne
Warwick, Dionne
Wilson, Anne and Nancy

Sacred, Hymnists, Religious, and Gospel

Dearie, Blossom
Grant, Amy
Jackson, Mahalia
Patty, Sandi
Staple Singers
Tharpe, Sister Rosetta

WOMEN AND MUSIC IN AMERICA SINCE 1900

L

La Barbara, Joan (1947–)

Joan La Barbara is a late-twentieth-century sound artist, composer, and performer who has devoted her career to extending the traditional limits of vocal performance. Her work has skillfully crossed stylistic boundaries, and she has worked in jazz, folk, rock, film, commercial, and contemporary classical music idioms. She has received numerous commissions as a composer, and many noted composers—John Cage, Morton Feldman, Philip Glass, Steve Reich, and James Tenney, to name but a few—have written compositions for her. She has perfected numerous extended vocal techniques, including glottal clicks, ululation, circular singing, and multiphonics, which she often incorporates into her performances and compositions.

Born on 8 June 1947 in Philadelphia, PA, La Barbara studied at the Syracuse University School of Music (1965–1968), and subsequently at the Berkshire Music Center, Tanglewood (1967–1968). She received a B.S. degree (1970) from New York University and debuted with Steve Reich and Musicians in 1971. For the next few years she performed with both Steve Reich (1971–1974) and Philip Glass (1973–1976). During the 1970s she also recorded with jazz musicians Hubert Laws, Jim Hall, Enrica Rava, and arranger Don Sebesky.

La Barbara's compositions, which typically feature multiple layers of electronic manipulation processing of her own voice, include *Berliner Träume* ([1983], Lovely Music 3001), *Rothko* (1986), *73 Poems* (1994) with text by Kenneth Goldsmith, and *Shamansong* ([1991, rev. 1998], New World Records 80545). Other recent works include *L'albero dalle foglie azzurre* for solo oboe and tape (1989), *To Hear the Wind Roar* for chorus (1989–1991), *Awakenings* for chamber ensemble (1991), and *Calligraphy II/Shadows* for voice, dizi, erhu, yangqi, and Chinese percussion (1995).

As a performer La Barbara has also worked with John Cage, premiering his *Solo for Voice 45*, *Atlas Eclipticalis*, and *Winter Music* with the Orchestra of The Hague. She performed in the Avignon premiere of Philip Glass's *Einstein on the Beach* and in the premieres of her husband Morton Subotnick's *Double Life of Amphibians* and *Jacob's Room* (Wergo 2014). She has also performed in the pre-

Joan La Barbara. *Photo © Jack Mitchell.*

mieres of several operas by Robert Ashley, including *Now Eleanor's Idea* (1994). Her own works have been performed by the Houston and San Francisco Symphonies, the Los Angeles Philharmonic, and the New York Philharmonic.

La Barbara has received numerous honors, including commissions from the National Endowment for the Arts and Meet the Composer. She continues her active career of both composing and performing and resides in Santa Fe, NM.

See also Experimental Music; Music Technology

For Further Reading

Cummings, David M. (ed.). *International Who's Who in Music and Musician's Dictionary, Sixteenth Edition*. Cambridge: Melrose Press, 1998.

Colby Leider

La Lupe (1936–1992)

Singer La Lupe was known for her frenzied and outrageous stage performances; her popularity in the United States peaked in the second half of the 1960s. She worked with some of the most important musicians of the century, including Mongo Santamaría and Tito Puente. Owing to her huge popularity, she performed live for thousands of people in the most prestigious public venues, including Carnegie Hall, Madison Square Garden, and the Manhattan Center.

Born Guadalupe Victoria Yoli Raymond in Santiago de Cuba, Oriente Province, Cuba, on 23 December 1936, La Lupe started her career in Havana in 1958 singing with the Trio Los Tropicubas while working as a schoolteacher.

Owing to her temperament and unconventional interpretation of the songs of that era, her relationship with the trio did not last long. In 1959 La Lupe made her solo debut singing at Havana nightclubs and cabarets. She became a great success and made several hit records as a result of her performances of rock and roll numbers in Spanish and far-fetched onstage behavior, including crying and screaming obscenities to her public. In 1960 she recorded her first album, *Con el diablo en el cuerpo* (*With the Devil in the Body*, Discuba LPD551). In addition to several Cuban *boleros* and ballads, this album included the songs "Crazy" by Paul Anka, "Alone" by Silma Craft, and "Fever" by Bavenpor-Cooley, all sung in Spanish. RCA Victor of Cuba awarded La Lupe the Disco de Oro de Popularidad (The Golden Record of Popularity) in 1960. In 1962 she moved to Mexico, where she failed to gain acceptance; she then relocated to New York in 1963.

In 1963 her career took an upturn when she recorded *Mongo Introduces La Lupe* (Milestone MCD-9210-2) with her compatriot, the already-famous conga player Mongo Santamaría. In that year she was also featured in Mongo Santamaría's Latin Top 10 cross-over hit "Watermelon Man." In 1965 she shot to stardom when she recorded with Tito Puente their Gold album *Tito Puente Swings, The Exciting Lupe Sings* (Tico 1121). With Tito Puente, La Lupe recorded three other albums for the Tico Record label: *Homenaje a Rafael Hernández* (Tico 1131), *The King and I* (1967), and *La pareja: T.P. and La Lupe* (1978). For her records sales in New York, Miami, Puerto Rico, Panama, and Venezuela, La Lupe was named singer of the year in 1965 and 1966 by the Latin Press of New York.

In addition to recording with Tito Puente, in the late 1960s and 1970s La Lupe collaborated with prominent Latin music artists such as Arturo "Chico" O'Farrill, Hector Rivera, Tite Curet Alonso, and Sonny Bravo, among others; she recorded for the Sony, Fania, Manzana, and Roulette record labels. Her albums include *They Call Me La Lupe* (Tico 1144), *La Lupe era/Le era de La Lupe* (Tico 1179), *The Queen Does Her Own Thing* (Roulette 42024), *Definitivamente La Yiyiyi* (Tico 1199), *The Queen* (Tico 1192), *Stop I'm Free Again* (CD Tico), *La Lupe en Madrid* (Tico 1229), and *One of a Kind* (Tico 1416).

In the early 1980s she retired from performing amid personal problems and public scandal. In the late 1980s she converted to evangelism and recorded Christian-oriented material until her death on 28 February 1992.

See also Latin American Musicians; Multicultural Musics

For Further Reading

Martínez, Rodríguez Raúl. "Lo trágico y lo controvertido en el canto y en la vida de Guadalupe Victoria Yoli Raymond, conocida como LA LUPE." *Revista Salsa Cubana* 1/4 (1998).

Francisco Crespo

LaBelle, Patti (1944–)

Rock and soul diva Patti LaBelle has enjoyed a career in the spotlight for over 30 years. Singing the Judy Garland (1922–1969) signature tune "Somewhere over the Rainbow," Patti LaBelle and the Bluebelles earned the respect of Atlantic Records, with whom they signed a recording contract in 1965. Her career is marked by a string of Top 5 hits, a Grammy Award, and her autobiography, *Don't Block the Blessings: Revelations of a Lifetime* (1996).

Born Patricia Holt on 24 May 1944 in

Philadelphia, PA, Patti LaBelle began performing in the local Baptist church. Her illustrious professional performing career began in 1961 when she teamed up with her friend Cynthia "Cindy" Birdsong to form the Ordettes. In 1962 two other singers joined the group, which was renamed the Blue Belles. The ensemble consisted of Patti LaBelle, Cindy Birdsong, Sarah Dash, and Wynona "Nona" Hendryx. The group was later renamed Patti LaBelle and the Bluebelles. Birdsong left in 1967 to join Diana Ross and the Supremes, and once again the group was renamed, this time shortened simply to Labelle. After the group signed with Epic Records, Labelle recorded its first number one hit, "Lady Marmalade." Although Labelle had five successive hits, Patti LaBelle opted to leave the group in 1977 to embark on a solo career. Her first solo album, *Patti LaBelle* (Epic ZK-34847), was released in 1977, with several of the songs becoming hits. She eventually left Epic Records to join Philadelphia International Records in 1981, only to leave again for MCA in 1984.

Musically, Patti LaBelle has explored soul, funk, disco, and rhythm and blues styles. She has made over 40 charted singles and released more than 20 albums during the course of her career. Her music has also been heard in several films, including *Beverly Hills Cop* (1985) and *License to Kill* (1989), and she was a featured performer at SuperBowl XXIX (Miami, FL).

Patti LaBelle has been nominated for a Grammy Award several times, and she won the coveted award in 1991 as Best Rhythm and Blues Female Vocal Performer. Additionally, she has been awarded the Martin Luther King Lifetime Achievement Award and the Ebony Achievement Award, and she is a two-time recipient of the National Association for the Advancement of Colored People (NAACP) Entertainer of the Year Award.

See also Rock and Popular Music Genres

For Further Reading

LaBelle, Patti. *Don't Block the Blessings: Revelations of a Lifetime*. New York: Riverhead Books, 1996.

Nathan, David. *The Soulful Divas: Personal Portraits of over a Dozen Divine Divas from Nina Simone, Aretha Franklin, and Diana Ross, to Patti LaBelle, Whitney Houston, and Janet Jackson*. New York: Watson-Guptill, 1999.

Kristine H. Burns

Lam, Bun Ching (1954–)

Composer Bun Ching Lam is one of the most important contemporary classical composers in the United States. In addition to many significant performances of her music, she has received a number of very prestigious grants and commissions. As a composer she relies heavily on her Chinese heritage to find inspiration for her works. In addition to composing, Lam continues to be active as a pianist and conductor.

Lam's music "integrates the chromatic harmony favored by postwar Western composers with an Asian sensitivity to timbre and the treatment of time" (Humphrey). In live and recorded performances of her works, she also combines the virtuoso talents of performers of traditional Chinese instruments and voice with those of performers of Western instruments. Her *Spring* cycle, including *After Spring*, *Another Spring*, and *Last Spring* (all available on Composers Recordings Inc. 726), is a series of works that feature the piano in a variety of ensemble settings, which contrast the full range of piano sonorities to that of the accompanying group. Lam looks to Chinese poetry in these works to explore the various meanings of the word "spring," including the season, as a source of water, a movement, and so on. Another composition, . . . *Like Water* (Tzadik 7021), is a study in 16 short pieces for piano, vibraphone, violin, and viola in which Lam explores musically the various forms that water can take such as ice, steam, and mist. Again, Lam turns to traditional Chinese proverbs as inspiration.

Bun Ching Lam was born in the Portuguese colony of Macau, China, in 1954. She began to study piano at age seven and presented her first solo recital at age 15. In 1976 she received a B.A. degree in piano performance from the Chinese University of Hong Kong. Lam then accepted a scholarship to study at the University of California at San Diego, where she earned a Ph.D. in composition (1981). Her teachers included Bernard Rands, Robert Erickson, Roger Reynolds, Barney Childs, Morton Subotnick, and Pauline Oliveros (b. 1932). In 1981 Lam accepted a position on the faculty at Cornish College of Arts in Seattle, WA, where she taught music composition, theory, and piano until 1986.

Lam has been the recipient of numerous awards, including the Rome Prize Fellowship (1991), the Hong Kong Conservatory Art Song Competition first prize, the Northwest Composer's Symposium and the Aspen Music Festival Composer's Contest. She received the highest honor at the Shanghai Music Competition, the first international composer's contest that took place in China. She was also a finalist in the Sixth Ancona Prize Competition in Italy and the Music Today Festival competition in Tokyo. Additionally, Lam has been awarded grants from the National Endowment for the Arts, the Seattle Arts Commission, Meet the Composer, and the New York Foundation for the Arts.

Her many commissions include *Saudades de Macau* for the Macau Cultural Institute; *Impetus* for the Hong Kong Chinese Orchestra; *Social Accidents* for the American Dance Festival; *Similia/Dissimilia* for the duo Trom-bown; *Sudden Thunder* for the American Composers Orchestra, *Last Spring* for pianist Ursula Oppens and the Arditti String Quartet, and *Klang* for Swiss percussionist Fritz Hauser.

Lam's critically acclaimed work *The Child God* (Tzadik 7031) was written as a shadow play with spoken narration in English, instrumental music, and tenor songs. This mini-opera has been described as a meeting of Western art music and Chinese troubadour traditions and has been compared to Igor Stravinsky's *L'histoire du Soldat* and Arnold Schoenberg's *Pierrot Lunaire*. The work includes three compositions based on Chinese texts from a Ming Dynasty mythical novel, *The Creation of the Gods*. Lam varies the tempo and style of the work throughout, often alluding to classic Chinese opera.

See also Asian American Music; Multicultural Musics

For Further Reading

Griffiths, Paul. "Chinese Songs, So Open Yet So Lyrically Opaque." *New York Times* (30 April 1997): 14.

Humphrey, Mary Lou. *CRI Exchange: Music at the Crossroads*. Available: http://www.composers recordings.com/cd/726.html

Scott Locke

Lamb, Roberta (1952–)

Music researcher and educator Roberta Lamb has been at the forefront of bringing gender research and feminist perspectives to the field of music education.

She wrote some of the first feminist analyses published in mainstream music education journals. According to Lamb, "feminist thinking provides a means for developing creative and critical spaces for all students and teachers" (Lamb, 2000). She has written articles incorporating music education and feminist theory and philosophy, and she has explored issues of sexuality in music and education. Lamb was involved in the first Feminist Theory in Music Conference in 1991. At that conference she, along with other researchers interested in gender issues in music education, established Gender Research in Music Education (GRIME). Through her leadership in GRIME since its inception, Lamb has helped to facilitate the creation of an open forum for the exploration of gender issues in music education and to encourage communication among those interested in gender research.

Born on 18 June 1952 in Lawrence, KS, Lamb possesses a perspective on gender research in music education that grew from her involvement in political activism as a young woman in the 1970s. She worked on political campaigns and lobbied for the Equal Rights Amendment. Lamb identifies her ideological roots as based in radical feminism, as described in Rosemarie Tong's *Feminist Thought*. Lamb, a flutist, received her bachelor's (1974) and master's (1979) degrees in music education from the University of Portland, OR. She then taught elementary school music for seven years. Wanting to combine her advocacy for women's rights from outside her academic life into her experience as a music educator and scholar, and in response to the absence of women in her musical experiences and studies as an undergraduate, Lamb began researching the topic of women in music. Her dissertation for her doctorate in music education from Teacher's College at Columbia University was entitled *Including Women Composers in Music Curricula: Development of Creative Strategies for the General Music Classes, Gr. 5–8*. Lamb received her doctorate in 1987.

From her interest in exploring ways to include women in music curricula, Lamb began to write articles from a theoretical feminist perspective. Working across the disciplines in music (e.g., musicology and feminist music criticism), Lamb presented feminist critiques and visions of music education. Her feminist perspective currently reflects a postmodern influence; her article "Aria Senza accompagnamento" (1994) demonstrates the postmodern practice of multiple-voiced texts. Using this perspective, she offers critiques of various approaches to music education. Lamb works to cross boundaries between fields within music education, and between music education and the wider community.

Lamb currently holds positions as an associate professor in music education at Queen's University in Kingston, Ontario, with cross-appointments to the Institute of Women's Studies and the Faculty of Education.

See also Gender and Curricula; Music Education

For Further Reading

Lamb, Roberta. "Feminism as Critique in Philosophy of Music Education." *Philosophy of Music Education Review* 2/2 (1994): 59–74.

———. "Feminist Influences in Music Education." *Orbit* 13/1 (Spring 2000): 38–39.

———. "The Possibilities of/for Feminist Criticism in Music Education." *British Journal of Music Education* 10/3 (1993): 169–180.

Julie Bannerman

LaPier, Cherilyn Sarkasian

See Cher

Larimer, Frances Hiatt (1929–)

Pianist and educator Frances Hiatt Larimer is one of several women who advanced the study of piano pedagogy in the second half of the twentieth century by developing graduate-level curricula in teacher training in piano. As a specialist in group instruction using keyboard laboratories, Larimer served as national group piano chair for the Music Teachers National Association and gave many presentations at national conferences on group teaching techniques.

Born in Tavares, FL, in 1929, Larimer received her bachelor's (1952) and master's (1954) degrees in piano performance from Northwestern University and taught in Northwestern's Preparatory Division. She later joined the piano faculty, developed courses and curricula in piano pedagogy, and developed instructional techniques for group piano lessons at the university level. Northwestern University was the first to offer the D.M. degree (1980) in piano performance and pedagogy.

She co-authored *The Piano Pedagogy Major in the College Curriculum* (1984, 1986), a set of case studies published by the National Conference on Piano Pedagogy that served as models for the establishment of pedagogy programs in colleges and universities. During the 1970s she spent several summers as a guest professor at the Rubin Academy of Music in Jerusalem. During the 1990s she developed educational exchanges with the St. Petersburg State Conservatory of Music in Russia, where she was the first American to lecture on piano pedagogy in the former Soviet Union.

Larimer directed the master's and doctoral programs in piano performance and pedagogy at Northwestern for over 25 years before her retirement in 1998. Her students hold teaching positions in colleges, universities, and community music schools throughout the United States and abroad.

See also Music Education; Piano Pedagogy

For Further Reading

Larimer, Frances, and Marienne Uszler. *The Piano Pedagogy Major in the College Curriculum. Part I: The Undergraduate Piano Pedagogy Major.* Princeton, NJ: National Conference on Piano Pedagogy, 1984.

———. *The Piano Pedagogy Major in the College Curriculum. Part II: The Graduate Piano Pedagogy Major.* Princeton, NJ: National Conference on Piano Pedagogy, 1986.

Uszler, Marienne. "Research on the Teaching of Keyboard Music." In *Handbook of Research on Music Teaching and Learning: A Project of the Music Educators National Conference*, ed. Richard Colwell. New York: Schirmer Books, 1992, 584–593.

Kenneth Williams

Larsen, Libby (1950–)

Libby Larsen is one of only a few active composers who succeed without being attached to a major academic institution. Larsen has been working strictly on commission since the mid-1980s and has become a highly sought-after contemporary composer. She is an outspoken advocate for the arts, working tirelessly throughout the 1980s and 1990s to promote widespread exposure of contemporary American concert music. With over 100 works, Larsen's compositions range from choral works to song cycles, and symphonic works to opera. The premiere of *Frankenstein: The Modern Prometheus*, commissioned by the Minnesota Opera, was selected by *USA Today* as one of the foremost classical music events of 1990. Her opera, *Eric Hermannson's Soul*, premiered in early 1999 by Opera Omaha.

Larsen was born on 24 December

1950 in Wilmington, DE. Her early experiences and exposure to music are as diverse as her compositions. As a child, Larsen was familiar with musical theater through her mother's collections of recordings and music. Larsen was a member of the Gregorian chant choir in Catholic grade school and the Southwest High School Lutheran Choir. For a short time she performed in a rock band.

As her background might indicate, Larsen's music shows stylistic versatility. Although classically trained, she includes elements of the American vernacular in her works such as rock and roll, gospel, and jazz. Larsen approaches music as a total sensory experience. Flowing from speech, it employs all senses, not just the auditory. Her music has been described as lyric, utilizing word painting and sound coloring. Larsen acknowledges Dominick Argento, her primary teacher during her doctoral work, as giving her confidence in orchestration and an understanding of the lyricism for which she strives throughout her works.

Larsen studied composition at the University of Minnesota with Dominick Argento, Eric Stokes, and Paul Fetler (B.A. 1971, M.A. 1975, Ph.D. 1978). Along with fellow student Stephen Paulus, Larsen co-founded the Minnesota Composers Forum (now the American Composers Forum), a composers advocacy group. Larsen worked with this nonprofit enterprise for 11 years raising funds and organizing concerts. The American Composers Forum has grown to be one of the largest and most important of its kind in the country. From 1983 to 1987, Larsen was composer-in-residence with the Minnesota Orchestra. Later she served in that capacity for the Charlotte Symphony. Most recently Larsen served as composer-in-residence with the Colorado Symphony. She has acted as advisor to the American Symphony Orchestra League, the American Society of Composers, Authors and Publishers (ASCAP), and the National Endowment for the Arts. Larsen has received awards, including a National Endowment for the Arts Composer Fellowship and an American Council on the Arts Young Artist Award. The Koch International release *The Art of Arlene Auger*, featuring Larsen's "Sonnets from the Portuguese," won a Grammy Award in 1994.

Larsen's principal publishers are E. C. Schirmer and Oxford University Press. Her music has been recorded on Angel/EMI, Koch International, Nonsuch, and Decca, and it appears on compact discs such as *Dancing Solo* (Innova, Bayside 512), *Incantation* (Delos 3184), and *Fabulous Femmes* (Centaur 2461).

See also American Composers Forum

For Further Reading

Boyer, Douglas R. "Musical Style and Gesture in the Choral Music of Libby Larsen." *Choral Journal* (October 1993): 17–28.

Briscoe, James R. (ed.). *Contemporary Anthology of Music by Women*. Bloomington: Indiana University Press, 1997.

Cheryl Taranto

Latin American Musicians

Women vocalists have had profound stylistic and social impacts on Latin American music in the United States. In fact, such influence has also affected non-Latin styles such as pop and jazz. One dominant example is that of Cuban-born Celia Cruz (b. 1924). After leaving Cuba for Mexico, where she appeared in a number of Mexican films and recorded extensively with the Cuban orchestra Sonora Matancera, she settled in New York City. By the mid-1960s she began to have a major impact on the Latin music being produced there, especially that of

Tito Puente, Johnny Pacheco, and Willie Colon, with all of whom she recorded. She also continued to record her own record albums as a solo artist, frequently with Sonora Matancera, which also relocated to New York, and her musical director and husband, Pedro Knight. She rapidly became recognized as the major stylist and most popular singer (or *sonera*) of the music that was now being called salsa, which was based on the Afro-Cuban forms of *son*, *mambo*, *cha cha cha*, and *bolero* that Cruz had been singing since her early career in Cuba. She eventually became known as the "Queen of Salsa," and her musical colleague and bandleader Tito Puente, with whom she so often worked, became known as the "King of Salsa." As of the year 2000, Celia Cruz continued to be recognized not only as the dominant vocalist among women in salsa but as the most dominant singer of the style in general. Younger women vocalists such as Gloria Estefan (b. 1957), Yolanda Duke, Millie P., and La India have used her as a model for their own styles. Male vocalists have also used her as a model, represented through the styles of Ismael Rivera, Hector Lavoe, Justo Betancourt, Oscar D'Leon, Ismael Miranda, Cheo Feliciano, Frankie Figueroa, Ruben Blades, Willie Colon, Lalo Rodriguez, Jose Alberto, and Tito Nieves, among many others.

Contemporary with Celia Cruz was another woman Cuban vocalist who also had a profound impact on the musical style of Afro-Cuban *son* and salsa. Known as "La Lupe," Lupe Yoli (1936–1992) was originally from Cuba and became highly popular within the context of Latin music from the late 1950s through the 1970s. Like Celia Cruz, she was also the featured *sonera* on a number of albums released by Tito Puente, in addition to her own albums as a solo artist. Her vocal style was quite different from that of Cruz, and she was recognized on the same level of artistic excellence. Her influence was a major one among many vocalists and continues to be one of the main models in the world of salsa. Yet another contemporary of both Cruz and La Lupe was Mexican-born Tonya "La Negra," who became highly recognized for her interpretations of the tropical (originally Cuban) *bolero* song style.

In the area of Mexican music, numerous women vocalists have had significant impacts on various musical styles in the United States. One of the first women to record Mexican music on either side of the U.S. and Mexican border was Lydia Mendoza (b. 1916) from southern Texas. By the 1930s Mendoza, who performed and composed a variety of Mexican styles, was recording on major American labels, and her recordings became highly popular throughout the U.S. Southwest and in Mexico. Her influence was one of the major determinants in the style that has become known as *tejano*. One of the more contemporary singers to partially emerge from this style is Tish Hinojosa (b. 1955). Other women vocalists contemporary with Lydia Mendoza who also had a major impact are Adelina Garcia and La Hermanas Padilla, all based in Los Angeles.

From 1988 through 1990, Linda Ronstadt (b. 1946), who had already achieved international acclaim with her recordings in English, began a series of Spanish-language albums, two in the mariachi style of Mexican music and one in the tropical style. All three albums were awarded Grammy Awards. Ronstadt's mariachi albums had a particular impact on what has been called the "Mariachi Renaissance" of the 1990s, especially among youth throughout the Southwest and among young women. By the year

2000 there were a number of highly successful women mariachis in the southwestern United States.

Young emergent women in the style include Nydia Rojas (b. 1981) from Los Angeles, and mariachis such as Mariachi Las Reynas de Los Angeles, Mariachi Las Adelitas, and Mariachi Las Alondras. Another major artist of Mexican American background is Vikki Carr (b. 1941), who since the 1960s has had major international success and influence in various musical styles, both in English and Spanish. Since the 1970s she has recorded a wide variety of Latin American styles ranging from the modern *bolero* to mariachi.

Contemporary popular singers such as Gloria Estefan (b. 1957), La India, Teresa Covarrubias, Alicia Armendariz, and Christina Aguilera (b. 1980) have impacted the contemporary music industry, recording in both English and Spanish and developing a style and market frequently referred to as "cross-over." Miami-based Estefan has represented the major impact in this area; she has recorded music that has attained phenomenal world recognition. She was awarded a Grammy Award for her *Mi Tierra* album (Epic 53807), a project through which she returned to her Cuban roots after a decade of major cross-over hits such as the single "Conga" of the early 1980s. After experimenting with punk rock in the early 1980s, Los Angeles–based Chicana singer-songwriters Teresa Covarrubias and Alicia Armendariz eventually formed a group called Goddess 13 and wrote songs incorporating feminist themes. New York–based La India has mixed the elements of hip hop, rhythm and blues, salsa, and jazz into a highly influential contemporary style. Pop singer Christina Aguilera, originally from Pittsburgh and of Ecuadorian and Irish American background, was awarded the 1999 Grammy Award for Best New Artist in the music industry.

As the Latina/o presence continues to grow in the United States, the role and influence of women artists have grown even faster in the music industry. Male domination in the field also continues to drop on a global basis.

See also Multicultural Musics

For Further Reading

Aparicio, Francis. *Listening to Salsa: Gender, Latin Popular Music, and Puerto Rican Cultures*. Hanover, NH: University Press of New England, 1998.

Loza, Steven. *Barrio Rhythm: Mexican American Music in Los Angeles*. Urbana and Chicago: University of Illinois Press, 1999.

Pena, Manuel. *Musica Tejana*. College Station: Texas A&M University Press, 1999.

Steve Loza

Lauper, Cyndi (1953–)

A video pioneer and singing superstar of the early and mid-1980s from songs such as "Girls Just Want to Have Fun" and "True Colors," Cyndi Lauper merged exuberant pop with new wave, punk, and rhythm and blues. Her candy-colored hair and outlandish fashion sense made her instantly recognizable, along with her four-octave range, quirky enthusiasm, and penchant for casting friends, family members, and wrestling stars (such as Lou Albano) in her videos.

She was born on 20 June 1953 in Queens, NY. After quitting high school because of dyslexia, she began her music career as a background singer, then sang in bands performing covers of the Beatles, Jefferson Airplane, and Bad Company. Her first notable contribution was as the lead singer for the band Blue Angel (named for the Marlena Dietrich film as well as the Roy Orbison song of the

Cyndi Lauper in performance c. 1984. *Photo © Neal Preston/CORBIS.*

same name), whose eponymous debut album failed commercially.

Her decision to go solo resulted in *She's So Unusual*, released in 1983 (Portrait RK-38930), which spawned not only the free-spirited anthem "Girls Just Want to Have Fun" but also the hits "Time after Time," "All through the Night," and "She Bop," a song in praise of women's masturbation. Her next effort was *True Colors* (Portrait RK-40313); though it did not have the explosive impact of her debut, it had hits with both the title track and "Change of Heart."

After an attempt at acting (*Vibes*, 1988) she released the album *A Night to Remember* (Epic EK-44318). That album's only hit was "I Drove All Night," and overall it was a decided commercial and critical disappointment. Lauper then took some time off, and then co-wrote and co-produced *Hat Full of Stars* (Epic 52878) in 1993. Critically acclaimed but her biggest commercial failure to date, she believes it to be her best work. The songs are intensely personal and singularly women-oriented, dealing in part with issues such as abortion ("Sally's Pigeon's") and abusive partners ("Broken Glass").

Her "greatest hits" album, *12 Deadly Cyns* (Epic 477363), included a reggae-style remixed remake of "Girls Just Want to Have Fun" (Sony 61104), which once again had significant airplay; but *Sisters of Avalon* (Sony 66433) and *Merry Christmas, Have a Nice Life* (Sony 69611) did not fare as well. The late 1990s found Lauper teaming up with Cher (b. 1946) on the "Believe" tour and generating her own version of the Trammps' "Disco Inferno."

See also Rock and Popular Music Genres

For Further Reading

Buckley, Jonathan (ed.) et al. *Rock: The Rough Guide*. London: Rough Guides, 1999.

Rees, Dafydd, and Luke Crampton. *VH1 Rock Stars Encyclopedia*. New York: DK Publishing, 1999.

Romanowski, Patricia, and Holly George-Warren (eds.). *Rolling Stone Encyclopedia of Rock and Roll*. New York: Rolling Stone Press, 1995.

Leslie Stratyner

Lawler, Vanett (1902–1972)

Music educator Vanett Lawler worked to develop policies for global music and education organizations and valued folk and vernacular materials for use in the American public schools. Lawler had substantive relationships with both American and international musical organizations during her lifetime. A leader in the Music Educators National Conference (MENC), she was involved from 1930 and supervised the transfer of its office to the Washington, DC, area in 1956. She held several key positions: assistant executive secretary from 1930 to 1942, associate executive secretary from 1942 to 1955, and executive secretary from 1955 to 1968. Under her leadership MENC's membership more than doubled. In the international arena Lawler was a founding member of the International Society of Music Education (ISME), serving as its first secretary general from 1953 to 1955 and as its treasurer from 1955 to 1970. Underscoring her global focus on music education, she was also a consultant on music education to the Pan American Union (PAU) during the 1940s and worked in the Arts and Letters section of the United Nations Educational, Scientific and Cultural Organization in 1947. Her activities throughout the world took her to areas of Central and South America and to the Soviet Union.

Vanett Lawler's professional association with the noted music scholar Charles Seeger illustrates another of her distinctive contributions to music education. She collaborated with both Charles Seeger and Ruth Crawford Seeger (1901–1953) to promote the use of American folksongs and the folk music from Latin America as teaching materials in the public schools. Upon her death on 16 February 1972, expressions from around the world gave tribute to her work and professional dedication. From Chile, Budapest, the Soviet Union, and Australia, colleagues wrote of her leadership and influence on music education worldwide. Ole Sand from the National Education Association summed up the sentiments of many: "when the history of music education is written, Vanett Lawler will head the list" (*Music Educators Journal*, 1972).

See also Music Education

For Further Reading

Izdebski, Christy Isabel. "Vanett Lawler (1902–1972): Her Life and Contributions to Music Education." D.M.A. diss., Catholic University of America, 1983.

McCarthy, Marie. "On 'American Music for American Children': The Contribution of Charles L. Seeger." *Journal of Research in Music Education* 43/4 (1995): 270–287.

"Vanett Lawler—Woman of Uncommon Gifts." *Music Educators Journal* 59 (September 1972): 78–79.

Nancy Uscher

LeBaron, Anne (1953–)

Composer and harpist Anne LeBaron is internationally recognized as one of today's most innovative and imaginative musicians. As a composer she expresses herself through a strikingly wide range of subject matter, genres, and musical styles. Her compositions reveal her interest in contemporary environmental and social issues, Greek mythology, theoretical physics, and religious history; they include orchestral, chamber, vocal, choral, opera and music theater, electronic works, dance and film scores, and the inaugural work for the Lyon and Healy Electric Harp. Her varied experience with academia, jazz, blues, and Asian music also enriches her work. As a performer, LeBaron's development of extended techniques and skill as an improviser earned her Ovation: The Arts Network's designation of "21st Century Harpist." Her performance techniques include bowing with a horsehair bow, steel tubing, and screen door springs; preparing strings with paper, chains, and alligator clips; and applying slide guitar techniques and electronic enhancements to the harp. She has also developed nontraditional notation for her techniques, aiding contemporary harp music composers and continuing the process of updating the harp. As an improviser LeBaron has performed and recorded with such noted improvising musicians as Muhal Richard Abrams, Anthony Braxton, and Davey Williams. Her Anne LeBaron Quintet (trumpet, tuba, electric guitar, harp, and percussion) highlights her talents as a jazz musician and bandleader.

LeBaron was born on 30 May 1953 in Baton Rouge, LA; she received degrees from the University of Alabama (B.A. 1974), State University of New York at Stony Brook (M.A. 1978), and Columbia University (D.M.A. 1989). She also studied harp with Alice Chalifoux at the Salzedo Harp Colony (1974, 1976), composition with György Ligeti as a Fulbright Scholar to Germany (1980–1981), and the kayagum (plucked zither) at the National Classical Music Institute of Korea (1983). LeBaron's numerous honors include several National Endowment for the Arts fellowships, a 1991 Guggenheim Foundation fellowship, the 1996–1997 CalArts/Alpert Award, and her 1993–1996 tenure under Meet the Composer's New Residencies program as composer-in-residence with the Washington, DC, Youth Orchestra Program, Horizons Theater, and the National Learning Center at the Capital Children's Museum. University of Pittsburgh grants helped to fund a new work, *Going Going Gone* for string quartet, tape, and live electronics, and a CRI recording of chamber ensemble work released in late 1999. Recent commissions include *American Icons* (National Symphony Orchestra, 1996); *Solar Music* for flute and harp (Fromm Foundation, 1997); *Bodice Ripper* for electric harp, clarinet/bass clarinet, and electroacoustic tape (Dance Alloy, Pittsburgh, premiered February 19–20, 1999); and *Nightmare* (Portland Gay Men's Chorus, premiered March 21, 1999).

LeBaron currently teaches at the California Institute of the Arts. Her *Traces of Mississippi* was featured in a PBS documentary about the Continental Harmony project of the American Composers Forum. She is working on an absurdist one-act opera, *The Vacuum Cleaner*, with libretto by Edward de Grazia. LeBaron's scores are published by Golden Croak Music and MMB Music; recordings are available on CRI, Ear-Rational, Mode, Music and Arts, and Tellus.

See also International Congress on Women in Music

For Further Reading

Gagne, Cole. "Anne LeBaron." In *Soundpieces 2: Interviews with American Composers*. Metuchen, NJ: Scarecrow, 1993.

May, Thomas. "Listening to the Silence of the Frogs: Anne LeBaron's Fable for Our Time." *Washington Post* (6 April 1997): G8.

Renée McBride

Lee, Brenda (1944–)

Brenda Lee is a cross-over country and rock and roll musician who was the sweetheart of a generation of teenagers in the 1960s. Her most popular songs include "I'm Sorry," "All Alone Am I" (both available on *The Brenda Lee Story (Her Greatest Hits)*, MCA 4012), and "Rockin around the Christmas Tree" (available on MCA 70090). Much of the credit for creating a pop-country crossover audience is often given to Patsy Cline (1932–1963). Owen Bradley produced both Cline and Lee in the early 1960s; however, Lee was still a teenager when success hit, so she was better able to draw in the younger audiences.

Born Brenda Mae Tarpley on 11 December 1944 in Lithonia, GA, Lee began performing at the age of 10. By age five she had won a trophy for singing "Take Me Out to the Ballgame," and her talent was discovered. At age seven she was a regular performer on the Atlanta radio show *Starmaker's Review*, and her name was changed to "Brenda Lee."

Although she concentrated on country music as a young performer, her early musical successes as a teenager were actually in the rock and roll genre, not in country music. In 1960 "I'm Sorry" became her first number one hit, and between 1961 and 1963 she had 25 pop chart hits. She toured extensively; when she went to England, the Beatles were her opening act. Dormant from the country music charts for 12 years, it was not until 1969 with "Johnny One Time" that Lee reclaimed her status on the country music scene.

Although her greatest success took place in the 1960s, Lee maintained an active career well into the 1990s. When her records failed to hit Top-20 spots, she turned to musical theater, television, and film. She starred in the huge production of *Music! Music! Music!* at the Acuff Theater in Opryland, USA, from 1988 through 1990. Her television credits include *Barbara Mandrell and the Mandrell Sisters*, *Nashville Alive*, and *The Dolly Show*; she also had a small role in the movie *Smokey and the Bandit* (1977).

Numerous performing and humanitarian awards have been bestowed upon Brenda Lee. In 1999 she was inducted into the Grammy Hall of Fame for her song "I'm Sorry." She was inducted into the Country Music Hall of Fame in 1997 and the Georgia Music Hall of Fame in 1983. With her engaging voice and commanding on-stage persona, Brenda Lee was dubbed "Little Miss Dynamite" despite her 4'11" stature. She is still considered one of the most influential women country-pop performers of the twentieth century.

See also Country Music; Rock and Popular Music Genres

For Further Reading

Erlewine, Michael (ed.), et al. *All Music Guide to Country*. San Francisco: Miller Freeman Books, 1997.

Kristine H. Burns

Lee, Peggy (1920–2002)

Blonde and sultry, Peggy Lee was a commanding figure among jazz vocalists; her stature as a performer belied her understated and heartfelt singing style. She was also a successful actress and composed many songs considered standards today, including "Manana," "Fever," and "It's a Good Day."

She was born Norma Dolores in Jamestown, ND, on 26 May 1920. Her mother died at an early age, and she was raised by her father and an abusive stepmother. Immediately following her high school graduation she left her unstable home and set out for Hollywood. However, she found little success singing in clubs there, so she returned to Fargo to sing on the *Hayloft Jamboree* radio show on station WDAY. It was there that she changed her name to Peggy Lee. She then moved to Minneapolis to sing and tour with the Will Osborne band.

Her first career break came when in 1941 Benny Goodman heard her perform at the Buttery Room in Chicago and chose her to replace Helen Forest. The next year Lee recorded "Why Don't You Do Right?" which became a hit, and "The Way You Look Tonight" as a ballad.

She married Dave Barbour, the guitarist in the Goodman band, in 1943, and with him began writing songs, including the hits "Manana" and "It's a Good Day." They were divorced in 1951. She was to marry and divorce three more times. During the 1950s Lee appeared in several television shows and motion pictures, including *Mr. Music* (1950) and *The Jazz Singer* (1953). In 1956 she received an Academy Award nomination for Best Supporting Actress for *Pete Kelly's Blues* (1955). Her most memorable film appearances, however, were as the

Peggy Lee. *Photo courtesy of Frank Driggs Collection.*

voices of Lady and several other characters in the Disney animated feature *Lady and the Tramp* (1955). She also contributed lyrics to several of the film's songs. Some of her hit recordings include "My Man," "Why Don't You Do Right?" and "Is That All There Is?" on Capitol (DCC 179), and "Black Coffee" and "Lover" for Decca (MCA 11122). The autobiographical Broadway show *Peg* (1983), a one-woman revue, ran for a week at the Lunt Theater.

In 1991 Peggy Lee won a lawsuit, filed in the late 1970s, against the Walt Disney Company claiming profits from the sale of the *Lady and the Tramp* videos. The judgment was for $3.8 million, but the award was later reduced to $2.3 million.

Suffering from diabetes, heart surgery, and a disastrous fall in 1967, Lee encountered frail health for many years. She passed away from a heart attack on 21 January 2002.

See also Jazz

For Further Reading

Lee, Peggy. *Miss Peggy Lee: An Autobiography*. New York: D. Fine, 1989.

Lees, Gene. *Singers and the Song*. Oxford and New York: Oxford University Press, 1987.

Stephen Fry

Lehmann, Lotte (1888–1976)

Although her career ended a half-century ago, dramatic lyric soprano Lotte Lehmann continued to influence opera houses and music schools throughout the world during the last half of the twenieth century. Best known for her interpretation of operatic roles and German *lieder*, she infused her characters with a life of their own and thus drew audiences into an intensely emotional musical experience. Lehmann's ability to convey text successfully brought operatic performance levels to new heights and influenced a new generation of singers as well as her contemporaries.

Born Charlotte Sophie Pauline Lehmann on 27 February 1888 in Perleburg, Germany, Lehmann had an innate musical ability that was discovered by a neighbor whose brother managed the cafeteria at the Royal High School of Music. This neighbor arranged for both an audition and a tutor. Cramming years of lessons into just six days, Lehmann auditioned and was accepted. Her first professional contract was with the Hamburg State Opera in 1910 at age 22, where she sang minor rolls. In May 1914 the director of the Vienna Opera attended Hamburg's production of *Carmen* with Lehmann singing the role of Micaela. His purpose was to audition the tenor for

Vienna, but he decided to sign Lehmann instead.

By the end of World War I, Lotte Lehmann was one of Europe's premiere performers. She sang under many leading conductors and composers, including Richard Strauss, Giacomo Puccini, Bruno Walter, and Arturo Toscanini, with whom she shared a close friendship until his death in 1957. Some of her most famous roles include those of Elisabeth in *Tannhäuser*, Sieglinde in *Die Walküre* (Grammofono Ita 78724), Elsa in *Lohengrin*, and the Marschallin in *Der Rosenkavalier* (Grammofono Ita 78794). Lehmann had her Metropolitan Opera debut in January 1934. Four months later, in April, she was banned from singing in Germany after a disagreement with a high-ranking Nazi official. When Hitler "annexed" Austria in 1938 she was driven from that country as well. She applied for American citizenship in 1939 and left Europe. When the United States entered World War II, Lehmann was declared an "enemy alien" by the American government and her professional engagements dropped from 29 in the 1941–1942 season to five in 1942–1943. During the 1943–1944 season Lehmann found a warming of public sentiment and a new agent. This final opera season also brought 30 bookings. She subsequently retired from the stage and performed recitals for the next seven years, ending her public career in 1951 at the age of 63. Her farewell concert was recorded on *Lotte Lehmann: The New York Farewell Recital* (Vai Audio 1038).

During her retirement Lehmann helped launch the American Music Academy of the West in Santa Barbara in 1951, where she conducted master classes and taught. Her students included Risë Stevens (b. 1913), Anne Brown (George Gershwin's original Bess), Jeanette MacDonald (1903–1965), Marilyn Horne (b. 1934), and Janet Baker. Lehmann died at age 88 on 26 August 1976 at her home in Santa Barbara, CA.

See also Classical Music; Performer, Vocal

For Further Reading

Jefferson, Alan. *Lotte Lehmann*. London: Julia MacRae Books, 1988.

Lehmann, Lotte. *Midway in My Song: The Autobiography of Lotte Lehmann*. New York: Bobbs-Merrill, 1938.

———. *My Many Lives*. New York: Boosey and Hawkes, 1948.

Lori Stevens

León, Tania (1944–)

Tania León has distinguished herself as a composer, conductor, educator, and new music advocate for over 30 years. Her accomplishments are numerous, and perhaps more remarkable because she is a Hispanic woman in a field dominated by white men. Her compositions are challenging for both performer and listener, although they are never inaccessible. In recent years her works have reflected musically syncretic qualities from the influence of "indigenous" musics of her homeland. These influences are well integrated and are frequently presented in a somewhat abstract manner.

Born in Havana, Cuba, in 1944, she immigrated to the United States in 1967 without family or fluency in English. After only two years she became the first musical director of the Dance Theatre of Harlem, where she founded the Dance Theatre's music department, music school, and orchestra. Although she had completed musical training as a pianist at the National Conservatory in Havana, León continued her studies in the United States. She obtained undergraduate and graduate degrees in music from New

Tania León conducting the Brooklyn Philharmonic in 1986. *Photo © Marbeth.*

York University while continuing her work with the Dance Theatre of Harlem. In 1978 León and two other colleagues began the Brooklyn Philharmonic's Community Concert Series. During the 10 years the series lasted, León conducted and helped present almost 1,000 concerts throughout most of New York.

In 1985 she began teaching at Brooklyn College, where she is now a distinguished professor of composition and director of the new music ensemble. She has taught, lectured, and served in residence at some of the most prestigious institutions, festivals, and centers in the United States and abroad, including Harvard University, Yale University, Cleveland Institute of Music, Hamburg Musikschule, Atlantic Center for the Arts, Bellagio, Berlin Biennial, Hamburg Begegnung, and American Academy in Rome. In 1993 she began a four-year position as musical advisor to Kurt Masur and the New York Philharmonic, during which time she became the first Hispanic woman to conduct the orchestra. In 1992 she co-founded the American Composers Orchestra's Sonidos Festival, an annual event that features music from different parts of the Americas. As a result of her artistic efforts, León received the New York Governor's Lifetime Achievement Award in 1998.

Although she has written numerous works in all genres, León's most successful work may be her first opera, *Scourge of Hyacinths*, based on a radio play by Nobel Prize–winner Wole Soyinka. Commissioned by the Munich Biennale in 1994, the opera won the BMW prize as the best new opera in the festival. In 1999 it was performed to great critical acclaim by the Grand Theatre de Geneve, the Opera de Nancy et de Lorraine in France, and the St. Polten Festspielhaus in Austria. The libretto for the opera is a statement against human oppression of all types. There is much conjecture regarding the parallels that can be drawn between the libretto's subject and the political situation in León's homeland. When asked, however, regarding such parallels, she responds that the listener should decide the meaning of the work. León's music shows excellent craft and is often rhythmically complex.

Other recordings of her music include the orchestral compositions *Batá* and *Carabali* (both on Louisville Orchestra First Edition 10), a solo compact disc entitled *Indígena* (Composers Recordings Inc. 662), and "Pueblo Mulato" on *Voces Americanas* (Composers Recordings Inc. 773).

See also Classical Music; Conductor, Instrumental and Operatic

For Further Reading

"Future Music." *Ear, Magazine of New Music* 11/4 (1986–87): 16.

Lundy, Anne. "Conversations with Three Symphonic Conductors: Dennis DeCoteau, Tania León, Jon Robinson." *Black Perspective in Music* 16/2 (1988): 213–226.

Orlando Jacinto García

Lesbian Music

Lesbian music is usually understood as a variant of "women-identified music" or "women's music" (and "womyn's music," around 1970), as the vast majority of the women performers, songwriters, producers, engineers, and audience of this music are lesbians. However, "lesbian music" can be understood as a much broader conceptualization of female homoeroticism in a wide variety of musical traditions, styles, genres, texts, and contexts. Lesbianism—loosely defined here as a range of sexual, emotional, and political passions and commitments between women—can be found in music in any number of ways: music by lesbian composers, musical settings of texts by lesbian writers or librettists, lesbian characters in opera or dramatic music, all-women musical ensembles, cabaret performers in lesbian bars, expressions of lesbian sexuality in blues and popular musics, "women's music," and lesbian-feminist choruses. Feminist scholarship in music argues compellingly that musical practices, repertories, theories, and interpretation are connected to the sexual politics of a given cultural context. Feminists have also maintained that musical performance and listening are embodied practices, complex physical and emotional processes that can both reflect and produce eroticism: as feeling, energy, sensation. Thus the concept of "lesbian music" deepens and expands constantly as lesbian scholars plunge into music history and reread (auto)biographical evidence, teasing out musical constructions of lesbianism, whether bold and explicit or barely discernible under the weight of institutionalized homophobia.

Women musicians performing together in the institutions of all-women's brass bands and symphony orchestras suggest sites of female homoeroticism and music that invite lesbian interpretation, listening, and speculation. The 1870s and 1880s saw the formation of several all-women brass bands, usually referred to as ladies' military bands, in various American cities. Such women flouted social convention of the Victorian era by playing wind instruments, especially brass, which was considered unseemly for respectable women. Active in Europe and North America since the late nineteenth century, all-women bands and orchestras provided women performers the opportunity to work professionally as musicians, though they were poorly paid. The orchestras were modeled on the Vienna Ladies Orchestra, which toured America in 1871 and usually played "light" classical and popular music under the direction of a male conductor. However, some of these orchestras were founded by women: the Boston Fadette Lady Orchestra, founded by Caroline B. Nichols and active from 1884 to 1920; the Philadelphia Women's Symphony, founded by Mabel Swint Ewer in 1921; and the New York Women's Symphony Orchestra, founded by Antonia Brico (1902–1989) in 1934. In 1908, 30 women's orchestras were active in the United States. Although the life span of the orchestras was from five to 20 years, most of them broke up as a result of the social and economic changes brought about by World War II. In the realm of popular music, all-women jazz and swing bands such as the International Sweethearts of Rhythm, the Darlings of Rhythm, Eddie Durham's All-Star Girls Orchestra, Queens of Swing, Ina Ray Hutton and Her Melodears, Harlem Playgirls, and the Prairie View College Co-Eds were popular in the 1930s and 1940s, traveled widely, and enjoyed some commercial success. With a few exceptions most bands were either all-black or all-white (with some band members passing as black or white) and played for segregated audiences. It is quite possible that some of the women in these all-women brass bands, orchestras, jazz and swing bands and their audience were lesbians: their bodily and sensory experiences of making music together as women remains a story in need of telling.

In the opera repertoire, the tradition of "breeches" or "trouser" roles—male characters sung by female singers—dates at least as far back as Orfeo in Christoph Gluck's *Orfeo ed Euridice* (1762) and functions as a rich and complex site of lesbian eroticism in music. Trouser roles and the divas who sang them support lesbian interpretations of these operas: the title role in Jules Massenet's *Le Jongleur de Notre Dame* (1902) and Octavian in Richard Strauss's *Der Rosenkavalier* (1911). Explicitly lesbian characters appear in Camille Erlanger's *Aphrodite* (1905), Alban Berg's *Lulu* (1929–1935), Paula Kimper's *Patience & Sarah* (produced at the Lincoln Center Festival, 1998), and Carla Lucero's *Wuornos* (1999). *Patience & Sarah* and *Wuornos* are possibly the only operas to focus on lesbian characters. Although none of British composer Ethel Smyth's six operas contain lesbian roles, her *Fantasio* (1894), *The Boatswain's Mate* (1914), and *Fête Galante* (1923) are intimately connected to Smyth's notions of lesbian desire and her passionate attachments to several of the women active in the British suffrage movement. Scholarly work by Terry Castle (on the mezzo-soprano Brigitte Fassbaender) and Elizabeth Wood (on "sapphonics") has opened up the concept of historically situated "lesbian audition" and invites a reexamination of the opera repertoire as a space for lesbian pleasure and for its connections and debts to lesbians—in life and in fiction—as composers, librettists, divas, listeners, and critics.

In musical theatre, lesbian spectators can readily identify with Maria in *The Sound of Music* (especially Mary Martin's creation of that role) as well as other "versions" of lesbianism portrayed by the characters of Sister Berthe, Frau Schmidt, and Elsa. Jonathan Larson's *Rent* (1996), a modern-day rewrite of the *La Bohème* story, includes several queer characters and features a sexy lesbian couple, Maureen and Joanne, who sing the duet "Take Me or Leave Me."

The earliest expressions of lesbian sexuality in American popular music are undoubtedly the songs of African American women blues singers, between 1920 and 1935, many of whom were lesbian or bisexual, both on and off the stage: Gertrude "Ma" Rainey (1886–1939), Bessie Smith (1894–1937), Alberta Hunter (1895–1984), Gladys Bentley (1907–1960), and Ethel Waters (1896–1977). Several blues songs address lesbianism. Ma Rainey's "Prove It on Me Blues" (1928) is a defiant and direct expression of lesbian identity and desire with lyrics that reference only having women friends and not liking men. Bessie Jackson (also known as Lucille Bogan [1897–1948]) recorded "B.D. Women's Blues" in 1935. In this song the singer identifies herself as a "B.D. Woman" (bulldagger or bulldyker) and criticizes their treatment by men by stating that women do not need men because men treat them poorly. Several variants of this song were recorded under the titles "B.D.'s Dream" or "B.D. Women." "Down on Pennsylvania Avenue" by Bertha Idaho portrays the sexual variety available in Baltimore, where the viewer will see outlandish sights because she cannot distinguish the men from the women. Lesbianism also appeared in a few songs by blues singers who were men. George Hanna celebrates the delights of lesbian sex in his "Boy in the Boat" (1930). The song's title is a slang phrase for the clitoris. Hanna's song also includes a call for social tolerance by asking the listener not to judge lesbians. In "Bad Girl Blues" Memphis Willie B. Borum sings about women loving each other out in the open. Working within a relatively tolerant social context of African American urban culture, these musicians and their songs created an important space for lesbian sexuality several decades before the second wave of feminism and lesbian/gay liberation.

Oral historical accounts of the lesbian subculture of Greenwich Village in the 1940s mention musical performances by lesbian entertainers, often in male drag, in cabaret shows in lesbian bars such as the 181 Club, Moroccan Village, Howdy Club, and 82 Club. These nightclubs held floor shows with lesbians (and sometimes gay men) singing in drag. A similar lesbian subculture thrived in Los Angeles in the 1950s. Lesbian historian Lillian Faderman reports that at the Club Laurel in North Hollywood, Beverly Shaw "would entertain in the style of Marlene Dietrich, perched atop the piano bar in impeccably tailored suits." Male impersonation had been a standard feature on the vaudeville stage since the mid-nineteenth century, but by the 1930s vaudeville was replaced largely by nightclub entertainment. Apart from popular songs and show tunes of the day, very little is known about the musical repertoire or the lesbian performers who sang in these nightclubs. One thing is certain: they were admired and well loved by their lesbian audience.

Since the 1960s the lesbian presence in American popular music has grown increasingly diverse and complex, especially in terms of the relationship between being a lesbian and being a musician, and how this relationship functions in a given performer's self-image, within the recording industry, and for the audience. The music of Azúcar y Crema, Melissa Etheridge (b. 1961), Melissa Ferrick, Girls in the Nose, Janis Ian (b. 1951), the Indigo Girls, Joan Jett (b. 1960), Nedra Johnson, k.d. lang (b. 1961), Connie Lofton, June Millington (b. 1949), the Murmurs, Random Order, Phranc, Toshi Reagon, Dusty Springfield (1939–1999), Tribe 8, and many others presents an extremely varied array of styles, genres, audiences, and identity politics.

The tradition of grass-roots feminist community choruses that began ca. 1975 in North America, Europe, and Australia is the most visibly lesbian context for music making. Influenced partly by the popularity of women's music or women-identified music, feminist and lesbian choruses perform choral arrangements of the folk-inspired "women's music" songs, but the bulk of their performance repertoire is comprised of historical music by women composers, new music by women, and music sung by women in non-Western cultures. Feminist and lesbian choruses also perform music with texts that express lesbian eroticism and seek choral music by men composers who set texts by women and/or lesbian poets. Many groups include both lesbians and straight women: Calliope Women's Chorus (Minneapolis), Anna Crusis

Women's Choir (Philadelphia), Muse: Cincinnati Women's Choir, Bread and Roses Feminist Singers (Maryland), the Portland Lesbian Choir (Oregon), Vox Femina (Los Angeles), Sound Circle (Boulder), and the Dallas Women's Chorus, to name only a few. Most of these choral ensembles belong to the Sister Singers Network and the Gay and Lesbian Association of Choruses. They are well known in the lesbian community, and some have produced compact discs. Feminist and lesbian choruses often volunteer their music as part of feminist activism and perform benefit concerts to raise money for battered women's shelters, rape crisis centers, lesbian health clinics, and the like. Moreover, some of these choruses strive to incorporate the aims of feminism into their organizational structures by using a consensus model of decision making and actively committing themselves to ending racism and ethnocentrism in musical performance.

In addition to choruses, the second wave of feminism inspired women in classical music to revive the tradition of all-women's professional orchestras. The New England Women's Symphony was co-founded in 1978 by lesbian composer-conductor Kay Gardner with Nancy Barrett Thomas and Leslie Judd. In 1981 flutist Nan Washburn helped establish the Bay Area Women's Philharmonic in San Francisco. Both groups hire women conductors and were formed with the purpose of employing professional women instrumentalists and performing music written by women composers, both historical and contemporary. Although nonprofessional, the Minnesota Philharmonia is the first lesbian and gay community orchestra in North America.

In the realm of contemporary classical or art music, lesbian composers and performers are becoming more visible and audible. The work of Ruth Anderson (b. 1928), Eve Beglarian (b. 1958), Madelyn Byrne, Linda Dusman (b. 1956), Jane Frasier, Lori Freedman, Kay Gardner, Sorrel Hays, Jennifer Higdon, Sharon Isbin, Laura Karpman, Paula Kimper, Marilyn Lerner, Annea Lockwood (b. 1939), Carla Lucero, Meredith Monk (b. 1942), Linda Montano, Pauline Oliveros (b. 1932), Naomi Stephan, Louise Talma (1906–1996), and Sheila Waller offers such a wide range of musical styles, genres, and aesthetics that the notion of "lesbian music" presents more questions than answers. But these are crucial questions that invite more nuanced and contextualized discussions of lesbian identity, sexuality, politics, and musical creativity.

See also Women-Identified Music; Womyn's Music

For Further Reading

Brett, Philip, Elizabeth Wood, and Gary C. Thomas (eds.). *Queering the Pitch: The New Gay and Lesbian Musicology*. New York: Routledge, 1994.

Fleming, Lee (ed.). *Hot Licks: Lesbian Musicians of Note*. Charlottetown, P.E.I., Canada: gynergy books, 1996.

Wolf, Stacy. "The Queer Pleasures of Mary Martin and Broadway: *The Sound of Music* as a Lesbian Musical." *Modern Drama* 39/1 (Spring 1996): 51–63.

Martha Mockus

Lewis, Laurie (1950–)

Blazing an individual pathway in bluegrass and folk since the 1970s, Laurie Lewis established herself as major artist, an endearing, vibrant performer, and a top talent as a fiddler, vocalist, songwriter, and bandleader. Although she is well versed in traditional forms and rarely strays from an all-acoustic instrumentation, her arrangements at times bring in elements of Western swing, jazz,

Cajun, Tex-Mex, funk, New Age, and gospel. Her music, from rousing bluegrass standards to ethereal ballads, is nonetheless convincing and cohesive for its depth of feeling and the clarity of her fiddling and singing voice.

Lewis was born on 28 September 1950 in Long Beach, CA, and was raised in Texas and Michigan. In her mid-teens her family returned to California, settling in Berkeley, where she is still based. Her entry into music was through the folk revival, and though she considers herself a vocalist first, in her youth she played piano, guitar, and banjo before concentrating on the fiddle. She eventually became a champion fiddler at music contests. Lewis has been part of several acclaimed bands, including Good Ol' Persons, which she formed in 1974 with Kathy Kallick. Her own band, called Grant Street, has backed her on most of her numerous albums, and she is a popular performer on the festival circuit.

There are many recordings available by Lewis, including *Restless Rambling Heart* (FLY 406), *Seeing Things* (ROUN0428), and *Laurie Lewis and Her Bluegrass Pals* (ROUN0461). The themes of her songs—her own compositions and ones selected from historic sources or contemporary singer-songwriters—often express emotions around love. Lewis has also sung of near-death experience, dancing bears, the impact of environmental deterioration, what the wood used to make a fiddle remembers about when it was a tree, the plight of Japanese Americans during World War II, and even tattoos. Her version of Kate Long's "Who Will Watch the Home Place?" won Song of the Year in 1994 at the International Bluegrass Awards, an organization that has twice named Lewis as Female Vocalist of the Year.

See also Bluegrass

For Further Reading

Bufwack, Mary A., and Robert K. Oermann. *Finding Her Voice: The Saga of Women in Country Music*. New York: Crown Publishers, 1993.

Willis, Barry R. *America's Music—Bluegrass: A History of Bluegrass Music in the Words of Its Pioneers*. Franktown, CO: Pine Valley Music, 1998.

Craig Morrison

Libraries and Archives

Libraries and archives serve many purposes, including the collection and preservation of materials so that current and future generations may learn about themselves and those who have come before. Some areas of study, such as women in music, were nearly nonexistent in most libraries until fairly recently. Through the efforts of dedicated archivists, there are a few women-in-music libraries in America, several in Europe, and increasing amounts of resources maintained on the World Wide Web. Many women-in-music organizations maintain libraries and archives that are known only to small or specifically focused groups or are regional, local, or private.

In the United States there are at least four places where women-in-music materials are housed. The American Music Center (AMC), located in New York City, is a clearinghouse for information on contemporary American classical music and jazz. Its mission is to build a national community for new American music. To accomplish this, there are grants, composition contests, workshops, World Wide Web network groups, electronic "chat" sessions, and an electronic mail group. The AMC publishes a directory of contemporary music ensembles, as well as other printed material. Internet users can search available works by composer, musical instruments, or media.

The American Women Composers Library has been housed at George Washington University's Gelman Library since 1995. This facility contains 1,670 scores and tapes of compositions written by women who were members of the American Women Composers (AWC) organization. There are works ranging from instrumental solos to major orchestral compositions.

The International Institute of Women in Music can be found at California State University, Northridge. Materials assembled by Aaron Cohen for the *Encyclopedia for Women Composers* and the *International Discography on Women in Music* are housed there, as well as thousands of scores, books, manuscripts, records scrapbooks, and other items of women who were members of the International Congress on Women in Music (ICWM).

Until 1990 the Women's Philharmonic had a National Women Composers Center that existed separately from the orchestra. The National Women Composers Center was organized as a means to address the increasing requests for information about compositions by women. Today it is an integral part of the Philharmonic. There are selected composition lists for orchestra and string orchestra available on the World Wide Web. At the end of 2000, Women's Philharmonic World Wide Web site became searchable and included resources for composers, conductors, and recommended repertoire.

Some libraries are devoted to a single individual, such as the Maud Powell Society for Music and Education. Maud Powell (1867–1920) was the first great American violinist to attain international status. The archives have existed in a Virginia home since 1995 and are gradually being transferred to the Library of Congress. It contains copies of most of Powell's music transcriptions, music composed for or dedicated to her, reviews, artifacts, scrapbooks, family background material, photos, and recordings.

In Europe there are at least five major archives for materials on women's music—the Centre for Women's and Gender Studies in Music in London; the Chard Festival Archives; Foundazione Adkins Chiti: Donne in Musica; European Female Composers Musical Archives; and the Stichting Vrouw en Muziek (the Foundation for Women in Music). The Centre for Women's and Gender Studies in Music in London is the first university-based organization of its kind. The purpose of the Chard Festival Archives is to promote music by women composers to the younger generation, and to educate teachers and conductors. Funding was awarded from the European Commission to continue work on the Archive of Music by Women Composers for Young People and Amateurs. In Italy, the nonprofit Donne in Musica foundation may have the largest physical library on women in music. Its mission is to "promote research, conservation, production and diffusion of musical documents in the classical, traditional, popular, electronic, and generally every type of music, and any type of support, as long as it is the fruit of feminine creativity." In Germany, Antje Oliver founded the European Female Composers Musical Archives in 1988. It houses a catalog of 5,000 compositions; over 500 records, compact discs, and tapes; literature in many languages; examination papers and dissertations; and newspaper articles. Formed officially in 1987, the Stichting Vrouw en Muziek "wishes to focus attention on the participation of women in music." It organizes professional concerts, lectures, projects, and exhibitions and also maintains a center for documentation to stimulate research on women and music.

Electronic "libraries" and archives are increasing in number on the World Wide Web in order to save the cost of printing and mailing catalogs, and to increase the speed of access and number of users. An example is the New York Women Composers' Internet catalog. Previously available in print, the Internet catalog has been in existence for over eight years. It provides links to information about compositions of women in the organization. Works listed are solos, duos, small and larger chamber ensembles, orchestra, concertos, opera, dance, theater, vocal, choirs, and electronic and computer music. Composer information and publishers are also listed.

In addition to women-in-music archives, general archives may be found in women's studies centers such as the Association of College and Research's Libraries' Women's Studies Section. The International Alliance for Women in Music (IAWM) World Wide Web site houses information about contemporary and historical women musicians, women-in-music course syllabi, and composition databases. Important academic libraries and archives of women musicians include those at the University of Wisconsin, Indiana University, Duke University, the College of St. Catherine, the University of Michigan, the University of Washington, the University of Rochester, and Arizona State University.

See also American Music Center; Internet Resources; Women's Philharmonic

For Further Reading

IAWM [International Alliance for Women in Music] Homepage. Available: http://www.iawm.org.

New York Women Composers. Available: http://www.ibiblio.org/nywc.

The Women's Philharmonic Home Page. Available: http://www.womensphil.org

Alicia RaMusa

Librettist

The librettist for a musical, being the person who constructs the "book" (or the storyline), is central to the success or failure of a show. If a show fails, no matter how brilliant the music, blame usually falls on the librettist. However, among the creators for a hit musical, it is generally the librettist who is most easily forgotten in the distribution of accolades. Broadway produced a number of significant women librettists during the twentieth century, from Rida Johnson Young (1869–1926) and Dorothy Donnelly (1879–1928) in the early decades, through Bella Spewack, Dorothy Fields (1905–1974), and Betty Comden (b. ca. 1917) in the middle ones, to Lynn Ahrens and Marsha Norman at century's end. Women have created (either alone or in collaboration) the librettos for such legendary Broadway shows as *Naughty Marietta*; *The Student Prince in Heidelberg*; *Annie Get Your Gun*; *On the Town*; *Kiss Me, Kate*; and *Beauty and the Beast*.

Rida Johnson Young and Dorothy Donnelly wrote the books for several of the principal operettas from the first third of the century. Young's librettos for *Naughty Marietta* (1910, music by Victor Herbert) and *Maytime* (1917, music by Sigmund Romberg) skillfully advanced a sentimental, escapist romantic plot accompanied by glorious music. Young also wrote the lyrics for both of these operettas, thereby devising every word heard from the stage. Donnelly's partnership with composer Sigmund Romberg resulted in four works: *Blossom Time* (1921), *The Student Prince in Heidelberg* (1924),

My Maryland (1927), and *My Princess* (1927). Donnelly, who also wrote the lyrics for each of these shows, garnered the huge responsibility of creating the words through which operetta would change from a European-based art form to a truly American one.

During the middle part of the century, the three most significant women librettists were part of collaborated teams. Writers such as Bella Spewack, Dorothy Fields, and Betty Comden were involved with the musical comedy genre (as opposed to operetta), where plots were contemporary and involved everyday characters. Bella Spewack joined her husband, Samuel Spewack, to create the books for the Cole Porter shows *Leave It to Me!* (1938) and *Kiss Me, Kate* (1948). Dorothy Fields, with her brother, Herbert Fields, wrote the librettos for Porter's *Let's Face It!* (1941) and *Mexican Hayride* (1944), Romberg's *Up in Central Park* (1945), and Irving Berlin's *Annie Get Your Gun* (1946). Betty Comden, with Adolph Green, wrote the books for Leonard Bernstein's New York celebrations *On the Town* (1944) and *Wonderful Town* (1953), Jule Styne's *Bells Are Ringing* (1956), and Charles Strouse's *Applause* (1970).

In the 1980s and 1990s women librettists continued to have a significant impact on Broadway. Lynn Ahrens wrote both the libretto and the lyrics for her first two stage collaborations with composer Stephen Flaherty: *Lucky Chance* (1988) and *Once on This Island* (1990). Pulitzer Prize–winner Marsha Norman won a Tony Award for Best Book of a Musical for *The Secret Garden* (1991, music by Lucy Simon), a show for which she also did the lyrics. Finally, Disney engaged women librettists for its first two Broadway endeavors: Linda Wolverton for *Beauty and the Beast* (1994), and Irene Mecchi, with Roger Alleri, for *The Lion King* (1997).

See also Musical Theater; Songwriter

For Further Reading

Engel, Lehman. *World with Music: The Broadway Musical Libretto*. New York: Schirmer Books, 1972.

Everett, William A. "Sigmund Romberg's Operettas 'Blossom Time,' 'The Student Prince,' 'My Maryland,' and 'My Princess.'" Ph.D. diss., University of Kansas, 1991.

William A. Everett

Lilith Fair

Lilith Fair was a traveling festival of women pop musicians founded in 1996 by Canadian musician Sarah McLachlan. The message of the festival was one of celebration and empowerment of women. In its three-year history the festival attracted over 100 acts, including Sarah McLachlan (b. 1968), the Indigo Girls, Sheryl Crow (b. 1962), the Dixie Chicks, and Suzanne Vega (b. 1959).

Although there are many derivations of the name "Lilith," the fair was named for the biblical Adam's first wife, Lilith. The festival was a women-oriented alternative to such male-dominated events as Lollapalooza and H.O.R.D.E. Critics attempted to dismiss the very existence of the festival by calling it "Chickapalooza" and "Estrofest." However, even in the first year of its existence Lilith Fair had a 35-city North American tour with many sold-out concerts.

The Lilith Fair organization sponsored local Lilith Fair talent contests and even a songwriting competition cosponsored by the American Society of Composers, Authors and Publishers (ASCAP) Foundation in alliance with Sarah McLachlan and Lilith Fair. The

During a June 1998 performance of the Lilith Fair in San Francisco, the stage is shared by (left to right) Amy Ray, Erykah Badu, Sarah Bettens (of the Belgian group K's Choice), Sarah McLachlan, and Tara Maclean. © *Tim Mosenfelder/CORBIS.*

ASCAP Foundation Lilith Fair Songwriting Contest: A Competition for New Women Songwriters was created to assist previously unrecognized performers and songwriters.

Although the Lilith Fair tours experienced great success, the festival ended with the 1999 tour. Perhaps Lilith Fair's most lasting contribution to late-twentieth-century popular music was its providing a forum for performance, composition, and the free exchange of ideas among women at various stages in their career and life development.

See also Women-Identified Music

For Further Reading

Jennings, Nicholas. "Songs of the Sirens." *Maclean's* 110/30 (28 July 1997): 50–51.

Taylor, Robin. "A Fair Mix of Spirituality, Music." *National Catholic Reporter* 34/43 (9 October 1998): 14–16.

Welcome to Lilith Fair! Available: http://www.lilithfair.com.

Kristine H. Burns

Liston, Melba Doretta (1926–1999)

Melba Doretta Liston was a pioneering jazz trombonist, composer, and arranger whose career spanned the 1940s through 1960s. In the course of her career, musicians including Count Basie, Duke Ellington, Dizzy Gillespie, Johnny Griffin, Milt Jackson, and Randy Weston performed her music.

Liston was born on 13 January 1926 in Kansas City, MO, and began her study of the trombone at the age of 12 as part of a program sponsored by the Works Progress Administration (WPA). After graduation from high school she joined the pit band at the Lincoln Theater (1942) in Los Angeles and then became a member of Gerald Wilson's orchestra (1943). Liston was a shy young woman who was interested, from the beginning of her musical career, in composing and arranging as well as performing.

In 1947 Liston played trombone with Dexter Gordon and then with Dizzy Gillespie's band. In 1949 she became Billie Holiday's (1915–1959) arranger and assistant director for a tour of the southern United States. During this tour Liston was upset and troubled by the racist treatment she experienced and decided to abandon her musical career. She returned to Los Angeles and found employment as a clerk for the Board of Education.

In 1955 Dizzy Gillespie convinced Liston to return to music in order to join his band for a U.S. State Department tour. She subsequently toured Europe with Quincy Jones before beginning her long association with Randy Weston in 1959. In 1973 Liston went to Jamaica and created a pop and jazz division of the Jamaica School of Music, thus introducing jazz to students whose musical knowledge was limited to reggae. She remained there until 1979, when she was persuaded to return to the United States for the Women's Jazz Festival in Kansas City. Her appearance there was followed by successful performances in Boston and New York, and Liston subsequently decided to relocate to New York City. She started her own band, Melba Liston and Company. In addition, she taught at Jazzmobile in New York City and the Pratt Institute Youth-in-Action Orchestra in Brooklyn.

Her original recordings and arrangements are numerous; they include performing on *African Waltz* (Original Jazz Classics OJC-258) with Cannonball Adderley, performing and arranging on *I Can't Help It* (GRP 114) featuring Betty Carter, and *And Her Bones* (SE-1013) with Slide Hampton. In 1985 Liston suffered a stroke that left her unable to play the trombone. She continued to work as a prolific composer and arranger. Melba Doretta Liston died on 23 April 1999.

See also Jazz; Jazz Education

For Further Reading

Dahl, Linda. *Stormy Weather; The Music and Lives of a Century of Jazzwomen*. New York: Pantheon Books, 1984.

Placksin, Sally. *American Women in Jazz, 1900 to Present: Their Words, Lives, and Music*. New York: Wideview Books, 1982.

Kimberly McCord

Little Coyote, Bertha (1912–)

Bertha Little Coyote is an Oklahoma Cheyenne singer whose range of musical experience extends from hymn singing to traditional war songs. A founder of the Fonda Seiling War Mothers Club, Bertha is one of the last women to remember the repertoire of that group, one of the many clubs of mothers and relatives of Native American soldiers who gathered to sing, dance, and raise money for the war effort during World War II. Little Coyote's skill as a singer of traditional songs was documented in the 1960s in a recording from Indian Records. Her reflective comments on these songs were recorded in 1993 for her mediated autobiography, *Leaving Everything Behind: The Songs and Memories of a Cheyenne Woman* (1997), which also contains descriptions of Plains song and dance styles. Her contributions were also included in *Southern Cheyenne Women's Songs* (1994).

Born on 2 February 1912 and raised in government boarding schools and converted to Christianity while still a child, Little Coyote was a consultant to the Mennonite Church for the compilation of the hymnbook *Cheyenne Spiritual Songs* (1982), and has long been a song and prayer leader at both Mennonite and Cheyenne traditional events. She has also served as a consultant to the Smithsonian

Institution, identifying Cheyenne artifacts for repatriation to the tribe. Her contribution to documenting Cheyenne music practice includes: descriptions of men's and women's musical behaviors; "lulu" (high-pitched ululation); mourning songs; dreams and spiritual revelation in the creation of songs; descriptions of the act of "catching" or learning a song; drum singing procedure; Native American church ("peyote") music; and Native American Christian spiritual songs.

See also Multicultural Musics; Native American Musicians

For Further Reading

Giglio, Virginia. *Leaving Everything Behind: The Songs and Memories of a Cheyenne Woman* (with compact disc). Norman: University of Oklahoma Press, 1997.

———. *Southern Cheyenne Women's Songs* (with audiocassette). Norman: University of Oklahoma Press, 1994.

Virginia Giglio

Lockwood, Annea (1939–)

Composer Annea Lockwood creates music that sounds at once very new and extremely old. Her approach to music centers on an intense interest in ecology and the sounds of the natural world. She challenges traditional notions of compositions by using raw recordings of natural phenomena such as rushing water, animal sounds, volcanic activity, and even a distant pulsar.

Lockwood was born in Christchurch, New Zealand, in 1939 and studied composition in England, Germany, and Holland. She lived for a time in London but eventually moved to the United States where she teaches composition at Vassar College.

Although Lockwood was trained in electronic composition, she has gradually simplified her compositional vocabulary through the minimal use of technology. In many instances her interest seems focused on the very nature of acoustic sound production. Several compositions are intended to be performed in very specific locations. For example, *Thousand Year Dreaming* (What Next? 0010) was performed and recorded in a highly resonant room. Inspired by the images of prehistoric cave paintings, the piece explores the interaction of ancient and modern instruments and the echoes and sonorities of the particular space. The resulting work is rich in overtones and delicate balances between the ancient percussion instruments, such as rattles and conch shells, and modern single- and double-reed woodwinds. The piece also includes four Australian didjeridus. An earlier work, *Nautilus* (1989), explored similar acoustic concerns and was compositionally based on the incremental structure of a chambered nautilus.

Lockwood's earlier work focused on raw sounds, as in the 1970 recording *The Glass World* (What Next? WN 21), which explored the unaltered sounds of various tubes, shards, and pieces of glass. *Tiger Balm* (1970) focused on the sounds of a purring cat with other sounds layered above. In 1966 Lockwood began the monumental and ongoing project *River Archive*, a collection of recordings of the world's rivers. The river sounds have been used in several installation works, such as *Play the Ganges Backwards One More Time Sam*, which utilized two rooms (one for slowly moving water, the other for rapids) and incorporated projected slide images of rivers. This same work was recreated outdoors with the speakers hanging from trees. *A Sound Map of the Hudson River* (Lovely Music 2081) was a similar installation piece, the recording of which has been released on compact disc.

Lockwood's installation works began in 1969 with the *Piano Transplants*. For these works Lockwood altered old pianos by installing them in natural settings or exposing them to a natural process such as burning. Pianos were submerged in bodies of water, buried, or positioned to be lifted into the air by a growing tree. The pianos were allowed to decay, decompose, and be "tuned" by the natural forces. While they remained playable, the results were recorded.

See also Experimental Music; Music Technology; Sound Installation Artist

For Further Reading

Oliveros, Pauline. *Software for People*. Baltimore, MD: Smith Publications, 1984.

Pendle, Karin. *Women and Music*. Indianapolis: Indiana University Press, 1991.

Jeffery Byrd

Los Angeles Women in Music

Los Angeles Women in Music (LAWIM) was founded in 1986 to increase awareness of women's contributions to the business and art of music. Its membership, currently around 150, includes performers and composers as well as members of the legal, technical, managerial, and representational sides of the music industry. Reflecting its location and membership, LAWIM sponsors workshops and conferences tailored to specific aspects of the business of music, such as music publishing, music software, home recording, writing for television and film, songwriting, and legal issues in the music business. More recently, smaller peer groups (goal-setting groups) have formed to provide members with a forum to share ideas in reaching short- and long-term goals.

The LAWIM *Newsletter* and World Wide Web site provide a calendar of events as well as job opportunities, conference and workshop summaries, and highlights from the LAWIM Soiree—an annual concert event featuring important rising songwriters from the Los Angeles area. Working in conjunction with the Berklee College of Music, LAWIM featured a Women in Music panel with Patrice Russian (composer, producer, and former music director for the Emmy Awards and People's Choice Awards). In 1996 LAWIM sponsored the first Music Resources Marketplace, a seminar on the creation, marketing, and release of an independent compact disc. Workshops on World Wide Web sales, self-promotion, and guerilla marketing skills have grown out of this initial project and mark the latest interests of the group.

The activities that LAWIM endorses reveal its foundational principle that "women and men working together in mutual respect, sharing abilities and expertise, will strengthen the music business and the music that is at its heart."

See also Organizations, Performer; Organizations, Regional Arts

For Further Reading

Cosola, Mary. "Resources for Women in Music." *Electronic Musician* 13/1 (January 1997): 96–102, 159.

Los Angeles Women in Music (LAWIM). Available: http://www.lawim.org

Gregory Straughn

Low, Henrietta G. Baker (1869–1960)

Henrietta G. Baker Low was an influential music educator in Baltimore in the early 1900s. She was supervisor of music in the Baltimore public schools, served as president of the Music Educators National Conference (MENC), and helped to found the Peabody Conservatory Department of School Music. Her administrative ideas were considered to be 20 years ahead of the times.

Low started out her career in general education teaching mathematics and English. However, she made continuous study of music her avocation and was organist and choir director at a Presbyterian church. This interest drew her attention to the need for school choruses, which she fostered with taste and enthusiasm. This initiative—combined with her understanding of young people—made her widely known, and she was recruited by the school district to become assistant director (1902–1904) and then director (1904–1914) of music for the Baltimore Schools. In this position she lectured, wrote, taught, trained choruses, and encouraged instrumental study, placing emphasis on the lasting recreational value of music in school and home.

During this period she encountered the administrative obstacles to students who wished to continue serious music study. She raised this concern to Dr. David Weglein, principal of the Western High School where she was chorus director. This led to the formation of an art course that enabled students to combine academic courses at the high schools with music study at the Peabody Conservatory. This led in 1912 to the inauguration of teacher-training courses.

In 1915 Low became head of the Department of School Music at the Peabody Conservatory, where she worked until 1940. She helped to provide a new program that furnished guidance to music teachers in all of the Baltimore County schools. In 1913 Low served as president of the Music Supervisors National Conference (MSNC), known as MENC since 1934. Her outstanding achievement in office was preparing a list of songs to be used in schools throughout the country, forging a standard repertoire to help unify Americans through promoting a shared musical heritage.

See also Music Education

For Further Reading

Luckett, Margie Hersh (ed.). *Maryland Women.* Baltimore, MD: Margie Hersh Luckett, 1931.

MENC Historical Center. *Henrietta Baker Low File.* College Park: University of Maryland Performing Arts Library.

"Mrs. Low, Pioneer Music Figure, Dies." *Baltimore Evening Sun* (10 March 1960): Section I, 4.

Kilissa M. Cissoko

LuPone, Patti (1949–)

Patti LuPone is one of the most important singing actresses of the late twentieth century. Her work on stage in both New York and London, and in film and on television, has garnered her great praise and numerous awards. Her first unqualified success was as the title role in the Broadway production of Andrew Lloyd Webber's *Evita* (1979). "Don't Cry for Me, Argentina," the show's central number, has become forever identified with LuPone. She won Tony and Drama Desk Awards for her performance.

Born on 21 April 1949 in Northport, NY, LuPone made her stage debut at age four as a tap dancer. She continued her dance studies with Martha Graham and subsequently studied acting at the Juilliard School, where she met Kevin Kline, with whom she starred in the short-lived Broadway musical *The Robber Bridegroom* (1975). She appeared in subsequent Broadway shows such as *The Baker's Wife* (1976) and *Working* (1978), neither of which was commercially successful.

In 1985 LuPone moved to London and appeared to great critical acclaim on

West End stages: first as Moll in a revival of *The Cradle Will Rock* and second as Fantine in the Royal Shakespeare Company's (RSC) initial production of *Les Miserables*. LuPone was the first American actress-singer to win a principal role with the RSC. She won the 1985 Olivier Award for Best Actress—the titles of both shows appeared on the award.

She returned to New York and starred in highly successful revivals of *Anything Goes* (1987) and *Pal Joey* (1995). LuPone returned to London to create the role of Norma Desmond in the world premiere of Lloyd Webber's *Sunset Boulevard* (1993), giving her the opportunity to introduce the songs "With One Look" and "As If We Never Said Goodbye."

In addition to her appearance in musicals, LuPone has enjoyed success with her one-woman shows and solo recordings. *Patti LuPone on Broadway* (1995) earned her an Outer Critics Circle Award. Her recordings *Patti LuPone Live* (RCA Victor 61834) and *Matters of the Heart* (Varese 6058) display the versatility of her craft.

LuPone has also made a name for herself outside of the musical realm. She played Maria Callas (a non-singing role) in Terrence McNally's *Master Class* in both New York and London and starred in David Mamet's *The Old Neighborhood*. LuPone's extensive film credits include *1941* (1979), *Witness* (1985), and *Driving Miss Daisy* (1989). She played Lady Bird Johnson in the NBC mini-series *L.B.J.: The Early Years* (1987) and Libby Thatcher in ABC's drama *Life Goes On* (1989–1993). LuPone sang the theme song to *Life Goes On*, and in later seasons of the series she frequently was given the opportunity to display her singing abilities.

See also Musical Theater; Tony Awards

For Further Reading

Driscoll, E. Paul. "Going to the Opera with Patti LuPone." *Opera News* 64/5 (1999): 46–48.

Green, Stanley. *Broadway Musicals Show by Show*, 5th ed. Milwaukee: Hal Leonard, 1996.

William A. Everett

Lynn, Loretta (1935–)

Country music superstar Loretta Lynn achieved career success previously unprecedented by a woman country entertainer. Her greatest successes came in the 1960s and 1970s; however, she maintained an active career throughout the second half of the twentieth century, with her latest solo album, *Still Country* (Audium/Koch 8119), being released in September 2000. With as many as 13 Top-10 hits from 1966 to 1970, she was honored as the first woman in country music to be named Country Music Association Entertainer of the Year (1972).

Lynn, the "Coal Miner's Daughter," was born on 14 April 1935 in Butcher Holler, KY. She was one of eight children raised in poverty in a log cabin built by her father. Married at age 13 to 21-year-old Oliver Mooney Lynn, Loretta was pregnant with her first child at age 14 and shortly thereafter moved to Custer, WA, where she bore three more children by age 18. She was a housewife and mother for 15 years before beginning her singing career.

Lynn's first guitar was a gift from her husband. She taught herself to play and was soon composing songs. Her singing career began in 1959 when Mooney recognized her musical talent and began taking her to local Washington honky-tonks and grange halls. Vancouver lumberman Norm Burley was impressed by one of Lynn's local television performances and financed her trip to Los An-

Loretta Lynn. *Photo courtesy of Frank Driggs Collection.*

geles in 1960. There she recorded her first record with a vocal style greatly influenced by Kitty Wells (b. 1918). "I'm a Honky-Tonk Girl" (1960), released on Burley's Zero Records, marked the beginning of a career that far surpassed the achievements of women country performers preceding her. The promotion for Loretta Lynn's first record was accomplished in a manner similar to that of other country performers of the era: Mooney Lynn mailed a photo of Loretta in a cowgirl outfit to 3,500 radio stations. They then traveled across the country to promote the record.

Based on the success of "I'm a Honky-Tonk Girl," Lynn moved to Nashville, TN, in 1961. She first appeared on the Grand Ole Opry in 1960 and became a permanent Opry member in 1962. Her career blossomed as she was befriended by performers Ernest Tubb, Patsy Cline (1932–1963), and the Wilburn Brothers. The latter featured Lynn in their television series beginning in 1963, where she rose to national fame.

Loretta Lynn's career is notable for its appeal to women, whose conditions she consciously represents in song. Until the 1960s, working-class women's lives and careers were subordinate to those of men, and Lynn's early songs mirror the sentiments of powerlessness heard in traditional women's country material. Her first hit, "Success," produced by Owen Bradley at Decca Records, stayed true to this course. Beginning in 1966, however, Lynn wrote and recorded a number of songs that made clear gender statements defying that earlier position. Songs like

"You Ain't Woman Enough to Take My Man" (MCA Special Products 22041), "Don't Come Home a Drinkin' (With Lovin' on Your Mind)" (MCA 11070), "Your Squaw Is on the Warpath" (Decca D17-5084), "Fist City" (MCA 11070), and "The Pill" (MCA Special Products 20261) illustrate sonically a newfound strength and rebellion against male domination that typified the growing feminist movement of the 1960s and signaled a new role for women country singers. Led preeminently by Loretta Lynn, country music feminism valued a new female strength and feistiness while continuing to espouse the importance of the family.

See also Country Music; Country Music Association; Grand Ole Opry

For Further Reading

Dew, Joan. *Singers and Sweethearts: The Women of Country Music*. Garden City, NY: Doubleday, 1977.

Lynn, Loretta, and George Vecsey. *Coal Miner's Daughter*. New York: Warner Books, 1977.

Tichi, Cecelia. *High Lonesome: The American Culture of Country Music*. Chapel Hill: University of North Carolina Press, 1994.

Amy Corin

M

MacArthur Fellows Program

Focused on creativity in the arts, the MacArthur Fellows Program is one of three programs administered by the John D. and Catherine T. MacArthur Foundation. The Foundation was created by John D. MacArthur (1897–1978), who owned Bankers Life and Casualty Company; Catherine (1909–1981), his wife, served as director of the Foundation. There are three criteria of selection for a MacArthur Fellowship: (1) the fellow must be an individual of exceptional creativity, (2) the fellow's work will probably have significant impact in human thought and action, (3) the fellowship must enable the creative individual to "break away" and work without restrictions.

This significant award has only been presented to a limited number of women since its inception in 1978. The Fellowship pays a stipend over a five-year period to qualifying individuals who show exceptional merit and demonstrate a potential to make significant contributions in their areas of creativity.

The MacArthur Fellowship remains one of the most prestigious awards offered to citizens and permanent residents of the United States. As of the 1999 awards, 28 percent of all recipients were women. Only a few of these women were in music disciplines: Bernice Johnson Reagon (1989), Marion Williams (1993), Meredith Monk (1995), Julie Taymor (1991), and Susan McClary (1995).

See also Prizes, Composer and Performer

For Further Reading

The MacArthur Foundation. Available: http://www.macfdn.org/index.htm

Stephen J. Rushing

MacDonald, Jeanette (1903–1965)

Singer and actress Jeanette MacDonald was the queen of operetta, voted the "Queen of Hollywood" by an Ed Sullivan poll in 1939, and was the biggest box-office draw in the concert world for her time. She made 30 films from 1929 through 1949, and her only real competition in film and light opera was Grace Moore (1898–1947). She was a soprano, and her voice was clear and vibrant. Although her voice was not well-suited for

Jeanette MacDonald ca. 1930. *Photo courtesy of Hulton/ Archive Photos.*

grand opera, Jeanette MacDonald and actor Nelson Eddy became America's favorite singing sweethearts during the 1930s and 1940s, singing movie versions of musicals and light operas.

Jeanette MacDonald was born in Philadelphia on 18 June 1903 (not 1907, as has been reported), and the original spelling of her first name was "Jeannette." She took voice and dance lessons as a child, and in 1920 her tap-dancing ability gained her a job in the chorus of Jerome Kern's *The Night Boat* on Broadway. She moved quickly from the back row of the chorus, and subsequently the won the title role in *Yes, Yes, Yvette* in 1927. In 1929 she was teamed with actor Maurice Chevalier for her first film, *The Love Parade*, director Ernst Lubitsch's first sound picture. Chevalier and MacDonald made three more successful operetta-style films together. Lubitsch also directed *The Cat and the Fiddle* ([1934], available on *San Francisco and Other Favorites*, RCA 60877), which included "Beyond the Blue Horizon," MacDonald's first hit recording. In 1935 Metro-Goldwyn-Mayer brought Jeanette MacDonald and Nelson Eddy together for the first time in *Naughty Marietta* ([1935] available on Demand Performance 121). They were enormously successful as America's singing sweethearts and made a series of films such as *Rose-Marie* (1936), *Sweethearts* (1938), and *New Moon* (1940), which audiences loved even though the films were criticized as being overly romantic and sweet. The successful *San Francisco* (1936) co-starred MacDonald with actors Clark Gable and Spencer Tracy. Eddy was her co-star again in *Girl of the Golden West* (1938).

Jeanette MacDonald married actor Gene Raymond in 1937; they had appeared together in *Smilin' Through* (1941). She sang for the troops in army camps and donated the proceeds from a concert tour in 1942 to the Army Emergency Relief Fund. MacDonald made her grand opera debut as Juliette in Charles Gounod's *Romeo and Juliette* first in Montreal in 1943 and later in Chicago in 1944. Even though singing at the Metropolitan Opera was a long-held goal, it was one she never attained. She made her last film, *The Sun Comes Up* (1949), with Claude Jarman Jr. and Lassie.

Ithaca College awarded her a Doctor of Music degree in 1953 for her many contributions to the field of music. She continued to sing for radio, concert, night club, and musical theater, in productions such as *Bitter Sweet* and *The King and I*. Although MacDonald had heart surgery in 1963, she died in Houston of congestive heart failure on 14 January 1965.

See also Musical Theater

For Further Reading

Parish, James Robert. *The Jeanette MacDonald Story*. New York: Mason/Charter, 1976.

Stern, Lee Edward. *Jeanette MacDonald*. New York: Jove, 1977.

Turk, Edward Baron. *Hollywood Diva: A Biography of Jeanette MacDonald*. Berkeley and Los Angeles: University of California Press, 1998.

Jeanne E. Shaffer

Maddox, Rose (1925–1998)

Despite humble beginnings, Rose Maddox had a career that ultimately spanned seven decades and clearly influenced performers in rock-a-billy, bluegrass, and country music styles. Rose Maddox had, in effect, three career incarnations. First she became wildly popular and integral to the success of the Maddox Brothers and Rose. She briefly joined Nashville's Grand Ole Opry in 1956, and when the family group disbanded in 1957, she became an important solo recording artist. Finally, during the folk revival of the 1960s, encouraged by bluegrass founder Bill Monroe, Rose gained prominence as a bluegrass vocalist.

Born Roselea Arbana Maddox on 15 August 1925 in Boaz, AL, Maddox began singing at 11 years of age as vocalist in her family's act, the Maddox Brothers and Rose. In 1933, as part of the Dust Bowl migration, the Maddox family hitchhiked and jumped freight trains from Alabama to Modesto, CA, where they found work as migrant laborers in the San Joaquin Valley's agricultural industry. The turning point from their poverty-stricken existence to eventual stardom as "America's most colorful hillbilly band" came when Rose's brother Fred, tired of back-breaking labor for pennies a day, convinced Modesto furniture store owner Jim Rice to sponsor the family on local radio station KTRB. The broadcasts made them an almost immediate success in the region. With Fred and Mama Lula acting as the group's managers, the Maddox Brothers and 11-year-old Rose began to use their radio broadcasts as a way to promote live appearances following the San Joaquin Valley rodeo circuit.

Their career was again furthered when, as a result of a talent contest they won at the Sacramento State Fair in 1939, the group began to perform on Sacramento station KFBK, whose range extended into a number of nearby states. When World War II erupted and her brothers were drafted, Rose continued to perform with other bandleaders. When her brothers returned, the group re-formed and once again contributed to shaping the West Coast's country music industry. Rose and her brothers defined, in many ways, what it meant to be a successful country group during that era. Mother Lula had extravagant, flashy, western costumes designed by famous Hollywood tailor Nathan Turk, and they always traveled to engagements in a caravan of shiny new Cadillacs.

Rose's recording career began in 1947 when, based on the group's tremendous postwar success, she and Lula traveled to Los Angeles to secure a recording contract. They recorded first for Pasadena-based Four Star Records and later for the more prestigious Columbia Records, where Rose also had a contract as a solo recording artist. Two important recordings, the provocative "Sally Let Your Bangs Hang Down" and Woody Guthrie's "Philadelphia Lawyer" (both available on *America's Most Colorful Hillbilly Band: Their Original Recordings 1946–1951, Vol. 1*, Arhoolie 437), were made during the group's first Four Star sessions. Rose's 1961 duets with fellow Californian Buck Owens not only launched his career but also established her as one of the most important women country performers of the era. Several recordings of the Buck Owens collaborations exist, including *On the Bandstand* (Sundazed 6044), *I Don't Care* (Sundazed 6046), and the compilation disc *The Buck Owens Collection (1959–1990)* (Rhino R2-71016).

Despite several heart attacks suffered during the later part of her life, Rose Maddox continued to perform at events throughout the country until shortly before her death near her home in Ashland, OR on 15 April 1998.

See also Country Music; Folk Music

For Further Reading

Dew, Joan. *Singers and Sweethearts: The Women of Country Music*. Garden City, NY: Doubleday, 1977.

Haslam, Gerald W. *Workin' Man Blues: Country Music in California*. Berkeley: University of California Press, 1999.

Whiteside, Jonny. *Ramblin' Rose: The Life and Career of Rose Maddox*. Nashville: Country Music Foundation and Vanderbilt University Press, 1997.

Amy Corin

Madonna (1958–)

Popular singer Madonna is perhaps best known for her chameleon-like character that continually changes, challenges, and captivates her audience. From the beginning of her career, journalists criticized Madonna for exploiting the men in her life for personal gain, denounced her singing voice, attributed her success to her producers, and focused almost completely on the overtly sexual character featured in her music videos. However, despite music criticism, Madonna thrived for close to 20 years, and her career is in no way slowing down.

She was born Madonna Louise Veronica Ciccone in Rochester, MI, on 16 August 1958. Madonna left a dance scholarship at University of Michigan to pursue ballet in New York City in 1977. Following a brief stint with a dance troupe in Paris, Madonna returned to New York to become the drummer and, later, lead vocalist of Breakfast Club, a band she formed with boyfriend Dan Gillroy. In 1980 Madonna formed Emmy with boyfriend Steve Bray, the last band she was to be involved with before moving on to a solo career that began in the dance clubs of New York. In 1982 Madonna was signed to Sire Records, her first major record label. Following the release of three dance club singles, her debut album, *Madonna* (Sire 2-23867), hit the record stores in 1983.

In 1984 Madonna released her second album, *Like a Virgin* (Sire 2-25157), and once again was criticized for her thin, squeaky, little-girl voice and her overemphasis on sex. Madonna began working with Patrick Leonard on *True Blue* (Sire 2-25442) in 1986; with its release the critics continued to express concern over her manipulative "sex sells" attitude, calling her everything from "mega-slut to bad girl" (O'Dair, 67). However, they seemed to be warming up to her vocals. In 1988 she released a relatively unknown remix album, *You Can Dance* (Sire 2-25535). With the release of *Like a Prayer* (Sire 2-25844) in 1989 the press began to take her seriously as a musician. In 1990, after seven years in the music industry, Madonna released a greatest hits album, *The Immaculate Collection* (Sire 2-26440). This seemed to begin the most sexually rebellious period in her career.

In 1991 she released the controversial *Truth or Dare* documentary of her Blonde Ambition tour. Madonna turned up the heat on her sexual image in her book *Sex*, featuring photographs of herself, models, and other celebrities. The public seemed to turn against her, citing *Sex* as disgraceful, and continued to scorn her with the release of *Erotica* (Maverick 2045154), an album entirely about sex. In 1994 with the rhythm and blues–style album *Bedtime Stories* (Maverick 45767), Madonna continued to feel the consumer backlash against her sexual image even though she proclaimed the album to be about love.

In 1995 Madonna began a transformation away from the overtly sexual image to a more "sophisticated" role, taking a lead role in the musical film *Evita* (1996). Also in that year she released *Something to Remember* (Maverick 46100), a nonprovocative album of ballads. With the birth of her daughter, Lourdes, in 1996, Madonna continued to move away from the sexual images she had portrayed in her early career. In fact, she viewed the birth of her daughter as a personal rebirth and a way of reclaiming her innocence. Madonna completely remade her image in 1997 with *Ray of Light* (Warner Brothers 46847), produced by William Orbit, a record encompassing themes of spirituality and motherhood. Madonna continued to work with William Orbit on her next studio album, *Music* (Warner Brothers 47598), in which she embraced the electronica genre and incorporated many electronic effects such as vocoders and synthesized sounds.

In 2000, Madonna gave birth to her second child, son Rocco, and married director Guy Ritchie.

See also Rock and Popular Music Genres; Rock Music

For Further Reading

Bego, Mark. *Madonna: Blonde Ambition*. New York: Harmony Books, 1992.

Benson, Carol, and Allan Metz (eds.). *The Madonna Companion: Two Decades of Commentary*. New York: Schirmer Books, 1999.

O'Dair, Barbara (ed.). *Madonna: The Rolling Stone Files*. New York: Hyperion, 1997.

Melissa West

Male Gaze

The term "male gaze" originated in art and film studies in the 1970s to refer to a way of seeing something from a male-gendered perspective. In accordance with the traditional binarisms of female/male and passive/active, the male gaze was characterized as coming from the position of one who acts. The term spread to advertising and other media studies, and it even entered public discourse along with other academic and feminist terms, although its common usage peaked sometime in the late 1980s when "male gaze" became a feminist euphemism for "male voyeurism."

Fortunately, gazing (male) and being-gazed-at (female) goes beyond this paradigm. For instance, the presence of the male gaze raises the question of what the female gaze could be. Because women, whether as actors, directors, or even viewers (women constitute an influential commercial market), have more or less control over what and how images are viewed, the gendered aspect of a normative gaze may change. As Susan Sontag writes in her introduction to Annie Leibovitz's photographic survey, *Women* (1999), "The imperial rights of the camera—to gaze at, to record, to exhibit anyone, anything—are an exemplary feature of modern life, as is the emancipation of women."

Still, whatever power a female model may yield in returning the gaze, or simply in posing, for that matter, we gazers (whether men or not) still have the power to gawk lasciviously at her. For their part, women, even liberated ones, still conform to stereotypes of what women are supposedly like—passive, submissive, and superficial.

One way to combat simplistic analysis of the gaze is through attention to viewers' purposes. Once this is acknowledged, analysis can distinguish a lustful gaze from an interested look from a peripheral glance. Further, one must analyze how the gaze is directed by the creators, or by the medium itself. A World Wide Web site works differently from a film in a dark theater.

The usefulness of the concept of male gaze is limited in studies of musical sound, of course, although it does arise in music iconography and in analyses of music videos, opera, and other forms of music theater. There may be some usefulness in the concept of the "male ear," although it raises similar problems to the male gaze in the gendering of hearing or listening.

See also Gender Issues

For Further Reading

Berger, John. *Ways of Seeing*. London: BBC/Harmondsworth, 1972.

Gamman, Lorraine, and Margaret Marshment (eds.). *The Female Gaze: Women as Viewers of Popular Culture*. Seattle: Real Comet Press, 1989.

Sontag, Susan. "A Photograph Is Not an Opinion. Or Is It?" In *Women* by Annie Leibovitz. New York: Random House, 1999.

Richard Rischar

Mandrell, Barbara (1948–)

Barbara Mandrell was one of the most influential women country performers of the 1970s and early 1980s. A multitalented, energetic performer who describes herself as assertive, aggressive, and organized, Barbara pushed traditional performance boundaries for women country artists, exhibiting a strong sense of showmanship and recording songs that crossed over from country to pop charts. An accomplished instrumentalist and singer, Barbara was one of the first women country artists to record songs depicting women in active relationship roles, including songs relating stories of women cheating on men. In an era when men dominated the world of country music, she modeled her career after other strong women performers such as Minnie Pearl (1912–1996), Martha Carson (b. 1921), Rose Maphis (b. 1922), and Rose Maddox (1925–1998). Drawing on the example set by Loretta Lynn (b. 1935), Barbara proved to reluctant concert promoters that women headliners

Barbara Mandrell performing ca. 1984.
Photo courtesy of Globe Photos.

could draw audiences as successfully as men.

Born in Houston, TX, on 25 December 1948 to strict Pentecostal parents, Barbara is the oldest of three daughters. Prior to her teenage years the family moved to Oceanside, CA, where she became a virtuoso instrumentalist, playing steel guitar, saxophone, mandolin, and banjo while appearing on stage shows and television programs. Barbara's sister Louise (b. 1954) played bass guitar and fiddle while baby sister Irlene played drums. Although her performing debut occurred at age five in her parents' church, Barbara's professional career began at age 11 when she accompanied her father, music store owner Irby Mandrell, to a Chicago convention to demonstrate the Standell amplifiers he sold. There she impressed guitarist Joe Maphis, who hired her to perform in his Las Vegas act and as a member of the cast on the Los Angeles television show *Town Hall Party*, billed as "The Princess of the Steel." By 1962 she was touring with country stars Johnny Cash and Patsy Cline (1932–1963).

In 1963 her parents formed a band, the Mandrells, featuring mother Mary on piano, Irby on guitar, Barbara on steel guitar, and Barbara's future husband, Ken Dudney, as the band's drummer. Barbara and Ken married in 1967, and she retired from the music business intending to be a housewife. However, when her parents relocated to Nashville and she visited them in 1968, Barbara made a trip to the Grand Ole Opry and was convinced to return to music.

While performing in Nashville's Printer's Alley, Barbara was approached by record companies and soon produced a string of hit records. She joined the Grand Ole Opry in 1972, and in 1979 she was named the Country Music Association's (CMA) Female Vocalist of the Year. In 1980 and 1981 she garnered the CMA's coveted Entertainer of the Year Award, and she won Grammy Awards for gospel performances in 1982 and 1983. In 1980 Barbara signed with NBC Television to do a national television variety series, *Barbara Mandrell and the Mandrell Sisters*. The show allowed Barbara and her sisters to again push performance boundaries for both women and country performers in general; this time incorporating choreographed dances and comedy skits.

Barbara left television in 1982 and returned to Las Vegas, where her show included polished choreography from her television experience, instrumental showmanship, and renditions of hit singles "I

Was Country When Country Wasn't Cool" (available on *Greatest Hits*, MCA MCAD-31302), "If Loving You Is Wrong (I Don't Want to be Right)" (available on *Moods*, MCA 1677), and her favorite song, "Battle Hymn of the Republic." A devastating automobile accident in 1984 nearly ended her life, but her determination again triumphed. She fought her way back to health and career success and continues to perform, recording for Capitol Records since 1987.

See also Country Music

For Further Reading

Dew, Joan. *Singers and Sweethearts: The Women of Country Music*. Garden City, NY: Doubleday, 1977.

Mandrell, Barbara, and George Vecsey. *Get to the Heart: My Story*. New York: Bantam Books, Mass Market Press, 1996.

Tichi, Cecelia. *High Lonesome: The American Culture of Country Music*. Chapel Hill: University of North Carolina Press, 1994.

Amy Corin

Martin, Mary Virginia (1913–1990)

Singer and actress Mary Virginia Martin was best known for her Broadway musical roles such as Peter Pan, Ensign Nellie Forbush (from *South Pacific*), and Annie Oakley (from *Annie Get Your Gun*). Martin was honored with an Emmy Award, several Tony Awards, and several New York Critics Drama Awards.

Martin was born in Weatherford, TX, on 1 December 1913. Her penchant for performing was encouraged by her parents, an older sister, and a supportive community. She first sang in public at age five. While attending Ward-Belmont Finishing School in Nashville she married Benjamin Hagman, a law student who worked for her father. Their son Larry (who became a successful television actor) was born in 1931.

Unhappy with domestic life, Martin opened the Mary Hagman School of Dance, with her family's support. Needing advanced instruction herself, she spent two summers at the Fanchon and Marco School of Theater in Hollywood and while there decided to pursue a show business career. She returned to Hollywood in 1935 while her father arranged an amicable divorce from Hagman. In 1937 a Broadway producer heard her in a nightclub and offered her a job in New York. Although unknown there, Martin landed the part of Dolly in the Cole Porter musical *Leave It to Me* in 1938. Her rendition of "My Heart Belongs to Daddy" became legendary and launched a Broadway career that spanned five decades.

A film contract with Paramount Pictures took Martin back to Hollywood in 1939, where she spent four years starring in such films as *The Great Victor Herbert* (1939), *Birth of the Blues* (1941), and *Kiss the Boys Goodbye* (1941). While there, she met and married Paramount executive Richard Halliday, who abandoned his own career to become Martin's agent and manager.

Preferring live performance, Martin returned to the stage in a series of Broadway runs and tours. She went on her first nationwide tour as Annie in Irving Berlin's *Annie Get Your Gun* in 1947–1948, and her young daughter, Heller, played Annie's younger sister. Martin returned to Broadway in 1949 as Nellie Forbush in the popular Rodgers and Hammerstein musical *South Pacific* (Sony 60722) and then took the show on tour to London for two years. Her next hit came in 1954 as Peter in a musical version of *Peter Pan* (RCA 3762), for which she won a Tony Award. *Peter Pan* was subsequently performed on live television, winning her an Emmy Award in 1955. In

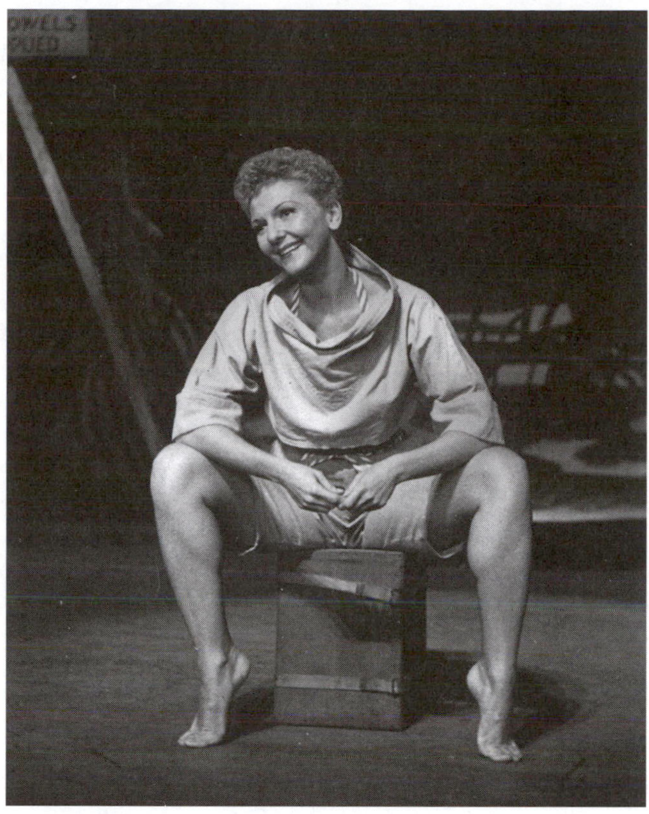

Mary Virginia Martin as Nellie Forbush in a December 1951 performance of *South Pacific* in London. *Photo courtesy of Hulton/Archive Photos.*

the following year the idea for *The Sound of Music* (Sony 60583) was born when Martin and Halliday saw a German film based on Baroness Maria von Trapp's book and persuaded their associates to produce a show. Rodgers and Hammerstein wrote the music; Martin traveled to Vermont to work with the Baroness herself; and in 1959 one of the most successful musicals of all time opened. Martin played the role of Maria until 1961 and was again awarded a Tony Award. In 1965–1966 she toured the United States and Asia, playing the title role in *Hello Dolly!*, then returned to Broadway in *I Do! I Do!* (RCA 1128-2-RC) from 1966 to 1968.

Taking a needed break, Martin retreated with her husband to their farm in Brazil until his death in 1973. After moving back to Palm Springs, she made several more television and stage appearances, hosted a PBS talk show, and embarked on a last national tour in 1986–1987 with Carol Channing in *Legends!* In 1989 Martin was honored by the Kennedy Center for lifetime achievement in the arts. She died of liver cancer on 3 November 1990 in Rancho Mirage, CA.

See also Musical Theater

For Further Reading

Martin, Mary. *My Heart Belongs*. New York: William Morrow, 1976.

Rivadue, Barry. *Mary Martin: A Bio-Bibliography*. New York: Greenwood Press, 1991.

Laurie Eagleson

Masaoka, Miya (1958–)

Miya Masaoka is a composer, performer, and performance artist at the center of the Asian American new music scene in San Francisco. Masaoka is a Sansei (third-generation Japanese American) whose political sensibilities were shaped during the ferment of the 1970s. She has traditional training on the Japanese koto and in the ancient Japanese court music called *gagaku* but chooses to play the koto in nontraditional ways: she has extended the instrument's possibilities not only through her base in jazz and new music but also through the innovative application of computer electronics.

She was born in born in Washington, DC, in 1958. In 1990 Masaoka graduated *magna cum laude* from San Francisco State University, receiving a B.A. degree in music; in 1994 she completed an M.A. in music composition from Mills College.

Masaoka's primary work is in free improvisation, drawn from the "revolutionary consciousness" that infuses the work of musicians linked with the Association for the Advancement of Creative Musicians (AACM). The AACM has been a fundamental inspiration for Masaoka and a circle of Asian American musicians in the San Francisco Bay Area. Mostly born in the late 1950s, these musicians participated in the Asian American political movement in the 1970s and brought its consciousness into their music. Over the years they have constructed an Asian American musical and political identity through their explorations of jazz, composition, and free improvisation. Masaoka has worked extensively with other improviser-composers in this group, including bassist Mark Izu, pianist Jon Jang, saxophonist Francis Wong, and pianist and shamisen player Glenn Horiuchi. In 1987 they formed their own nonprofit recording label entitled Asian Improv, thus pointing to the two shared characteristics of their music: its base in Asian American identity and in improvised musical techniques.

In 1993 Improv produced Masaoka's solo album, *Compositions/Improvisations* (X Dot 25 13). The title points to the creative tension between the improvisational process and Western ideas of composition. Masaoka has noted that the challenges of improvisation are made more complicated for her by issues of intercultural musical experimentation, suggesting that her own position as a Sansei artist must be taken into consideration and that her commitment to improvisation is not coincidental (Masaoka 1996).

Masaoka has had several residencies at STEIM (Studio for Electro Instrumental Music), an electronic music studio in the Netherlands dedicated to live performance. Working closely with technicians, she has developed a unique technology for her koto that dramatically extends its vocabulary. Masaoka also employs a sensor system combining pickups for the koto bridges, foot pedals, and ultra-sound sound-rings for her hands that capture gestures of movement, transforming them into gestures of sound. She calls this new instrument "KOTO-monster," playfully and ironically acknowledging its new possibilities as well as its challenges.

Masaoka has also experimented with performance art, creating such multimedia works as *Ritual* (for koto and Madagascar roaches), *Bee Project #1* (for violin, koto, percussion, and live beehive), and *What Is the Sound of Ten Naked Asian American Men?* (in progress). Masaoka's album *What Is the Difference between Stripping and Playing the Violin?* (Victo 1998) features sounds drawn from a site-specific work performed on Market Street in San Francisco, inspired by the murders of five prostitutes. The album weaves together the sounds of the 16-piece Masaoka Orchestra with street interviews with passersby about stripping and the sex industry.

See also Asian American Music; Multicultural Musics

For Further Reading

Masaoka, Miya. "Koto No Tankyu (Koto Explorations)." *Institute for the Study of American Music Newsletter* 25/2 (1996): 8–9.

Deborah Wong

Maud Powell Society for Music and Education

The Maud Powell Society for Music and Education (formerly the Maud Powell Foundation) was founded in 1986 and is dedicated to educating the public about the life and art of Maud Powell and furthering her musical ideals by encouraging young people to perform and appreciate music.

Maud Powell (1867–1920) was America's first great master of the violin to achieve international rank. Her appearance on American concert platforms from 1885 to 1920 exerted a pivotal influence on the tradition of violin playing and on the development of audiences and institutions for classical music in North America.

The Maud Powell Society co-published (with Iowa State University Press) the definitive biography *Maud Powell, Pioneer American Violinist* by Karen A. Shaffer and Neva Garner Greenwood (1988) and reissued Powell's recordings (1904–1917) on three compact discs, *The Art of Maud Powell* (MPF-1, 2, 3), both to international critical acclaim. In 1994 the Society published the first in its *Women in Music* series of books for children—*Maud Powell, Legendary American Violinist* by Powell biographer Karen A. Shaffer. California composer Elinor Remick Warren (1900–1991) will be the subject of the next book in the series. These books complement the Society's *Music and Your Child* program designed to educate parents about the importance of music in the lives of their children. Additionally, the Society sponsored an exhibit, *Maud Powell, American Musical Pioneer*, at the Indianapolis Children's Museum in 1994. It was the first major exhibition in the world featuring a woman musician and the visual centerpiece of the 1994 Indianapolis International Violin Competition. The Society awarded a $5,000 Maud Powell Prize for the Best Performance of a Romantic Violin Concerto at the Competition.

The Maud Powell Signature is the Society's subscription magazine devoted to the achievements of women in classical music, past and present. Five issues were published from 1995 to 1997, when publication was suspended. *Signature* serves as a point of reference for teachers, students, composers, and performers throughout the world.

The work of the Society gave impetus to the realization of an 8-foot bronze statue of Maud Powell in the city of her birth—the only statue to an American woman musician in the United States. The Society encouraged, advised, and supported the efforts of the city of Peru, IL, which dedicated the statue on 1 July 1995. Maud Powell artifacts in the possession of the Society are on display at the public library, and there is an annual Maud Powell Music Festival in her hometown.

The Maud Powell Society offers lectures, seminars, and school programs and assists teachers, students, and performers in research on Maud Powell, American music of her era, the history of classical music in the United States, and the achievements and contributions of women in music. The Society also assists violinists in giving Maud Powell commemorative concerts. In 1998 the Society began transferring the Maud Powell Archive to the Library of Congress. The Society is a nonprofit, tax-exempt corporation operated exclusively for educational, charitable, and literary purposes.

See also Performer, String

For Further Reading

Shaffer, Karen A. "Perpetual Pioneer." *The Strad* (November 1987).

Shaffer, Karen A. and Neva Garner Greenwood. *Maud Powell, Pioneer American Violinist*. Ames: Iowa State University Press, 1988.

Karen A. Shaffer

McElwee (Gonzales), Ileane (1920–2000)

Throughout her career, music educator Ileane McElwee (Gonzales) had an active interest in working with handicapped and gifted children. Her clinics for trainable mentally handicapped–gifted instrumental students beginning in 1976 earned her the reputation as a national authority and pioneer in this field. Of these clinics, one of the most notable was presented in Chicago at the National Music Educators National Conference (MENC) Convention in 1978. Consequently, many school districts adopted the teaching format advocated by McElwee at these clinics. In addition to her work with handicapped and gifted students, McElwee spent several summers teaching at the Navajoland Festival of the Arts on the Navajo Indian Reservations.

Ileane McElwee (Gonzales) was born on 19 October 1920 in East Liberty, OH. McElwee began her musical career at the age of five, taking piano lessons. Through the encouragement of her mother, these piano lessons were soon supplemented with violin lessons, and she later played clarinet as well as violin in high school. McElwee received her Bachelor of School Music degree (1943) from Capital University in Columbus, OH. Over the course of her teaching career, subsequent postgraduate work was pursued at Ohio Northern University (1954), Grand Canyon College (1964), Arizona State University (1968–1970), the University of Arizona (1972–1973), the University of Southern California (1974), and the University of Hawaii (1975).

A devout pedagogue, McElwee taught instrumental music in the public schools for more than 57 years. Her teaching career began in 1943 at East Liberty Schools (OH). McElwee spent the next 17 years teaching in Ohio with tenures at West Mansfield and Indian Lake Consolidated Schools. In 1960 McElwee and her family moved to Phoenix, AZ, where she remained active as a teacher of instrumental music. Tenures in Phoenix included John F. Kennedy Junior High School and Indian High School. After 24 years of teaching in the Phoenix public school system, McElwee spent two years teaching in Zuni, NM, and the last 14 years of her career teaching in Payson, AZ.

McElwee's commitment to education and pioneering work in the field of special learners earned her many distinctions and honors. These included: Outstanding Woman Band Director of the Year (1972), Outstanding Leader in Elementary and Secondary Education in the United States of America (1976), One of the 10 People Making America Musical (1977), the Silver Baton Award, and the Sousa Foundation Citation of Honor.

Her professional memberships were numerous, including the National Education Association, the Ohio Education Association, the Ohio Music Education Association, the Arizona Education Association, the Arizona Band and Orchestra Association, and the Music Educators National Conference. McElwee was a charter member of the National Band Directors' National Association, in which she served as Arizona state chairman (1961–1963) and National Directory chairman (1962–1964). She also was a charter member of the Women Band Directors' National Association, in which she served as Arizona state chairman, Western States chairman, 2nd vice-president (1975–1976), 1st vice-president (1976–1977), and national president (1977–1978).

McElwee died on 30 March 2000 in Payson, AZ.

See also Band Music Education; Music Education

For Further Reading

McElwee, Ileane. "Colored-Coded Band." *School Musician* 46/8 (1975): 60–61.

———. "Indian High School Band: A New and Interesting Challenge." *School Musician* 53/10 (1982): 34–35.

———. "Memoriam for Rafael Mendez." *School Musician* 53/9 (1982): 25.

———. "Navajoland Festival of the Arts." *School Musician* 48/8 (1977): 45.

———. "We All Learn Together." *School Musician* 49/4 (1977): 68–69.

Daryl Kinney

McEntire, Reba (1954–)

Reba McEntire, one of the most successful women country music recording artists of the 1980s and 1990s, is also one of the industry's few authentic cowgirls. In the early 1990s, as country music fans and record companies eschewed women vocalists in favor of their honky-tonk influenced male counterparts, McEntire remained a force to be reckoned with. She consciously chose to record songs by women writers that speak to and for her women fans who are women: songs that depict the plight of poor, working-class women and that provide them with an otherwise unavailable "three minute rebellion."

Reba McEntire. *Photo courtesy of NBC/Globe Photos.*

Born on 28 March 1954 and raised on an Oklahoma cattle ranch, Reba was one of four children born to Jackie and Clark McEntire. When they were young, McEntire and her siblings followed the paternal family tradition of rodeo competition, but they were also strongly influenced by their mother's musicality. By the time McEntire had reached high school age, the siblings had formed a family performing group called the Singing McEntires. They won numerous local talent contests and, in 1971, wrote and recorded a locally successful record.

In 1974 country star Red Stegall heard Reba sing the national anthem at the

Oklahoma City National Rodeo Finals. Impressed with her voice, he invited her to Nashville and financed a recording session that resulted in a Mercury Records contract. During the remainder of the 1970s, Reba McEntire married bulldogger and steer wrestler Charlie Battles and finished college. She continued her recording efforts but achieved only minimal success until 1980, when her recording career began to show promise.

McEntire's true ascent to country music stardom began when her 1980 recording of "(You Lift Me) Up to Heaven" reached number eight on the country music charts. Her first number one record, however, did not come until 1982 with the release of "Can't Even Get the Blues" on her *Unlimited* album (Mercury 822882-2). Dissatisfied with the approach taken toward her development by Mercury Records, Reba took charge of her career in 1984, moving from Mercury to MCA Records. From this point forward, Reba's rise to stardom was meteoric. During the period 1984–1987 she won a Grammy Award and was inducted into the Grand Ole Opry. She earned a record-breaking four consecutive Country Music Association awards as Female Vocalist of the Year and one as Entertainer of the Year.

Beginning in 1986, McEntire's stage productions became increasingly elaborate as she steered other aspects of her career in a more dramatic direction. Following the trend in the country music industry, she began producing elaborate mini-movie-like music videos of her hit records. The success of her videos brought Reba acting roles in films, a television movie, and the soap opera *One Life to Live*. She pushed other boundaries too, adding pop and rock–influenced production to her recordings.

McEntire divorced Battles in 1987 and married Narvel Blackstock, her road manager and steel guitarist, two years later. Together they continued to direct her career into an empire that includes a publishing company, booking agency, fan club, and a business that leases private jets.

See also Country Music; Country Music Association

For Further Reading

Bufwack, Mary A., and Robert K. Oermann. *Finding Her Voice: The Saga of Women in Country Music*. New York: Crown, 1993.

Dew, Joan. *Singers and Sweethearts: The Women of Country Music*. Garden City, NY: Doubleday, 1977.

McEntire, Reba. *Comfort from a Country Quilt*. New York: Bantam Doubleday Dell, 1999.

Amy Corin

McLean, Priscilla Anne (1942–)

Priscilla Anne (Taylor) McLean is a composer and performer of electro-acoustic music. Known for her multimedia concerts with her husband, Barton, as part of the McLean Mix, Priscilla has served as an instructor at Indiana University, Kokomo (1971–1973); composer-in-residence at the Electronic Music Center, St. Mary's College, Notre Dame (1973–1976); and visiting professor at the University of Hawaii (1985). She has received numerous grants and awards and maintains a concert schedule filled with international performances.

She was born on 27 May 1942 in Fitchburg, MA, and at age 11 began her study of music. McLean received degrees from the Fitchburg State College (B.Ed. 1963), the University of Massachusetts in Lowell (B.M.E. 1965) and the Indiana University (M.M. 1969). Her composition teachers include Richard Kent, Thomas Beversdorf, and Bernhard Heiden.

She was greatly influenced by the music of Iannis Xenakis, who was composer-in-residence and director of the Electronic Music Center during her stay at the Indiana University. She met and married fellow student and composer Barton McLean in 1967. She and her husband formed the McLean Mix, a duo that has performed numerous multimedia concerts and interactive installation exhibits on four continents.

Her awards include three National Endowment for the Arts (NEA) Composer Grants; Martha Baird Rockefeller Fund for Music Grant; an NEA Media Arts Grant; four MacDowell Colony Fellowships; and composer-in-residence positions at Gaudeamus Musiekweek, Holland (1979), Indiana State National Orchestral Symposium (1975), and Louisville Orchestra at Kennedy Center (1978). Additionally, McLean was on the Executive Committee of the Society of Composers from 1978 to 1983, creating with Barton McLean two series of 13 radio programs, *Radiofest: New American Music*.

McLean's works include orchestral, chamber, vocal, and electro-acoustic music. Her music is unique for its use of nature sounds combined with electronics, the creation of special sound worlds, and her masterful singing and use of extended vocal techniques. Selected works include: *Variations & Mosaics on a Theme of Stravinsky* for orchestra (1967–1969, revised 1975); *Dance of Dawn* for tape (1974); *Invisible Chariots* for tape (1975–1977); *Beneath the Horizon I* for four tubas and tape (1977–1978); *The Inner Universe* for piano and tape (1979–1982); *A Magic Dwells* for orchestra and tape (1982–1984); *Voices of the Wild* for electronic music soloist and orchestra (movement two by Barton McLean, 1986–1988); *Rainforest*, an audience-interactive multimedia installation, a collaboration with Barton McLean (1989–1990); *The Dance of Shiva* for stereo computer music and slides (1989–1990); and *Rainforest Images II* for tape, a collaboration with Barton McLean (1992).

See also Experimental Music; Music Technology

For Further Reading

McLean Mix Duo/Media Duo. Available: http://members.aol.com/mclmix2/index.html

Mary Simoni

McPartland, Marian (1918–)

Marian McPartland, with her elegant and swinging style, is one of the best known and loved jazz pianists playing today, but she is equally well known for her popular radio interview series *Piano Jazz*, and for her articulate advocacy of jazz music. Continually contributing articles and reviews to *Down Beat* and other jazz journals, McPartland received the *Down Beat* Lifetime Achievement Award in 1994. Her other awards include the Peabody Award from the University of Georgia, the Southern Educational Communications Association Lifetime Achievement Award (1992), and the American Society of Composers, Authors and Publishers Deems Taylor Broadcasting Award (1991), and she has been honored by many colleges and universities.

Born Margaret Marian Turner on 21 March 1918 in Slough, Buckinghamshire, England, the young Marian studied both piano and violin from an early age. Because of her prodigious talent she was soon transferred from a boarding school to the Guildhall School of Music in London, where she studied primarily classical piano and composition. Having discovered jazz from the recordings of Duke Ellington, Fats Waller, and other pian-

Marian McPartland. *Photo courtesy of Frank Driggs Collection.*

ists, she began playing with a vaudeville team in England. Around the age of 20, during World War II, she played for British and American troops with the British United Service Organization. While entertaining troops in Belgium she met the young American cornet player Jimmy McPartland. They were married in 1945, and soon after the war they moved to New York.

In her autobiography, *All in Good Time* (1987), McPartland alludes to discrimination against her as a woman, white, and British, in the jazz world. But she often performed with her husband, a well-known musician, and in 1951 created a successful trio with Bill Crow (bass) and Joe Morello (drums) to play at Condons, the Embers, the Hickory House, and other New York clubs.

McPartland became friends with composer Alec Wilder in the 1960s, and Wilder, from time to time, would write jazz pieces and songs for her. Such Wilder tunes as "Jazz Waltz for a Friend," and "Why?," written specifically for her, and others, including "Who Can I Turn To," "It's So Peaceful in the Country," "While We're Young," and "I'll Be Around," have become staples in her repertoire.

In the late 1960s she formed her own record label, Halcyon, and began issuing recordings of jazz groups and soloists. She issued many recordings of her own jazz compositions, including the *Ambience* album (The Jazz Alliance Discography, TJA-10029) and the singles "Twilight World," "With You in My Mind," and "In the Days of Our Love." In 1978 Alec Wilder recommended to South Carolina Educational Radio that McPartland, who already had established a reputation teaching jazz in the public schools, host a jazz show on the radio. National Public Radio (NPR) distributed the show, and McPartland's format of interviewing and playing with major jazz performers was a resounding success. Still continuing today, it has become the longest-running show on NPR, and many of the best programs (e.g., interviews with Teddy Wilson, Dave Brubeck, Bill Evans, etc.) have been issued by the Jazz Alliance on compact disc. McPartland's more recent programs have included interviews with non-pianist jazz artists, including Tony Bennett, Wynton Marsalis, Milt Hinton, and Rosemary Clooney (1928–2002).

Although the McPartlands were ultimately divorced, they remained friends, often performing together, and in 1991 they remarried, just prior to Jimmy

McPartland's death. Now in her eighties she continues to broadcast her NPR radio show and to perform.

See also Jazz Education; Music Programmer/Host

For Further Reading

Bash, Lee. "The Jazz Pioneer." *Jazz Educators Journal* 30/4 (January 1998): 143–145.

McPartland, Marian. *All in Good Time*. New York: Oxford University Press, 1987.

Stephen Fry

McRae, Carmen (1920–1994)

Carmen McRae, legendary song stylist, was a classically trained pianist and a jazz singer noted for her impeccable musicianship. Her voice was certainly a strong instrument, but what gained her the reputation as a remarkable performer was her behind-the-beat phrasing and interpretation of lyrics. Her long and distinguished career spanned nearly 60 years and was highlighted in 1994 when McRae was named a Master of Jazz by the National Endowment for the Arts.

McRae was born on 8 April 1920 in New York to West Indian immigrant parents. In 1937 she won an amateur talent contest at the Apollo Theater in Harlem. At about the same time she met her idol and muse, Billie Holiday (1915–1959). Two years later Holiday recorded "Dream of Life," a song written by Carmen McRae. Although strongly influenced by Billie Holiday, McRae did not imitate her. McRae had a very recognizable contralto voice and scatted, whereas Holiday did not. McRae was greatly influenced by the bebop instrumentalists, whereas Holiday's influential jazz instrumentalist was Louis Armstrong, who predates the bebop stylists by more than 20 years. Both singers, however, used "blues" shadings in their styles. Additionally, McRae was a great interpreter of many popular standards.

By the mid-1940s McRae had begun her career as a singer, first as a band singer for Benny Carter from 1944 to 1946, and then with Count Basie and Mercer Ellington from 1946 to 1948. After her initial career as a band singer, she moved to Chicago in the late 1940s to begin a solo career. She married and quickly divorced bebop drummer Kenny Clarke in the mid-1940s. Then she returned to New York, where she worked as an intermission singer and pianist at Minton's Playhouse in Harlem, and began recording her music. Her first album, issued in 1954 on the Bethlehem label, garnered her "New Star" honors in *Down Beat* magazine in 1955. She continued recording with Decca for four years but then issued her work on a variety of other labels, large and small, including Kapp, Columbia, Mainstream, Groove Merchant, Catalyst, Blue Note, Buddah, Atlantic, and Concord. The Decca recordings are available on compact disc sets such as *I'll Be Seeing You* (Decca 2647); later McRae recordings are found on *Live: Take Five* (Columbia Special Products 9116), *At the Great American Music Hall* (Blue Note 709), and *Fine and Mellow: Live at Birdland West* (Concord Jazz CCD-4342).

With the support of such jazz critics as Leonard Feather and John Gammond, McRae successfully toured Europe and Asia in the late 1960s and 1970s. She also continued recording and performing in the United States. She received rave reviews for her recordings with the Dave Brubeck Quartet in the 1970s, and again for her *Carmen Sings Monk* album (Jive/Novus 3086-2-N13). A longtime sufferer of asthma, in May 1991 she collapsed while performing at the Blue Note in New York City. She never performed again. She continued in ill health, and following a stroke in October 1994 she died on 10 November 1994 at her home in Beverly Hills, CA.

See also Jazz

For Further Reading

Dahl, Linda. *Stormy Weather: The Music and Lives of a Century of Jazzwomen*. New York: Pantheon Books, 1984.

Friedwald, Will. *Jazz Singing: America's Great Voices from Bessie Smith to Bebop and Beyond*. New York: Scribner, 1990.

Gourse, Leslie. *Louis' Children: American Jazz Singers*. New York: William Morrow, 1984.

Monica J. Burdex

Meet the Composer

A national, not-for-profit organization, Meet the Composer supports the music of living American composers by (1) providing funds for composers of all genres to create new musical pieces, and (2) facilitating direct contact between composers and audiences. The organization was founded in 1974 by the New York State Council on the Arts and New York–born composer John Duffy. The organization also encourages collaborative networks between U.S.-based composers and artists living in and outside the United States, and it creates educational programs that increase public awareness of composers and their work.

Since its inception, the goals of Meet the Composer have been met through a variety of programs. Applications to specific Meet the Composer programs are submitted by a sponsor on behalf of a composer. Eligibility varies by program, and each program has its own application process and deadline. Women composers are well represented on the Board of Directors by Chen Yi (b. 1953) and Julia Wolfe. Additionally, Heather Hitchens, current president of Meet the Composer, and much of the senior staff of Meet the Composer are women.

Meet the Composer Fund (1974–present), the founding program of Meet the Composer, enables composers to interact with audiences at performances of their works. Participation may include performing, conducting, speaking to audiences, presenting workshops, giving interviews, and coaching rehearsals.

Orchestra Residencies Program (1982–1992) was established to strengthen the relationship among American composers, American orchestras, and symphony audiences. During its 10-year history the Orchestra Residencies Program enabled 65 new musical works to be commissioned, 19 musical recordings to be produced, 15,000 scores to be reviewed, and 500 musical works to be commissioned. Following the conclusion of the Orchestra Residencies Program, the New Residencies (1992–present) program was established with the intent of uniting composers, professional arts institutions, and community-based organizations. Within this program, resident composers create musical works that focus on the history and culture of a specific community. Resident composers are also responsible for organizing local cultural events, teaching, and promoting local heritage, in the hopes of creating sustained and direct artistic ties for a community.

Commissioning Music/USA (1996–present), a partnership between Meet the Composer and the National Endowment for the Arts, supports not-for-profit organizations that wish to commission new works by providing funds for composer and librettist commissioning fees and copying costs, as well as assistance in generating support for future commissions. The establishment of the Commissioning Music/USA program was facilitated by two previous Meet the Composer commissioning programs—Meet the Composer/Lila Wallace–Reader's Digest Commissioning Program (1988–1995) and Meet the Composer/Rockefeller Foundation/AT&T Jazz Program (1989–1992).

New Music for Schools (1988–present) supports composer residencies in primary and secondary schools, whereby the composer creates new works for student ensembles and works with teachers, students, and their families.

Music Alive (1999–present) is a nationwide composer residency program designed to bring American orchestras and composers together to boost audience attendance for new music performances. Activities of resident composers include public presentations, collaboration with artistic staffs on new music programming, and preparation for the performances of newly composed works.

Composers who have benefited from the various Meet the Composer programs include Libby Larsen (b. 1950) and Shulamit Ran (b. 1949). Over the course of its history Meet the Composer has received a number of awards, including the Business Committee for the Arts Award, the New York State Governors Award, the American Composers Alliance's Laurel Leaf Award, the American Symphony League's Gold Baton Award, and the Duke Ellington Philanthropy Award.

See also National Endowment for the Arts Composers Program

For Further Reading

Meet the Composer. Available: http://www.meetthecomposer.org

Erin Stapleton-Corcoran

Mendoza, Lydia (1916–)

Guitarist and singer Lydia Mendoza is one of the most outstanding and influential figures in Mexican American music. Dubbed "La Alondra de la Frontera" (the Meadowlark of the Border) and "La Cancionera de los Pobres" (the Songstress of the Poor), she was one of the first Spanish-language vernacular singers and recording stars of the southwestern United States. She toured extensively around the Mexican-U.S. border and other parts of the southwestern United States, performing music for the poor and the working class. Later she became the first Mexican-American woman performer to achieve stardom throughout Latin America.

Born on 21 May 1916 in Houston, TX, Mendoza did not receive formal musical training but grew up in a performing musical family from an impoverished rural background. Music was her family's main means of survival. Mendoza first recorded in 1928 for the Okeh label, performing on the mandolin with her parents and sister under the collective artistic name of Cuarteto Carta Blanca. Later, Mendoza and her family recorded several tracks for Blue Bird Records in 1934. Mendoza was also given the opportunity to record another six solo songs, among them the tango "Mal Hombre" (available on *Mal Hombre and Other Original Hits from the 1930s*, Arhoolie 7002), which became her signature song and a major hit among the migrant labor and working-class people throughout the Spanish-speaking community in the United States. The success of this recording led to a contract with the Bluebird Record label, for which she recorded close to 200 songs between 1934 and 1940. In most of those recordings she accompanied herself on a 12-string guitar. Her first name is consistently spelled "Lidya" on all Bluebird Record label releases from the 1930s. Later releases include *La Gloria de Texas* (Arhoolie CD-3012), *First Queen of Tejano Music* (Arhoolie 392), and *Texas-Mexican Border Music, Vols. 15 and 16* (Arhoolie C-219).

Over her long, groundbreaking career, Mendoza recorded for a great number of labels, including RCA Victor of Mexico, Columbia Records of Mexico, Discos Azteca, Aguila, Colonial, Corona, Globe, Imperial, Ideal, and Falcon, among others. Her repertoire included *corridos*, *canciones rancheras*, *canciones*, *valses*, *sones*, *tangos*, *rumbas*, and *boleros*, among other genres. In 1976 she was featured in Les Blank's border music film classic *Chulas Fronteras*. She performed at the Smithsonian Bicentennial Festival of American Folklife and at the Jimmy Carter presidential inauguration. In 1982 she was one of the first recipients of a National Heritage Fellowship. Mendoza was inducted into the Tejano Music Hall of Fame and the Conjunto Music Hall of Fame. In 1999 she was presented with the National Association for Chicana and Chicano Studies Lifetime Achievement Community Award, and President Clinton presented her the Medal of Arts for her outstanding contributions to the field of music in the United States.

See also Latin American Musicians; Multicultural Musics

For Further Reading

Gil, Carlos B. "Lydia Mendoza: Houstonian and First Lady of Mexican American song." In *Chicano Border: Culture and Folklore*, ed. Jose Villarino. San Diego, CA: Marin Publications, 1992, 181–194.

Mendoza, Lydia. "*La alondra de la frontera*/The Lark at the Border." *In Ethnic Recordings in America: A Neglected Heritage, Studies in American Folk Life*, vol. 1. Washington, DC: American Folklife Center, Library of Congress, 1982, 105–131.

Strachwitz, Chris, and James Nicolopulos. *Lydia Mendoza: A Family Autobiography*. Houston: Arte Público Press, 1993.

Francisco Crespo

Merchant, Natalie (1963–)

Natalie Merchant was the primary lyricist and singer on seven releases by the group 10,000 Maniacs, and she has had continued artistic and commercial success with her two solo albums. Merchant wrote most of the music for the 10,000 Maniacs album *Our Time in Eden* (Elektra 61385-2) and all of the music on her two solo studio albums, *Tigerlily* (Elektra 61745) and *Ophelia* (Elektra/Asylum 62196). She met the musicians that ultimately formed the group 10,000 Maniacs in 1980 at Jamestown Community College (NY). The group released *Human Conflict Number Five* (Mark MC 20247) and *Secrets of the I Ching* (LP Christian Burial Music) on its own independent label before it was signed with Elektra in 1985.

Merchant was born on 26 October 1963 in Jamestown, NY. She graduated from high school at the age of 16 and enrolled at Jamestown Community College. She received an associate degree at age 18, the same year she joined 10,000 Maniacs.

Though the sound of the 10,000 Maniacs subtly evolved over time, it never strayed far from its folk/pop/rock sound. As a lyricist, Merchant wrote about subjects that included child abuse, war, and environmental concerns. Her socially conscious writing, joined with the smooth production values on 10,000 Maniac's fourth album, *In My Tribe* (Elektra 60738-2), helped bring the group its first commercially successful recording. The

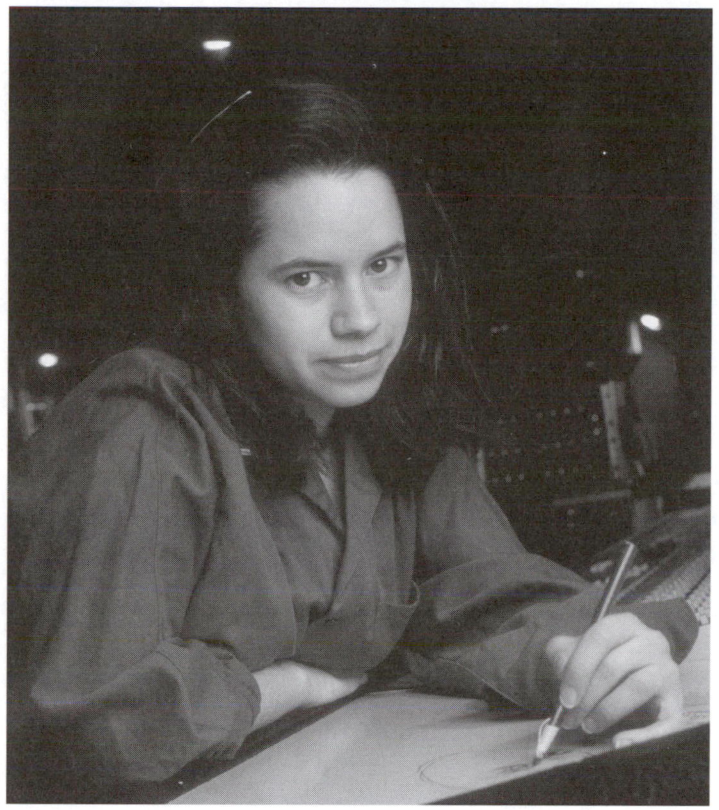

A 1989 photo of Natalie Merchant, former leader sing of the group 10,000 Maniacs. *Photo courtesy of Deborah Feingold/ Archive Photos.*

single "Trouble Me" from the group's fifth album, *Blind Man's Zoo* (Elektra 60815-2), helped the album achieve Gold status. *Our Time in Eden* is notable for the addition of horns and a shift in emphasis from politically and socially relevant lyrics to more personal writing.

In 1993 Merchant left the 10,000 Maniacs and released her first solo album, *Tigerlily*. The album was more sparsely orchestrated than her work with 10,000 Maniacs and relied more on her piano playing for textural backing. The single "Carnival" helped the album break into the Top 20. In her album, *Ophelia* (1998), Merchant created numerous personas for the title character.

See also Rock and Popular Music Genres; Singer-Songwriter

For Further Reading

AMG: All Music Guide. Available: http://allmusic.com

O'Dair, Barbara (ed.). *Trouble Girls: The Rolling Stone Book of Women in Rock*. New York: Random House, 1997.

Garth Alper

Merman, Ethel (1909–1984)

Ethel Merman was one of the most celebrated entertainers and denizens of the Broadway stage. Her legendary theatrical style, punctuated by a loud, gutsy voice,

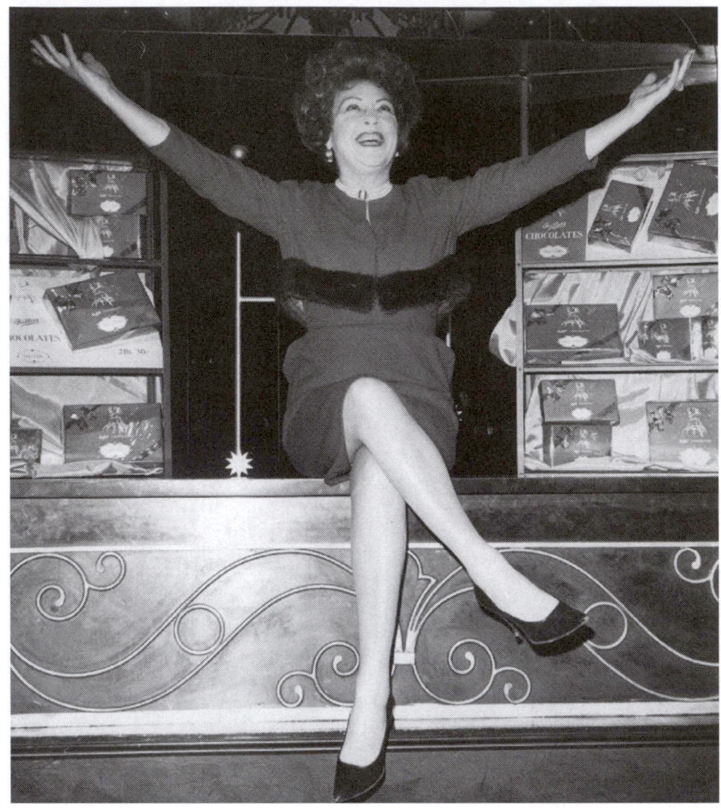

Ethel Merman in February 1964. *Photo courtesy of Hulton/Archive.*

earned her a lasting legacy in her field of entertainment.

Born in Astoria, NY, as Ethel Agnes Zimmermann on 16 January 1909, Merman was singing in the Brooklyn Paramount Nightclub when she was discovered by producer Vinton Freedley. He signed her for the Broadway production of the George Gershwin's *Girl Crazy* (1930). Merman was so successful in her role and her rendition of "I've Got Rhythm" that the song became forever associated with her.

Successive accolades followed for two years after her Broadway debut, with *Scandals* (1931), where she starred with Rudy Vallee, and *Take a Chance* (1932). Beginning in 1934, Merman was cast in the starring roles for five successful Cole Porter shows. The first, *Anything Goes*, subsequently led to her being cast for the film version of the show in which she co-starred with Bing Crosby. Merman joined Bob Hope and Jimmy Durante to star in Cole Porter's *Red, Hot, and Blue!* (1936), followed by the Porter shows *DuBarry Was a Lady* (1939), *Panama Hattie* (1940), and *Something for the Boys* (1943).

In 1946, Merman was cast as Annie Oakley in Irving Berlin's *Annie Get Your Gun* (MCAD-10047). Her longest-running Broadway musical, *Annie Get Your Gun* had 1,147 performances. The show's "There's No Business Like Show Business" became yet another song inextricably associated with Merman throughout her career. Her second Berlin show, *Call Me Madame* ([1950] MCAD-10521), like *Anything Goes*, was later made into a film (1953). Merman was cast for the film along with Donald O'Connor, Vera-Ellen, and George Sanders.

Jule Styne's and Stephen Sondheim's score of *Gypsy* (1959) provided Merman the vehicle and the challenge to make her performance as the overbearing stage mother, Mama Rose, the pinnacle of her career. Following *Gypsy* she performed in a replacement engagement in *Hello, Dolly!* and a short revival of *Annie Get Your Gun*. After these performances Merman left the Broadway musical stage.

Merman was cast in a number of Hollywood movies, some of which were filmed during her Broadway stage career. Prior to her film version of *Anything Goes*, Merman appeared in *We're Not Dressing* (1934) and *Kid Millions* and *Strike Me Pink*, both produced in 1935 starring with Eddie Cantor. She was cast in *Alexander's Ragtime Band* (1938) with Don Ameche, Alice Faye, and Tyrone Power. In 1954 she co-starred with Dan Dailey, Donald O'Connor, and Marilyn Monroe in *There's No Business Like Show Business*.

Although the aforementioned were all singing roles, Merman also appeared in films that were not musical comedies. She had non-singing roles in *It's a Mad, Mad, Mad, Mad World* (1963), *The Art of Love* (1965), and *Airplane* (1980). She also appeared in television shows and specials. Notable was her performance with Mary Martin (1913–1990) for the Ford 50th Anniversary Show, a portion of which was released for sale on the Decca record label. Merman also recorded a two-volume work for Decca entitled *Musical Autobiography* (Dxl-153). She also had an ancillary career as a recording artist. Along with hit numbers from her various Broadway shows, Merman recorded four duets with Ray Bolger and some solo songs, including the very successful "How Deep Is the Ocean" and "Move It Over." Her final major performance was in 1982 at a Carnegie Hall benefit. Ethel Merman died on 15 February 1984.

See also Musical Theater

For Further Reading

Bryan, George B. *Ethel Merman: A Bio-Bibliography*. Bio-Bibliographies in the Performing Arts, No. 27. New York: Greenwood Press, 1992.

Merman, Ethel, and George Eells. *Merman*. New York: Simon & Schuster, 1978.

Merman, Ethel, and Pete Martin. *Who Could Ask for Anything More*? Garden City, NY: Doubleday, 1955.

Suzanne L. Gertig

Mid-America Arts Alliance

See Organizations, Regional Arts

Mid-Atlantic Arts Foundation

See Organizations, Regional Arts

Midler, Bette (1945–)

From her 1966 New York debut as Tzeitel in *Fiddler on the Roof* to her 1999 *The Divine Miss Millennium Tour*, Bette Midler continues her career as a singer, actress, and sometimes outrageous comedian. In additional roles of author and activist, she has written two books and founded an urban renewal effort, the New York Restoration Project. Midler's best-selling book, *A View from a Broad* (1980), chronicling her world *Divine Madness* tour, and *The Saga of Baby Divine* (1982), a children's book, are both out of print.

Born on 1 December 1945 in Patterson, NJ, but raised in Hawaii, Midler

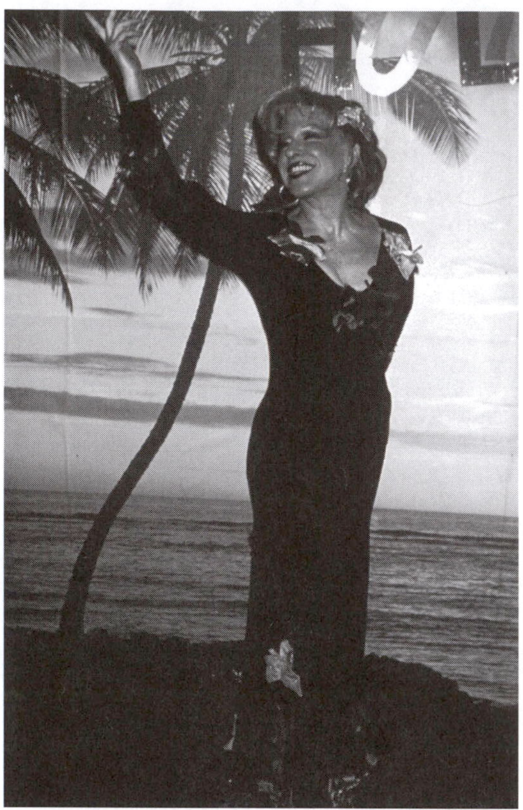

Bette Midler at the "Hula-ween" fundraiser in New York City in October 2000. *Photo courtesy of John Barrett/Globe Photos.*

studied theater at the University of Hawaii before moving to New York. After leaving *Fiddler on the Roof* she launched her career in a somewhat unlikely venue, singing to gay men dressed in bath towels at the Continental Baths in Manhattan. Midler's bizarre cabaret incorporating rock, blues, torch songs, and other novelties resulted in more mixed audiences being allowed in to experience the show. From this point until the early 1980s her career flourished, with frequent New York appearances, a contract with Atlantic records, and a Grammy Award for her debut album, *The Divine Miss M* (Atlantic SD-7238-2). Her performance in the 1979 film *The Rose* (a fictional account of Janis Joplin's life) resulted in an Oscar nomination, with the title track becoming a Top 10 hit.

In 1982 her career sagged with a box office disaster and subsequent nervous breakdown. She married Martin Von Haselberg in 1984 and signed on with the Walt Disney Studios for a strong comeback with the movie *Down and Out in Beverly Hills* (1986). Instead of touring, for the next 10 years she threw her seemingly limitless energy into a series of uproarious comedy movies: *Ruthless People* (1986), *Outrageous Fortune* (1987), and *Big Business* (1988). In the early 1990s Midler revived her musical career with *Experience the Divine*, a three-hour Radio City Music Hall stage show extravaganza. In October 1999 Midler embarked on her 31-city *The Divine Miss Millennium Tour*, including performances of past hits such as "From a Distance" (from *Some People's Lives*, Atlantic 82129-2), "The Rose"(Atlantic 82778), and "Wind beneath My Wings" (Atlantic 84896).

Over the course of her virtuosic career as an entertainer, to date Midler has won four Golden Globe Awards, four Grammy Awards, two Emmy Awards, and a Tony Award. Her broadly based, out-of-control comedy features spectacularly unexpected shocks. According to entertainment columnist Liz Smith, "her greatest talent is the ability to use her voice to convey any emotion, to make you laugh out loud, and weep with remembered pleasure and pain. Nobody, but nobody sings anything at all like Bette Midler" (The Official Bette Midler Site, 2000).

See also Rock and Popular Music Genres

For Further Reading

Mair, George. *Bette: An Intimate Biography of Bette Midler*. Secaucus, NJ: Carol Publishing, Group, 1995.

O'Dair, Barbara (ed.). *Trouble Girls: The Rolling Stone Book of Women in Rock*. New York: Random House, 1997.

Yahoo! Presents: The Official Bette Midler Site. Available: http://promotions.yahoo.com/promotions/bette/

Anita Hanawalt

Military Music

As long as there have been military forces, there have been military musicians and military music. From the ancient mariners who used drums and singing to synchronize oarsmen to the ceremonial brass of Rome; from reveille that begins a soldier's workday, to taps that sounds as comrades are buried: music has always been an integral part of military life. At its inception the American military borrowed the tradition of bands and their duties from the English. Individual regiments maintained their own musicians according to the regiment's needs, desires, and financial resources, subject to local command. Buglers signaled daily activities such as wake-up, inspection, meal times, lights out, and so on. Drummers and fifers regulated marching. Some units also supported dance bands for entertainment and to perform for visiting dignitaries.

Today, although the mission statement of each branch's bands varies somewhat, its components are essentially the same: support military ceremonies, enhance morale, promote a positive image, and improve international relations. To accomplish this, the Army, Navy, Air Force, and Marine Corps maintain a network of bands at locations throughout the United States and overseas, with premiere groups at their respective academies and around the nation's capitol. Additionally, the Navy and the Air Force also sponsor North Atlantic Treaty Organization (NATO) bands, comprised of musicians from other countries as well as Americans. After almost two centuries, all band programs are now open to women musicians who meet the requirements for military service.

Introducing women into Army bands followed the typical pattern of first serving in auxiliary status. In 1943 the 400th, 401st, 402nd, 403rd, and 404th Army Bands were completely staffed by members of the Women's Army Corps (WAC). The 14th Army Band at Fort McClellan remained an all-women unit until 1975. Because of previous WAC designations, it is difficult to pinpoint when the first women enlisted in full standing. But in 1977 the Army commissioned two women to serve as bandmasters: Nancy Bodenhammer and Ginny Allen. With the logistical difficulties of shipboard travel, the Navy's inclusion of women took longer to implement. Evangeline Bailey Taylor first enlisted as a musician in 1972. Because Navy bandmasters are promoted from within, there was also a lag until a woman candidate reached an eligible rank. Lorelei Conrad became the fleet's first woman bandmaster in 1991. Branching off from the Army around World War II, the Air Force also initially had women serving with, rather than in, its ranks. Karen Erler entered the premiere Concert Band in 1972; there may have been two women in regional bands prior to this date. In 1980 Melinda Richards became the first woman commander of a regional band. Amy Mills served as commander/conductor of the premiere band from 1990–91. The Marine Corps Band admitted its first woman member in 1973. The Coast Guard, which falls under the jurisdiction of the Navy during wartime, differs from the other branches in maintaining only one band in New Haven, CT. In 1974 Constance Coghlan enlisted. There have been no women bandmasters to date.

See also Performer, Brass

For Further Reading

Gender Gap and the Military. Available: http://www.gendergap.com/military/Warriors.HTM.

Wadsworth, Cherilee. "Being a Female Composer in the U.S. Navy." *IAWM Journal* 3/2 (1997): 10–12.

———. "Musicians, ahoy!" *Triad* 62/6 (1995): 27–28.

Cherilee Wadsworth Walker

Minnelli, Liza (1946–)

Since her screen debut before she was three years old, singer, dancer, and theater and movie actress Liza Minnelli continues as a leading world entertainer. Her famous parents—Judy Garland (1922–1969) and Vincente Minnelli—divorced in the early 1950s and told Minnelli that she would have to build her career on her own. Based in New York City, she proceeded to do just that, traveling with touring productions and winning a recording contract with Capitol Records for her debut album, *Liza! Liza!* (Capitol ST-2174). At age 19 she became the youngest actress to win a Tony Award, for her Broadway debut in *Flora, the Red Menace* (RCA 60821).

Born on 12 March 1946, Minnelli gave serious consideration to other career possibilities but started apprenticing in musical theater by age 16. After she became the only singer to sell out Carnegie Hall for three weeks straight, her skills as a singer and vocal interpreter confirmed her status as an artist in her own right. Her skilled dramatic portrayals of social

Liza Minnelli during a 1972 performance at the London Palladium before Queen Elizabeth and Prince Philip. *Photo courtesy of Hulton/Archive.*

outcast characters in films such as *Charlie Bubbles* (1967), *The Sterile Cuckoo* (1969), and *Tell Me That You Love Me, Junie Moon* (1970) confirmed her consistently solid acting abilities. From 1967 to 1972 Minnelli was married to entertainer Peter Allen.

In 1972 she won an Academy Award for *Cabaret* and an Emmy Award for her television special *Liza with a Z*. From 1974 to 1979 Minnelli was married to producer Jack Haley Jr. Further dramatic roles included *New York, New York* (1977) and the *Arthur* films with Dudley Moore in the 1980s. The Broadway musical *The Act* ([1977] Allegiance 90329) won Minnelli another Tony Award, but she collapsed from exhaustion during its run. Later, rumors about substance abuse circulated in the press, though Minnelli returned to perform on Broadway in *The Rink* ([1984] Jay 1328), earning another Tony nomination. She dropped out of that show to seek treatment for substance abuse at the Betty Ford Clinic. Coming back in 1985, she performed a sold-out concert at the London Palladium and won a Golden Globe Award for Best Actress for *A Time to Live*. From 1979 to 1992 she was married to stage manager and sculptor Mark Gero.

In the late 1980s Minnelli substituted for Dean Martin in a series of live concerts with Frank Sinatra and Sammy Davis Jr., both of whom she had known since birth. She also filled in for Julie Andrews in the Broadway show *Victor/Victoria* in 1997. In 1994 she had hip replacement surgery, after living and performing in pain for 10 years. Her substance abuse problems could well have been exacerbated by coping with this pain. In 1999 Minnelli still reported battling substance abuse problems, though she continued her career in music and film and even opened a new Broadway show, *Minnelli on Minnelli* ([2000] Angel 24905).

See also Academy Awards

For Further Reading

Larkin, Colin (ed.). *The Encyclopedia of Popular Music*. London: MUZE UK, Ltd., 1998.

Luft, Lorna. *Me and My Shadows: Living with the Legacy of Judy Garland*. New York: Pocket Books, 1998.

Anita Hanawalt

Minnesota Composers Forum

See American Composers Forum

Miranda, Carmen (1909–1955)

Prominent singer and actress Carmen Miranda settled in the United States in 1939, where she captivated audiences for more than a decade with her sparkling personality, delightful “stiletto-staccato” singing style, and characteristic samba dancing. Miranda’s hallmark costume included “tutti-frutti” turbans, platform sandals, and exotic dresses, which during the 1940s helped transform her into a stereotyped symbol of the Latin American women in Broadway shows and Hollywood movies. Singing mostly in Portuguese, Miranda brought a large repertory of Brazilian sambas to the United States, becoming the first to internationalize Brazilian popular music.

Born on 9 February 1909 in Marco de Canaveses, Portugal, and raised in Rio de Janeiro, Brazil, Miranda grew up in Rio de Janeiro, where she started singing while still a child. Owing to her family’s financial problems, Miranda started work as a salesgirl in a hat shop at age 15. During this time she also sang at her mother’s restaurant, entertaining customers alongside other popular musi-

Carmen Miranda in a publicity photo for the 1946 film *If I'm Lucky*. *Photo courtesy of Frank Driggs Collection.*

cians. In 1929 Miranda met Josué de Barros, who became her friend and mentor and introduced her to influential people at radio stations and recording studios.

Miranda's first recording came out in 1930 in Brazil, followed by her first hit, "Taí (P'ra você gostar de mim)," recorded by Victor for the 1930 Carnival season. Starting in 1933 she took part in five Brazilian films, but it was in *Banana da terra* (1938), produced by the North American Wallace Downey, that she first appeared in the *bahiana* outfit with the fruit-bearing turban, stereotyping the black women of the northeast Brazilian state of Bahia.

In 1939, while performing in Rio de Janeiro's nightclub Casino da Urca, Miranda was spotted by Lee Shubert, who signed her to sing in his Broadway musical *The Streets of Paris* (1939). Miranda left Brazil in May 1939 and started a career in the United States that rapidly took her to an unexpected stardom. Always accompanied by her own band, the Bando da Lua (The Moon Gang), Miranda immediately captivated U.S. audiences, singing Brazilian popular songs and other hits such as "South American Way." She had roles in no fewer than 14 U.S. films, mostly Technicolor musicals, including *Down Argentine Way* (1940), *That Night in Rio* (1941), *Weekend in Havana* (1941), *Spring Time in the Rockies* (1942), *The Gang Is All Here* (1943),

Greenwich Village (1944), and *Something for the Boys* (1944). By 1944 Miranda was the best-paid woman in U.S. show business.

In 1940 Miranda returned to Rio de Janeiro but was disappointed when Brazilian audiences accused her of having become too "Americanized." She then returned to the United States and settled in Hollywood, where in 1945 she married David Sebastian, the producer of her last film, *Copacabana* (1947). In 1954 a busy performance schedule and an unhappy marriage drove Miranda to a nervous breakdown. She fled to Brazil in that year to recover her health and to be among former friends and family. Miranda returned to Hollywood in 1955, where she died on 5 August 1955 of a heart attack at age 46.

There are several recordings of Miranda's most popular songs, including *Carmen Miranda* (Milan 052424), *South American Way* (Saludos Amigos 62063), and *The Lady in the Tutti Frutti Hat* (Harlequin 133). Carmen Miranda's last U.S. appearance was on the *Jimmy Durante Show*, where her performance lacked the joviality of previous years. However, Miranda's image remains to this day as one of the hottest Latin exports who fulfilled with vigor and pride her role in the U.S. "Good Neighbor" propaganda of the early 1940s.

See also Latin American Musicians; Multicultural Musics

For Further Reading

Consiglio, Dulce Damasceno de Brito. *O ABC de Carmen Miranda*. São Paulo: Companhia Editora Nacional, 1986.

Gil-Montero, Martha. *Brazilian Bombshell: The Biography of Carmen Miranda*. New York: D. I. Fine, 1989.

Saia, Luiz Henrique. *Carmen Miranda*. São Paulo: Brasiliense, 1984.

Cristina Magaldi

Mitchell, Joni (1943–)

Three decades of bold and varied work have established Joni Mitchell as one of the most enduring and influential singer-songwriters in American popular music. From the intimate imagery of her early songs to the experimentation of her jazz excursions, she has followed a fiercely personal trail. Her 19 albums have won critical acclaim, chart success, and Grammy Awards. Yet her deepest significance may be found more in the general impact of her music than in her specific achievements. Her guitar tunings, which initially seemed strange, are basic to any guitarist's technique today. Her use of the piano as a "folk" instrument has been widely adopted. Her attention to poetry, approaching an art song sensibility, is echoed in the text-centered songs of many current songwriters.

Born Roberta Joan Anderson in Western Canada on 7 November 1943, she grew up dancing to Ray Charles records, singing in the church choir, and learning folk songs from the early Judy Collins (b. 1939) albums. Mitchell taught herself guitar for fun but went to college to major in art. As she began singing at folk music clubs during her freshman year, her focus turned away from art classes. After performing (as Joni Anderson) at the Mariposa Folk Festival in 1965, she remained in Toronto, developed a following there, and married American folksinger Chuck Mitchell. The couple moved to Detroit; in 1967, after their marriage ended, Joni moved to New York to pursue a solo career.

In 1968 Mitchell's startlingly original first album, *Song to a Seagull* (Reprise 6293), was released on Reprise Records. The lyrics were introspective and autobiographical, and the cover featured

Joni Mitchell, posing with her guitar as part of a *Vogue* magazine photo shoot in November 1968. *Photo courtesy of Jack Robinson/Archive Photos.*

Mitchell's artwork. Her clean and elaborate guitar playing highlighted her trademark open tunings, and her melodic lines soared across an unusually wide range. The highly original poetry and artwork, technical mastery, and boldness of gesture in her first album have remained hallmarks of Mitchell's work.

Several artists recorded covers of Mitchell's songs, but it was Judy Collins's 1968 chart success with the single "Both Sides Now" that brought Mitchell national exposure. Mitchell's own version of "Both Sides Now" appeared later on her 1969 album, *Clouds* (Reprise 2-6341).

Mitchell released a new album almost every year until 1982, when her pace started to slow. Her 1971 album, *Blue* (Reprise 2-2038), has drawn particularly positive response and is still considered by many to be her best work. Several of her later albums feature collaborations with jazz musicians such as Tom Scott and Charles Mingus. Her 1975 album, *The Hissing of Summer Lawns* (Asylum 2-1051), features a song in which her vocals unfold over Burundi drumming, years before any general interest in world music had arisen. As her work moved in such unexpected directions, Mitchell sometimes had to weather negative response from both critics and fans.

In the 1990s Mitchell enjoyed renewed success, including two Grammy Awards for her 1994 album, *Turbulent Indigo* (Warner Brothers 45786). She continues to write fresh songs, as other artists continue to enjoy chart success with their own recordings of her songs from years past. In 1995 Mitchell was awarded *Billboard* magazine's Century Award, given for "the uncommon excellence of one artist's still-unfolding body of work."

See also Rock and Popular Music Genres; Singer-Songwriter; Songwriter

For Further Reading

Briscoe, James R. *Contemporary Anthology of Music by Women*. Bloomington: Indiana University Press, 1997.

The Joni Mitchell Homepage. Available: http://www.JoniMitchell.com/

O'Dair, Barbara. (ed.). *The Rolling Stone Book of Women in Rock: Trouble Girls*. New York: Random House, 1997.

Kathleen Pierson

Miyamoto, Nobuko Joanne (1939–)

A Sansei (third-generation Japanese American), Nobuko Miyamoto has been a driving force in the Asian American arts since the early 1970s. Her work as a dancer, composer, performance artist, and producer has consistently addressed the politics of ethnicity in the United States.

Born on 14 November 1939 and trained as a dancer, Miyamoto appeared in such Orientalist classics as *The King and I*, *Flower Drum Song*, and *Kismet*; she also appeared as a Puerto Rican in the movie *West Side Story*, one of the few times she broke the color line. In New York City during the 1960s and 1970s, Miyamoto was deeply involved in the civil rights and antiwar movements and developed her guiding belief in the power of the arts to transform self and society. In the 1970s she was swept up in the emergent Asian American movement and collaborated extensively with musicians Chris Iijima and Charlie Chin. Their album, *A Grain of Sand* (1973, Paredon; 1997, Bindu reissue), now part of the Smithsonian Institution collection, has been regarded as a seminal work of Asian American music; it includes such original songs as "Yellow Pearl," "Warriors of the Rainbow," "Somos Asiaticos (We are Asians)," and "Free the Land."

In 1975 Miyamoto left New York and returned to her native Los Angeles, where in 1978 she founded Great Leap, Inc., a nonprofit arts organization dedicated to the promotion of multicultural awareness. Originally based at Senshin Buddhist Temple, Great Leap has been explicitly community-based from its inception and received the President's Award from the Los Angeles Human Relations Commission in 1998, recognizing 20 years of artistic activity with a focus on interethnic awareness. Great Leap has been the home base for A Slice of Rice, Frijoles, and Greens, a troupe of Asian American, Latino, and African American performance artists who tour extensively. In 1995 Miyamoto developed *A Grain of Sand*, her one-woman performance artwork incorporating video, slides, song, stories, and dance. Intensely autobiographical, the show focuses on Miyamoto's political and artistic work during the 1960s and 1970s and incorporates many of her songs from the album of the same name. It is a centrally important work in Asian American women's performance art.

Miyamoto's ties to Senshin Buddhist Temple inspired a series of songs written for Bon Odori, a Japanese Buddhist traditional song/dance performed in the summer. These songs are the first written in English for Japanese American Buddhists. The song/dance "Yuiyo" (1984), the first in the series, was featured in the film *Karate Kid II* (1986). *Gaman*, a short film shown on PBS, was created around a song Miyamoto wrote about a child growing up in a Japanese concentration camp during World War II.

Miyamoto has also written several other musical theater works, including *Joanne Is My Middle Name* (1990), *Talk Story, I and II* (1987–1989), and *Chop Suey* (1980–1981) (composed with Benny Yee), and two solo albums, *To All Relations* (1997, Bindu Records) and *Best of Both Worlds* (1985, Great Leap). Whether dramatic, musical, or both, her work is consistently accessible and proactive and is based on an Asian American sensibility developed through close and continued contact with African American, Latino, and Native American activism and the arts.

See also Asian American Music; Multicultural Musics

For Further Reading

Nobuko's home page at Bindu Records. Available: http://bindurecords.com/nobuko/

Deborah Wong

Monk, Meredith (1942–)

Meredith Monk creates music and art on the edges of several media. Her goal has always been to produce art that blends theater, movement, and music into a unified form. She was among the first to successfully combine film with live performance, and she has won many awards, including two Guggenheim fellowships and the prestigious MacArthur fellowship.

Monk was born on 20 November 1942 in New York City into a family of singers. In 1964 she graduated from Sarah Lawrence College, where she had studied dance under Bessie Shoenberg. She was a frequent presenter at Judson Church in New York City, a focal point for experimental interdisciplinary art during the late 1960s. She later incorporated singing into her pieces and developed a style that connected movement and sound in a very direct and personal manner. For Monk, there seems to be no distinction between singing and moving.

Over time she has developed a highly individualized vocabulary of sounds that draws on African and Asian singing styles and extended vocal techniques such as ululation, nasal resonance, chirps, yips, yodels, and howls. *Light Songs* (1988) features Monk humming at the same time as she produces clicking sounds with her teeth and tongue. This distinctive approach includes the adaptation of traditional Western European forms (opera, requiem, and oratorio) to suit her individual needs. Monk frequently dismisses text in favor of a chant-like vocalise based on vowel sounds and vocal percussive effects. When words are used, they are most often ambiguous and impressionistic rather than rationally narrative.

In the late 1970s Monk formed The House ensemble to perform her work. She sought ways to emphasize the qualities and character of each voice without establishing a style to which the other must adhere. With the ensemble, she was able to explore a wider range of possibilities through the interaction of different voices. An early work for the ensemble was *Dolmen Music* (ECM New Series, CD, 78118-21197-2).

Although Monk's works often seem rather abstract, they do deal with specific ideas and content. She frequently addresses themes of spirituality and revelation. The characters in many pieces are driven by mystical visions. Joan of Arc was the subject of *Vessel* (1971). *Book of Days* features a young Jewish girl in a medieval village who sees images of the future such as planes, bombs, and people using cameras. In *Atlas: An Opera in Three Parts* (ECM New Series, CD

Meredith Monk. *Photo courtesy of Massimo Agus.*

78118-21491-2), an explorer goes on a quest to seek the unknown only to find meaning, in the end, in the mundane activities of her everyday life.

Monk produced several film works during the 1980s. *Ellis Island* (1981), *Paris* (1982), and *Book of Days* (1988) were elaborate productions that also included musical scores written for voices and various combinations of instruments. Monk also addresses contemporary social issues, albeit metaphorically. *Ellis Island* depicted the "cataloguing" of Eastern European immigrants entering America during the nineteenth century. *Book of Days* presented a story of how Jews were blamed for plagues that occurred in the Dark Ages. In both instances Monk selected tales that serve as allegories for current concerns such as racism and AIDS.

See also Experimental Music; Music Technology; Performance Art

For Further Reading

Banes, Sally et al. *Art Performs Life: Merce Cunningham / Meredith Monk / Bill T. Jones*. Minneapolis, MN: Walker Art Center, 1998.

Jowitt, Deborah (ed.). *Meredith Monk*. Baltimore and London: Johns Hopkins University Press, 1997.

Jeffery Byrd

Monsour, Sally A. (1929–)

Sally Monsour is well known for her national and international contributions to music education, having been at the forefront of significant developments in the profession over the course of her 45-year teaching career. She was one of four music education consultants to the 1962 Juilliard Repertory Project; primary team member for the 1979 Ann Arbor Symposium; author of computer software programs for primary age students; and researcher, author, and clinician in teaching general music and music with multicultural content and perspectives (Middle Eastern emphasis) from 1965 to 1995.

Born in Valentine, NE, in 1929, Monsour holds degrees from Manhattanville College and Teachers College, Columbia University in New York (M.A. 1952) and the University of Michigan (D.Ed. in music and education 1959). It is her excellence as a teacher of teachers for which she is best remembered. Guided by the philosophies of her teachers James Mursell and Lilla Belle Pitts (1884–1970) at Columbia University (1950–1952), Marguerite Hood (1903–1992), and Allen Britton at the University of Michigan (1954–1959), Sally Monsour's teaching practice is rooted in the belief that "there are innumerable positive benefits from a life enhanced by musical participation on any level and at any age; music should be for all and not only for the few." Monsour taught general and choral music in the primary and secondary schools of Winter Park, FL, and Ann Arbor, MI, and has held faculty positions at Rollins College (FL), the University of Michigan, the University of Colorado at Boulder, and Georgia State University. The challenge of developing a graduate degree program in music education took her to Georgia State, where she served as professor of music and education from 1970 until her retirement in 1995.

Sally Monsour has visited 85 colleges, universities, and school districts as curriculum consultant, workshop clinician, and lecturer, and she has presented workshops at more than 60 state, regional, national, and international music education conferences. She has served as a visiting professor at the University of Hawaii Conservatory of Music, in Sydney (Australia), and at several Canadian universities.

Monsour has authored or co-authored more than 10 books, including *A Junior High School Music Handbook*, *Music in Recreation and Leisure*, and *Songs of the Middle East*. She has published nearly 20 articles, was a contributing author of *Sing!* choral text, and created teaching strategies for *Sounds of the World* (Persia, Arab, Turkey) and an audiotape lecture in the *Voice of Experience Series* "Viewing Music Education in a Global context," both for the Music Educators National Conference (MENC).

In 1987 Monsour was named "Trendsetter in Music Education" by the Colorado Music Educators Association, and in 1989 she was designated a distinguished doctoral recipient by the University of Michigan Graduate School. Retirement has not slowed down this trendsetter in general music education. Sally Monsour's spirit of sharing "who we are and the talents we've been given" continues into her retirement, which finds her traveling to underdeveloped countries to help native people with organic farming and building schools on behalf of the Global Volunteers organization.

See also Music Education

For Further Reading

Department of Public Relations, Georgia State University. "Sally Monsour Biography." Atlanta: Georgia State University, Department of Public Relations, 2000.

Monsour, Sally, and Margaret Perry. *A Junior High School Music Handbook*. Englewood Cliffs, NJ: Prentice-Hall, 1963.

Kathy M. Robinson

Montaner, Rita (1900–1958)

A most versatile Cuban vocalist, Rita Montaner was internationally recognized for her interpretation of Cuban music during four decades beginning in the 1920s. She combined her outstanding musical and dramatic talents, personal charm, and beauty as she performed in opera and *zarzuela*, film and theater, and the popular genres of Afro-Cuban music.

Born on 29 August 1900 in Guanabacoa, near Havana, Rita Montaner began piano lessons at age four and later received vocal training. By 1919 she was singing for charity events in Havana cultural institutions, and in 1922 she sang in the first broadcasts of Cuban radio. In the 1920s Montaner appeared on the principal stages of Havana, singing operatic arias and Cuban *zarzuelas*, notably Ernesto Lecuona's *Niña Rita*, in which she sang what would become the international hit "Ay Mamá Inés" (available on Musica Latina CD55028). She popularized other Cuban tunes such as "Siboney" and "The Peanut Vendor."

Montaner traveled to New York in 1927, where she worked with the Shubert Follies review, and again in 1928 when she made her first recordings. In the next few years she traveled extensively, again to New York and several times to Paris, where she performed at the Palace Theater, with the Josephine Baker show and the Follies Bergère. In the United States she appeared in Al Jolson's musical production *The Wonder Bar* in 1931.

In the late 1930s and early 1940s Rita Montaner maintained an intense pace singing and recording Cuban popular songs, appearing in opera and *zarzuela* in Havana, and taking a leading role in a number of films, while continuing to tour extensively throughout Latin America. With the development of the sumptuous nightlife of Havana in the 1940s, she became one of the star attractions and the featured artist at the famed Tropicana Cabaret. Montaner returned to New York in the late 1940s to sing with the accompaniment of the Xavier Cugat orchestra. In the 1950s she remained active in Havana theaters, and with the advent of television to Cuba in the early 1950s she sang and performed successfully in the new medium.

In a career spanning four decades, Rita Montaner excelled as a vocalist in opera, *zarzuela*, and popular Cuban music. She possessed superb voice and acting ability and an engaging personality. Montaner became a national institution in Cuba where she was universally admired and loved by the mass public. In the United States she helped spread the sounds of Cuban and Latin American music in the 1920s and 1930s. With the Shubert Follies review she sang Spanish songs in a nationwide tour that took her to every state in the Union. In the early 1930s her recording of "The Peanut Vendor" became immensely popular. The tune became a national hit and was interpreted by numerous U.S. artists, notably jazz trumpetist Louis Armstrong. Furthermore, Montaner's *zarzuela* performances and recordings had a lasting impact on the small but durable *zarzuela* and Spanish opera public in New York and other major U.S. cities.

See also Latin American Musicians; Multicultural Musics

For Further Reading

Muguercia, Alberto, and Ezequiel Rodríguez. *Rita Montaner*. Cubana, La Habana: Editorial Letras, 1984.

Raúl Fernández

Moore, Undine Smith (1904–1989)

Best known for her choral compositions, Undine Smith Moore experienced teaching as an art, with a valuable reciprocal relationship to composition. Though Moore is best known for her shorter choral works, such as *Lord, We Give Thanks to Thee* (1971), *Daniel, Daniel, Servant of the Lord* (1952), and *The Lamb* (1958), she also wrote extended cantatas and an oratorio, *Scenes from the Life of a Martyr*, which premiered in 1982, based on the life of Martin Luther King Jr., which was nominated for a Pulitzer Prize in 1981. Her best-known instrumental compositions are the *Afro-American Suite* (1969) for flute, cello, and piano, and *Soweto* (1987) for violin, cello, and piano, written in memory of the South African massacre at Soweto township in 1976.

Born on 25 August 1904 in Jarrat, VA, Moore began private piano study at age five with Lillian Allen Darder, a graduate of Fisk University. At Darder's encouragement Moore also enrolled at Fisk, graduating in 1926. She earned an M.A. at Teachers College, Columbia, in 1931, with additional study at the Manhattan School of Music and the Eastman School of Music. Most of Moore's extensive teaching career was spent at Virginia State College, Petersburg (1927–1971), although she also taught at Virginia Union University, the College of St. Benedict, St. John's College, and Carlton College. Moore's compositional career began through her desire to fulfill the needs of Virginia State College's laboratory school chorus. From 1969 to 1972 she co-founded with Alton Trent Johns the Black Music Center of Virginia State College. After retiring from Virginia State College in 1972, Moore remained active as a teacher, composer, lecturer, and consultant until her death on 6 February 1989.

Recordings include *The Negro Speaks of Rivers* (Musicians Showcase 1011) and *Art Songs by Black American Composers* (University of Michigan Records, SM 0015). Honorary doctorates were conferred on Moore in 1972 by Virginia State College and in 1976 by Indiana University. Her association with the Afro-American Arts Institute at Indiana University was a strong motivating force in her life. Moore's visit to West Africa, including slave-trading centers in Senegal and Ghana, was also a strong formative influence. Her many awards include the National Association of Negro Musicians Distinguished Achievement Award (1975); the proclamation of Undine Smith Moore Day on 13 April 1975 by the mayor of Petersburg, VA; and the Governor's Award in the Arts. She was also a cultural laureate for the State of Virginia. Moore taught many musicians at Virginia State University who went on to achieve national prominence. Her wide circle of influence also included students seeking less prestigious, yet vital, musical leadership positions in smaller communities.

See also African-American Musicians; Classical Music

For Further Reading

Baker, David N., Lidea M. Belt, and Herman C. Hudson (eds.). *The Black Composer Speaks*. Metuchen, NJ, and London: Scarecrow Press, 1978.

Walker-Hill, Helen. *Piano Music by Black Women Composers: A Catalog of Solo and Ensemble Works*. Westport, CT: Greenwood Press, 1992.

Anita Hanawalt

Moorman, Charlotte (1933–1991)

Charlotte Moorman was a cellist who specialized in nontraditional performance techniques. Her experimental work explored the ways in which the specific characteristics of the performer (dress, setting, manner) can influence the content of the music.

Charlotte Moorman in concert in 1964. *Photo by Peter Moore. © Est. Peter Moore/Vaga, New York, NY.*

Moorman grew up in Little Rock, AR, and was classically trained at the University of Texas and at the Juilliard School. She eventually became a member of the American Symphony Orchestra under the direction of Leopold Stokowski. After growing tired of playing the standard classical selections, Moorman discovered the work of John Cage and other experimental composers, including video art pioneer Nam Jun Paik, who became her frequent collaborator. Both were associated with the Fluxus movement that flourished internationally during the 1960s and 1970s.

In Paik, Moorman found a kindred spirit with a passion for new and progressive ideas about music and performance. This common interest fueled an intense and prolific working relationship that lasted for many years. Paik wrote several pieces that symbolically attacked the Western musical tradition, including *Violin with String* (1961), which required the performer to drag the instrument on the street, and *One for Violin Solo* (1962), which demanded that the instrument be completely smashed.

Paik wrote many pieces for Moorman that required her play in unusual locations or wear special costumes. Paik covered her with electronic gizmos in works such as *TV Glasses* (1971), in which two tiny monitors were placed next to Moorman's eyes and *TV Cello* (1971), in which a cello made from television sets with strings taught across the screens was used. Moorman could alter the video images on the screens as she bowed the instrument. Moorman also played cellos made from ice and chocolate; and in a rather erotic interpretation of John Cage's *26'1.1499"* for a string player (1955), she held Paik against her breast and stroked his back with her bow.

The idea of bringing eroticism to music culminated in Paik's scandalous *Opera Sextronique* (1967). This piece required Moorman to play her cello while doing a strip tease that left her nude from the waist up and led to her arrest for indecent exposure in 1967. She was found guilty, but this judgment later led to a change in New York laws regarding nudity in performances. After the trial, Paik produced *TV Bra for Living Sculpture* (1969) for Moorman; two TV monitors were worn over her breasts, and a foot pedal was used to manipulate the video images. The title of this piece speaks volumes of Moorman's power as a performer. She was able to embody a composer's ideas, fully giving of herself and her body to complete the composition.

Moorman was an enthusiastic promoter of the works of other artists as well. She founded the New York Avant-Garde Art Festival, which ran from 1963 to 1982. She also performed works by numerous other composers, including Yoko Ono (b. 1933), Joseph Beuys, and Mieko Shiomi. She died of cancer on 8 November 1991.

See also Experimental Music; Fluxus; Performance Art

For Further Reading

Battcock, Gregory, and Robert Nickas (eds.) *The Art of Performance: A Critical Anthology*. New York: E. P. Dutton, 1984.

Hanhardt, John G. *Nam Jun Paik*. New York: W. W. Norton, 1982.

Jeffery Byrd

Morissette, Alanis (1974–)

An international icon of popular music, Alanis Morissette has earned tremendous critical and public acclaim. *Jagged Little Pill* (Warner Brothers 45901), her 1995 debut album for Madonna's Maverick Records, was for two years the best-selling record by a woman artist of all time and has enjoyed 28 million worldwide sales to date. Her music, most typically co-written with and produced by former Michael Jackson collaborator Glen Ballard, combines the raw delivery of unadulterated, chiefly autobiographical lyrics with a paradigmatic alternative rock sound that continues to inspire a host of imitators. *Supposed Former Infatuation Junkie* (Warner Brothers 47094) and *Unplugged* (Maverick 47589) are characterized by a softening of Morissette's trademark confrontational tone in songs of greater depth and subtlety permeated by "a sense . . . of tranquility."

Morissette was born Alanis Nadine Morissette on 1 June 1974 in Ottawa, Canada. At the age of 10 she landed a role on Nickelodeon Cable Network's "You Can't Do That on Television." She achieved a respectable measure of commercial success in her native Canada by the age of 16 following the release of her Canadian debut record, *Alanis*, and the 1992 follow-up, *Now Is the Time* (both released on MCA Canada). A move to Los Angeles in 1993 precipitated her association with Madonna and Ballard. The stunning popular success of *Jagged Little Pill* was reflected at the 38th annual Grammy Awards, at which she was awarded Album of the Year, Best Rock Album, Best Rock Song, and Best Female

Rock Vocal. *Jagged Little Pill*'s performance was followed similarly at Canada's Juno Awards. There also, Morissette won the 1997 International Achievement Award, and in March 2000 *Supposed Former Infatuation Junkie* (Wea International 47239) was awarded Best Album.

Beyond strictly musical pursuits, Morissette has occupied herself with a widely publicized interest in Yoga and Vedantic philosophy, new means of music distribution (such as MP3 and other Internet-friendly formats), and both stage and film acting. She played God in 1999's religious comedy *Dogma* and received excellent reviews for her off-Broadway work in Eve Ensler's *The Vagina Monologues* (2000).

See also Rock and Popular Music Genres

For Further Reading

The Alanis Morissette Internet Hub. Available: http://www.maverickrc.com/alanis

Cantin, Paul. *Alanis Morissette: A Biography*. New York: St. Martin's Press, 1998.

Coles, Stuart. *Alanis Morissette: Death of Cinderella*. London: Plexus Publishing, 1998.

Edward John Coffey III

Motown

In 1959 Berry Gordy Jr. started Motown recording company in his hometown of Detroit; the name presumably came from Detroit's sobriquet, "The Motor City." Over the next two decades Gordy's firm launched some of the most popular stars of the 1960s and 1970s; many of the label's victories were the achievements of the women he had put under contract. Dressed in bouffant wigs, glittering gowns, and spike-heeled shoes, these African American women made recording and radio and television broadcast history by producing some of the first songs that crossed over from what was considered race music into mainstream pop.

The first woman whom Gordy signed was Mable John (b. 1930), sister of rhythm and blues star Little Willie John. She was introduced to Gordy, then recording under the Tamla label, by his mother, with whom John had worked selling insurance. Although John signed with Tamla in 1959, her first record was not released until 1961. By that time Gordy was aiming for a cross-over sound, and John, whose voice was more a blues instrument, left Motown to become one of Ray Charles's Raelettes.

The next woman Gordy signed was Claudette Robinson, a member of the Miracles, back-up group for her husband, Smokey Robinson. Her voice was so like her husband's that when he became ill on tour, she was able to step in to lead the group until he recovered. Gordy's first real star was Mary Wells (1943–1992). Named "The First Lady of Motown," she recorded hits like "My Guy" that helped to take the label from the realm of rhythm and blues into pop. Wells, whose career was marred by poor management and drug addiction, reportedly signed her recording rights over to Gordy. Motown histories disagree over whether Gordy acted in Wells's interests or whether he took what was rightfully hers to promote the group that would ultimately become the Motown favorite—the Supremes.

The first number one hit for Motown was "Please Mr. Postman" by the Marvelettes, credited as the first African American group to make the cross-over for which Gordy strove. Originally a quintet, the Marvelettes were the only group to feature two women who sang lead: Gladys Horton ([b. 1944] "Postman") and Wanda Young ([b. 1944] "Don't Mess with Bill"). Other members included Georgeanna Tillman (1944–1980), Juanita Cowart (b. 1944), and Katherine Anderson (b. 1944). Cowart was the first to leave the group; Tillman eventually followed, leaving the others to perform as a trio.

While other women singers were being signed to record, Martha Reeves (b. 1941) patiently waited her turn by working as secretary for Motown executive Mickey Stevenson (who later married Kim Weston). Reeves, backed up by the Vandellas—Rosalyn Ashford (b. 1943) and Betty Kelley (b. 1944), the latter of whom came from the Velvelettes)—eventually was put under contract and performed some of Motown's most dynamic hits: "Dancing in the Street," "Heat Wave," and "Nowhere to Run." As was the case with many groups, members of the Vandellas changed as women left to marry or move on; subsequent members included Annette Beard and Reeves's sister, Lois. Sandra Tilley was the last to join before Reeves went solo.

Easily the most famous—and surely the most controversial—of Motown's girl groups was the Supremes, Gordy's ultimate cross-over stars. Originally called the Primettes, a sister-group to the Primes (later the Temptations), this quartet was composed of Florence Ballard (1943–1976), Mary Wilson (b. 1944), Barbara Martin (b. 1950), and Diane (later Diana) Ross (b. 1944). Martin left after the group signed with Motown. Originally less popular in the Detroit area than the Velvelettes, against whom they were often pitted in mock "Battles of the Groups," the Supremes became Gordy's favorites. In a market that would promote only so many African-American girl groups, Gordy pulled support from other performers and put it behind the Supremes. Growing jealousy over his obvious favoritism for Ross led to Ballard's dismissal. Cindy Birdsong (b. 1939), one of Patti LaBelle's (b. 1944) Blue Belles, replaced her, and shortly after that the group became Diana Ross and the Supremes. Jean Terrell (b. 1944) replaced Ross when the latter left to solo. Other women, including Lynda Laurence, Sherrie Payne, Susaye Green, and Sundray Tucker, joined and rejoined (as did Birdsong) the group in its various reincarnations. Laurence, Payne, and another addition, Freddie Poole, toured as FLOS, "Former Ladies of the Supremes," although Wilson sued them for use of the original group's name.

The Velvelettes made Motown history with "Needle in a Haystack." Perhaps the least well remembered of all the girl groups, its members included Mildred Gill, Norma Barbee, Carolyn "Cal" Gill, Bettey Kelley (who later joined the Vandellas), and Bertha Barbee. Filling in when members left were Annette Rogers, Sandra Tilley (also later in the Vandellas), and Carolyn Street. Gordy also signed solo stars including Agatha Weston (later Kim Weston), "It Takes Two"; Brenda Holloway (b. 1946), "Every Little Bit Hurts"; and Tammi Terrell (1946–1970), who partnered Marvin Gaye in "Ain't No Mountain High Enough."

Behind the scenes at Motown were women like executive Suzanne DePasse and charm school owner Maxine Powell, whom Gordy hired to teach group members modeling techniques, etiquette, grooming, and movement. Because many of the singers were minors when Gordy signed them, other women, including Holloway's mother, served as chaperones when the groups did summer tours as the Motown Revue or with Dick Clark's Caravan of Stars. Not only did these women make Motown famous with their distinctive sounds; some, like Wells and

Holloway, actually composed the music they performed.

When Motown moved to Los Angeles in the 1970s, many of the groups were left professionally stranded in Detroit. Some of the women had already left performing to begin families or different careers; others soon followed. Some groups like FLOS, the Velvelettes, and the Vandellas (with Reeves) occasionally re-form for club appearances, benefits, and tours.

See also Rock and Popular Music Genres

For Further Reading

Reeves, Martha, and Mark Bego. *Dancing in the Street : Confessions of a Motown Diva*. New York: Hyperion, 1994.

Ross, Diana. *Secrets of a Sparrow: Memoirs*. New York: Villard Books, 1993.

Smith, Suzanne E. *Dancing in the Street : Motown and the Cultural Politics of Detroit*. Cambridge, MA: Harvard University Press, 2000.

Wilson, Mary Supreme Faith. *Dreamgirl and Supreme Faith*. New York: Cooper Square, 2000.

Denise Gallo

Multicultural Musics

In the twentieth century, multicultural musics—music influenced by a wide range of cultures and ethnicities—expanded into many genres of music, including jazz, popular, and classical forms, and throughout the twentieth century women helped to create diverse and rich subcultures within the larger cultural melting pot of the United States. The driving force of women helped to diversify musical practices in particular, and women's participation in music making resulted in styles that crossed community boundaries and were embraced by mainstream U.S. audiences.

Women musicians who immigrated to the United States in the twentieth century were mostly performers, and predominantly vocalists. They brought with them the music from their own countries and usually started their musical careers in the United States by performing songs and dances familiar to their compatriots, using music to reinforce their identity. Outside their own communities, immigrant women had to continuously battle for inclusion and recognition in the U.S. musical world. Although some continued to perform in restricted venues, others were successful in adapting their music to appeal to larger audiences. These women ultimately succeeded in regenerating U.S.-established musical genres and styles. For instance, early in the twentieth century Venezuelan pianist and composer Teresa Carreño (1853–1917) glowed on the stages of the United States and Europe with her brilliant performances of her own piano virtuoso pieces. Carreño taught extensively in the United States, influencing U.S. composers such as Edward MacDowell and guiding an entire generation of performers.

Latino Influences. Women played a crucial role in shaping a Latino identity in the United States. Performers like Celia Cruz (b. 1924), identified with the emergence of salsa in New York City, unified different Afro-Cuban and Puerto Rican forms to build a singing style that brought together several Latino communities in the United States. Collaborating with prominent Latin artists such as Tito Puente, Cruz, and others like Cuban singer La Lupe (1936–1992) contributed to the current popularity of Latin jazz and other Latin musics in the United States. More recently, Gloria Estefan (b. 1957) and Albita Rodríguez (b. 1962) were able to unify Latinos in Miami through the performance of songs of their native Cuba. Estefan has successfully crossed over and reached mainstream audiences by adapting her own music to the U.S. environment. As these women achieve widespread success in the United States, they not only engender large-scale acceptance in their home countries but also ultimately start to represent the U.S. Latino community to the outside world.

In the Southwest, where a strong Mexican American presence prompted mariachi to become emblematic of the local culture, women have also played significant roles in shaping the local identity. Texan guitarist-singer Lydia Mendoza (b. 1916), one of the most influential figures in Mexican American music, was one of the first Spanish-language vernacular singers and recording stars of the Southwestern United States. Her songs reached the poor and working-class people throughout the Spanish-speaking community of the Southwestern United States. Her wide repertoire of Latin American genres also made her well known and respected throughout Latin America. Another native of Texas, Vikki Carr (b. 1941), has built one of most successful careers among Mexican American vocalists. Singing in both English and Spanish, she has reached audiences both in Latin America and in the Hispanic areas of the United States.

Just as Latin women have had to continuously fight to have their voice in the United States, they have also had to battle gender distinctions, although in most cases groups' solidarity has been valued above gender differences. Overcoming gender barriers, Mexican American Laura Sobrino (b. 1954) pioneered as a woman professional mariachi musician in the United States, a field traditionally and predominantly occupied by men. Focusing on teaching and giving workshops on mariachi, today Sobrino is the musical director of the all-women mariachi Mujer 2000 in Los Angeles. Linda Ronstadt's (b. 1946) famous mariachi albums impacted what has been called the "Mariachi Renaissance" of the 1990s. This revival especially influenced youth throughout the Southwest, particularly young women.

Early in the twentieth century, when immigrant women singers started to appear on U.S. stages, they mostly represented the local stereotyped view of their homelands. In the 1920s, Cuban Rita Montaner (1900–1958) worked with the Shubert Follies review singing Spanish songs and helping spread the sound of urban Latin American music throughout the United States with her *zarzuela* performances. But it was singer and actress Carmen Miranda (1909–1955), a native of Portugal raised in Brazil, who took a leading position in U.S. show business. During the 1940s Miranda's hallmark costume, including "tutti-frutti" turbans, platform sandals, and exotic dresses, helped transform her into a stereotyped symbol of the Latin American women in Broadway shows and Hollywood movies. Singing mostly Brazilian sambas in Portuguese, Miranda was undoubtedly one of the most successful Latin exports in U.S. show business. Although to some she helped perpetuate the image of the Latin exotic, Miranda opened doors to other immigrant women to be accepted in the U.S. music industry.

Asian Influences. The growing presence of immigrants from Asia in the twentieth century deeply impacted U.S. culture and music. As with their counterparts from Latin America, Asian American women musicians had an active role in building an Asian American identity. One of the first Asian American women to take a starring role in American musical theater, Japanese American Pat Suzuki (b. 1930), pioneered in a field almost totally dominated by Anglo-American women. Despite the pervading negative attitudes toward Americans of Japanese descent in the post–World War II years, Suzuki rose to stardom through her talent and perseverance; her performances were compared to those of such great artists as Judy Garland (1922–1969), Ella Fitzgerald (1917–1996), Billie Holiday (1915–1959), and Sarah Vaughan (1924–1990).

More recently, Asian American women have aggressively used the arts and music not only to shape their own identity but also to address the politics of ethnicity in the United States. A militant in the civil rights movement, Nobuko Miyamoto (b. 1939) has been a driving force in creating an Asian American movement and in promoting multicultural awareness in the United States since the 1970s. A composer of songs and dramatic pieces, as well as works of performance art, she has produced seminal works that not only address the Asian American identity but also open artistic activity to focus on interethnic awareness.

The growing presence of Asian American women musicians in the United States has been manifested recently in the innovative sounds they have brought to established American forms such as jazz, as well as the new possibilities they are opening to experimental music. Miya Masaoka (b. 1958), Sumi Tonooka, and June Kuramoto have incorporated Japanese traditional instruments in the performance of jazz and new music, as well as in innovative applications of computer electronics.

Born in China, composer Chen Yi (b. 1953) has been considered one of the most prolific composers living in the United States today. Trained in Western art music repertoire, Chen Yi came to the United States in 1986, where she completed a D.M.A. (1993) and was appointed to several distinguished positions in U.S. orchestras and universities.

African American Influences. The force of women to enrich and renew twentieth-century music in the United States was not restricted to those bringing their culture from distant lands. Women musicians have been crucial in the strengthening of local subcultures from within. Particularly in the realm of popular music, African American women have played substantial roles as innovators while at the same time using music to address social, ethnic, and gender issues. Mamie Smith (1883–1946), Gertrude "Ma" Rainey (1886–1939), and other classic blues singers in the 1920s and 1930s brought to the blues traditions a high sense of drama by expressing the everyday experiences of black women in the United States in their music and lyrics. African American women musicians such as gospel singer Mahalia Jackson (1911–1972) have also been pioneers in the struggle for racial equality and recognition in the United States. In addition to asserting their ethnic, social, and political positions through music, African American women have had to continuously fight to break gender barriers. Whereas Mary Lou Williams (1910–1981) succeeded in the male-dominated world of jazz, recently women have emerged as strong performers and composers in genres like rap, which has also been traditionally mostly dominated by men.

Native American Influences. Native American women musicians have been engaged in the preservation of their culture by studying, archiving, and reviving their traditional songs and dances. Joanne Shenandoah's commitment to the preservation of her culture resulted in the founding in 1992 of Round Dance Productions, a Native American traditional music archive and arts center. Bertha Little Coyote (b. 1912) has also made vital contributions to documenting Cheyenne musical practices. Although some Native women remain committed to building careers in music that reflect their native cultures, others have chosen to cross boundaries and to participate in the development of musical styles and genres that appeal to a larger spectrum of the diverse U.S. audiences. Buffy Sainte-Marie (b. 1941), for example, has left the realm of her native culture to create classics of the folk, country, and popular genres.

Other Influences. Women continue to mark their presence in music making in the United States even when they are part of ethnic groups that have not yet attracted widespread interest from the music industry. Active within the boundaries of their ethnic communities, most of them have not reached stardom and are away from the appeal of larger audiences. As performers and singers, however, they come to play significant roles in the preservation and innovation of traditional and popular musics of communities such as Arab Americans, Czech Americans, and Jewish Americans. Although the music activities of women in these communities have not yet received an in-depth study, they have played substantial roles in preserving their cultural institutions as well as in supporting musical activities within their own communities.

Although several women musicians played important roles in building identity images for various immigrant groups and local subcultures in the United States during the twentieth century, some chose to follow career patterns that shunned specific roles within the politics of identity. Perhaps because of pressures in the music industry, some women preferred to produce and perform within a more flexible framework, one that could satisfy both their community and the mainstream. And as some choose to not subscribe to the role of cultural activists, their claim of self-representation may in the end directly or indirectly contribute to building a more diverse and reinvigorating mainstream U.S. music.

See also African American Musicians; Asian American Music; Jewish Musicians; Latin American Musicians; Native American Musicians

For Further Reading

Aparicio, Francis. *Listening to Salsa: Gender, Latin Popular Music, and Puerto Rican Cultures*. Hanover, NH: University Press of New England, 1998.

Keeling, Richard (ed.). *Women in North American Indian Music: Six Essays*. Bloomington, IN: Society for Ethnomusicology, 1989.

Koskoff, Ellen (ed.). *Women and Music in Cross-Cultural Perspective*. New York: Greenwood Press, 1987.

Lornell, Kip, and Anne K. Rasmussen (eds.). *Musics of Multicultural America: A Study of Twelve Musical Communities*. New York: Schirmer Books, 1997.

Loza, Steven. *Barrio Rhythm: Mexican American Music in Los Angeles*. Urbana and Chicago: University of Illinois Press, 1999.

Cristina Magaldi

Multifocal History

Multifocal history, or relational history, is the last, ideal phase of the historiography in Gerda Lerner's 1975 classification in which women and men receive equal consideration in a kind of "universal" history. This phase supersedes compensatory history (women judged by male standards), bifocal history (women overcoming patriarchal oppression), and feminist history (women's history). Applied to music, the concept of multifocal history involves interdisciplinary work in much the same ways as historical studies in feminist musicology and feminist music theory. Multifocal history involves considering the musical score or performance and its cultural context and subtext. The historian analyzes gender, along with race, ethnicity, class, marital status, and sexual preference, as determining factors in musical creation. Ideally, the multifocal approach results in both genders being represented in the academic and performing canon, and the work of women and men is seen as contributing equally to musical life.

The multifocal approach is sometimes evident in studies of specific institutions and genres. Peter Dykema's "Musical Fraternities and the Development of Music in America" (1933) explores women's music clubs, men's music fraternities, and honorary fraternities with women and men members. Venise T. Berry's "Feminine or Masculine: The Conflicting Nature of Female Images in Rap Music" (1994) compares women and men rappers' depictions of women, showing how texts and structures of rap videos express contemporary and traditional female roles. Biographies such as Catherine Smith and Cynthia Richardson's *Mary Carr Moore, American Composer* (1987), Judith Tick's *Ruth Crawford Seeger* (1997), and Adrienne Fried Block's *Amy Beach, Passionate Victorian* (1998) are multifocal in that they depict their subjects as influenced by mainstream standards as well as feminine values, and they show how these women were both discouraged by patriarchal traditions and supported by established institutions. Susan McClary in "Different Drummers" (1999) considers how three prominent American composers—Pauline Oliveros, Meredith Monk, and Joan Tower—"have made vastly different uses" of the mainstream heritage and have "responded to what it can mean to be a woman artist in a wide variety of ways." So far, no multifocal historical surveys or chronologies of long spans of time have appeared that summarize women's work along with men's.

See also Feminist Music History; Feminist Musicology; Historiography

For Further Reading

McClary, Susan. "Different Drummers: Theorising Music by Women Composers." In *Musics and Feminisms*, ed. Sally Macarthur and Cate Poynton. Sydney: Australian Music Centre, 1999.

Treitler, Leo. "Gender and Other Dualities of Music History." In *Musicology and Difference: Gender and Sexuality in Music Scholarship*. Berkeley: University of California Press, 1993, 23–45.

Deborah Hayes

Multimedia

The desire to construct an artistic event that educates an audience about herself, her questions, her answers, and her experience leads many women already engaged with music technology to cross the line to the interdisciplinary realm and add "visual instruments" to their audio world, creating a multimedia art form. More immediately recognizable visual images serve to enhance musical meaning, allowing composers to communicate effectively without resorting to cliché in either medium. Additionally, multimedia may be used in a purely abstract manner, enabling the composer to experiment with her interests and abilities in the visual arts. The majority of women composers utilizing multimedia technology today share a thorough knowledge of both music and art, as well as an understanding of the absolute usefulness and necessity of these media in much of their current work. This work has led to beneficial interdisciplinary collaborations, greater involvement in performances, the exploration of the correlation between color and sound, and the documentation of personal experience.

Perhaps the most well known woman pioneer in multimedia art and performance is Laurie Anderson (b. 1947), who has become the model for anyone interested in incorporating all media and meaning into her work. Described by *WIRED* magazine as "America's Multi-Mediatrix," Anderson has designed and performed multimedia works for three decades beginning with her 1972 *Automotive*, an outdoor concert for car horns, and culminating with the more recent CD-ROM *Puppet Motel* (1995) and the opera *Moby Dick* (1999). Receiving training in art history at Barnard College and sculpture at Columbia University, Anderson combined this education with her skills as a violinist and keyboardist to create her often large-scale and multipart concert works. Among the most popular of these is her 1983 *United States I–IV* (excerpts of which are featured in the 1986 video *Home of the Brave*) and the commercially successful released single *O Superman*, which climbed to number two on the British pop charts in 1981.

Several writers and researchers have observed and analyzed Anderson's sexual ambiguity in performance, with musicologist Susan McClary (b. 1946) giving one of the most thorough commentaries on this aspect of the artist's creativity. In her 1991 text *Feminine Endings*, McClary outlines performance, visual, and musical aspects of Anderson's art that underline a theme of oppositions and dichotomy in society. Observing that initially the artist is perceived as illustrating standard Western relationships of male and female, authenticity and corruption, and truth and fiction, McClary then emphasizes Anderson's ability to transcend these basic ideas and "tilt them slightly." McClary illustrates her ideas with examples from Anderson's texts, performances, and music.

Anderson has often been cited as a "cultural ethnographer," and much of her work contains humorous and insightful aural and visual observations of her own life and artistic experience. This tendency to utilize multimedia as a documentary device is also evident in the audiovisual works of composers Elizabeth Hinkle-Turner (b. 1964), Alicyn Warren (b. 1955), Jennifer Masada, and Megan Roberts. For her CD-ROM *Full Circle*, Hinkle-Turner created a straightforward yet nonsimplistic documentary of her cancer survivorship and the urgent social, political, and emotional issues resulting from these personal experiences. These events are also a common theme in other works by the composer, including her *Parable of Pre-existing Conditions* (1994), *Antigone's Peace* (1995), and *An Object of*. . . (1997). With the recently completed *A Stitch in Time* (1999), Hinkle-Turner continues to draw inspiration from life experience. A chronicle of quilt making and quilt giving among the women in her family, the work features audio and video mixed in real-time and utilizes the *Image/ine* software application that allows for MIDI (Musical Instrument Digital Interface—a communications protocol for synthesizers and computers) control of digital visual images. Hinkle-Turner currently works as a computer network manager and teaches multimedia and music at the University of North Texas.

Alicyn Warren serves on the music technology faculty of the University of Michigan. Her 1997 *Molly* is an intriguing 13-minute allegorical video reflection upon her mother's death. Using home movies of her family dog and inventing an audio "character" of the animal, Warren creates a subtle work that gradually transforms from a simple autobiography to a more profound commentary on love, family, and dying. Both Warren and Hinkle-Turner have received awards from the prestigious Institut International de Musique Electroacoustique de Bourges competition for their multimedia works.

Equally subtle and powerful is the work of Jennifer Masada, a Japanese American composer living in Iowa City, IA. Her *Kimono* (1993) presents a "loop" of aural and visual events filled with images suggesting body function, internal struggle, family history, Japanese tradition, and feminine duty all evident in the simple act of constructing and wearing a single garment. By performing this act of dressing live and recording and arranging the event later on videotape, Masada is able to construct her piece from two entirely different viewpoints. As both the composer and performer of the work and its witness, she uses the camera to create a piece *about* one of her pieces.

This self-critiquing device is also used by upstate New York's Megan Roberts, who collaborates closely with sculptor Raymond Ghirardo in the creation of large-scale installations involving her videos and soundtracks. *Inflated Ruins* (1989), *Ghost Rocks* (1988), and *Badlands* (1988) all were initially presented as sound and video constructions, ultimately dismantled as needed. However, Roberts's short video "documentaries" of the larger events function as engaging stand-alone works that offer the audience a personal view of what the creator herself perceived as significant in her creation. An early video piece, *Life with Ray* (1980)—a discussion of life in Minnesota, collegial interactions, and a Radio Shack remote-controlled tank—served a similarly effective purpose, allowing the viewer to witness some of the composer's perceptions of her collaborator.

Other composers actively involved in multimedia are Maggi Payne (b. 1945), Sylvia Pengilly (b. 1935), Kristine H. Burns (b. 1966), and Ann Warde. These women share a common interest in photography and film, as well as a desire for a close correlation of aural and visual aesthetics in their works. Payne is a distinguished faculty member at Mills College, and both her electro-acoustic and multimedia works contain gradually unfolding sonic and visual textures. *Liquid Metal* (1994) utilizes a visual exploration of water patterns encountered by the composer while canoeing. The accompanying soundtrack is comprised of transformed reflections of intrusive human-made sounds that threatened to ruin Payne's nature experience. The composer transformed these sounds into something she found more acceptable and less annoying. An additional example of close musical and visual aesthetic mapping is evident in Ann Warde's work. Her *Chromosonics: Alexander Lake* (1991) and *Chromosonics: The Lady That's Known as Lou* (1993) were created using a computer system she developed for the Amiga computer. Warde's creative algorithms allow the transformation of sound to be directly influenced by video color information.

Sylvia Pengilly's initial incentive to develop her visual interests in correlation with her musical creations was the desire to incorporate live performance with video technology. Retired after serving on the faculty of Loyola College, the composer currently resides in California and has an active career as a guest artist and performer. Much of Pengilly's work utilizes the Mandala system developed for the Amiga computer.

With the Mandala system, a real-time image of a performer is digitized and introduced into an Amiga computer, where it becomes a functional part of the program that is able to trigger visual events by "touching" specific icons incorporated into the camera space. Pengilly actually creates her pieces in real-time by using this system and can chose a different presentation with each performance. Her *Dark Places* (1995) consists of the composer triggering alternatively disturbing and fanciful video footage with her dance-like motions. Elements of war films, the suffering of the homeless, and other violence are interspersed with symmetrical animations of shapes and colors. All this activity is viewed only through the silhouette of the composer's body, enabling her to make the choice of what is actually witnessed. This device gives the work a strongly feminist slant, emphasizing a woman's perspective on a world that should be changed.

Kristine H. Burns, director of the electronic music studios at Florida International University (Miami), combines her interests in vocal and instrumental experimentation with her multimedia work. Her *Earlobe* (1993–1995) for five bodies, video, and stereo tape contained footage of choreography rehearsals of the performers who were given a series of instructive scores long before the final completion of the work. In this way Burns is able to produce an environment in which rehearsals serve as an integral part of the creative process rather than simply as a means to perfect a performance of an already rigid set of composed notations. A more recent work, *Underwear* (1998, text by Lawrence Ferlinghetti) for video and contrabass, required the performer not only to play the bass but also to explore the text in a series of elaborate vocalizations. In the 1995 CD-ROM *Dido and Anaïs*, Burns also reflected on her research into opera and literature. Here the audience was introduced to the work of Henry Miller and Anaïs Nin, the correspondence between the two writers, and the title characters in the Henry Purcell opera *Dido and Aeneas*. Containing bio-bibliographical information as well as external sound elements, information about the opera and the literary figures is presented; then, for an interesting added aspect, three music and video compositions are included. By viewing the pieces, the user is provided with the composer's critical commentary expressed in the medium with which she best communicates.

Multimedia technology has also provided many women with an artistic outlet via the Internet. Carla Scaletti (b. 1956), owner of Symbolic Sound Corporation and co-inventor of the Kyma sound composition environment, received a 1995 commission from the International Computer Music Association for her World Wide Web work *Public Organ*. Additionally, more groundbreaking multimedia experimentation done at the M.I.T. Media Lab has involved women at several levels. Most notable is the work of visual coordinator Sharon Daniel and production manager Maggie Orth on Tod Machover's *Brain Opera*, (1996), one of the more large-scale multimedia works developed at the Lab.

Unusual media combinations and experiments are also found in the work of California's Barbara Golden. Golden incorporates humorous and often banal words and melodies with ironically contrived visual situations to create film works that have the subtle impact of the well-conceived political cartoon. Her *Clit Envy* (1994) features a repetitive background chant over which more serious discussions of male and female sexuality and gender misunderstandings are heard. The inclusion of expertly filtered, processed, and abstracted visual images also serves as a balance between the insightful and the ridiculous. Other works, such as *Lap Pool* (1987) and *Trashy Girls* (1986), allow the listener/viewer to witness the interactions of women and draw their own conclusions about their significance or silliness. Fans of Golden's are also able to incorporate her pieces into their daily lives by purchasing the composer's *Home Cooking*, a book containing recipes accompanied by music, visuals, and lyrics from her multimedia works. In many ways Golden's pieces are similar to those of Laurie Anderson, whose wry ethnographic pieces about social life thoughtfully inform while they thoroughly entertain.

The majority of current multimedia creativity by women has been confined to North American artists and composers, a reflection of the greater accessibility of affordable multimedia technology in the United States and Canada and the widespread instruction available in this area at the colleges and universities of these countries. As video production, three-dimensional modeling, and digital animation hardware and software become more affordable and available internationally, it is evident that they will be increasingly utilized on a worldwide scale by composers in general and women in particular. As an effective aide in the communication of musical messages to a larger audience, the advantages of multimedia as an artistic tool are obvious to many women already, and their fine work continues to inform their colleagues about the medium and its possibilities. As a result, multimedia has emerged as a powerfully feminine and feminist art form, and the continued work of women in the field should serve to further integrate them as equally valid participants in the practice of musical composition with technology, an area still often traditionally associated with the male gender.

See also Experimental Music; Music Technology

For Further Reading

Hinkle-Turner, Elizabeth. *Crossing the Line: Women Composers and Music Technology in the United States*. New York: Electronic Music Foundation, 2000.

McClary, Susan. "This is not a story my people tell: Musical Time and Space According to Laurie Anderson." In *Feminine Endings*. Minneapolis: University of Minnesota Press, 1991.

McCorduck, Pamela. "America's Multi-Mediatrix." *WIRED* 2/3 (March 1994): 79–83, 136–137.

Elizabeth Hinkle-Turner

Musgrave, Thea (1928–)

Composer Thea Musgrave is one of the most significant opera composers of the second half of the twentieth century. She won the Koussevitsky Award in 1974, two Guggenheim Fellowships (1974 and 1982), and received an honorary doctorate from Glasgow University (1995). Not only is she a highly respected composer, but she has also conducted many of her own works and even written the libretto to her opera *Mary, Queen of Scots*.

Musgrave was born on 27 May 1928 in Narnton, Edinburgh, Scotland. She began her study at the University of Edinburgh in medicine, but she eventually switched to music and received her B.M. (1950). Additional studies with Nadia Boulanger took place in Paris from 1950 to 1954.

In 1970 Musgrave served as guest professor at the University of California, Santa Barbara, and began to spend much of her time in the United States. She eventually emigrated to the United States in 1973, when she accepted a teaching position at Queen's College, City University, New York.

She has composed in nearly every medium, including symphonic, operatic, and choral. Musgrave has undergone many stylistic changes throughout her career, including expanded tonality and chromaticism, and even strict serialism. Although several of her compositions are abstract (e.g., *From One to Another* for solo viola and prerecorded tape), Musgrave is primarily known for her programmatic, theatrical characteristics.

Perhaps her most significant contribution to classical music of the twentieth century are her many historically based operas, including *Simón Bolívar* (1995), *Harriet, the Woman Called Moses* (1985), *Mary, Queen of Scots* ([1977] Moss Music Group MMG-301), and *The Voice of Ariadne* (1973). Thea Musgrave's music is published by Novello and Company and Chester Music, and her recordings include "Orfeo III": An Improvisation on a theme, for flute and strings (available on *Women of Note*, Koch International Classics 703), "Narcissus" (available on *Narcissus and Kairos*, Neuma 45095), and *Thea Musgrave: Clarinet Concerto, The Seasons, Autumn Sonata* (Cala Records 1023).

See also Classical Music

For Further Reading

Briscoe, James R. (ed.). *Historical Anthology of Music by Women*. Bloomington and Indianapolis: Indiana University Press, 1987.

Hixon, Donald L. *Thea Musgrave: A Bio-Bibliography*. Westport, CT: Greenwood Press, 1984.

Kristine H. Burns

Music Critic

Attempting to define the role of the music critic is difficult at best—a music critic's opinions are sought as to taste, correctness, and the success or failure of a recording or performance. Music critics are expected to educate their readers, through both their opinions and command of music history and their understanding of musical style. Toward this end, women in American music have contributed to the evolution of music criticism as a definitive discipline.

Some of the earliest examples of music criticism by American women are found in periodicals geared specifically toward men. One such periodical is the equine sporting journal *Spirit of the Times: A Chronicle of the Turf, Field Sports, Literature, and the Stage* (1831–1902). Recognizing a need for a comprehensive sporting journal, founder William T. Porter included reviews of opera, orchestra, and recital activity in major U.S. and European cities. Frequently, those writing reviews of musical events left their columns unsigned. Though it is impossible to determine the identities of many of the correspondents with any certainty, many of the reviews took the form of "letters" from exotic locations. As *Spirit* was a periodical for men, some of the women writing the reviews were careful to note that they attended certain performances "in the company of" a brother, husband, or other suitable male escort.

Periodicals like *Spirit* moved music criticism into the twentieth century, and they were quickly followed by more journals, many of which completely discounted the contributions of women. The *Musical Review*, eventually with a reputation for solid articles, included essays about women composers and performers.

One of the earliest and most influential women music critics in America was Claudia Cassidy (1899–1996). Dubbed "Acidy Cassidy" by those with whom she found disfavor, she was music and drama critic for the *Chicago Tribune*. Her reputation as a straightforward, no-nonsense writer, with an elaborate and ornate style of prose, caused difficulty with some of her subjects, including Belgian conductor Désiré Défauw and Rafael Kubelik.

Nora Holt (1885–1974), a somewhat eccentric and vivid writer, served as critic for the *Chicago Defender* until 1921 and, after 1940, for the *New York Amsterdam News*. She produced a radio show entitled "Nora Holt's Concert Showcase" on New York's WLIB-FM, and she was the only black member of the New York Music Critics Circle from 1940 until 1960. Holt's career found her working primarily in African American circles, never shifting to a wider audience.

One of the most versatile music critics of the late twentieth century was Joan Peyser. After pursuing a degree in historical musicology at Columbia University, she began writing essays and articles for magazines and newspapers and served as a freelance contributor to the *New York Times* Sunday edition. She acted as a champion of serialist music and published psychoanalytic studies of Pierre Boulez, George Gershwin, and Leonard Bernstein. Her success with these biographies acted as a catalyst for her continued success with the popular press, including periodicals such as *People* magazine.

See also Music Programmer/Host; Musicologist

For Further Reading

Grant, Mark N. *Maestros of the Pen: A History of Classical Music Criticism in America*. Boston: Northeastern University Press, 1998.

Saffle, Michael, "Promoting the Local Product: Reflections on the California Musical Press, 1874–1914." In *Music and Culture in America, 1861–1918*. New York: Garland Publishing, 1998.

Stauffer, Kristen K. "Spirit of the Times: Music Criticism as an Exegesis of Public Opinion and History of Reception." Ph.D. diss., University of Kentucky, 1998.

Kristen Stauffer Todd

Music Education

Music education generally falls into four categories: general music teacher, band director, choral director, and orchestra director. However, in many respects all women musicians are music educators to the extent that in their music making they are teaching listeners about music and about women's place in music. However, there is an official category and title of "music educator" attained through undergraduate, master's, and doctoral levels of education. Depending on the wealth and commitment of a school district, the district may employ elementary general music, band, and string teachers; middle school general music, choral, band, and orchestra directors; and high school band, choral, and orchestra directors.

The function of music education in kindergarten through 12th grade schools (K–12) is primarily to teach about and prepare students to become musicians in the Western classical music tradition. It is to prepare students to participate in bands, choirs, and orchestras as well as appreciate listening to and attending concerts of Western classical music. Because music education is predicated on the values of Western classical music, music teachers teach musical literacy; how to play instruments from Western ensembles such as strings, brass, woodwinds, and percussion; how to sing according to the principles of *bel canto*; and how to listen to and appreciate classical music. Composition and improvisation skills are often components of elementary music education programs. In most states, music education is required at the elementary school level, and the profession has developed numerous creative methodologies for preparing children for and training them in notated-musical skills. Training in ensembles generally does not begin until the fourth grade, when opportunities to play stringed or band instruments, or to sing in a choir, are made available.

Most states require all students to study music in the middle school, which means that those students who have not studied an instrument or are not adept at singing in a chorus continue taking general music courses. By high school, few states require music for graduation. As a result, only students who have learned to play instruments or enjoy singing in a chorus continue with music. Some high schools offer music electives such as music theory, music history, or general music. At the high school level, ensemble opportunities are expanded and may include marching band, jazz band, jazz choir, swing choir, strolling strings, and musical theater. Musical competitions sponsored by state music organizations play a major role in many high school music programs. The adjudicated events available for soloists, small ensembles, and large ensembles are "noncompetitive" in that musicians perform for a numerical rating and not a ranking. Show choirs and marching bands tend to compete in competitive contests that do result in rankings and trophies.

One of the ongoing challenges of music education has been to incorporate diverse, non-Western musical styles in ensembles and general music classes. Since the Tanglewood Symposium in 1967, music educators have agreed that popular music should be included in the curriculum. However, few teachers have training in the genre and, therefore, find including it in the curriculum difficult. The same issue surrounds teaching music from non-Western countries; most music educators have little training in these musics. The teachers who have been most successful in incorporating "world musics" or multicultural musics have been those who teach general music and choir.

Although music is taught at most universities and colleges, music education again pertains to a specific degree through which students become music educators. The degree consists of studying music theory and history; a primary instrument; conducting; methods courses for teaching specific grade levels and concentrations such as vocal or instrumental; psychology; general education courses; and ensemble participation. On average, it takes four to five years to complete a bachelor's degree in music education.

The role of women in music education mirrors the role of women in general education. Teaching music is considered an "appropriately feminine" profession, and therefore women have been teaching in K–12 schools throughout the entire twentieth century. There are many pioneering women educators whose stories have not been told in mainstream textbooks, including Alys Bentley (1869–1951), Frances Elliott Clark (1860–1958), Julia Ettie Crane (1855–1923), Mabelle Glenn (1881–1969), Marguerite Hood (1903–1992), Lilla Belle Pitts (1884–1970), Alice Inskeep (1875–1942), Vanette Lawler (1902–1972), and Emma Hackley (1867–1922). Although women music teachers have outnumbered men music teachers, the profession of music education has been slow to accept women in leadership roles such as presidents of professional organizations (such as the Music Educators National Conference or the International Association of Jazz Educators) or as professors of music education. The profession has sorted teachers into gendered categories wherein women are predominantly elementary general music teachers and choral directors, whereas men tend to be the band and orchestra directors. Throughout the twentieth century, however, there have always been notable exceptions, again excluded from the conventional history of music education. These important women include Ileane McElwee Gonzales (1920–2000), Rebekah Covell (b. 1939), Pamela Tellejohn Hayes (b. 1947), Phyllis Young (b. 1925), Mary Lou Williams (1910–1981), Melba Liston (1926–1999), and Ellen Rowe (b. 1958).

Women's work in music education has provided the groundwork for prevalent theories of learning and research, although they have not always received the credit due to them. Philosophy of music education is an area where women such as Estelle Jorgensen (b. 1945) and Roberta Lamb (b. 1952) have had a significant impact on the profession. Beginning in the 1980s a group of feminist and gender researchers emerged and brought important issues to the forefront that significantly impacted some policies and practices in music education, such as the representation of women in music textbooks and sex-stereotyping of instruments.

Although conversations about gender have become more prevalent in music education, numerous gender issues continue to dog the profession. Although girls participate in music in abundant numbers, they encounter discrimination in every area of music education. In elementary music class, students encounter unflattering stereotypes in the music they sing (Koza, 1994); and even though elementary music textbooks now include a few women conductors and women playing nontraditional instruments such as tubas or percussion, they fail to teach how women historically have been excluded from a musical education, from many professional performing opportunities, and from music history textbooks. This lack of information about women's historical treatment and presence in music suggests to young girls that women do not compose, conduct, and professionally perform on most instruments. Therefore, young girls often are not educated about or encouraged to explore a diversity of musical opportunities and career choices.

In instrumental music education there are few women orchestra conductors and even fewer women band directors at high school, college, or professional levels. Instrumental music teachers have taken precautions to limit sex-stereotyping of instruments (i.e., girls play flutes, boys play tubas) as they encourage young students to choose their first instrument (Zervoudakes, 1994). However, change is slow to occur. For example, consider the scenario for membership in the Texas State Honor ensembles. Roughly 1,275 flute players audition for 100 positions in the five All-State Bands and the two All-State Orchestras. Likewise, 375 tuba players audition for the 30 band and orchestra positions. This means that 1,175 flutists (mostly girls) will be rejected, whereas only 345 tubas (mostly boys) will be rejected. Clearly, there are liabilities to one's instrument choice.

Further, the historical belief lingers among professional musicians that men are better musicians than women are. This is exemplified by auditions for professional orchestras wherein instrumentalists must play from behind a curtain so that gender will not taint the audition outcomes. Although orchestras have decreased gender bias in hiring practices (women hold 36 percent of orchestra positions in American symphonies), it is disheartening that many professional musicians still cannot interpret performances divorced from gender biases (Allmendinger and Hackman, 1995).

In choral programs girls outnumber boys three to one, and because boys are rare commodities they are afforded numerous privileges for which girls, again, have to compete fiercely (O'Toole, 1997). Choral directors primarily desire a balanced, mixed-voice ensemble, which limits the participation of women to the number of available male singers. Because of the competition only girls face for membership in ensembles, they will more than likely be better musicians than the boys and therefore find their musical education limited by the ability of the male singers.

Female singers also confront limitations in how they are permitted to use their voices. Boys are encouraged to develop the full extent of their ranges (falsetto to bass), but girls' ranges are limited to the higher registers (soprano/alto ranges as opposed to tenor/bass ranges). Although women with low vocal ranges perform in jazz and popular music, the choral profession does not acknowledge this range as appropriate for women and, therefore, positions women singers to be dependent on men singers for full participation in choral singing. Another limitation confronted by women who sing in choirs is in the lack of music about women and by women composers. Unfortunately, the vast majority of repertoire written for mixed-voice and women's choirs is by male composers, from the male perspective, and about male experiences (O'Toole, 1998). This suggests to women singers that only men compose and only men's experiences are worth singing about.

The best way to keep abreast of new research, articles, books, and conferences regarding gender issues in music education is by joining the Special Research Interest Group (SRIG), Gender Research in Music Education (GRIME). Members of the GRIME SRIG participate in discussions and announcements and are a part of an international group of educators interested in gender issues. GRIME has become an invaluable resource to the profession of music education.

There is great difficulty in presenting the research and developments of only a handful of the thousands of women music educators in the United States. For every woman included in this volume, there are five others who should have been represented. In this regard, it is imperative that the profession recognize and document women's work in music education so that a fuller history of music education in America may be constructed.

See also Choral Education; General Music; Instrumental Education; String Education

For Further Reading

Delzell, Judith. "Variables Affecting the Gender-Role Stereotyping of High School Band Teaching Positions." *Quarterly Journal of Music Teaching and Learning* IV-V/4, no. 1 (1994): 93–103.

Green, Lucy. *Music, Gender, Education*. Cambridge: Cambridge University Press, 1997.

Koza, Julia. "Females in 1988 Middle School Music Textbooks: An Analysis of Illustrations." *Journal of Research in Music Education* 42/2 (1994): 145–171.

O'Toole, Patricia. "A Missing Chapter from Choral Method Texts Books: How Choirs Neglect Girls." *Choral Journal* 39/5 (1998): 9–34.

———. "What Have You Taught Your Female Singers Lately?" *Choral Cues* 27/2 (1997): 12–15.

Patricia O'Toole

Women Presidents of MENC

President	Dates of Service
Frances Elliott Clark	1907–1908
Henrietta G. Baker Low	1913
Elizabeth Casterton	1914
Mabelle Glenn	1929–1930
Lilla Belle Pitts	1942–1944
Marguerite V. Hood	1953–1954
Frances M. Andrews	1971–1972
Mary E. Hoffman	1981–1982
Dorothy A. Straub	1993–1994
Carolynn Lindeman	1997–1998
June Hinckley	1999–2000

Music Educators National Conference

The Music Educators National Conference (MENC) was formed to advance music education as a profession and to ensure that every child in the United States has access to a balanced, sequential, high-quality education that includes music as a core subject of study. Founded in 1907 with 69 members—and known through 1934 as the Music Supervisors National Conference—the current membership has grown to nearly 85,000. MENC has an extensive history of advocacy in music education, from publishing in 1940 the first recommendations for kindergarten through 12th grade music curricula, to developing in 1994 the National Standards for Music Education, part of the first comprehensive set of educational standards for K–12 arts instruction.

MENC's publications range from practical resource guides and periodicals offering articles on teaching approaches and philosophies, current trends and issues in music education, classroom techniques, and updates on products and services, to cutting-edge journals reporting on research in the music education field. The Conference's educational programming includes the Music in Our Schools Month, the World's Largest Concert, the Fund for the Advancement of Music Education, the SingAmerica! Campaign, and the National Biennial In-Service Conference for music teachers.

From MENC's inception in 1907, 11 outstanding women music educators have held the helm. Although only 13 percent of MENC's presidents have been women, they have made indelible contributions to the organization's mission of service to the American Public.

See also Music Education

For Further Reading

MENC Homepage. Available: http://www.menc.org/information/advocate/glance.html

Kilissa M. Cissoko

Music Learning Theory

Music learning theory, a powerful and relatively recent development in music education, provides an explanation of the process through which students of all ages learn music. Understanding the process provides a theoretical framework on which teachers can plan effective music instruction.

Edwin E. Gordon defines music learning theory as "the analysis and, synthesis of the sequential manner in which we learn when we learn music" (Gordon, 1997). He asserts that music is learned in much the same way as we learn language, an opinion that resembles Suzuki's idea that children learn musical instruments in the same way they learn to speak. Gordon discusses the four vocabularies of music, stating that as with language development, the music vocabularies are hierarchical—listening, speaking, reading, and writing. Moreover, he contends that an individual acquires these vocabularies in accordance with his or her music aptitudes. Gordon sets up a sequence for how these vocabularies are developed within the context of "audiation," a term coined by him to mean "the sound of music that is heard and formally comprehended in one's mind but that is no longer or may never have been physically present." Gordon maintains that audiation is different from discrimination, recognition, imitation, and memorization; he identifies eight types and six stages of audiation. He uses the analogy that "audiation is to music, what thought is to language" and speculates that children begin to audiate when they are about five years old. Before that age, Gordon claims that children "pass through developmental stages of Preparatory Audiation—i.e., they subjectively hear and informally comprehend in the mind the sound of music that is no longer or may never have been physically present" (Gordon, 1997).

Music learning theory has evolved over the course of Gordon's professional life, beginning in Iowa as reported in the monograph "How Children Learn When They Learn Music" and continuing to the present as he gains new insights from his research and that of others. Based on empirical evidence from research in the psychology of music and associated disciplines, Gordon credits many individuals with inspiration and assistance over the years as the development of music learning theory and its practical applications evolved. That help has taken many forms: from persons asking thought-provoking questions in class, to the conduct of independent relevant research. Among those individuals, he credits several women: his wife, Carol Gordon; his former colleague at the State University of New York (SUNY) at Buffalo, Maria Runfola; and most recently his co-authors of the *Jump Right In Music Curriculum*, Beth Bolton, Alison Reynolds, Cynthia Taggart, and Wendy Valerio.

Carol Goodridge Beccue Gordon played a significant role in the advancement of music learning theory by organizing the Sugarloaf Seminars in Philadelphia during the 1980s, as well as Professor Gordon's initial European lectures. The Sugarloaf Seminars were the first major thrust to bring music learning theory to teachers and musicians across the country. Many ideas for the practical applications of music learning theory were outgrowths of these seminars. Because of some resistance to music learning theory, especially in the hierarchy of the Music Educators National Conference, Mrs. Gordon arranged and accompanied her husband on lecture tours of several European countries and commented that "the European academics seemed far more curious and open to Professor Gordon's research and writings than the professoriate seemed in many U.S. educational institutions." She continues to encourage, support, and promote music learning theory and believes "if one embraces the tenets of music learning theory and diligently pursues its practice, the degree of improvement in musicianship for students AND teacher can be not only gratifying, but motivating and inspiring" (personal communication with author, 22 February 2000). Many of the materials in the Edwin E. Gordon Archive housed in the Music Library at the University of South Carolina were collected and preserved by Mrs. Gordon. Mrs. Gordon (b. 1927) received her bachelor's degree from Denison University, where she studied music methods with Dr. Robert John, and her Master of Music degree from Northwestern University, Evanston, IL. For 25 years she taught music in various schools in Lake Forest, IL, and western New York, including Newfane Central School, the Buffalo Seminary, and the Nichols School. In addition to teaching, she has been an organist and choir director for several churches in western New York. Dr. and Mrs. Gordon were married in Buffalo, NY, on 18 August 1976.

Maria Runfola attended Nazareth College of Rochester, the Eastman School of Music, and SUNY Buffalo, where she earned a Ph.D. (1976) under the guidance of Edwin E. Gordon. During her graduate study Runfola worked closely with Gordon, providing critical feedback and input as he uncovered groundbreaking knowledge of how young children develop an understanding of music. An important aspect of Gordon's theory is student acquisition of a vocabulary of tonal patterns and rhythm patterns; Runfola assisted with research that led to the development of a taxonomy of tonal patterns and rhythm patterns. Born in Buffalo, NY, on 26 January 1941, she studied piano with Florence Rose Pelton and gave her first public recital at age five. The Felician Sisters, who, along with Pelton, nurtured her musical development, encouraging her to pursue a college degree in music, guided her elementary and secondary education. A member of the faculty at the State University of New York at Buffalo for over 30 years, Runfola has held posts of director of music education (1978–1988), Department of Music chair (1984–1987), and associate dean of the university's Graduate School (1989–1992). In 1999 she relocated the music education program to the Graduate School of Education in order to become affiliated with the Fisher Price Endowed Early Childhood Research Center. Before teaching at the State University of New York at Buffalo, Runfola taught general music in several public junior high schools. She is currently the music chair of the New York State Education Department's ASSETS (Assessments, Standards, Staff Education and Technology Systems) Project, whose mission is to develop arts assessments for high school students throughout the state.

Beth Bolton is on the faculty at the Esther Boyer College of Music, Temple University, Philadelphia, PA. Her publications include an innovative scoring procedure for use with the Gordons' *Primary and Intermediate Measures of Audiation.* Born Beth Marie Scholle in Ashland, KS, on 2 March 1950, Bolton attended public schools in Dodge City, KS. In 1973 she completed undergraduate studies in music education at Ft. Hays State University, Hays, KS. After serving two years as a band director, Bolton entered graduate school, earning a master's degree in bassoon performance from Emporia State University, Emporia, KS. In 1977 she returned to public school teaching, this time as an elementary general music teacher, and in 1989 she accepted a teaching position at Temple University. She completed her Ph.D. in music education under the tutelage of Edwin Gordon in 1995. As a child, Bolton was raised in a rich musical environment. Her grandfathers and parents played and sang in the home, practicing for performances with local bands; her mother, a singer and violist, majored in music at the Conservatory of Music, University of Missouri, Kansas City. Both parents encouraged participation in music, affording her the opportunity of ballet lessons, private studio instruction on several instruments, attendance at summer band camp, and travel to Europe as the first bassoonist in the 1966 School Band of America.

Alison Mist Reynolds was born in Albuquerque, NM, on 14 December 1961. She attended music kindergarten in Portland, OR, and at age four moved to Texas, where she began piano lessons. Reynold's primary music influences included experience in public school choral groups as well as the Central Texas Girls Choir. In 1985 she received her bachelor of music education degree from Texas Christian University in Ft. Worth, TX, with Ruth Whitlock as her mentor and Tamas Ungar as her piano instructor. Reynolds taught K–5 general music in Round Rock, TX, until 1988, when she returned to school to study music learning theory and research with Edwin Gordon and Darrel Walters at Temple University. She earned her Master's of Music degree in 1990 and her Ph.D. in music education research in 1995. Reynolds completed Kodály Level I certification at Westminster Choir College and Orff Level I certification at St. Thomas University. From 1993 to 1998 she was a member of the faculty at Ashland University in Ashland, OH. The Music Play classes for young children that she established there are continued under the sponsorship of the Ashland Community Arts School. Currently she is a member of the music faculty at the University of Southern Mississippi, Hattiesburg.

Cynthia Crump Taggart, associate director of graduate studies for the School of Music, has been on the faculty at Michigan State University (MSU) since 1993. She received MSU's prestigious Teacher-Scholar Award and the Undergraduate Teaching Excellence Award while on the faculty at Case Western Reserve University (1985–1993). Born in Madison, WI, on 22 March 1957 to Patricia Ann Neubauer and Phillip Edgar Crump, Taggart attended public schools in Brookfield, WI. Though her mother, a music teacher, provided a stimulating musical environment in the home, Taggart's serious interest in music evolved as she began to study French horn in fourth grade. Throughout her education she participated in bands, choirs, and many curricular and extracurricular music activities. In summer 1979 she attended Interlochen National Music Camp, performing as a singer and hornist. Her teaching experience includes classroom and instrumental music in public and private schools. Taggart holds B.M. and M.M. degrees from the University of Michigan, where she initially majored in French horn performance and later in music education. With James Froseth as her advisor, she completed research on the history and analysis of solmization systems used in music education. As a Ph.D. student at Temple University, Taggart was coordinator and instructor for the Children's Music Development Program, where her research focused on the hierarchical nature of the stages of tonal audiation. This research was important because it supported Gordon's study of audiation and its relationship to music learning theory.

Wendy Hicks Valerio was born in Ottawa, KS, on 5 January 1961. She participated in small midwestern town church and school music groups for the first 18 years of her life and studied flute with her father. In 1984 she earned a B.M.E. at her father's alma mater, Baker University, a small private Methodist university. She completed student teaching under the mentorship of Beth Bolton, who introduced Valerio to Gordon and his music learning theory. Valerio taught elementary general music in Lawrence, KS, until 1987, when she began graduate study at Temple University. Under the guidance of Walters and Gordon, her research focused on the initial stages of preparatory audiation. She completed her Master's degree in 1991 and a Ph.D. in music education in 1993. Valerio completed Kodály certification Level I at Hamline University and Orff certification Level I at the University of Illinois Champaign—Urbana. Before becoming a member of the faculty at the University of South Carolina, Columbia, where she is currently teaching, she taught at Rutgers University (1990–1992), and the University of North Carolina at Charlotte (1992–1995).

These women continue to support music learning theory as members of the Gordon Institute for Music Learning (GIML) Executive Board: Bolton, editor of the *GIML Research Monograph Series*; Valerio, editor of *Audea*; Taggart, chair of the Education Committee; Runfola, treasurer. They write extensively for professional journals and appear frequently as clinicians/consultants throughout the world. They continue to teach early childhood music classes in research or development centers at their respective universities, investigating, through interactive classroom observation, how young children learn music and how their potential for music learning can be increased. Several have received research grants from MBNA, the Presser Foundation, and the Texaco Foundation.

See also Kodály Method; Music Education

For Further Reading

About Music Learning Theory. Available: http://unm.edu/audiate/learning.htm

Gordon, Edwin E. *Learning Sequences in Music*. Chicago: G.I.A. Publications, 1997.

———. *A Music Learning Theory for Newborn and Young Children*. Chicago: G.I.A. Publications, 1997.

Maria E. Runfola

Music Librarian

The music librarian administers libraries consisting of music scores and parts, books about music, periodicals about music, multivolume sets of the collected works of individual composers, recorded music in many formats, musically related photographs, and archives of music materials. These materials are presented in varying degrees of completeness in historically oriented academic music libraries, performance-oriented conservatory libraries, general service public libraries, and various types of specialized music libraries. Music libraries may be independent subject libraries housed in an academic music department or conservatory building, a subject department in a public library, or a free-standing special library such as the American Music Center in New York City, which promotes contemporary American music. Present in most music libraries is foreign language material: texts of songs and operas, some biographies, reference materials, and periodicals.

The music librarians who administer such collections are musicians with undergraduate and graduate degrees in music and a Master of Library Science degree from an American Library Association (ALA)-accredited library school. Many ALA-accredited library schools include courses taught by the university's music librarians that introduce the students to the basics of music librarianship. The Music Library Association issues periodic lists of such programs; the most recent is *Directory of Library School Offerings in Music Librarianship*, 6th ed., compiled and edited by Raymond A. White, (Education Committee, Music Library Association, 1996). A committee of the Music Library Association has prepared a statement of Qualifications of a Music Librarian, which was published in 1974 (*Fontis Artis Musicae* 21 (Summer 1974): 139–43. *Journal of Education for Librarianship* 15/2 (Summer 1974): 53–59; and *College Music Symposium* 15 (1975): 87–93. Such an individual selects music materials for purchase, processes them for use, and services the library's clientele. Today some librarians specialize in a particular aspect of music librarianship, for example, selecting materials to be purchased, cataloguing, servicing recorded music, providing reference service to the library's clientele, and processing and servicing archival materials.

The Music Library Association, founded in 1931, is the umbrella professional organization for all American music librarians. Its journal, *Notes*, publishes scholarly articles of interest to music librarians and reviews of literature, music, and recorded music. The Association's *Newsletter* includes news of the organization and its regional chapters.

Unlike many of their male counterparts, America's first women music librarians were musicians whose library skills were learned from their work experience. From that group, a few rose above the ranks to achieve "stardom." Barbara Duncan, perhaps the first woman music librarian, began her career in 1907 at the Boston Public Library, where she worked extensively with the Allen A. Brown collection of music; in 1922 she became librarian of the Sibley Music Library of the Eastman School of Music, where she selected and purchased the foundation of that library's unique collection. Her cataloguer was Elizabeth Schmitter, a graduate of the Springfield (MA) Library's training program.

When the new San Francisco Public Library building opened in 1917, Jessica Fredricks became head of the Music Department. In 1938 Fredricks founded the San Francisco/Northern California Chapter of the Music Library Association. Gladys Caldwell was made head of the Art and Music Department of the Los Angeles Public Library in 1922, a position she retained until her retirement in 1948. Caldwell was the first chairperson of the Southern California Chapter of the Music Library Association, founded in October 1941.

In 1924 Eva Judd O'Meara became the first music librarian of the School of Music Library, Yale University. She had been supervisor of the library on a part-time basis from 1917. O'Meara's suggestion led to the founding of the Music Library Association in 1931; she began and edited its journal, *Notes*, from 1934 until 1940. She chaired the Music Library Association committee that produced a *Code* for cataloguing music, published 1941–1942.

Three women built the New York Public Library's Music Library in the 58th Street branch: Dorothy Lawton, 1920–1945, Gladys Chamberlain, 1945–1955, and Catharine Keyes Miller, 1951–1965. Miller was one of the first American music librarians to hold both music and library science degrees. She also taught a highly respected course in music librarianship at Columbia University.

In 1943 Gretta Smith of the Enoch Pratt Library in Baltimore produced a pamphlet for the Music Library Association entitled *The Public Library Music Department*. It discussed administration, acquisitions, technical processes, equipment, and circulation problems, the first publication of its type for music librarians. Irene Millen built the Music Division of the Carnegie Library of Pittsburgh; her career, begun in 1938, ended with her retirement in 1974. An academic music librarian (North Texas State University and Texas Christian University), Anna Harriet Heyer (b. 1919) published a book of great value to all music librarians—*Historical Sets, Collected Editions, and Monuments of Music*—that proceeded through three editions (1957, 1969, 1980) before passing to other compilers. Virginia Cunningham, New York Public Library, Columbia University, and, most significant, music cataloguer at the Library of Congress from 1942 to 1972, influenced music libraries nationwide. She was also a president of the Music Library Association and acted as informal liaison between the Library of Congress and the Music Library Association. Others of significance were Elizabeth Olmsted of the Oberlin Conservatory, and Ruth Watanabe of the Sibley Music Library, Eastman School of Music. Olmsted edited a significant two-volume compilation of music cataloguing data: *Music Library Association Catalog of Cards for Printed Music, 1953–1972; Supplement to the Library of Congress Catalogs* (Totowa, NJ: Rowman and Littlefield, 1974). From 1957 until the mid 1970s, Watanabe and the staff of the Sibley Music Library conducted summer workshops of continuing professional education for music librarians. Active in the Music Library Association, she was president from 1979 to 1981.

See also Musicologist; Organizations, Research

For Further Reading

Adamson, Danette Cook, and Mimi Tashiro. "Servants, Scholars, and Sleuths: Early Leaders in California Music Librarianship." *Notes* 48 (1992): 806–835.

Bradley, Carol June. *American Music Librarianship: A Biographical and Historical Survey*. New York: Greenwood Press, 1990.

——— (ed.). *Manual of Music Librarianship*. Ann Arbor, MI: Music Library Association, 1966.

Carol June Bradley

Music Management

American women working in various types of music management, in small to large nonprofit or for-profit music organizations, have begun at the bottom of the music ladder and climbed up as far as they have wished, by learning management skills that enabled them to use their love, imagination, and knowledge of music to enrich other peoples' lives. Clear goals, enthusiasm, dedication, perseverance, new ways to look at challenges, ability to learn from others, and courage to fund-raise are qualities needed to begin a music organization.

The highly respected, beloved role model for women, general director of the Lyric Opera of Chicago from 1981 to 1997, the late Ardis Krainik (1929–1997), began her ascent to the top of the opera company beginning as a clerk-typist and mezzo-soprano singing supporting roles for the Lyric Opera in 1954. Under Krainik's leadership the Lyric Opera became one of the world's most artistically and financially successful performing arts organizations. Krainik launched an artistic initiative to produce two twentieth-century operas each season during the 1990s. In 1993 she directed the purchase and renovation of the Civic Opera House, supported by a $100 million "Building on Greatness" capital campaign. During her last eight years of tenure, the concert seasons were sold out.

Her endless energy inspired everyone around her.

Deborah Borda, former executive director of the New York Philharmonic, and later executive vice president and managing editor of the Los Angeles Philharmonic, began her music life as an accomplished violist. Switching to management, she learned the art of music business by holding positions with various orchestras, slowly working her way to the top in 1993 and becoming one of the most knowledgeable and influential people in the business. Her sense of vision, passion, innovation, and knowledge led the New York Philharmonic to new artistic growth with financial and organizational stability. In addition, Borda is a well-respected international lecturer and consultant for artistic and orchestral management.

Born and raised in New York City's Harlem, earning a B.S. degree in economics from the Wharton School of the University of Pennsylvania, Sylvia Rhone (b. 1952), chairperson of the Elektra Entertainment Group, began her popular music management career as a secretary with Buddah Records in 1974. Rhone was directly involved in launching new artists such as Third Eye Blind and Natalie Cole (b. 1950).

Warm, personable, and a professionally trained soprano, Loraine Bernstein (b. 1929), assistant director of the Peggy and Yale Gordon Charitable Trust, heads the music aspects of the Baltimore-based foundation dedicated to presentation of high-quality classical music concerts and helping young artists further their music careers. Bernstein oversees more then 50 concerts a year. Artist managers, individual musicians, and music organizations from around the world contact Bernstein hoping to secure a performance in a Peggy and Yale Gordon Charitable Trust concert.

One of the early actions of composers Libby Larsen (b. 1950) and Stephen Paulus, co-founders of the Minnesota Composers Forum (renamed American Composers Forum), one of the largest organizations in the United States to promote music by American composers, was to secure a grant from the Minnesota State Arts Board. This paid performers' expenses, office maintenance, and staff remuneration.

The Baltimore Museum of Art paid for the first concert expenses of Res Musica Baltimore (renamed Res MusicAmerica). Vivian Adelberg Rudow (b. 1936) was the artistic director of this successful American new music organization, which performed creative concerts mostly from 1980 to 1991 to packed houses. Although the goal of Res Musica Baltimore was to bring the music audience closer to music composed in their time, the original concerts of music by American composers were related to museum art exhibitions. Because of its rapid growth, Res Musica needed additional funds, and volunteer Renee Cohen became the principal fundraiser.

Women who love the music cause, work hard, listen, and persevere can learn effective management skills, become leaders, and enjoy success in their music management endeavors.

See also Patronage; Production Manager

For Further Information

Abruzzo, James, and Stephen Langley. *Jobs in Arts and Media Management*. New York: ACA Books, 1990.

Vivian Adelberg Rudow

Music Programmer/Host

Music programmer/host, program host, announcer, DJ: these are some of the titles applied to people whose voices are heard during music broadcasts on radio. The job varies from station to station. Often the management of commercial radio stations admonishes hosts not to speak, except to read prewritten scripts—including advertisements, weather reports, public affairs items, news—and, of course, to introduce the music. Usually hosts at commercial stations have little or no voice in choosing the music. However, on many public radio stations (those belonging to National Public Radio, for example), the host plans the entire program: selecting the music to be aired, developing her commentary, and possibly inviting guests to appear on the program. However, she may not even be physically present at the station; instead she has recorded her comments in advance, and a technician in the station's control room plays the prerecorded commentary, cues up the music selections, and plays the selections at the appropriate time.

Classical women composers and musicians have historically appeared in small numbers on radio station playlists. However, in the last decade of the twentieth century, more and more women composers and performers were added to the playlists. With a lot of hard work, a small station's music collection may be turned into what may be the largest assembly in the country of compact discs containing music written by women. That is just one example of what can be accomplished by an enthusiastic, self-motivated, and determined volunteer program host.

Some well-known women who are or have been DJs are jazz musicians Marian McPartland (b. 1918), Carol Sloane, and Nancy Wilson (b. 1937); classical pianist Virginia Eskin; and composers Elinor Remick Warren (1900–1991) and Jeanne Shaffer (b. 1925).

Any girl or woman who wants to be a music host and is interested in having a position of some autonomy might contact the National Federation of Community Broadcasters in San Francisco to obtain a list of college and community stations in her area. There are approximately 143 community stations and many more college stations currently broadcasting in the United States.

See also McPartland, Marian; Wilson, Nancy

For Further Reading

National Federation of Community Broadcasters. Available: http://www.nfcb.org/

Jeanne Brossart

Music Psychology

Women in the field of music psychology find it a particularly rewarding arena of research. It is truly interdisciplinary in that composers, performers, theorists, and musicologists interact with psychologists, computer scientists, neurologists, and others in the pursuit of common interests. It is also a field in which women have been particularly influential. For example, Diana Deutsch (b. 1938) founded the major society for the field, the Society for Music Perception and Cognition; at present the society's president is Carol Krumhansl (b. 1947) and its secretary-treasurer is Marilyn Boltz. Diana Deutsch, who served as its first editor for 13 years, founded the major journal in the field, *Music Perception*. Other women in the field whose work is very influential include Mireille Besson, Helen Brown, Lola Cuddy, Caroline Palmer, and Sandra Trehub.

For composers in the field of computer music, many questions in perceptual psychology are particularly interesting. For example, how can you set about synthesizing a tone that sounds first like a violin and then gradually evolves to sound like a trumpet? What characteristics of a tone pattern cause the listener to perceive a single melodic line, or instead multiple lines in parallel? In searching for answers to such questions, the most productive approach is to invent sound patterns and shape them in various ways—rather as a composer might shape sound patterns in order to achieve certain results. In the process, one can come across striking and unexpected illusions. Some of these illusions show that there can be surprising differences among listeners in the way that certain musical patterns are perceived.

Another subfield where there is strong interdisciplinary interaction lies at the interface of music theory and cognitive psychology. The writings of theorists such as Heinrich Schenker, Arnold Schoenberg, and Leonard Meyer have had profound influences on the thinking of psychologists who are studying ways in which musical structures are represented in the brain. Interestingly, important recent advances in this area have come from people who approached it as music theorists rather than as psychologists.

The input of musicians is also particularly valuable for research into the brain regions involved in various aspects of music perception and performance. One branch of this field involves the study of patients who have suffered loss of some musical capacity through brain injury. Such losses are often confined to a particular aspect of musical processing, such as the ability to recognize melodies, rhythms, or timbres, to sight-read, or to perform on an instrument. Other patients have lost their ability to speak even though their musical capacities have remained intact. Related work on normal subjects employing brain-scanning methods has indicated that different regions of the brain are involved in carrying out particular musical tasks.

Another area in the psychology of music concerns the striking differences in musical talent that exist among individuals. There is little doubt that musical talent runs in families. Opinions differ, however, concerning the relative contributions of genetic and environmental factors in the development of such talent. Many researchers believe that musical training in early childhood is particularly important, although this has not been fully documented. Another intriguing question concerns relationships between musical ability and mathematical, scientific, linguistic, and other abilities. Although we have learned much about such relationships, many questions remain unanswered.

See also Organizations, Research

For Further Reading

Deutsch, Diana (ed.). *The Psychology of Music*, 2d ed. San Diego: Academic Press, 1999.

Krumhansl, Carol L. *Cognitive Foundations of Musical Pitch*. New York: Oxford University Press, 1990.

Music Perception. A quarterly journal published by the University of California Press, Berkeley.

Diana Deutsch

Music Technology

The arts have historically remained separate from the sciences, and the sciences were fields of study generally accessible only by men; this two-fold division accounts for the relatively small number of women involved in music technology, the uniting of the arts and sciences, until the late twentieth century. Women have traditionally been relegated to the arts, the more "feminine" side of expression. In her now-famous article "And Don't Call Them 'Lady' Composers," Pauline Oliveros (b. 1932) pointed out: "What kind of self-image can little girls have, then, with half their peers despising them because they have been discouraged from so-called masculine activity and wrapped in pink blankets?" (Oliveros, 47). Certainly the blending of arts and technology is not a new practice. However, it was not until the late twentieth century that women in the United States were able to establish themselves as important developers and innovators in music technology.

Technology has been used in many ways for the creation, modification, and dissemination of music. Although women are currently involved in all aspects of technological music production, some fields have been more open to women whereas others largely still remain closed. Contemporary music involving the use of music technology has been called electronic music, computer music, electroacoustic music (EA), electronica, and electronic dance music (EDM). The combination of computer programming and knowledge of music is necessary for a career in music technology.

Many professional organizations are devoted to technology, to music, and to music technology. To date, however, there are no organizations devoted entirely to women in music technology. Some of the U.S. national organizations for music technology include the Society for Electro-Acoustic Music in the United States (SEAMUS), the National Association of Recording Arts and Sciences (NARAS), and the Society of Professional Audio Recording Services (SPARS). Key international organizations include the International Computer Music Association (ICMA) and the Audio Engineering Society (AES). Several prominent women serve in leadership roles on the boards of national and international music technology organizations. Shirley Kaye became the executive director of SPARS in the late 1990s; and in 1999 Mary Simoni was elected president of the ICMA, the first woman to serve in that office. Thus far, only the AES has developed a subcommittee expressly devoted to women in the field; Cosette Collier became chair of the AES Women in Audio committee in 1999.

A number of awards are sponsored by the various music technology organizations. Some of the more prestigious composition awards are presented by the International Electroacoustic Music Competition, Bourges; Prix Ars Electronica; and SEAMUS. Bourges not only supports composition awards but also has sponsors' awards in computer music programming. In 1986 Vivian Adleberg-Rudow (b. 1936) became the first American woman to win a first prize in the program division of the prestigious International Electroacoustic Music Competition, Bourges, for her composition *With Love*. In 2000 Elainie Lillios (b. 1968) became the first woman student composer awarded the ASCAP/SEAMUS Student Commission for her electro-acoustic composition *Arturo*.

Although the vast majority of electronic music studios in Europe were housed in radio stations (e.g., West Deutscher Rundfunk, Studio di Fonologia di Milano, Swedish Radio) in the 1940s and 1950s, colleges and universities supported many of the electronic music studios in the United States. In the mid-1980s many academic institutions in the United States began offering training, and even degrees, in a wide range of music technology majors including recording engineering, electronic and computer music composition, and even multimedia production. Even the early studios in the United States had women associated with them. Established in 1955, the Columbia-Princeton Electronic Music Studios was one of the first studios in the United States, and there were women working in these facilities almost from the start, including Alice Shields (b. 1943), Daria Semegen (b. 1946), and Pril Smiley.

Several important electronic and computer music studios in the United States have been founded by women. Although the majority of studios were in academic institutions, there were several women working independently of academic institutions. Bebe Barron and her husband, Louis, worked in New York as film scorers. Their score to *Forbidden Planet* (1956) was the first all-electronic score. The film studios did not even characterize their sound design as "music" but rather labeled it as "electronic tonalities" in the opening credits. Pauline Oliveros helped to establish the San Francisco Tape Music Center in 1961. This facility was available to anyone who wanted to develop electronic music. In 1966 the facility moved to Mills College and later was renamed the Center for Contemporary Music.

Electronic and computer music studios continued to find a stronghold in the academic music community. The Peabody Electronic Music Studio (Peabody Conservatory of Music, Johns Hopkins) was founded by Jean Eichelberger Ivey (b. 1923) in 1967. Over the following two decades, several important women established studios in the United States. In 1976 Beverly Grigsby (b. 1928) established the California State University, Northridge, Computer Music Studio. Throughout the 1980s studios for both composition and recording were established by prominent women, including the Center for Research in Electronic Art Technology (1986) by Joann Kuchera-Morin, and the Virginia Center for Computer Music (1988) by Judith Shatin (b. 1949).

Performance art, although difficult to formalize and define, usually combines multiple art forms into a live performance presentation. Music, theater, visual art, and even poetry and prose are intertwined to create a unique art form. Multimedia integrates music with visual elements and may take the form of video, film, or installations. This may be in collaboration with a visual artist, or the composer may work with the visual herself. Laurie Anderson (b. 1947) was one of the earliest and most significant performance art and multimedia artists. When her "O Superman" hit number two on the British pop charts, Anderson clearly established herself as a cross-over composer between art music and popular music. Other multimedia artists include Maggi Payne (b. 1945) and Sylvia Pengilly (b. 1935). Payne has worked in a variety of venues. Her music often is comprised of slowly evolving textures with thoughtful processing of elements. Pengilly has the unique position of being both a composer and a dancer. Her music and movement are inexorably intertwined, as she is the creator of both artistic expressions. Several women multimedia and performance artists developing at the close of the twentieth century are Carla Scaletti (b. 1956), Elizabeth Hinkle-Turner (b. 1964), and Kristine H. Burns (b. 1966).

The sound installation artist is one who creates a sound environment which the audience moves through in order to experience it. Installation artists such as Maryanne Amacher (b. 1946), Liz Phillips (b. 1951), and Annea Lockwood (b. 1939) have all created music that while seemingly ambient on the first listening, becomes more complex on further evaluation. Lockwood's *A Sound Map of the Hudson River* (1983) made use of river recordings to create an enviromental space that was reminiscent of water moving on the river. Amacher coordinates multiple rooms, or even entire buildings, into one unified sonic environment in which the listener is guided through the space. Phillips combines audio and visual elements, and the audience is often encouraged to touch various sculptures, actions that cause changes in the sonic evolution of the composition.

The scientific development of tools in music technology has largely been a male-dominated field. Although there are rare instances of women in this area (such as the English scientist Ada Lovelace, daughter of Lord Byron), the vast majority of women have been unable to break into this field until fairly recently. Joan Miller was a breakthrough programmer working at one of the most prestigious institutions in the United States—the Bell Telephone Laboratories. She and computer programmer Max Mathews wrote the MUSIC4 computer music language in the late 1950s; this language served as the impetus for the development of computer music for the next 50 years. Laurie Spiegel (b. 1945) also worked at Bell Labs from 1973 to 1979. Spiegel established the electronic music studio at New York University and developed the Music Mouse program, one of the first interactive computer music composition programs. Carla Scaletti cofounded the Symbolic Sound Corporation with her husband, Kurt Hebel. She developed the Kyma Sound Synthesis system, which has been used extensively in both commercial and art music fields. Another composer and programmer, Mara Helmuth has authored a variety of programs, including StochGran, a program for granular synthesis.

The field of audio production, including recording engineering, has long been dominated by men. However, there have been a few notable exceptions. Shirley Kaye and Cosette Collier have worked to establish themselves in the audio industry while also mentoring younger women interested in the field. Kaye served as a panelist for the AES—Women in Audio project; and Cosette Collier is chair of the AES Women in Audio committee, one of the few such professional audio engineering committees devoted entirely to women's issues.

Although not all film composers make use of technology in the creation of sound, certainly the sound designer makes great use of music technology in the creation of sound effects. The knowledge of computer programs, acoustics, and music is necessary, as well as a creative mind for creating imaginary sounds. Wendy Carlos (b. 1939), is one such designer, her diverse credits range from *Switched-On Bach* (CBS/Sony MK 7194), the first classical album to reach Platinum status, to film scores including *The Shining* (1980) and *Tron* (1982). Brenda Hutchinson (b. 1954) and Frankie Mann (b. 1955) are both sound designers working with sound effects in video games, television and film, and installations.

Live electronic performance is a field that has been evolving since the early part of the twentieth century. With the advent of inexpensive computer and electronics systems, individuals could develop performance paradigms at home. Clara Rockmore (1911–1998), the most famous theremin performer and perhaps the first woman involved in live electronic performance, began concertizing in the mid-1930s. Laetitia Sonami (b. 1957) makes use of a pair of gloves outfitted with sensors that are able to measure motion and translate those motions into music. Eve Beglarian (b. 1958) and Kathleen Supové founded the group Twisted Tutu and perform exclusively with a wide range of electronic sounds. Joan La Barbara (b. 1947) and Diamanda Galás (b. 1955) have developed techniques of mixing voice and electronics. Having performed much of the music of her husband, Morton Subotnick, La Barbara has also written a number of compositions for herself with live processing and effects. Galás, on the other hand, has devoted a great deal of her composition and performance to bringing about greater awareness of sociopolitical issues such as those related to AIDS. Mary Lou Newmark (b. 1964), violinist and composer, and Beth Wiemann (b. 1959), clarinetist and composer, have developed specialized performance techniques with acoustic instruments and electro-acoustic music.

Musicians developing electro-acoustic music, recording engineering, audio production, sound installations, and live electronic performance usually, but not always, have a background in traditional music. They are also required to know the basics of acoustics, recording, and computer programming. Although the different fields within music technology have been relegated to men for decades, women involved in this arena have had a great deal of success in recent years.

See also Organizations, Professional Audio; Performer, Live Electronics; Sound Design

For Further Reading

Burns, Kristine H. *WOW/EM: Women On the Web/ElectronMedia*. Available: http://eamusic.dartmouth.edu/~wowem

Chadabe, Joel. *Electric Sound: The Past and Promise of Electronic Music*. Upper Saddle River, NJ: Prentice-Hall, 1997.

Oliveros, Pauline. "And Don't Call Them 'Lady' Composers." *New York Times* (13 September 1970). Reprinted in *Software for People*, Baltimore, MD: Smith Publications, 1984, 47–51.

Kristine H. Burns

Music Theorist

A music theorist studies the structure of music through the analysis of melody, rhythm, harmony, counterpoint, timbre, and form. Theorists traditionally study Western art music, but a growing trend in recent years has been toward extending the scope of materials studied to include non-Western art music as well as jazz and popular music. In the most general sense, the practice of music theory involves the contemplation of music wherein the observation of the general behavior of one or more aspects of a specific repertoire is succeeded by the speculation of principles or rules that describe the behavior of the musical elements under consideration.

The practice of music theory dates back to ancient Greece, where philosophers such as Plato discussed music's function in an ordered society and mathematicians such as Pythagoras and Aristoxenus recorded the acoustical properties of musical intervals in terms of their mathematical ratios. Music theorists have provided insight into compositional practices throughout recorded history, and many of the treatises that were originally written using early Greek or Latin texts as well as the more recent treatises that were written in modern European languages have been interpreted and translated into contemporary English thanks to the work of modern theorists and musicologists who study the history of theory. The study of the history of theory may be broken down according to historical periods (Medieval, Renaissance, Baroque, Classical, Romantic), geographical regions (Greek, Latin,

French, German, Italian, etc.), or speculative descriptions of the music (rhythm, harmony, counterpoint, form, etc.). Prominent women scholars concentrating on this area of inquiry include Nancy Baker (for her work on the writings of Heinrich Koch), Patricia Carpenter (for work on both Renaissance modal theory and the theoretical writings of Arnold Schoenberg), and Maria Rika Maniates (for her work on Nicola Vicentino and sixteenth-century Italian music).

The majority of contemporary music theorists are, at least to some degree, involved in the analysis of music that may be divided into three subcategories: pretonal theory (Western art music written before 1600); tonal theory (Western art music from 1600 to 1900 as well as jazz and popular music); and post-tonal theory (Western art music written after 1900). The distinction between tonal and non-tonal music is largely determined by the harmonic language used and often predetermines the analytic approach that the theorist will use. Many of the field's more prominent figures have made important contributions to more than one area of research. The growing list of prominent women theorists who regularly publish research in the area of musical analysis includes: Jane Piper Clendinning (for her work on the music of György Ligeti and the theoretical writings of Gioseffo Zarlino); Martha Hyde (for her work on the music of Arnold Schoenberg and Igor Stravinsky); Christie Collins Judd (for her work on the music of Josquin des Prez and prebaroque music); Marianne Kielian-Gilbert (for her work on the music of Igor Stravinsky and Frederic Chopin); Elizabeth West Marvin (for her work on the music of Anton Webern as well as contour theory); Ann McNamee (for her work on the music of Franz Schubert and Karol Szymanowski); Severine Neff (for her work with Arnold Schoenberg's music and theoretical writings), Janet Schmalfeldt (for her work on the music of Ludwig van Beethoven and Alban Berg); and Susan Tepping (for her work on the music of Wolfgang Amadeus Mozart and Schenkerian pedagogy).

In addition to publishing research, most theorists are also involved in teaching music theory at the postsecondary level. As a result, another area of research in recent years is music theory pedagogy, or the study of how to teach music theory. This area of study involves research into both conventional teaching techniques as well as computer-aided instruction methods. Many of the scholars involved in this discipline also produce textbooks or computer software as teaching aids for both rudimentary and advanced levels of education. Some of the women theorists involved in this area of research include: Joyce Conley (for her work with John Clough on programmed learning), Rosemary Killiam (for her work in computer-assisted instruction), Dorothy Payne (for her work with Stefan Kostka on tonal harmony pedagogy), and Mary Wennerstrom (for her work on form and style analysis instruction).

Finally, several emerging interdisciplinary areas of study are attracting scholars from various outside disciplines to the scholarly study of music theory. These include the union of music theory with such diverse fields as ethnomusicology, cognitive psychology, mathematics, linguistics, literary criticism, semiology, hermenuetics, and phenomenology. See, for example, the work of Carolyn Abbate, Jeanne Bamberger, Elaine Barkin (b. 1932), Judith Becker, Diana Deutsch (b. 1938), Marion Guck, Carol Krumhansl (b. 1947), Janet Levy, Susan McClary, Mary Louise Serafine, and many others whose work is shaped by an interdisciplinary approach.

See also Feminist Music Theory; Music Psychology; Musicologist

For Further Reading

Beach, David et al. "The State of Research in Music Theory." *Music Theory Spectrum* 11/1 (1989): 1–94.

Bent, Ian, and William Drabkin. *Analysis*. New York and London: W. W. Norton, 1987.

Brown, Matthew. "Theory." In *The New Harvard Dictionary of Music*, ed. Don Randel. Cambridge, MA: Harvard University Press, 1986, 844–854.

Cook, Nicholas. *A Guide to Musical Analysis*. New York and London: W. W. Norton, 1987.

Dunsby, Jonathan, and Arnold Whittall. *Music Analysis in Theory and Practice*. New Haven, CT: Yale University Press, 1988.

Palisca, Claude V. "Theory, Theorists." In *The New Grove Dictionary of Music and Musicians*, vol. 18, ed. Stanley Sadie. London: Macmillan, 1980, 741–762.

John Cuciurean

Music Therapy

Music therapy is the practice of using music (performance, composition, and other forms of participation) for mental, emotional, or physical healing purposes. Several American women were very influential in the promotion and development of music therapy as a career during the early twentieth century. Eva Vescelius is credited with creating the first journal on the topic of music therapy in 1903. She also founded a professional group, the National Therapeutic Society of New York, which unfortunately did not last.

In 1919 Margaret Anderton instituted the first college course work in music therapy at Columbia University. Isa Maud Ilsen wrote articles about music therapy for the American Red Cross in 1926, and Harriet Seymour was noted for advocating the use of music in hospital settings during this period (Davis, Gfeller, and Thaut, 1992).

Most historians attribute the beginning of the modern music therapy career to volunteer musicians who gave concerts in veterans hospitals for traumatized soldiers immediately following World War II. The first official degree programs began in United States in the 1940s. Currently the profession is widely developed in the United States with over 70 colleges and universities providing degree programs at the bachelor's, master's, or doctoral levels. Today, approximately 85 percent of the nation's music therapists are women.

The common goal for all types of music therapy is to achieve beneficial change in an individual or group through special music techniques. A large body of research during the last 50 years has resulted in a wide variety of music therapy applications and types of jobs. Currently music therapists work in the fields of mental health, special education, infant stimulation and early intervention, gerontology, general and rehabilitative medicine, hospice, counseling, substance abuse, and juvenile justice. Some music therapists have established private practices emphasizing a clinical specialty area.

Music therapy combines the human responses to music with principles of psychology, education, medicine, and rehabilitation. Research has shown that music can relax or stimulate, reduce the perception of pain, shorten labor in childbirth, alter moods, communicate ideas and express emotions that people hesitate to speak of, facilitate recall of paired memories, enhance learning, build self-esteem, promote social skills, prolong physical exertion, and provide leisure, recreational, celebratory, and aesthetic experiences. Music therapy techniques include the full gamut of human interactions with, and thoughts about, music: playing, singing, discussing, moving to, and composing or creating. People of all ages respond to music therapeutically, and the individual's preference for type of music is very important in its therapeutic benefit. To be optimally effective for the widest range of people, the music therapist, therefore, combines classical music training with functional knowledge of music from many tastes and cultures.

A qualified music therapist completes at least a four-year bachelor's degree, including a six-month internship in a clinical music therapy program. The curriculum consists of liberal studies, music, psychology, special education, anatomy and physiology, and music therapy research, techniques, and practical experiences. Following completion of the undergraduate degree, the music therapist may then take a national exam to become Board Certified. A master's degree in music therapy is often sought for clinical specialization, and a doctorate is desirable for college teaching in this field.

See also Music Education; Organizations, Research

For Further Reading

Davis, William B., Kate E. Gfeller, and Michael H. Thaut (eds.). *An Introduction to Music Therapy Theory and Practice*. Dubuque, IA: William C. Brown, 1992.

Journal of Music Therapy. Lawrence, KS: National Association for Music Therapy.

Standley, Jayne M. *Music Techniques of Therapy, Counseling, and Special Education*. St. Louis, MO: MMB, 1991.

Jayne Standley

Musical Theater

Musical theater uses elements of live vocal and instrumental performance, drama, dialogue, costumes, and sets to create a world in which people move freely from speaking to singing and back again. The first musical theater work of record in America was *Flora*, a ballad opera, performed in Charleston in 1735. In the early days of musical theater, women often started in burlesque and vaudeville. Later, some of them took over other aspects of theater from fathers or husbands who died. Women have participated in greater numbers than theater history books indicate because histories usually mention only those who distinguished themselves by rising to the upper echelons of Broadway productions. Historically women had three major problems to overcome: the patriarchal prejudice against allowing women to deal with big money, the Victorian prejudice that women were too emotional and weak to be trusted with decision making, and the puritanical bias that anyone in theater was morally suspect. In spite of the difficulties, many women overcame these obstacles and became successful in every field related to musical theater.

The Girl from Up There, the twentieth century's first musical, opened at the Herald Square on 7 January 1900 and starred Edna Mae. Women have been stars in musical theater from the time of Lillian Russell (1861–1922) in *Fiddle-dee-dee* (1900) and Aileen Stanley (1893–1982) in *Pleasure Bound* (1927) to Pearl Bailey (1918–1990) in *Hello Dolly* (1967) and Bernadette Peters (b. 1948) in *Sunday in the Park with George* (1984).

Some women are associated with the roles they created and are adored by the American public in those particular roles. Early examples are Fannie Johnston in *Florodora* (1900), Marie Cahill in *The Wild Rose* (1902), Ida Brooks Hunt in *The Chocolate Soldier* (1909), Marilyn Miller (1898–1936) in *Sally* (1920), Edith Day in *Irene* (1919)—the first of many to play the lead, Beatrice Lillie in *Charlots Revue* (1924), Mary Ellis in *Rose Marie* (1924), Louise Groody in *No! No! Nanette!* (1925), Helen Morgan (1900–1941) as Julie and Norma Terris as Magnolia in *Show Boat* (1927), Lois Moran in *Of Thee I Sing* (1931)—the first musical to win a Pulitzer Prize, Claire Luce in *Gay Divorce* (1932), and Fay Templeton and Tamara Geva in *Roberta* (1933). Fanny Brice (1891–1951) is in a category by herself, having performed in Florenz Ziegfeld's *Follies* from 1910 to 1923. *Porgy and Bess* (1935) also claims its own category as an American folk-opera with no place to play except Broadway; Anne Brown played the first Bess.

A few more successful women and the shows in which they starred include Mary Martin (1913–1990) in *The Sound of Music* (1959), Ethel Merman (1909–1984) in *Annie Get Your Gun* (1946) and *Call Me Madam* (1950), Carol Channing (b. 1921) in *Hello Dolly* (1964), Gertrude Lawrence in *The King and I* (1951), Gwen Verdon (1926–2000) in *Damn Yankees* (1955), Julie Andrews in *My Fair Lady* (1956), Judy Holliday (1922–1965) in *The Bells Are Ringing* (1956), Carol Lawrence and Chita Rivera (b. 1933) in *West Side Story* (1957), Carol Burnett (b. 1935) in *Once Upon a Mattress* (1959), Barbra Streisand (b. 1942) in *Funny Girl* (1964), Lauren Bacall (b. 1924) in *Applause* (1970), Glynis Johns in *A Little Night Music* (1973), Angela Lansbury in *Sweeney Todd* (1979), Betty Allen and Kathleen Battle (b. 1948) alternating in *Treemonisha* (1975), and Bernadette Peters in *Dames at Sea* (1968) and the *Annie Get Your Gun* revival in 1999.

Broadway has been slow to allow women to direct or produce, but women have done both in other parts of the country with great success. After directing effective experimental theater productions at Grinell and Vassar Colleges, and winning a Guggenheim Fellowship, Hallie Flannagan Davis was appointed national director of the Federal Theater Project (FTP) in 1935. She invited Rose McClendon, a respected African American actress, to direct the Negro Unit; but fearing her inexperience as a director, McClendon declined and recommended John Houseman. Although Houseman tried, he could not persuade the play selection committee to produce plays condemning racism. Hallie Flannagan Davis was influential in establishing viable regional theater that was artistic and educational as well as popular; but because of the FTP's refusal to address the race issue substantively, it had less impact on African American playwrights. Unfortunately, the FTP was eliminated after four years by a Congress that objected to its radicalism. *Bubbling Brown Sugar* (1976), the creation of Rosetta LeNoire, was important as the first musical to portray the history of African American music both on Broadway and in Harlem.

The only woman in her directing class at Yale Drama School, Lynne Meadow was a director at the Manhattan Theater Club for more than 15 years. Her *Ain't Misbehavin'* (1978), with Nell Carter (b. 1948), was the club's big revenue maker. Julianne Boyd directed a series of off-Broadway productions. Her *Eubie*, on the life of Eubie Blake, ran with great success in 1978. Boyd's *A . . . My Name is Alice* grew out of a benefit for the National Abortion Rights Action League and had an extended run in Greenwich Village at the Top of the Gate.

Cheryl Crawford produced *Brigadoon* (1947) and *Love Life* (1948) and was one of the producers for *Celebration* (1969). Diana Krasney co-produced *Anyone Can Whistle* (1964), and Margo Lion produced *Jelly's Last Jam* (1992).

Women have written for musical theater from its genesis. Anne Nichols wrote the books for several musicals in 1919, three years before her play *Abie's Irish Rose* ran for 2,327 consecutive performances and became a national institution with touring companies. She earned $1 million as the playwright and millions more as producer. Because she failed to get anyone else interested in producing her work, she mortgaged her home and did it herself. Nichols's musical *Linger Longer Letty* was revived by its star, Charlotte Greenwood, throughout the 1920s and 1930s. Under the name *I Want a Sailor*, it became Bob Hope's first big hit. Dorothy Fields (1905–1974) is certainly one of musical theater's most successful and prolific librettists. Her credits include *Annie Get Your Gun*, *Mexican Hayride*, *Up in Central Park*, *Something for the Boys*, *Seesaw*, *A Tree Grows in Brooklyn*, *Hello Daddy*, *Let's Face It*, and *Sweet Charity*. Betty Comden (b. ca. 1917) and Adolph Green comprised a brilliant writing team who produced many fine shows, including *The Bells Are Ringing*, *On the Town*, and *Applause*. Carolyn Leigh wrote lyrics for the early version of *Peter Pan*, but when Jerome Robbins decided to add more music, he called on Comden and Green, who were more experienced. In spite of this, Leigh's *Peter Pan* songs are the more memorable, and her career continued with her work in *Wildcat* and *Little Me*. Dorothy Donnelly (1879–1928) was the lyricist for many of Sigmund Romberg's most popular operetta-style musicals, such as *Blossom Time*, *Poppy*, *My Maryland*, and *The Student Prince*. Susan Birkenhead is noteworthy for her lyrics for *Triumph of Love*, *High Society*, and *Jelly's Last Jam*. Many other women wrote successfully for musical theater but were not as prolific as those previously mentioned. Bella and Samuel Spewack wrote the book for *Kiss Me Kate*, and Gertrude Stein for *Four Saints in Three Acts*. Lillian Hellman wrote the stage version of *Candide*, and Rida Johnson Young adapted *Wie Einst in Mai* into *Maytime* for Sigmund Romberg.

Even though many women compose for musical theater and have their work produced regionally, few have made it to Broadway. An early exception is Liza Lehman. Her *Sergeant Brue* opened in London in 1904 and came to New York in 1905. She became furious when producer Frank Curzon added some American popular songs. Other exceptions are Kay Swift (1897–1993), with the solid hit *Fine and Dandy* (1930); the French composer Marguerite Monnot, with her *Irma la Douce* (1960); and Lucy Simon, with *The Secret Garden* (1991). *The Secret Garden* was a women's team effort, with book and lyrics by Marsha Norman based on the novel by Frances Hodgson Burnett. Scenery was by Heidi Landesman, who was also one of the producers. The musical was directed by Susan H. Schulman, with costumes by Theoni Aldredge and Tharon Musser. It starred Daisy Eagan and Rebecca Luker. Composer Elizabeth Swados (b. 1951) received her first critical notice for the La Mama experimental theater *Trilogy: Medea, Electra and the Trojan Woman*. Swados was music director of the International Theater Group for several years after *Trilogy*. She returned to New York as resident composer at La Mama, where *Nightclub Cantata* won her one of several Obies in 1978. She teamed with Julie Taymor in *Haggadah* (1981) and with Garry Trudeau in the off-Broadway revue *Rap Master Ronnie* (1984).

Some women constitute a category unto themselves. In 1934, Sophie Treadwell anticipated multimedia-integrated musical theater works with *For Saxo-*

phone. This work included almost unbroken musical accompaniment, off-stage voices from people never seen on-stage, and 14 scenes in different pools of light on a dark stage. It was never produced on Broadway, however. Founded in Minneapolis by eight lesbians in 1973, the Lavender Cellar Theater produced musicals and dance revues for two years about the lesbian experience. The musical parody *Scene at the Center* and dance revue *Isadora Is Arisen* reflected artistic interaction and activity at the Lesbian Resource Center. The first feminist choreopoem was Ntozake Shange's *For Colored Girls Who Have Considered Suicide When the Rainbow Is Enuf* (1975). *Getting My Act Together and Taking It on the Road*, with book by Gretchen Cryer and music by Nancy Ford, proved to be a successful off-Broadway feminist musical. Cryer and Ford fared less well on Broadway, where their *Shelter* ran only for a month in 1973.

As a whole, theater has never recovered totally from the devastating blows delivered by McCarthyism. The wedge between art and politics is driven even deeper by continuing suspicion of the National Endowment for the Arts, which remains one of the few possible sources of funding for nontraditional performance art theater. Women often write, direct, design, and act in their own works of performance art. Three such women are JoAnne Akalaitis of Mabou Mines, Liz LeCompte of the Wooster Group, and Meredith Monk (b. 1942) of the House. Meredith Monk received two prestigious Obie awards for *Vessel* (1972) and *Quarry* (1976). She won first prize in the Musical Theater category at the 1975 Venice Biennale for *Education of the Girlchild*. Monk uses all forms of music, dance, and theater, transforming them into a uniquely personal voice. She calls her work theater cantatas, opera epics, or opera.

The examples cited are a small sample of women who have worked with Broadway musicals and include almost none of those involved in academic, local, and regional theater and touring companies. Historically, directors who are men have directed shows by and about women, whereas women directors seldom have been hired to direct shows by and about men. The smaller the theater and the lower the pay, the more likely it is that women will be directing and managing all aspects of production. That situation has been slow to change.

In the early part of the twentieth century, the musical theater focus was on women as bodies. Gradually, after the beginning of the first women's movement, they were portrayed in relation to the men in their lives. Musical theater struggled with allowing women to emerge from the bedroom, then the kitchen, and finally, with the second wave of the women's movement, to speak honestly about themselves. During the 1980s many musical theater productions became technical spectacles, concentrating more on the set and special effects than on the lives of the characters. As women have become more involved in all aspects of production, the musical has tended toward an ensemble effort about the human condition. It is heightened by aspects of music, dance, set, costumes, and lighting, not overpowered by them.

See also Librettist

For Further Reading

Brown, Janet. *Feminist Drama: Definition and Critical Analysis*. Metuchen, NJ: Scarecrow Press, 1979.

Chinoy, Helen Krich, and Linda Walsh Jenkins. *Women in American Theater*. New York: Theater Communications Group, 1987.

Green, Stanley. *The World of Musical Comedy*. New York: A. S. Barnes, 1974.

Hay, Samuel A. *African American Theater: A Historical and Critical Analysis*. New York: Cambridge University Press, 1994.

Jackson, Arthur. *The Best Musicals from Showboat to A Chorus Line: Broadway. Off-Broadway*. New York: Crown Publishers, 1977.

Philips, Julien. *Stars of the Ziegfeld Follies*. Minneapolis: Lerner Publications, 1972.

Roth, Moira. *The Amazing Decade: Women and Performance Art in America: 1970–1980*. Los Angeles: Astro Artz, 1983.

Jeanne E. Shaffer

Musicologist

A musicologist engages in the scholarly study of music. Music as a field of academic inquiry was born in nineteenth-century Europe, as the founders of the discipline discovered (or rediscovered) and analyzed scores, examined treatises, compiled biographies, and developed systematic cataloguing procedures. Current musicological pursuits include not only historical studies (biography and music history) but the study of acoustics, music editing, style, music theory, manuscripts and notation, textual criticism, archival research, lexicography (terminology used in the discipline), organology (the study of musical instruments), iconography (the study of visual materials related to music), performance practice (the study of the way music was performed in times past), and aesthetics and criticism. Ethnomusicology (the study of music in a larger cultural context), in the past considered a subset of musicology, is now viewed as a related, but separate, field of inquiry.

A recent study indicates that between 1823 and 1970 several hundred women were active as music professors, bibliographers, and librarians. Pioneering women musicologists include Pauline Alderman (1893–1983), Louise Cuyler (1908–1998), and Anna Harriet Heyer (b. 1909). Alderman was notable for her early work on women and music, Cuyler as the first woman to receive a doctorate in musicology from an American university, and Heyer for her valuable *Historical Sets, Collected Editions, and Monuments of Music*. Edith Borroff's (b. 1925) treatment of American music and Eileen Southern's (b. 1920) research in Renaissance and black American music necessitate their inclusion in any study of contributions to the discipline.

The late 1980s and early 1990s produced a windfall of musicological studies that (1) probed the historical and social circumstances under which women composers and performers worked (or were prevented from doing so), and (2) belatedly acknowledged their highly significant musical contributions. Carol Neuls-Bates, Karin Pendle (b. 1939), Diane Peacock Jezic, Jane Bowers (b. 1936), Adrienne Fried Block, Nancy Reich, and Judith Tick (b. 1943) were among those whose research sparked interest in this now-vital field of inquiry. The number of musicological research articles by women scholars in the discipline's premier periodicals such as the *Journal of the American Musicological Society* also gradually increased during this time.

Other recent musicological research has questioned the current musical canon, analyzed works from a feminist perspective, developed gay and lesbian musicology, and scrutinized the relationship among and implications of gender, music, and women. Prominent scholars in this area of musicology include Susan McClary (b. 1946), Marcia J. Citron (b.

1945), and Elizabeth Wood (b. 1939).

See also Feminist Musicology; Music Librarian; Organizations, Research

For Further Reading

Brett, Philip, Elizabeth Wood, and Gary C. Thomas (eds.). *Queering the Pitch: The New Gay and Lesbian Musicology*. New York and London: Routledge, 1994.

Citron, Marcia J. "Feminist Approaches to Musicology." In *Cecilia Reclaimed*, eds. Susan C. Cook and Judy S. Tsou. Urbana and Chicago: University of Illinois Press, 1994.

Journal of the American Musicological Society. Chicago: University of Chicago Press.

Ellen Grolman Schlegel

National Academy of Recording Arts and Sciences

See Organizations, Professional Audio

National Association for Music Education

See Music Educators National Conference

National Endowment for the Arts Composers Program

This program is actually a collection of programs funded by the National Endowment for the Arts to provide financial assistance for activities related to the composition and performance of new musical works from 1966 to 1995. During its 30-year history, the Composers Program functioned under several different names and was comprised of a variety of granting subcategories that provided over $7.3 million in funds to composers.

The program was called Composers Assistance Program from 1966 to 1970 (assisted by the American Symphony Orchestra League and the American Music Center), the Composer-Performer Commissioning Program in 1971, and Composer Assistance in 1972, all of which provided funds for copying and completing scores and parts for orchestral presentation, as well as for commissioning and preparing works for performances. The program was named Composer/Librettist Fellowship from 1973 to 1978, during which time it assisted composers and librettists in composing new musical works, completing works in progress, and establishing careers in the profession. Composers who received grants through the Composer/Librettist Fellowship include Barbara Kolb (b. 1939), Margaret Garwood, Vivian Fine (1913–2000), Miriam Gideon (1906–1996), Ada Lasansky, Lucia Dlugoszewski (b. 1931 or 1934), Joyce Mekeel (b. 1931), Louise Talma (1906–1996), Suzanne Ciani, Caroline Lloyd, Shulamit Ran (b. 1949), Patricia Brant, Gail Godwin, and Elaine Barkin (b. 1932).

In 1979 the program was renamed the Composers Program and consisted of five subcategories of grants—Composer Fellowships, which provided funds for the creation or completion of musical works or for related research activities; Collaborative Fellowships, which supplied funds to composers and their collaborators for the creation or completion of new works; Centers for New Music Resources, which were awarded to music facilities to support collaborations between composers and other artists; Services to Composers, which were given to organizations for projects that assisted composers on a national or regional basis; and Consortium Commissioning, which enabled consortia of three or more performing or presenting organizations to commission and perform new works.

From 1984 the Composers Program was reduced to two granting subcategories—the Composers Fellowships and the Collaborative Fellowships. Composers who received grants through the Composers Program from 1984 to 1995 include Ann Callaway, Pauline Oliveros (b. 1932), Marilyn Shrude, Cindy Cox, Jane Ira Bloom, Chaya Czernowin, Mary Jane Leach, Janis Mattox, Cindy McTee (b. 1953), Sheila Silver, Jennifer Stasack, Marghreta Cordero, and Clare Shore.

See also American Music Center

For Further Reading

"Compositions, Libretti, and Translations Supported by the National Endowment for the Arts Composer/Librettist Program." New York: The Center, 1978.

"Generation of Fellows: Grants to Individuals from the National Endowment for the Arts." Washington, DC: National Endowment for the Arts, 1993.

"The National Endowment for the Arts Composer/Librettist Program Collection at the American Music Center." New York: The Center, 1979.

Erin Stapleton-Corcoran

National Federation of Music Clubs

The National Federation of Music Clubs (NFMC), a philanthropic and educational organization dedicated to music education and promotion of the creative and performing arts, was founded in America in 1898. Endorsed by the Music Teachers National Association (MTNA), the NFMC held its first convention on 3 May 1899 in St. Louis, MO. The Music Clubs, branches of the Federation, function and represent individual states to this day.

Beginning with the Second Biennial Convention in 1901, the NFMC has distributed thousands of dollars each year in scholarships and awards, given in divisions of piano, voice, strings, organ, opera, composition, music education, music therapy, music for the blind and handicapped, summer music camps, and so on. The NFMC was the first to offer large prizes to American composers. Starting in 1932, when John Powell was commissioned an orchestral work on authentic Anglo-Saxon material, commissioning works from American composers became a continuous major contribution and encouragement of the NFMC to the musical culture of America.

The NFMC holds a large number of competitions for musicians of various levels and ages. For example, the Young Artists Competition exemplifies the Federation's mission; it biannually selects four young artists in categories of piano, strings, and men's and women's voice and provides them a large monetary award and concert management. The artists perform in various Music Clubs around the country, thus developing and increasing performing and touring experience. Past winners include such internationally renowned figures as pianist Van Cliburn and soprano Kathleen Battle (b. 1948).

The NFMC is the only music organization accredited as a non-governmental organization (NGO); it was chartered by the U.S. Congress on 9 August 1982.

The mission of the Federation is to support and develop American music and musicians. The organization publishes the *Music Club Magazine* quarterly.

See also International Alliance for Women in Music; Prizes, Composer and Performer

For Further Reading

The Artistic Guide to Chicago and the World's Columbian Exposition. Washington, DC: Chicago Archives of the NFMC in the Library of Congress, 1982.

Ward, Lucile Parrish. *Musical Legacy of 100 Years: The Story of the National Federation of Music Clubs*. Greenville, SC: A Press Pub., 1995.

Inna Faliks

National Women Composers Resource Center

See Women's Philharmonic

Native American Musicians

In the first half of the twentieth century Native American women musicians were neglected in academic scholarship, and reports were often marred by misinterpretations of Native American culture. Charges of gender inequity prevailing in early writings were based on observations such as (1) the fact that the use of the drum and flute in many tribal communities was restricted to men only, and (2) the configuration of singers at powwows, whereby men form a circle and play the drum while women sit behind them. Although these statements might indicate that a lesser value was placed on women's contributions to the musical whole, recent scholarship raises objections to assumptions of inequity and highlights principles of gender balance emanating from the tribal cultures themselves.

At the end of the twentieth century scholars agreed that to understand gender and music relationships in Native American culture, a grasp of tribal mythological and social principles was essential. Studies of southwestern tribes' girls' puberty ceremonies (Frisbie, 1967; Farrer, 1989), for example, reveal these musical ritual dramas as reenactments of creation mythology wherein balance between male and female forces is sought as menses is celebrated. Recent research also shows that the imperative of women's musical/spiritual support to ensure the success of soldiers persists in Plains music as demonstrated by "war mothers songs" (Hatton, 1989; Giglio, 1994, 1997). Furthermore, music behavior in Canadian Algonkian tribes exhibits a principle of gender "complementarity" rather than separation, although studies of Shoshone and Cheyenne music indicate that there are still areas in which women's roles are defined by restriction (Diamond Cavanaugh, 1989; Vander, 1988; Giglio, 1994, 1997).

Notwithstanding past controversies, the close of the twentieth century found Native American women achieving considerable critical and popular acclaim in commercial venues. Fusion of traditional texts and melodies with contemporary harmonic, instrumental, and rhythmic colors has highlighted the careers of Buffy Sainte-Marie (b. 1941), Joanne Shenandoah, and the vocal trio Ulali. Since 1995, the Aboriginal Arts Program (Banff, Alberta, Canada) has provided professional development opportunities for Native Women singers, increasing musicianship and professional knowledge levels. In the United States, the Smithsonian Institution's Folkways Recordings *Heartbeat: Voices of First Nations Women* (Smithsonian Folkways 40415) and *Heartbeat 2: More Voices of First Nations Women* (Smithsonian Folkways 40455) have made available to a wide audience a variety of musical selections performed by women, including traditional social and ceremonial music, story songs, jazz, and contemporary songs. With performance and recording opportunities increasing, the ensuing decades promise a new era of creative expression for Native American women.

See also Multicultural Musics; Sainte-Marie, Buffy; Shenandoah, Joanne; Ulali

For Further Reading

Diamond Cavanaugh, Beverley. "Music and Gender in the SubArctic Algonkian Area." In *Women in North American Indian Music: Six Essays*, ed. Richard Keeling. Bloomington, IN: Society for Ethnomusicology, 1989.

Farrer, Claire R. "Singing for Life: The Mescalero Apache Girls' Puberty Ceremony." In *Southwest Ritual Drama*, ed. Charlotte Frisbie. Prospect Heights, IL: Waveland Press, 1989.

Frisbie, Charlotte J. *Kinaalda: A Study of the Navajo Girl's Puberty Ceremony*. Middletown: Wesleyan University Press, 1967.

Giglio, Virginia. *Leaving Everything Behind: The Songs and Memories of a Cheyenne Woman*. With compact disc. Norman: University of Oklahoma Press, 1997.

———. *Southern Cheyenne Women's Songs*. With audiocassette. Norman: University of Oklahoma Press, 1994.

Hatton, Orin T. "Gender and Musical Style in Gros Ventre War Expedition Songs." In *Women in North American Indian Music: Six Essays*, ed. Richard Keeling. Bloomington, IN: Society for Ethnomusicology, 1989.

Vander, Judith. "From the Musical Experience of Five Shoshone Women." In *Women in North American Indian Music: Six Essays*, ed. Richard Keeling. Bloomington, IN: Society for Ethnomusicology, 1989.

Virginia Giglio

New Age Music

One of the most eclectic categories of music to emerge in the last quarter of the twentieth century was the genre commonly known as New Age. Indeed, the tremendous diversity of this music makes precise definition of the style difficult. Ambient soundscapes intended to promote relaxation or meditation; quiet acoustic instrumentals inspired by folk, world, and classical sources; and experimental electronic essays have all been called New Age music. However, even such a broad category as New Age may be characterized by its essential values—expressed in what the music emphasizes and what it eschews—and these values will provide a helpful introductory profile.

Taken as a whole, New Age music favors simplicity over complexity and prefers smooth continuity to sharp contrasts. It tends to be calm and contemplative, rather than passionate or profound. More about mood than drama, New Age music seeks to free the imagination instead of captivate it, offering diversion in place of challenge. And unlike virtually any genre before it, New Age music tries to project impressions of optimism, inclusion, equality, social responsibility, and multicultural diversity. It is music meant for the new millennium, invested with the qualities of peace and synergy that its authors hope the new era will bring.

The term "New Age" may be traced to a loosely formed philosophical and spiritual movement oriented toward the renewal of Western culture through the adoption of various Eastern and Middle Eastern attitudes, principles and practices, as well as the reconsideration of traditional patterns of religious behavior. Mysticism, metaphysics, transcendentalism, astrology, psychic phenomena, and even the paranormal played roles in the New Age movement, and followers felt free to select and pursue the elements that appealed to them. Unifying the movement was the belief that humanity was entering a new age, one that was to bring enlightenment, positive personal and social transformation, and a harmonious planet. This movement experienced increased interest during the late 1960s and early 1970s, a period of profound social and cultural change, and it attracted the attention of many performers and composers, particularly those living on the West Coast of the United States and in Europe.

Some adherents of New Age philosophy responded with music meant to facilitate meditation; others produced recordings designed to help relieve stress and enhance psychological well-being; a few even offered compositions said to have healing properties. Much of this early New Age music emphasized repetitive rhythmic figures; consonant and long-sustained harmonies; improvisatory melodies; warm, rich, reverberant timbres; and free-flowing formal structures—all of which combined to create soothing, atmospheric, and even hypnotic effects. Some of the mental and physical benefits claimed on behalf of New Age music have since come under scrutiny and even some sharp criticism, most notably by Lisa Summer in her book *Music: The New Age Elixir* (1996). Even so, the optimism, self-awareness, and humanism advocated by the New Age movement, as well as many of the techniques and traits of early New Age music, seem to have appealed to countless musicians, including many with no formal and personal ties to the movement. In fact, some of the most prominent artists popularly associated with New Age music, including Irish-born Enya (b. 1961) and Canadian-born Loreena McKennitt (b. 1957), have not publicly claimed to represent New Age philosophy and may not acknowledge the link or even the label. Likewise, many listeners have little or no awareness of the movement that gave rise to this music. In lieu of a better alternative, however, the term "New Age" appears to adequately characterize much light, contemporary contemplative music for many people.

New Age is a Library of Congress cataloging keyword, a Grammy Award category, and a widely used marketing term in the music industry. Nevertheless there are increasing indications that the appellation may come to refer to a much smaller repertoire, perhaps limited to music explicitly associated with the New Age spiritual movement, and that new terms may be coined to represent some of what is now known as New Age music.

Women in the United States have been deeply involved with New Age music since its inception. As composers, performers, and promoters, they have profoundly shaped the genre's development and enriched its repertoire. Among the true pioneers of New Age music is Suzanne Doucet, whose meditative recordings use drones, ostinati, arpeggios, simple melodies, and even natural sounds to lead listeners to less stressful states. Constance Demby, a composer dedicated to developing new timbral resources, has offered music of remarkable dimensionality and visuality, often organized around spatial and futuristic themes. Pianists Suzanne Ciani, Liz Story, and Lorie Line reveal classical, jazz, and popular influences in their work; and harpist Georgia Kelly and flutist Radhika Miller incorporate elements of folk and world music in original compositions and arrangements. Finally, the group Angels of Venice, whose members have included harpist Carol Tatum, keyboardist Joanne Paratore, cellist Sarah O'Brien, and flutists Suzanne Teng and Susan Craig Winsberg, combines features of medieval, baroque, and classical music with Middle Eastern, African, and Celtic resources to create a truly unique New Age style.

See also Asian American Music; Grammy Award; Multicultural Musics

For Further Reading

Berman, Leslie. "New Age Music?" In *Not Necessarily the New Age: Critical Essays*, ed. by Robert Basil. Buffalo, NY: Prometheus Books, 1988, 250–268.

Summer, Lisa. *Music: The New Age Elixir*. Amherst, NY: Prometheus Books, 1996.

Werkhoven, Henk. *The International Guide to New Age Music*. New York: Billboard Books, 1998.

James William Sobaskie

New England Foundation for the Arts

See Organizations, Regional Arts

New York Women Composers, Inc.

The New York Women Composers, Inc. (NYWC), organization was formed in 1984 for the purpose of promoting "serious concert music" by living women composers and, more specifically, by its own members. Ultimately its goal is for music by women to succeed because of merit, regardless of a composer's gender. The NYWC is a not-for-profit corporation that is controlled by its own members. Since its inception, there have been around 100 members in the NYWC, approximately 60 of whom are composers; the balance of the membership is made up of performers and musicologists. The NYWC chooses to remain a local organization, comprised of women from New York State as well as the New York City metropolitan area.

The organization presents concerts and festivals, recognizes outstanding service to the area of women in music, and catalogs music by women composers in the New York area. Concerts in and around the New York City area are of great importance, as are outreach concerts in national and international venues. Exchange concerts have been presented in such diverse cities as Cincinnati, OH, and Moscow, Russia.

The NYWC sponsors an award for Distinguished Service to Music by Women that includes a plaque and recognition. Past recipients include Joseph Blu, Esq., Sylvia Glickman, JoAnn Falletta (b. 1954), Nan Washburn, and the sharing of an award by Max Lifchitz and Judith Tick (b. 1943). In February 1998, at the suggestion of composer-member Eva Wiener, the NYWC presented a conference in collaboration with Barnard College entitled "Celebration of Women Composers, a New York Soundscape." Included at this event were lectures by musicologists, two concerts including contemporary and historical compositions by women, and panel discussions on various aspects of music presentation.

One of the most significant projects of this organization is its publication *The New York Women Composers' Catalog of Composers of Concert Music*. This catalog lists nearly 1,200 compositions from 60 NYWC members, including compositions for solo instruments, chamber ensembles, voice, choral (*a cappella* and accompanied), opera, dance, theater, orchestral, and electronic and computer works. Short biographies of the composers and program notes are also provided.

The NYWC has undergone many changes in its administration owing to the recent retirement of longtime administrator Bob Friou and his wife, secretary-treasurer and membership coordinator composer Elizabeth Bell. Marilyn Bliss is the current president; Beth Anderson is the treasurer; and Eve Orenstein is the membership coordinator. Former and current members of the NYWC include Lydia Ayers, Elizabeth Bell, Marilyn Bliss, Adrienne Fried Block, Victoria Bond (b. 1945), Ann Callaway, Laura Carnibucci, Lucy Coolidge, Robert Friou, Katherine Hoover (b. 1937), Dorothy Indenbaum, Elena Ivanina, Binnette Lipper, Ursula Mamlok, Alla Pavlova, Judith Rosen, Judith Ste. Croix, Ruth Schonthal (b. 1924), Linda Seltzer, Jeanne Singer, Mira Spektor, Elizabeth Wood, Susan Withrop, Chen Yi (b. 1953), and Judith Lang Zaimont (b. 1945).

See also American Women Composers, Inc.; International Alliance for Women in Music

For Further Reading

New York Women Composers. Available: http://www.ibiblio.org/nywc

Weiner, Barry. "A Celebration of Women Composers—A New York Soundscape." *IAWM Journal [International Alliance for Women in Music]* (June 1997): 26–27.

Holly Schwartz

Nicks, Stephanie "Stevie" (1948–)

Stephanie "Stevie" Nicks—bohemian singer-songwriter, mystical gypsy, California folk-pop-rock icon of the mid-1970s—is one of the most significant rock and pop musicians of the twentieth century. Nicks's psychic goddess stage persona, over-the-top hippie-gypsy fashion sense, and wildly unbalanced vibrato combined to allow for a unique and definitive female erotic identity and lyric. She serves as an artistic and philosophical link between tough women rockers of the 1960s like Janis Joplin (1943–1970) and Grace Slick (b. 1939) and current women in alternative rock genres.

Nicks was born in Phoenix, AZ, on 26 May 1948. For a time, she was the vocalist (and her boyfriend, Lindsey Buckingham, was the lead guitarist) for the San Francisco band Fritz. After leaving Fritz, Nicks and Buckingham moved to Los Angeles and recorded the aptly titled album *Buckingham-Nicks* (Polydor 5058) at Second City Studio, later used as a demo to pitch their talents to Mick Fleetwood. Hired in 1975 to replace Fleetwood Mac's exiting drummer, Bob Welch, the Nicks and Buckingham team proved a fortunate addition, providing the band with almost immediate and overwhelming commercial success. A talented and autobiographical songwriter, Nicks penned many of the band's best-known songs, including "Dreams" (from *Rumours*, Reprise 3010]) and "Rhiannon."

After five years and several album releases with Fleetwood Mac, Nicks recorded and released a successful solo album, *Bella Donna* (Modern MR-38139-2)—a 1980 Platinum release that stayed at the top of the charts for over two years and produced two U.S. Top *Billboard* singles: "Stop Dragging My Heart Around" (a soulful duet with Tom Petty) and "Leather and Lace" (featuring Eagles drummer Don Henley). Nicks's second solo album, *The Wild Heart* (Modern 90084-2), included the hit songs "Nightbird" and "Stand Back." *Rock a Little* (Modern 90479-2), her third solo album, did not fare as well commercially or artistically as her two previous releases. A victim of rock and roll excess, Nicks subsequently entered the Betty Ford Clinic for treatment of addiction to cocaine and, later, for addiction to Lonopin (a tranquilizer).

Nicks got clean and sober and returned to Fleetwoood Mac to record *Tango in the Night* (Reprise 25471) and then released several more solo albums, including *The Other Side of the Mirror*

(Modern 91245-2), *Street Angel* (Modern 92246-2), and a compilation album, *Time Space: The Best of Stevie Nicks* (Modern 91711-2). Her tune "Landslide" from the 1980 self-titled Fleetwood Mac release (Reprise 2-2281) was recently re-recorded by the California-based folk-pop foursome Venice on its album *Spin Art* (Vanguard 79529)—the only cover tune on the 13-track album. Nicks recently completed a U.S. tour to promote her first boxed-set release, *Enchanted: The Works of Stevie Nicks* (Atlantic 83093), a 46-track retrospective (which includes eight unreleased cuts) of songs selected from her six solo albums.

Married briefly to Kim Anderson and reputed to have had relationships with Don Henley and Joe Walsh, among others, Nicks is now content to be single, drug-free, healthy, and concentrating on writing good songs.

See also Rock and Popular Music Genres; Rock Music

For Further Reading

Dickerson, James. *Women on Top: The Quiet Revolution That's Rocking the American Music Industry*. New York: Billboard Books, 1998.

Dougherty, Steve. "High Priestess." *People* 49/2 (1 January 1998): 67.

Fornatale, Pete. *The Story of Rock 'N' Roll*. New York: William Morrow, 1987.

Paraire, Philippe. *50 Years of Rock Music*. New York: Chambers, 1992.

Judith A. Coe

Nigro, Laura

See Nyro, Laura

Norman, Jessye (1945–)

Jessye Norman is a world-renowned opera and recording star and a soprano recitalist. In spite of the segregated world around her, her teacher-mother, Janine

Jessye Norman performing in the title role of Strauss's *Ariadne auf Naxos*. *Photo by Winnie Klotz/Metropolitan Opera.*

King Norman, and insurance broker father, Silas Norman, created a secure home life for her and her four siblings that fostered Norman's talent and intellect. Her majestic height, large vocal compass, language facility, professional attitude, and even temperament commend her to conductors and directors. Her recitals (often in the language of the audience and sometimes in extraordinary locations) and recordings of works by European and American composers, and also of spirituals and folk songs, all show her amazing range.

Born of African American parents in Atlanta, GA, on 15 September 1945, Norman excelled in school and gave early evidence of vocal ability, singing in her local Baptist church. Educated at Howard University, the Baltimore Conservatory, and the University of Michigan, Norman won the Munich International Music Competition in 1968. Her operatic debut was in Berlin as Elisabeth in *Tannhäuser* in 1969. She has triumphed in many operatic roles, including those of Guiseppe Verdi's *Aïda* and *Don Carlo*, Richard Wagner's *Parsifal* (Deutsche Grammophon 37501) and *Der Ring Des Nibelungen* (Deutsche Grammophon 45354), Giacomo Meyerbeer's *L'Africaine*, Wolfgang Amadeus Mozart's *La finta giardiniera*, *Idomeneo* and *Le nozze di Figaro*, Hector Berlioz's *Les Troyens* and *Cléopâtre*, Richard Strauss's *Ariadne auf Naxos* (Philips 22084) and *Salome* (Philips 32153), Carl Maria von Weber's *Euryanthe* (Berlin Classics 1108), and Gabriel Fauré's *Pénélope*.

Her adventurous, risk-taking spirit is noticeable in some of her projects, such as *Great Day in the Morning* with Robert Wilson, which used spirituals in a non-operatic depiction of a woman's progression through a day. The result was disappointing to many in the audience. Norman's video and television credits include *Jessye Norman at Notre Dame*, *Amazing Grace* (with Bill Moyers et al.), *Spirituals in Concert*, *Meet the Met*, *Stravinsky: Oedipus Rex*, and the movie *Diva*, a semi-biographical tribute.

Norman's honors and awards include honorary doctorates from universities in the United States (her alma mater Howard University; the Boston Conservatory; the University of the South; the University of Michigan) and in the United Kingdom (the Universities of Cambridge and Edinburgh). She has had named after her the Augusta (GA) Riverwalk Amphitheater and Plaza, and (owing to the efforts of the French Museum of Natural History) a species of orchid, *Phalaenopsis Jessye Norman*. In 1984 France made her a Commander of the prestigious Order of Arts and Letters. During France's bicentennial celebration in 1989, she sang "La Marseillaise" at the Arc de Triomphe. She is a dedicated worker for civil rights, dance, and AIDS victims. As a result, she has served on the Board of Directors of such institutions as New York City's City-Meals-on-Wheels, Botanical Gardens, and Public Library, as well as those of the National Music and Lupus Foundations, the National Advisory Board of Dance, and the renowned Theatre of Harlem. Norman lives in London but maintains a home in New York.

See also Classical Music; Performer, Vocal

For Further Reading

Castle, Terry. "In Praise of Brigitte Fassbaender: Reflections on Diva-Worship." In *En Travesti: Women, Gender Subversion, Opera*. New York: Columbia University, 1995.

Karsh, Yousuf. *Karsh: American Legends*. Boston: Bullfinch, 1992.

Story, Rosalyn M. *And So I Sing: African-American Divas of Opera and Concert*. New York: Warner, 1990.

Murl Sickbert

Nyro, Laura (1947–1997)

Laura Nyro achieved great success as a songwriter but failed to win a place on the charts with a song of her own. Her soulful and revelatory compositions stand as a paradoxical aspect of her life, which she kept highly secretive. As a result, her significant and inventive contributions to rock have been largely overlooked until very recently. A recent issue of a two-CD career retrospective has promoted a renewed appreciation for her genius.

Born Laura Nigro on 18 October 1947 to musical parents of Jewish and Italian descent, Nyro was influenced by urban jazz, rhythm and blues, and the beloved doo-wop music that she grew up with in her Bronx neighborhood, music that fashioned itself out of Italian and Latin impulses fused with black gospel and white pop. Nyro's early songs were brutally thoughtful, honest, and highly original; many of them portrayed metaphorical oppositions of romance and sexuality, sin and redemption. All of them were sensuous and stunning. Her style changed after the death of her mother in 1976 and the birth of her son, Gil, in 1978. She began to write distinctively intense, introspective, and brutally honest lyrics, in which social and personal issues intersected and global concerns connected with the conflicting emotions of maternal love. She managed to accomplish this at a time when feminism was just beginning to be defined and the relationships among mothers, fathers, and children and notions regarding the role and status of the family were dramatically shifting.

Wholly unwilling to adapt her art to fit the contours of mass culture, and fully satisfied with her own abilities as an artist and a woman, Nyro lacked overwhelming commercial success. Indeed, her present obscurity is ironic. On one hand, she tended to be reclusive, and her voice, though haunting and sometimes memorable, was also sometimes less than technically perfect; on the other hand, she wrote songs that many celebrities made famous, including "Stony End," recorded by Barbra Streisand (b. 1942), "And When I Die," a signature piece written for the horn funk band Blood, Sweat and Tears, and "Wedding Bell Blues," a song popularized by the Fifth Dimension. Remarkably, all three of these tunes were written by the time Nyro was 19 years old, and they and appeared on her first album, *More Than a New Discovery* (Verve/Forecast FTS-3020), which had very little popular or critical success on its own. Perhaps her determination to retain her privacy, made possible by the royalties from her album covers, was simply out of sync with the no-holes-barred, celebrity-driven musical culture of the period. Her 11 albums were produced from 1966 to 1993, most of them on the Columbia label. Critics point to *Christmas and the Beads of Sweat* (Columbia CK-30259) as tour de force of stylistic fusion. Nyro died of ovarian cancer in 1997 at the age of 49.

See also Rock and Popular Music Genres; Singer-Songwriter

For Further Reading

Claghorn, Charles Eugene, and Mary Louise VanDyke. *Women Composers and Songwriters: A Concise Biographical Dictionary*. Lanham, MD: Scarecrow Press, 2000.

Grattan, Virginia L. *American Women Songwriters*. Westport, CT: Greenwood Publishing, 1993.

Leanne Fazio

O

Oliveros, Pauline (1932–)

Pauline Oliveros is one of the most accomplished and well respected composers in contemporary music. Her compositional output includes works for chamber ensembles, chorus, electronic tapes, film scores, works for dancers (including collaborative projects with Merce Cunningham, Elizabeth Harris, Deborah Hay, and Paula Josa-Jones), compositions for herself as accordionist, meditations for people with or without formal musical training, and improvisational multimedia works for musicians, dancers, and actors.

Born on 30 May 1932 in Houston, TX, Oliveros grew up in a musical household. Her mother and grandmother were both piano teachers. Oliveros studied composition and accordion at the University of Houston (1949–1952), and in 1957 she earned her B.A. degree in music from San Francisco State College, where she studied composition with Robert Ericson. From 1967 to 1981 she taught in the Department of Music at the University of California at San Diego, where she also directed the Center for Music Experiment and Related Research. In 1981 she resigned, and since 1985 she has been the artistic director of the Pauline Oliveros Foundation: Anchor for the Arts, which supports artists internationally in the creation of new works in musical, literary, and performing arts.

Based on her lifelong fascination with the sonic environment, her work, most notably the *Sonic Meditations* and *Deep Listening* pieces (New Albion NA 022), often involves a heightened sensitivity to many different kinds of sounds: musical, technological, environmental, bodily, remembered, and imagined. The primary element of Oliveros's creativity is "deep listening," that is, listening in every possible way to everything possible to hear no matter what one is doing. As a result, timbre and texture form the structural and highly sensuous components of her music, whereas melody, harmony, and rhythm are secondary.

Oliveros often maximizes unusual acoustics and has worked as an accordionist with natural spaces (caves and cisterns with long reverberation times) as well as virtual acoustics achieved through the electronically "expanded instrument system." Oliveros's music challenges

Pauline Oliveros. *Photo courtesy of Gisela Gamper.*

many traditions of Western art music, as her pieces rarely use conventional music notation. She relies heavily on improvisation and prefers collaborative work over the notion of composer as sole creator; in performance she often invites the audience to join her in making sound.

A committed feminist, Oliveros has written several essays exposing the historical and institutional marginalization of women in the music professions as well as the gender bias of much traditional thinking about music. In 1971 she came out in her profession as a lesbian; some of her most compelling pieces were created in collaboration with other women artists such as Linda Montano (*Living Arts*), Deborah Hay (*The Well and the Gentle*, *Tasting the Blaze*), Susan Marshall (*Contenders*), Paula Josa-Jones (*Skin*, *Ghostdance* [Deep Listening DL7]), and Ione (*Njinga the Queen King*). Her recordings include *Deep Listening* (New Albion 22), *Sanctuary* (Mode 46), *Crone Music* (Lovely Music 1903), and *Alien Bog/Beautiful Soup* (Pogus 21012).

Oliveros is the recipient of the Pacifica Foundation Prize (1961), Gaudeamus Foundation Award (1963), Guggenheim Fellowship (1973), Beethoven Prize, City of Bonn (1977), National Endowment for the Arts Composer's Fellowship (1983, 1988, 1990), New York Foundation for the Arts Award (1989), Bessie Award (1991), Society for Electro-Acoustic Music in the United States Award for Lifetime Achievement (1999), and numerous other awards.

See also Experimental Music; Music Technology

For Further Reading

Oliveros, Pauline. *The Roots of the Moment*. New York: Drogue Press, 1998.
———. *Software for People: Collected Writings 1963–80*. Baltimore: Smith Publications, 1984.
Pauline Oliveros Foundation. Available: http://www.artswire.org/pof

Martha Mockus

Ono, Yoko (1933–)

Composer and performer Yoko Ono was already a prominent figure in the alternative art scenes of both London and New York when she met John Lennon in 1966. She had presented her work in several galleries and had performed at Carnegie Recital Hall in 1961. The work of Yoko Ono spans many disciplines. A composer of popular music and experimental jazz as well as a visual and conceptual artist, Ono participated in the Fluxus movement during the 1960s and organized exhibitions and performances of new work in her Soho loft. It was, however, her relationship with Lennon that made her a widely known celebrity.

Yoko Ono performs at the One on One Festival in New York's Central Park in August 1972. *Photo courtesy of Brian Hamill/Archive Photos.*

Ono was born on 18 February 1933 Tokyo, Japan. Her father was a banker; her mother played several instruments and sang in traditional Japanese vocal styles. Ono studied piano and Western music theory from a very early age. The melding of these influences is evident in her music, which features conventional song structures with unusual vocal techniques. Ono studied for a time at Sarah Lawrence College but dropped out to move to New York City and become an artist.

In the early 1960s she began making "instruction" pieces. These works existed primarily as texts, that could be performed and might result in an object or in an action. Most of the pieces urged the interpreter to think of the everyday activities of life in a creative or structured way. *Mending Piece I* (1966) instructs the performer to glue pieces of a broken cup together while thinking of a personal problem that also needs mending. *Tape Piece III* (1963) instructs one to record the sounds of falling snow and then use the tape itself for tying up packages. Other scores provide instructions for making paintings by leaving canvas on the ground for people to walk on or by cutting holes in canvas to shake hands through. The texts themselves are poetic and suggestive rather than specific, reading much like a haiku or Zen koan. Ono's artistic creations have much in common with these ancient forms of poetry in that she, too, emphasizes attentiveness and contemplation. Ono interpreted many of the instruction pieces herself and showed the results in several gallery exhibitions in America and Europe.

Ono has recorded albums of popular and free jazz music. She collaborated with John Lennon on many recordings, such as *Two Virgins* (Rykodisc 10411), a collection of experimental tape pieces, and *Double Fantasy* (Capitol C2–91425), which featured popular music and was Lennon's last work before he was killed in 1980. Throughout Ono's musical career the common element has been her distinctive voice. Widely criticized as "screaming," Ono's vocal work is actually a composite of various influences ranging from Alban Berg's operas to Japanese styles such as *hetai*, used in Kabuki theater. Ono uses the voice as a wide-ranging expressive instrument and does not ignore the vocal sounds that are traditionally considered non-musical.

See also Experimental Music; Fluxus

For Further Reading

Haskell, Barbara, and John G. Hanhardt. *Yoko Ono: Arias and Objects*. Salt Lake City, UT: Peregrine Smith Books, 1991.

Ono, Yoko. *Instruction Paintings*. New York and Tokyo: Weatherhill, 1995.

Jeffery Byrd

Orff Approach

The Orff Approach to music education has enjoyed widespread acceptance in many countries during the half-century that has followed the first publication of *Das Schulwerk*. Many women in the United States and Canada have been involved in the documentation and implementation of this important pedagogical approach to music.

Composer Carl Orff (1895–1982) conceived the Orff approach as a means for ensuring a holistic approach to the development of the artist in each person. Orff long held an interest in language and poetry, and this is reflected in the artistic use of the spoken word. Impressed by the work of Jacques-Dalcroze and Laban, as well as the dancing of Mary Wigman, Orff developed the idea of "elemental music"—a music that does not separate speech, movement, dance, and drama from music making. Orff was convinced that dance, especially modern dance, held essential keys to unlocking the musicianship of the individual. The opportunity to explore and experiment with these ideas came in a partnership with Dorothee Gunther, a dancer who had a vision of a school for movement and rhythmic and dance training. The years at the Guntherschule (1924–1930), where Orff served as music director, were a time of incubation for the Orff approach. The dance students were taught to make their own music by using body rhythms and simple percussion instruments to accompany their movement. It was through the Guntherschule that Orff met dancer Maja Lex and his lifetime colleague, Gunild Keetman (1904–1990). These two women had a profound influence on the development of the Orff approach to music education.

Women have indeed played an important role in the development of the Orff approach. It was often through women that pedagogy and specific cultural materials were developed. After meeting Orff at the Guntherschule in 1925–1926, Lex and Keetman became dedicated to the principles of the approach. In 1930 these two women formed a dance and instrumental ensemble based on the ideals of the Guntherschule. Lex was a major force in the development of the dance component of this artistic education, and Keetman was key to the development of the Orff ensemble, composing repertoire for the ensemble as it grew and developed. In 1948 Keetman began to transfer Orff's musical and pedagogical ideas into practice for classes of young children. Keetman was a gifted teacher, and in 1951 she joined the faculty of the Mozarteum in Salzburg. As the Orff approach became known internationally, students were drawn from many parts of the world. Doreen Hall (Canada), Daniel Hellden (Sweden), and Minne Lange (Denmark) were among the first to travel to study with Orff and Keetman. Each returned to their country and became founders of the Orff movement there. The first English adaptation of the Orff Schulwerk was Doreen Hall and Arnold Walter's *Music for Children*, followed by Margaret Murray's British edition. Each of these series follows the original instrumental work faithfully but adapt the speech exercises and use traditional North American or British folksongs in place of the German material.

After working closely with Keetman and Orff, Doreen Hall set up the first children's classes and teacher-training classes in North America. Classroom teachers and university professors came to Toronto to watch Hall work with the children. In 1962 the first teacher course in North America was held at the University of Toronto, with Carl Orff, Liselotte Orff, Barbara Haselbach, and Gunild Keetman teaching. Later that year these three traveled to Japan for a lecture and demonstration tour.

Other prominent women who have guided the evolution of the approach include Margaret Murray, Jane Frazee, Arvida Steen, Isabel McNeil Carley, Brigitte Warner, Gertrud Orff, Lois Birkenshaw-Fleming, Sr. Marcelle Corneille, Ruth Boshkoff, and Mary Goetze (b. 1943). There are Orff associations in countries around the world, and the Orff materials have been translated into over 20 languages. In addition to the original five volumes, teachers and composers have developed materials in many different cultural and linguistic contexts, from Ewe to Japanese. Teacher-training centers have developed worldwide. In addition to the international courses offered at the Mozarteum, it is now possible to study Orff pedagogy at the graduate level in several universities.

See also Music Education; Organizations, Music Education

For Further Reading

American Orff-Schulwerk Association. Available: http://www.aosa.org/

Carl Orff Foundation. *Carl Orff Homepage*. Available: http://orff.munich.netsurf.de/orff/start_e.html

Keetman, Gunild. *Elementaria*. Trans. Margaret Murray. London: Schott and Co., 1974.

Warner, Brigitte. *Orff-Schulwerk: Applications for the Classroom*. Englewood Cliffs, NJ: Prentice-Hall, 1991.

Lori-Anne Dolloff

Organizations, Music Education

Professional music education organizations tend to fall under the larger organization of the National Association for Music Education (MENC), formerly known as the Music Educators National Conference. Each of these organizations has a relationship with MENC and has the purpose of promoting music education. All organizations are open to a variety of constituencies and have various criteria for membership.

The American Choral Directors Association (ACDA) is a nonprofit professional organization including choral musicians from schools, colleges, universities, communities, industrial organizations, churches, and professional groups.

ACDA encourages the finest in choral music, performance, composition, publication, and research. It publishes the *Choral Journal* 10 months a year. ACDA is an MENC auxiliary organization. Women who have served as the national president include Colleen Kirk and Diana Leland.

The American Guild of English Handbell Ringers (AGEHR), Inc., is dedicated to improving ringing skills, providing education and aids for directors, promoting excellence in performance, and improving the quality of handbell music. AGEHR sponsors massed ringing at conferences, director's seminars, reading sessions, and workshops, and it produces publications and other resources. AGEHR is a MENC-associated organization. Women who have served as president include Karen Leonard, Ginny Fleming, Marilyn Hines, D. Linda McKechnie, Mary Kettlehut, Mary McCleary, Nancy Poore Tufts, Bessie Erb, and Margaret Shurcliff.

The American Orff-Schulwerk Association (AOSA) is comprised of music and movement educators dedicated to the creative teaching approach developed by Carl Orff and Gunild Keetman. They are united by the belief that learning about music should be an active and joyful experience. Membership benefits include a subscription to the quarterly magazine, access to research grants and scholarships funds, an annual conference, teacher-training courses, and information on career development. AOSA is a MENC-associated organization. Women who have served as president include Ruth Pollock Hamm, Konnie Saliba, Jacobeth Postl, Jane Frazee, Nancy Ferguson, Mary Shamrock, Lillian Yaross, Arvida Steen, Millie Burnett, Carolyn Tower, Janice Rapley, Judith Thomas, Virginia Ebinger, Judy Bond, Marilyn Davidon, Carol Erion, Carolee Stewart, and Linda Ahlstedt.

The American String Teachers Association (ASTA) with National School Orchestra Association (NSOA) is the professional organization of string and orchestra players. Members include studio teachers, college faculty, schoolteachers, performers, students, and members of the string and orchestra business community. ASTA with NSOA publishes *American String Teacher* and holds conferences and workshops of specific interest to its membership. ASTA with NSOA sponsors the Biennial National High School Honors Orchestra and its Biennial National Solo Competition as well as other clinics, competitions, and workshops. Carol Smith, director of orchestral studies and conductor at the Sam Houston State University, is the ASTA's current secretary. Additionally, Pamela Tellejohn Hayes (b. 1946), outstanding string educator, orchestra clinician, and consultant, and Judy Palac, associate professor of music education at Michigan State University, serve as members-at-large.

Chamber Music America is a national service organization established to promote professional chamber music. It offers grant programs; consulting and technical assistance; education initiatives, including *Flying Together*, a chamber music education newsletter; and awards for excellence in chamber music teaching. Chamber Music America is a MENC auxiliary organization. B. J. Bucker was the first woman to hold the position of executive director.

The College Band Directors National Association (CBDNA) helps its members grow as musicians, educators, conductors, and administrators. It presents conferences, publishes the journals *CBDNA Report* and *CBDNA Journal*, maintains a state-by-state network of university and college band conductors, and supports commissioning projects to generate new works by significant composers. The CBDNA is a MENC auxiliary organization. The Ethnic and Gender Committee of the CBDNA "calls into focus historical patterns of social interaction, socioeconomic factors that have been in place for decades and the confusing and even contradictory rhetoric that permeates our contemporary consciousness" (Mission Statement). Of the national officers, only one is a woman: Patricia Hoy, director of bands at Northern Arizona University, serves as the treasurer.

The Dalcroze Society of America is a nonprofit organization that promotes the teachings of Emile Jaques-Dalcroze. Membership, which is open to anyone interested in the Dalcroze teaching approach, includes a subscription to the *American Dalcroze Journal*, which contains articles of interest, news, and schedules of courses and workshops. The Society is affiliated with the Federation Internationale des Enseignants de Rhythmique (FIER), a worldwide association of Dalcroze teachers with headquarters in Geneva, Switzerland. Mary Michalka Egan currently serves as the society's secretary, and Leslie Mills is the editor of the *American Dalcroze Journal*.

The Gordon Institute for Music Learning (GIML) was founded in 1987 to promote Edwin E. Gordon's pioneering research in music aptitude and theories on how children learn music. It encourages the application of Gordon's music learning theory in classrooms across the country. GIML sponsors summer seminars and an annual conference that includes sessions specifically devoted to music learning theory. GIML is a MENC auxiliary organization. Many women have been involved in the development of this institute, including Carol Gordon, Maria Runfola, Beth Bolton, Alison Reynolds, Cynthia Taggart, and Wendy Valerio.

The International Association of Jazz Educators (IAJE) promotes the appreciation of jazz and its artistic performance, helps organize jazz curricula in schools, and fosters the appreciation of jazz principles at all levels of education. The IAJE cooperates with organizations dedicated to the development of musical culture; IAJE is a MENC-associated organization. The Women's Caucus was founded in 1984 to provide support for women members of the IAJE. Soon thereafter, Julie Hudson was elected to the Executive Board, and sexist language was removed from IAJE journal and literature. Currently there are several important women members of the Executive Board, including Dianthe Spencer (San Francisco Jazz Organization), vice-president; Yvonne Tost Ervin (Western Jazz Presenters Network), recording secretary; and Mary Jo Papich (Peoria Public Schools), treasurer.

The National Association of College Wind and Percussion Instructors (NACWPI) includes university, college, and conservatory teachers. This organization encourages the effective teaching of wind and percussion instruments on the college level, serves as a forum for information, and supports fine music and instruments in wind and percussion. NACWPI also coordinates activities with other groups and encourages the performance of solo and chamber music. NACWPI is a MENC-associated organization.

The MENC: the National Association for Music Education is the premier organization for music educators, founded in 1907. Its mission is to advance music education as a profession and to ensure that every child in America has access to a balanced, sequential, high-quality education that includes music as a core subject of study. MENC played a key leadership role in the development of the National Standards for Music Education. The National Standards, developed in 1994, represent the first comprehensive set of educational standards for K–12 arts instruction. MENC publishes the following journals; *Music Educators Journal*, *Teaching Music*, *Journal of Music Teacher Education*, *General Music Today*, *Journal of Research in Music Education*, and *UPDATE*. MENC also sponsors the following educational programs: Music in Our Schools Month, World's Largest Concert, Fund for the Advancement of Music Education, National Biennial In-Service Conference, and Sing America! The following women have served as president: Henrietta Baker, Elizabeth Casterton (1877–1946), Mabelle Glenn (1881–1969), Lilla Belle Pitts (1884–1970), Marguerite Hood (1903–1992), Frances Andrews, Mary Hoffman, Dorothy Straub (b. 1941), Carolynn Linderman, and June Hinckley.

The National Band Association (NBA) is the largest band organization in the world. Members can receive the *NBA Journal* and the *Instrumentalist*, a selective music list for band, and adjudication forms. Activities include a biennial convention, numerous regional conventions, a composition contest, the National High School Honors Concert and Jazz Bands, and the NBA Community Band. The NBA is a MENC-associated organization. Although there has never been a woman elected as NBA president, there are currently several important women affiliated with the NBA, including Paula Crider (b. 1944), president (director emeritus, Longhorn Band, University of Texas at Austin); and Linda Moorhouse, second vice-president (associate director of bands, Louisiana State University).

The National Association for the Study and Performance of African American Music (NASPAAM) serves as a voice for the concerns of black music educators throughout the United States; promotes, preserves, and advances the tradition of black music throughout the African diaspora; encourages the participation of black musicians in all areas of musical activity; and promotes the advancement of black music through MENC. NASPAAM is a MENC-associated organization.

The North American Steel Band Association (NASBA) is a nonprofit organization dedicated to the development, support, and the promotion of the steel drum art form, its history, instrument development, and cultural heritage as it pertains to music education. NASBA is a MENC-associated organization.

The Organization of American Kodály Educators (OAKE) is an organization designed to promote the concept of "Music for Everyone" through the improvement of music education in schools. It is a MENC-associated organization. Ann Kay was the 1999 executive director. The current executive committee is comprised mainly of women: Jill Trinka, president; Sandra Mathias, president elect; Susan Tevis, vice president; Jeanne Wohlgamuth, secretary; John Dahlin, administrative director; and Anita McLaughlin, treasurer.

Opera for Youth, Inc., is a national nonprofit service organization that was founded in 1978 for the encouragement of the creation of operas to be performed by children, young adults, and adults, and to support the composers and librettists of these works. A quarterly journal and a bibliography of works support this purpose. The organization is a MENC auxiliary organization. Barbara Lockard-Zimmerman is the current president.

The Percussive Arts Society (PAS) is a not-for-profit service organization. Its purpose is educational, promoting drums and percussion through a viable network of performers, teachers, students, enthusiasts, and sustaining members. PAS accomplishes its goals though publications, a worldwide network of chapters, the World Percussion Network (WPN), the Percussive Arts Society International Headquarters/Museum, and the annual Percussive Arts Society International Convention (PASIC). PAS is a MENC-associated organization. Currently, Kristin Shiner-McGuire (Nazareth College of Rochester) is the PAS secretary. Several women serve on the Board of Directors, including Kay Stonefelt and Lisa Rogers.

The Society for the Preservation and Encouragement of Barber Shop Quartet Singing in America (SPEBSQSA) is an organization for those who share a love of close harmony singing. Through educational services, music publishing, public performance, and competition, SPEBSQSA preserves a rich heritage of uniquely American music for future generations. SPEBSQSA is a MENC auxiliary organization. Sweet Adelines International is a worldwide organization of women singers committed to advancing the musical art form of barbershop harmony through education and performances. "Harmonize the World" is its motto. This organization is a MENC auxiliary organization. Edna Mae Anderson (1903–1959) was the first president.

The Technology Institute for Music Educators (TIME) provides in-service training and certification in music technology, helping music teachers learn how to integrate the tools of technology in the music curriculum in support of the National Standards for the Arts. Although none of the TIME directors is a woman, there are many women who serve on the National Advisory Board, including Joy Cardin, June Hinkley, Valerie Pippin, and Kimberly Walls.

See also Choral Education; Instrumental Education; Jazz Education; Music Education; Music Educators National Conference; String Education

For Further Reading

National Association for Music Education. Available: http://www.menc.org/connect/allies.html

Marla Butke

Organizations, Performer

Performer organizations are nonprofit professional service societies for performers, teachers, and students of specific musical instruments, instrument makers, and other interested parties. Such groups exist for most standard modern orchestral instruments, as well as for vocal and choral performance, conducting, and historic instruments. These organizations advance artistic excellence and pedagogy in the playing and teaching of the instrument and foster communication among performers, increasing knowledge about the instrument and its history and literature. Some organizations encourage new compositions for the instrument and work to develop audiences and encourage appreciation of the instrument. Associations may adopt official bylaws to assist in achieving their purposes and managing the organization. Groups may be national or international in scope, and some are divided into regional chapters or maintain online branches. Some preserve diplomatic relations with similar organizations from other countries. Some U.S. organizations are sections of worldwide organizations, and some have been founded as an alliance of various national or worldwide associations.

Performer organizations host conventions, providing a forum for performers and others interested in the instrument. Attendees have opportunities for solo and chamber performance and for lectures pertaining to the instrument. They share performance techniques and discuss the furtherance of performance practice. Discourse at these meetings may also address pedagogical issues, as well as the examination of new critical editions and the review of recent articles about the instrument. Conventions also serve as a venue for the dissemination of new literature. A highlight of conventions is frequently one or more performance competitions, which may feature the winning composition of a contest sponsored by the organization.

Performer societies provide other services as well. Most promote research and publication regarding the instrument, and they also publish a scholarly journal or magazine, newsletters, and bulletins. Many groups support educational efforts to edify the general public and to encourage and assist young performers in establishing their careers; some even identify themselves as principally educational organizations. Some are also active in arts advocacy. Societies frequently sponsor events such as festivals, concerts, seminars, workshops, and master classes. Many groups present awards to performers, sometimes but not always in conjunction with competitions. Grant programs and the issuance of recordings are further activities of certain organizations. Some groups house archives and electronic databases of music written for the instrument. Most maintain official Web sites, which provide current information about the ongoing activities of the organization.

The role of women in performer organizations has changed over time. In addition to holding membership, women are now more able to become active members, participating in functions. Many hold leadership positions as officers or directors. They may act as liaisons to other national or worldwide organizations, serve on committees, act as referees or staff members for the journal, or work as adjudicators in performance or composition competitions.

The major performer societies in the United States may be classified according to instrument type. Associations for woodwind instruments include the National Flute Association (NFA), the International Double Reed Society (IDRS), and the International Clarinet Association (ICA). The NFA has several key woman who serve on the Board of Directors, including Nancy Andrew, Teresa Beaman, and Katherine Hoover, (b. 1937). Nancy Ambrose King, Norma Hooks, and Andrea Merenzon all serve on the board of the IRDS. Julie DeRoche, president; Kelly Burk, treasurer; Maurita Murphy Mead, secretary of the ICA.

Brass organizations include the International Horn Society, the International Trumpet Guild (ITG), the International Trombone Association, and the International Tuba and Euphonium Association (TUBA), board members include Mary Ann Craig, vice president; Velvet Brown, secretary; Kathy Aylsworth Brantigan, treasurer. Although few women serve on any of the boards of directors for the major brass organizations, there are a few notable exceptions. ITG Board of Directors includes Joyce Davis and Laurie Frink. Mary Ann Craig (secretary) and Kathy Aylsworth Brantigan (treasurer) both serve on the board of TUBA. The International Women's Brass Conference (IWBC) was founded in 1990 to offer support, education, and development for women brass musicians. Its first president and founder was Susan Slaughter.

Groups for percussive and keyboard instruments include the Percussive Arts Society, the American Guild of Organists (AGO), and the American Harp Society (AHS). Dorothy Remsen serves as the executive secretary of the AHS, and Shirley S. King serves as the secretary of the AGO.

For stringed instruments, organizations include the Violin Society of America (VSA), the American Viola Society (a section of the International Viola-Gesellschaft, or International Viola Society), the International Viola Society, the World Cello Congress (an event as well as an organization), the International Cello Society, and the International Society of Bassists. A major performance association for chamber musicians is Chamber Music America. Helen M. Hayes (president) and Joan E. Miller (treasurer) both serve on the board of the VSA.

The main vocal and choral organizations in the United States are the National Association of Teachers of Singing and the International Federation for Choral Music (representing singers and choral directors). NATS has on its board Darleen Kliewer-Britton, vice-president for the NATS Artist Awards competition, and Martha Randall, vice-president for membership.

Conducting and directing groups include the Conductors Guild and the American Choral Directors Association (ACDA). Mitzi Groom, president-elect and Maxine Asselin serves as treasurer on the executive committee of the ACDA. Historical performance associations include Early Music America, the American Recorder Society, the Historic Brass Society, the Historical Harp Society, and the Viola da Gamba Society of America. Societies designed to help launch the careers of young performers include Young Concert Artists, Inc., and the American Pianists Association.

See also Committees; International Women's Brass Conference; Organizations, Music Education; Organizations, Research

For Further Reading

American Choral Directors Association. Available: http://www.acdaonline.org.

American Harp Society. Available: http://harpsociety.org

International Clarinet Association. Available: http://www.clarinet.org/

International Trombone Association. Available: http://www.ita-web.org/

International Trumpet Guild Web Site. Available: http://www.trumpetguild.org/

National Flute Association: NFA online. Available: http://nfaonline.org/

T.U.B.A. Homepage. Available: http://www.tubaonline.org/

Welcome to IDRS. Available: https://www.idrs.org

Dawn Williams

Organizations, Professional Audio

Although there are many organizations with members whose work involves sound and music, there are few professional audio organizations. More common are organizations with an audio subcommittee or section within the larger body of the group. As is the case in many technical fields, women have historically been greatly underrepresented in these organizations.

The two primary professional audio organizations are the Audio Engineering Society (AES) and the National Academy of Recording Arts and Sciences (NARAS). The AES is the more technical of the two, and it plays an important part in the dissemination of current technical information and research. This is largely through its monthly publication of the *Journal of the Audio Engineering Society* (the only peer-reviewed journal devoted exclusively to audio technology) and the paper sessions, exhibits, demos, and workshops presented at the annual AES Convention (2000 saw the 108th convention.) The AES is an international organization, and its members include engineers, scientists, executives, educators, and students. Although women represent less than 10 percent of its membership, the AES has taken a proactive role in increasing opportunities for women in the organization and in the audio industry in general. At its annual convention in 1995 the AES Women in Audio subcommittee initiated a project called "Women in Audio: Project 2000." The goals of the project include examining the challenges women face when entering or engaged in the field of audio engineering; recommending initiatives that will encourage women to pursue careers in audio-related fields; actively soliciting new AES members; providing networking opportunities for women in the AES; and focusing on successful women working in the field. Perhaps the most visible indication of the desire of the AES to increase the number and visibility of its women members is the fact that two of its recent presidents have been women: Elizabeth Cohen and Marina Bosi.

The National Academy of Recording Arts and Sciences, Inc. (NARAS), (also known as the Recording Academy) is an organization with members drawn from all areas of musical and sound production, including performers, producers, composers, and engineers. Although there are technical aspects to the NARAS, it tends to focus more on the business, cultural, and public relations side of things, often dealing with issues such as intellectual property rights, record piracy, the archiving and preservation of recordings, and censorship concerns. NARAS is also actively involved in raising public awareness of and support for music education. NARAS is best known publicly as the organization that gives the Grammy Awards each year for achievements in a variety of artistic and technical categories, including Song of the Year, Best New Artist, and Best Engineered Album.

There are a number professional organizations not specifically focused on audio but whose members may be involved in various aspects of the audio industry. The Society of Motion Picture and Television Engineers, Inc. (SMPTE), is an international professional organization for the motion picture and television industries. SMPTE members are drawn from almost every discipline in the motion-imaging industry, and they work with a wide range of motion-imaging technologies including film, television, video, computer imaging, and telecommunications. There is no specific committee or category of women members. The Institute of Electrical and Electronics Engineers, Inc. (IEEE), helps coordinate engineering activities around the world and is instrumental in establishing protocols and standards for emerging technologies, many of which are audio-related. The IEEE has a Women in Engineering Committee (WIE) dedicated to issues specifically related to women engineers; it offers professional development, educational, and mentoring programs.

The Academy of Motion Picture Arts

and Sciences is an organization that brings together professionals from all parts of the motion picture industry. Although it is best known as the entity that presents the Academy Awards each year (in both artistic and technical categories), it also actively supports and enables artistic and technical progress and research related to motion pictures.

There are also various organizations oriented toward the broad topic of multimedia, which generally includes an audio component. Among them, the Special Interest Group on Computer Graphics (SIGGRAPH) organization is perhaps the most "audio friendly," and the annual SIGGRAPH convention often features papers, exhibits, and presentations that deal with audio issues. SIGGRAPH also stands out as having had substantial involvement from women throughout the organization, on both the general membership and leadership levels.

There are many other professional organizations whose members include audio specialists and engineers. And as all media become multimedia, the number of such organizations is growing. Although the number of organizations devoted specifically to audio will most likely remain small, there is, and will be, no shortage of support for interested audio professionals.

See also Audio Production; Music Technology

For Further Reading

Cosola, Mary. "Resources for Women in Music." *Electronic Musician* 13/1 (January 1997): 96–102, 159.

Journal of the Audio Engineering Society. New York: Audio Engineering Society.

National Academy of Recording Arts and Sciences. Available: http://www.naras.org

Douglas Repetto

Organizations, Regional Arts

There are seven regional nonprofit arts organizations, excluding national, state, and composer and/or performer-oriented arts organizations, that provide funding opportunities and are committed to the improvement and dissemination of the arts in the United States. Although women are present on the boards of directors for many of these regional organizations, the vast majority of people holding positions of authority are men.

Arts Midwest. Formed in 1985 through the merger of the Affiliated State Arts Agencies of the Upper Midwest and the Great Lakes Arts Alliance and based in Minneapolis, MN, Arts Midwest has distributed over $8,000,000 to artists and arts organizations in support of over 5,100 projects and artistic events. Its mission is to maintain its initial commitment to the performing arts touring and jazz services while considering other programs and initiatives. Serving Iowa, Illinois, Indiana, Michigan, Minnesota, North Dakota, Ohio, South Dakota, and Wisconsin, one primary area of focus is the Midwest Arts Conference, an annual cooperative education and booking conference that draws attendees from throughout the United States. The Heartland Arts Fund, a joint venture with the Mid-America Arts Alliance, supports presenters of public performances and educational events. Arts Midwest is estimated to bring arts and arts education events to almost one million people in its target communities each year.

Consortium for Pacific Arts and Cultures (CPAC). The primary goal of the Consortium is to "promote and cultivate increased global awareness and appreciation of Pacific cultures" throughout its member region and the United

States. Its dedication to the preservation of the traditional cultures of its members is cultivated through the "presentation and encouragement of opportunities for the growth and exchange of both traditional and contemporary arts" as well as by "fostering and perpetuating the arts within the Pacific region." The Consortium's focus on the arts, both traditional and contemporary, is particularly directed at stimulating new aesthetic directions and posing new means for artistic inquiry. CPAC is committed to providing technical assistance, regional programming, and financial resources to its member constituents in the U.S. territories of American Samoa and Guam and to the Commonwealth of the Northern Mariana Islands from its base of operations in Honolulu, HI. Members of the Board of Directors include Simona Lauti (chairperson, American Samoa Council on Arts, Culture and Humanities), Leala Pili (executive director, American Samoa Council on Arts, Culture and Humanities); and Deborah Bordallo (executive director, Guam Council for Arts, Culture and the Humanities Agency).

Mid-America Arts Alliance (M-AAA). Founded in 1972 to "bring the arts and audiences together," the Mid-America Arts Alliance promotes arts education and partnerships to "provide accessibility, assure affordability, broaden understanding, cultivate skill development, and nurture communities," both culturally and creatively. Its mission is to "transform lives and build communities by uniting people with the power of art." Based in Kansas City, MO, the organization serves diverse communities of various sizes in Arkansas, Kansas, Missouri, Nebraska, Oklahoma, and Texas. Its primary activities are to introduce both emerging and well-known artists to member communities, provide opportunities for communities to interact with artists, bring performances and exhibitions to underserved communities, and promote the arts in education. M-AAA's Community Catalysts program provides mini-grant opportunities that "broaden and deepen public participation in the arts" (including Meet the Composer funding). To date, the organization has designated its considerable funding resources (and an economic impact estimated at over $232,000,000) to support over twelve thousand exhibitions and performances reaching an audience estimated at over 25 million people. June Freeman, Joy Pennington, and Frances Shackelford all serve on the Board of Directors for Arkansas. Marianna Beach, Carolyn Dillon, and Judith Sabitini serve in Kansas. Karen Holland, Anne Liberman, and Noree Byrd serve in Missouri. Marian Andersen (emeritus), Ruth Keene, Marilyn Mitchell, and Jennifer A. Severin serve in Nebraska. Linda S. Frazier, Kay Goebel, Nancy E. Meinig, and Betty Price are on the Board of Directors in Oklahoma. Alejandrina Drew, Suzy Finesilver, Adair Margo and Lillie Fontenot serve in Texas.

Mid-Atlantic Arts Foundation (MAAF). The Mid-Atlantic Arts Foundation works to serve both the most highly developed and underserved communities in the United States. Founded in 1979 and based in Baltimore, MD, MAAF is dedicated to the growth and appreciation of the arts throughout its region and beyond. MAAF programs encourage the creation of original works of art, promote interrelationships throughout its performing arts communities, build audiences, and advocate increased arts in education programs in its nine-member community. Its primary areas of support include artist residency programs, individual artist fellowships, and leadership development. Specific projects include touring artist programs, community arts programs, peer assistance and mentoring, traditional arts, and jazz education. With funding primarily through private, corporate, and foundation contributions, donors have the option of assigning donations to specified foundation activities. Serving Delaware, the District of Columbia, Maryland, New Jersey, New York, Pennsylvania, the U.S. Virgin Islands, Virginia, and West Virginia, MAAF serves an estimated 24 percent of all artists living in the mainland United States. The Board of Directors includes Laura Seanlan (executive director of the Delaware State Arts Council), Peggy Baggett (executive director of the Virginia Commission for the Arts), Nicolette Clarke (executive director of the New York State Council on the Arts), Barbara F. Russo (executive director of the New Jersey State Council on the Arts), and Kitty Carlisle Hart is the honorary chair.

New England Foundation for the Arts (NEFA). Formed to both promote and leverage regional arts on a national level, NEFA has worked since 1975 to be a premier disseminator of state and national arts funding as well as to promote its own unique funding programs. Serving Connecticut, Massachusetts, Maine, New Hampshire, Rhode Island, and Vermont, NEFA currently promotes three large-scale funding programs. The Creation and Presentation, Culture in Community, and Connections funds are specifically designed to support and disseminate new works, link the arts to community development, and promote research and technology-based cultural awareness programs in New England, respectively. Funded through the National Endowment for the Arts, by member states, and by corporations, foundations, and private individuals, the Foundation has an annual budget of $5,000,000. Based in Boston, MA, NEFA has initiated several projects to measure the economic impact of cultural activities on local communities, setting new standards and defining research and evaluation strategies to support its funding efforts. Of particular interest to musicians are NEFA's Presenter Travel Fund, New England States Touring Program, Meet the Composer New England fund, and NEON fund for technical and touring assistance. The Board of Directors includes Mary Kelley (executive director, Massachusetts Cultural Council).

Southern Arts Federation. Based in Atlanta, GA, the Southern Arts Federation serves nine member states: Alabama, Florida, Georgia, Kentucky, Louisiana, Mississippi, North Carolina, South Carolina, and Tennessee. The Federation was formed in 1975 to "enhance the professional skills of southern arts organizations and artists and broaden the appreciation and support of the arts in the South among policy makers and audiences." The Federation is particularly interested in funding arts education in its nine-state region. Focus areas include arts partnership opportunities that promote and nurture collaborations between artists and arts organizations, and professional development funding that provides technical assistance and training. The remaining foci of its funding activities are designed to support southern arts and culture and arts education/arts advocacy. Important funding partners include the Lila-Wallace Reader's Digest Fund and Meet the Composer South, both of which support a variety of regional touring initiatives in dance, music, theater, and opera. Programs include Arts Education, Folklorists of the South, Southern Connections, American Traditions, **Jazz**

Touring, and JazzSouth Radio. The Board of Directors includes Judee Pettijohn (executive director, Florida Arts Council), Mary B. Regan (executive director, North Carolina Arts Council), Suzette Surkamer (executive director, South Carolina Arts Commission). Betsy Baker (executive director, Georgia Council for the Arts), Gerri Combs (executive director, Kentucky Arts Council), and Pam Breaux (executive director, Louisiana Division of the Arts).

Western States Arts Federation (WESTAF). Serving 12 member states (Alaska, Arizona, California, Colorado, Idaho, Montana, Nevada, New Mexico, Oregon, Utah, Washington, and Wyoming), WESTAF is a nonprofit arts service organization "dedicated to the creative advancement and preservation of the arts." Based in Denver, CO, the federation engages in projects that focus on arts research and policy development, information-systems development, and the convening of arts experts and leaders to "benefit the future health of the arts community of the West." Founded in 1974, WESTAF is supported by the National Endowment for the Arts, member state arts agencies, and private/corporate foundations. It is governed by a 22-member Board of Trustees drawn from arts professionals in the member states, and it administers an estimated $1,500,000 budget annually. Through this funding, WESTAF achieves its organizational goals by "engaging in innovative approaches to programs and services and focusing its efforts on strengthening the financial, organizational, and policy infrastructure of the arts" among its constituents. The focus of its programs is in four areas: TourWest (presenting and touring support), TumbleWords (literature presenting and residencies), regional folk arts, and Native American arts in a variety of disciplines.

See also Committees; Organizations, Music Education; Organizations, Performer; Organizations, Research

For Further Reading

Arts Midwest Homepage. Available: http://www.artsmidwest.org

Consortium for Pacific Arts and Cultures. Available: http://www.nasaa-arts.org/new/nasaa/gateway/CPAC.html

Mid-America Arts Alliance. Available: http://www.maaa.org

Mid-Atlantic Arts Foundation. *Homepage 1*. Available: http://www.midatlanticarts.org

New England Foundation for the Arts Homepage. Available: http://www.nefa.org

Southern Arts Federation. Available: http://southarts.org

Western States Arts Federation. *Arts Resources*. Available: http://www.westaf.org

Michael Remson

Organizations, Research

Organizations or societies of scholars or artists with common research goals whose interests are categorized according to their academic discipline include musicology (including music history and music theory), composition, performance, music education, and jazz studies. The activities of these organizations include annual meetings for the exchange of ideas, the publication of journals and monographs, and the promotion of performances of new or recently discovered works. A charter, constitution, or set of by-laws usually governs these activities. Each organization retains an executive committee including a president, vice-president, secretary, and treasurer; in addition, organizations that publish a journal appoint an editor. Some of the larger societies create subcommittees to study specialized issues, including women's studies, gender issues, cultural diversity, awards, and professional development. The earliest musical organizations date back to medieval Europe for the performance of music and have been a part of musical life since that time. Two of the earliest and still existing American organizations to achieve international prominence were the Handel and Haydn Society in Boston (est. 1815) and the Philharmonic Symphony Society in New York (est. 1842).

The following list provides a select catalog of prominent active national organizations in the United States in their respective areas of research. For each organization, the founding date, organization purpose, and name of the primary research journal are listed. The current mailing and World Wide Web addresses are listed in the organization's journal or in the *International Directory of Music Organizations*, an annual index published by the College Music Society. Additionally, many of the national organizations have regionally affiliated organizations that are also listed on the World Wide Web pages. Information pertaining to prominent women members of organizations listed in this entry is based on searches of the respective organization's World Wide Web sites at the time of writing.

Musicology. The American Musicological Society (AMS), established in 1934, is a learned society whose objective is the advancement of research in the various fields of music as a branch of learning and scholarship. Its primary journal is the *Journal of the American Musicological Society*, 1948– . AMS has several women on its executive committee, including Jessie Ann Owens, president, and Elaine Sisman, vice-president.

The Society for American Music (SAM), formerly known as the Sonneck Society, was established in 1975 and is dedicated to the encouragement and study of all aspects of American music and music in America. Its primary journal is *American Music*, 1983– . SAM has several women on its executive committee, including Katherine K. Preston, secretary, and Marva G. Carter, Emily Good, Linda Pohly, and Mary DuPree, members at large.

The Society for Ethnomusicology (SEM), established 1955, promotes the research, study, and performance of music in all historical periods and cultural contexts. Its primary journal is *Ethnomusicology*, 1957– . SEM has several women on its executive committee, including Ellen Koskoff, president; and Anne K. Rasmussen, first vice-president; Beverly Diamond, second vice-president; Laurel Sercombe, treasurer; and Deborah Wong, secretary.

The Society for Music Theory (SMT) was established in 1978 to support scholarship, pedagogy, and other interests in the field of music theory. Its primary journal is *Music Theory Spectrum*, 1979– . SMT has several women on its executive committee, including Elizabeth W. Marvin, president; Gretchen Horlacher, secretary; and Candice Brower, treasurer.

There are a number of specialized organizations dedicated to research of a single composer. One representative example of this type of organization is the American Brahms Society (ABS), which was established in 1983 to foster and disseminate research into the life, music, and historical context of Johannes Brahms. Its journal is *Brahms Studies*, 1994– . ABS has Elaine Sisman as secretary on the executive committee.

Composition. The Society of Composers, Inc. ([SCI] formerly American Society of University Composers (1966–1988), est. 1989), is a professional society dedicated to the promotion of composition, performance, understanding, and dissemination of new and contemporary music. Its primary journals are the *ASUC Journal of Music Scores*, 1973–1988, and *SCI Journal of Music Scores*, 1989– . SCI does not have any women on its executive committee at this time, although there are women actively involved in the society's operations.

The Society of Electro-Acoustic Music in the United States (SEAMUS), established 1984, seeks to provide a broad forum for those involved in electro-acoustic music and to increase communication among the diverse constituency of this relatively new music medium. Its primary journal is *Journal SEAMUS*, 1985– . SEAMUS has several women on its executive committee, including Elainie Lillios (b. 1968), vice-president for membership, and Elizabeth Hinkle-Turner (b. 1964), treasurer.

Performance. A thorough discussion of the diverse performance organizations that presently exist is beyond the scope of this entry. There are organizations that support virtually every instrument that is studied today, as well as performing societies dedicated to antiquarian instruments. A few select performance organizations deserve mention here owing to the nature of the scholarly or pedagogical research undertaken. The American Choral Directors Association (ACDA), established 1959, is a nonprofit organization whose central purpose is to promote excellence in choral music through performance, composition, publication, research, and teaching. Its primary journal is the *Choral Journal*, 1959– . ACDA has Mitzi Groom, president-elect and Maxine Asselin as treasurer on the executive committee.

The American String Teachers Association (ASTA), established in 1950, is an organization that promotes excellence in string and orchestra teaching and playing. Its primary journal is *American String Teacher*, 1951– . ASTA has several women on its executive committee, including Carol Smith, secretary, and Pamela Tellejohn Hayes (b. 1946), member-at-large.

The National Association of Teachers of Singing (NATS), established in 1944, encourages the highest standards of singing through excellence in teaching and the promotion of vocal education and research. Its primary journal is the *Journal of Singing*, 1995– . The association has several women on its executive committee, including Darleen Kliewer-Britton, vice-president for NATS Artist Awards competition, and Martha Randall, vice-president for membership.

The National Opera Association (NOA), established in 1955, seeks to promote a greater appreciation of opera and music theater, to enhance pedagogy and performing activities, and to increase performance opportunities by supporting projects that improve the scope and quality of opera through collegiate and regional productions and publication of scholarly articles. Its primary journal is *Opera Journal*, 1968– . NOA has several women on its executive committee, including Patricia Heuerman, president, Penelope Speedie, vice-president for resources, and Carol Notestine, secretary.

Music Education. The College Music Society (CMS), established in 1957, exists to support its members in their professional and pedagogical goals by creating forums in which individual disciplines can expand, interact, and communicate with one another and by gathering, considering, and disseminating ideas on the philosophy and practice of music. Its primary journal is *College Music Symposium*, 1960– . CMS has several women on its executive committee, including Barbara Bennett, vice-president, and Karen Garison, secretary. CMS administration is further divided into 16 specialized committees. There are women chairing several of these committees, including Judith Coe (Committee on Music, Women, and Gender), Gail Woldu (Committee on Musicology), Pamela Poulin (Committee on Music Theory), Nancy Barry (Committee on Mentoring), and Nanette Kaplan Solomon (Advisory Committee on Performance).

The Association for Technology in Music Instruction (ATMI), established in 1992, formerly the Association for the Development of Computer-Based Instructional Systems (1975–1991), serves as a forum for the scholarly presentation of technical information by and for specialists as well as nonspecialists in the field of computer-assisted instruction (CAI) in music. Thus ATMI cultivates the development of music CAI and disseminates information about the evolution and application of technology in music instruction. Its primary journal is the *ATMI Technology Directory*, 1992– . ATMI has Judith Bowman as secretary on the executive committee.

The Music Educators National Conference (MENC), established in 1907, seeks to advance music education as a profession and to ensure that every child in America has access to a balanced, sequential, high-quality education that includes music as a core subject of study. Its primary journal is the *Journal of Research in Music Education*, 1953– . Owing to its enormous size (85,000+ members), MENC has a vast administrative organization that features women at all levels of governance, including Virginia C. Bennett, North Central Division president; Barbara Geer, Southern Division president; Gayle C. McMillen, Southwestern Division president; and Lynn Brinckmeyer, Northwest Division president.

The Music Teachers' National Association (MTNA), established in 1876, was formed to promote the professional growth and development of members and to further the art of music by providing programs that encourage and support teaching, performance, composition, and scholarly research. Its primary journal is the *American Music Teacher*, 1951– . MTNA has several women on its executive committee, including Phyllis I. Pieffer, president-elect; Sue H. Holder, vice-president of membership; and Kathryn B. Huel, vice-president of professional activities.

Jazz Studies. The International Association of Jazz Educators (IAJE), formerly the National Association of Jazz Educators (1968–1988), was established in 1989 as a voluntary organization whose primary focus is to foster the understanding, study, and appreciation of jazz and its artistic performance. Its primary journal is the *Jazz Educators Journal*, 1969– . IAJE has Dianthe Spencer, vice-president; Yvonne Tost Errin, recording secretary; and Mary J. Papich, treasurer.

The American Federation of Jazz Societies (AFJS), established in 1985, is an international resource and networking organization serving jazz societies, festivals, presenters, and related jazz organizations by disseminating research on current trends affecting jazz societies and festivals. Its primary journal is the *AFJS Journal*, 1985– .

Miscellaneous. There are many noteworthy organizations that are involved in research about an aspect of music other than those mentioned above. The American Music Therapy Association (formerly the National Association of Music Therapy, 1950–1970, and the American

Association of Music Therapy, 1971–1997), established in 1998, promotes public knowledge of the benefits of music therapy and increases access to quality music therapy services. Its primary journal is the *Journal of Music Therapy*, 1964– . AMTA has several women on its executive committee, including Andrea Farbman, executive director.

The Center for Black Music Research (CBMR), established in 1983, documents and preserves information about black music throughout the world. The Center promotes and advances scholarly knowledge and thought about black music and disseminates it through its publications. Its primary journal is the *Black Music Research Journal*, 1980– . CBMR has several women on its executive committee, including Marsha Heizer, associate director of operations and coordinator of publications; Suzanne Flandreau, librarian and archivist; and Rosita M. Sands, director designate.

The International Alliance for Women in Music (IAWM), established in 1995, is a coalition of professional composers, conductors, performers, musicologists, educators, librarians, and lovers of music that encourages all activities integrating women and music by encouraging the publication and distribution of music by women composers, supporting performances and recordings of women composers, fostering scholarly research on women-in-music topics, and facilitating communication among members and with other organizations. Its primary journal is the *IAWM Journal*, 1995– and *Women and Music: Journal of Gender*, 1997– . IAWM has several women on its executive committee, including Kristine H. Burns, president; Sally Reid, past-president; and Francis Norbert, vice-president.

The International Association for the Study of Popular Music (IASPM), established in 1981, is an international network of educators, researchers, journalists, musicians, activists, and industry professionals who promote inquiry, scholarship, and analysis in the area of popular music. Its primary journal is the *Review of Popular Music*, 1982– . Anahid Kassabian, chair of executive committee and Claire Larry, general secretary serve on the executive committee.

The Music Library Association (MLA), established in 1931, exists to further and consolidate the concerns of music librarians and music bibliographers. MLA provides a forum for study and action on issues that affect music libraries and their users, and its members make significant contributions to librarianship, publishing, standards and scholarship, and the development of new information technologies. The association's primary journal is *Notes*, 1934– . MLA has several women on its executive committee, including Paula Matthews, president, and Laura Gayle Green, treasurer.

See also Organizations, Music Education; Organizations, Professional Audio; Organizations, Regional Arts

For Further Reading

International Directory of Music Organizations, 5th ed. Missoula, MT: College Music Society, 1999.

Randel, Don (ed.). *The New Harvard Dictionary of Music*. Cambridge, MA: Harvard University Press, 1986. S.v. "Societies," by Harold E. Samuel.

John Cuciurean

Owens, Dana Elaine

See Queen Latifah

P

Parker, Alice (1925–)

For more than five decades Alice Parker has made significant contributions to choral music in America as an arranger, composer, conductor, teacher, and author. Parker has produced hundreds of other choral arrangements and original compositions in all vocal forms, including 26 cantatas and four operas. While producing a steady stream of vocal and instrumental compositions throughout her career, Parker has authored several books. *Creative Hymn Singing* and *Folksong Transformations* provide tune selections with discussion and ideas for their use in a variety of situations. *Melodious Accord: Good Singing in Church* offers Parker's views on the importance of melody and singing in creating community.

Born in Boston on 16 December 1925, she began piano lessons at age five and began composing when she was eight. While in seventh grade, Parker began private music theory lessons at the New England Conservatory with Mary Mason, and in high school she wrote two compositions for orchestra. She went on to study composition at Smith College, earning her B.A. there (1947). The summer following graduation, Parker attended the Berkshire Music Festival at Tanglewood, where she sang in the festival chorus and first met Robert Shaw and Julius Herford. She considered attending the Eastman School of Music for graduate study in composition, but the expectation that she study and compose serial music caused her to change her plans and attend the Juilliard School to major in choral conducting. At Juilliard, Parker worked closely with Herford in piano, Shaw in choral conducting, and Vincent Persichetti in theory and improvisation. Her second year at Juilliard was the first year of the Robert Shaw Chorale and the beginning of her long collaboration with Shaw. Together they produced a large body of choral arrangements (both in print and recording) that include a wide range of American spirituals, folk songs, carols, and hymn tunes that have become standards in the American choral repertoire. Many of these arrangements have been recorded and are available on *A Treasury of Easter Songs* (RCA LM 1201), *Christmas Hymns and Carols, Vol. I* and *II* (RCA LM 2139 and RCA LM 1711), and *Deep River* (RCA LM 2247).

Alice Parker. *Photograph by Roy Lewis.*

Graduating from Juilliard in 1949, Parker taught full-time for two years at the North Shore Country Day School in suburban Chicago and then returned to New York to resume piano study with Herford. He assisted her in securing a part-time job with Helen Bender at the Summit School of Music, where she learned much about the art of teaching. During summers, Parker assisted Herford at San Diego State College. In 1954 she married Thomas Pyle, an assistant to Shaw as well as a baritone in the chorale, and during the next eight years they had five children.

Parker has offered an annual week-long workshop, "Writing for Voices," at Westminster Choir College since the 1960s. She maintains a rigorous schedule of lectures and workshops around the country, and she conducts "Sings," an opportunity for people of various levels of musical ability to join in the joy of community singing. Examples of these sessions can be seen in her videos, including *Shall We Gather: Singing Hymns with Alice Parker* (LTP 374) and *When We Sing: Conversations with Alice Parker and Friends* (LTP 375). Parker now lives in northwestern Massachusetts.

See also Arrangers; Conductor, Choral

For Further Reading

Alice Parker Home. Available: http://www.aliceparker.com

Gresham, Mark. "Alice Parker: Who Sings?" In *Choral Conversations: Selected Interviews from Chorus! Magazine*. San Carlos, CA: Thomas House Publications, 1997.

Parker, Alice. *The Reason Why We Sing: Community Song with Alice Parker*. Video. Chicago: Liturgy Training Publications, 1995.

Richard AmRhein

Parton, Dolly (1946–)

From humble beginnings, singer and songwriter Dolly Parton became one of the wealthiest, most respected figures in the entertainment industry and was the first woman to cross over from country music celebrity into contemporary popular culture superstardom. Her flamboyant appearance, sporting large extravagantly styled wigs and clothes clearly designed to emphasize her ample bustline and hourglass figure, and her fearless forays into business domains previously unexplored by women country music performers, have earned her a reputation as a daring and talented singer, songwriter, and actress, and a tough-minded businesswoman.

Born on 19 January 1946, country music superstar Dolly Rebecca Parton was the fourth of 12 children born to Lee and Avie Lee Parton. Dolly Parton's life story provides an example of an authentic rags-to-riches saga that began in early childhood. Her mother sang, played guitar, and taught Dolly the old ballads she had learned from her own mother, Lindy Owens. Her grandfather, the Reverend Jake Owens, played fiddle and composed gospel songs as did Avie Lee's sister, evangelist Dorothy Jo Hope. Parton began to compose new songs as a child, and at age seven she received her first guitar from her uncle, songwriter Bill Owens.

By the time she was 10, Parton was performing regularly on the Cas Walker radio broadcast on Knoxville station WIVK. She made her first Grand Ole Opry appearance at age 12; recorded her first record, "Puppy Love," for the Goldband label the following year; and signed with Mercury records at age 14. In 1964 Parton became the first member of her family to graduate from high school, and on the following day she moved to Nashville, where she found early success as a songwriter with Fred Foster's Combine Music. She subsequently signed with Monument Records, where her first two singles attracted the attention of country star and syndicated television performer Porter Wagoner, who hired her to appear on his widely distributed television series. Wagoner persuaded his recording company, RCA Records, to sign her, and during the following six years the two recorded a series of hit duets earning them the Country Music Association's (CMA) 1968 Vocal Group of the Year designation.

Parton's solo recording career began to flourish in 1970 when Wagoner produced her version of Jimmie Rodgers's 1930 country classic "Mule Skinner Blues." During the 1970s her records, including *Coat of Many Colors* (RCA Victor 4603), *Jolene* (RCA 55980), *I Will Always Love You* (Sony 67582), and *The Bargain Store* (RCA 10950), consistently charted in the country Top 10, and at least eight of her efforts reached number one. She ended the partnership with Wagoner in 1975, was named CMA Female Vocalist of the Year in 1975 and 1976, launched a groundbreaking ABC television network series, *Dolly!*, in 1976, and began to achieve cross-over pop success with her 1977 recording *Here You Come Again* (DCC 162).

Dolly Parton's career soared throughout the 1980s, when she had 12 Top 10 hits and became particularly controversial when she appeared on the cover of *Playboy* and in *Rolling Stone*, *People*, *Time*, and *Good Housekeeping* magazines. The 1980s also saw her begin an acting career, appearing first in *Nine to Five* (1980). Parton wrote the film's Academy Award–nominated title song, which became her first number one single on the pop charts. The year 1985 saw the opening of another Parton project, a theme park she called Dollywood.

Parton's songwriting has been acclaimed for both thematic range and emotional depth and clarity. Her compositions often approach women's issues from unconventional perspectives and frequently examine and dignify the plight of poor and working-class women.

See also Country Music; Country Music Hall of Fame; Grand Ole Opry; Singer-Songwriter

For Further Reading

Bufwack, Mary A., and Robert K. Oermann. *Finding Her Voice: The Saga of Women in Country Music*. New York: Crown, 1993.

Elison, Curtis W. *Country Music Culture: From Hard Times to Heaven*. Jackson: University of Mississippi Press, 1995.

Haslam, Gerald W. *Workin' Man Blues: Country Music in California*. Berkeley: University of California Press, 1999.

Amy Corin

Patronage

Since the nineteenth century, patronage has been the chief means of support for the American musical establishment. Working either singly or collectively in guilds, clubs, or boards of directors, generous donors have spent time and money founding and funding musical organizations, underwriting concert and opera seasons, and ensuring the livelihood of composers and performers. It is significant in the history of twentieth-century American music that women were far more dedicated arts benefactors than were men.

Some who have done research on this issue are loathe to use the word "patron," for it implies privilege and money—hence, only the participation of the wealthy white upper class. Terms such as "supporter" and "activist" have been proposed instead, for many women of modest means, by volunteering time and energy, were able to secure musical resources for their churches, schools, and communities. It still remains, however, that a number of women with access to substantial monetary resources, either from their husbands' incomes or their inheritances, purposefully functioned in the traditional role of musical patron, offering direct financial support to composers and musicians by paying them grants and stipends or giving indirect help by contributing to the musical organizations and establishments that employed them. Even with little or no experience in finance, the majority of these women developed a keen sense of business and were able to administer projects, in some cases well enough to assume the roles of impresarios and entrepreneurs. Although they may have been novice financiers, these women were knowledgeable observers and cultivators of the music scene.

Some, like Elizabeth Sprague Coolidge (1864–1953) and Hazel Harrison (1883–1969), were themselves accomplished performers; others, such as Mary L. Europe (1884–1947) and Ella Sheppard Moore (1851–1914), were choir directors and teachers. The latter three demonstrate that patronage in America was not only the province of whites; Harrison, Europe, and Moore, along with other African Americans such as Harriet Gibbs Marshall (1869–1941) (founder of the Washington [DC] Conservatory of Music and School of Expression), Mary Cardwell Dawson (1894–1962), founder of the National Negro Opera Company, and Lulu Vere Childers (founder and dean of the School of Music at Howard University), are only a few of many activists who supported the careers of African American performers and composers. Moreover, whereas white patrons tended to devote their energies to light classical and art music, Marshall and others like Maud Cuney-Hare (1872–1936) and Emma Azalia Hackley (1867–1922) worked to preserve the heritage of African American folk music.

Patrons of means found various outlets for their assistance. Marjorie Merriweather Post (1887–1973), Ima Hogg (1882–1975), and Adella Prentiss Hughes (1869–1950) helped to found or to support symphony orchestras. Coolidge, Elise Hall (1851–1924), and Betty Freeman commissioned works from composers. Jeannette Meyer Thurber, Antonin Dvorák's American patron, attempted to found a national opera company that would offer productions at affordable ticket prices; Eleanor Robson was the force behind the Metropolitan Opera Guild. Others, like Gertrude Clark

Whittall (1867–1965), endowed concert series; Whittall was also responsible for purchasing and donating five Stradivarius instruments and a substantial collection of autograph manuscripts to the Library of Congress. Louise M. Davies not only helped sponsor the San Francisco Symphony but was also responsible for funding construction of the concert hall in which the group performs. Catherine Filene Shouse (1896–1994) founded the Wolf Trap festival park, which features a summer concert season of symphony, opera, dance, and popular music. Although many of these patrons ensured venues and underwrote performances, others provided institutions where composers and musicians could learn their professions. Mary Louise Curtis Bok (1876–1970), for example, founded the Curtis Institute of Music (Philadelphia); and Thurber established the National Conservatory, a remarkably democratic institution that eventually folded because her pleas for government funding met perpetual resistance in the U.S. Congress. Alma Morgenthau Wertheim (1887–1953) founded and was sole support for Cob Cos Press, which published the scores of young American composers. Even Helen Herron Taft (1861–1943), wife of William Howard Taft, was an involved patron, serving as the first president of the Board of Directors of the Cincinnati Symphony before her husband took office as president of the United States. Later in the century, another First Lady, Jacqueline Kennedy Onassis (1929–1994), founded the Kennedy Center, a showcase for national and international performing arts organizations.

Although some of these patrons may be better known for one musical cause, quite frequently they took part in a variety of activities. For example, in addition to building the auditorium at the Library of Congress that bears her name (purported to be one of the finest acoustical venues for chamber music performances in the country), Coolidge commissioned new works (including Aaron Copland's *Appalachian Spring*), sponsored composition competitions, founded music festivals, and supported musicians, including the members of the Pro Arte Quartet, one of whom she was able to bring to the United States from Nazi-occupied Belgium. Also, her donation of all the autographed scores of Coolidge commissions and prizewinners significantly enriched the holdings of the Music Division of the Library of Congress. On a personal level, Coolidge and other patrons offered those they supported encouragement and, in many cases, close friendship.

Women, whether wealthy or not, often joined together in clubs and guilds to foster the arts. In the late nineteenth and early twentieth centuries, music clubs were important as group patrons, for members combined their efforts in order to raise money to support musical organizations. During the Great Depression of the 1930s, for example, the women of the Friday Club of Chicago purchased season tickets to the Chicago Symphony that were then donated back to the community; thus these women, at one and the same time, saved the orchestra's season, kept its members off unemployment, and ensured an audience (who could otherwise not have afforded to attend). Other clubs like the Saturday Morning Musical Club (Tucson, AZ) and the Women's Club of Columbus, OH, sponsored and booked concert series. African American women also joined together as musical patrons in groups such as the Treble Clef Club of Washington, DC, and the punningly named B-Sharp Club of New Orleans; the latter, still active, counts as one of its main functions the funding of scholarships for aspiring young talents.

Not all of the concerts sponsored by women were aimed for public consumption. Patterning their brand of patronage on the idea of the nineteenth-century salons, some of the wealthier women planned concerts in their homes, inviting select members of fashionable society for an audience. Often these programs served the dual purpose of supporting musicians and raising funds for charities. Setting the standards in Boston, for example, was Isabella Stewart Gardner (1840–1924), whose legendary programs in the music room of her home at Fenway Court might feature the Boston Symphony Orchestra or an appearance by a touring star such as soprano Nellie Melba (1861–1931). Socialites fortunate enough to be invited might receive a program handwritten on an original art print; then they would be treated to a program that featured a mix of Gardner's favorites: selections from the classics, nineteenth-century German works, and pieces by contemporary French composers. Indeed, one of the consequences of patronage is that those controlling the money help determine the repertoire that they program or commission. However, all told, the sum total of music that resulted from the support of twentieth-century patrons reflects a balanced variety of tastes. Although some women such as Whittall took an interest in reviving older music, the majority encouraged new composers, some giving voice to those who wrote in daring and experimental styles. Freeman, for example, supported John Cage, LaMonte Young, and Steve Reich.

The extent of the support of women patrons is perhaps best understood by mentioning some of the composers who benefited from their aid, either directly or indirectly. Among the composers were Arnold Schoenberg and his students Alban Berg and Anton Webern, Claude Debussy, Vincent d'Indy, Ferruccio Busoni, Samuel Coleridge-Taylor, Victor Herbert, Jan Sibelius, George Antheil, Roy Harris, Walter Piston, Roger Sessions, Amy Marcy Cheney Beach (1867–1944), Carl Ruggles, and Ruth Crawford Seeger (1901–1953). Performers included Marian Anderson (1897–1993), Olga Samoroff, Ignace Paderewski, Lilli Lehmann, Pablo Casals, Charles Martin Loeffler, and the Trapp Family Singers. A glance at the composers listed, however, demonstrates the undeniable fact that although the majority of patrons were women, they generally failed to give financial support to composers of their own gender.

Although some patrons simply handed over checks to those whom they supported, many became social and political activists, campaigning against the government's refusal to actively assist the arts. Unfortunately, no permanent government assistance was arranged until the creation of the National Endowment for the Arts in the mid-1960s; and today, many fear that arts funding is in danger of being eliminated altogether. Because more women are now in the work force (many in musical professions such as conductor, arts manager, and administrator, which had not traditionally been open to them), fewer are available to devote hours and energy comparable to that expended by their twentieth-century precursors. Nevertheless, it is significant that of those who do volunteer their time and contribute their money in support of music in America, the majority are still women.

See also Gender Issues; National Endowment for the Arts Composers Program

For Further Reading

Barr, Cyrilla. *Elizabeth Sprague Coolidge: American Patron of Music*. New York: Schirmer, 1998.

Blair, Karen. *The Torchbearers: Women and Their Amateur Arts Associations in America, 1890–1930*. Bloomington: Indiana University Press, 1994.

Locke, Ralph P., and Cyrilla Barr (eds.). *Cultivating Music in America: Women Patrons and Activists since 1860*. Berkeley: University of California Press, 1997.

Denise Gallo

Patty, Sandi (1957–)

Known as "The Voice," Sandi Patty is one of the biggest recent stars on the contemporary Christian music scene. She has earned five Gold albums, three Platinum albums, five Grammy Awards, and 33 Dove Awards.

Born on 14 July 1957 in Oklahoma City, Sandi Patty made her singing debut at the age of two, singing "Jesus Loves Me." With her two brothers, Sandi performed gospel music across the country as a member of the Ron Patty Family. She studied voice at San Diego State University and Anderson College (IN). She married John Helvering after graduating from Anderson College, and he helped her with her first album, *For My Friends*, which sold over 11 million copies. Her name has been printed as "Sandi Patti" as well as "Sandi Patty" on various albums throughout the years.

When *Sandi's Song* (Word EK-48572) was released in 1979, she began a series of musical ministry tours that led to her first two Dove Awards in 1982 for *Lift Up the Lord* (Word EK-48570). Her *Songs from the Heart* (Word EK-48573) album was promoted on her 1984 U.S. musical tour. In 1988 Sandi sang at the Republican National Convention. By the early 1990s she had become a role model and inspiration to millions of Americans for what a good Christian wife should be. Unfortunately, she filed for divorce from her husband in June 1992, and she admitted in 1995 to having had two affairs while married to Helvering. Thereafter many radio stations would not play her music, and her record company postponed the release of her 1995 Christmas album. Her career never recovered.

See also Church Music

For Further Reading

Cusic, Don. *Sandi Patti: The Voice of Gospel*. New York: Doubleday, 1988.

Home Page. Available: http://www.sandipatty.com/

Brad Eden

Payne, Maggi (1945–)

Composer, flutist, and video artist Maggi Payne is not only trained as a musician; she also holds a degree in computer engineering from the University of Illinois. Payne has received many honors, including two Composer's Grants and an Interdisciplinary Arts Grant from the National Endowment for the Arts as well as video grants from the Mellon Foundation and the Western States Regional Media Arts Fellowships Program, and she was a second prize winner in the Third International Luigi Russolo Competition for Electronic Music in 1982.

Born on 23 December 1945 in Temple, TX, and raised on the High Plains of Texas, Payne returned to the familiarity of a desert landscape by moving to California in 1970. She spent some time away, however. Her education eventually took her to both coasts as well as to the middle of the United States. She received her B.M. degree from Northwestern

University (1968), and after study at Yale University in the following year, she completed a master's degree in music (in flute) at the University of Illinois (1970). At Illinois, Payne studied composition with both Ben Johnston and Salvatore Martirano; while there, she began to compose electronic music. After her move to California later in 1970, she pursued studies at Mills College, earning an M.F.A. degree (1972). She continues her Mills tenure in various capacities today.

After earning her degree at Mills, Payne stayed on as a recording engineer. For 10 years she was the recording engineer at the Mills College Center for Contemporary Music, and she served as a production engineer at a major San Francisco Bay area radio station for a decade. In her capacity as recording engineer, Payne has helped to commit to tape or disc the works of many other contemporary composers and performers, including Alvin Lucier, Roger Reynolds, Barbara Kolb (b. 1939), Igor Kipnis, and John Zorn. In 1980 she began teaching courses at Mills College in recording engineering (techniques for audio, video, and film) and in electronic music. And in 1992 she became co-director of the Mills Center for Contemporary Music.

Her 1991 *Desertscapes* for two spatially separated choirs describes four desert images: Pyramid Lake, Death Valley, Bryce Canyon, and the Devil's Playground/ Kelso Dunes. The forces for the composition include only women's voices, and as in many of her works, issues of spatial distance and metaphors of vast empty spaces take center stage. Payne's 1987 electro-acoustic work *Airwaves (realities)* can be presented with a video the composer shot of some of Nevada's static desert landscapes. The aural images in the work attempt to contrast the lives and perspectives of San Francisco Bay Area urbanites and the residents of the nearby Nevada desert. There are only two unprocessed sounds in the piece: two airplanes that pass over, and cars driving by. Payne derives all the other sounds from major sources of "unrealities": television and radio broadcasts.

See also Experimental Music; Multimedia; Music Technology

For Further Reading

Claghorn, Charles Eugene, Gene Claghorn, and Mary Louise VanDyke. *Women Composers and Songwriters: A Concise Biographical Dictionary*. Lanham, MD: Scarecrow Press, 1996.

Cohen, Aaron. *International Encyclopedia of Women Composers*, 2d ed. New York: Books and Music, 1987.

Sadie, Julie Anne, and Rhian Samuel. *The Norton/ Grove Dictionary of Women Composers*. New York: W. W. Norton, 1995.

Alan Shockley

Performance Art

Performance art, by its very nature, defies definition—it is a forum used by artists to combine elements of many different media and art forms, incorporating aspects of theater, music, and the visual arts. Many performance artists are also interested in crossing the perceived boundary between art and life by thinking of everyday activities in an artistic manner. Performance art is an ever-changing, often controversial form. There are some very general characteristics that may describe some (but probably not all) performance art. One such characteristic is the emphasis on time. Performances exist in real space and time, and the ephemeral nature of the work is often integral to understanding its meaning. The fact that the performance lasts for a definite amount of time and will exist only in the memories of its audience is a radical notion in the context of painting and sculpture, which are usually made with longevity in mind. Like performances of music, works of performance art can be recorded, but unlike music, performance art often involves interaction between the artist and spectator, and therefore a document is unable to fully capture the piece.

Another characteristic is symbolic action. In performance art, the emphasis is on action and doing. This often extends to include the body of the artist as a kind of material not unlike marble or clay in a traditional sculpture. When the body does something or something is done to the body, it can have metaphoric potential. Performance art is frequently compared to theater, which it only superficially resembles. Performance art, however, rarely communicates its content in the same manner as a play. It usually lacks the plot or character development that is often associated with a play. Theater frequently requires a willing suspension of disbelief that is not a part of performance art. In performance art, the emphasis is on the here and now; it attempts to eliminate artifice. Philosophically, performance art also questions the roles of artist and audience, and in many cases it blurs the distinction between what is an aesthetic experience and an ordinary life experience.

Historians have traced the history of performance art as far back as the Renaissance, when Leonardo and Bernini staged interdisciplinary pageants. It was not, however, until the twentieth century that performance art really took shape as a distinct medium. In many ways, performance art can be seen as a reflection of the turbulence and cultural upheaval of the century. For example, the Futurists and Dadaists found performance to be a valuable tool when facing the political landscape of their time. The Futurists, led by F. T. Marinetti, a poet and master publicist, celebrated speed, war, and technology as ways of freeing Italy from the burdens of the past. In the *Futurist Manifesto* (1908), Marinetti urged that museums, libraries, and other storehouses of history be destroyed. He compared the beauty of a speeding motorcar to that of the Nike of Samothrace and claimed that salvation lay in looking only forward. Luigi Russolo wrote *The Art of Noises* (1913), outlining a method of creating music through the use of machines and other nontraditional devices. Hugo Ball, a philosophy student, and Emmy Hennings, a cabaret performer and accused forger, founded the Cabaret Voltaire in Zurich, Switzerland, in 1916. Several others including Tristan Tzara, Marcel Janco, and Hans Arp joined them, and the Dada movement was born. The name itself is significant in that this was one of the few movements in art history named by the artists themselves. Irate critics named most other groups, such as the Impressionists. "Dada" was likely chosen because it sounds like random nonsense, but it does mean various things in several languages, such as "hobbyhorse" and "yes, yes."

Early Dada performances were variety shows including lectures, songs, dance pieces, and poetry readings with sets designed and painted by the performers themselves. Their poetry was devised using several methods, including a chance method created by Tzara whereby the poet pulls random words from a hat. Ball and others created poetry from abstract sounds created by the mouth, foreshadowing both the vocal works of the Fluxus movement and extended vocal techniques of contemporary artists such as Meredith Monk (b. 1942) and Joan La Barbara (b. 1947).

Performance art was also a major part

of the curriculum at the Bauhaus School in Germany. The theater workshops of Oskar Schlemmer provided a place where students could explore two- and three-dimensional design principles in real space and time. Schlemmer's personal work dealt with covering the human form through unusual costumes that altered and restricted the movements of the performer. Made from various industrial materials, the costumes looked like bizarre mechanical/human hybrids. The Bauhaus closed in 1932. Labeled "degenerate" by Adolf Hitler, many modern artists fled Europe during World War II and came to America, where they passed on their avant garde ideas to an entire generation of young students.

Among this younger group of students was John Cage. He briefly studied under composer Arnold Schoenberg and became one of the most influential people in late-twentieth-century performance art. Cage was also influenced by Marcel Duchamp, a Dadaist who had challenged conventional notions of creativity by suggesting that art was an act of selection rather than creation and that the artist need only choose what is to be art rather than fabricate it. Cage adapted this to music by taking a nonhierarchical attitude toward sounds. To Cage, all sounds were musical. Cage augmented this idea with the Zen Buddhist tenet of suppression of the ego. The composer would no longer play the supreme role in the creation of music. Cage shared this philosophy through his teaching at the experimental summer institute Black Mountain College, NC, and at the New School of Social Research, NY. His goal was to erase remnants of his personal biases from his music, composing through the use of chance operations in which he would allow uncontrollable factors to determine the sequence of pitches and their duration. His later work was concerned with giving more creative control to the performers of his music. Many artists associated with the Fluxus movement attended Cage's classes in New York, including Allan Kaprow, who created *Happenings* in the 1960s—loosely scripted events that turned all participants into artists.

The 1960s and 1970s were a vigorous time for performance art. Many artists embraced performance as a means of undermining the notion of art as a commodity to be bought and sold and also as a way of working with content beyond the formalist concerns that had been paramount in the art world for some time. The body, sexuality, and issues of autobiography and identity became common topics in performance art. Many women artists felt that performance art provided uncharted territory to explore, as men had long dominated painting and sculpture.

Among the innovative artists of this time was Carolee Schneeman, whose work explored the previously taboo issue of women's sexuality. In *Interior Scroll* (1975), she provided a scathing critique of how women were treated in the art community. Another artist whose work focused on issues related to women's identity was Elenor Antin. Her work delves into the notion of what actually constitutes an individual identity. Antin created several characters (The Ballerina, The Nurse, and The King), and she literally became a different person operating in the real world for a period of time. Each persona had a history and memories different from Antin's. Her work foreshadowed the work of many later artists such as Cindy Sherman, who elaborately costumes herself and makes photographic self-portraits.

Linda Montano's art focused on ritual

and giving structure to her daily life. She made pieces by obsessively recording the food that she ate or photographing her smile on a daily basis. From 1984 to 1991 she performed *Seven Years of Living Art*, which included a demanding regimen of daily rituals based on the seven *chakras* (energy centers) of the body. In 1982–1983 she spent an entire year tied to performance artist Tehching Hsieh with an eight-foot piece of rope. They did not touch one another for the duration of the piece.

One common factor in the performance work of the 1960s and 1970s was its interest in finding uncommon venues. Performances took place in every type of place imaginable. Recently performance art has seen a move toward decidedly more theatrical works with overt political content. Artists such as Laurie Anderson (b. 1947) and Rachel Rosenthal all produce work that fits nicely on the stage, assembling recorded and live music, projected slides, films, and videos that complement the live action. Anderson focuses on the technology itself, exploring how machines are affecting the human experience. Others, such as Guillermo Gomez-Pena, James Luna, and Adrian Piper, use their personal experience to comment on racism in America.

Performance art was the center of a national debate when the National Endowment for the Arts (NEA) retracted four grants given to performance artists an account of their controversial content. The NEA 4 (Karen Finley, John Fleck, Holly Hughes, and Tim Miller) produced work that, through autobiographical narrative, frankly examined such subjects as incest, rape, homosexuality, and lesbianism. The artists sued and eventually the funding was reinstated, but the controversy made clear that performance art remains a polemical force.

Performance art continues to threaten dearly held notions of what art should be and how it should behave. Through its ephemeral and immaterial nature, it challenges the position of art within the capitalist marketplace; and through its emphasis on the body and life of the artist as a conduit for meaning, it exposes the power structure of the greater sociopolitical realm.

See also Experimental Music; Fluxus; Music Technology

For Further Reading

Goldberg, Roselee. *Performance Art: From Futurism to the Present*. New York: Harry N. Abrams, 1988.

Schimmel, Paul. *Out of Actions: Between Performance and the Object 1949–1979*. New York: Thames and Hudson, 1998.

Jeffery Byrd

Performance Ensembles, Classical

Professional classical performance ensembles range from vocal and instrumental chamber groups to symphonic orchestras and choruses. The professional category exposes a contradiction in music performance of the late twentieth century. Whereas many smaller instrumental ensembles have a roster of paid musicians, there are many trained, but unpaid, women singing in choruses performing and recording at the professional level.

Women's choral music has been, and continues to be, an active force across the country. The groups are long-lasting and award-winning. Their continued excellence in performance has helped to further promote women's artistry in the twentieth century. Most of the choirs tend to address social, political, and gender issues in their concerts. They perform music written by women and for women, commissioning works by contemporary composers of both sexes.

Historically the Gena Branscombe Choral (1933–1954) was an early success in women's vocal music. The New York–based choir, founded by Branscombe, performed her works and her arrangements of other music. The New York Treble Singers, founded in 1980, is a 12-voiced professional ensemble. Directed by Virginia Davidson, they perform music written specifically for women, including music by women. Today the most prominent professional women's vocal ensemble is Anonymous 4, founded in 1986. The list of amateur vocal organizations is long and includes such groups as Cincinnati's MUSE, founded by Catherine Roma in the 1980s. Most impressive is the Peninsula Women's Chorus, founded by Marjorie Rawlins in 1966, a 60-voice choir. Under the direction of Patricia Hennings, the group has garnered much praise and has commissioned works from Libby Larsen (b. 1950), Nancy Telfer, and Victoria Ebel-Sabo.

The acceptance of women in the symphony orchestra has been a difficult one. By the 1920s numerous women musicians had trained at established conservatories. However, except for the women harpist, orchestral opportunities for all-women groups were often confined to restaurant and hotel work. One of the earliest all-women American orchestras was the Boston Fadette Lady Orchestra, founded in 1888 by Caroline B. Nichols, who led the group for 32 years. By 1920, Nichols's orchestra had provided professional work for nearly 600 women. Nichols received her training under Julius Eichberg at the Boston Conservatory. Eichberg also founded an all-women orchestra using his own students. The Eichberg Lady Orchestra, organized in 1884, provided important training to young women as professional musicians.

In the early twentieth century all-women orchestras were organized across the country from the East Coast to the West Coast. Besides Nichols, many outstanding women conducted all-women orchestras. Their hard work and perseverance created opportunities for women to be heard on the symphonic concert stage. The most prominent conductors and groups were Antonia Brico's New York Women's Symphony Orchestra (1934–1938) and the Women's Symphony Orchestra (WSO) of Chicago (1924–post World War II), with conductors Ethel Leginska (1927–1929) and Ebba Sundstrom (1929–1938). The WSO of Chicago performed works by women in the late 1920s and 1930s, including those of Gena Branscombe (1881–1977), Amy Marcy Cheney Beach (1867–1944), Eleanor Everest Freer (1864–1942), and Florence Price (1887–1953). Leginska also led the Boston Woman's Symphony Orchestra (1926–1930) and the National Women's Symphony Orchestra in 1932. Also noteworthy was the Long Beach Woman's Orchestra (1925–1948), led by Eva Anderson, and Frederique Petrides's Orchestrette Classique, aka Orchestrette of New York (1932–1943). Although each conductor found some professional satisfaction with the all-women orchestras, the podium of the all-men orchestra was an impenetrable tower. The women orchestral player fared better, as the century progressed, than the woman conductor did.

By the 1930s women's organizations in New York and Chicago were making public the need for equality in the orchestra, and women were beginning to make their way into the chairs of the secondary all-men orchestras. However, it was World War II that served as a catalyst in forming today's mixed orchestra. Successful individual players left most of the all-women orchestras in precarious situations with fewer qualified musicians. Many groups disbanded by the 1940s, although a few continued into the 1950s and 1960s. The Detroit Women's Symphony Orchestra gave concerts until 1971, and the Cleveland Women's Symphony Orchestra was active until 1985. Today the successful all-women orchestra is exemplified in the Women's Philharmonic (1980), founded by conductor Elizabeth Seja Min, Miriam Abrams, and Nan Washburn. Guest conductors have included Antonia Brico (1902–1989), Laurie K. Steele, J. Karla Lemon, and Jeanine Wager. JoAnn Falletta (b. 1954) became conductor in 1985; Apo Hsu (b. 1956) is in her fourth season as conductor.

In the last 50 years or so the string quartet has provided many opportunities for the woman professional. The history of professional women in this genre reaches back into the last few decades of the nineteenth century. Once again Eichberg figures into the picture. The Eichberg Quartet, originally formed in 1878 from his studio, was "the first all-female quartet in America" (Schaffer, 1988). This ensemble, with a constantly changing roster, had favorable performances in New York, Philadelphia, Boston, Canada, and the southern United States through the 1890s. Maud Powell (1867–1920), internationally renowned violinist, formed her own string quartets; an all-women group in 1891, and the Maud Powell Quartet, in 1894, for which Powell sat first violinist, flanked by three men. The enterprising Powell went on to form a piano trio with cellist May Mukle and pianist Ann Ford, Mukle's mother. Their tour of small western towns in America during the 1908–1909 season ended in a well-received New York concert. Other early-twentieth-century quartets included the Morgan Quartet (1901), founded by Geraldine Morgan, with her brother playing cello and two other players who were men. Olive Mead, a student of Eichberg, formed the Olive Mead Quartet around 1903, an all-women group that remained active through 1917. Giving concerts throughout the East, this quartet is touted as being "one of the finest ensembles of its time."

The second half of the century saw more string quartet performances. Often formed at the university to continue on to professional status, all-women ensembles acquired momentum through prize-winning performances at national and international competitions. Among the current groups enjoying rewarding careers are the Lark Quartet and the Cassatt String Quartet. Another active ensemble is the DaVinci Quartet, formed in 1980. DaVinci performed and recorded compositions by women and commissioned several pieces by women during the 1990s. A short-lived but successful Vieuxtemps String Quartet (1973–1977), founded by Marnie Hall, consisted of professional freelance players. The all-women ensemble performed in various venues, including Lincoln Center's Out-of-Doors Festival.

Women members of mixed string quartets also furthered the professional status of women artists in the twentieth century. Joan Jeanrenaud, cellist for the Kronos Quartet, exemplifies the professional woman whose exceptional artistry is recognized in this field dominated by men. Julia Adams, violist for the Portland (ME) String Quartet (PSQ), also has established herself as an equal to her male counterparts. Adams relates that "being the only woman in the quartet has been a fascinating experience—perhaps more so than if I were in an all female group" (personal communication). The orchestra's conductor established the PSQ, formed with principal players of the Portland Symphony Orchestra, in 1969. This ensemble remains one of the nation's oldest and top-ranking regional string quartets. Along with traditional repertoire, they have performed works by Amy Marcy Cheney Beach, Rebecca Clarke (1886–1979), and Ruth Crawford Seeger (1901–1953).

Other successful ensembles mix vocal and instrumental mediums. There is wide variety in the repertoire, but most focus on early music by women or on music of contemporary women composers. Groups of mixed gender, such as the Kentucky-based Ars Femina, perform works by women before 1800. Their recordings include the music of Isabella Leonarda, a sixteenth-century Ursuline nun. All-women ensembles include the Urban Sky Consort, based in Pittsburgh, which began as a mixed ensemble in 1989 and reorganized in 1991 as an all-women group. The ensemble performs medieval, Renaissance, baroque, and twentieth-century vocal music. Bimbetta, a five-woman ensemble in which all members have graduate degrees from the Early Music Institute at Indiana University's School of Music, specializes in music of the seventeenth and eighteenth centuries.

The woman composer/performer has promoted herself and her music by putting together an ensemble of musicians. Pauline Oliveros (b. 1932) founded the Sonics, later called the San Francisco Tape Music Center, in 1961. Meredith Monk (b. 1942) formed her own performance ensemble to present her theatrical works. Joan Tower (b. 1938) is the founder, and was pianist from 1969 to 1984, of the Da Capo Chamber Players, which commissioned and premiered many of Tower's works.

The efforts of these and many other women of the late nineteenth and twentieth centuries have benefited the woman musician. The performances of music by women have helped to promote knowledge and acceptance of a long-existing but unknown and unappreciated repertoire. The support and encouragement given to the living woman composer through commissions has helped to ensure future generations of a musical resource that includes works by women.

See also Conductor, Choral; Conductor, Instrumental and Operatic; Performer, Choral and Vocal Ensemble

For Further Reading

Bowers, Jane, and Judith Tick (eds.). *Women Making Music: The Western Art Tradition, 1150–1950.* Urbana: University of Illinois Press, 1987.

Neuls-Bates, Carol (ed.). *Women in Music: An Anthology of Source Readings from the Middle Ages to the Present*, rev. ed. Boston: Northeastern University Press, 1996.

Pendle, Karin (ed.). *Women and Music: A History.* Bloomington: Indiana University Press, 1991.

Nan Childress

Performer, Brass

Women brass performers faced much opposition at the beginning of the twentieth century. Although it was becoming more common to see women playing piano and violin in the concert halls, women were steered away from wind and brass instruments that might require them to contort their faces and supposedly abandon their good looks while playing. Among other complaints were that women lacked the breath capacity and lip power to play brass instruments, therefore the instruments would always be out of tune; that women could not be depended on to put in the hard work required to attain proficiency on a brass instrument; and that women were not aggressive enough. Another possible reason why few women played brass instruments was the sex stereotyping of instruments. Trumpets were identified with the military, and French horns were identified with hunting; thus both were seen as masculine instruments, fit only for a man to play.

Once women began to learn to play brass instruments, their only classical music performance outlet in the 1920s and 1930s was in all-women orchestras. Even then there were often gaps in the low brass section, and men were substituted. However, the pay in the women's orchestras, if any, was much lower than what the men were earning in the major orchestras. These brass-playing women were described as challenging notions about what was appropriately female. When World War II started, many male musicians went into the military. Just as in other labor forces, women were asked to take their places in the previously all-men's orchestras. The St. Louis Symphony had Dorothy Ziegler as principal trombone from 1944 to 1958; Ethel Merker was principal horn of the NBC Symphony Orchestra from 1943 to 1949; and Betty S. Glover was principal trombone of the Kansas City Philharmonic Orchestra from 1944 to 1948. Women were slowly making their way into a previously all-male playing field.

Women were still struggling for equality in major orchestras. In a 1952 issue of *Etude Magazine*, Raymond Paige, the director of Radio City Music Hall, noted that there were women playing the heavier brass instruments but their chances for employment were lower because when they played it looked forced and incongruous. He felt that playing the French horn was as far as women should wander into the brass section. In the 1960s the International Conference of Symphony and Opera Musicians decreed that all union orchestras must publicly advertise any open positions and that the selection of a player could not be left up to the conductor alone. This was an effort to reduce the cronyism that was responsible for most orchestra seatings. In the 1970s orchestras began the practice of auditioning prospective players behind a screen. This opened up opportunities not only for women but for minorities as well. Some brass sections gained many women. For example, in 1940 out of 47 orchestras surveyed, 18 percent of the horn players were women. By 1980 out of 44 orchestras surveyed, 27 percent of the horn players were women. However, in all other brass categories (trumpet, trombone, and tuba) the percentage dropped. Trumpets dropped from 8 percent in 1940 to 5 percent in 1980, trombones dropped from 6 percent to 3 percent, and tuba from 7 percent to 2 percent.

As college music faculty, women brass performers have seen percentages go up and down as well. In 1976 out of 1,078 brass music faculty tenure track positions, only 5.4 percent were women; however, in 1986 out of 1,199 positions only 5.2 percent were women. For non–tenure track brass music faculty, the numbers increased. Out of 1,032 positions in 1976 7.4 percent were filled by women; in 1986 out of 1,846 positions 12.6 percent were filled by women. The reduced number of tenure track women brass faculty could be attributed to continued sex stereotyping of instruments at the grade school level, thereby producing fewer women brass musicians. Or it could be attributed to sexism at professional levels.

In 1990 trumpeter Susan Slaughter responded to a survey she had issued to more than 1,400 women brass players and formed the International Women's Brass Conference. The organization holds conferences every three to five years in order to give women the opportunity to exchange information, support each other, and inspire all women brass players. These conferences have spawned an all-women trombone quartet, the Aurora Trombone Quartet.

There are many notable women brass performers. Abbie Conant (b. 1955) is a very prominent trombone player who received a lot of attention in the 1980s and 1990s owing to her 13-year battle to secure her position as solo trombone in the Munich Philharmonic. Another notable trombone player is Rebecca Bower Cherian, who has been co-principal trombone of the Pittsburgh Symphony since 1989, as well as a faculty member of Carnegie Mellon University. Janice Elaine Robinson is a trombone player who is at home in the jazz band as well as in the symphony orchestra, having played with Chuck Mangione, Gil Evans, and the Rochester Philharmonic. Julie Landsman has been principal horn of the New York Metropolitan Opera Orchestra since 1985 and on the faculty at the Juilliard School since 1989. Before her appointment with the Met she was co-principal horn of the Houston Symphony. Gail Williams was assistant principal horn in the Chicago Symphony from 1979 to 1984, when she was appointed associate principal horn. She retired from the orchestra in 1998 but still teaches at Northwestern University. Barbara Butler was professor of trumpet for 18 years at the Eastman School of Music and currently teaches at Northwestern University. She is co-principal and soloist with Chicago's Music of the Baroque and the Chicago Chamber Musicians. Susan Slaughter has been principal trumpet of the St. Louis Symphony since 1973. As well as founding the International Women's Brass Conference (IWBC), she founded the Monarch Brass, an all-women brass ensemble, in 1995. The first woman trumpet player in a major symphony orchestra was Marie Speziale. She was associate principal trumpet of the Cincinnati Symphony Orchestra from 1964 to 1996. She has taught at the University of Cincinnati College-Conservatory of Music since 1979. Velvet Brown is best known as a tuba soloist, having performed with both the St. Louis and Detroit Symphonies. She has also been principal tuba with the New Hampshire Music Festival Orchestra since 1989. Brown is currently associate professor of Tuba and Euphonium at Bowling Green State University.

See also Discrimination; International Women's Brass Conference; Military Music

For Further Reading

Block, Adrienne Fried. *Women's Studies/Women's Status*. Boulder, CO: College Music Society, 1988.

Handy, D. Antoinette. *Black Women in American Bands and Orchestras*. Metuchen, NJ: Scarecrow Press, 1981.

Macleod, Beth Abelson. "'Whence Comes the Lady Tympanist?' Gender and Instrumental Musicians in America, 1853–1990." *Journal of Social History* 27/2 (1993): 291–308.

Stacie Lorraine

Performer, Choral and Vocal Ensemble

Even though women participate extensively as choral and vocal ensemble performers, most of this activity has been as amateurs (i.e., unpaid). Professional or paid opportunities are virtually all part-time with modest financial compensation. Such opportunities include jobs with religious organizations, often as section leader and/or soloist with a choir; symphony or festival choruses (e.g., the Chicago Symphony Chorus founded in 1957 by Margaret Hillis [1921–1998], who continued to conduct the chorus until her retirement in the spring of 1994); professional opera choruses, and independent professional choirs such as the Robert Shaw Chorale or Dale Warland Singers. In 2000, Chorus America, an organization that serves a variety of independent choirs as well as professional ensembles, had about 110 member choruses in the United States and Canada that pay some or all of their singers. In 1997, singers in some professional choruses were paid around $30 for a two- or three-hour rehearsal and from $30 to $85 for a performance. In some cases all members are paid, but in other ensembles only a small fraction receive financial compensation.

Some small vocal ensembles—often specialized in terms of repertoire—offer women musical opportunities at a professional level. In Chicago's *a cappella*, where four of the nine members are women, classically trained soloists focus on repertoire from what they call choral singing's first "golden age" (1480–1620) and music composed since 1970. Among the most widely known vocal ensembles is Anonymous 4, an all-women group founded in 1986 to explore the sound of women's voices performing medieval chant and polyphony. These four singers (Marsha Genensky, Susan Hellauer, Johanna Maria Rose, and Jacqueline Horner, who replaced Ruth Cunningham in 1998) have appeared in concerts and on radio broadcasts throughout North America and Western Europe; they have also performed in Poland, Japan, Australia, and New Zealand and have created award-winning recordings. *An English Ladymass* (Harmonia Mundi 907080), their first of eight recordings on the Harmonia Mundi USA label, became the first medieval music to appear on *Billboard*'s classical album chart, where it spent much of 1993. In November 1994, Anonymous 4 had three albums simultaneously on *Billboard*'s classical chart. Bimbetta, another all-women chamber ensemble, is comprised of three sopranos, harpsichordist, and cellist. They perform seventeenth-century music with a "risqué sense of humor, rock and roll lighting, a heady helping of feminism and even the occasional somersault" (Evenson 1999). Established in 1993, Bimbetta has performed concerts and residencies throughout the United States and Europe; their educational outreach programs are geared for people of all ages from elementary school students through adults. Their debut compact disc, *War of Love: La guerra d'amore* (D'Note Classics 1023), includes music by Barbara Strozzi and Claudio Monteverdi, among others.

Education and experience needed for a profession with a choral or vocal ensemble are generally developed through ensemble participation and musical study in high school, college and university settings, and religious institutions, along with private voice study. Important skills include accurate intonation, sight reading, general musicianship, good vocal production and diction, ability to blend with other voices, and a vocal timbre consistent with the ideals of the ensemble or conductor. Preparation in language study, historical research, performance practice, and music editing are also beneficial for this career. For a person planning to found an ensemble, managerial expertise such as grant writing, publicity and public relations, and organizational skills are especially important during the early years.

Throughout the twentieth century, women participated in choral singing in increasing numbers; and at least during the second half of the century, women wishing to engage in choral singing generally outnumbered men. These unpaid ensembles of adult singers included, for example, community or company choruses, Sweet Adelines (barbershop), town-gown choirs, and members of GALA (Gay and Lesbian Association of Choruses). Formed in 1982 by 14 choruses, GALA now includes approximately 10,000 singers in 200 member choruses (e.g., MUSE Cincinnati's Women's Choir with founder and artistic director Catherine Roma, or Vox Femina Los Angeles under the artistic direction of Iris S. Levine). In many choirs, members pay a fee or provide their own music; moreover, they participate in the organization in other ways such as fundraising and selling tickets. Earlier in the twentieth century, women were also active in choral singing at suffrage movement meetings and marches, at women's music clubs (e.g., the Treble Clef Club founded by Mamie Hilyer in 1897 within Washington, DC's, black community), and for patriotic activities during wartime. Choral singing in the United States—in contrast to some European choral endeavors—remains largely an amateur activity or one with nominal stipends, even for trained singers who are professional soloists in other contexts.

See also Anonymous 4; Barbershop Quartet; Sweet Adelines

For Further Reading

Bucker, William Robert. "A History of Chorus America—Association of Professional Vocal Ensembles." D.M.A diss., University of Missouri, 1991.

Morrow, Phillip Jeffery. "The Influence of the Robert Shaw Chorale, the Roger Wagner Chorale and the Gregg Smith Singers on the Professional Chorus in the United States." D.M.A. diss., Southern Baptist Theological Seminary, 1993.

Roma, Catherine. [Chapter on History of the Women's Choral Movement]. In *Radical Harmonies: A History of Women's Music*, ed. Boden Sandstrum. Urbana: University of Illinois Press, forthcoming.

Waleson, Heidi. "Anonymous No More." *Early Music America* 2/4 (Winter 1996–97): 19–22.

J. Michele Edwards

Performer, Keyboard

In the twentieth century women held a variety of keyboard performer positions, amateur and professional, and full- and part-time. Performing on the keyboard has been socially acceptable for women at least since the Renaissance period. Today keyboard performers can choose to specialize on the organ, harpsichord, piano, synthesizer, or all of them. Although women participate in all phases of keyboard music such as performance, recording, teaching, composition, research, writing, and instrument building, men by and large control the music industry.

Churches and synagogues are the main employers of organists, and most church positions are part-time; relatively few full-time organist positions are available. To qualify for a church position an organist usually studies piano as well as organ, and an undergraduate degree is necessary. Many women in the second half of the twentieth century pursued advanced studies in organ and earned a master's degree and a doctorate. The combined position of organist and choir director provides more full-time opportunities, although additional conducting skills are needed. Organists often add to their income by playing for weddings, funerals, and other religious ceremonies, or by substituting.

A performance career as an organ soloist, chamber musician, or staff organist for a chamber ensemble or orchestra is usually only a part-time occupation. Possible venues for performance include churches, colleges, universities, cultural centers, orchestras, concert series, radio, and television. Although audiences often enjoy hearing traditional repertoire for organ, most performers have also chosen a specialty such as contemporary music, women organ composers, or transcriptions from the orchestral literature. Many organists specialize in lecture recitals on various topics such as early music, new techniques of organ composition, Jewish music, or multicultural organ music.

The twentieth century heard many excellent organ performers and recording artists, such as Marie-Claire Alain, Cherry Rhodes, Barbara Harbach, Diane Bish ([b. 1941] also a composer and television personality), Christa Rakich (who specializes in women organ composers), Diane Belcher, Kimberly Marshall (also a writer and researcher on women composers), Janice Beck, Christina Harmon (also a gifted arranger), Carol Williams, and Marianne Webb. Carole Terry performs and records on both the organ and the harpsichord.

In a more popular vein, theater organ concerts are a thriving field of entertainment with a larger and more diverse membership than the American Guild of Organists. Also, a few pizza parlors in the United States have magnificent theater organs in good repair available for performance. Before the last quarter of the twentieth century, organists were needed for entertainment at baseball games, and in the first half of the century, organists accompanied silent movies.

In the twentieth century women were always involved with the teaching of keyboard, either in a private studio, as a public school teacher, or as a teacher or professor at a college or university. Teaching often augments the income from a part-time church position or performing career. A doctorate is now required for an academic position at a college or university, although a master's degree with several years of teaching experience may suffice. Few full-time organ teaching positions are available. Therefore, a second area of specialty such as music theory or literature is needed. Teaching in the public school system requires an undergraduate degree in music education, additional study for a master's degree, and often a teaching certificate. A large number of excellent women teachers (who also perform and record) teach in many schools today. Marilyn Keiser, Wilma Jensen, Sandra Soderlund, Margaert Evans, Anita Eggert Werling, Judith Hancock, Roberta Bitgood (also a composer and the first woman president of the American Guild of Organists), Roberta Gary, Emma Lou Diemer (b. 1927), Marilyn Mason, and Joyce Jones are a few examples of outstanding teachers.

Several women have started successful agencies for organists: Ruth Plummer with her *Artist Recitals*; *Karen McFarlane Artists*; Phyllis Stringham *Concert Management*; and Beth Zucchino (director) of *Concert Artist Cooperative*.

By specializing in the performance on all three main keyboards (piano, organ, and harpsichord), many women are accomplished soloists, chamber musicians, keyboardists for an orchestra, or accompanists.

Because the audience for harpsichord music is even smaller than the audience for organ performance, harpsichord performers usually require another means of financial support in addition to performing, recording, and teaching. Today, the harpsichord is utilized as part of the continuo in early music performance, and it has had a resurgence of popularity in early music performance as well as contemporary music. Instruction on the harpsichord and organ is usually necessary to develop a professional technique on the harpsichord.

Several women were influential in reviving interest in the harpsichord in the twentieth century. The legendary Wanda Landowska (1879–1959) was a performer and teacher who created a great deal of interest in historical harpsichord literature and inspired many contemporary composers to write for the harpsichord. Lotta Van Buren (1877–1960) was a performer and teacher. Alice Ehlers (1887–1981) was born in Vienna and came to the United States as a teacher and performer; she even appeared as a harpsichordist in William Wyler's film *Wuthering Heights*. Yella Pessl (1906–after 1952), born in Vienna, was also a performer and teacher in the United States. The next generation of performers and recording artists included Sylvia Marlowe (1908–1981) and Antoinette Vischer (1909–1973). Contemporary harpsichordists who perform, record, or teach include Elaine Comparone, Vivienne Spiteri, and Frances Bedford. All these performers and recording artists (as well as many others) premiere new works for the harpsichord, commission and inspire new works, and stimulate interest in the harpsichord.

With some additional study, women have other career options, such as becoming a keyboard critic for trade publications like *The American Organist Magazine* or *The Diapason*, as well as writing compact disc reviews, articles on keyboard technique, literature, or analyses of various repertoire styles. Instrument building or repair and maintenance usually require an apprenticeship with a master builder.

See also Church Music; Organizations, Performer

For Further Reading

The American Organist Magazine. New York: American Guild of Organists.

The Diapason: The Official Journal of the International Society for Organ History and Preservation. Des Plaines, IL: Scranton Gillette Communications.

Barbara Harbach

Performer, Live Electronics

Twentieth-century innovations such as the vacuum tube, transistor, and microprocessor have allowed performers the opportunity to assume a new creative role—that of live electronics performer. Since its inception as an art form, electronic music has fallen into one of two general categories. The first category, called tape music, involves playback of audio that has been stored on tape or disc. Tape music is generally fixed in form and content. The second category, live electronic music, consists of a live concert realization of a musical composition on electronic equipment. By adding a performance aspect to electronic music, live electronics can bridge the gap between fixed tape music and traditional classical music performance.

The earliest electric musical instruments—the Singing Arc (1899), Telharmonium (1901), Theremin (1920), and the Ondes Martenot (1928), to name a few—adopted the player-instrument model of traditional classical music in which a performer, acting on the instrument, obtains an immediate, predictable response for a given output. For example, just like on a violin, these early instruments yielded the same musical output for a given gestural input, time after time. The most prominent of these early instruments is the Theremin, in which the performer's hand positions in space are used to control the amplitude and pitch of the instrument. The greatest thereminst in history, Clara Rockmore (1911–1998), emigrated to the United States and devoted her career to expanding the repertoire of the instrument, concertizing extensively. Her legacy and technique lives on in contemporary thereminsts, particularly Moscow-born Lydia Kavina.

The invention of the transistor in 1956 made it possible to build electronic instruments much more inexpensively than previous vacuum tube–based models. The transistor also made possible the development of more portable electronic hardware. Once computer became more commonly available, engineers and composers began to approach live electronic music in one of two ways: using electronic gadgeting and custom-built hardware, or using software on a general purpose computer.

Pioneers of the hardware-based approach include David Tudor and Gordon Mumma, who built their own analog hardware for live electronic music. More recently, Pauline Oliveros (b. 1932) has helped develop the EIS (Expanded Instrument System) for simulating virtually any acoustic space in any room. For example, using the EIS system, a small room could be made to respond to instruments and reverberate like a large cathedral.

Another leader in the hardware-based approach to live electronic music is Laetitia Sonami (b. 1957). In 1991 she retrofitted rubber kitchen gloves with sensors to make a new controller for live electronic music. The controller is an important contribution to live electronic music: using a controller, which typically tracks some gestural action by a human performer, performers are able to intuitively control various electronic hardware, such as MIDI (Musical Instrument Digital Interface—a communications protocol for synthesizers and computers) synthesizers, effects units, and computers. Other performers such as Eve Beglarian (b. 1958) often employ an entire arsenal of electronic hardware in their live electronic music. Twisted Tutu, a duo consisting of Beglarian and pianist Kathleen Supové, uses synthesizers and samplers in their live electronic music.

The software approach to live electronic music is a somewhat newer phenomenon, as powerful computers have become more available and affordable. Laurie Spiegel (b. 1945), working at Bell Laboratories in the 1970s on the GROOVE system, wrote software routines for live performance that enabled her to improvise entire pieces. The software-based approach to live electronic music is also exemplified in the music of composers like Mari Kimura (b. 1962). Kimura employs computer software to alter the sound of her violin in performance, creating sounds in realtime that would otherwise not be possible.

See also Experimental Music; Music Technology; Software Designer/Programmer

For Further Reading

Chadabe, Joel. *Electric Sound: The Past and Promise of Electronic Music.* Upper Saddle River, NJ: Prentice-Hall, 1997.

Colby Leider

Performer, Percussion

Percussion performers, generally referred to as percussionists, require tenacity and versatility; the possibilities for women in the late twentieth and early twenty-first centuries are limitless. One can pursue a career in the orchestral, contemporary chamber, electronic, pop, jazz, performance art, or recording industries. The percussionist must have a broad knowledge of many different musics and be able to perform on the various percussion instruments that are at their foundation. It is important to find a professor that one respects and feels can not only teach technique but inspire musicality, in a university or conservatory. It is best to study as many types of world musics as possible. Most universities now offer, at the very least, African, Indian, and Indonesian music studies; four years of study in each is a strong start, as is a bachelor's degree in all-around percussion performance.

No musician is required to have a degree to perform, but being in an intense musical environment for several years at a time can accelerate musical development. Learning to swing in a jazz situation as well as getting a true sense of "groove" in a pop band is very important. It is preferable to either form small groups to play with on a regular basis, or to secure a job in a Top 40 band in order to learn many different drummers' styles. Listening and playing along with recordings of other jazz "greats" is also helpful. Those performers with interests in symphonic performance usually first perform with local community orchestras, often for little pay.

Several outstanding women percussionists are Amy Knoles, Nancy Zeltsman (b. 1958), Julie Spencer (b. 1962), and Sheila E. (b. 1957). Knoles is the percussionist for the California Ear Unit and Basso Bongo, in addition to performing solo percussion. Nancy Zeltsman teaches at the Berklee School of Music and the Boston Conservatory, a university that offers the rare degree in marimba performance. Julie Spencer is a mallet improviser who uses her own special four-mallet technique to amaze and confound the listener. Finally, performer Sheila E. not only plays Latin percussion but is particularly adept at drum-set technique.

See also Organizations, Performer

For Further Reading

Modern Drummer. Clifton, NJ: Modern Drummer Publications.

Percussive Notes. Lawton, OK: Percussive Arts Society.

Amy Knoles

Performer, Strings

Traditionally, preparation for a career as a string performer involves applied studies that begin early, sometimes at four or five years of age. Advanced training at a conservatory or school of music follows, with a curriculum that includes music theory, solfeggio, form and analysis, music history, conducting, and ensemble experience. If the ultimate goal is a solo career, the string player seeks performance opportunities that include solo recitals and concerti and may enter competitions to assess her potential as a concert or recording artist. The soloist often engages professional representation to arrange scheduling, travel, and promotion. An early violin soloist was Maud Powell (1867–1920), who enjoyed international acclaim and left a lasting legacy on violin playing in this country. Newcomers Hilary Hahn (b. 1979) and Sarah Chang (b. 1980) possess levels of technical and musical maturity on the violin that show great promise. Violists Kim Kashkashian (b. 1952) and Lillian Fuchs have carved out admirable solo careers, yet surprisingly few American women cellists in the twentieth century have achieved prominence as solo artists. The almost exclusively male-dominated field of double bass has, in the last 20 years, been breached by outstanding soloists such as Diana Gannett of the University of Iowa, and Linda McKnight of the Manhattan School of Music.

An orchestral career involves the same early training, followed by auditions with desired ensembles. Depending on the symphony's season, this may be a full- or part-time position. The artist may supplement her income with private teaching and/or outside performances. Concertmistress of the Minnesota Orchestra, Jorja Fleezanis often showcases contemporary music in her solo performances. Violist Cynthia Phelps is principal violist of the New York Philharmonic, and Sabrina Thatcher is her counterpart in the St. Paul Chamber Orchestra. Orchestral cellists include Martha Babcock, currently assistant principal cellist with the Boston Symphony Orchestra, and Anne Martindale Williams, principal cellist of the Pittsburgh Symphony. The New York Philharmonic boasts bassist Orin O'Brien, and the St. Louis Symphony has Carolyn White Buckley.

Only the rare string player has exclusively a chamber music career. Following rigorous training, a chamber performer with an established ensemble and an active recording schedule may also hold a faculty position at a conservatory of music. Such an institution may create a residency program specifically for a successful ensemble, with the expectation that the group perform, coach, present master classes, and do outreach to local public schools. Equally respected on both violin and viola and currently violinist of the Beaux Arts trio, Ida Kavafian has had a stellar career as a chamber musician. Violinist Pamela Frank is another chamber player in great demand. Ani Kavafian, viola, has a solid recording career, much of it as one-half of a duo with her sister Ida. Early in the twentieth century, Eleanor Aller was the founding member and cellist of the famed Hollywood String Quartet. More recently, Sharon Robinson has produced numerous chamber recordings with some of the world's finest artists. The paucity of bass chamber music explains the absence of any prominent chamber bass performer. Less traditional string performance careers, outside the purview of this entry, may occur in the realm of jazz or popular music, as in the case of violinist Alison Krauss (b. 1971) or bassist Christine Korb.

See also The Maud Powell Society for Music and Education; Organizations, Performer; Performance Ensembles, Classical; Prizes, Composer and Performer

For Further Reading

Shaffer, Karen. *Maud Powell, Pioneer American Violinist*. Ames: Iowa State University Press, 1988.

Stowell, Robin (ed.). *Cambridge Companion to the Cello*. Cambridge and New York: Cambridge University Press, 1999.

Ellen Grolman Schlegel

Performer, Vocal

At the turn of the twentieth century, the "golden age" of opera was at its height; many of the greatest women vocal performers of the era were American-born but European-trained. The leading Wagnerian soprano at the Metropolitan Opera was Lilian Nordica, born Lilian Norton (1857–1914) in Farmington, MN. Her principal musical training took place in Milan. Lyric sopranos Suzanne Adams (1872–1953), Estelle Liebling (1880–1970), and Emma Eames (1865–

1952) studied with Mathilde Marchesi in Paris before embarking on their careers. Edyth Walker (1867–1950) studied in Dresden and sang most of the German roles for soprano and mezzo-soprano. Geraldine Farrar (1882–1967) and Louise Homer (1871–1947) began their studies in the United States but went to Europe for their final polish. An exception was Minnie Hauk (1851–1929), entirely trained in the United States and the most celebrated Carmen of her time.

Each of these women were born in the latter half of the nineteenth century into a country that lacked its own tradition of lyric theater. This lack of tradition proved to be an advantage for all of them. Country and cultural tradition did not trap them into singing only one type of repertoire. They were obliged to absorb all styles and idioms, enabling them to move readily from one repertoire to another. This is not to say that their work or their careers were easy. In addition to their native talent, these women brought to the opera world ambition, determination, tenacity, and the American capacity for hard work.

Three great American singers of the era were born on foreign soil. Ernestine Schumann-Heink (1861–1936) was born in Austria, and Mary Garden (1874–1967) was born in Scotland. Renowned for her rich contralto voice, Schumann-Heink was closely identified with Bayreuth for nearly 20 years. She fell in love with America on her first visit in 1898 and became a naturalized citizen shortly thereafter. She endeared herself to American audiences by giving yearly cross-country tours. For many years, until the outbreak of World War II, her recording of "Stille Nacht, heilige Nacht" was an American Christmas tradition. Olive Fremstad (1871–1951) was born in Stockholm of humble origins. She was adopted by an American couple and brought to Minnesota. She studied in New York before going to Berlin for study with Lilli Lehmann. During the first 10 years of her career, she sang soprano and mezzo roles in all the major European theaters. She made her Metropolitan Opera debut in 1903 and continued there for the next 11 seasons. Mary Garden came to America as a child and first studied singing in Chicago. She became closely identified with the heroines of the French repertoire. Debussy personally chose her to create the role of Melisande. She eventually returned to Chicago, where she began a long association with the Chicago Grand Opera. In 1921 she became the company's director and during her tenure was responsible for many artistic successes.

Two more New Englanders belonged to the next generation. Geraldine Farrar was born in Melrose, MA, and received her training in Boston and New York. She studied briefly with Marchesi in Paris before seeking guidance from Lilli Lehmann in Berlin. It was there, at the Royal Opera House, that she made her debut as Marguerite in *Faust*. Beautiful, tempestuous, and an outstanding actress, she captured the imagination of her audiences. Throughout her 20-year career at the Metropolitan Opera, the roles of Carmen and Madame Butterfly were virtually her private property. One of the most beautiful voices of the twentieth century belonged to Rosa Ponselle (1897–1981). Born in Meriden, CT, she studied with her mother and sang in vaudeville before making her operatic debut at age 23 as Leonora (*La Forza del destino*) opposite Enrico Caruso at the Metropolitan Opera. For the next 20 years she dominated the Italian repertoire, singing in all the capitals of the world. One of the most difficult of soprano roles, Norma, was probably her greatest. She retired in 1937 and became an equally legendary teacher. Many of her former students were still singing at the end of the twentieth century on stages throughout the world.

Another great American contralto, Marian Anderson (1897–1993), was born in Philadelphia, and though she lacked formal schooling, the outstanding qualities of her voice were recognized and she received excellent training from her teachers La Forge and Boghetti. As an African American she found it difficult to be accepted as a serious artist in her homeland. However, concert tours of Europe brought her success and recognition.

The Great Depression years and the years prior to World War II saw a brief decline in the number of quality American singers. The influx of European stars fleeing the political and economic turmoil of their homelands left little room for Americans to develop their talents on their home turf. One of the immigrants was the mezzo-soprano Jennie Tourel (1900–1973). Born in Belo-Russia, she studied in Paris and made her debut there before coming to the United States. She eventually became an American citizen and, following her retirement, a respected voice teacher at the Juilliard School and the Aspen School. Another immigrant was the great German soprano Lotte Lehmann (1888–1976). Although she was in the latter stages of her magnificent career when she immigrated, she was still one of the greatest interpreters of vocal music. She concertized regularly throughout the United States and established a private voice studio at her home in Santa Barbara. Some of the greatest singers of the latter half of the twentieth century studied with her at her institute.

This period also saw the rise of radio and film as popular and inexpensive forms of entertainment. The soprano Grace Moore (1898–1947) was a star in both media, as well as opera, and maintained her success until her tragic death in an airplane crash in 1947. Helen Traubel (1899–1972), the outstanding dramatic soprano of her generation, also enjoyed success in popular entertainment. This, however, led to a dispute with the Metropolitan Opera and a release from her contract. The mezzo-soprano Risë Stevens (b. 1913) was the greatest Carmen of her generation. Her name and her voice became even better known after she sang with Bing Crosby in *The Bells of St. Mary's*.

With the onset of World War II, the number of singers from Europe declined and American opera houses were forced to rely more on homegrown talent. Margaret Harshaw (b. 1909) began her career as a mezzo-soprano and won the Metropolitan Opera Auditions on the Air in 1942. Following the war she became a dramatic soprano and replaced Helen Traubel as the leading Wagnerian soprano at the Metropolitan Opera. Other outstanding singers during the war years were: the mezzo-soprano Martha Lipton (b. 1916), famous for her trouser roles; soprano Dorothy Kirsten (b. ca. 1907), who specialized in Puccini heroines; and Eleanor Steber (1914–1990), a Mozart and Strauss specialist. She also created the title role in Barber's *Vanessa*.

The postwar years saw the rise of a generation of American singers trained on their home soil and polished by their European-born teachers. Lili Chookasian (b. 1921), Irene Dalis-Loinaz (b. 1925), and Rosalind Elias (b. 1929) were the mezzo-sopranos of this generation. Chookasian, a contralto, studied with Rosa Ponselle. The sopranos who made their reputation in this period were Patrice Munsel (b. 1925), Evelyn Lear (b. 1926), and Beverly Sills (b. 1929), a student of Estelle Liebling. All of them were outstanding exponents of the traditional repertoire, but Evelyn Lear created many roles by twentieth-century American and European composers. She was also closely identified with the role of Berg's *Lulu*.

Probably the most remarkable singer of this generation was the African American soprano Leontyne Price (b. 1927). A graduate of the Juilliard School, she initially found work in a touring group of *Porgy and Bess*. She created the role of St. Cecilia in Thomson's *Four Saints in Three Acts* and sang in the American premiere of Poulenc's *Dialogues des Carmelites*. She eventually made debuts in San Francisco, Vienna, Verona, and Covent Garden. Her Metropolitan Opera debut took place in 1961 as Leonora in *La Forza del destino*. Best known for her interpretation of Aida, she was one of the finest lirico spinto sopranos in the latter half of the twentieth century.

Another singer in the postwar generation was the soprano Roberta Peters (b. 1930). Born and trained in New York, she made her professional debut at the Metropolitan Opera on very short notice at the age of 20. She remained a beloved member of the company for another 35 years.

The late 1950s and early 1960s saw more and more American-trained singers going to Europe for professional experience. Some, like Reri Grist (b. 1932) and Anna Moffo (b. 1932), who found success on both continents, chose to remain in Europe and make their homes there. This period also saw the rise of three outstanding mezzo-sopranos. Mignon Dunn (b. 1931), a native of Memphis, studied in New York and sang nearly every major mezzo role in her long career. Marilyn Horne (b. 1934) and Grace Bumbry (b. 1937) both studied with Lotte Lehmann in Santa Barbara. Horne's remarkable technique and her partnership with the Australian soprano Joan Sutherland led to a revival of the great *bel canto* repertoire in opera houses throughout the world. Grace Bumbry began as a mezzo but soon added important dramatic soprano roles to her repertoire. Her debut at the Bayreuth Festival in 1961 created a sensation, and she was hailed throughout the world as the "Black Venus."

Other fine sopranos of this generation were: Benita Valente (b. 1934), a student of Lehmann and Harshaw; Judith Blegen (b. 1941), long-time coloratura soubrette at the Metropolitan Opera; Carole Farley (b. 1946), a graduate of Indiana University, who became closely identified with twentieth-century vocal music; and Jessye Norman (b. 1945), who specialized in roles that suited her dark-hued voice and were shrewdly chosen to accommodate her generous physique. A popular recitalist, she was also one of the most frequently recorded singers of her generation.

The final decades of the century saw the emergence of many more African American singers. Among them, Barbara Hendricks (b. 1948), Kathleen Battle (b. 1948), Roberta Alexander (b. 1949), and Florence Quivar (b. 1944) all have firmly established their reputations. The younger generation is represented by Harolyn Blackwell (b. 1960), who succeeded Kathleen Battle as the soubrette of choice at the Metropolitan Opera, and Michelle Crider (b. 1963), who appears to be the outstanding lirico spinto soprano of her generation.

A popular mezzo-soprano in the final decades of the twentieth century was

Fredericka Von Stade (b. 1945). She was particularly successful in trouser roles, especially these of Cherubino and Octavian. Jennifer Larmore (b. 1958) inherited the mantle of Marilyn Horne in the *bel canto* repertoire, and Gail Gilmore (b. 1950) is the outstanding dramatic mezzo-soprano of her generation. One of the most exciting singers from this group is Denyce Graves (b. 1963). Her smoldering interpretations of Carmen and Dalilah have captured the imagination of audiences around the world. In addition to Graves, the mezzos who show the most promise for the twenty-first century appear to be Susanne Mentzer (b. 1957) and Susan Graham (b. 1960).

Outstanding sopranos in the final decades of the twentieth century include Catherine Malfitano (b. 1948), June Anderson (b. 1952), and Carol Vaness (b. 1952). Malfitano has combined strong vocal technique with a committed stage presence and has been particularly successful in psychologically complicated characterizations. June Anderson has a beautiful, lyric soprano voice and was a favorite of the conductor Leonard Bernstein. Carol Vaness has been very successful in a variety of roles, from lyric coloratura to lirico spinto. In the final decade of the century, Renee Fleming (b. 1959), Dawn Upshaw (b. 1960), and Sylvia McNair (b. 1956) have emerged as the most popular sopranos of their generation. They all have strong international reputations, and they have made numerous recordings. Other sopranos who show promise for the twenty-first century are Heidi Grant Murphy (b. 1962), Barbara Bonney (b. 1956), and Ruth-Ann Swenson (b. 1957).

See also Classical Music; Organizations, Performer; Performer, Choral and Vocal Ensemble

For Further Reading

Pleasants, Henry. *The Great Singers: From the Dawn of Opera to Our Own Time*. New York: Simon & Schuster, 1966.

Robinson, Francis. *Celebration: The Metropolitan Opera*. Garden City, NY: Doubleday, 1979.

Robert B. Dundas

Performer, Woodwind

In the early part of the twentieth century in United States there were very few professional woodwind performers on any of the wind instruments, including flute, oboe, clarinet, and bassoon. It was considered most unseemly and indecent for a woman to play a wind instrument in public. There was even a Massachusetts state law that made it possible for a woman to be arrested for playing a wind instrument in public. However, when the American Musicians' Union formed in the early part of the twentieth century, women were allowed to join.

Now there are many more women studying to be professional flutists and oboists than men, even though a much higher proportion of the well-paid orchestra positions are still held by men. The number of women studying to be professional clarinetists and bassoonists has grown steadily to almost 50 percent during recent years. However, men also still hold most of the important positions for clarinet and bassoon in the orchestral world. Currently, women woodwind players play many of the freelance music jobs, and many more women woodwind specialists hold important faculty teaching positions in U.S. conservatories and universities.

One of the most significant events for women woodwind players was the appointment of Doriot Anthony Dwyer (b. 1922), flutist, teacher, and granddaughter of Susan B. Anthony, as principal flute of the Boston Symphony Orchestra (BSO) by Pierre Monteux in 1952. Dwyer was the first woman appointed principal chair of a major U.S. orchestra, and she remained the only woman principal of the BSO until 1980. She was the first orchestral player to be awarded the Sanford Fellowship from Yale University (1975) and an honorary doctorate from Harvard University (1982). She taught at the New England Conservatory of Music, Boston University, and the Berkshire Music Festival at Tanglewood in Lenox, MA.

A number of women woodwind performers have held important U.S. symphony orchestra positions in the latter part of the twentieth century. Jean Baxstresser was formerly principal flute of the New York Philharmonic and the Toronto and Montreal Symphonies. Jean Birkenstock is principal flute of the Lyric Opera of Chicago Orchestra, principal flute of the Grant Park Orchestra, and co-artistic director of the Door County Chamber Music Festival, WI, and a faculty member of Chicago College of the performing Arts, Roosevelt University. Zart Dombourian-Eby is piccolo flute with the Seattle Symphony and champion of new music and a board member of the National Flute Association, the principal organization for professional flutists. Anne Giles is principal flute of the Los Angeles Philharmonic. Leone Buyse, flutist with the Boston Symphony, is on the faculty at Rice University and also a champion of new music.

Women oboists were inspired by the famous British oboist Lady Evelyn Rothwell Barbirolli, a student of Leon Goossens and an international soloist. She was a member of the Covent Garden touring orchestra and gave the first performance of the rediscovered Mozart Concerto K314. Her writings include important books for players: *Difficult Passages from Orchestral Repertoire* (London 1953), *Oboe Technique* (1953), *Difficult Passages from Bach* (1955), and *The Oboist's Companion* (1974).

Lois Wann, former oboist of the Metropolitan Opera Orchestra and teacher at the Juilliard School for many years, was a student of the legendary Marcel Tabuteau at the Curtis Institute of Music. Elaine Douvas is principal oboe of the Metropolitan Opera Orchestra and a faculty member of the Juilliard School. Gladys Elliott was principal oboe of the Houston Symphony and then of the Lyric Opera of Chicago Orchestra, before a tragic accident ended her performing career. Elizabeth Camus, oboist with the Cleveland Orchestra, is also a teaching associate of John Mack, principal oboe of the orchestra. Marilyn Zupnik is principal oboe of the Minneapolis Symphony; Sara Watkins played principal oboe with the National Symphony Orchestra in Washington, DC; and Carolyn Hove plays English horn with the Los Angeles Philharmonic and is an important recording artist.

Clarinetists in the twentieth century have excelled at performing contemporary literature by living composers. There are many women role models, including Laura Ardan, principal clarinetist of the Atlanta Symphony; Marilyn Lauriente, former principal clarinet of the Lyric Opera of Chicago Orchestra until her death in 1995; and her successor, Charlene Zimmerman, who currently holds the position.

Women bassoonists have achieved some of the most important orchestral positions. Betty Johnson, mentor to many bassoonists throughout the United States, was the original principal bassoonist in the first Oklahoma City Symphony, which was founded in 1936. She retired briefly in 1985 after 50 seasons and later returned to play for a few years in the newly formed Oklahoma City Philharmonic. The principal bassoonists of both the New York Philharmonic and the Metropolitan Opera orchestra are women: Judith LeClair and Patricia Rogers. LeClair, principal bassoonist with the New York Philharmonic, won the audition while she was a student at the Juilliard School in the early 1980s. Rogers is principal bassoon of the Metropolitan Opera Orchestra. Nancy Goeres, another contemporary orchestral bassoonist, performs with the Pittsburgh Symphony. Isabelle Plaster, contrabassoon specialist, has played with the Boston Symphony Orchestra as an extra player for the last 30 years and has been very involved in promoting new music.

Many women woodwind specialists have chosen to concentrate on chamber music or teaching rather than pursuing orchestral careers, and several have achieved international reputations. Eugenia Zuckerman and Carol Wincenc are among the most important flutists in the United States. Both are international flute concerto soloists, chamber musicians, and recording artists. A champion of new music, Patricia Spencer is the flutist with Speculum Musicae in New York. Mary Stolper, principal flute of Chicago Sinfonietta and piccolo specialist, is a founding member of American Women Composers Midwest and the past president of the Chicago Flute Club. Additionally, Stolper has recorded the chamber music of composer Shulamit Ran on the Erato label and frequently performs with the Chicago Symphony. Flutist Paula Robeson is a member of the Marlboro Festival Chamber Players and a noted recording artist. Janice Misurell-Mitchell is a flutist, composer, and performance artist. She is also a faculty member of DePaul University Music School, co-artistic director of CUBE Contemporary Music Ensemble, and a founding member and one of the past presidents of American Women Composers Midwest.

There are a number of significant women flute educators at various academic institutions in the United States. These include Judith Bentley, nationally recognized flute teacher at Bowling Green State University (OH), and Claudia Anderson and Jill Felber of the Anderson/Felber Flute Duo, both champions of new music. All support new music performance. Amy Rice Young is a flutist and publisher of the largest selection of flute choir music by Alray Publications. Kathleen Goll Wilson is editor of *Flute Talk Magazine*, the largest magazine in circulation for flutists. Katherine Hoover (b. 1937), composer and flutist, is a prolific composer of music for the flute. Her compositions are published by Papagena Press. Nancy Toff is a flutist and historical scholar specializing in pre-modern flutes and historical flute performance. With over 6,000 members, the National Flute Association is the largest organization for flutists in the United States; Nancy Andrews, Teresa Beaman, Katherine Hoover, Stephanie Jutt, and Mary Possess are all on the Board of Directors.

Laila Storch has been an important role model for many oboe educators and chamber music performers. Storch was the first woman to be admitted to the legendary class of Marcel Tabuteau at the Curtis Institute of Music, Philadelphia. Jennifer Paull is widely regarded as the most important oboe d'amore soloist and recording artist in the world. Nancy Ambrose King was the winner of the 3rd New York International Solo Oboe Competition and is a professor of oboe at the University of Illinois, Champaign. Andrea Gullickson is an oboe and oboe d'amore player with WIZARDS! virtuoso double reed consort, Iowa City. Oboe and English horn performer Patricia Nott is a chamber music specialist who performed for many years with the Lincoln Center Chamber Players. She is also the organizer of the John Mack Oboe Camp and the executive director of the New World Symphony (Miami, FL).

Peggy Pearson is a Johann Sebastian Bach specialist, soloist, and chamber musician. She has been the winner of the Naumberg award for chamber music and the recipient of the Radcliffe Bunting Grant to promote the composition of new music for oboe, and she has organized group commissioning of a work (1999) by Yehudi Wyner for oboe and string trio by a consortium of oboists including Patricia Morehead and Sara Bloom. Bloom, professor of oboe at the Cincinnati Conservatory of Music, is the editor of the Robert Bloom Collection of oboe literature. Nora Post was the first woman woodwind faculty member at Darmstadt New Music Festival in 1982 and 1984. She holds a Ph.D. in music history and a D.M.A. in oboe, and she is the owner of one of the most successful oboe shops in the United States. She performed with the Buffalo Group for New Music and is the author of many notable articles on the oboe for the *Journal of the International Double Reed Society*. Nancy Fowler hosted the 25th Anniversary Festival of the International Double Reed Society (IRDS) at Florida State University, Tallahassee, and is a professor of oboe and a promoter of new music. Patricia Morehead, oboist, composer, and co-artistic director of CUBE, has been one of the few oboists to specialize in extended techniques and has premiered over 40 works, many of them by women.

Women woodwind players have been especially supportive of new and experimental music. This is especially true of clarinetists. Suzee Stevens (Evanston, IL), American virtuoso clarinetist and performance artist, has been a longtime associate and collaborator of the Karlheinz Stockhausen Group as soloist and performer in the opera *Licht*. She has an enormous repertoire of clarinet, basset clarinet, and bass clarinet pieces written especially for her by Stockhausen. Julie DeRoche is on the clarinet faculty of DePaul University School of Music and is president-elect of the International Clarinet Society and an active performer. Laura Flax is clarinetist with Speculum Musicae, NYC, specializing in new music performance and the commissioning of new works. Christie Vohs is clarinetist and founder of the Chicago Chamber Music Collective, as well as founder of the Hinsdale Music School. Kathy Pirtle is founder and clarinetist of the Orion Chamber Ensemble, Chicago. Orion tours nationally and promotes living composers. Esther Lamneck, of New York University, and a champion of new music, has commissioned numerous compositions by contemporary composers.

Among the significant women bassoonists are Andrea Merenzon, Norma Hooks, Susan Nigro, and Julie Feves. Merenzon is a bassoon soloist who hosted the IDRS convention in the year 2000 in Buena Aires, Argentina. Hooks is a bassoonist, secretary of the IRDS, and a faculty member of Western Maryland College. Nigro is a noted contrabassoon soloist and active commissioner of new music for the contrabassoon, a frequent player with the Chicago Symphony Orchestra woodwind section, and a recording artist with Bassoon Heritage Editions. Feves is a bassoonist and a full-time faculty member of the California Institute of the Arts.

See also Organizations, Performer; Prizes, Composer and Performer

For Further Reading

The Clarinet. The Official Publication of the International Clarinet Association.

The Double Reed. International Double Reed Society.

Flutist Quarterly: The Official Magazine of the National Flute Association. Tucson, AZ.

The Journal of the International Double Reed Society. International Double Reed Society.

Patricia Morehead

Performing and Mechanical Rights Organizations

Performing and Mechanical Rights Organizations safeguard the creations of lyricists and composers and pay these musicians for public performances. The principal organizations providing this service in the United States are the American Society of Composers, Authors and Publishers (ASCAP); Broadcast Music, Inc. (BMI); the Society of European Stage Authors and Composers (SESAC); and the National Music Publishers Association/Harry Fox Agency (NMPA/HFA). These agencies collect monies from customers and pay members.

ASCAP. ASCAP was the first performing rights organization. It was founded in 1914 by a small group of songwriters led by Victor Herbert. He was joined by Irving Berlin, John Philip Sousa, James Weldon Johnson, and 100 people from the music community who met to establish a way for creators to get paid. The Society exists to "protect rights of its members by licensing and paying royalties for the public performance of their copyrighted works."

Several women hold prominent positions at ASCAP. Marilyn Bergman is the current president and chairman of the board of ASCAP. She is the first woman ever elected to the ASCAP Board of Directors, and she has received three Academy Awards, three Emmy Awards, two Grammy Awards, and one Cable Ace Award. Additionally, Frances Richard is vice-president of concert music. Prior to her service with ASCAP, Richard was a founding director and the vice-president of Meet the Composer.

The Society has reciprocal agreements with 55 similar societies internationally. A full spectrum of genres are represented, including pop, rock, alternative, country, rhythm and blues, rap, hip hop, film and television music, new age, theater and cabaret, contemporary Christian, symphonic, and concert. Women in ASCAP include Madonna (b. 1958), Melissa Etheridge (b. 1961), Amy Grant (b. 1960), the Dixie Chicks, and songwriter Betty Comden (b. ca. 1917).

BMI. Broadcast Music, Inc., was started in 1940 "as a non-profit-making corporation to open the door to performing rights representation for songwriters and composers of all types of music." It is incorporated as a nonprofit organization, except for operating expenses. Members believe that creators have the right to be fairly paid. They support music and musicians. Because of BMI's Open Door Policy, those who had written blues, jazz, rhythm and blues, gospel, folk, country, Spanish-language, and eventually rock and roll music, who had often not been paid, were welcomed and are well represented today. Reciprocal agreements were made with similar organizations around the world.

As current president and chief executive officer, Frances W. Preston is one of the most significant women in the performing and mechanical rights industry. She joined the organization in 1954 and was named vice-president in 1964. Additionally, Frances Preston was elected president of the ICSAC (International Confederation of Societies of Authors and Composers) Canada/USA Committee in 1998.

Membership in BMI is over 200,000. Members have won the Pulitzer Prize, the Oscar, and the Grammy, Emmy, Soul Train, Dove, Tony, and American Music Awards for modern classical music composers. BMI states that it has the largest number of songwriters, composers, and publishers in any performing rights organization. There are more than 60,000 publishers and more than 140,000 writers. More than 75 percent of those in the Rock and Roll Hall of Fame, 80 percent in the Country Music Hall of Fame, and 90 percent of those who have received the Pioneer Award by the Rhythm and Blues Foundation are BMI members. Popular musicians such as Shania Twain (b. 1965), Sarah McLachlan (b. 1968), Mariah Carey (b. 1970), Sheryl Crow (b. 1962), Faith Evans, and Patti LaBelle (b. 1944) belong to BMI.

Other performing and mechanical rights organizations include the National Music Publishers Association (NMPA), established in 1917; the Harry Fox Agency (associated with the NMPA), established in 1927; and the Society of European Stage Authors and Composers (SESAC), founded in 1930. The HFA represents over 20,000 music publishers, and it licenses music globally for uses in all audiovisual media, including background music, music on airplanes, radio, MIDI (Musical Instrument Digital Interface), karaoke, and multimedia. SESAC was initially limited to European and gospel music but has diversified to include dance hits, rock classics, adult contemporary, rhythm and blues, Latin, jazz, country, contemporary Christian, new age, film, television theme music, advertising jingles, and commercials.

See also Country Music Hall of Fame; Rock and Roll Hall of Fame

For Further Reading

ASCAP: The American Society of Composers, Authors and Publishers. Available: http://www.ascap.com

BMI [Broadcast Music Inc.] Home Page. Available: http://www.bmi.com

Welcome to SESAC! [Society of European Stage Authors and Composers]. Available: http://www.sesac.com

Alicia RaMusa

Perry, Julia (1924–1979)

Successfully melding the music of her African American heritage with twentieth-century European influences of her teachers Nadia Boulanger and Luigi Dallapiccola, Julia Perry's compositions are a significant contribution to American music. Perry's only extant piano piece, *Prelude*, appears in *Black Women Composers: A Century of Piano Music (1893–1990)* (Walker-Hill, 1992). It reveals a richly intense keyboard compositional style. Four other piano compositions remain unlocated. Her more experimental large-scale work, *Homunculus C.F.* (available on CRI-252), the *Stabat Mater* (available on CRI-133), and *A Short Piece for Orchestra* (available on CRI-145) have been recorded. Several songs by Perry have been published by Galaxy Publishing Company. Facsimile editions of many chamber and orchestral works are available from Peer-Southern Concert Music through Theodore Presser, Bryn Mawr, PA. The American Music Center in New York City also holds works by Perry. Her style has been referred to as "neoclassic" but also "eclectic," because her style did change over her lifetime.

Born in Lexington, KY, on 25 May 1924 to a musical family, Perry knew from an early age that she wanted to become a composer. In 1948, after completing bachelor's and master's degrees at Westminster Choir College, studying piano, voice, violin, conducting, and composition, Perry moved to New York to continue studying composition at the Juilliard School. Composition was her greatest skill, but conducting was her chosen medium of performance. Conducting afforded Perry opportunities to experiment with sounds, exploring the musical effects of her compositions in performance.

Between 1952 and 1958, Perry studied conducting at the Accademia Chigiana in Siena and composition with Nadia Boulanger, in Paris, where she won a Boulanger Grand Prix for her Viola Sonata. She was also awarded 1952 and 1955 Guggenheim Fellowships to study with Luigi Dallapiccola in Italy. In 1957 Perry organized and presented a concert tour of Europe, sponsored by the U.S. Information Agency. After returning to the United States in 1959, Perry continued to compose, winning the American Academy and National Institute of Arts and Letters award in 1964. From 1967 to 1968 she taught at Florida A&M College, and she was a visiting lecturer at Atlanta College Center from 1968 to 1969.

In 1971 Perry suffered a series of severe strokes, which left her paralyzed on her right side. Eventually she taught herself to write with her left hand, continuing to compose, before moving back to Akron, OH, where she died on 24 April 1979.

See also African American Musicians; Classical Music

For Further Reading

Green, Mildred Denby. *Black Women Composers: A Genesis*. Boston, MA: Twayne, 1983.

Walker-Hill, Helen. *Black Women Composers: A Century of Piano Music (1893–1990)*. Bryn Mawr, PA: Hildegard Publishing, 1992.

———. *Piano Music by Black Women Composers: A Catalog of Solo and Ensemble Works*. Westport, CT: Greenwood Press, 1992.

Anita Hanawalt

Peters, Bernadette (1948–)

From love goddess to wicked witch, to sharp-shooting cowgirl, Broadway singer Bernadette Peters has been dazzling audiences and critics for more than four decades. She is one of the most versatile film and stage actresses and singers of her time. She is best known for her interpretations of songs by Stephen Sondheim. With her clear, girlish voice, she is able to move quickly from belting Broadway

Bernadette Peters. *Photo courtesy of Nat Solomon/Globe Photos.*

melodies to more rhythmically complex and jazzy tunes.

Bernadette Lazzara was born on 28 February 1948 in Ozone Park, NY. She made her professional debut at age three as a television contestant on the game show *Juvenile Jury*. By age nine she had joined Actor's Equity. Soon thereafter she changed her name from Lazzara to "Peters," after her father's first name, to avoid being typecast in ethnic roles. Her theatrical debut came at age ten in Otto Preminger's *This Is Goggle* (1957). While still in her teens she appeared in *The Most Happy Fella* and *The Penny Friend* and toured nationally at age 13 for eight months in *Gypsy*. Following the *Gypsy* tour Peters took a break from performing and attended the Quintana School for Young Professionals in New York City.

She made her Broadway debut in 1967 in *Johnny No-Trump* and starred with Joel Grey in the 1968 production of the musical *George M!* Peters's portrayal of Josie Cohan won her a Theatre World Award; the same year also brought her first Drama Desk Award, for her performance in *Dames at Sea*. Peters received both the Tony Award and Drama Desk Award for her performance in Andrew Lloyd Webber's musical *Song and Dance* (1985) and a second Tony Award, and Drama Desk Award, for the 1999 revival of the musical *Annie Get Your Gun*. She received Tony nominations for her work in *The Goodbye Girl* (1992) and Stephen Sondheim's Pulitzer Prize–winning musical *Sunday in the Park with George* (1983). Tony nominations also came for *Mack and Mabel* (1974) and Leonard Bernstein's musical *On the Town* (1971). Although early in her career Peters was often cast in mediocre shows, critics have consistently commented on the fine quality of her performances. In 1995 she became the youngest inductee into the Theater Hall of Fame.

Bernadette Peters's impressive career also boasts nearly a dozen television appearances, several recordings, and 20 motion pictures. Some of her acclaimed works for television include *Shelley Duvall's Fairy Tale Theater-Sleeping Beauty* (Fanlight Productions 1987), *The Last Best Year* (ABC movie 1990), and *The Odyssey* (NBC miniseries 1997). Her Grammy-nominated recordings include *I'll Be Your Baby Tonight* (Angel 54699) and *Sondheim Etc.: Bernadette Peters Live at Carnegie Hall* (Angel 55870). She is probably best known, however, for her portrayal of the witch in the filmed stage version of Stephen Sondheim's smash hit musical *Into the Woods*. The musical's mix of comedy and drama draws on the full spectrum of Peters's abilities as an actress and stage performer. She has been married to investment advisor Michael Wittenberg since 1996.

See also Musical Theater; Tony Awards

For Further Reading

Bordman, Gerald (ed.). *American Musical Theater: A Chronicle*, 2d ed. New York: Oxford University Press, 1992.

Miller, Marc. "Shooting Star." *In Theater* (March 1999): 18–23.

Moritz, Charles (ed.). "Peters, Bernadette." *Current Biography Yearbook 1984*. New York: H. W. Wilson, 1984.

Lori Stevens

Phillips, Liz (1951–)

Liz Phillips is internationally recognized as an interactive multimedia installation artist. Her installations combine visual and sonic material in a multidimensional space that responds to the audience. The audience plays the sculpture like a musical instrument by moving through the space and causing intriguing sonic events. The audience explores the relationship between their movement and the response of the installation. Total strangers have been known to dance duets with complete delight in a Phillips installation. Phillips has received numerous awards, including a Guggenheim Fellowship (1987) and grants from the National Endowment for the Arts and the New York State Council on the Arts.

Liz Phillips was born on 13 June 1951 in Jersey City, NJ. In 1973 she received a B.A. degree from Bennington College. She has taught courses in light and sound sculpture at the State University of New York at Purchase. In 1981 she collaborated with five other media artists to found the Parabola Arts Foundation, a nonprofit organization committed to the creation and exhibition of new media.

Her works often use light, infrared, electromagnetic, and ultrasonic sensors. As people enter the installation space, their body positions are recognized by the system and sonic events are directed toward them. Phillips uses Serge and Kurzweil, in addition to synthesizers she herself has made. She has received additional technical support from Michael Wu, a graduate of the MIT Media Lab.

Phillips's sound installations include *T.V. Dinners* (1971), *Sound Structures* (1971), *Windspun* (1981), *Sunspots* (1982), *Zephyr* (1984), *Sound Syzygy* (1985), *Graphite Ground* (1987), *Koi* (1998), and *Echo Evolution* (1999). Her installations have been exhibited at the Whitney Museum of American Art, Ars Electronica, Creative Time, the Spoleto Festival USA, the Kitchen, the Walker Art Center, Jacob's Pillow, the Capp Street Project, the San Francisco Museum of Modern Art, the Clocktower, Brown University, and New Music America (Los Angeles, San Francisco, Minneapolis, and Chicago). Phillips has collaborated with the Merce Cunningham Dance Company, and her works have been presented by the Cleveland Orchestra, IBM Japan, and the World Financial Center.

See also Multimedia; Music Technology; Sound Installation Artist

For Further Reading

Ahlstrom, David. "Liz Phillips: Sunspots." *Computer Music Journal* 6/3 (1982): 83–85.

Zaimont, Judith Lang. "Composers Speaking for Themselves: An Electronic Music Panel Discussion." In *The Musical Woman: An International Perspective, Vol. II.* New York: Greenwood Press, 1985, 280–312.

Mary Simoni

Phranc (1957–)

Born Susan Gottlieb, Phranc's music combines protest songs of the 1960s with punk, new wave, and folk-rock idioms. Her homosexuality is a common theme in her music, often manifesting itself in lyrics espousing personal identity and sexual freedom. She bills herself as an "all-American, Jewish lesbian folksinger" and continues to hold fast to her beliefs of individual expression and independence. Phranc strives to reduce the marginalization and ghettoizing of women's music by recording on labels that exist largely outside of the women's music community, most notably, Rhino and Island.

Born in 1957, Phranc grew up in Santa Monica, CA, as the daughter of a dental assistant and an insurance salesman; her childhood allowed her the freedom to explore her sexuality. By 1974 she began performing in coffeehouses and clubs. She quickly discovered the Los Angeles punk-rock culture and became involved with several local bands. Eventually her desire for more textual clarity superceded her punk tradition, and she turned toward a more folk-rock sound. Her songs are essentially autobiographical, and they feature diverse subject matter such as apartheid, women's mud-wrestling, and pop culture trends.

To date, Phranc's solo releases include *Folksinger* (Island 422-846358-2), *I Enjoy Being a Girl* (Island 422-842579-2), *Positively Phranc* (Island 422-848282-2), *Goofyfoot* (Kill Rock Stars 233), and *Milkman* (Phancy 1).

See also Lesbian Music; Rock and Popular Music Genres

For Further Reading

Phranc. Available http://www.phranc.net

Warren, Holly George, and Patricia Romanowski (eds.). *The New Rolling Stone Encyclopedia of Rock and Roll*. New York: Fireside Press, 1995.

Kristen K. Stauffer

Piano Pedagogy

Piano pedagogy evolved during the twentieth century in response to the need for teacher training focused specifically on piano studies. The field developed from an early emphasis on teaching children to encompass a broad range of issues relating to piano teaching, including the particular needs of preschool and older adult students, techniques for group teaching, and applications of computer technology in piano teaching. Women have long been involved as some of the most significant innovators in the field of piano pedagogy.

The art of piano performance has been transmitted through generations of teachers and students by way of tutorial teaching—a tradition of apprentices learning from master teachers. Teacher training during the nineteenth and early twentieth centuries was limited to the study of repertoire, technique, and musical interpretation. The production of pianos and the number of piano students grew rapidly during the early decades of the twentieth century. Traditional studies with master teachers and performers, although appropriate for training virtuoso performers, was not adequate preparation for pianists who would teach the growing number of amateur musicians. Piano study was considered especially important for girls because making music was an important part of homemaking. Twentieth-century pioneers of piano pedagogy, a field traditionally dominated by women, reformed teacher training by developing innovative materials for piano students and new modes of teacher training. Modern piano pedagogy incorporated studies in learning theory and adopted practices from classroom teacher training, such as observation of model teaching and supervised intern teaching experiences, and applied them to training pianists for individual and group teaching.

The focus of piano pedagogy was originally on the elementary level of study. Twentieth-century pedagogues developed materials that promoted comprehensive musicianship with particular attention to the process of teaching reading. Authors of method series for beginners designed piano courses that would lead young students from prereading musical experiences at the piano to the works of the master composers. By the end of the century, piano pedagogy encompassed teacher preparation for all levels of study using the traditional tutorial approach as well as innovative techniques for group teaching and teaching applications for computer technology. Given the importance of teaching in the careers of most pianists, studies in piano pedagogy became widely available for piano students in colleges and universities during the second half of the century. Women dominated the field from its inception because music study and education were considered appropriate fields for women. Over the course of the century, however, women continued to make significant contributions to piano pedagogy through performing and teaching; publishing and editing educational materials, textbooks, and journals; holding leadership positions in professional organizations; founding music schools and preparatory departments; and instituting pedagogy courses and degree programs in colleges and universities. In some cases, the expertise that women had developed in home piano studios created career opportunities for them in academia and the music industry.

During the early decades of the twentieth century, women made important contributions to piano pedagogy by carrying on the celebrated traditions of the European master teachers and by establishing music schools in America's industrial and cultural centers. Amy Fay (1844–1928), a native of Mississippi, taught in New York and Chicago after six years of study with some of the most respected pianists in Germany. A collection of letters written to her sister and published under the title, *Music Study in Germany* remains one of the most valuable documents on the teaching of the great pianists and teachers of the nineteenth century: Franz Liszt, Friedrich Wieck, Clara Schumann, Carl Tausig, Theodore Kullak, and Ludwig Deppe.

Women founded several music conservatories that continue to train pianists today. Clara Baur established the Cincinnati Conservatory of Music in 1867 and taught there until her retirement in 1930. Only three years after founding the school, she established a preparatory division offering piano instruction for children. The Manhattan School of Music grew out of the Neighborhood Music School in New York, founded by Janet Daniels Schenck (1883–1976). May Garrettson Evans and her sister Marion Dorsey Evans founded a school of music for children in Baltimore that eventually became the Preparatory Division of the Peabody Conservatory. Women who founded other schools of music include Angela Diller (Diller-Quaille School of Music in New York) and Julia Ettie Crane ([1855–1923] the Crane School of Music at Potsdam, New York).

For more than a century, women have made significant contributions to piano pedagogy through the production of educational music and materials. Important contributors from the early part of the twentieth century include Mrs. John Spencer Curwen (*The Child Pianist* and *The Pianoforte Method*); Mrs. Crosby Adams (*Very First Lessons at the Piano*); Antha Minerva Virgil (*The Virgil Method*); Julia Caruthers (*Piano Technique for Children*); and Florence Goodrich (*Synthetic Series of Piano Pieces*).

Frances Clark (1905–1998) raised the standard in materials available for piano instruction by compiling and editing music by master composers and commissioning new pedagogical works by outstanding contemporary composers for the Frances Clark Library published in 1955. Whereas materials had traditionally included folk songs, Clark introduced young students to contemporary idioms in the music of composers such as Béla Bartók, Dmitri Kabalevsky, Aleksander Tansman, and Alexander Tcherepnin. Frances Clark collaborated with co-author Louise Goss on (b. 1926) *The Music Tree*, a method series for beginners featuring the classic intervallic approach to reading. Pupils developed skills in reading by intervals on a limited staff before learning the grand staff and note names. Many of the materials developed in the late twentieth century incorporated features of intervallic reading.

Frances Clark also introduced major reforms in teacher training by incorporating concepts from educational philosophy and psychology to better understand how the teaching and learning process applies to piano study. Clark set a precedent in training piano teachers by creating a format that combines studies in learning theory with observations of demonstration teaching and practicum teaching with critique from a master teacher. Clark taught piano pedagogy at Kalamazoo College and Westminster Choir College before founding The New School for Music Study in Princeton (NJ) in 1960. The New School became the first professional training center for piano teachers, producing not only successful piano teachers but many students who went on to establish courses in piano pedagogy in U.S. colleges and universities.

Other women who have contributed to method series for beginners include Jane Smisor Bastien (*Music through the Piano*), Louise Bianchi (*Music Pathways*), Barbara Kreader (*The Hal Leonard Student Piano Library*), and Amanda Vick Lethco (*Alfred's Basic Piano Library*). Prominent composers, editors, and publishers of piano music for children include Katherine Beard, Mary Elizabeth Clark, Emma Lou Diemer (b. 1927), Jane Magrath, Elvina Truman Pearce, and Eugenie Rocherolle. Several women have collaborated with their husbands in producing pedagogical materials: Jane Smisor Bastien and James Bastien, Nancy and Randall Faber, Walter and Carol Noona, and Gayle Kowalchyk and E. L. Lancaster. The practice of presenting workshops on teaching techniques and materials has served not only to promote sales of educational materials but also to raise the level of professionalism among independent music teachers.

During the second half of the twentieth century, piano pedagogy flourished as a specialized discipline in academic degree programs in colleges and universities throughout the United States. Many women brought the expertise they had gained from teaching in private studios and preparatory divisions to universities, where they established courses and degree programs in piano pedagogy. Women directed many of the successful pedagogy programs in colleges and universities: Louise Bianchi at Southern Methodist University, Martha Hilley at the University of Texas; Frances Larimer at Northwestern University; Barbara English Maris at the Catholic University of America; Joanne Smith at the University of Michigan; and Marienne Uszler at the University of Southern California.

Directors of pedagogy programs formed a professional organization, the National Conference on Piano Pedagogy, that met biennially beginning around 1980 to exchange ideas on the teaching of piano pedagogy and to develop guidelines for developing coursework and degree programs in piano pedagogy. The conference published two reports in the mid-1980s offering guidelines for establishing pedagogy programs at the undergraduate and graduate levels. These reports were based on information collected from model programs around the country. Subsequent Conference Proceedings became the primary source of collecting and publishing information and research on piano pedagogy.

Advances in computer technology and digital instruments had an important impact on the field beginning in the 1970s. Many colleges and independent studios purchased piano laboratories with multiple pianos and equipment for communications between instructors and students. The technology facilitated group instruction for secondary piano and classes for functional keyboard skills. Pedagogues developed specific techniques for group instruction for music majors who needed basic keyboard skills. The growing popularity of teaching laboratories for piano enabled teachers to incorporate ensemble activities at the piano. Many teachers found that teaching and learning in group environments, with or without a keyboard laboratory, enhanced musicianship and motivation. Toward the end of the twentieth century, piano pedagogy included training for teachers in how to use synthesizers and computer software to enhance piano instruction.

See also Organizations, Music Education; Performer, Keyboard

For Further Reading

Allen, Doris. "Women's Contributions to Modern Piano Pedagogy." In *The Musical Woman: An International Perspective. Volume II*, ed. by Judith Lang Zaimont. New York: Greenwood Press, 1985, 411–444.

Bastien, James. *How to Teach Piano Successfully*, 3rd ed. San Diego: Neil A. Kjos Music, 1988.

Uszler, Marienne. *The Well-Tempered Keyboard Teacher*. 2d ed. New York: Schirmer Books, 2000.

Kenneth Williams

Pitts, Lilla Belle (1884–1970)

Lilla Belle Pitts was an outstanding contributor to the music education profession. Pitts published numerous journal articles on general music, classroom music, and opera. She was the single author of books on music reading, singing, and curriculum. With music educators Mabelle Glenn (1881–1969), Lorrain E. Watters, and Louis Wersen, she edited *Our Singing World* (1949–1954), a popular textbook series published by Ginn. This series included student textbooks, teaching guides, and recordings. Along with music educator Gladys Tipton, Pitts wrote notes for teachers for many recordings produced by RCA Victor in the 1940s. She was on the Board of Directors of the Metropolitan Opera Guild (1950–1964) and helped prepare music education materials on opera.

Pitts was born in Aberdeen, MO, on 26 September 1884. The eldest of seven children, she grew up in Mississippi. Pitts studied piano, voice, and violin at Ward Seminary in Nashville, TN, receiving a diploma in 1904. She studied piano at North Texas Female College in Sherman, TX, at the Chicago Conservatory of Music, and at Northwestern University; and she taught piano privately in Leesville, LA, for one year. In Texas, Pitts taught in the public schools of Amarillo (1910–1914). In Dallas, she was an elementary music teacher and the assistant supervisor of music (1914–1922), working under Sudie Williams. She then spent two years traveling as the educational representative in the South for Columbia Phonograph Company. Then Pitts moved north, where she taught in Elizabeth, NJ (1924–1938), specializing in junior high school general music. She studied with Charles H. Farnsworth and Peter W. Dykema at Teachers College, Columbia University, receiving a B.S. degree in 1935. Pitts was on the faculty at Columbia Teachers College (1938–1954) where she taught courses on general music and music methods.

In the Music Educators National Conference (MENC), Pitts was second vice-president (1938–1940), a member of the Executive Committee (1940), president (1942–1944), and first vice-president (1944–1946). She was a member of the

MENC Research Council (1950–1956) and chairman of the Golden Anniversary Commission in 1956. The MENC conference in 1944 was held in St. Louis, MO, with a theme of "Widening Horizons for Music Education." MENC met in conjunction with the National Catholic Music Educators Association for the first time that year. Articles written by Pitts during her presidency reflect the concerns of a nation at war. Under the Schools at War program, children were encouraged to create patriotic songs. Pitts urged educators to be aware of the significance of new technologies (phonographs and sound-films) and to expand the curriculum to relate music to the current world.

At the end of her career Pitts taught at Florida State University (1957–1958). After retirement she was an important clinician at state and national MENC meetings. She received an honorary doctorate from Elon College, NC, in 1949 and became professor emeritas at Columbia in 1959. She died in Nashville, TN, on 24 January 1970.

See also Music Education; Music Educators National Conference

For Further Reading

Blanchard, Gerald L. "Lilla Belle Pitts: Her Life and Contributions to Music Education." Ed.D. diss., Brigham Young University, 1966.

Sondra Wieland Howe

Powell, Jane (1929–)

Singer, dancer, and actress Jane Powell was one of the most popular Hollywood musical performers of the mid-twentieth century. Receiving great acclaim for her singing at an early age, she was invited to perform on Stars Over Hollywood, a radio show hosted by Janet Gaynor, when she was only 14 years old. The success of this single appearance led to Jane's signing a seven-year contract with Metro-Goldwyn-Mayer (MGM) the very next day and appearing in *The Edgar Bergen–Charlie McCarthy Show.* She made her screen debut later that same year in *Song of the Open Road* (1944), where she played a young movie star named Jane Powell—a name that she would take professionally.

Jane Powell. *Photo courtesy of Bernard/Globe Photos.*

Born Suzanne Lorraine Burce on 1 April 1929, Jane Powell began dance lessons at the early age of two. Her parents, sure of their daughter's natural musical talent, spent the early years of Powell's childhood encouraging her to pursue singing, dancing, and acting lessons to better prepare for a career in Hollywood. When she was just six years old, Powell moved with her family to California in order to attend a dance school promising stardom for children, only to return to Portland, OR, several months later. There she was given, at age 11, her own local radio show, where she sang a mixture of classical and popular songs.

The 1940s and 1950s saw Jane Powell starring in a number of movies and musicals including *Delightfully Dangerous* (1945), *Three Daring Daughters* (1948), *Two Weeks with Love* (1950), *Rich, Young, and Pretty* (1951), *Hit the Deck* (1955), and *The Girl Most Likely* (1958). Her best-loved musicals are *Royal Wedding* (1951) [available on CBS CD47028] in which she co-starred as Fred Astaire's sister and later released the duet "How Could You Believe Me When I Said I Love You When You Know I've Been a Liar All My Life?" that became a million-selling album, and *Seven Brides for Seven Brothers* (1954) [available on Rhino CD 71966] co-starring Howard Keel. Each of these films was marked by her beautiful voice and youthful vivacity, and it was not long before she, like fellow actresses Debbie Reynolds (b. 1932) and Doris Day (b. 1929), became Hollywood's beloved "girl-next-door."

As the golden age of the musical drew to a close in the mid- to late 1960s, Powell turned to the theater, touring in musicals such as *South Pacific*, *Oklahoma!*, *Carousel*, *The Sound of Music*, *The Unsinkable Molly Brown*, *Brigadoon*, and *My Fair Lady*. In 1974 she made her Broadway debut in the revival of *Irene*, succeeding Debbie Reynolds in the leading role. Her television appearances include three films—*Wheeler and Murdoch* (1970), *The Letters* (1973), and *Mayday at 40,000 Feet* (1978)—as well as a nine-month stint (beginning in August 1985) on the ABC soap opera *Loving*. In 1988 Jane Powell published her autobiography, *The Girl Next Door . . . And How She Grew*, titled after her nationally acclaimed one-woman show.

See also Musical Theater

For Further Reading

Buckley, Michael. "Jane Powell." *Films in Review* (June/July 1987): 322–338.

Powell, Jane. *The Girl Next Door . . . And How She Grew*. New York: William Morrow, 1988.

Maria Purciello

Price, Leontyne (1927–)

Leontyne Price was one of the first African American opera singers to enjoy an international reputation. Although she began her operatic career with the traditional role of Bess in George Gershwin's *Porgy and Bess*, she soon developed an affinity for both contemporary music and for the heroines of Giuseppe Verdi and Giacomo Puccini. Since retiring from the operatic stage in 1985 she has performed exclusively on the concert stage to resounding critical acclaim. She is considered by many to be one of the greatest sopranos of the twentieth century. Her voice was pure, yet opulent from top to bottom, rich and dusky in the lower register and velvety on top. She had flawless transitions throughout all her vocal registers.

Mary Violet Leontine (later Leontyne) Price was born in Laurel, MS, on 10 February 1927. Price's parents, both amateur musicians, encouraged their daughter's interest in music from the very beginning. At age nine Price saw singer Marian Anderson (1897–1993) perform, an event that left a lasting impression on the young woman, who was already singing and playing the piano at school, church, and community functions. Price studied music education in Wilberforce, OH, at the College of Education and In-

Leontyne Price. *Photo courtesy of the Metropolitan Opera Archives.*

dustrial Arts (now Central State University). She graduated with a B.A. degree (1948) and proceeded to New York to begin vocal studies with Florence Page Kimball at the Juilliard School of Music. As a result of her performance in a student production of *Falstaff*, composer Virgil Thomsom invited her to perform in a production of his *Four Saints in Three Acts*. After the production she spent two years touring the United States and Europe in *Porgy and Bess*. In 1954 she married opera singer William Warfield, her co-star in *Porgy and Bess*. They separated in 1959 and were divorced in 1973.

In 1955 Price performed the title role of Floria in an NBC production of *Tosca*, becoming the first African American to appear in an opera on television. Performances with the San Francisco Opera, the Vienna State Opera, Covent Garden, and La Scala followed. She made her Metropolitan Opera debut in 1961 as Leonora in *Il Trovatore*. Between 1961 and 1969 she appeared in 118 productions at the Metropolitan Opera, including Samuel Barber's *Antony and Cleopatra*, the work commissioned for the opening of the Metropolitan Opera House at Lincoln Center in 1966. During the 1970s she reduced the number of her operatic performances in favor of concert and recital appearances. Price retired from the operatic stage altogether in 1985 following a televised performance of *Aida*.

She has numerous recordings from her long career. The most recent operas and recorded collections include Giuseppe

Verdi's *Aida* (UNI/London Classics 17416), Giacomo Puccini's *Tosca* (UNI/London Classics 452620), and *The Essential Leontyne Price* (BMG, RCA Victor 68153). Price has received numerous awards, including the Medal of Freedom (1964), the National Association for the Advancement of Colored People Spingarn Medal (1965), the Order of Merit (Italy, 1965), Kennedy Center Honors for lifetime achievement (1980), the National Medal of Arts (1984), and 15 Grammy Awards, including a Lifetime Achievement Award in 1983.

See also Classical Music; Performer, Vocal

For Further Reading

Lyon, Hugh Lee. *Leontyne Price: Highlights of a Prima Donna*. New York: Vantage Press, 1973.

Sargeant, Winthrop. "Leontyne Price." In *Divas*. New York: Coward, McCann and Geoghegan, 1973.

David L. Bruner

Prizes, Composer and Performer

Prizes for composers and performers each fall into two broad categories: awards for which the musician competes, and awards made by panels via a nomination process. For composers, prizes can be a cash award, a performance or a commission, a recording, or some combination of these things. For performers, prizes range from certificates of achievement to the opportunity to perform in public, as in many local concerto competitions for students, to some combination of prize money, representation and concert bookings, and recording contracts. In the popular music world, prizes are most often awarded for work already completed, as in the Grammy Awards, although there are competitions in the form of songwriting contests and battles of the bands. Although some of the more elite prizes have been slow to make awards to women, significant strides were made during the twentieth century.

The major financial awards for composers in the classical field include the Grawemeyer Award, grants from the MacArthur and Guggenheim Foundations, and the Charles Ives Living Award from the American Academy and Institute of Arts and Letters. Other important awards include the Pulitzer Prize and selection for membership in the American Academy and Institute of Arts and Letters, an organization annually making several awards in music to nonmembers, ranging from the Gold Medal to recording grants. Approximately 28 percent of the MacArthur Fellowship winners have been women, whereas the only woman to ever win the Grawemeyer Award has been Joan Tower (b. 1938). Since its inception in 1943, the Pulizter Prize in music has been awarded to only three women: Ellen Taaffe Zwilich (b. 1939), Shulamit Ran (b. 1949), and Melinda Wagner (b. 1957). Awards more specifically for emerging or mid-career composers include the Brandeis Creative Arts Award; commissions from the Koussevitsky, Fromm, and Barlow Foundations, and the Rome Prize. Vivian Fine (1913–2000), Pauline Oliveros (b. 1932), Thea Musgrave (b. 1928), and Joan Tower (b. 1938) have been among the winners of these important awards.

Major awards for band music include the ABA/Ostwald Award (est. 1956) and the Sudler Award from the John Philip Sousa Foundation. In composition, designations such as "emerging," "mid-career," and "senior" have more to do with professional achievement than with age and, in the absence of objective guidelines (such as age limits), are self-designations. Composer Loretta Jankowski (b. 1950) is the only woman thus far to receive the ABA/Ostwald Award.

The Kennedy Center Honors, established in 1978 to recognize excellence and life achievement in the performing arts, has annually honored a number of composers, conductors, instrumentalists, and singers in nationally televised broadcasts. Since 1978 more than 30 women have won the award, including Marian Anderson (1897–1993), Ella Fitzgerald (1917–1996), Betty Comden (b. ca. 1917), and Jessye Norman (b. 1945).

There are a number of well-established awards programs and competitions for student composers. Both Broadcast Music, Inc. (BMI), and the American Society of Composers, Authors and Publishers (ASCAP) Foundation annually make awards to students; in addition, ASCAP in 1998 joined with the Society of Composers, Inc. (SCI), and the Society for Electro-Acoustic Music in the United States (SEAMUS) in creating a commissioning program for students affiliated with those organizations. In 2000 composer Elainie Lillios (b. 1968) became the first woman to win the ASCAP/SEAMUS commission. Additionally, programs such as First Music in New York and reading sessions sponsored by the American Composers' Orchestra and the Chicago Civic Orchestra, among others, offer younger composers the opportunity to hear their orchestral works and sometimes also include a commission for a new work. The American Academy and Institute of Arts and Letters annually award several Charles Ives Scholarships to promising composers. Selection for seminars and master classes sponsored by the Atlantic Center for the Arts, the Bloch Festival, the Aspen Music Festival, and the Tanglewood Music Festival also serve to bring the younger composer to the attention of the music world.

Major events include New York–based competitions sponsored by the Walter Naumberg Foundation and the Young Concert Artists International Auditions, student competitions sponsored by major orchestras, and admission to summer programs at the Aspen Music Festival, Tanglewood, and the Music Academy of the West. Although the emphasis in the summer programs is on advanced study and not on opportunities for concert engagements or artist management, admission is competitive and prestigious and carries in each case a full scholarship. The Naumberg award rotates among piano, violin, viola, cello, flute, and classical guitar performers; previous winners include Shirley Verrett, Carol Brice, and Lucy Shelton.

Auditions sponsored by the Federation of Music Clubs are among the oldest programs in the United States, with Young Artist Auditions established in 1915 and the Young Composers Contest in 1943. Instrumentalists, vocalists, and composers compete at the local, regional, and national levels. Similar programs are sponsored by the Music Teachers National Association (MTNA) and the Piano Guild. Committed to supporting the creation of new works by American composers, MTNA has a commissioning program designed to give state associations financial support for commissioning and performing new works. Although the Piano Guild also sponsors competition at local, regional, and national levels, the organization's attitude toward the auditions is that every pupil becomes a winner of an award commensurate with achievement.

Among educators, there is some disagreement as to the absolute value of competitions to the development of the "whole musician," some perceiving an over-emphasis on playing the instrument perfectly rather than demonstrating a consummate musicianship. Others believe that competitions can be valuable to a musician's development, so long as the events are carefully chosen and timed to best meet the student's needs. Despite some drawbacks, high-profile competitions continue to be important as a way of attracting and holding the attention of the general public, supporters, and concert management; winning one can literally make a career. Local and regional events are an important performance outlet as well as a potential source of scholarship support. As most of these events have an upper age limit of 35, this emphasis on identifying and rewarding performers at a young age works very much against the mature musician.

Important exceptions are the Avery Fisher Prize, established in 1975, and the Avery Fisher Career Grants. Not competitions, these awards were established to assist instrumentalists who have already demonstrated that they deserve wider attention, a determination made by a board of nationally known conductors, instrumentalists, educators, and so on with final selection made by an executive committee. One of the first to be honored with the Avery Fisher Prize was pianist Ursula Oppens, in 1976; a recipient of a Career Grant was violinist Pamela Franks.

In the popular music world and in the area of recording, awards are much more likely to be made on the basis of past performance rather than a specific competition. The Grammy Awards, established in 1958, recognize achievement in recording in all areas of music. Performers and composers can also be recognized for their achievements by the National Academy of Recording Arts and Sciences, the Country Music Awards, the Academy Awards, and the Tony Awards. Publications such as *Downbeat*, *Rolling Stone*, and *Billboard* magazine regularly make awards to performers and composers, both by panels and through readers' choice polls. Winners of these popular awards include Lauryn Hill (b. 1975), Leann Rimes (b. 1982), Bette Midler (b. 1945), and Carly Simon (b. 1945), Rachel Portman (b. 1960), Carole Bayer-Sager (b. 1946), and Barbra Streisand (b. 1942), and Mary Martin (b. 1913), Ethel Merman (1909–1984), Carol Channing (b. 1921), and Liza Minnelli (b. 1946).

See also Grawemeyer Award for Music Composition; Guggenheim Award; MacArthur Fellows Program

For Further Reading

Jezic, Diane. *Women Composers: The Lost Tradition Found*. Second edition prepared by Elizabeth Wood. New York: Feminist Press, 1994.

Kenneson, Claude. *Musical Prodigies: Perilous Journeys, Remarkable Lives*. Portland, OR: Amadeus Press, 1998.

Locke, Ralph P., and Cyrilla Barr (eds.). *Cultivating Music in America: Women Patrons and Activists since 1860*. Los Angeles: University of California Press, 1997.

Leslie Hogan

Production Manager

The significant increase in concert touring, regional professional events, and music festivals nationally and internationally in the twentieth century gave rise to the role of a production manager in the music industry. The need came about in the theatrical circle. Even as far back as the third century B.C., groups of performers toured, basically managing themselves as well as their props, sets, and costumes. Centuries later, stage managers were hired to assist directors during auditions, casting, rehearsals, and performances. Although men dominate this profession, there have been a handful of important women working in the field. Tammy Bowman is the production manager for Walt Disney World Entertainment, a job of immense importance and exposure. Tami Drury-Smith works as the guest talent and education program manager for Magic Music Days, a part of Walt Disney World Entertainment. Judy Joseph is the production manager and technical director at the Broward Center (FL) for the Performing Arts. Finally, Tanya Grubich is in production management for TMG Marketing.

Contemporary concerts and productions are more event oriented and require more technological expertise than was needed in previous years. This is where the production manager comes into play. Not only does a conductor or artistic director need assistance during rehearsals and performance, but the concert itself as a separate entity needs someone to make it run smoothly. The production manager ultimately supervises all aspects relating to the creation and execution of a concert, event, or production. The production manager needs to coordinate all of the persons who make up the creative team and set up what are called production meetings. These are usually held on a weekly basis, commencing anywhere from four to six weeks prior to performance. In these meetings the artistic director's concept or conductor's wishes are discussed and executed by the creative and production teams. In these meetings all rehearsal requirements are discussed and any special requests during the concert are brought up so the production crew has adequate time to prepare.

The creative team includes the artistic director, the conductor, and any light and scenery designers. The production team includes the stage manager, production crew, and the production manager. The production manager usually delegates the majority of all concert performance–related duties to a stage manager. A stage manager is the person in charge of (1) making sure that all musicians are on time and all rehearsal requirements are met, and (2) overseeing light, sound, and stage cues for the actual performance. A production manager's work begins as soon as any artist is contracted for a concert. It is the production manager's responsibility to ensure that the artist's contract is executed and all necessary technical requirements within the contract are met. The production manager controls all related production costs including but not limited to: artist salaries, appropriate royalties, marketing, publicity, technical costs, and design fees—such as those for lighting and scenery. She or he is also responsible for setting up all rehearsal schedules, including those of the technical and creative team, throughout the production life cycle. A production life cycle is the groundwork and foundation hub where all concert production elements are placed. It is a comprehensive calendar that includes all the timelines and deadlines for all aspects of the concert, from initial contract negotiations to post-production work. The production manager is the central person during a concert whom all artistic, design, and production personnel go to in order to coordinate their schedules and is, at times, the communicating voice of the artistic director and conductor in executing the artistic concept.

See also Music Management

For Further Reading

Abruzzo, James, and Stephen Langley. *Jobs in Arts and Media Management*. New York: ACA Books, 1990.

Langley, Stephen. *Theatre Management and Pro-*

duction in America. New York: Drama Book Publishers, 1990.

Stern, Lawrence. *Stage Management*. 7th ed. Boston, MA: Allyn and Bacon, 1995.

Vasey, John. *Concert Tour Production Management*. Woburn, MA: Butterworth-Heineman, 1997.

Karen Fuller

Professionalism

Fundamentally, professionalism is working for pay, that is, for gain or livelihood. Professionalism is distinguished from amateurism, which is unpaid. In music, a person may achieve professional status in many activities, including performing, conducting, composing, teaching, research, music criticism, arts administration, and recording-industry positions such as recording engineer or producer. Professional status enhances the person's authority and recognition. It also implies certain standards for the quality of work, conduct, and aims. Professional work may be full-time or part-time. However, the fact that women often choose to work at music part-time, owing to the demands of home and family, has sometimes placed them at a disadvantage in achieving professional status. Faced with the competing ideologies of biologically or culturally-defined gender roles and professionalism, many women experience an identity crisis and may choose a career for its compatibility with a personal life.

American women have often been excluded from prerequisites for professionalism in music, including education, performance, publication, and critical reception. The following examples of barriers to women in orchestras, in composition, and in academia represent only a small sample of the difficulties. The Musicians Union excluded women until 1904, when it affiliated with the American Federation of Labor; thus women were excluded from symphony orchestras. Even with union membership, women could be denied orchestra positions. Women's orchestras were formed after World War I to provide employment and experience for women instrumentalists and conductors. During World War II, with many men overseas, women performed in major orchestras, and when the war ended they demanded mixed orchestras.

Traditionally, women have been considered supporters of composers, not creators with their own professional capabilities. Anecdotal accounts abound of compositions rejected when submitted under the woman's name but accepted for performance and publication when resubmitted under a male pseudonym. Women composers joined forces for mutual support and encouragement and to promote new works. In 1924 the Society of American Women Composers was founded with Amy Marcy Cheney Beach (1867–1944) as its president. In 1975 Nancy Van de Vate (b. 1930) founded the International League of Women Composers.

Academic professional organizations excluded women, especially in the early decades of the twentieth century. In 1930 Ruth Crawford Seeger (1901–1953) was excluded from the founding meeting of the New York Musicological Society; she was placed in an adjoining room, and the door to the meeting room was closed. Since the 1980s many organizations have formed committees on the status of women that address issues of professionalism, including promotion and tenure.

With increased professionalism, women began to win important competitions. Crawford Seeger was the first woman to receive a Guggenheim Fellowship (1930). Ellen Taaffe Zwilich (b. 1939) became the first woman awarded a D.M.A. in composition from the Juilliard

School (1975) and the first woman to win the Pulitzer Prize in music (1983).

Professionalism remains an important goal for many American women musicians. Despite obstacles, some of which remain, women have made significant strides in achieving professional status in many areas of music.

See also Gender Issues

For Further Reading

Citron, Marcia J. "Gender, Professionalism and the Musical Canon." *Journal of Musicology* 8/1 (1990): 102–117.

———. "Professionalism." In *Gender and the Musical Canon*. Cambridge: Cambridge University Press, 1992, Chapter 3.

Neuls-Bates, Carol (ed.). *Women in Music: An Anthology of Source Readings from the Middle Ages to the Present*. New York: Harper and Row, 1982. Rev. ed., Boston: Northeastern University Press, 1996.

Diane Follet

Pseudonyms

Musicians' pseudonyms—fictitious names used by the creator—serve many purposes. Women composers have used male pseudonyms when seeking publication, because publishers have assumed women's work to be inferior. Women students have submitted work under male pseudonyms when applying to a school to study composition. Established composers have used pseudonyms when offering music in an atypical style or genre. Performers and composers have devised pseudonyms to express different aspects of their musicianship and personality. Women members of 99-percent-male groups such as bands or drum and bugle corps have been rostered under male pseudonyms. Musical "stars" and other performers of popular music, jazz, rock, and techno often adopt pseudonyms or stage names. Pseudonyms have been common in the recording industry for vocal and instrumental soloists and groups. In some cases more than one artist has recorded under the same pseudonym, usually on different record labels; an individual artist may have recorded under several pseudonyms, sometimes to suggest that more artists are working for that label than is actually the case. Although bibliographers take care to reveal the name behind the pseudonym, some researchers believe such information should remain secret.

The list of pseudonyms in Aaron Cohen's *International Encyclopedia of Women Composers* (1987) includes many women active in art music in the United States since 1900. Twelve different male pseudonyms are listed for the Philadelphia musician Frances McCollin: Alfred, Atticus, Awbury, Canonicus, Garrett, Karlton, Mayfair, Pastor, Pilgrim, Selen, Wendel, and Wheelwright. The list also identifies Lyle de Bohun as Clara Lyle Boone of Arisis Press; Paul Ducelle as Carrie William Krogmann; Sidney Forrest as Louise E. Stairs; Bernard Haigh as Clara Edwards; Juan Masters as Juanita Eames; Francesco Nogero and Francisco di Nogero as the musician and critic Emilie Frances Bauer; and Edgar Thorne as Marie E. Merrick.

Rebecca Clarke (1886–1979) used the pseudonym Anthony Trent for the 1918 premiere of *Morpheus* (unpublished). Because she thought it a somewhat inferior work, she was amused when critics paid more attention to it—presumably because its composer was apparently a man—than to her other works. Ruth Crawford Seeger (1901–1953) published a popular song, "Lollipop-a-Papa," under the name Fred Karlan. With its blues harmonies and old-fashioned vaudeville ragtime rhythms, it represented a different compositional persona from her ultra-modern concert music. Virginia Eskin invented an alter ego in the musicologist Rawle Dryson and interviewed "him" in the liner notes to one of her albums of Amy Marcy Cheney Beach's (1867–1944) piano music.

Some women have retained their family name while changing the given name to one identifiably male: Priscilla A. Beach became Alden Beach, and Sister John Joseph Bezdek became Jan Bezdek. Women have often used initials to conceal their gender, as when they are composing in a traditionally male-identified genre. Nancy Van de Vate (b. 1930) recalled having an orchestral work by N. Van de Vate accepted for performance, only to have the conductor at the run-through inquire after her husband, the composer.

Women have used female pseudonyms, such as Rosemary Hadler, pseudonym for Ellen Jane Lorenz, and Jane Murdock for Amber Roobenian. Frances Gumm used the stage name Judy Garland. Van de Vate occasionally wrote music as Helen Huntley or William Huntley. Liliuokalani, Queen of Hawaii, disguised her royal status in the pseudonym Mme Aorena. Some pseudonyms are shorter or simpler versions of the musician's given name: Henrietta Elizabeth Bassett became Beth Bassett, Grace Marschal-Loepke became Grace Cotton-Marshall, and Augusta Zuckermann became Mana-Zucca.

As an illustration of the association of genre with gender, men writing in woman-identified genres have taken women's names. Septimus Winner published parlor songs such as "Listen to the Mockingbird" under the pseudonym Alice Hawthorne.

See also Gender Issues

For Further Reading

Baker, Glenn. *The Name Game: Their Real Names Revealed*. Sydney: Weldon, 1984. London: GRR, 1986.

Cohen, Aaron I. "List of Pseudonyms." In *International Encyclopedia of Women Composers*. 2d ed. New York: Books and Music, 1987, Appendix 5.

Sutton, Allan (cop.). *A Guide to Pseudonyms on American Records, 1892–1942*. Westport, CT: Greenwood Press, 1993.

Deborah Hayes

Ptaszynska, Marta (1949–)

Marta Ptaszynska is a Polish composer and percussionist, active in the United States since 1972. Ptaszynska's academic credentials are coupled with an impressive track record of awards that include prizes from the Percussive Arts Society (1974, 1976, 1987), a medal from the Polish Composers' Union (1988), second prize at the UNESCO International Rostrum of Composers (Paris, 1986, for *Winter's Tale*), and a Lifetime Achievement Award from the Jurzykowski Foundation (1996). Ptaszynska's music can be described as an individual brand of "sonorism"—with the best examples provided by her percussion works. Her affinity for percussion timbres is apparent in her choice of percussion instruments as soloists in her concerti and as important elements in her chamber works. Although percussion is often seen as a source of rhythmic drive, in Ptaszynska's music the timbral variety of percussive instruments takes a priority. Ptaszynska has the synaesthetic ability to hear "in color" not only pitches and chords, but also percussive timbres; indeed, her music is often inspired by painting and colorful images from poetry.

Born on 29 July 1949, Ptaszynska studied at the State Highest School of Music in Warsaw (now the Chopin Academy of Music) from 1962 to 1968 and received degrees in composition, percussion, and music theory. From 1969 to 1970 she studied with Nadia Boulanger in Paris on a scholarship from the French government, and from 1972 to 1974 she continued her studies at the Cleveland Institute of Music, where she received an Artist Diploma Degree in percussion.

In 1977–1978 Ptaszynska served as a guest professor at the University of California, Berkeley, and in 1979–1980 she was a composer-in-residence at the University of California, Santa Barbara. In the 1980s she taught composition and percussion at Northwestern University and at the University of Chicago. In 1997 Ptaszynska became a tenured professor of composition at Indiana University, Bloomington; since 1998 she has been a tenured professor of composition at the University of Chicago.

Her choice of texts for song settings includes poems by Paul Verlaine, Rainer Maria Rilke, William Shakespeare, Leopold Staff, and Frederico Garcia Lorca. Her chamber music "sparkles" with a kaleidoscopic array of colors and subtle sound effects often supported by traditional formal models of the sonata-allegro form, concerto, rondo, or variations. Since 1965 she has composed 10 collections of children's pieces and coauthored a percussion textbook in five volumes, as well as a children's opera, *Mr. Marimba* (1995). This light-hearted opera highlights her fascination with Asia and has few precedents in her dramatic works, including the television opera *Oscar of Alva* (POLTEL 1988).

The list of Ptaszynska's politically-oriented works includes a composition dedicated to the feminist cause (*Ode to Praise All Famous Women* for orchestra, 1992), a series of compositions on Polish themes, and a monumental *Holocaust Memorial Cantata* (Accord ACD 016) to Leslie Woolf Hedley's "Chant for all the People on Earth." Despite the focus of her large-scale "public" works on issues of current patriotic and political relevance, her lasting contribution to twentieth-century Polish music consists of her imaginative expression associated with percussive instruments. Ptaszynska's chamber music demonstrates a marked preference for subtle sonorities of the harp, flute, and voice, often joined by a marimba or vibraphone and a variety of exotic percussion instruments. She frequently selects titles relating to space, dreams, light, imagination, the charming domains of decorative arabesques, and the living beauty of nature. Her music is published by PWM Edition in Poland and by Theodore Presser in the United States.

See also Multicultural Musics

For Further Reading

Chan, Philip Hong. "A Study of Marta Ptaszynska's Holocaust Memorial Cantata." D.M.A. diss., University of Cincinnati, 1996.

Harley, Maria Anna. "Percussion, Poetry and Color: The Music of Marta Ptaszynska." Musicworks 74 (Summer 1999): 34–47.

Szwarcman, Dorota. "The Colourful World of Marta Ptaszynska." *Polish Music* 23/2–3 (1988): 25–31.

Maja Trochimczyk

Publication Awards

Several organizations honor authors of scholarly studies through publication awards. Although women authors continue to constitute a small percentage of honorees, the 1990s saw a slight increase in the number of studies about women receiving these acknowledgments.

The International Alliance for Women in Music (IAWM) gives the most important award dedicated to women in music. Since 1986 the Pauline Alderman Prize has honored the authors of published and unpublished books and articles dealing with women in music. Three awards are given periodically: one for a book-length study, one for a journal article, and one honoring a bibliographic study. Past winners have included articles on specific composers as well as works dealing with issues of gender and feminist theory, such as Marcia J. Citron's *Gender and the Musical Canon* and Susan McClary's *Feminine Endings: Music, Gender and Sexuality*.

American Musicological Society (AMS). The AMS presents two publication awards. The Alfred Einstein Award honors an article written by an American or Canadian musicologist in the early stages of his or her career. Although no articles specifically about women have won this award, a number of women authors have been honored. Of the 34 honorees between 1967 and 1999, 10 have been women, beginning with Ursula Kirkendale in 1968, and more recently Pamela Potter in 1997. The Society's Otto Kinkeldey Award, also inaugurated in 1967, recognizes a distinguished book by a member of the Society. No monographs about women have won, and only four women authors have been recognized: Rulan Chao Pian (1968), Vivian Perlis (1975), Margot Fassler (1994), and Jane Bernstein (1999).

Society for Music Theory (SMT). The SMT presents three annual publication awards: the Wallace Berry Award for a book by an author of any age; the Outstanding Publication Award for an article by an author of any age; and the Emerging Scholar Award for a book or article published within five years of the author's Ph.D. None of these awards has ever been granted to a book or article about women, and only three women authors have been honored: Elizabeth West Marvin, Naomi Cumming, and Cristle Collins Judd.

Society for American Music: Sonneck Society (SAM). The SAM has presented the Irving Lowens Award to the authors of one book and one article since 1983. On five occasions women have been honored. Two of these, Judith Tick's *Ruth Crawford Seeger: A Composer's Search for American Music*, and Adrienne Fried Block's, *Amy Beach, Passionate Victorian* are specifically about a woman composer.

American Society for Composers, Authors and Publishers (ASCAP). A number of women authors and studies of women have been honored with the ASCAP Deems Taylor Award, including Ralph Locke's article "Paradoxes of the Woman Music Patron in America" as well as Adrienne Fried Block's book *Amy Beach: Passionate Victorian*. Women have not yet won the major general literary awards in significant numbers.

Since its inception in 1950, the National Book Award has never been awarded to a woman author on music. Only one woman has won a Pulitzer Prize for her writing on music, Manuela Hoelterhoff of the *Wall Street Journal* for arts criticism.

See also International Alliance for Women in Music; International Congress on Women in Music

For Further Reading

32nd Annual ASCAP-Deems Taylor Award Winners Announced. Available: http://www.ascap.com/press/deems-120999.html

Crawford, Richard. *The American Musicological Society, 1934–1984: An Anniversary Essay*. Philadelphia: American Musicological Society, 1984.

Fry, Stephen M. "The Pauline Alderman Award." *IAWM [International Alliance for Women in Music] Journal* (Fall 1997): 20–21.

Patrick Warfield

Publication Awards

Award	Author/Publication	Year
Alfred Einstein Award	"Negotiating Culture Allies; American Music in Darmstadt, 1946–1956." *Journal of the American Musicological Society* 53 (2000): 105–140.	2001
Alfred Einstein Award	"Late-Nineteenth-Century Chamber Music and the Cult of the Classical Adagio." *Nineteenth-Century Music* 23 (1999): 33–61.	2000
Alfred Einstein Award	Pamela Potter "Musicology under Hitler: New Sources in Context," *Journal of the American Musicological Society* 49 (1996): 70–113	1997
Alfred Einstein Award	Anne C. Shreffler, " 'Mein Weg geht jetzt voruber': The Vocal Origins of Webern's Twelve-Tone Composition," *Journal of the American Musicological Society* 47 (1994): 275–339	1995
Alfred Einstein Award	Anne Maria Busse Berger, "The Myth of Diminutio per tertium partem," *Journal of Musicology* 8 (1990): 398–426	1991
Alfred Einstein Award	Anne Walters Robertson, "Benedicamus Domino: The Unwritten Tradition," *Journal of the American Musicological Society* 41 (1988): 1–62	1989
Alfred Einstein Award	Paula Higgins "In Hydraulis Revisited: New Light on the Career of Antoine Busnois," *Journal of the American Musicological Society* 39 (1986): 36–86	1987
Alfred Einstein Award	Elaine R. Sisman "Small and Expanded Forms: Koch's Model and Haydn's Music," *Musical Quarterly* 68 (1982): 444–475	1983
Alfred Einstein Award	Eugene K. Wolf and Jean K. Wolf, "A Newly Identified Complex of Manuscripts from Mannheim," *Journal of the American Musicological Society* 27 (1974): 379–437	1975
Alfred Einstein Award	Rebecca A. Baltzer, "Thirteenth-Century Illuminated Miniatures and the Date of the Florence Manuscript," *Journal of the American Musicological Society* 25 (1972): 1–18	1973
Alfred Einstein Award	Sarah Fuller, "Hidden Polyphony—a Reappraisal," *Journal of the American Musicological Society* 24 (1971): 169–192	1972
Alfred Einstein Award	Ursula Kirkendale, "The Ruspoli Documents on Handel," *Journal of the American Musicological Society* 20 (1967): 222–273	1968
Irving Lowens Award	Adrienne Fried Block, *Amy Beach, Passionate Victorian*. Oxford University Press, NY, 1998.	1998
Irving Lowens Award	Judith Tick, *Ruth Crawford Seeger; A Composer's Search for American Music*. Oxford University Press, NY, 1997	1997
Irving Lowens Award	Ingrid Monson, *Saying Something: Jazz Improvisation and Interaction*. University of Chicago Press, Chicago, IL, 1996	1996
Irving Lowens Award	Judith Tick, "Charles Ives and Gender Ideology" *Music and Difference*. Smithsonian Institution Press, Washington, DC, 1991	1993
Irving Lowens Award	Susan Porter, *With an Air Debonair: Musical Theatre in America*. Smithsonian Institute Press, Washington, DC, 1992.	1991
Irving Lowens Award	Vivian Perlis, *Copland: Since 1943*. St. Martins Press, New York, 1989.	1989

Pugh, Virginia Wynette

See Wynette, Tammy

Publishers, Women's Music

Despite historical adversity, the history of women's music publishers has a long and esteemed tradition. Maddalena Casulana's first collection of madrigals was published in Venice in 1568 by Girolamo Scotto, the first publication of a volume of music by a woman. The event had special significance because music publication was still in its early days. Francesca Caccini published *Il primo libro delle musiche a una e due voci*, an extensive collection of monody, in 1618 (Florence: Zanobi Pignoni), and Barbara Strozzi published her first book of madrigals, *Il primo libro de madrigali*, in 1644 (Venice: Alessandro Vincenti) with seven other publications of cantatas and arias in years to come. In about 1655 Isabella Leonarda's first book of motets was published in Milan, followed by an astonishing 19 additional volumes of her music. After the initial publications of women's music in Italy, other European centers saw similar activity. Jacquet de la Guerre published her first book of *pièces de clavecin* in Paris in 1687 and a short score of her opera *Cephale et Procris* in 1694. Elisabetta de Gambarini's three volumes of harpsichord music and songs, *Lessons for the Harpsichord*, were published in 1754 in London. Breitkopf published the opera *Il trionfo della fedeltà* by Maria Antonia Walpurgis in Leipzig after its first performance in 1754, and Artari published Marianna von Auenbrugger's *Sonata per il Clavicembalo o Forte pian* in Vienna around 1781. By 1794 Mary Ann Pownall was publishing her songs in the United States.

Noteworthy publications of women's music early in the twentieth century from Europe are: Ethel Smyth's opera *The Wreckers*, published by Universal Edition in 1904; Alma Mahler's *Fünf Lieder* in 1910; and the historical *Die Kompositionen der heiligen Hildegard* in a facsimile edition in 1913. As now, some women found publishers to carry much of their music. Lili Boulanger, for example, had a contract with Ricordi, but many women composers found barriers to publication. It is in this context that presses devoted exclusively to women's music arose in the last quarter of the twentieth century.

There have been a number of significant U.S. companies that specialize in music by women. Founded in 1976, Arsis Press is the oldest publisher of women's chamber music and choral works still in existence, printing music primarily by living composers. In its first years founder Clara Lyle Boone published just a handful of composers besides herself: Emma Lou Diemer (b. 1927), Ruth Lomon, Nancy Van de Vate (b. 1930), and Elizabeth Walton Vercoe. The catalog now numbers about 150 works by over 40 composers, including one man. Because the press was established to provide exposure to women's music that was largely unavailable elsewhere, the goal was to show the work at its best: engraved or hand-copied (now computer-printed) on high-quality paper, with biographical information and program notes along with covers featuring photographs of contemporary artwork. Several issues have received Paul Revere Awards for excellence from the Music Publishers Association. In 1977 Arsis Press affiliated with the International League of Women Composers. A groundbreaking three-volume series of recordings of women's music by pianist Rosemary Platt in the 1970s included a number of the first publications of Arsis Press for piano solo.

In 1988 Sylvia Glickman founded Hildegard Publishing Company in Bryn Mawr, PA, with a similar broad mandate to print music in all genres by both historical and contemporary women composers. With its reciprocal agreement with Furore Verlag, a German publishing company founded by Renate Matheu, and others, the catalog contains over 450 entries ranging from pieces by Hildegard of Bingen, the eleventh-century abbess who is the company's namesake, to those of Glickman herself and reprints from the 12-volume G. K. Hall *Women Composers* series. The company also acts as distributor for the Casia Publishing Company, Classical Vocal Reprints, Songflower Press, and Arts Venture, and it publishes compact discs. Additionally, a nonprofit institute and performing ensemble are associated with the press.

There are other small presses that focus on niche markets for women's music and many desktop publications by composers distributing their own music. ClarNan Editions, founded in 1984 by American musicologist Barbara Garvey Jackson, publishes early music by women primarily from Europe. The computer-printed editions indicate editorial additions, offer print translations of texts, and provide historical information and bibliographical resources.

Vivace Press in Wisconsin, publisher of the *Women of Note Quarterly* and compact discs on the Hester Park label, publishes mostly keyboard music, about two-thirds of which is by women. The music is from the eighteenth century to the present and includes such figures as Anna Amalia, Clara Schumann, and Judith Lang Zaimont (b. 1945). Organist and composer Barbara Harbach and Jonathan Yordy established the press in 1990 to further the work of underrepresented composers.

Another small press devoted primarily to women composers is Treble Clef Music Press in North Carolina, which publishes choral music for treble voices from a medieval conductus to works of Cécile Chaminade and Mary Howe. Ars Femina, a press associated with a performing group of the same name, has published about 70 pieces by women composers before 1800. The group has also produced several compact discs. A Canadian publisher called Avondale Press located in Vancouver, British Columbia, has a catalog with about 20 pieces by contemporary Canadian women, including Violet Archer, Barbara Pentland, and Jean Coulthard. Finally, Da Capo Press issued a Woman Composers Series beginning in 1979 that contains such important works as the Rebecca Clarke piano trio.

In addition to small presses devoted to women's music, many large, established publishers began to acquire significant listings of women composers in recent years. Edition Peters is among those with a dozen or more women composers in its catalog, including Cathy Berberian (1925–1983), Miriam Gideon (1906–1996), and Peggy Glanville-Hicks (1912–1990). E. C. Schirmer also lists a substantial number of women composers, including Libby Larsen (b. 1950), Alice Parker (b. 1925), and Clare Shore. Most of this music is in the rental catalog. Oxford University Press publishes the music of Ruth Crawford Seeger (1901–1953), Emma Lou Diemer, and Hilary Tann, among others. G. Schirmer also has many women composers listed in its catalog, including Sofia Gubaidulina, Nicola LeFanu, Thea Musgrave (b. 1928), Joan Tower (b. 1938), and Judith Weir. Because G. Schirmer has acquired the rights to Margun Music, the press established by Gunther Schuller in Massachusetts, Schirmer now owns Ellen Taaffe Zwilich's (b. 1939) Pulitzer Prize–winning composition Symphony No. 1, available only as a rental. Boosey and Hawkes lists a handful of women composers, including Barbara Kolb (b. 1939). MMB Music lists over a dozen women composers in its catalog of 150 contemporary composers, among them Anne LeBaron (b. 1953), Cindy McTee (b. 1953), and Judith Shatin (b. 1949).

Finally, music distributor Theodore Front maintains an extensive list of over 1,000 titles of music by women composers from various publishers around the world. The Theodore Front list contains works by both historical and contemporary women composers and may be viewed as a resource for finding some current publishers of women's music.

See also Arrangers; Copyist; Gender and Repertoire

For Further Reading

Briscoe, James R. (ed.) *Historical Anthology of Music by Women*. Bloomington: Indiana University Press, 1987.

Neuls-Bates, Carol (ed.). *Women in Music*. Boston: Northeastern University Press, 1996.

Elizabeth Vercoe

Pulitzer Prize

The Pulitzer Prize was first awarded in 1917, established by a provision in the 1904 will of newspaper publisher Joseph Pulitzer. Pulitzer, an immigrant from Hungary, had been the shrewd and innovative publisher of the New York *Herald* and the St. Louis *Post-Dispatch*. His unwavering passion for challenging dishonest government while maintaining a fierce competitive stance against his business rivals left a lasting influence on the nature of American journalism. Pulitzer's vision for the prize bearing his name was that such an award should inspire excellence by recognizing superior achievement in American journalism, arts, and letters.

The Pulitzer Prize in Music was first awarded in 1943; it was not until 40 years later that Ellen Taaffe Zwilich (b. 1939) became the first woman to win this coveted award. The 1983 jury consisted of three composers: Miriam Gideon (1906–1996), who served as chair, Leon Kirchner of Harvard University, and Robert Ward of Duke University. Out of 80 submitted compositions, this jury selected Zwilich's Symphony No. 1 (subtitled *Three Movements for Orchestra*) as its recommendation to the Pulitzer Board. This work had been commissioned by the American Composers Orchestra and the National Endowment for the Arts, and it was premiered by that orchestra under Gunther Schuller's direction on 5 May 1982 at Alice Tully Hall in New York.

Shulamit Ran (b. 1949) was awarded the Pulitzer Prize in Music in 1991 for her Symphony. Born in Tel Aviv, Israel, Ran came to the United States to study at the age of 14. Six years after graduating from the Mannes College of Music, she was invited to teach at the University of Chicago. In 1989–1990, Ran took a year's leave of absence from this post to compose her three-movement Symphony, which had been commissioned by the Philadelphia Orchestra. It then premiered this work on 19 October 1990, with Gary Bertini conducting. After winning the Pulitzer Prize in 1991, Ran's Symphony also received a first-place Kennedy Center Friedheim Award in 1992.

The final Pulitzer Prize in Music of the twentieth century was awarded in 1999 to Melinda Wagner (b. 1957), for

Twentieth-Century American Women Who Were Awarded the Pulitzer Prize in Music

Composer	Year	Composition
Ellen Taaffe Zwilich	1983	Symphony No. 1
Shulamit Ran	1991	Symphony
Melinda Wagner	1999	Concerto for Flute, Strings, and Percussion

her Concerto for Flute, Strings, and Percussion. This work was commissioned by the Barlow Endowment for Music Composition for the Westchester Philharmonic in 1997. It was then premiered by that orchestra under the direction of Paul Lustig Dunkel (who also served as the flute soloist) in Purchase, NY, on 30 May 1998.

See also Prizes, Composer and Performer; Ran, Shulamit; Zwilich, Ellen Taaffe

For Further Reading

Kozinn, Allan. "Composer's Pulitzer Malas the Telephone Her New Instrument." *New York Times* (11 April 1991): C15, C19.

The Pulitzer Prizes. Available: http://www.pulitzer.org

Rockwell, John. "Ellen Zwilich Considers Pulitzer Double Victory." *New York Times* (4 May 1983): C17.

Seitz, Don C. *Joseph Pulitzer, His Life and Letters*. New York: AMS Publishers, 1974.

Wetzler, Cynthia Magriel. "Orchestra Fostered Pulitzer Prize." *New York Times* (18 April 1999): XIV–NJ, 9.

Jeremy Beck

Purim, Flora (1942–)

Singer Flora Purim emerged in the 1970s as one of the most influential singers of the jazz-fusion movement in the United States. Her innovative improvisations dispense with the usual bop-style scat syllables favored by most jazz singers and instead use a wide range of vocal effects: guttural moans, squeals, swooping glissandi, and ethereal cries. Purim also possesses an uncanny ability to imitate and blend with brass and woodwinds, often employing her voice as a lead instrument in a horn section. Singing in both English and Portuguese, Purim has a repertoire that includes her own compositions and songs by Brazilian artists such as Hermeto Pascoal, Milton Nascimento, and Djavan and by Americans such as George Duke and Chick Corea.

Born in Rio de Janeiro, Brazil, on 6 March 1942, Purim studied guitar and piano as a child and was first exposed to jazz through her parents' recording of Errol Garner and Miles Davis, among others. Her Rumanian-born father was a violinist, her mother a pianist. Purim began singing professionally at age 20 and in 1964 recorded her first album, *Flora é M.P.M* (RCA BBL-1304, 1964), a record consisting primarily of bossa nova songs.

Purim moved to São Paulo in 1966, where she met her future husband and collaborator, drummer and percussionist Airto Moreira. In 1968 she moved to the United States, first to Los Angeles and then to New York, where she performed and recorded with Duke Pearson, Cannonball Adderley, Gil Evans, and Stan Getz. In 1972 she married Airto, and the couple became widely known through their work with pianist Chick Corea. Along with Corea's groundbreaking quintet "Return to Forever," Purim and Airto recorded two commercially and critically successful records, *Return to Forever* (ECM 811978-2) and *Light as a Feather* (Polydor 827148-2).

Purim's career suffered a blow when she was arrested for cocaine possession in 1971, for which she served 18 months in California's Terminal Island Federal Prison from 1974 to 1975. It was during this period that she released her first U.S. recording, *Butterfly Dreams* (Original Jazz Classics OJCCD-315-2), and received the first of three consecutive *Down Beat* awards for female vocalist of the year (1974–1976). Upon her release from prison, Purim recorded one of her most successful albums, *Open Your Eyes* (Milestone M-9065), a recording that signaled a more commercial, less jazz-oriented musical direction.

Except for a brief period from 1978 through the early 1980s when they each pursued separate careers, Purim and Moreira have maintained a musical partnership, co-leading a series of touring bands. They have recorded both as a duo and as solo artists, often appearing on each other's recordings. The couple's two Concord compact discs, *Humble People* (Concord Jazz CCD-43007) and *The Magicians* (Crossover CCD-45001), are representative samples of Purim's work during the 1980s. Since 1990 Purim and her husband have performed and recorded primarily with their group, Fourth World. As of the date of this publication, Purim has released over 25 recordings as a leader or co-leader and has appeared as a guest artist on at least 75 others.

See also Jazz; Latin American Musicians; Multicultural Musics

For Further Reading

Lyons, Len. "Flora Purim: Dreams of a Brazilian Butterfly." *Down Beat* 41 (19 December 1974): 17–18.

McGowan, Chris, and Ricardo Pessanha. *The Brazilian Sound: Samba, Bossa Nova, and the Popular Music of Brazil.* New York: Billboard Books, 1991.

Nolan, Herb. "Flora Purim: Flying High on Freedom." *Down Beat* 45/16 (5 October 1978): 23, 57, 64.

Andrew M. Connell

Q

Queen Latifah (1970–)

Dana Elaine Owens, also known as Queen Latifah, is a successful hip hop artist, entrepreneur, television host, and movie star. Her music is characterized by strong, empowering lyrics, and a highly personalized style, which has blended rap, hip hop, reggae, rhythm and blues, and jazz.

Born on 18 March 1970 in Newark, NJ, Owens chose the Arabic name "Latifah" at age 8 in response to a trend among black youth to adopt the nomenclature of the growing Nation of Islam movement. Interpreted as "sensitive" and "delicate," the name "Latifah" represented for Owens a sense of freedom and individuality. On the heels of her first success, *Wrath of My Madness* (Tommy Boy 916), Latifah searched for a new identity. She added "Queen" to Latifah to emphasize an ideal of strength and womanhood. In the wake of the apartheid controversy in late 1980s and the release of Nelson Mandela from prison, the connection of "Queen" with African heritage and the motherland was not lost. Aside from these social influences, Queen Latifah attributes her self-confidence to a strong family background, specifically crediting her mother, Rita Owens, as a role model. Her father, Lancelot Owens, and brother Lancelot "Winki" Owens she credits for instilling in her a belief in the equality of men and women.

These images of independence, strength, and womanhood came to define Queen Latifah's music as suggested in her first compact disc, *All Hail the Queen* (Tommy Boy TBCD-1022), and her second compact disc, *Nature of a Sista* (Tommy Boy TBCD-1035). Her third album, *Black Reign* (Motown 37463-6370-2), came out on the Motown label and reflected even more her confident independence. Although she does not embrace the term "feminist," her self-assured nature, and matter-of-fact, often pro-woman messages tell a different story.

Queen Latifah's authoritative role extends beyond the realm of music performer to entrepreneurship with her own management company, Flavor Unit Entertainment. Flavor Unit supports major personalities in the hip hop industry such as Naughty by Nature, Monie Love, Outkast, N.E.X.T., L.L. Cool J., and

Queen Latifah in a publicity photo for the 1998 film *Living Out Loud. Photo courtesy of Merrick Morton/New Line Cinema/Globe Photos.*

SWV. Her most recent compact disc, *Order in the Court* (Motown 530895), inaugurated the newest division of the Flavor Unit enterprise with its own record label.

In yet another way, Queen Latifah illustrates a positive self-image and control, especially for women, on television and in movies. Her autobiography, *Ladies First: Revelations of a Strong Woman*, was not intended as a self-help book but rather as a means of revealing the lessons and experiences that shaped Dana Elaine Owens into Queen Latifah and offers a genuine perspective on life for today's generation.

See also Rap

For Further Reading

Berry, Venise T. "Feminine or Masculine: The Conflicting Nature of Female Images in Rap Music." In *Cecilia Reclaimed: Feminist Perspectives on Gender and Music*, ed. Susan C. Cook and Judy Tsou. Urbana: University of Illinois Press, 1994.

Green, Rebecca. "Queen Latifah" In *Popular Musicians*, vol. 3, ed. Steve Hochman. Pasadena, CA: Salem Press, 1999.

O'Brien, Lucy. *She Bop: The Definitive History of Women in Rap, Rock, and Soul.* New York: Penguin Books, USA, 1995.

Roxanne Reed

Quintanilla-Perez, Selena

See Selena

R

Radio DJ

See Music Programmer/Host

Rainey, Gertrude "Ma" (1886–1939)

Gertrude "Ma" Rainey, "the Mother of the Blues," was acclaimed as the greatest of the Classic Blues singers of the 1920s. She was inducted into the Blues Foundation's Hall of Fame in 1983 and into the Rock and Roll Hall of Fame in 1990, and she was honored among Georgia Women of Achievement in 1993.

She was born Gertrude Pridgett on 26 April 1886 in Columbus, GA. Her parents were minstrel performers. Rainey first appeared onstage as a singer and dancer with them in 1900. She married the minstrel trouper William "Pa" Rainey in 1904, and the couple toured as "Ma and Pa Rainey" or "Rainey and Rainey" in tent shows throughout the South, including the Moses Stokes Troupe, the Rabbit Foot Minstrels, and Tolliver's Circus and Musical Extravaganza. On these tours Rainey allegedly met and tutored a young Bessie Smith (1894–1937). She separated from Pa Rainey in 1916 and toured on her own as Madam Gertrude Ma Rainey and Her Georgia Smart Sets.

In the 1920s Rainey became a featured performer on the TOBA (Theater Owners' Booking Association) circuit, and in 1923 she signed a recording contract with the Paramount label. By then, at the age of 38, she was a mature performer, and her recordings, including such classics as "Bo-Weevil Blues," "Yonder Comes the Blues" (recorded with the young Louis Armstrong), and "See See Rider," one of the most recorded blues of all times, were wildly popular. Her humorous song "Ma Rainey's Black Bottom" was especially well liked. Her recording career ended in 1928. During her five years of studio work she recorded about 90 songs, drawing on the talents of Fletcher Henderson, Willie "The Lion" Smith, Buster Bailey, Coleman Hawkins, and other outstanding young musicians.

There are numerous recordings of Ma Rainey that have been digitally remastered and preserved. *Ma Rainey* (Milestone 47021) includes many of her most popular songs, including "See See Rider Blues," "Ma Rainey's Black Bottom," and "Jealous Hearted Blues." At various

Gertrude "Ma" Rainey in 1923. *Photo courtesy of Frank Driggs Collection.*

times, Riverside (RLP-1003, RLP-1016), Black Swan (12001, 12002) and Document (5581, 5582, 5583, 5584) have published multivolume sets documenting many of Rainey's performances.

Rainey's popularity with southern audiences came from the glamour she displayed with lavishly sequined gowns and ostentatious jewelry, and from her songs, steeped in country culture and dealing with the plights of sharecroppers and poor Southern blacks as well as with the pain of sexual mistreatment. Rainey's career ceased in the 1930s, but she had been a shrewd businesswoman and her earnings enabled her to retire from touring in 1935. Rainey returned to her hometown, Columbus, GA, where she managed two theaters until she died of a heart attack on 22 December 1939.

See also Blues; Jazz

For Further Reading

Davis, Angela Yvonne. *Blues Legacies and Black Feminism: Gertrude "Ma" Rainey, Bessie Smith, and Billie Holiday*. New York: Pantheon Books, 1998.

Lieb, Sandra. *Mother of the Blues: A Study of Ma Rainey*. Amherst: University of Massachusetts Press, 1981.

Stewart-Baxter, Derrick. *Ma Rainey and the Classic Blues Singers*. London, Studio Vista, New York: Stein and Day, 1970.

Stephen Fry

Raitt, Bonnie (1949–)

Bonnie Raitt is an acclaimed blues, and blues and rhythm, singer and guitarist. Her accolades are many; they include winning several Grammy Awards and being inducted into the Rock and Roll Hall of Fame. Raitt has been influenced by many people, but she has developed a style all her own. In high school she was caught up in the musical protest movement and learned to play the guitar emulating folk singers like Pete Seeger and Joan Baez (b. 1941), and blues artists like Muddy Waters. She learned to play "bottle-neck" style as well as "picking" style guitar. While attending a local music camp, she developed an emotional husky style singing blues and folk music.

She was born Bonnie Lynn Raitt on 8 November 1949 in Burbank, CA; her father was famed Broadway star John Raitt. She entered Radcliffe College in Cambridge, MA, in 1967 but was drawn to a musical career in the Boston area. Dick Waterman, the famed blues historian and photographer, introduced her to legendary blues musicians and managed her career when she dropped out of college in 1969. In a recent interview she said, "I loved the blues, and one of the great thrills of my life was that early in my career I got to live with and hang out with some of the greatest country and Chicago blues artists alive; people like Skip James, Arthur "Big Boy" Crudup, Mississippi Fred McDowell, Buddy Guy" (*Los Angeles Times*, March 6, 2000, F1, F13).

Raitt signed a recording contract with Warner Brothers in 1971 and brought out her initial album, titled simply *Bonnie Raitt* (Warner Brothers 2-1953). She issued a new album each year for the next five years, but with little commercial success. Her recorded music, which included mostly covers and songs by other writers, along with a few of her own songs, was admired but only generated mediocre sales. Her 1977 album, *Sweet Forgiveness* (Warner Brothers 2-2990), turned Gold, but a few years later Warner Brothers dropped her, although the label issued *Nine Lives* (Warner Brothers 2-25486) in 1986 to little acclaim. She faced many emotional ordeals during this period, including the increasing use of alcohol.

However, in 1983 she signed with Capitol Records and began to work with producer Don Was. Their collaboration brought a commercial breakthrough in 1989 with *Nick of Time* (Capitol C2-91268). The album sold four million copies, won four Grammy Awards, and produced several hit singles, including "Nick of Time" and "Thing Called Love." Raitt and Was collaborated on *Luck of the Draw* (Capitol C2-96111) in 1991, which also included the hit songs "Something to Talk About" and "Not the Only One," which received extensive air play and earned her more Grammy Awards. Her appearance on John Lee Hooker's album *The Healer* (Chameleon D2-74808) won a Grammy Award for Best Duo. With her revitalized career on

Bonnie Raitt in concert in September 1992. *Photo © Henry Diltz/CORBIS.*

Capitol Records, and subsequent Grammy Awards for her recent recordings, Bonnie Raitt has earned a place among the most admired guitarists, singers, and songwriters. She is also active in political and environmental causes. She was inducted into the Rock and Roll Hall of Fame on 6 March 2000.

See also Rock and Roll Hall of Fame; Singer-Songwriter; Songwriter

For Further Reading

Bego, Mark. *Bonnie Raitt: Just in the Nick of Time.* Secaucus, NJ: Carol Pub. Group; A Birch Lane Press Book, 1995.

Stephen Fry

Ran, Shulamit (1949–)

Shulamit Ran is a prominent classical composer of the late twentieth and early twenty-first centuries. In 1991 she won the Pulitzer Prize in Music for her Symphony, and in 1992 she won the Kennedy Center Friedheim Award for the same composition. She has served as composer-in-residence for the Chicago Symphony Orchestra and the Lyric Opera of Chicago. Additionally, Ran has served on the faculty of the University of Chicago since 1973. When she won the Pulizter Prize in Music for her Symphony, she became one of three women ever to receive this award since its inception in 1943. The *Chicago Sun-Times* said of her Symphony that "[it] is immediately notable for its energy. It has a thrust to the thematic ideas that sets her phrases moving over a compelling pulse." Her music is freely atonal but at the same time very lyrical and expressive.

Shulamit Ran was born on 21 October 1949 in Tel Aviv, Israel. Her parents encouraged her musical development by providing her with piano lessons beginning at age eight. In 1963 Ran and her mother left for the United States to study piano with Nadia Reisenberg and composition with Norman Dello Joio at the Mannes College of Music. She later continued her studies on piano with Dorothy Taubman. In 1973 Ran ceased performing to concentrate on composing and to embark on a teaching career. She met Ralph Shapey, then a faculty member at the University of Chicago. Impressed by her composition *O the Chimneys* (Erato Disques 0630-1278702), Shapey invited Ran to join him on the composition faculty.

Her most recent compositions have explored her Jewish heritage, including *Between Two Worlds* (*The Dybbuk*), an opera that premiered in 1997, based on Yiddish writer Shloime Ansky's 1916 play, and *Vessels of Courage and Hope*, a six-part symphonic poem recalling the SS *President Warfield*, a ship in the formation of the state of Israel. The latter work was premiered in 1999 and commemorated the fiftieth anniversary of the founding of the State of Israel.

Her compositions are featured on many compact discs. The *Concerto da Camera II* was recorded by the Contemporary Chamber Players of the University of Chicago (CRI 609); *East Wind* for solo flute was recorded on Bridge Records (BCD 9052); and her String Quartet No. 1 was recorded by the Mendelssohn String Quartet on Koch International Classics (3-7269-2H1). Additionally, Ran has won numerous awards and commissions from various organizations, including the Rockefeller Fund, the Ford Foundation, the National Endowment for the Arts, the Fromm Music Foundation, and the Guggenheim Foundation.

See also Guggenheim Award; Pulitzer Prize

For Further Reading

Shulamit Ran. Available: http://www.presser.com/ran.html

White, C. B. "Equilibria: Shulamit Ran Balances." *ILWC [International League of Women Composers] Journal* (October 1994): 1–4.

Kristine H. Burns

Rao, Doreen (1950–)

Conductor, teacher, lecturer, author, editor, and consultant Doreen Rao is best known for her role in establishing the children's choir movement in the United States. Her career has continued to impact the choral profession in the late twentieth and early twenty-first centuries. Rao has had significant philosophical influence among practitioners by articulating connections between choral art as performance and the goals of choral education. Her commitment to providing professional development for aspiring conductors and teachers has influenced a generation of young artists to pursue their craft.

Rao was born on 14 November 1950 in Chicago to Doreen Merritt and Donald Dunlap, two promising singers. Her childhood was filled with music as she listened daily to opera and symphonic music, as well as her parents' singing and practice. She studied piano and voice from an early age and was closely guided by her mother.

Mentors were central to Rao's development; they include noted choral pedagogues Colleen Kirk and Harold Decker at the University of Illinois during the late 1960s. Sir George Solti and Margaret Hillis (1921–1998), conductors of the Chicago Symphony Orchestra and Chorus, were primary mentors during the next two decades as she entered the professional arena. Eventually she became assistant conductor to the Chicago Symphony Chorus, and it was this long-term association that positioned Rao to have national impact in the area of children's voices.

From 1972 to 1988 she was music director of the Glen Ellyn Children's Chorus, a community-based children's choir in the western suburbs of Chicago. During her tenure the chorus participated with the Chicago Symphony Orchestra and Chorus in four Grammy Award recordings and a Grand Prix du Disque. Through awards, touring, recording, and media attention, the children's chorus enjoyed an international reputation of artistic excellence. Subsequently Rao formed the first national committee on children's choirs through the American Choral Directors Association (ACDA) and effectively launched the children's choir movement in the United States. Prior to her work with the Glen Ellyn Children's Chorus, few notable children's choirs existed in the United States. Currently, communities large and small throughout North America support children's choirs, many conducted by Rao's former students.

Doreen Rao's career as a conductor has been informed by her wider interests in choral education. Her influential publications include choral textbooks, an extensive choral music series through Boosey and Hawkes, and ongoing collaborative research projects with public school systems. In 1988 Rao was appointed director of choral programs at the University of Toronto and was awarded the Elmer Iseler Chair in Conducting in 1999. Rao guides major choral music research projects and provides international professional development opportunities for conductors and teachers through the Choral Music Experience International Center for Conducting, Teaching, and Research in Choral Music Education.

See also Children's Choir; Choral Education

For Further Reading

Elliot, David J., and Doreen Rao. "Musical Performance and Music Education." *Design for Arts in Education* 91/5 (1990): 23–34.

Rao, Doreen. "Children and Choral Music: The Past and the Present—the Challenge and the Future." *Choral Journal* 29/8 (1989): 6–14.

Sandra Snow

Rap

Women rap musicians draw on traditions in music they inherited from their forebears in blues, jazz, gospel, rhythm and blues, and soul. They also share in a legacy familiar to many women who built careers in the male-dominated industry of popular music. Women rappers address a diversity of issues in their music, ranging from racism to sexism in popular culture. Although the nature of rap is ephemeral and women are continuing to establish themselves in the rap industry, women rappers can be discussed according to their period of activity and the themes most prominent in their music.

Period of Activity. By most accounts rap began in the late 1970s with the commercial success of "Rapper's Delight" by the Sugarhill Gang. Women's participation in rap as solo or group artists came shortly thereafter. Salt-N-Pepa, Queen Latifah (b. 1970), MC Lyte, and Roxanne Shanté were among the earliest group of women rappers to achieve popular success. Their peak popularity was in the late 1980s and early 1990s. Roxanne Shanté is best known for her "revenge" raps. In *Roxanne's Revenge* (Pop Art 8801), Shanté challenged the sexual ability of male rappers and bragged about her abilities as an MC (emcee). She played by the same rules as her male counterparts in rap—infusing her music with profanity, sexual hyperbole, and aggressive bragging—and in so doing claimed a space for women in the misogynist world of rap in the mid-1980s. MC Lyte infiltrated hip hop as a 17-year-old in 1988. Some of her music, like "10% Dis" (First Priority 90905), is marked by the competitive, ego-boosting style characteristic of much male rap in the 1980s. In other music, Lyte touches on important social issues, particularly those that explore heterosexual relationships. Her "Paper Thin" (First Priority 90905) is a powerful rap about men's infidelity and women's vulnerability.

Salt-N-Pepa and Queen Latifah address the complex intersection of race and gender in late twentieth-century African American popular culture. Latifah, whose name is Arabic for "delicate" and "sensitive," challenges rap's notions of womanhood and femininity. Her pride in her intelligence and looks, which are manifest in her powerful and assertive style of rapping, commands attention and forces the question of rap's caricatures of women as weak and submissive. Latifah's "Ladies First" (Tommy Boy TB1022) is rap's womanist anthem. It became a rallying cry for black female empowerment and unity in the early 1990s. In this rap, Latifah derides the male-dominated rap industry for its sexist stereotypes and demands that the world of hip hop treat women with respect.

Known as the divas of hip hop and rap, Salt-N-Pepa are anomalous among rap groups, male or female, in that they have sustained a career in rap. They started their careers as rappers in 1985, during the infancy of rap's music industry, and helped shape the direction of what would become the business of rap. Their music is an organ for talking candidly about sex. In their best-known rap, "Let's Talk about Sex" (Next Plateau 1019), Salt-N-Pepa exhort women to differentiate between sex and money, and sex and love. The rap also ridicules men's views of sex, chiding men for not understanding the difference between making love and having sex. In another rap, "None of Your Business" (PolyGram 28392), the group challenges the double standards in sexual relationships for men and women and boldly proclaims women's right to be sexually promiscuous. Their video *Tramp* (1986) is a story about sexual politics in the 1990s that warns men and women to be circumspect in their dating and mating.

Women's rap in the mid- to late-1990s was dominated by Lil' Kim (b. 1975), Foxy Brown (b. 1979), and Missy Elliott. Sex is discussed openly in much of this music. Kim and Brown use explicit language to define their own sexuality, defend their sexual needs, and denigrate a partner's sexual performance. Kim's compact disc *Hard Core* (Atlantic 92733) and Brown's *Ill Na Na* (Def Jam 533684) are scatological how-to manuals for their would-be lovers, full of instructions describing how they want to be treated sexually. In "Not Tonight" and "We Don't Need It" (Atlantic 92733), Kim berates inept lovers and heralds the quid pro quo nature of her lovemaking.

The music of Lauryn Hill (b. 1975) is also important, although it is not limited to rap. Largely devoid of prurient lyrics, Hill's music is a panoply of Afrodiasporic musical styles—rap, reggae, rhythm and blues, soul, and gospel—whose messages are intended to empower African Americans. Her "Doo Wop" (Sony 69035) sends a strong message to black men and black women about black pride, responsibility, and self-respect.

Themes in Women's Rap. The most prevalent themes in women's rap are those that address sexist stereotypes of black women in the rap industry, black women's sexuality, and to a lesser extent, race. The music of the Lady of Rage is aggressive and angry, recalling the swagger and bravado of her male counterparts on the Death Row label, Tupac, Dr. Dre, and Snoop Dogg. Rage explains her confrontational style in the title track of *Necessary Roughness* (Interscope 90109).

Sex as a theme is as dominant in the music of women in rap as it was in the music of the blues queens who were active in the 1920s. Like blues women Ida Cox (1896–1967), Gertrude "Ma" Rainey (1886–1939), and Bessie Smith (1894–1937) some 70 years earlier, women rappers use sex in their performances and recordings to challenge notions of black women's sexuality and femininity. Many women in rap flaunt their bodies, demand parity in sexual relationships, and state they have the right to be as sexually aggressive as men. "Foxy's Bells" (Polygram International 4465) is unique among women's raps. In it, Foxy Brown boasts about her sexual abilities as she touts her skills as a rapper. Race is often addressed in the music of Lauryn Hill. In "Forgive Them Father" and "Doo Wop," both from *The Miseducation of Lauryn Hill* (Sony 69035), Hill tells black men and women to value each other more than money and fame and to take pride in their African heritage.

See also Blues; Gospel Music; Jazz

For Further Reading

George, Nelson. *Hip Hop America*. New York: Viking, 1998.

Souljah, Sister. *No Disrespect*. New York: Times Books, 1994.

Gail Woldu

Raymond, Guadalupe Victoria Yoli

See La Lupe

Researchers in Music Education

Women researchers in music education were highly prolific during the twentieth century. Since the publication of journals such as the *Journal of Research in Music Education* (JRME), *Music Supervisors Journal* (MSJ), *Music Educators Journal* (MEJ), and *Bulletin of the Council for Research in Music Education* (CRME), women have researched, documented, and published papers on various topics of music education.

The first issue of the JRME included Nan Cooke Carpenter, Viola A. Brody, and Mrs. Jessie L. Fleming as contributing authors. Prior to this publication, however, and before 1934, concerns, ideas, and research findings shared by music educators were published in the MSJ, founded in 1914 through the initiative of the Music Supervisors National Conference (MSNC). The MSNC was the forerunner of what from 1934 on was and still is called today the Music Educators National Conference (MENC). Prior to 1914, issues concerning music education and the teaching of music in the schools primarily had been reported in the *Journal of Education*. Its cursory review of music-related contributions between 1900 and 1914 shows C. H. Congdon and Elizabeth Fairweather as one of the first women authors, and W.S.B. Mathews from Chicago and Constance Barlow-Smith from the University of Illinois as repeat authors. Although today any of these authors' articles would be labeled editorial pieces or articles of interest, their significance as forerunners of later, more research-based writings should be noted. For example, the 1905 article by Elizabeth Fairweather, a teacher at Norwood High School, OH, addressed the ethical value of music. It might be considered a precursor to philosophical discourse specific to music education.

From its inception in 1914, the MSJ carried a variety of articles, informational items, editorials, and columns of interest, and women contributed mostly through editorials, "opinion pieces," and letters to the editor. The first women authors to report the results of what today might be referred to as survey research were Bessie M. Whiteley and Gladys Arthur Brown. Initially read as a paper at the Missouri State Teacher's Association in 1914, Whiteley described the responses of 23 major cities across the United States (out of 26 contacted) on the establishment of orchestral practice in the elementary schools in those cities. Brown provided a status report on instrumental education in 200 schools.

A second area of research published in the MSJ from its inception encompassed extensive bibliographies on different subjects relevant to music teaching. One such published bibliography, spanning over six issues of the MSJ, was the result of Vivian Gray Little's master's thesis at the University of Wisconsin Library School, edited and expanded by MSJ editor P. W. Dykema. Soon to follow were the bibliographic projects of Florence Lampert, supervisor of music in Lena, IL, and Maude E. Glynn, both studying at the University of Wisconsin.

Later the MSJ, renamed in 1934 as the MEJ, devoted space to what was called a School Survey Section. Over the years, several women researchers contributed to reports in that section, among them Stella R. Root from State Normal School, St. Cloud, MN, and Catharine E. Strouse, and Florence M. Wallace from the Arthur Jordan Conservatory of Music, Indianapolis, IN. Perhaps owing to past editor Dykema's interest in issues concerning testing and measurement, a section devoted to such topics was initiated and edited by him and included the works of a number of women. They were Hazel M. Stanton, Sarah Rachel Isbel, Esther Church, Margaret Harrison from Columbia Teachers College, Hannah M. Cundiff, and Clara E. Lawrence, formerly director of public school music at the State Teachers College, Valley City, ND. Julia Emery reported on a survey concerning leisure and music reading.

What today may be labeled as reports on qualitative case studies were published first by Helen Leavitt, Helen Schwinn, and Marian Nelson; early studies were reported by Mary Browning Scanlon in 1938 and 1940, respectively. In 1942 acoustical aspects of music performance were addressed by Oleta L. Benn, and several articles on music as therapy, one of them a survey report, were published by Esther Goetz Gilliland in 1944 and 1945.

The first truly experimental study reported as a two-page abstract in the MEJ in 1948 was done by Viola A. Brody. She had conducted the study, supervised by John H. Muyskens, professor of phonetics, in partial fulfillment of her Ph.D. requirements in education at the University of Michigan. As stated in the abstract, she had tested "[a] voice-training program based entirely upon effective motor coordination for the production of tone" with "a group of thirty-four children, ranging in age from nine to seventeen and including grades four through twelve" (Brody, 23).

A number of other articles of interest published by women writers in the MEJ, but not necessarily classifiable as research articles, deserve mention here. They reflect topics that continue to be of interest today and have been dealt with in various forms of scholarly writing since that time. Particular mention in this regard should go to such noted music educators and prolific writers as Mabelle Glenn (1881–1969), Lilla Belle Pitts (1884–1970), and Elizabeth A. H. Green, who are discussed more extensively elsewhere in this encyclopedia. Perhaps lesser known writers were Dorothea Doig, a music psychologist from Cleveland, OH, interested in matters concerning the testing of music capacities; Marguerite Ullman, who published a literature review on stage fright as early as 1939, and Johanna Anderson, who addressed music appreciation for college students. Particularly in and around war times, an interest in international music education led to a number of brief articles and "travelogues" by such authors as Helen M. Hosmer, Margarita Mendendez, Mary Santos, and Stella Marie Graves.

Clearly, the Music Supervisors (later Educators) National Conference and its official publication were important to the history of music education research and scholarship. This is not to say, though, that there were not women researchers who published elsewhere and were listed as competent researchers by Schneider and Cady in their review of early research in music education. They particularly mentioned Grace V. D. More and Mary T. Whitley, both of whose work had appeared in the *Review of Education Research* in 1932 and 1934, respectively. Neither of these names appear at any time in the MEJ or in subsequent research publications in music education.

Of importance for the future of research in music education itself was the MSNC/MENC's organization of past presidents, first called the Educational Council, then renamed the National Council for Research in Music Education, and finally changed to the Music Education Research Council (MERC).

Through the initiative of the MERC, the *Journal of Research in Music Education* (JRME) was founded in 1954. Because of the academic positions of its first editor, Allen Britton, the editorial office was housed at the University of Michigan. As stated at the beginning of this entry, women researchers contributed from the beginning. In the first 10 years, notably among and in addition to those cited above was Kate Hevner from Indiana University, who as early as 1940 had contributed a chapter on aesthetics in J. P. Guilford's *Fields of Psychology*. Her work as a psychologist and researcher with a keen interest in music was most prominent in her contributions to the Oregon Tests of Musicality. Between 1963 and 1972 two more names, Frances Andrews and Marilyn Pflederer (Zimmerman), appear prominently in the JRME. It should also be noted that an analysis of all women contributors in the JRME since its inception until today, when done in 10-year units of analysis, reveals a considerably lower number of women between 1953 and 1982 than it does for the years since 1983.

Ten years after the JRME appeared on the scene, another publication, the CRME, was launched by the University of Illinois through its School of Music, the College of Education, and the Curriculum Laboratory in cooperation with the Office of the Superintendent of Public Instruction. Unlike the JRME, it had a format of invited feature articles, refereed articles of interest, and critical and analytical reviews of dissertations. One such feature article was provided by Marilyn Pflederer in 1966. Based upon her 1963 dissertation, she reported her research on how children conceptually organize musical sounds.

With the existence of both the JRME and the CRME, music education researchers now had two important outlets not only for publishing their studies but also for serving on editorial boards and councils. A total of five names appeared on both lists. These included (in alphabetical order): Alice-Ann Darrow, Laura Dorow, Kate Hevner-Mueller, Janet Gilbert, Marilyn Pflederer-Zimmerman, and Cornelia Yarbrough. However, in light of prolific and consistent contributions either as published researchers or as women active as leaders on research boards and editorial committees, an additional number of names deserve mention: Betty Atterbury, Ruth Brittin, Patricia Shehan Campbell, Jane Cassidy, Eugenia Costa-Giomi, Patricia Flowers, Hildegard Froehlich, Joyce Eastlund Gromko, Harriet Hair, Carol Harrison, Gretchen Hieronymous (Beall), Judith Jellison, June Jetter, Joyce Jordan, Carol Scott Kaessner, Janice Killian, Sue Malin, Claire McCoy, Jan McCrary, Carol Pemberton, Carol Prickett, Roseanne Rosenthal, Deborah Sheldon, Carolyn Sherrill, Melanie Stuart, Wendy Sims, Patricia Sink, Jayne Standley, Cecilia Chu Wang, Lizabeth Wing, and Annette Zalanowski.

Finally, a number of important research contributions to music education have been made by women researchers whose focus has been outside the editorial policies of the research journals and boards mentioned here. Their work became known through feature articles in other music or music education journals, through books and monographs. Hence the reliance on a person's publication record either in the JRME or CRME *Bulletin* might not adequately describe a person's role as researcher in music education. This would certainly be true for such eminent music educators and scholars as Estelle Jorgensen from Indiana University; Barbara Reeder Lundquist, professor emerita from the University of Washington; and Carol P. Richardson from the University of Michigan. In addition, when reviewing the names of contributing authors and editors of the 1992 *Handbook of Research on Music Teaching and Learning*, such leaders in U.S. music education scholarship as Maria Runfola, Joanne Rutkoswki, and Nancy Whitaker deserve special mention.

Research in music education is a multifaceted pursuit with a diverse array of procedures and methodologies. Whether one engages in empirical-experimental investigations or prefers an anthropological approach toward field study and participant observation often determines the type of publication by which one becomes known. Therefore, the lines between what does or does not constitute research in music education are blurred. Thus the answer to whether or not a music educator deserves to be called a researcher is similarly blurred. This has been the case from the beginnings of music education when the Music Supervisors National Conference began its publication; it still is the case today. As a result, there are many more women music educators than listed in this entry who have championed the cause of music education in their work as teachers and scholars. Not always, though, have their voices been heard and acknowledged as they should have been. Further study certainly is warranted.

See also Choral Education; Early Childhood Music Educators; General Music; Instrumental Education; Music Education

For Further Reading

Brody, Viola A. "The Emergence of Song: An Experimental Study of the Evolving Song According to Biological Principles." *Music Educators Journal* 35/1 (1948): 22–24.

Hildegard Froehlich

Reynolds, Debbie (1932–)

Debbie Reynolds. *Photo courtesy of Globe Photos.*

Over the years, singer and actress Debbie Reynolds has become synonymous with the cheerful, bouncy "girl-next-door" who spent her first years in Hollywood working on comedies and musicals such as *June Bride* (1948), *Three Little Words* (1950), and *Two Weeks with Love* (1950). These early films paved the way for Debbie's greatest successes both on film and in recordings. In what may be her most memorable role—*Singing in the Rain* (1952), in which she co-starred with Gene Kelly and Donald O'Connor—Reynolds secured her position as one of the biggest box office draws in America in the 1950s and early 1960s.

Born Mary Frances Reynolds on 1 April 1932, Debbie Reynolds spent the first seven years of her life in El Paso, TX, before moving with her family to Burbank, CA, where her father, a carpenter for the Southern Pacific Railroad, had been transferred. In 1948 Mary Frances entered and won a Miss Burbank Pageant with her imitation of Betty Hutton. Several days later her parents were contacted by a talent scout for Warner Brothers who had seen Mary Frances's performance in the pageant and wanted to arrange a screen test. Her success during the test led to a contract with Warner Brothers and a new name: "Debbie Reynolds."

Reynold's performances during the 1950s and 1960s, included *Tammy and the Bachelor* ([1957] original soundtrack available on Crl-57159), *How the West Was Won* ([1962] available on MGM S1E-5), *The Unsinkable Molly Brown*

([1964] available on MGM SE-4232), for which she received an Oscar nomination, and *The Singing Nun* (1966). As Hollywood began to move away from the musical genre that had launched her career, Reynolds turned to other venues, starting with a Broadway debut in the 1973 revival of *Irene*. This was soon followed by her own television series (*The Debbie Reynolds Show*, 1969–1970), numerous nightclub revues, and appearances in Las Vegas (often together with many of her former film co-stars).

One of America's enduring sweethearts, Debbie Reynolds has spent much of her life in the limelight—from her first marriage to Eddie Fisher in 1955 and their difficult divorce in 1959, two subsequent marriages to Harry Karl and Richard Hamlett, financial problems, and difficult relationships with her daughter, actress Carrie Fisher. Through it all, Reynolds has remained buoyant, opening her own casino and nightclub in Las Vegas, making several cameo appearances in films from the early 1990s, and finally returning to the screen in Albert Brooks's *Mother* (1996) and *In and Out* (1997).

See also Musical Theater

For Further Reading

Chambers, Andrea. "Debbie Reynolds, Hollywood's Perennial Girl-Next-Door, Looks Back on a Life of Broken Promises." *People Weekly* 24 (October 1988): 83–86.

Reynolds, Debbie, and David Patrick Columbia. *Debbie—My Life*. New York: William Morrow, 1988.

Maria Purciello

Richter, Marga (1926–)

Marga Richter is an important composer whose career spanned the better part of the twentieth century. The number of commissions, performances and published works of Richter attests to the stature of this pioneering composer: 60 orchestral performances in the United States and abroad, eight American publishers, and commissions by notable soloists and performing groups. Richter considers *Qhanri: Tibetan Variations* for cello and piano (Leonarda LE337) her most significant work. The extensive variations are performed without pause and include a chant that Richter heard while traveling in Tibet. *Riders to the Sea*, Richter's recent chamber opera based on J. M. Synge's play, retains her characteristic style in a more tonal atmosphere. The accompanying instruments include Celtic harp, penny whistle, bodhran (Irish drum), free-bass concert accordion, and string quintet. Melody is the primary element in Richter's music. Her rhapsodic style frequently employs variations; repetitive accompanying figures (ostinati, drones, and pedal points); intervals of seconds, sevenths, and ninths; and propulsive rhythms.

Born on 21 October 1926 in Wisconsin, Richter began piano lessons at age four, and at age 11 she started composing. Her American mother, Inez Chandler, had an operatic career in Germany, where she met and married Paul Richter, son of a conductor and composer. The family moved to New York in 1943 to facilitate their daughter's piano study with Countess Helena Morsztyn. In 1945 Richter entered the Juilliard School (B.S. 1949, M.S. 1951) as a piano student of Rosalyn Tureck. She studied composition with William Bergsma and Vincent Persichetti beginning in 1946. Following a brief first marriage, Richter married Alan Skelly, professor of philosophy at C. W. Post College, in 1953. He died in 1988.

In 1972 Richter and Herbert Deutsch founded the Long Island Composers Alliance. She also served on the original

Board of Directors of the League of Women Composers, and in 1975 she organized their milestone concert at New York's Museum of Modern Art.

Richter's 126 compositions fall into three distinct periods. Early works include the song cycle *Transmutation* (1949), *Sonata for Piano* (1954), *Concerto for Piano and Violas, Cellos, and Basses* (1955), *Lament* for strings (1956), and *Aria and Toccata* for viola and strings (1957). All these works were recorded in the 1950s by MGM Records. She also composed several scores for the Dance Associates (1950–1953) and *Abyss*, a 1964 reworking of *Aria and Toccata* (commissioned and performed worldwide by the Harkness Ballet). The second period includes a group of miniatures: *Eight Pieces* for piano (1961), *Fragments* for piano (1963), *Suite* for violin and piano (1964), and *Soundings* for harpsichord (1965). Unlike the expansiveness of the first and third periods, in these pieces Richter explores composing without development. The third period commences with the pivotal *Landscapes of the Mind I* (1968–1974), a piano concerto with full orchestra and electric guitar, electric bass, electric sitar or tamboura, and a battery of percussion including three Indian drums. Inspired by two Georgia O'Keeffe paintings, the composition shows influences of Charles Ives's Fourth Symphony and Indian music (stimulated by sitarist Maureen Skelly, Richter's daughter). *Landscapes I* and *II* (1971) were written simultaneously and are "cross-pollinated." *Landscapes II* (Leonarda LE337) was written for violinist Daniel Heifetz and was recorded with pianist Michael Skelly, Richter's son. Materials in these pieces were used in several orchestral works over a 10-year period, including *Blackberry Vines and Winter Fruit* (1976), *Spectral Chimes/Enshrouded Hills* ([1980] MMC Recordings, MMC2066), and *Out of Shadows and Solitude* (1985).

For Further Reading

Fuller, Sophie. *The Pandora Guide to Women Composers: Britain and the United States, 1629–Present*. San Francisco: Pandora, 1994.

Jezic, Diane Peacock. *Women Composers: The Lost Tradition Found*. New York: Feminist Press, 1988.

LePage, Jane Weiner. *Women Composers, Conductors, and Musicians of the Twentieth Century*. Metuchen, NJ: Scarecrow Press, 1980.

Vivian Taylor

Rimes, LeAnn (1982–)

Country music star LeAnn Rimes has followed in the footsteps of earlier country music child stars Brenda Lee (b. 1944) and Tanya Tucker (b. 1958), who also saw their initial record releases achieve remarkable success. As several women country stars preceding her, Rimes continues to transcend barriers between music genres and commercial styles. She recorded a duet with country music legend Eddy Arnold and has sung duets with pop music superstar Elton John. She has begun to write some of her own material and has earned various awards: the 1996 Grammy Awards for the Best New Artist and Best Country Vocal Performance, and the Country Music Association's (CMA) 1996 honors for Top New Female Vocalist, Song of the Year, and Single of the Year. In 1997 LeAnn Rimes was honored as the TNN/Music City News woman Star of Tomorrow, received the CMA Horizon Award, and was named Favorite New Artist at the American Music Awards.

Rimes was born on 28 August 1982 in Jackson, MS. She began singing before age two and, at five, entered and won her first talent contest. She then announced to her parents that she wanted a career in the entertainment business. The family moved to the Dallas suburb of Garland, TX, the following year, so she could pursue her dream. At the age of seven Rimes debuted in a Dallas production of *A Christmas Carol* and competed for two weeks on the national television series *Star Search* when she was eight. She appeared as a regular on Johnnie High's local Fort Worth television show *Country Music Review* and performed *a cappella* renditions of the "Star Spangled Banner" at Dallas Cowboy football games. Mirroring the early career of country singer Reba McEntire (b. 1954), LeAnn also performed at rodeos and cutting horse championships.

Her first album was produced by her father and recorded in Clovis, NM, when LeAnn was 11 years old. During the same year the album was released on the independent Nor Va Jak label. Although sources differ, some state that this album included a version of the song "Blue" (Curb 77821) that would later become LeAnn's first big hit. The story behind her recording of "Blue" is informative in terms of both the history of Rimes's career and the process of mythologizing that occurs often within the culture of country music. Dallas promoter and disc jockey Bill Mack, impressed by the young singer, sent her the song "Blue" and began to promote her career. Central to his plan to bring LeAnn wider recognition was Rimes's recording of the song written by Mack in the 1960s. LeAnn attracted the attention of executives at Curb Records, who signed her to a contract and released "Blue" as a single. Label promotion stated that Mack had waited patiently for over 30 years to find the right person to record the song, originally written for Patsy Cline (1932–1963), who died before she could record it. However, other sources report that "Blue" had actually been recorded and released by three other singers, including Mack's own version from the 1960s on the Starday label. Regardless, the Curb Records 1996 release of 13-year-old LeAnn Rimes's rendition of the song catapulted her to virtually instant stardom, casting her in the role of successor to the career of the late Patsy Cline.

Other recent Rimes recordings include *You Light up My Life: Inspirational Songs* (Curb 77885), *Sittin' on the Top of the World* (Curb 77901), and *LeAnn Rimes* (Curb 77947).

See also Country Music

For Further Reading

Rimestimes.com: The Official Website of LeAnn Rimes. Available: http://www.rimestimes.com

Amy Corin

Riot Grrrl

See Underground Music

Ritchie, Jean (1922–)

Folk performer and composer Jean Ritchie is a living embodiment of the Appalachian folk music tradition. With half a century's performing and recording to her credit, and still performing on traditional instruments, she has been the subject of television documentaries, has published numerous books and articles, and has been featured on Smithsonian/Folkways recordings. Ritchie also writes original songs in the traditional style that talk about life in the Cumberland Mountains where she was born and raised. Presently living in Port Washington, NY, she and her husband of 50 years, George Pickow, run their own music-related companies, Greenhays Recordings and the Folklife Family Store.

Born on 8 December 1922 in Viper,

Jean Ritchie. *Photo by George Pickow.*

KY, Ritchie was the youngest of 14 children. In the Ritchie home music was learned through oral tradition, and singing accompanied daily chores. In the evenings the family gathered to sing hymns, popular songs, and traditional music. Folklorist Cecil Sharp visited the family in 1917 and wrote down the over 300 songs that the family knew by heart. In the 1930s, pioneering ethnomusicologists in the United States John A. and Alan Lomax made field recordings of the Ritchie family for the Archive of Folk Song of the Library of Congress.

Ritchie's first public performances were at 4H Club meetings and at the local county fair. She attended Cumberland College in Williamsburg, KY, and went on to graduate Phi Beta Kappa from the University of Kentucky with a degree in social work. When she left Kentucky for a job at the Henry Street Settlement in New York City, she sang her Appalachian songs and played the little-known dulcimer for the children at the Settlement, gradually attracting attention and invitations to perform in more formal settings.

The year 1950 was a landmark one for Ritchie. In a single year she signed a recording contract with Elektra records, became a regular on Oscar Brand's WNYC radio show *Folksong Festival*, and married Pickow. In 1955 Oxford University Press published her book, *Singing Family of the Cumberlands*. As a Fulbright scholar (1952–1953), Ritchie traveled to the British Isles to trace the roots of American folk music. She was asked to serve on the first board of the Newport

Folk Festival along with Theodore Bikel, Bill Clifton, Clarence Cooper, Eric Darling, Pete Seeger, and Peter Yarrow. Through her performing, recording, advocacy, and research activities, she so successfully popularized the dulcimer that for a time she and her husband were building and selling dulcimers from their basement.

Ritchie's activities as musician, writer, and businesswoman have continued to the present day, and she is generally regarded as one of the most significant characters in the history of American folk music. Her album *None But One* (Greenhays 0708) received the 1977 Rolling Stone Critics' Award, increasing her visibility within popular music. Other recordings include *Jean Ritchie and Doc Watson at Folk City* (Smithsonian/Folkways SF 40005), *Mountain Born* (Greenhays 725), and *American Folk Tales and Songs* (Flying Fish 70717).

In 1996 PBS affiliate station KET filmed *Mountain Born: The Jean Ritchie Story*, an hour-long documentary of her life. In 1998 Ritchie was awarded the Folk Alliance Lifetime Achievement Award, acknowledging her enduring contributions to the preservation and promotion of traditional music.

See also Folk Music

For Further Reading

Briscoe, James R. *Contemporary Anthology of Music by Women*. Bloomington: Indiana University Press, 1997.

Ritchie, Jean. *Celebration of Life*. Port Washington, NY: Geordie Music Publishing, 1971.

Kathleen Pierson

Rock and Popular Music Genres

At the beginning of the twenty-first century, interest in and awareness of the significant contributions of women in rock and popular music genres has greatly increased, largely owing to the discerning efforts of contemporary researchers and scholars of popular culture. These scholars have endeavored to deconstruct male-centered accounts of the history of rock and popular music by challenging assumptions about a woman's "proper" role in the music industry, and by calling into question every established societal attitude about women's artistic, political, and business aptitudes, roles, and contributions. This interest and awareness parallels current social and cultural shifts that examine and filter aspects of power and privilege, authority and legitimacy, convention and revolt, sex and romance, and censorship and creative passion—through the lens of gender. Women have been present in vigorous and varied roles in rock and pop music for at least 50 years, beginning with the women who sang the blues, to the girl groups, Motown, and the folk rock and counterculture scene of the 1960s; the feminist music movement, singer-songwriter phenomenons, and punk rebellion of the 1970s, to the bad girl bands of the 1980s to the women rappers and hip hop artists; and underground and indie artists and business-savvy megastar pop icons of the 1990s.

Today, women artists work in diverse genres and comment on a wide variety of issues in their songs—racism, sexism, censorship, class, violence, poverty, AIDS, homelessness, homophobia, drug and alcohol addiction, gender identity, and political oppression—controversial subject matter that was deemed neither ladylike nor artistically appropriate for women artists in the 1950s. Contemporary women artists continue to exercise an emerging authorship in their work, writing much of their own material. They are intimately involved in the business aspects of producing and marketing their own work, which empowers them with greater artistic control and freedom for personal artistic and political expression.

Popular music is a colossal genre, a vast and steadily evolving art form, with many subgenres and cross-over categories, styles, and overlapping elements. These include rock and pop, urban and hip hop, alternative, electronica, jazz and blues, country and folk, new age, world, inspirational, soundtracks, children's, experimental, spoken word, and performance art. The variety and influence of popular musics is broad and notable, shaped by the style, attitudes, and fashions of society itself, and most recently by the digital and computer idioms of the 1990s, a ubiquitous force as society becomes increasingly globally intertwined.

The origins of rock are embedded in the African rhythms transported to North America by way of the slave trade. Slaves—and subsequently sharecroppers—used field hollers as a means of both communicating with other workers and controlling work animals. Descended from functional African musical traditions, this style of vocal declamation was later appropriated by blues musicians. The pioneers of rock and roll were the women of the blues, including Mamie Smith (1883–1946), Gertrude "Ma" Rainey (1886–1939), Bessie Smith (1894–1937), Ida Cox (1896–1967), Memphis Minnie (1897–1973), La Vern Baker (1929–1997), Sippie Wallace (1898–1986), Ruth Brown (b. 1928), Victoria Spivey (1906–1976), Willie Mae "Big Mama" Thornton (1926–1984), Bonnie Guitar (b. 1924, Bonnie Buckingham), Wanda Jackson (b. 1937), and Koko Taylor (b. 1935). Early rock and roll women included Kay Starr (b. 1922) and Gogi Grant (b. 1924).

The jazz tradition was enriched through the contributions of women such as Billie Holiday (1915–1959), Ivie Anderson (1905–1949), Peggy Lee (1920–2002), Sarah Vaughan (1924–1990), and Ella Fitzgerald (1917–1996). Gospel's legends included Sister Rosetta Tharpe (1915–1973), Clara Ward (1924–1973), Mahalia Jackson (1911–1972), Marion Jackson, and Marion Williams (1927–1994); and early rhythm and blues artists included Ruth Brown (b. 1928) and Etta James (b.1938). Brenda Lee (b. 1944) was a major early rockabilly star, and country music performers included the Carter Family, Kitty Wells (b. 1918), Patsy Cline (1932–1963), Loretta Lynn (b. 1935), Tammy Wynette (1942–1998), Dolly Parton (b. 1946), and Emmylou Harris (b. 1947).

The pop, folk, Motown, and rock women of the 1950s and 1960s—including Nancy Sinatra (b. 1940), Cher (b. 1946), Dionne Warwick (b. 1940), Carole King (b. 1942), and Aretha Franklin (b. 1942)—were the original "rebel girls," flouncy and feisty, singing about love, power, and sex. They testified to women's condition and transformed themselves from "cute little girl singers" and "rock chicks" to confident and powerfully sexy women performers and artists.

Folk and protest singers and singer-songwriters who came to the forefront were Joan Baez (b. 1941), Odetta (b. 1930), lesbian folk singer Alix Dobkin, Tracy Nelson (b. 1944); and Connie Francis (b. 1938). Other prominent women during the 1950s and 1960s included Rita Coolidge, Carla Thomas (b. 1942), Judy Collins (b. 1939), Peggy Seeger (b. 1935), Laura Nyro (1947–1997), rockabilly icon Wanda Jackson (b. 1937), and bad girl hard-rocker Grace Slick (b. 1939).

Early girl groups included the Chantels, the Ronettes, the Shangri-las, the Crystals, and the girls groups of the 1960s—including the Shirelles, the Chiffons, the Angles, Reparta and the Delrons, the Exciters, the Cookies, the Supremes, Martha and the Vandellas, the Marvelettes, and Patti LaBelle and the Blue Belles—were a phenomenon that was initiated in the 1950s by groups like the Blossoms, the Clickettes, the Joytones, and the Bobbettes. These groups began to produce songs that effectively mingled "doo wop" harmonies with rhythm and blues music. The "girl group" sound was comprised of a lead vocalist with a supporting background trio or quartet, and this genre and its era exemplified an important aspect of early rock and roll and the history of women in popular music. The emergence of the new "girl group" sound established, for the first time, a distinct performance style that audiences associated with women and helped to change the direction of popular music.

The girl group sound was masterminded and manufactured by producers who were men: songwriters and managers who exploited individual artists as mere vehicles for hit songs, establishing and repeating formulaic devices for creating Top 40 tunes. Additionally, most of the women in these groups were very young and relatively inexperienced. Consequently they were routinely taken advantage of and allowed virtually no control over their artistic output. They rarely wrote their own material and never played instruments; they were merely allowed to perform in acceptable roles as singers, a musical role deemed proper for women throughout history.

Teen magazines and television shows essentially ignored girl groups, severely limiting strategic exposure and opportunities for promotion. Aside from the prevailing sexism, racism within the music industry limited the success of many performers. Mostly black, the girls in the groups came from New York City, Long Island, New Jersey, and Detroit. Allowed only minimal media coverage, the artists who made up the girl groups were compelled by rapacious and self-serving producers to record the same basic song (somewhat but not substantially reworked) over and over again, repeating the formula until the public wearied of the similarity of their tunes. Once public regard—and therefore the possibility of commercial and fiscal success—diminished, the producer discarded the group and moved on to another project, another group, and another formula.

Typical of the experiences of women in music (and of black musicians in general), the girl groups were exploited and their artistic aptitudes and contributions devalued and marginalized. Their songs generally portrayed women as submissive, needy, and clinging. Nevertheless, this first major rock style associated with girls provided a voice for a generation of young girls. These groups enjoyed only fleeting success, but their sound exerted significant influence on their musical contemporaries, and it continues to inspire emerging performers.

During the 1960s, the single most significant decade for popular music, diverse pop genres developed independently but also merged and intersected with each other, creating unique blended and fused genres. This period initiated the aesthetic cross-fertilization and multifaceted music that exist and thrive today. Rock women in the 1960s and 1970s, including Janis Joplin (1943–1970), Tina Turner (b. 1938), Joni Mitchell (b. 1943), Bonnie Raitt (b. 1949), Linda Ronstadt (b. 1946), and Bette Midler (b. 1945), were a small but tough and talented group of artistic dissidents, some often facing isolation and scorn while pursuing careers in rock, clearly a professional objective outside of the conventional societal expectations for women in a "bad boy rockers" world. As the popularity of disco and punk intensified in the late 1970s, the singer-songwriter movement lost momentum and popular appeal. A decade later, the momentum resurfaced and intensified in the works of Suzanne Vega (b. 1959) and Tracy Chapman (b. 1964), and later, Tori Amos (b. 1963), Shawn Colvin (b. 1956), Sheryl Crow (b. 1962), Melissa Etheridge (b. 1961), and Liz Phair (b. 1967).

Pop and punk women from the 1970s included Chaka Khan (b. 1953), Gladys Knight (b. 1944), Debby Boone, Cher (b. 1946), Kiki Dee (b. 1947), Roberta Flack (b. 1939), Crystal Gayle (b. 1951), Gloria Gaynor (b. 1949), Nina Simone (b. 1933), Karen Carpenter (1950–1983), Patti Smith (b. 1946), Janis Ian (b. 1951), Rickie Lee Jones (b. 1954), Dolly Parton (b. 1946), the Pointer Sisters, Carly Simon (b. 1945), Phoebe Snow (b. 1952), Barbra Streisand (b. 1942), Deborah (Debbie) Harry (b. 1945), Yoko Ono (b. 1933), Jennifer Warnes (b. 1947), Tina Weymouth (b. 1950), Exene Cervenka (b. 1956), Chrissie Hynde (b. 1951), and Donna Summer (b. 1948). These women championed the ideals of initiative over technique and commercial viability over artistic representation. Many were outspoken feminists, refusing to play by the rules. Some were androgynous interpreters or poets and journalists. Others were not interested in conventional song structures, some intentionally returned to the comfort and monotony of three-chord song structures, some were accused of possessing a somewhat superficial approach to pop music, some were hotheads, some were cool and self-possessed, and some merged the prevalent dance obsession with sex and concepts of autonomy and power to rewrite an entire generation's response to dominance and submission.

As women rock and pop musicians gained acceptance in the late 1970s and 1980s, rap and heavy metal, previously exclusively male genres, increased in vogue and created a gender conflict that ushered in women's adaptations of hard, guitar-driven rock with women at the helm. Moreover, numerous diverse genres began to exist side-by-side. Women artists were found in all arenas of popular music, as represented by bohemian renegades Stevie Nicks (b. 1948) and Heart, Cyndi Lauper (b. 1953), the Roches, and Sarah McLachlan (b. 1968). Other prominent rock and pop women of the 1980s included Madonna (b. 1958), Salt-N-Pepa, Queen Latifah (b. 1970), Rickie Lee Jones, Suzanne Vega (b. 1959), Deborah (Debbie) Harry (b. 1945), Joan Jett (b. 1960), Tina Turner, Cyndi Lauper, Tracy Chapman (b. 1964), Stevie Nicks, Carole King (b. 1942), Pat Benatar (b. 1953), Natalie Merchant (b. 1963), Alanis Morissette (b. 1974), Janet Jackson (b. 1966), Whitney Houston (b. 1963), Mariah Carey (b. 1970), Mary J. Blige (b. 1971), and TLC, to name a few.

The 1990s saw an even greater abundance of women in rock and pop. Laurie Anderson (b. 1947), Kim Gordon (b. 1953), Janet Jackson, Madonna, and Mariah Carey reinvented themselves from previous decades and thereby liberated themselves and their audiences. Toni Braxton (b. 1967) was one of the most significant breakout artists of the decade. Rebel Grrls, Bikini Kill, Tribe 8, and the Indigo Girls could be considered ambassadors of "responsible girlism." The year 1996 was a veritable turning point as women artists out-charted their male counterparts on the Top 20 charts for the first time in history.

Popular music is starting to enjoy a long overdue and well-merited legitimacy, worthy of scholarly consideration. Indeed, vast numbers of brilliant, insightful, and skillfully constructed books on popular music and its hosting culture have been written in the past decade. Critical analyses of American popular music have focused on issues of race, class, gender, and sexuality, utilizing the filter of mass media. Entire journals and individual columns that focus on philosophical and cultural issues related to women in rock and pop music have migrated to the Internet, opening up a whole new world for women in music, providing access, information, and validation. With the advent of feminist theory and scholarship three decades ago, thoughtful and essential documentation has chronicled the contributions of women in rock and pop music who have influenced the culture in powerful ways. More women now front their own bands, play lead guitar or drums, compose their own music, pen their own lyrics, and produce and market their own albums. Women are resisting and overthrowing all manner of long-standing traditions, including the oppression of sexism, to establish themselves at the cutting edge of contemporary popular music.

Even though censorship of the work of women artists continues by the dominant culture, as a method for suppressing and oppressing the voices of women (along with other minority groups) who "don't know their place," some positive changes have transpired in the music industry. Women performers, particularly in alternative arenas, have been easily integrated into bands, an important aspect of the punk music scene and one that is patently absent from the mainstream rock and pop scene. Additionally, some bands have comfortably crossed over from indie to major labels, and many performers in the alternative rock scene have collaborated on various projects. The independent domain has also largely cast aside banal notions about women musicians and their roles, admonishing the public to quit marginalizing women musicians as women musicians, and to simply accept them as good musicians.

Women in rock and popular music genres continue to evolve into power positions as business people and artists, imposing tremendous changes in the male-dominated American music industry scene—as key recording artists, label executives including Frances Preston, president of Broadcast Music, Inc.; Tracey Edmonds, chief executive officer of Yab Yum Entertainment; and Sheila Shipley Biddy, senior vice-president and general manager of Decca Records. Women's active and continuous participation in the rock and pop music industry, in spite of extensive obstacles and the experiences they have faced as women working in a male-dominated industry, has served and will continue to help them find their own voices as artists and as essential revolutionary catalysts for generating positive and equitable social and political change.

See also Bands, Pop Rock; Garage Rock and Heavy Metal Bands; Indie-Rock; Motown; New Age Music; Rap; Rock Music; Singer-Songwriters

For Further Reading

Evans, David. *Big Road Blues: Tradition and Creativity in the Folk Blues*. Berkeley: University of California Press, 1982.

Juno, Andrea. *Angry Women in Rock*, Vol. 1. New York: Juno Books, 1996.

McClary, Susan. *Feminine Endings: Music, Gender,*

and Sexuality. Minneapolis: University of Minnesota Press, 1991.

Steward, Sue, and Sheryl Grant. *Signed, Sealed and Delivered: True Life Stories of Women in Pop*. Cambridge, MA: South End Press, 1984.

Judith A. Coe

Rock and Roll Hall of Fame

The Rock and Roll Hall of Fame Foundation was established in 1983 to honor the contributions of performers, producers, songwriters, and others who have had a significant impact on the evolution, development, and perpetuation of rock and roll. The Hall of Fame inducts in four categories: Performers, Nonperformers, Early Influences, and Sidemen. The careers of the inductees must span at least 25 years.

The first inductions took place in 1986. No women were inducted that year in any category. In 1987 Aretha Franklin (b. 1942) became the first woman inducted into the Rock and Roll Hall of Fame. Franklin, who has to date charted more million-sellers than any other woman in recording history, was inducted in the Performer category. She was quickly followed in 1988 by the Supremes, the most popular girl group of the 1960s.

All of the following women have been inducted into the Rock and Roll Hall of Fame in the Performer category: Tina Turner (b. 1938) and Ike Turner, known for high-energy performances on the soul circuit during the late 1960s and early 1970s and chart-topping hits in the 1980s and 1990s; LaVern Baker (1929–1997), the versatile vocalist whose blending of blues, jazz, and rhythm and blues, was influential in the emergence of the rock and roll idiom. Etta James (b. 1938), a blues singer whose raw vocals and pioneering hits from the 1950s influenced singers ranging from Janis Joplin to Bonnie Raitt. Ruth Brown (b. 1928), rhythm and blues singer who dominated the rhythm and blues charts during the 1950s and helped Atlantic Records secure its footing in the record industry.

Janis Joplin (1943–1970) was an influential blues singer and embodiment of the psychedelic generation of the 1960s. Martha and the Vandellas was a leading pop soul Motown group with rhythm and blues edges popular during the 1960s. Martha Reeves was backed up by the Vandellas—Rosalind Ashford and Annette Beard. Betty Kelly replaced Beard in 1964. Gladys Knight (b. 1944) led one of the outstanding all-woman groups of the Motown era and one of the longest-established soul vocal groups, with hits spanning four decades.

Grace Slick (b. 1939) with Jefferson Airplane made up a San Francisco psychedelic rock band popular during the 1960s. Its lineup consisted of singers Grace Slick and Marty Balin, guitarists Jorma Kaukonen and Paul Kantner, bassist Jack Casady, and drummer Spencer Dryden. The Shirelles were one of the first girl groups of the late 1950s and early 1960s. The members were Shirley Alston Reeves, Addie "Micki" Harris, Doris Kenner Jackson, and Beverly Lee. Joni Mitchell (b. 1943), folk singer/songwriter who began her career during the late 1960s, incorporated elements of jazz and classical music. She continues to record eloquent songs of personal revelations and sociopolitical commentary.

Stevie Nicks (b. 1948) and Christine McVie (b. 1943) were vocalists and songwriters for Fleetwood Mac, the popular 1970s group whose album *Rumours* (Reprise 3010) is the third best-selling album of all time. It is a classic lineup that also included songwriter/vocalist Lindsey Buckingham, drummer Mick Fleetwood,

Women Inductees in the Rock and Roll Hall of Fame

Year	**Performer**
2000	Bonnie Raitt
1999	The Staple Singers
1999	Dusty Springfield
1998	Mamas and Papas
1998	Stevie Nicks and Christine McVie
1997	Joni Mitchell
1996	The Shirelles
1996	Gladys Knight and the Pips
1996	Grace Slick
1995	Janis Joplin
1995	Martha and the Vandellas
1993	Ruth Brown
1993	Etta James
1991	LaVern Baker
1991	Tina and Ike Turner
1988	The Supremes
1987	Aretha Franklin
Year	**Early Influences**
2000	Billie Holiday
1997	Mahalia Jackson
1990	Gertrude "Ma" Rainey
1989	Bessie Smith
1993	Dinah Washington
Year	**Non-Performer**
1990	Carole King and Gerry Goffin

and bassist John McVie. The Mamas and the Papas were a folk-based, harmony-rich pop group popular in the 1960s who mixed men's (John Phillips, Denny Doherty) and women's (Cass Elliot, Michelle Phillips) voices, with songwriting and arrangements from Phillips. The British pop diva Dusty Springfield (1939–1999) helped the Motown sound take root in the United Kingdom. Her career was remarkably long-lived, as she enjoyed hits in each of the last four decades of the twentieth century. The Staple Singers were a gospel-based soul group who have recorded songs of social activism and religious conviction since the 1950s. The group consists of patriarch Roebuck "Pops" Staples and daughters Mavis, Cleotha, and Yvonne Staples. The most recent inductee, Bonnie Raitt (b. 1949), is a popular singer/guitarist whose work includes pop, rock, and ballads with a serious rooting in the blues. Since she began recording in the 1970s, Raitt has been the recipient of numerous Grammy Awards.

In all, five women performers have been inducted in the Early Influences category. These women are Bessie Smith (1894–1937), Gertrude "Ma" Rainey (1886–1939), Dinah Washington (1924–1963), Mahalia Jackson (1911–1972), and Billie Holiday (1915–1959). Smith was the legendary singer who sang raw, uncut country blues inspired by life in the South. Ma Rainey was one of the first women blues singers. She began recording memorable songs in 1923 about the harsh realities of life in the Deep South. Washington was the most popular black woman recording artist of the 1950s; her music skirted the boundaries of blues, jazz, and popular music. Jackson was a pioneer interpreter of gospel music whose career began in the mid-1930s. Holiday was the pre-eminent jazz singer of her day; she performed and recorded from 1933 to 1958.

In the Non-Performer category, the only woman inductee is Carole King (1990, with Gerry Goffin). Songwriting partners Goffin and King composed a string of classic hits for a variety of artists during the 1960s. During the 1970s King pursued a successful solo career as a singer-songwriter. There are no women inductees in the Sidemen category. The Rock and Roll Hall of Fame and Museum is located in Cleveland, OH.

See also Rock and Popular Music Genres

For Further Reading

Welcome to the Rock and Roll Hall of Fame and Museum. Available: http://www.rockhall.com

Susanna P. Garcia

Rock Music

Despite the comparatively recent arrival of rock music, contemporary women rockers owe a large debt of their success to the early women artists of vaudeville and of the later speakeasies and honky-tonks. In times where working women could choose between the professions of nursing and teaching, these women artists not only secured a place for themselves in the entertainment industry but also publicly assaulted entrenched racial and sexual barriers. Such icons include Tin Pan Alley singer and "Last-of-the-Red-Hot Mammas" Sophie Tucker (1884–1966), and blues singers Gertrude "Ma" Rainey (1886–1939), and Bessie Smith (1894–1937). Jazz singers Ella Fitzgerald (1917–1996) and Billie Holiday (1915–1959) brought the soulful female voice to a genre of music previously dominated by men. Fitzgerald's "scat" vocal technique remains a mainstay of vocal jazz even today. Country singer Patsy Cline (1932–1963) brought women to a place of unprecedented popularity in her genre, although it was Kitty Wells (b. 1918), singing in response to a moralistic Hank Thompson, who emphasized the fact that women would not return to the kitchen in barefooted obedience after the boys returned home from World War II.

Initially, rhythm and blues and rock were identical musics categorized as separate genres only by the race of the band members. Nonetheless the wholesale emancipation of women in "rock" began with the black women "doo-wop" groups of the 1950s. Essentially this music was the "barbershop" music of the black community. It was heavily influenced by blues and gospel and although originally sung *a cappella*, it was hardly ever recorded in this fashion. What is doubly significant is that not only were the singers in these groups black, they were black women. By the end of the decade, girl groups—with or without the doo-wop—were no longer a novelty, and groups such as the Angels, the Ronettes, the Shangri-Las, and the Shirelles enjoyed great success in cross-over markets. But while this music was enjoying wider acceptance, this music also remained politically correct. Good girls were still expected to sit politely at home, "wishing and hoping"—as the song goes. Nevertheless, these girl groups of the 1950s and early 1960s brought women into the performance arena in far greater numbers than ever before. Women were in the front of the band, regardless of what they were singing.

It is precisely what these women sang about that changed so dramatically in the next decade. During the political and social turbulence of the 1960s and into the following decade, front women like Janis Joplin (1943–1970) of Big Brother and the Holding Company and Grace Slick (b. 1939) of Jefferson Airplane did not limit themselves to "proper ladies' topics." These women, often in emotional and electrifying stage performances, took on issues ranging from politics to drugs to sexual freedom. As one might imagine, these artists were both embraced by a generation disillusioned with Vietnam and Watergate and shunned by those not quite ready to hear the criticism and definitely not ready to hear it from women.

Many mainstream recording companies promoted a softer female personality during the 1970s. Following the unashamed commerciality of Connie Francis (b. 1938) and Brenda Lee (b. 1944), who enjoyed a much greater pop following than her counterpart, Patsy Cline, and the interpretive singing of Joan Baez (b. 1941) and Judy Collins (b. 1939) in the early 1970s, boy-girl duos such as Sonny and Cher (b. 1946), Karen (1950–1983) and Richard Carpenter, and the Captain and Tennille kept their material mainstream and profits high. Teaming a woman with her husband or brother lent an air of respectability to women in the music business. These middle-of-the-road duos, as well as solo performers such as Debby Boone (b. 1956), Anne Murray, and Olivia Newton-John, became so mainstream that rock became acceptable even for bubblegum television (*The Partridge Family*) and movie roles (*Grease* [1978] and *You Light up My Life* [1977]).

In spite of this, women musicians of the late 1970s and early 1980s continued to push the envelope. Australian-born singer Helen Reddy (b. 1942) and Linda Ronstadt (b. 1946) continued to sing about equality and the emergence of women into the white-collar work force. Cross-over country-pop star Dolly Parton (b. 1946) both sang the theme song and co-starred in the movie *9 to 5* (1980), a mainstream film about three women who outclass and outsmart their chauvinistic boss. Donna Summer (b. 1948) and Diana Ross (b. 1944), formerly a member of the Supremes and star of the film biography of Billie Holiday, sang of the sexual freedom so associated with the disco era. Women such as Pat Benatar (b. 1953) and the garage-rocking sister-duos Ann and Nancy Wilson (Heart) and Debbi and Vicki Peterson (the Bangles) exhibited an even more aggressive attitude. Not content with merely singing and fronting the group, these women echoed the behavior of early rock pioneers who were men. They slung guitars over their shoulders, and they took center stage with music that they themselves had written.

The decade of the 1980s was perhaps the most significant for women in terms of discovery and experimentation, coinciding with a technological revolution in the music industry. Microchips led to affordable and portable computers and synthesizers, which were readily adopted by professional musicians. Gone were the days of the requisite Hammond B-3 and its Leslie speakers that weighed more than all of the band members combined. Gone, likewise, was the large supporting cast of back-up musicians. The digital age in music had begun, and women were at the forefront. The Eurythmics, a

United Kingdom–based duo fronted by the gregarious and sometimes androgynous Annie Lennox, is credited with the first video presentation of the use of a computer keyboard capable of producing music. Today, with far superior technology available even in the elementary school classroom, the significance is almost impossible to grasp.

In the early stages, music videos were largely concert footage edited for television or stilted scenarios with limited special effects. Almost immediately, however, women musicians featured themselves in positions of power in video storylines and unashamedly broke the rules of propriety and obedience for all to see. Donna Summer sang about an independent woman struggling to make it on her own in "She Works Hard for the Money," Madonna (b. 1958) depicted sexually and financially liberated women in "Like a Virgin" and "Material Girl," and Cyndi Lauper (b. 1953) and Christina Amphlett of the Divinyls programmed songs and videos that ranged from thwarting authority to masturbation in "She Bop," "Girls Just Wanna Have Fun," and "I Touch Myself." These portraits of self-assurance demonstrate how far women had come in a very short period.

The 1980s provided a marriage of music technology and video, fostering a wide variety of experimentation in musical styles and "eye candy"—all delivered directly into our homes by Music Television (MTV). But by the end of the decade, MTV apparently forgot (or, in its defense, purposely turned its back on) the idea of being primarily a purveyor of music video. If video had truly killed the radio star, it was music that was increasingly based on cheap message and novelty that killed the video star. By the late 1980s, women were no longer secondary to their male counterparts. Women artists were seldom seen as part of a boy-girl duo, and many of those who had fronted popular girl groups in the 1980s, such as Belinda Carlisle (b. 1958) of the Go-Go's and Natalie Merchant (b. 1963) of 10,000 Maniacs, pursued successful solo careers.

Contemporary women artists who formerly opened concerts for men artists are now the featured performers and produce cover versions of songs by their male counterparts, like Madonna with the Don McLean song "American Pie." Their lives are documented on screen, in the tabloids, and on VH1; and women artists regularly promote and manage the careers of younger performers and stage their own concert tours such as Lilith Fair. Growth from the confining traditions of the past was necessary and inevitable. Younger emerging women artists like Meredith Brooks continue to sing about the developing persona of women in society in songs such as "Bitch" and artists such as Alanis Morissette (b. 1974) and Melissa Etheridge (b. 1961) continue to write and perform songs that actively resist and overthrow patriarchal and misogynist notions in their exploration of controversial social and cultural themes.

See also Bands, Pop Rock; Barbershop Quartet; Lilith Fair; Rock and Popular Music Genres

For Further Reading

Campbell, Michael. *And the Beat Goes On*. New York: Schirmer Books, 1996.

Szatmary, David. *A Social History of Rock 'n' Roll*. New York: Schirmer Books, 1996.

Thomas Sovík
Donna Dupuy

Rockmore, Clara (1911–1998)

The theremin has enjoyed a recent resurgence of popularity, owing largely to the work and legacy of its primary proponent, performer Clara Rockmore (née Reisenberg). A violin prodigy, at the age of four she became the youngest musician to ever gain admission to the St. Petersburg Conservatory. Later in life Rockmore moved to New York City, where she studied the violin and became interested in the theremin, an early electronic music instrument. She studied the theremin with its inventor, Leon Theremin.

Born on 9 March 1911 in Vilnius, Lithuania, Rockmore was able to apply some of her violin technique to the mastery of this new instrument, but because the theremin is played without being touched directly, she had to invent and develop a unique method of playing. Rockmore was a true virtuosa of the theremin, as much as one can be of any instrument. She was able to command from it passages of extreme subtlety, nuance, and vibrato across all dynamic ranges, and her technique is still taught today. At her suggestion, Leon Theremin made several structural modifications to his designs to improve its articulation.

One of her earliest performances on the theremin was a concert in New York City's Town Hall on 30 October 1934, in which she performed an arrangement of César Franck's Violin Sonata. Her talent brought the theremin into the public spotlight and led to the composition of new works for the instrument, including a concerto by the composer Anis Fuleihan. Her career included performances with the New York Philharmonic, the Philadelphia Orchestra, and the Toronto Symphony. More recently, Rockmore was featured extensively in the documentary *Theremin: An Electronic Odyssey* (1994) by filmmaker Steven M. Martin. Additionally, many of Rockmore's early performances are documented on *The Art of the Theremin* compact disc (Delos DE 1014).

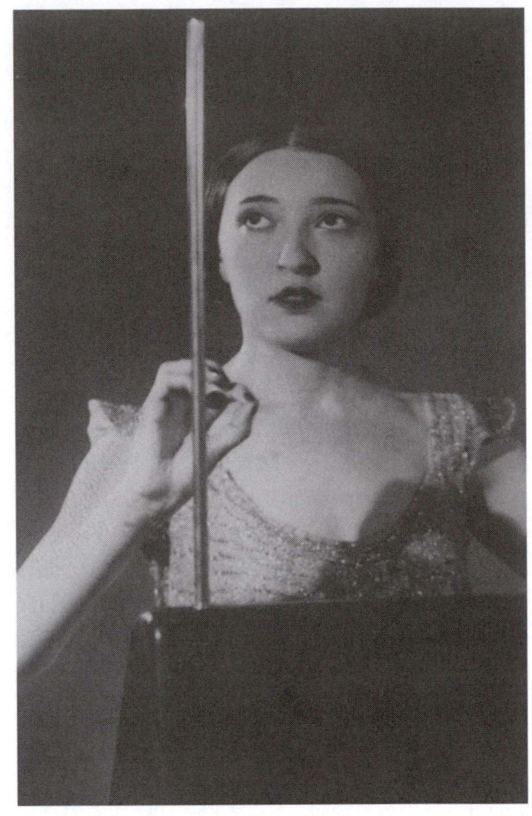

Clara Rockmore. *Photo courtesy of International Piano Archives of Maryland.*

Rockmore passed away in her home in Manhattan on 10 May 1998. The varied repertoire, international interest, and public awareness of the theremin serve as lasting reminders of the legacy and lifetime devotion of its greatest performer.

See also Music Technology; Performer, Live Electronics

For Further Reading

The Art of the Theremin. Delos, 1977. (LP, rereleased on CD later).

Martin, Steven M. *Theremin: An Electronic Odyssey*. Hollywood, CA: Orion Classics, 1994.

Colby Leider

Rodríguez, Albita (1962–)

Cuban singer and songwriter Albita Rodríguez has refashioned the traditional styles of Cuban *guajiro*, or country music. Albita's first recording, *Habrá Música Guajira* (Egrem), was released in Havana in 1988. She moved to Colombia in 1991, where she became very popular and continued to record and even ventured into Colombian genres such as the *cumbia*. In 1993 Albita and her band settled in the United States. An outstanding live performer, Albita became something of a celebrity in Miami, where her performances at a tiny restaurant attracted enthusiastic crowds and show business celebrities.

Born on 6 June 1962, Rodríguez began playing at age 15, and by age 19 she had appeared on Havana's television program *Palmas y Cañas*, which features country-style musicians. Supported by a group that included several women instrumentalists, Albita followed in the tradition of Celina González (b. 1928) but took the music one step further. She altered the traditional country music ensemble by adding a flute, and she produced her own fusion of *guajiro* country music with the Cuban *son*.

In 1995 Albita released her first album in the United States, *No se parece a Nada* (Crescent Moon/Epic 66966). Soon thereafter she and her band began to tour the United States, Spain, Mexico, Colombia, Venezuela, Panama, and Puerto Rico. A second album, *Dicen que* (Sony 67757), followed as Albita's appearances became de rigueur at salsa and Latin jazz venues and festivals throughout the United States.

Albita Rodríguez has developed a very unique sound, which while being faithful to its roots in Cuba's Afro and Spanish traditions has rejuvenated the style of the *guajiro* country genre. She is an excellent singer with a distinct contralto voice, a sound songwriter, and an outstanding performer.

Albita Rodríquez during a 1995 performance. *Photo courtesy of Rose Hartman/Globe Photos.*

See also Latin American Musicians; Multicultural Musics

Raúl Fernández

Ronstadt, Linda Maria (1946–)

Since she began singing professionally at age 14, Linda Maria Ronstadt has won innumerable awards, including seven Grammy Awards in Latin, rock, country, and popular genres. Today, Ronstadt has remained a popular artist for nearly three decades and has sold more than 30 million albums.

Born on 15 July 1946 in Tucson, AZ, of Mexican and German descent, singer-

Linda Maria Ronstadt. *Photo courtesy of Globe Photos.*

songwriter Ronstadt has produced most of her recordings from the Los Angeles area. Ronstadt moved to Los Angeles in 1969 while still a member of the trio the Stone Poneys, but soon thereafter she embarked on a successful solo career. In the early 1980s Ronstadt took time out from her recording career and made her Broadway debut in the production of Gilbert and Sullivan's *Pirates of Penzance* and later starred in the movie production. In 1983 she came back to the recording market with *What's New* (Asylum 60260-2), a collection of pop standards that sold over two million copies. By 1988 she was one of the first rock artists ever to reach Double Platinum sales. During that period she also became the highest-paid woman in rock and roll. Her rock songs "Heart Like a Wheel," "Hasten Down the Wind," and "Living in the U.S.A." became instant classics in the 1970s.

An eclectic artist who has explored various genres of popular music, including country rock, big band, country, rock and roll, standards, opera, and white soul, among others, she began to experiment with the mariachi style in the PBS television production of Luis Valdez's *Corridos* (filmed in San Francisco in 1985) and in guest appearances with mariachis at the annual Tucson International Mariachi Conference. Her fondness for mariachi music stems from the influence of her part-Mexican father, Gilbert Ronstadt, who listened to Mexican *ranchera* songs interpreted by Mexican legends such as Lola Beltrán and Lucha Villa as she was growing up. With her mariachi performances she has brought to the mariachi style an even greater, international level of commercial recognition and diffusion.

Ronstadt's 1988 album *Canciones de mi Padre* (Asylum 60765-2) includes performances by members of three Los Angeles–based mariachi bands: Los Camperos de Nati Cano, Los Galleros de Pedro Rey, and Mariachi Sol de México de José Hernández. A fourth mariachi band involved in the recording, Mexico-based Mariachi Vargas de Tecalitlán, has been recognized as the most longstanding and successful group in the history of mariachi music. This album received a 1989 Grammy Award in the Mexican American category. Her second album of Mexican music, *Más Canciones* (Asylum 61239), was released in November 1991. Mariachi Los Camperos de Nati Cano toured extensively with Ronstadt throughout the United States in 1991. In 1992 she released another album with Spanish material entitled *Frenesi* (Asylum 61383–2).

During her career Ronstadt has recorded with a number of U.S. pop artists, including Aaron Neville, Don Henley, Glen Frey, Bernie Leadon, and Randy Meisner. The trio she formed with Dolly Parton (b. 1946) and Emmylou Harris (b. 1947) has been the most productive and rewarding collaboration for Linda Ronstadt.

See also Latin American Musicians; Multicultural Musics; Rock and Popular Music Genres

For Further Reading

Bego, Mark. *Linda Ronstadt, It's So Easy*. Austin, TX: Eakin, 1990.

Loza, Steven. *Barrio Rhythm: Mexican American Music in Los Angeles*. Urbana and Chicago: University of Illinois Press, 1993.

Orloff, Katherine. *Rock 'n Roll Woman*. Los Angeles: Nash, 1974.

Steve Loza

Ross, Diana (1944–)

Pop diva Diana Ross started on the road to fame as a singer in the Supremes. She later embarked on a solo career that has included singing, recording, and acting and has elevated her to superstar status. Ross, one of the most successful recording artists of all time, is known for her seductive vocal style and outrageous and highly stylized appearance, complete with a wide array of wigs and sequined gowns.

Born on 26 March 1944 in Detroit, MI, Diane Ernestine Ross joined a girl musical group called the Primettes while still in high school. After recording for the Lu-Pine label in 1960, the Primettes were signed to Berry Gordy's Motown Records in 1961. Originally named the Primettes as a sister group to the all-male Primes, they were renamed the Supremes (the Primes had previously signed on with Motown and had been renamed the Temptations). The group included Ross, Florence Ballard (1943–1976), and Mary Wilson (b. 1944). Under Gordy's direction, Ross became the lead singer of the group; and with songs written by Brian and Eddie Holland and Lamont Dozier, the group had a long string of hits throughout the 1960s including "Baby Love," "Where Did Our Love Go?," and "Love Child." In 1967, with the departure of Ballard and the addition of Cindy Birdsong (b. 1939), the group was renamed Diana Ross and the Supremes.

Diana Ross performing in Central Park in July 1983. *Photo © Bettmann/CORBIS.*

Ross left the Supremes in 1970 to pursue a solo career, and she performed frequently in nightclubs and jazz festivals. She landed several movie musical roles in the 1970s, appearing in *Lady Sings the Blues* (1972), *Mahogany* (1975), and *The Wiz* (1978). Her role as Billie Holiday in

Lady Sings the Blues garnered her an Academy Award nomination.

Well known for her glamorous pop and soul persona, Ross has often been criticized for her ultra-theatrical, extravagant performances. The 1981 musical *Dreamgirls* is broadly based on her life with the Supremes and subsequent solo career. Despite these criticisms, Ross has remained very popular to the present day and continues to perform, record, and act. She has written her memoirs, *Secret of a Sparrow*, and a children's book, *When You Dream*. The numerous awards Ross has been honored with include a Grammy in 1970, the 1970 National Association for the Advancement of Colored People Female Entertainer of the Year award, a special 1977 Tony Award, and a 1988 induction into the Rock and Roll Hall of Fame.

See also Rock and Popular Music Genres; Rock and Roll Hall of Fame

For Further Reading

Brown, Geoff. *Diana Ross*. London: Sidgwick and Jackson, 1981.

Ross, Diana. *Secrets of a Sparrow: Memoirs*. New York: Villard Books, 1993.

Taraborrelli, J. Randy. *Call Her Miss Ross: The Unauthorized Biography of Diana Ross*. New York: Carol Publishing, 1989.

Kristina Lampe Shanton

Rowe, Ellen H. (1958–)

Ellen Rowe was the first woman director of jazz studies of a major university program. She began her teaching career in 1981 as a graduate assistant for Rayburn Wright at the Eastman School of Music. In 1984 she was appointed assistant professor of music and director of jazz studies at the University of Connecticut. Rowe joined the faculty of the University of Michigan as associate professor of music and coordinator of the undergraduate jazz studies program in 1996. In addition to her career as a jazz educator, she has been active as an arranger, composer, and jazz pianist. In a field overwhelmingly dominated by men, Rowe emerged not only as a leader in jazz education at the university level but also as a conductor and clinician in the secondary schools.

Rowe was born on 11 November 1958 in Norwalk, CT, and was the daughter of a high school band director, Robert Arnold Rowe, and flutist, Page Grosenbaugh Rowe. Her interest in music began at a young age in a house full of pianists and pianos, and by the time she reached high school she was playing flute and bassoon. While in high school, Rowe studied jazz piano with John Mehegan and began composing.

Rowe's musical influences are Rayburn Wright, who mentored her as a jazz composer and arranger, and Marian McPartland (b. 1918), jazz pianist, who has also mentored Rowe since they first met in 1981. McPartland frequently commissions Rowe to compose and arrange music for her special projects. As a pianist Rowe leads a trio and has also performed with jazz artists Kenny Wheeler, Gene Bertoncini, Tom Harrell, John Clayton, Harvie Swartz, and Jiggs Whigham. She has been a guest on Marian McPartland's *Piano Jazz* show on National Public Radio.

Rowe's compositions include commissions for the Frankfurt Radio Big Band, DIVA Big Band, New Haven Symphony, West German Big Band, Aequalis Chamber Ensemble, London Symphony Orchestra, Rochester Philharmonic, Concordia, and the New York Pro Arte Chamber Players. Compositions by Rowe appear on recordings by DIVA (Leave it to DIVA), the Andrei Ryabov Quartet, the Eastman Jazz Ensemble, and the University of Michigan Jazz Ensemble led by Rowe. Her compositions number over 165 and range from jazz ensemble compositions to film scores.

Rowe has been active as a clinician for jazz workshops for high schools and universities and has presented at the Music Educators National Conference, International Association of Jazz Educators, and the Connecticut Music Educators, Association conferences. In addition, Rowe has adjudicated at numerous high school and college jazz festivals. She has been a member of the jazz faculty at the Banff Centre for the Arts since 1994.

See also Jazz Education; Music Education

For Further Reading

McCord, Kimberly. "The State of the Art Today." In *Sung and Unsung Jazzwomen*. New York: Smithsonian Institution and 651, An Arts Center, 1996.

Kimberly McCord

S

Sacred Music

See Church Music

Sager, Carole Bayer (1947–)

Reportedly the youngest lyricist on Broadway in 1970, Carole Bayer Sager began writing songs when she was 15 years old. She had her first hit at age 19 when Patti LaBelle (b. 1944) and the Bluebells recorded "A Groovy Kind of Love." She went on to win both an Academy Award for Best Song ("Arthur's Theme—Best That You Can Do") in 1982 and a Grammy Award for Song of the Year ("That's What Friends Are For") in 1986. She was voted the Best New Artist in France and Germany by the German Record Academy in 1977. Her Hollywood Walk of Fame star was unveiled on 15 February 2000.

Carole Bayer Sager was born on 8 March 1947 in New York City. She graduated from New York's High School of Music and Art, and in 1967 she completed her B.S. degree in speech and dramatic art at New York University. She married Andrew Sager in 1970, but they subsequently divorced.

She maintained both a professional and romantic relationship with Marvin Hamlisch for several years. Critics reported that their 1979 Broadway hit musical comedy *They're Playing Our Song* was autobiographical and that its story of the crazy personal and professional relationship between a popular composer and his lyricist lover reflected the life of its songwriters. In 1982 Bayer Sager married composer Burt Bacharach and had one son, Christopher Elton. They divorced in 1991. In addition to her songwriting, Sager released several albums of her works, including *Carole Bayer Sager* (Wea International 60617), *Too* (Import 18960), and *Sometimes Late at Night* (Boardwalk 37069). In 1987 she authored the novel *Extravagant Gestures.*

See also Academy Awards; Grammy Award; Singer-Songwriter

For Further Reading

Ganzl, Kurt. *The Musical: A Concise History*. Boston: Northeastern University Press, 1997.

Gottfried, Martin. *More Broadway Musicals since 1980*. New York: Harry N. Abrams, 1991.

Frieda Patrick Davison

Sainte-Marie, Buffy (1941–)

A writer of protest and love songs in the 1960s, Buffy Sainte-Marie (Cree, Piapot

First Nation, Saskatchewan, Canada) is perhaps most widely known for her high-profile television presence representing Native America on the public television program *Sesame Street* in the 1970s. Sainte-Marie's early style was marked by her swift vocal vibrato accompanied by her guitar, with occasional usage of traditional instruments such as the mouth bow. Composer of the 1982 Academy Award–winning song "Up Where We Belong" (from the film *An Officer and a Gentleman*), Sainte-Marie has written many songs that have become classics of folk, country, and popular genres: "Until It's Time for You to Go," "He's an Indian Cowboy in the Rodeo," "Bury My Heart at Wounded Knee," "Moonshot," and "Universal Soldier," which was adopted as an unofficial anthem of the peace movement of the 1960s.

Born on 20 February 1941, Sainte-Marie has a Ph.D. in fine art from the University of Massachusetts. As both a musician and a visual artist, she has served as adjunct professor at York University (Toronto), Indian Federated College (Saskatchewan), and Evergreen State College (WA). She is also artist-in-residence, digital art, at the Institute for American Indian Arts, Santa Fe, NM. Sainte-Marie lectures on women's issues, native government, songwriting, film scoring, digital art, and electronic music.

A dual citizen of both the United States and Canada, Sainte-Marie helped establish a Juno Awards category for the Music of Aboriginal Canada and has received an Award for Lifetime Musical Achievement from the First Americans in the Arts (U.S.). Her enthusiasm for computer technology resulted in her first electronically produced compact disc, *Coincidence and Likely Stories* (Chrysalis F2-21920), and the development of her digital artistic skills, currently displayed both on the World Wide Web and in museums. Sainte-Marie is also the founder of the Cradleboard Teaching Project, a curriculum resource for children designed to deliver accurate cultural information about Native Americans. In 1997 Sainte-Marie received the Order of Canada in recognition for her outstanding lifetime achievement and service.

See also Native American Musicians; Songwriter

For Further Reading

Buffy Sainte-Marie. Available: http://aloha.net/~bsm/

Virginia Giglio

Salt-N-Pepa

The late 1980s witnessed the rise of a new trend in women's rap with the unprecedented style of rap duo Salt-N-Pepa and their DJ, Spinderella. Salt-N-Pepa's first compact disc, *Hot, Cool, & Vicious* (London 422-828363-2), laid the foundation for their tough but feminine image. They followed up with *A Salt with a Deadly Pepa* (London 422-828364-2), *Black's Magic* (London 422-828362-2), and *Very Necessary* (PolyGram 28392), all of which in some way typify the group's dual persona. Although they earned a Grammy Award for the hit "None of Your Business" in 1994, other singles such as "Let's Talk about Sex," "Whatta Man," and "Expression" provide a better example of the positive, pro-feminist message the group espouses.

Cheryl "Salt" James (b. 1964) was raised in Brooklyn, NY; Sandra "Pepa" Denton (b. 1961) was born in Jamaica; and Spinderella, Deidre "Dee Dee" Roper was raised in Queens, NY. Although they were not the first women rappers, Salt-N-Pepa was the first all-women rap group to make a lasting im-

Sandra "Pepa" Denton and Cheryl "Salt" James of the hip hop group Salt-N-Pepa perform at Woodstock '94 in Saugerties, New York, in August 1994. *Photo © Neal Preston/CORBIS.*

pression on the male-dominated rap scene, boasting their own girl DJ, a rarity in itself. Spinderella joined the group in 1987, assuming the stage name from the group's first DJ, Latoya Hanson.

What started out as a college class project launched these girls into the rap spotlight. While attending Queens Burough Community College for a degree in nursing, James and Denton were drafted by Hurby Azor to provide vocals for his class project, a rap recording called "The Showstopper." This recording was a response to the popular rap "The Show," by artist Doug E. Fresh. "The Showstopper" set a precedent for women rappers as equals with their male counterparts. Salt-N-Pepa, self-proclaimed feminists, reveled in their ability to challenge male rappers without sacrificing their femininity.

Their most recent compact disc release, *Brand New* (Red Ant/London 828959), was a collaborative effort featuring such artists as Queen Latifah (b. 1970), Kirk Franklin, Sounds of Blackness, and Sheryl Crow (b. 1962). In addition to a wealth of video, soundtrack, and even movie credits, Salt-N-Pepa are a community-conscious trio using their music to promote AIDS awareness and financial assistance.

Their evolution as a group took a turn in the early 1990s when Salt-N-Pepa assumed creative control over their music. They have continued the trend of drawing on a variety of genres and musical styles, as evidenced by *Brand New*, and they also have continued their positive message of femininity and womanhood in a voice uniquely their own.

See also Rap

For Further Reading

Berry, Venice T. "Feminine or Masculine: The Conflicting Nature of Female Images in Rap Music." In *Cecilia Reclaimed: Feminist Perspectives on Gender and Music*, eds. Susan C. Cook and Judy Tsou. Urbana: University of Illinois Press, 1994.

O'Brien, Lucy. *She Bop: The Definitive History of Women in Rap, Rock, and Soul*. New York: Penguin Books, USA, 1995.

Powell, John. "Salt n Pepa." In *Popular Musicians*, vol. 3, ed. Steve Hochman. Pasadena, CA: Salem Press, 1999.

Roxanne Reed

Scaletti, Carla (1956–)

Composer, harpist, and computer scientist Carla Scaletti has served as principal harpist for both the Lubbock and New Mexico symphony orchestras and is the president of her own music software and equipment corporation. Scaletti has served as a guest professor, composer, and lecturer at Vienna's Universtät für

Musik und darstellende Kunst, at the University of Oregon, at Stockholm's Electronic Music Studio, and at Dartmouth College, and she served as composer-in-residence at the California Institute of the Arts in 1994. Her Kyma Sound Design Station received *Electronic Musician Magazine*'s 1998 Editor's Choice Award, and she has received many other honors, including the International Computer Music Association's Commission Award in 1998 and performances at the Banff, Canada; Aarhus, Denmark; Urbana, IL; and Columbus, OH, International Computer Music Conferences.

Born on 28 April 1956 in Ithaca, NY, she received her B.M. degree from the University of New Mexico (1977), a master's degree in music from Texas Tech University (1979), and subsequently received two advanced degrees from the University of Illinois: a master's degree in computer science, and a doctorate in music composition. Scaletti is the designer of the Kyma language, a sound design computer language, and is also the co-founder (as well as president) of a maker of computer music equipment and software located in Champaign-Urbana's "silicon prairie."

Although her early years of musical study were spent pursuing traditional musical instrument performance, Scaletti has since become much more widely known for her electronic music and for her computer software and language design work. Scaletti credits the *Computer Music Journal* with sparking her interest in computer programming: she discovered the journal in 1978, and frustrated by the issue's articles being beyond her technical grasp, she enrolled in her first programming class and eventually found her way to the University of Illinois.

Her musical output is an interesting mix of pure tape compositions and interactive works for live performer and electronics. Her works in both categories often exhibit their foundation in complexities uncovered in environmental or natural phenomena. For example, *Lysogeny* (1983), for harp and Music 360 generated tape, is based on lysogenic viruses and the spread of information. *Levulose* (1986), a work composed for IMS digital synthesizer and contrabass, is likewise based on the idea of left-handed sugars. In *sunSurgeAutomata* (CDCM Computer Music Series, Vol. 3, Centaur Records, CRC 2045), a tape composition based on cellular automata, various clicks are grouped together into recognizable pitches and rhythms through the use of one-dimensional cellular automata. In the composer's notes to the work she connects this organization to Lewis Thomas's proposal of the thermodynamic inevitability of life on earth and Thomas's suggested correlation between the desire to make music and some sort of recreation of the genesis of life on earth.

See also Music Technology; Software Designer/Programmer

For Further Reading

Scaletti, Carla. "Composing Sound Objects in Kyma." *Perspectives of New Music* 27/1 (1989): 42–69.

———. "Reflections on the 20th Anniversary of CMJ." *Computer Music Journal* 20/3 (1996): 31–35.

Alan Shockley

Schonthal, Ruth (1924–)

Ruth Schonthal is a very significant composer whose career has spanned the second half of the twentieth century. Her compositional style includes traits from both twentieth-century romanticism and twentieth-century trends. This is one of its great strengths; however, her lack of association with a particular school or style of composition has tended to keep her on the musical periphery. Despite this fact and a history of considerable personal hardship, her music is gradually assuming the secure place in the repertoire it deserves.

Ruth Schönthal (she dropped the umlaut when she came to America) was born in Hamburg, Germany, on 27 June 1924. Her family moved to Berlin a year later. Her parents were Viennese and had amateur music backgrounds. As a result, her musical talents were noticed early, and at the age of six she entered the Stern Conservatory. Five years later she was expelled, a victim of increasing German anti-Semitic repression. In 1938 the family emigrated to Stockholm. There she was admitted to the Royal Conservatory, although she met neither the age nor citizenship requirements. Three years later the family emigrated again, this time to Mexico City, where she studied composition with Manuel Ponce. In 1946 she met composer Paul Hindemith, who arranged a scholarship for her at Yale University. Schonthal received her A.B. degree (1948), one of the few Hindemith students to graduate with honors.

In finding her own voice, Schonthal overcame two well-meaning but limiting influences. Her father supported her early career but wanted her to write in a late romantic style. Although she benefited greatly from Hindemith's instruction in terms of harmonic vocabulary and technical facility, his method of composition—planning a movement's structure, then melody and bass line, then filling in the inner voices—was essentially foreign to her. In contrast, Schonthal found it more natural to let inspirations derive from one another in the course of a work. This principle informs such larger works as her First String Quartet. She is able to draw on an astonishing variety of styles and techniques when the need arises: cabaret and operetta in the *Totengesäng*, Latin American music in the *Fiestas y danzas* (available on *Character Sketches by 7 American Women*, Leonarda Records 334), prepared piano sonorities in *Nachklänge*, the Americanisms of the composers Aaron Copland and Roy Harris in the Walt Whitman settings of *By the Roadside*. More often than not, however, these are subsumed into rich textures that simultaneously employ dissonant vertical lines with parallel thirds and sixths, or passionate, improvisatory textures that tend to the nonmetrical. Her compositions are available on several compact discs, including *Diverse Settings—New Works for Clarinet* (Capstone 8641), *Margaret Mills Plays Piano Works by Liebermann and Schonthal* (Cambria Records 1094), and *Vive la Difference* (Leonarda Records 336).

In Mexico City and at Yale, Schonthal had to play piano in bars in order to make ends meet, but she found that the music and the atmosphere inhibited her musical imagination. Settling in New York after graduation, she gradually gave up such work in favor of a strenuous schedule of teaching piano and composition, both privately and at universities, in addition to her own creative work. Her disinclination to self-promotion was compensated for by appreciative colleagues such as composer Paul Creston, who facilitated her professional memberships and publication opportunities. Recognition has come in the form of numerous honors, including the American Society of Composers, Authors and Publishers (ASCAP) awards, Meet the Composer grants, and a finalist place for her opera *The Courtship of Camilla* in the New York City Opera competition. Today she holds appointments at the

Westchester Conservatory, New York University, and State University of New York at Purchase.

See also Classical Music; Jewish Musicians

For Further Reading

Jezic, Diane Peacock. "Ruth Schonthal (b. 1924): Emigré Composer and Teacher." In *Women Composers: The Lost Tradition Found*. New York: Feminist Press, 1988, 183–192.

LePage, Jane Weiner. "Ruth Schonthal: Pianist, Teacher." In *Women Composers, Conductors, and Musicians of the Twentieth Century: Selected Biographies*, vol. 3. Metuchen, NJ: Scarecrow Press, 1988, 235–249.

Steve Luttmann

Selena (1971–1995)

Her talent, endearing personality, and unprecedented level of mainstream success made Selena a role model for many young Mexican American and Latino artists across the United States. Her success in the recording industry helped attract major record labels, which provided opportunities for other aspiring Latino women. She made her first recordings for various small labels when she was a teenager, and in 1986 she was voted Best Female Performer of the Year at the Tejano Music Awards. In 1990 Selena had her first big break when she signed a contract with the Capitol/EMI Latin label.

Born on 16 April 1971 in Lake Jackson, TX, Selena Quintanilla-Perez had a short and tragic but very fruitful and influential career in the United States. Selena made her first public appearances at age nine at her family's restaurant with her own group, Selena and Los Dinos, consisting of Selena and her brothers and sisters. In 1993 and 1994 Selena was awarded the Premio Lo Nuestro prizes for Best Regional Mexican Album, Best Female Singer of the Year, Best Song of the Year, and Best Album of the Year, for her recordings *Entra A Mi Mundo* (EMI Latin 42635) and *Amor Prohibido* (Capitol/EMI Latin H2-28803). Selena also won a 1993 Grammy Award for Best Mexican/American Album for *Selena Live* (EMI Latin 42770). In 1995 she was preparing for her first English-language album when she was shot by the president of her fan club in Corpus Christi, TX. Selena died on 31 March 1995.

Selena at the Grammy Awards in New York City in 1993. *Photo courtesy of S. Moskowitz/Globe Photos.*

The first single released from her English album, *Dreaming of You* (EMI Latin 34123), "I Could Fall in Love," hit number one on the *Billboard* chart in July 1995. This tune, sung predominantly in Spanish, became the best-selling chart debut by a woman artist and is among the 10 best-selling debuts of all time. On

9 March 1999, EMI Latin released a comprehensive greatest-hits package of Selena classics entitled *All My Hits: Todos Mis Exitos* (EMI International 97886), including such hits as “Amor prohibido,” “I Could Fall in Love,” “Tu solo tu,” “I'm Getting Used to You,” “Como la flor,” and “Dreaming of You.” *All My Hits: Todo Mis Exitos, Vol. 2* (EMI International 23332) was released on 29 February 2000 and contains 16 songs, two of which were recorded live from the now-celebrated Astrodome concert in 1995: “No me queda más,” and “Bidi Bidi Bom Bom.”

Two years after Selena was murdered, a major Hollywood feature film about her life opened in theaters around the United States. Directed by Gregory Nava, *Selena* was the first Hollywood film that cast solely Latino actors playing Latino roles. Abraham Quintanilla, Selena's father, made this movie with the help of the Esparza/Katz productions to preserve his daughter's memory. The film earned $27.7 million in ticket sales after a two-week run in U.S. theaters. In 1998, the Quintanilla family built a museum in Corpus Christi, TX, as a memorial to Selena.

See also Latin American Musicians; Multicultural Musics

For Further Reading

Patoski, Joe Nick. *Selena Como la Flor*. Boston: Little, Brown, 1995.

Willis, Jennifer L., and Alberto Gonzalez. “Reconceptualizing Gender through Dialogue: The Case of the Tex-Mex Madonna (Media Representations of Singer Selena Quintanilla-Perez).” *Women and Language* 20/1 (1997): 9–13.

Francisco Crespo

Sembrich-Kochanska, Marcella (1858–1935)

Marcelina Prakseda Sembrich-Kochanska (stage name “Marcella Sembrich”) was a coloratura soprano who triumphed on the operatic stages, especially at the Metropolitan Opera in New York. In her performances Sembrich-Kochanska juxtaposed the highest degree of virtuosity with profound expressiveness. Her enormous repertoire of vocal parts in seven languages included primarily early Italian operas, as well as compositions by Wolfgang Amadeus Mozart, Giacomo Meyerbeer, Giuseppe Verdi, Richard Wagner, and Giacomo Puccini. While performing as a recitalist in Poland, she accompanied herself on the piano in the songs of Frederic Chopin, Wladyslaw Zelenski, Aleksander Zarzycki, and other Polish composers.

She was born on 18 February 1858 in Poland and began studying music with her father, Kazimierz Kochanski, and then continued her education in Lwów, majoring in piano and violin, and graduated from the Conservatory in 1873. Sembrich-Kochanska began her vocal studies on the advice of Franz Liszt; in Vienna she studied piano with J. Epstein and voice with V. Rokitanski. Sembrich-Kochanska also studied voice with G. D. Lamperti and with his father, M. Lamperti, in Milan. Her operatic debut took place in 1877 in Athens as Elvira in *I puritani*; she then performed in Dresden, Vienna, Berlin, Paris, St. Petersburg, Stockholm, London, and Madrid.

In 1883 Sembrich-Kochanska sang at the Metropolitan Opera House in New York for the first time. After touring Europe in 1884–1898 she received a permanent contract from the Metropolitan and performed there from 1898 to 1909. Following her retirement from the operatic stage she taught singing at the Juilliard School of Music in New York and at the Curtis Institute of Music in Philadelphia. She also continued to give song recitals until 1917. At present, two vocal competitions are organized yearly to commemorate her name: one by the American Council for Polish Clubs in Washington, DC, and the other sponsored by Kosciuszko Foundation, An American Center for Polish Culture, in New York.

Numerous historical recordings have been made of Sembrich; among them are *Marcella Sembrich—The Rare Recordings 1903–1919* (Minerva Ita 40), *Marcella Sembrich—The Victor Recordings 1904–08* (Romophone UK 81026), and Prima Voce (Nimbus 7901). Marcella Sembrich-Kochanska died on 11 January 1935.

See also Multicultural Musics; Performer, Vocal

For Further Reading

Arnim, G. *Marcella Sembrich und Herr Prof. Julius Hey*. Leipzig, Germany: 1898.

Damrosch, Walter. *My Musical Life*. New York: Charles Scribner's Sons, 1926.

Owen, H. Goddard. *A Recollection of Marcella Sembrich*. New York: Marcella Sembrich Memorial Assoc., 1950.

Maja Trochimczyk

Semegen, Daria (1946–)

Daria Semegen is internationally recognized as a composer of chamber, orchestral, vocal, dance, electronic, and film music. Her music has received numerous awards and international performances. These include two Broadcast Music, Inc. (BMI), awards, including first place in the Western Hemisphere; six National Endowment for the Arts composition fellowships and interarts grants; a National Academy of Recording Arts and Sciences prize; fellowships to Yaddo, MacDowell Colony, Tanglewood Summer Music School, and the Chautauqua Music School; a National Chamber Music Competition prize; an International Society of Contemporary Music, International Electronic Music Competition prize; and the Pennsylvania Institute for the Arts and Humanistic Studies award. In 1987 she was the first woman to be awarded the McKim Commissions from the Library of Congress for a work for the Theater Chamber Players of Kennedy Center, Washington, DC.

She was born on 27 June 1946 in Bamberg, West Germany. She immigrated to the United States in the early 1950s and became a citizen in 1957. In 1965 she composed *Six Plus*, a pioneering work for six instruments and *musique concrète* sounds on tape while she was a student at the Eastman School of Music (B.M. 1968). During 1968–1969 she was a Fulbright scholar in Warsaw, Poland, studying with composer Witold Lutoslawski. She studied Cologne Radio Studio techniques with Wlodzimierz Kotonski at the Polish Radio Studio. From 1969 to 1971 she studied electronic music with Bülent Arel at Yale University on a fellowship (M.M. 1971). During 1971–1975 she assisted Vladimir Ussachevsky at the Columbia-Princeton Electronic Music Center and worked on the teaching staff at the Center. She joined the faculty of the University of New York at Stony Brook in 1974, where she now serves as professor of composition and director of the electronic music studio.

Semegen's electronic music is orchestral in its conception, characterized by a wide dramatic range with shifting tone colors. She often uses the spatial placement of sound as an organizing element in her work. Her music is often atonal but does not strictly adhere to the rules of 12-tone composition. Her sense of humor is evident in her music, which has been described as avoiding electronic cliché through lighthearted inventiveness. Her recorded compositions include *Mu-*

sic for Violin Solo (Opus One 59), *Electronic Composition No.1* (New World Records 80521), *Spectra Studies* (CRI 443), *Arc: Music for Dancers* (Finnadar SR 9020), and *Electronic Composition No. 2* (1979).

See also Classical Music; Experimental Music; Music Technology

For Further Reading

Hinkle-Turner, A. Elizabeth. "Daria Semegen: Her Life, Work and Music." D.M.A. diss., University of Illinois, 1991.

Semegen, Daria. "Electronic Music: Art beyond Technology." In *On the Wires of Our Nerves: The Art of Electroacoustic Music*, ed. Robin Julian Heifetz. Lewisburg: Bucknell University Press; London and Cranbury, NJ: Associated University Presses, 1989.

Mary Simoni

Separate Spheres—Sexual Aesthetics

The metaphor of separate spheres—sexual aesthetics describes the dualism of private versus public domains. Traditionally, women's activities have been linked to the private, domestic sphere, whereas those of men have been located in the public. The designation of private and public spheres refers not only to physical location and status within a society, but also to epistemology. The private sphere, with its restrictions and limitations, suggests boundaries to knowledge, whereas the public sphere implies unbounded knowledge and freedoms. The idea of women's and men's contrasting "worlds" is not limited to a single generation or society, nor was it new to the twentieth century; the division between private and public was present in ancient Greece. American usage of the term became common after World War II, when Alexis de Tocqueville's *Democracy in America* (1840) was widely reprinted and read as a classic history text. The second volume of this work considers the status of women and asserts that American women's activities occurred within a narrow domestic circle. Historians during the 1940s found de Tocqueville's ideas helpful in explaining American antebellum society, and separate spheres, became a "historical trope" or figure of speech used to discuss women's role in American history (Kerber, 10).

The approach to the term has changed since the 1950s. During the 1960s and early 1970s, some historians viewed separate spheres as a significant theme in women's historical experiences. In the later 1970s, ideas of "sisterhood" became prominent, along with the sentiment that a separate sphere or differentiated "women's culture" was potentially empowering for women. Since 1980, although still in common usage, the metaphor of separate spheres has been recognized as a rhetorical construction and its utilization as a metaphor has been questioned. Unfortunately, "separate spheres" is often used carelessly, employed simultaneously to mean "an ideology *imposed on* women, a culture *created by* women and a set of boundaries *expected to be observed* by women" (Kerber, 17). Explanations behind the separation of women's and men's spheres are numerous. Some argue that biological facts such as childbirth and lactation, together with the woman's traditional role as nurturer, have accounted for women's relegation to the home. Others employ a Marxist approach, viewing women's domestic "place" as a social construction that serves the interest of the dominant class while hiding the inequality of social and economic benefits for women and men.

The making of Western art music, which occurs in both private and public spheres, has also been traditionally linked to gender; women's musical participation has been viewed as taking place in the private sphere. Since the mid-nineteenth century the public realm in Western art music has been elevated in esteem and privilege over the private, which leads to several problems. First, women's association with the "lower" and less auspicious level of musical activity is disputable. Many women have had success in the public musical sphere. Further, those who remain private musicians, whether or not by choice, are not necessarily less talented or ambitious than their male counterparts in the public sphere. Second, the private sphere often goes unrecognized as a positive, flourishing musical space. Many American parlors at the turn of the twentieth century were egalitarian atmospheres for both women and men performers and listeners. Moreover, the family tradition of a musical parlor was often passed matriarchally from mother to daughter to granddaughter, instituting an important legacy of musical learning. Third, the field of musicology has often underscored the hierarchy of public over private musical production, in affirming the values of public structures and canonical (male) composers and their works while deemphasizing or ignoring more private ventures that often involve women. The above issues have led feminist musicologists like Marcia J. Citron (b. 1945) to suggest an "elimination of public and private as realms of normative or prescribed societal activity" (Citron, 102). Indeed, what constitutes public and private today is blurred. Even as more women become professional performers, conductors, and composers, there are many women whose so-called "public" roles remain fairly private, in a gray area of positions such as music librarian, patron, or educator.

In music criticism the notion of separate spheres, extended to genres, has particularly affected women composers via sexual aesthetics, which associates symphonies, operas, and other large-scale genres with the public sphere of men, and songs, chamber music, and small-scale genres with women and the private domestic sphere. Women who compose music deemed "outside" their sphere traditionally had to face criticism that linked both musical virtues and vices to their female gender. A 1903 critique of the New York Metropolitan Opera's performance of the opera *Der Wald* by the English composer Ethel Smyth praises her for successfully composing "like a man." Smyth's strong, meritorious foray in the operatic genre was not acceptable as a woman's creation, so it was framed in male terms. Sexual aesthetics also plays out in criticism of the American composer Amy Marcy Cheney Beach's (1867–1944) works, which include a mass, an opera, a piano concerto, and the *Gaelic Symphony in E Minor*, op. 32 (1896). Hearing the premiere of the *Gaelic Symphony* by the Boston Symphony Orchestra, critics who were men described it as overly virile and strenuous, both features supposedly endeavoring to compensate for the innate femininity of its composer. Beach's career also reflects patriarchal notions of woman's place based on marital status. During her marriage to a prominent Boston physician, Beach concentrated on composition and wifely duties, leaving aside her public performing career as a pianist. After her husband's death she returned to a more public career on the performing stage, embarking on concert tours in Europe and the United States.

Today, women's musical activities often continue to be shaped by the metaphor of separate spheres and judged in terms of sexual aesthetics. An imbalance persists between women and men in private and public positions alike; the majority of high-profile positions, particularly those of conductors, music scholars, and composers, continue to be held by men. One public arena openly and successfully occupied by women is the realm of popular music. Powerhouses like Madonna (b. 1958) produce successive hits, and Sarah McLachlan (b. 1968) instituted Lilith Fair, a tremendously popular musical event that spotlighted the woman musician and celebrated women's musical culture.

Ultimately, private and public spheres do not form a factual dualism that explains or summarizes women's and men's activities, musical or otherwise. Complicated by issues of power, commerce, and social convention, the metaphor of private and public spheres is tenuous and should be used with caution. More important for women in music today is the choice of musical activity according to their own desires and talents, not according to a constructed paradigm of private versus public.

See also Music Education; Music Librarian; Patronage

For Further Reading

Borroff, Edith. "An American Parlor at the Turn of the Century." *American Music* 4/3 (1986): 302–308.

Citron, Marcia. J. *Gender and the Musical Canon.* Cambridge: Cambridge University Press, 1993.

Kerber, Linda K. "Separate Spheres, Female Worlds, Woman's Place: The Rhetoric of Women's History." *Journal of American History* 75/1 (1988): 9–39.

Lynette Miller Gottlieb

Sexual Aesthetics

See Separate Spheres—Sexual Aesthetics

Shenandoah, Joanne

Composer, songwriter, and singer Joanne Shenandoah is one of the most significant Native American musicians in the twentieth century. She attributes her musical gift to her upbringing as a member of the Wolf Clan, Oneida Nation, Iroquois Confederacy. Having received the Oneida name Tekalihwa: khwa (TEK-YA-WHA-WHA), meaning "She Sings," her music consists for the most part of peaceful, accessible arrangements of Iroquois-rooted melodies and texts. Her mellow, flute-like voice combined with traditional instruments such as drum, rattles, and flute became familiar to audiences in the 1980s through the popular television program *Northern Exposure* and the film *Indian in the Cupboard* (1995). Her music was also a feature of *How the West Was Lost* (Discovery Channel) and the Public Broadcasting System's productions "Honorable Nations," "This Land Is Our Land," "Everything Has a Spirit," and "Fly with Eagles."

Shenandoah's commitment to the preservation of First Nations music resulted in the founding in 1992 of Round Dance Productions, a Native American traditional music archive and arts center. A featured performer at President Clinton's inaugurations in 1993 and 1997, Shenandoah was also honored with a Pulitzer Prize nomination for her 1994 song "Ganondagan." Additional recordings include *Peacemaker's Journey* (Silver Wave SD/SC 923), *Matriarch* (Silver Wave SD 913), and *Life Blood* (Silver Wave SD/SC 809). In 1998 she won the Native American Music Award in the category of Best Female Artist and contributed to a collection of Iroquois traditional stories. Her compact disc *Orenda* (Silver Wave SD 918) won the 1999 Native American

Music Award for Best Traditional Recording.

See also Native American Musicians

For Further Reading

Joanne Shenandoah: Native American Singer, Songwriter, and Performer. Available: http://www.joanneshenandoah.com

Shenandoah, Joanne. *Skywoman: Legends of the Iroquois*. Santa Fe, NM: Clear Light Publishers, 1999.

Virginia Giglio

Shields, Alice Ferree (1943–)

Alice Ferree Shields distinguished herself as one of the earliest and most significant women composers of electro-acoustic music in the United States. Any list of the people working at the Columbia-Princeton Electronic Music Center (EMC) reads like a roll call of the pioneers of electronic music: names of composers like Otto Luening, Vladimir Ussachevsky, Milton Babbitt, Mario Davidovsky, and Charles Wuorinen always appear. But what is missing from many of these descriptions are the names of women who were also instrumental to the New York electronic music world and to the Columbia-Princeton Center. Foremost among these is Alice Shields.

Born on 18 February 1943 in New York City, Shields entered Columbia as an undergraduate studying music and literature in 1961 (B.S. in music). From 1965 to 1982 she served first as a technical instructor and later as associate director of the Columbia-Princeton EMC. She received her D.M.A. in composition from Columbia in 1975 (in all likelihood making her the first woman at Columbia to do so); and in the early 1970s while she was composing and performing her own works such as her electronic piece *The Transformation of Ani* (available on *American Master—Pioneers of Electronic Music*, Composers Recordings Inc. 611) and her chamber operas *Odyssey 2* and *Odyssey 3*, Shields was also singing in standard opera repertoire. She performed roles in operas by Wolfgang Amadeus Mozart, Guiseppe Verdi, Richard Wagner, and Richard Strauss. Eventually she served as soloist in many illustrious companies, including the New York City Opera, the Opera Society of Washington, DC, Wolf Trap Opera, Yale University's prestigious Yale-at-Norfolk Festival, and the Metropolitan Opera's Studio.

Alice Shields's 1970 tape composition *The Transformation of Ani* makes clear the cross-over between her career as a mezzo-soprano and her work as a composer, and this early work aptly displays many of the common traits of her work even to the present day. *The Transformation of Ani* takes its text from an ancient culture's ritual practice—here, from the Egyptian *Book of the Dead*. Nearly all the sounds used in the composition are derived from the composer's own voice: she manipulates recordings of her own performances (singing and reading) of the text. Each letter of E. A. Wallis Budge's English translation of the hieroglyphic text is assigned a pitch, and each hieroglyph is linked to a short phrase of more indefinite pitch. With these two foundations for the piece defined, Shields improvised on them to create the non-text elements in the piece.

Since 1990 Shields has immersed herself in classical Indian music, making significant use of the traditional Bharata Natyam dance-drama (from South India) in several ways: borrowing metrical cycles and choreography, and using texts in Sanskrit and in Hindi in many of her chamber and operatic works. Shields's 1993 opera *Apocalypse* (Composers Recordings Inc. 647) is an electronic opera for both live and recorded singers, choreographed with movement patterns taken from the Bharata Natyam.

For Shields, singing and composing seem to be one; there is no clear demarcation of a division between performing and writing music. Almost all of her works, whether composed for live performers or intended to be sounded by tape over loudspeakers, include the human voice in some way; usually the vocal source is Shields herself. She has composed nine opera or music theater pieces and a significant number of vocal works and electronic pieces using processed vocal sounds as the primary sound source. Shields's work as a singer and composer has been recognized in many ways, including a New Jersey Council on the Arts grant, two National Endowment for the Arts grants, and residencies at Brooklyn College and at New York City's Pass Studio.

See also Classical Music; Music Technology

For Further Reading

Cohen, Aaron. *International Encyclopedia of Women Composers*, 2d ed., rev. and enl. New York and London: Books and Music, 1987.

Alan Shockley

The Shirelles

The Shirelles, the first of the internationally successful and influential American all-girl vocal groups, defined the girl-group sound of the late 1950s and early 1960s and placed six singles on the Top 10 charts between 1960 and 1963. They bridged both the uptown New York pop-soul and "doo-wop" styles, combining rhythm and blues with pop rock.

As high school classmates in Passaic, NJ, the Shirelles sang together and were discovered and later managed by Florence Greenberg, the mother of a classmate. Their early songs, on the Scepter label, featured the writing of Luther Dixon as well as top Brill-Building songwriters like Van McCoy, and the Bacharach-David and Goffin-King teams. Their biggest hits include "Dedicated to the One I Love," "Baby It's You," "Mama Said," "Foolish Little Girl," "Soldier Boy," and their best-known song, "Will You Love Me Tomorrow?" There are numerous albums by the Shirelles, including *Tonight's the Night* (Scepter 501), *Baby It's You* (Collectables 9204), and *Foolish Little Girl* (Sundazed 6017).

Their tunes "Boys" and "Baby It's You" were featured by the Beatles on their first album, and the film *It's a Mad, Mad, Mad, Mad World* (1963) included their songs. But after 1963 the Shirelles were unable to come up with megahits. However, they recorded well into the 1970s, sometimes as a trio without Doris Kenner, and adopting a more soul-oriented sound. In 1982 Addie Harris died from a heart attack, and the remaining members separated, each forming their own versions of the Shirelles, which toured sporadically into the 1990s.

See also Rock and Popular Music Genres; Rock Music

For Further Reading

Hitchcock, H. Wiley, and Stanley Sadie (eds.). *New Grove Dictionary of American Music*. New York: Grove's Dictionaries of Music, 1986.

Brad Eden

Shocked, Michelle (1962–)

Singer-songwriter Michelle Shocked is one of the most versatile popular musicians of the twentieth century. Throughout her career she has performed in styles ranging from punk to bluegrass. Shocked came to fame in 1986 when Peter Lawrence, a British producer, heard her at the Kerrville Folk Festival (TX). He asked if she would perform a few songs so he could record them on his Sony Walkman. This recording became *The Texas Campfire Tapes* (Mercury 834581-2), her first album, which soared to the top of British charts and caught the attention of the Mercury recording label.

Shocked was born Karen Michelle Johnston on 24 February 1962 in Dallas, TX. The daughter of a schoolteacher, "Dollar" Bill Johnston, who played mandolin, and a Mormon fundamentalist mother, Shocked lived with her mother and stepfather until 1979. At the age of 16 she ran away from the family's Gilmer, TX, home to San Francisco to live with her father, through whom she became familiar with the music of Leadbelly, Doc Watson, Big Bill Broonzy, Randy Newman, Guy Clark, and others. Her father also took her to blues jams and bluegrass festivals. She spent 1981–1983 studying at the University of Texas at Austin, but in 1983 she dropped out of school, moved to San Francisco, and became involved in squatter activity and hardcore punk music. She returned to Austin, where her mother had her admitted for a month to a psychiatric hospital. She was released, homeless, institutionalized again, and eventually jailed for political protesting. She changed her name and moved to New York in the mid-1980s. In 1984 she continued on to Amsterdam as a political protest to Ronald Reagan's re-election. However, her experience in Europe turned brutal when she was raped, and Shocked returned to the United States in 1986.

Shocked has always included her political ideologies in her songwriting. She has retained autonomy in her career and has been leery of allowing others to determine which direction her music should take. She was initially untrusting of Pete Anderson, who produced her first Mercury recordings, *Short Sharp Shocked* (Polygram 834924) and *Captain Swing* (Polygram 838878). Michelle Shocked has always had an interest in diverse musical genres that have precluded her from being pinpointed as a singer-songwriter of only one particular style. Her album *Arkansas Traveler* (Polygram 512101) features this diversity as well as the works of other well-known musicians like Doc Watson, Norman Blake, the Red Clay Ramblers, Bela Fleck, Taj Mahal, Clarence "Gatemouth" Brown, and Alison Krauss (b. 1971). Shocked produced this album herself. She has lived in Los Angeles and in New Orleans and claims an interest in gospel, blues, creole, funk, rhythm and blues, soul, and jazz. In 1995 she filed a lawsuit and left her contract with Polygram/Mercury Records, which refused to release her music because of its stylistic diversity. She claimed that Mercury only had an interest in promoting her as a folk-pop artist. During a concert she gave on 9 November 1996 at Irving Plaza in New York, she performed a variety of styles from funk to bluegrass, boldly claiming that she would never look back. She released *Kind Hearted Woman* (Private Music 82145) on her own. Her latest album is *Good News* (Mood Swing 162044-4W1-8049), released in 1998.

See also Rock and Popular Music Genres; Singer-Songwriter

For Further Reading

Larkin, Colin (ed.). *Encyclopedia of Popular Music*, vol. 6, 3rd ed. London: MUZE UK, Ltd., 1998.

Romanowsi, Patricia, Holly George-Warren, and Jon Pareles (eds.). *The New Rolling Stone Ency-*

clopedia of Rock and Roll. New York: Fireside Rockefeller Center, 1995.

Susan Epstein

Sills, Beverly (1929–)

Soprano Beverly Sills revolutionized the American opera scene by becoming one of the most prominent opera stars from the United States who did not first establish a reputation in Europe or with the Metropolitan Opera. A born actor with a soaring coloratura voice, she paved the way for future young American singers to build a career in the United States. In addition, through her efforts, opera in America has gained more acceptance and popularity.

Born on 25 May 1929 in Brooklyn, NY, as Belle Silverman, Beverly Sills exhibited her performing talent as early as age three when she sang on commercial radio. At the age of seven Sills began voice training with Estelle Liebling and decided very early that she wanted to be an opera singer. At age 16 she traveled with a Gilbert and Sullivan repertory tour, and in 1947 she made her operatic debut with the Philadelphia Opera Company. Sills actually began her career in 1951 when she sang the role of Violetta in *La Traviata* with impresario Charles Wagner's traveling opera company. She sang with the San Francisco Opera Company (1953) and made her debut with the New York City Opera in *Die Fledermaus*

Beverly Sills performing a scene from the opera *Manon* in 1969. *Photo courtesy of Bernard Gotfryd/Archive Photos.*

(1955). Although she sang many different roles with the New York City Opera, the turning point of her career occurred when she sang Cleopatra in Georg Friederich Handel's *Giulio Cesare* (1966). This performance established her as a star.

Following Sills's triumph at the New York City Opera, she was offered the role of Pamina in Gioacchino Rossini's *Le siege de Corinthe* at La Scala (1969). Her performance was such a success that she was asked to sing in major opera houses all over the world. On 8 April 1975 she made her debut as Pamina at the Metropolitan Opera in a new production of *Le siege de Corinthe*. Numerous recordings have been made of Sills's many performances; historical compact disc reissues include *Beverly Sills—Plaisir d'amour* (Sony Classics 60576), *Handel: Julius Caesar* (BMG/RCA Victor 6182), and *Verdi: La Traviata* (EMD/EMI Classics 69827).

Although she was an extraordinarily busy and successful performer, Sills decided to retire from singing in 1979 at age 50 to become director of the New York City Opera. Unaware of the City Opera's serious financial problems when she accepted the position, she was forced to spend much of her first few years raising money for its support. During those first years as the director, Sills introduced the projection of English supertitles over the stage to help American audiences understand the words and action onstage. By 1986 the New York City Opera was financially secure. In 1994 Sills accepted a new challenge as co-chairperson for the Lincoln Center for the Performing Arts, the first performing artist to serve in this position. Here she has worked with the Lincoln Center's various opera companies, theaters, ballets, orchestra, library, and film society and has contributed to artistic decisions. She is also active outside of music, serving as a director or member on several corporations and boards and working with the March of Dimes.

See also Performer, Vocal

For Further Reading

"Beverly Sills: The Fastest Voice Alive." *Time* 98 (22 November 1971): 74–76, 81–82.

Blumenthal, Ralph. "Beverly Sills, at 66, Stars in her Grandest Role." *New York Times* (13 February 1996): Sec. C: 13, 18.

Sills, Beverly. *Bubbles: A Self-Portrait*. Indianapolis: Bobbs-Merrill, 1976.

Jenny Williams

Silverman, Belle

See Sills, Beverly

Simone, Nina (1933–)

Nina Simone is an eccentric, feminist, politically active jazz singer, and pianist. Known as "The High Priestess of Soul," Simone is actually adept at jazz, gospel, rhythm and blues, and popular music styles, all of which she incorporates into her eclectic but individual performances. Her most admired recordings include many songs covered from other sources: "I Loves You Porgy" (from George Gershwin's opera *Porgy and Bess*), "Forbidden Fruit" (Oscar Brown Jr.), "To Love Somebody" (BeeGees), and "My Baby Just Cares for Me" (Walter Donaldson and Gus Kahn).

Nina Simone was born Eunice Waymon, on 21 February 1933 in Tyron, NC. She grew up in a middle-class family and took piano lessons as a child with prominent local piano teachers. Music became important to her, and she accompanied at church and in school. After high school Simone studied piano at the

Juilliard School with Vladimir Sokhaloff and others on a scholarship. She moved to Philadelphia in the mid-1950s, performing in jazz clubs, and then moved to New York to perform and record there and in Atlantic City. She released *Little Girl Blue* (Bethlehem 3004) on Bethlehem Records in 1958, then *The Amazing Nina Simone* (Colpix SCP-407) on the Colpix label the next year. She recorded with Phillips in 1963 and with RCA in 1966.

As her fame grew she began performing in New York City's Town Hall, in Carnegie Hall, and in smaller clubs in Greenwich Village. She traveled extensively, performing throughout Europe and in Nigeria. She had married and divorced in 1958, but she married Andrew Stroud in 1961 and gave birth to a daughter, Lisa. Simone's growing political militancy and concern with racism contributed to her divorce in 1970 and brought her into self-imposed exile in Europe. She settled in southern France, where she currently lives. Simone acted in and performed music for the film *Point of No Return* (1993).

Rhino Records recently reissued Simone's Colpix recordings under the title *Anthology—The Colpix Years* (Rhino 72567), and RCA issued *Saga of the Good Life and Hard Times* (RCA 66997), which includes many of her previously unreleased live and studio performances from the late 1960s.

See also Blues; Jazz

For Further Reading

Moroff, Diane. "Nina Simone." In *Contemporary Musicians*, vol. 11. Detroit: Gale Research, 1994, 228–231.

Simone, Nina, and Stephen Cleary. *I Put a Spell on You: The Autobiography of Nina Simone*. New York: Pantheon Books, 1991.

Stephen Fry

Singer-Songwriter

A singer-songwriter writes and performs his or her own music, frequently employing subdued, understated scoring such as solo voice with either piano or acoustic guitar accompaniment. Lyrics tend to be literate and sometimes poetic—often emotive, confessional, romantic, and highly personal in subject matter and feel. Although some of these individuals have enjoyed significant chart success, well-crafted albums, not hit singles, are normally the artist's primary goal.

The initial heyday of singer-songwriters spanned a 10-year period lasting from approximately 1968 to 1977. Performers during this era primarily fell into two categories: those influenced by Tin Pan Alley genres such as the Broadway and the Brill Building pop, and those influenced by folk and allied genres. The major women exponents of the Tin Pan Alley style were Carole King (b. 1942) and Laura Nyro (1947–1997). Nyro experienced minimal chart success with her self-performed work, but her best albums, such as *Eli and the 13th Confession* (Columbia CK-9626) and *New York Tendaberry* (Columbia CK-9737), garnered significant critical acclaim and proved influential on singer-songwriters of the early 1980s. King (in tandem with then-partner Gerry Goffin) was in fact one of the most important of the Brill Building tunesmiths. In the late 1960s she moved to Los Angeles and embarked on a highly successful solo career, releasing perhaps the best-selling singer-songwriter album of all time, *Tapestry* (Epic EK-34946), and a host of charting singles, including "It's Too Late," "So Far Away," and "Jazzman." Other notables in this style included Melissa Manchester (b. 1951) and Dory Previn (b. 1929).

The second group of women singer-songwriters, those influenced by folk and allied genres, may be considered direct descendents of Bob Dylan, Joan Baez (b. 1941), Judy Collins (b. 1939), Buffy Sainte-Marie (b. 1941), and Peter, Paul, and Mary. The most important exemplars of this approach were Joni Mitchell (b. 1943) and Carly Simon (b. 1945). Mitchell, a Canadian who relocated in California, produced a lengthy string of first-rate albums, including *Blue* (Reprise 2-2038), *For the Roses* (Asylum 2-5057), and *Court and Spark* (Asylum 2-1001), and charted with such singles as "Big Yellow Taxi," "You Turn Me On, I'm a Radio," and "Help Me." Simon had even more commercial success than Mitchell, especially with the songs "Anticipation," "You're So Vain," and "The Right Thing to Do"; her finest album was *No Secrets* (Elektra 75049-2). Other North American notables in this vein included Americans Janis Ian (b. 1951), Phoebe Snow (b. 1952), and Wendy Waldman, and Canadians Kate and Anna McGarrigle. Some of Bonnie Raitt's (b. 1949) earlier work, despite notable blues influence, also belongs here, as does the proto-Goth *oeuvre* of former Velvet Underground chanteuse Nico (1938–1988).

The late 1970s saw significant erosion in popularity of the singer-songwriter movement, mainly because of the ascendancy of disco and punk. At this point, Mitchell's output lessened and became highly jazz-influenced, Simon's work turned increasingly toward pop and film music, King's later albums showed a slackening in sales, and Nyro experienced lengthy dry spells. Despite this, a few U.S. artists found success between 1977 and 1985. Carole Bayer Sager (b. 1947), one of the last Tin Pan Alley–style singer-songwriters, released three highly respected albums: a self-titled debut (Elektra 1100), *Too* (Elektra 151), and *Sometimes Late at Night* (Casablanca 33237), and a few of her self-performed singles, "Stronger than Before," and "You're Moving Out Today," attained popularity. The work of Rickie Lee Jones (b. 1954) proved highly eclectic, showing influences of Nyro, Tom Waits, jazz, beat poetry, and other entities; albums such as *Rickie Lee Jones* (Warner Brothers 2-3296) and *Pirates* (Warner Brothers 2-3432) received critical and commercial notice, and she charted with the single "Chuck E.'s in Love."

A second important groundswell of singer-songwriters, mainly American and mostly women, began in the late 1980s and continues today. From a purely musical standpoint, this generation of artists as a rule showed significant kinship to the 1970s folk ethos of Joni Mitchell and partial affinity to the do-it-yourself aesthetic of U.S. college radio bands; over time, the latter approach became increasingly prominent. A few were more strongly influenced by blues, pop, rock, or country styles. They frequently wrote socially conscious, sometimes overtly feminist lyrics as well as ones about personal matters—the latter at times expressed in an earthy, not romantic, manner. The first notables of this later period had relatively sparse outputs but strongly prosperous careers. Suzanne Vega's (b. 1959) literate, highly regarded initial albums, one self-titled (A&M 75021-5072-2), the other *Solitude Standing* (A&M 75021-5136-2), spawned singles such as "Luka" and "Tom's Diner." Like Vega's, Tracy Chapman's (b. 1964) first two albums, *Tracy Chapman* (Elektra 60774-2) and *Crossroads* (Elektra 60888-2), had significant chart impact, featuring the songs "Fast Car" and "Talkin' 'Bout a Revolution;" Chapman and Britain's Joan Armatrading (b.

1950) were the two major women singer-songwriters of color.

The success of Vega and Chapman opened the door for a wide range of performers in the genre, especially America's Tori Amos (b. 1963), Shawn Colvin (b. 1956), Sheryl Crow (b. 1962), Melissa Etheridge (b. 1961), and Liz Phair (b. 1967), as well as Canada's Sarah McLachlan (b. 1968) and Alanis Morissette (b. 1974). Amos's intense songs displayed clear affinity to that of Mitchell and England's Kate Bush; her albums *Little Earthquakes* (Atlantic 82358-2) and *Under the Pink* (Atlantic 82567) gained much attention, as did the songs "Me and a Gun," "God," and "Cornflake Girl." Mitchell's work also notably influenced Colvin's estimable Grammy Award–winning albums *Steady On* (Columbia CK-45209) and *A Few Small Repairs* (Columbia 67119); her best-remembered singles were "Sunny Came Home" and "I Don't Know Why." McLachlan's music owed more to alternative rock and pop than these two; her albums *Fumbling Towards Ecstasy* (Arista 18725) and *Surfacing* (Arista 18970) sold well, as did the singles "I Will Remember You" and "Possession;" she also organized the first of several Lilith Fair package tours, which would become a spotlight for important and up-and-coming acts in the genre. Containing some of this style's most ribald lyrics, Phair's work was even more obviously indebted to the indie-rock movement; her first album, *Exile in Guyville* (Matador 51), was praised by critics and aficionados and contained the single "Never Said." Morissette transformed herself from a dance-pop stylist to a singer-songwriter, and her work thereafter betrayed a frothy pop sensibility; her best-selling album *Jagged Little Pill* (Maverick/Reprise 45901) sported hits such as "You Oughta Know," "Hand in My Pocket," and "All I Really Want." Crow's work also had a strong ear for popular success but showed more of a blues and country influence; her most notable albums, *Tuesday Night Music Club* (A&M 314-540126-2) and *Sheryl Crow* (A&M 540587), contained such charting singles as "All I Wanna Do," "Strong Enough," and "If It Makes You Happy." Etheridge's gutsy music aspired to a more rootsy rock-oriented approach that proved equally chart-friendly; albums such as *Brave and Crazy* (Island 422-842302-2) and *Yes I Am* (Island 422-848 660-2) gained notice, as did the singles "If I Wanted To" and "I'm the Only One." Mitchell's career experienced a renaissance at this time with *Night Ride Home* (Geffen GEFD-24302) and *Turbulent Indigo* (Warner Brothers 45786).

Other notable U.S. singer-songwriters of varying types include Fiona Apple (b. 1977), Tracy Bonham, Edie Brickell (b. 1966), Jonatha Brooke, Kate Campbell (b. 1961), Rosanne Cash (b. 1955), Paula Cole, Catie Curtis, Iris DeMent (b. 1961), Ani DiFranco (b. 1970), Kristin Hersh (b. 1966), Jewel (b. 1974), Lucy Kaplansky (b. 1960), Patty Larkin, Christine Lavin, Mary Lou Lord, Laura Love, Lois Maffeo, Aimee Mann (b. 1960), Barbara Manning, Natalie Merchant (b. 1963), Joan Osborne, Holly Palmer, Sam Phillips (b. 1962), Rosanne Raneri, Patti Rothberg, Michelle Shocked (b. 1962), Kendra Smith, Syd Straw, Tanita Tikaram (b. 1969), Norma Waterson, Ilene Weiss (b. 1953), Cheryl Wheeler (b. 1951), Dar Williams, Lucinda Williams (b. 1953), and Victoria Williams; and Canada's k.d. lang (b. 1961), Mary Margaret O'Hara, and Jane Siberry (b. 1955). Mention should also be made of all-women groups whose work lies within this style, such as the Indigo Girls and the Roches.

See also Lilith Fair; Rock and Popular Music Genres; Songwriter

For Further Reading

Berman, Leslie. "Charmed Circle: Folksingers and Singer-Songwriters." In *Trouble Girls: The Rolling Stone Book of Women in Rock*, ed. Barbara O'Dair. New York: Random House, 1997, 125–135.

Mellers, Wilfrid. *Angels of the Night: Popular Female Singers of Our Time*. New York: Basil Blackwell, 1986.

Woodworth, Marc (ed.). *Solo: Women Singer-Songwriters in Their Own Words*. New York: Delta, 1998.

David Cleary

Ska

Ska was originally a Jamaican dance music, fusing American rhythm and blues with a traditional style, *mento*. However, starting in the early 1960s, ska spread to the United Kingdom through West Indian immigration and is now popular in many countries. Rocksteady and reggae are two later styles that are rooted in ska. Ska is generally considered to have enjoyed three "waves" of popularity. The third wave, which at the end of the 1990s was in full swing, is strongest in the United States and Canada. Women are well represented in all roles in third wave ska, including instrumentalists, vocalists, songwriters, and producers. Second wave ska, centered in England, was less gender-balanced, though a number of all-women bands were prominent; and first wave ska, which was based in Jamaica, featured few women, almost exclusively as guest vocalists with all-male groups.

Millie Small (b. 1946) is perhaps the best-known women exponent of first wave ska. Her international hit "My Boy Lollipop" (Smash 67055) introduced ska to listeners outside of Jamaica. Rita Anderson, who was later to back future husband Bob Marley as a member of the vocal trio I-Threes, was a major rocksteady artist in the 1960s as a member of the Soulettes. More typical, though, was Marguerita, who recorded "Woman a Come" with the all-male Skatalites in 1965 as a guest vocalist. Most women in early Jamaican ska sang as guest duet partners for male artists.

Second wave ska, which brought together racially mixed groups in England in the wake of the punk movement, was significant for the number of important all-women or women-fronted bands. The Bodysnatchers were a seven-woman lineup from London who toured with the Selecter. The Selecter, a legendary second wave group, was fronted by Pauline Black and released five full-length albums, including *Prime Cuts* (Magnum 4), a rarity in a singles-dominated genre.

In the 1990s the primary locus of ska migrated to the United States and Canada, and women found more flexible roles in the scene. All-women bands like the Deltones continued to flourish, but women also began to appear in mixed-gender bands as instrumentalists, such as Paula Richards, bassist with the Potato 5, and Denise Butler, saxophonist with the British band the Loafers. Women also appeared prominently in popular ska-influenced pop bands like No Doubt and Dance Hall Crashers. By the late 1990s, Shanachie Records had released two volumes of a retrospective compilation, *Ska Down Her Way—Women of Ska* (Shanachie 5725 and 5733).

See also Blues; Underground

For Further Reading

Willis, Tomas. *Questions and Answers about Ska Music*. Available: ftp://rtfm.mit.edu/pub/usenet/news.answers/music/ska-faq/part1

Mike Daley

Slick, Grace (1939–)

Grace Slick was one of the most important rock "divas" of the 1960s and 1970s. Musically, she came to represent the psychedelic counterculture that swept across the nation from Haight-Ashbury. In the end, however, what her fans remember most is her powerhouse, metallic-before-heavy-metal, audience-baiting voice.

Slick was born on 30 October 1939 in Chicago, IL. After attending Manhattan's Finch College, Slick spent time as a model before forming the band the Great Society with her film-maker-student husband and her brother-in-law. Although the band's time together was brief, it produced songs for which Slick would eventually become celebrated. Marty Balin formed San Francisco's pioneering psychedelic band Jefferson Airplane in 1965, comprised of Paul Kantner, Jorma Kaukorean, Skip Spence, Signe Anderson, and Bob Harvey, who was soon replaced by Jack Casady. Slick arrived in 1966 and immediately became Balin's on-stage protagonist. Her performing personas challenged traditional female performing aesthetics, by creating outlaw archetypes such as acid priestess, mother superior, revolutionary warrior, Hitler drag, alien queen, cosmic witchy woman, and bitch. These images reinforced female sexuality and power and utilized rock and roll as a revolutionary, political tool with which to dismantle censorship.

Recording and performing, including gigs at the legendary Woodstock and Altamont festivals, Slick was up-front and aggressive and, to detractors, often obscene. Ariel Swartley (1997) describes Slick's voice as "a pipe organ crossed with an electric drill . . . the first singer to cut through a mix with the sustained steel authority of an electric guitar." In the

Grace Slick performing with Jefferson Starship at the Save the Cable Cars benefit in San Francisco in September 1981. *Photo © Roger Ressmeyer/CORBIS.*

periods from 1967 to 1972 and 1987 to 1993, Slick and Jefferson Airplane recorded eight albums on the RCA label, including their first album, *Surrealistic Pillow* (RCA PCD1-3766), which introduced the songs for which the band is still best known—"Somebody to Love" and "White Rabbit"—written during their "Great Society" days; a greatest hits album, released in 1970 as *The Worst of the Jefferson Airplane* (RCA 4459-2-R); and the 1992 three-disc set *Jefferson Airplane Loves You* (RCA 61110-2).

In 1971 and by now separated from her husband, Slick had a daughter, Chris, with Paul Kantner; Chris would later become an MTV VJ (video jockey). In 1972

Jefferson Airplane disbanded, and Slick tried working with numerous bands, various musicians, and as a solo singer. None of these activities proved fulfilling, and this fact provoked Slick's steady descent into alcoholism. In 1974 she and Kantner formed the Jefferson Starship, a revamping of Jefferson Airplane, and later the band became the self-parodying Starship. With this group, Slick rebounded and recorded eight more albums, most of them on Starship's own label, Grunt. Chart-topping songs included "We Built This City," "Sara," and "Nothing's Gonna Stop Us Now."

Known for her excessive drug use and sexual escapades with the rich and famous of the rock and roll scene of the 1960s, Slick prevails now as an elder stateswoman for a turbulent time and music, the powerhouse lead singer and determining force of the Jefferson Airplane, and the pioneering, fearless, mouthy, and authoritative woman who carved a gutsy and powerful path for women in rock and roll.

See also Rock and Popular Music Genres; Rock Music

For Further Reading

Perry, Charles, Parke Puterbaugh, James Henke, and Barry Miles. *I Want to Take You Higher: The Psychedelic Era 1965–1969*. San Francisco: Chronicle Books, 2000.

Slick, Grace, and Andrea Cagan. *Somebody to Love? A Rock and Roll Memoir*. New York: Warner Books, 1998.

Swartley, Ariel. "Red Blue Jeans: Wanda Jackson and Grace Slick." *Rolling Stone Book of Women in Rock*. New York: Random House, 1997.

Leanne Fazio

Smith, Bessie (1894–1937)

Bessie Smith was the seminal blues and early jazz singer of the twentieth century. Called the "Empress of the Blues," Bessie

Bessie Smith in 1923. *Photo courtesy of Frank Driggs Collection.*

Smith had a powerful voice and imposing range. She sang with excellent phrasing and intonation. With her growling style, dexterous use of "blue notes," and ability to convey the meaning of the lyrics of her songs, Bessie emerged as the pinnacle of blues singing from the 1920s.

Smith was born in Chattanooga, TN, on 15 April 1894. The actual year is unverifiable; 15 April 1894 is the birth date she listed on her application for marriage in 1923, but her birth was unregistered. She was born into an impoverished, uneducated, and large family. Her parents died while she was a young child, leaving Bessie's older sister to raise her younger siblings. Bessie, with her younger brother Andrew accompanying her on guitar, sang and danced for money tossed to them by onlookers in their hometown. Bessie's brother Clarence had joined one of the many minstrel tent shows traveling throughout the South, and he brought Bessie into the show primarily as a dancer. She toured throughout the South and Midwest with various troupes starting around 1912. Other prominent cast members in some of these shows were Gertrude "Ma" Rainey (1886–1939), the future "Mother of the Blues" and the first recorded blues singer, and Thomas A. Dorsey, later Rainey's accompanist and the "Father of Gospel Music" in African American churches. Smith became good friends with Rainey and developed skills as a singer and comedienne.

Bessie's recording career did not begin until 1923, when she contracted with Columbia Records. Her first recording on the label, "Down Hearted Blues," was issued in 1923 and became phenomenally successful. She continued to issue recordings for the next 10 years. About 45 of the 180 songs she recorded had been written by Bessie, including her famous "Empty Bed Blues," and "Yellow Dog Blues." The musicians who recorded with her, including Fletcher Henderson, Louis Armstrong, Coleman Hawkins, and Sidney Bechet, represented the best of the jazz world. Many retrospective recordings exist from Smith's long career, including *The Essential Bessie Smith* (Columbia/Legacy 64922), *Any Woman's Blues* (Columbia 30126), and *The Empress* (Columbia CGT-30818).

Smith married her business manager, Jack Gee, in 1923, and they adopted a son in 1926. But the marriage ended in 1929, and alcoholism and dismal personal relationships plagued her. She also faced financial problems arising from the Great Depression of 1929. However, she continued to perform in nightclubs and arena shows and also starred in the motion picture *St. Louis Blues* (1929). In the early morning of 26 September 1937, on her way to fulfill a contract in Clarksdale, MS, Smith sustained injuries from a car accident and subsequently died later that morning. Controversy continues to surround her death. In 1960 the playwright Edward Albee wrote a brief, poignant drama based on this incident.

See also Blues; Jazz

For Further Reading

Brooks, Edward. *The Bessie Smith Companion: A Critical and Detailed Appreciation of the Recordings*. Wheathampstead, Herts: Cavendish Pub. Co.; New York: Da Capo Press, 1982.

Feinstein, Elaine. *Bessie Smith*. New York: Viking, 1985.

Friedwald, Will. *Jazz Singing: America's Great Voices from Bessie Smith to Bebop and Beyond*. New York: Scribner, 1990.

Monica J. Burdex

Smith, Kate (1907–1986)

With a career spanning the 1920s to the 1970s, Kate Smith was one of the most popular women vocalists and personalities of the twentieth century. Quintessentially American, she proved, despite her large figure (at times the object of ridicule), that talent is worth more than appearance. Loved for her singing, heard by countless millions on recordings, radio shows, and in concert, she was also so highly regarded that in the 1930s she had a daytime radio program on which she voiced her opinions on various topics. A friendly, motherly woman who never married, Smith had a warm, clear, comforting soprano voice that exuded sincerity. Her singing came naturally: she never took lessons and did not read music.

Smith was born on 1 May 1907 in Greenville, VA, and was raised in Washington, DC, where she sang at church and military camps. In 1926, at the urging of her family, she began training to

Kate Smith in 1935. *Photo © Bettmann/ CORBIS.*

become a nurse, but she quit after a year to focus on entertaining. The vaudeville show led to the Broadway production, and she made her first recordings soon thereafter for Columbia Records. Smith started in radio in 1929; two years later she had her own show, which featured "When the Moon Comes over the Mountain" as her theme song, with lyrics of her own composition. Her long association with her manager, Ted Collins, began at that time. From the offerings of music publishers he would select material for her, and she introduced to the public hundreds of songs, including a large number that became standards.

Through the Great Depression years and beyond, her commercially sponsored network radio shows attained great popularity. She also toured and appeared in several movies. In 1938 President Franklin D. Roosevelt presented her to the king and queen of England in a concert at the White House. In that year she recorded "God Bless America," composed by Irving Berlin in 1918 (available on *God Bless America*, Delta 15380); it made her a symbol for her country and was a hit several times over. During World War II she helped raise a record amount of money through drives for the purchase of war bonds.

Kate Smith recorded for major labels, had many hit records, and influenced other singers, notably England's Vera Lynn. In 1950 she began a very successful television show. She retired five years later following the death of her manager but returned to radio in 1958 and television in 1960. A triumphant Carnegie Hall concert in 1962 was recorded and issued (available on Special Music 2587).

Ill health caused her to stop performing in the mid-1970s. In 1982 she was given two awards: an Emmy for her television achievements, and the prestigious U.S. Medal of Freedom, presented by President Ronald Reagan. In the same year her "God Bless America" was inducted into the Grammy Hall of Fame as one of the most important of all recordings. She wrote two autobiographies: *Living in a Great Big Way* (1938) and *Upon My Lips a Song* (1960).

See also Grammy Award

For Further Reading

Parish, James Robert, and Michael R. Pitts. *Hollywood Songsters*. New York: Garland Publishing, 1991.

Pitts, Michael R. *Kate Smith: A Bio-Bibliography*. Westport, CT: Greenwood Press, 1988.

Whitcomb, Ian. *After the Ball: Pop Music from Rag to Rock*. New York: Simon & Schuster, 1973.

Craig Morrison

Smith, Patti (1946–)

Patti Smith is a punk poet, underground singer-songwriter, and performing artist.

Although Smith struggled during her first few years living in New York in the 1960s, she devoted herself to all sorts of artistic pursuits, including co-authoring the play *Cowboy Mouth* with Sam Shepherd. Shortly thereafter she began performing her poetry publicly, at times appearing with guitarist Lenny Kaye, who has since worked with her for the majority of her musical career. Smith and Kaye later teamed with pianist Richard Sohl, and the group found a willing audience at the famous rock and punk music club CBGB's. In 1974 the trio recorded their first single, "Hey Joe," executive-produced and funded by Robert Mapplethorpe. By the middle of 1975 they signed a seven-record deal with Arista. With the help of the Velvet Underground's John Cale as producer and a now-famous cover photograph of Smith by Mapplethorpe, Patti Smith's debut album, *Horses* (Arista ARCD-8362), was released in late 1975. On the album, often considered one of the forerunners of punk rock, Smith's songs touched on a wide range of topics, including lesbianism, suicide, and religion, all delivered in her quasi-improvisational singing style.

Smith was born on 30 December 1946 in Chicago, IL, but was raised in Woodbury, NJ. Despite her considerable intellectual and artistic abilities, she never quite fit into either her high school or college academic environment, eventually dropping out of Glassboro State College to move to New York City in the late 1960s. Soon after her arrival, she met and befriended the fledgling artist Robert Mapplethorpe, with whom she remained friends for many years.

Smith's group recorded three more albums over the next few years, including *Radio Ethiopia* (Arista ARCD-8161), *Easter* (Arista ARCD-8166), and *Wave* (Arista ARCD-8546), gradually building a devoted following. While recuperating from an accident she suffered on her tour in support of *Radio Ethiopia*, Smith also published a book of her poetry entitled *Babel*. Of the various songs released by the band in the late 1970s, notable among them is the radio hit from *Easter*, "Because the Night," co-penned by Bruce Springsteen. Over the years, Smith has also worked with other major recording artists, including Blue Oyster Cult and Michael Stipe of REM.

At the height of her popularity, Smith decided to step back from public life in 1979 to begin living a quieter family life in Detroit with her new love, Fred "Sonic" Smith of the rock band MC5. The two Smiths wed in March 1980 and had two children, Jackson and Jesse. Together, the husband and wife team recorded *Dream of Life* (Arista ARCD-8453) in 1988, while Patti Smith continued to write her own poetry, releasing both *Early Work* and *Woolgathering*.

Although Smith hinted at a return to the stage with several readings of her poetry in the early 1990s, it was not until the untimely deaths of both her husband and her brother in the mid-1990s that she more significantly returned to the public performance of her work. Since then she has released three more albums, *Gone Again* (Arista 18747), *Peace and Noise* (Arista 18986), and *Gung Ho* (Arista 14618) in early 2000.

See also Rock and Popular Music Genres; Singer-Songwriter; Underground

For Further Reading

Smith, Patti. *The Coral Sea*. New York: Norton, 1997.

———. *Patti Smith Complete: Lyrics, Reflections, and Notes for the Future*. New York: Doubleday, 1998.

Jeff Herriott

Sobrino, Laura Garciacano (1954–)

Classically trained violinist Laura Garciacano Sobrino is considered one of the pioneer professional women mariachi musicians in the United States. She has been described as the "Mariachi Queen" by the *Los Angeles Times*. Sobrino is the former director and lead violinist for the all-women professional show group Mariachi Reyna de *Los Angeles*. Throughout her professional career Sobrino has been a positive role model and teacher for a great number of new women mariachi musicians. She was the first teacher for professional recording artists such as Tatiana Bolaños and Nydia Rojas.

Born on 25 September 1954 in Watsonville, CA, Sobrino began her musical education at age eight, playing violin in elementary school. Her career as a semiprofessional mariachi violin musician began in 1975 when she played for weddings and restaurants while studying for her B.A. in music at the University of California in Santa Cruz, specializing in Mexican traditional music. Her senior thesis was devoted to the mariachi violin style. After finishing her studies she moved to Los Angeles to perform mariachi music professionally, becoming the first woman to play with the Mariachi Los Galleros de Pedro Rey and the Mariachi Sol de México de José L. Hernández, two of the nation's most prestigious mariachi groups. Mariachi Sol de México has been recognized as one of the best mariachi music ensembles in the world. Laura Sobrino's recording credits with the Mariachi Sol de México include Linda Ronstadt's *Canciones de mi Padre* (Asylum 60765-2), Lucha Villa's 25th anniversary album (WEA International 55118), Juan Gabriel's album *Todo* (RCA 6001-2-RL), and a music video for Charo. Sobrino's first job as a professional mariachi was given to her in 1978 by University of California Los Angeles (UCLA) ethnomusicologist Mark Folquist, who was the director of the mariachi Ucatlán, a UCLA student group that had just turned professional.

Sobrino has taught mariachi music classes at the Mariachi Heritage Society's youth program at the Los Angeles Music and Art School in East Los Angeles, California State University at Northridge, Plaza de La Raza cultural center in East Los Angeles, North Ranchito Elementary School in Pico Rivera, Magnolia Elementary School in Los Angeles, and Maxwell Elementary School in Duarte. She also has been a featured instructor at workshops at many of the well-known mariachi music festivals throughout the United States. Sobrino has also initiated her own mariachi music publishing company, the Mariachi Publishing Company. Some of her mariachi music transcriptions can also be found at the Southern Music Company in Texas. Today, Sobrino is the musical director of the all-star women mariachi Mujer 2000.

See also Latin American Musicians; Multicultural Musics

For Further Reading

Laura Sobrino. Available: http://www.sobrino.net/music/LSobrino.html

Mariachi Publishing Company. Available: http://www.mariachi-publishing.com

Quintanilla Michael. "Mariachi Queen." *Los Angeles Times*, Sunday Profile, Life and Style (17 September 1995).

Francisco Crespo

Social Darwinism

Social Darwinism (c. 1870–1910) is a set of theories about the evolution of humans and their societies, and their changes through prehistory and history, as it was applied to the role of American women as makers of music. This entry is in four parts: (1) a summary of social Darwinist theory, (2) applications of the theories to women, (3) applications to women in music, and (4) responses of feminists to social Darwinism.

Social Darwinism (sD) applies Darwinian principles of natural selection to human societies. Included in sD theory are ideas from the writings of not only Charles Darwin (1809–1882) but also Herbert Spencer (1820–1903), who believed that human evolution from lower to higher forms was a result of the survival of the fittest, with its corollary that those on the lowest strata of society were doomed to failure whether or not society assisted them: society benefited only by their demise. The dominant ideology of the period, sD was nowhere more influential than among the middle and upper classes in the United States from c. 1870 to 1910. Basing their deductions on fragmentary archeological evidence and observation of a few tribal societies, social Darwinists such as the American William Graham Sumner (1840–1910) reconstructed human prehistory as a mirror of Victorian social organization, including its racism, imperialism, materialism, and gender ideology, and then used that construction to justify gender roles in the Victorian period, among them the status of "woman," a category that superseded all differences among women.

Social Darwinists believed that within each social group the women were inferior to the men because they were less highly evolved both physically and intellectually. Spencer stated that women's inferiority had a biological basis: the "earlier arrest of individual evolution in women than in men [was] necessitated by the reservation of vital power to meet the costs of reproduction" (Conway, 48), an idea based on the theory of the conservation and transformation of energy. These presumed sex-linked characteristics, by no strange coincidence, made the contemporary woman highly adapted to domestic life. Further, Sir Patrick Geddes theorized that such differences could be traced to the beginning of life: cell metabolism was the biological explanation for men's social dominance, based on the differentiation of male and female reproductive cells into the "hungry and active . . . flagellate sperm" and the "quiescent, well-fed . . . ovum" (Conway, 51). Geddes generalized from that difference to explain male aggression and rationality and female passivity and intuition.

Many of these ideas were circulating before the publication of Darwin's *The Origin of Species* (1859). For example, in 1843 an article in an American publication presented contrasting characteristics of men and women, respectively: cognition vs. intuition and emotion, action vs. reaction, justice vs. mercy, talent vs. genius (where genius was defined as an unschooled, intuitive gift); in other words, "the womanly virtues of wisdom and understanding have conclusions reached through intuition, while the male virtues of truth and knowledge come from the intellect" (Welter, 77). Social Darwinism not only reinforced these notions but also gave them "scientific" validity.

The influential Boston physician Edward Hammond Clarke applied the principle of the conservation of energy to women's physical and mental development. He declared that in order for a woman to carry out her "divinely appointed" domestic tasks, conservation of her energy was required, especially during puberty, to allow for physical development of the sex organs. Attempting to train girls like boys risked injury to health; brain work interfered with physiological development, caused incomplete, even faulty sexual maturation, and had "almost extinguished them as girls" (Clarke, 45). Girls who had professional ambitions of any kind were warned they would be at risk physically at the very time when education and training for a career are traditionally undertaken. Regarding women's intellectual development, Spencer believed that "the male capacity for abstract reason had been evolved along with the attachment to abstract justice and this was a sign of highly evolved life." Intellectually, "woman," being "the lesser man" (Brower, 334), lacked that ability.

The assumption of relative weakness, placidity, and arrested mental development of the women became the explanation for women's lesser musical achievements vis-à-vis men in music of the Western art tradition. Whereas amateur music making at home was prescribed for middle- and upper-class women, professional careers in music were proscribed. Music was a socially advantageous accomplishment for women before marriage, but following marriage they were warned in 1865 not to let it "interfere with the practice at the kneading trough, the washboard, or any other duty" of a true woman. At the same time, the doctrine of separate spheres denied gifted and talented women professional careers in music: women who performed in public risked social degradation.

The debate on women composers was launched by the music critic George Putnam Upton, who, like the social Darwinists, believed that women's lesser abilities in music were genetic, a result of intellectual inferiority, with its attendant reliance on intuition and inability to use abstractions. This limited their capacity to compose large-scale abstract music, the varieties of which constituted crucial tests of musical skill and talent. Upton defined women's primary role as muse to composers who were men. He posed the question, Why have women, who are more emotional than men, not succeeded as composers even though music is the language of the emotions? Despite the fact that more girls than boys study music, why do women remain inferior to men as musical creators? The answers almost always refer to inborn, presumably sex-linked characteristics—women are emotional, not intellectual; they write from intuition; they are receptive, not creative; and they cannot master the scientific, the "mercilessly logical and unrelentingly mathematical" aspects of music (Upton, 27). Lacking virility and "active emotional force," even their presumed greater emotionality is flawed, because "strong emotions go with strong intellect" (Brower, 335).

American women had models of professionalism, however, among the many fine women musicians—especially singers and pianists—from Europe and Great Britain, most of whom were trained and initiated into professional life by family members. By the latter part of the nineteenth century, some American women took the daring step of becoming professional musicians. Among the earliest of the native-born artists were the soprano Clara Louise Kellogg (1842–1916) and the violinist Maud Powell (1867–1920), both of whose parents provided a supportive environment, musical training, and encouragement despite societal censure. Kellogg, who anticipated losing her respectability once she sang in opera, bade her friends goodbye before making her debut. Following both women's debuts, critics praised their talent and musicality yet claimed that the two women were aberrant (i.e., exceptions who proved the rule of woman's genetic musical deficits). Powell, typically, was criticized for lacking man's strength. The pianist Anton Rubinstein stated that in music, women also lacked men's "power of thought, breadth of feeling, freedom of stroke" (Rubinstein, 118). When these women did play with strength, critics accused them of trying too hard and playing harshly. The Venezuelan pianist Teresa Carreño (1853–1917) was called the "Brünnhilde of the piano" (Milinowski, 4), a sobriquet that implies the abnormal development Clarke predicted for women who exceeded societally prescribed roles. Yet their careers were affirmations of women's capacities as professional performers.

Regarding the composition of music, the women-identified genres were hymns, parlor songs, and piano pieces. All the remaining genres—symphony, oratorio, string quartet, sonata, fugue, as well as band music, etc.—were identified with men. Large-scale abstract works, especially, were declared beyond women's mental capacities. Upton wrote, "There is a natural aptitude among musical women for the writing of songs and ballads . . . but their work never survives. When they try for larger forms, they fail to win performances. . . . Having had equal advantages with men, they have failed as creators. . . . Women have neither time nor disposition for the theoretical application which musical composition requires" (Upton, 20). Further, Upton stated that whereas woman is emotional by nature, man is also emotional but controls his emotions and can give outward expression to them. Men are able "to treat emotions as if they were mathematics, to bind and measure and limit them within rigid laws of harmony and counterpoint, and to express them with arbitrary signs . . . a cold-blooded operation . . . possible only to the sterner and more obdurate nature of man" (Upton, 22).

Contemporary arguments refuting the idea that women are less highly evolved than men include those of Antoinette Brown Blackwell, who in 1875 stated that the reasoning of social Darwinists was androcentric and that no scientific tests had proven that women are less highly evolved than men. Until such time as they do, "it is difficult to perceive what self-adjusting forces . . . have developed men everywhere the superiors of women" (Blackwell, 358). She questioned why female offspring do not inherit from the same gene pool as their brothers.

The performance in 1892 of Amy Marcy Cheney Beach's Mass in E-flat, op. 5, a 75-minute composition involving large performing forces, touched off further controversy over women as composers. Julia Ward Howe, writing in the *Woman's Journal* (February 1892), stressed the intellectual aspect of the Mass's composition: the work "made evident the capacity of a woman's brain to plan and execute a work combining great seriousness with unquestionable beauty." A second feminist, Alice Stone Blackwell (niece of Antoinette Brown Blackwell), citing the example of Beach's Mass, came to the defense of all other women as composers, using the arguments of nurture vs. nature: "when the climate of opinion, the support, and the training were the same for women as men, and when those conditions endured for decades if not centuries, then such comparisons would be apt if women did not rise to men's levels as composers" (Ibid.).

By the second decade of the twentieth century, sD began to be displaced by reformist programs in support of the needy. Nevertheless, ideas of women's inferiority as music makers persisted until the 1970s, a time when more and more women were playing in orchestras, and when composers began to be accepted without distinction of gender.

See also Discrimination; Female Inferiority, theories of; Professionalism; Separate Spheres—Sexual Aesthetics

For Further Reading

Blackwell, Antoinette Brown. "Sex and Evolution." [1875]. In *The Feminist Papers: From Adams to de Beauvoir*, ed. Alice S. Rossi. New York: Columbia University Press, 1973, 356–377.

Brower, Edith. "Is the Musical Idea Masculine?" *Atlantic Monthly* 73 (March 1894): 332–339.

Clarke, Edward Hammond. *Sex in Education, or, A Fair Chance for Girls*. Boston: James R. Osgood, 1873.

Conway, Jill. "Stereotypes of Femininity in Theory of Evolution." *Victorian Studies* 14 (September 1970): 47–61.

Hofstadter, Richard. *Social Darwinism in American Thought*, rev. ed. New York: George Braziller, 1955.

Milinowski, Marta. *Teresa Carreño: "By the Grace of God."* New Haven: Yale University Press, 1940. Reprint, New York: Da Capo Press, 1977.

Rubinstein, Anton. *A Conversation on Music*. Trans. Mrs. John P. Morgan. New York: Charles F. Tretbar, 1892.

Tick, Judith. "Passed Away Is the Piano Girl: Changes in American Musical Life, 1870–1900." In *Women Making Music: The Western Art Tradition, 1150–1950*, eds. Jane Bowers and Judith Tick. Urbana: University of Illinois Press, 1986, Chapter 13.

Upton, George Putnam. *Woman in Music*. Boston: James R. Osgood, 1880.

Adrienne Fried Block

Society of Motion Picture and Television Engineers, Inc.

See Organizations, Professional Audio

Software Designer/Programmer

A software designer/programmer creates compositional environments and instruments for the computer music composer or performer, and develops techniques for analysis, synthesis, and processing. A skilled programmer has the ability to invent highly configurable tools, limited only by her imagination and platform capabilities. Women who program have both music and computer science skills, as computer music is a hybrid field. They may be composers dissatisfied with tools available, or engineers researching techniques or developing applications. A designer of software can be employed in academic positions in universities, or by companies distributing commercial software or products involving music. Programming languages that are used include low-level assembly languages and higher-level C, C++, LISP, Smalltalk, or, for World Wide Web audio, Java. Many women use programs such as Opcode's Max and Macromedia's Director for multimedia composition and teaching, which can be considered programming, but not generally software design.

Obstacles have so far kept the number of women software designers in music low. The two main areas music programmers emerge from, music composition and engineering, have been traditionally dominated by men, with few women role models. Bias in educational experiences, lack of acceptance by peers, security concerns for studio use, and family demands may derail women from computing careers. While these factors operate in some situations, intelligent women also may find that the computer is a bias-free collaborative partner to realize her most unique musical dreams, and that she may bypass more obstacles with the control technology offers. Laurie Spiegel (b. 1945) and Carla Scaletti (b. 1956) have successfully created and marketed music software for use by a devoted and active group of users.

Composing the tools that composers and performers use requires the creativity and musical knowledge to envision and use new forms of musical expression as well as technical skills. Facility with C or other languages and some knowledge of digital signal processing and audio are essential. Object-oriented programming skills, such as in C++, are desirable. To obtain a composition or music technology academic position, a doctorate is usually necessary. For software engineering or development jobs at top companies, at least a B.S. in electrical engineering or computer science and some experience are usually required, along with familiarity with particular protocols, operating systems, or applications.

After early work at Bell Laboratories, Spiegel developed and marketed her Music Mouse software for Macintosh, Amiga, and Atari. Scaletti created the Kyma music language in connection with Kurt Hebel's Capybara hardware, which she markets through Symbolic Sound. Acoustics researcher and mathematician Joan Miller contributed to the development of Music IV and V at Bell Laboratories in the 1960s, and she later developed software for stringed instrument sound analysis. Elizabeth Cohen (Cohen Acoustical, Inc., Stanford University) programmed acoustics, audio, and Internet applications. Marina Bosi (Digital Theater Systems, president of the Audio Engineering Society) worked extensively with audio compression. Mara Helmuth (University of Cincinnati) created several applications for the NeXT and Silicon Graphics platforms, including Patchmix, a code-writing object-oriented graphical instrument builder for the Cmix music programming language StochGran, a granular synthesis application used in *Abandoned Lake in Maine*, the *SoundColors* installation, and its high band-width Internet version, Internet Sound Exchange. For *Elements 1.1: sulphur, phosphorus; diamond*, Judy Klein (b. 1943) programmed algorithms in C based on physical properties of the elements. Insook Choi (National Center for Supercomputing Applications) designed chaotic circuit models for tone generation and contributed to the development of the Manifold Control high-dimension interactive control system and the virtual sound server software environment for virtual reality applications. K. Romana Machado contributed to JI Calc, the just intonation calculator. Other programmers are Robin Goldsmith (Digidesign), Emily Laugesen, Linda Seltzer (AT&T), Belinda Thom, and Tarynn Witten.

See also Experimental Music; Music Technology; Organizations, Professional Audio

For Further Reading

Grigsby, Beverly. "Women Composers of Electronic Music." In *The Musical Woman; An International Perspective*, ed. Judith Lang Zaimont. Westport, CT: Greenwood Press, 1984.

Helmuth, Mara. "Gender and Computer Music." *ARRAY* 13/2 (1993): 15–18.

Mathews, Max. *The Technology of Computer Music.* Cambridge, MA: MIT Press, 1969.

Mara Helmuth

Songwriter

A songwriter is the composer *and* lyricist of a vocal composition, usually with accompaniment, in a popular style. In operatic arias, greater emphasis is placed on music than on words; popular songs treat words and music equally. In art songs, accompaniments often incorporate the melody, but popular song accompaniments generally do not. Women songwriters have contributed to all genres of popular song, including pop, rock, jazz, blues, folk, country, and musical theater.

In the early 1900s women composers often wrote art songs and, like Mary Earl ("Beautiful Ohio," 1918), the occasional popular or parlor song. By the 1920s composers including Lily Strickland ("Mah Lindy Lou," 1920) and Kay Swift ([1897–1993] "Can We Be Friends," 1929) had moved firmly into popular forms. The 1930s were fruitful for women songwriters, including Swift ("Fine and Dandy," 1930), Ann Ronell (who wrote the music and lyrics for "Willow Weep for Me," 1932), Maria Grever, Bernice Petkere, and lyricist Doris Tauber. Lyricist Dorothy Fields (1905–1974) wrote many songs with Jerome Kern that have become standards, including "I Won't Dance" (1935) and "A Fine Romance" (1936).

Significant women songwriters of the 1940s include Evelyn Danzig ("Scarlet Ribbons," 1949) and lyricist Nancy Hamilton ("How High the Moon," 1940). The 1940s saw the rise of Broadway "book" musicals and their film counterparts. The lyricist team of Betty Comden (b. ca. 1917) and Adolph Green, with composer Leonard Bernstein, created the Broadway shows *On the Town* (1945) and *Wonderful Town* (1953); they later wrote with Jule Styne ("The Party's Over," 1956) and others. Film musicals' popularity through the 1950s was bolstered in part by the works of such songwriters as Sylvia Fine (1913–1991) and lyricist Carolyn Leigh.

The late 1950s and early 1960s saw the rise of rock and roll and an interest in folk music. Songwriters in New York City's Brill Building, including the teams of Carole King (b. 1942) and Gerry Goffin ("Up On the Roof," 1962), and Cynthia Weil (b. 1937) and Barry Mann, continued to turn out music for singers to record. Still, the era of the self-contained singer-songwriter had arrived. Singer-songwriter Judy Collins (b. 1939) also promoted the music of others, including Joni Mitchell (b. 1943) and Malvina Reynolds (1900–1978). Mitchell's songs are often jazz oriented, although the folk-pop song "Both Sides Now" (1967) is her best known; Reynolds's songs are folk in approach ("Little Boxes," 1962). Songs written by Carole King in 1971, alone or with Toni Stern, became instant classics, including "I Feel the Earth Move." Women singer-songwriters in pop and rock have included Melissa Etheridge (b. 1961), Joan Jett (b. 1960), Janis Joplin (1943–1970), Madonna (b. 1958), Bonnie Raitt (b. 1949), Carly Simon (b. 1945), and Suzanne Vega (b. 1959).

Women jazz and blues performers often wrote their own material. Billie Holiday (1915–1959) composed few but notable songs, including "Fine and Mellow" (1940). "Empress of the Blues" Bessie Smith (1894–1937) wrote "You've Been a Good Ole Wagon" (1925), among several blues classics.

From June Carter Cash (b. 1929)—"Ring of Fire," with Merle Kilgore in 1962—to Dolly Parton (b. 1946), women songwriters have greatly contributed to country music. The team of Felice (b. 1925) and Boudleaux Bryant wrote many hits, including "Bye Bye Love" (1957). Other country music songwriters included Loretta Lynn (b. 1935), Shania Twain (b. 1965), and Dottie West (1932–1991).

See also Librettist; Musical Theater; Singer-Songwriter

For Further Reading

Citron, Stephen. *Songwriting: A Complete Guide to the Craft*. New York: Limelight Editions, 1985.

Frankel, Aaron. *Writing the Broadway Musical*. New York: Drama Book Publishers, 1977.

Wong, Dr. Herb (ed.). *The Ultimate Jazz Fake*

Book. Milwaukee: Hal Leonard Publishing, 1988.

Steven L. Rosenhaus

Sound Design

Sound design has paralleled the developments of sound-generating technology and computers. Faster computer processing time, less expensive hardware, and larger, more efficient storage capacity have driven the development of computer technology. This progression has enabled computers to take over the function of many electronic musical instruments from analog synthesizers to samplers. However, even the fastest computers and most elegant synthesizers are mindless machines. The skills, ideas, and imagination of the people working with the technology bring it to life. The diversity of background and aesthetics of the sound designers themselves has greatly enhanced and expanded the field. Computer programmers, sound artists, composers, performers, and sound engineers have all found their way into sound design, and the field has expanded because of their diversity and creative energy.

Atari's "Pong," from the 1970s, was one of the earliest electronic games. The palette for creating sounds for games paralleled those used in synthesizers of the time. Through clever programming and imaginative use of limited equipment, sound designers created remarkable audio backdrop with analog oscillators, noise generators, and envelope generators. In general, however, sound design was limited to sound effects.

However, by the early- to mid-1980s, the field of sound design had changed significantly, and several of the leaders in this field were women. In the early 1980s large samplers like the Fairlight Computer Music Instrument (CMI) and the Synclavier from New England Digital came onto the commercial music scene. Faster, smaller, cheaper led to more portable and affordable samplers made by Casio, Emu, and Akai among others. Eventually, computers were fast, small and cheap enough to store and process the sounds themselves. This was an important step in sound design for computer games. Samplers brought into the purely electronic world, the sounds from everyday life. Instrumental, human, animal, machine, and environmental sounds—an enormous variety of sounds were added to the designer's palette. According to Brenda Hutchinson (b. 1954), through the skillful use of sound design, listeners can disassociate these everyday sounds from their original context, and create new meanings and magical environments.

Frankie Mann (b. 1955) wrote "Orphie," a music and sound effect interpreter for the computer games developed by Children's Television Workshop, in 1984. Orphie enabled the user to use independent voices associated with individual graphic animation frames or specific game characters. Mann believes that her classical music background influenced her software development and implementation.

Additionally, by the mid-1980s MIDI (Musical Instrument Digital Interface—a communications protocol for synthesizers and computers) made it possible to access small groups of sounds preset or pre-stored in the computer or game. Long melodies and entire musical pieces could be played in real time through the use of MIDI. Sound effects could now be played against a continuous background of music which in turn defined a mood or accompanied the on-screen action.

Maggi Payne (b. 1945), Co-Director of the Center for Contemporary Music at Mills College, has realized "how much sound design can affect the tone of visuals/dialog. The atmosphere can change from innocent to ominous within an instant. The power of both worlds—visual and aural—to create a new 'reality' can be astounding" (Payne, 2000). People were able to create more interesting relationships between the images and/or action and the sounds that accompanied them. By and large, sound design was (and still is) a visually driven process.

Until the early 1990s most of the games were action/adventure games, and the sound designers were predominately men. Many of the games (and sounds) were related to war, killing, fighting, etc. The type of interactivity was often limited to quick reaction time, navigation, and strategy. The sounds of grunting, smacking, gunfire, explosions, etc. were the sound effects heard over a bed of some repetitive music generated by stored sounds played by MIDI. The arcades were full of these games. The manner by which Lisa Kadet Kuhne uses specialized sound effects and audio processing techniques to create an "other-worldly landscape in ordinary objects" (Kuhne, 2000).

As personal computers became even faster, cheaper, and able to handle larger amounts of information in real-time. CD-ROMs became a new means of delivering the sounds, images, and animations for games. Storage capacity increased, so sound quality improved. More subtle and intricate sound design was now possible. People were no longer limited to sound effects and simple layering or looping of sounds. The increased speed of the computers made more interactivity possible. It became possible to create a sound design for the player of the game to actually choose and create the soundscape. Interactivity itself is part of the sound design. The manner in which Lisa Kadet Kuhne approaches sound design is to use "sound effects and personalize them so as to make them . . . unique, specialized creations [by] putting sound effects through various processing techniques and by exploring the myriad of ways signal paths can be manipulated. This approach has been described as something like hanging a photograph upside down so as to see other-worldly landscapes in ordinary objects."

Women have been involved in sound design since the earliest days. However, with the advent of more varied subject matter for games, an expanded range of interactivity, and the opportunity to expand the sound, more women have become attracted to sound design than ever before. These women are composers, sound artists, installation artists, instrument makers, software designers, and performers. They bring a vast breadth of experience and range of aesthetics to sound design. According to Elise Baldwin (b. 1969), "Sound design in games serves firstly a basic narrative function, much as it does in theater or film: the creation of an environment through aural perception and establishing the position of the 'audience/user' relative to that space. In film and theater, sound design reinforces the emotional subtleties of both location and narrative. . . . Sound design for games possesses another dimension, and that is the . . . most interesting bit of designing for games or any interactive experience" (e-mail interview with author, 2000).

Sound design is no longer about sound effects or even mood. It has become a compositional medium with a broad range of possibilities. Recently some games have been sound driven. That is, the timing of the animation and development of the story lines have depended on the sound design being created first. Entire cohesive sound worlds are being created. Players can move through spaces that are not only visually beautiful and interesting but also sonically stunning. Designers not only design the sounds and their relationships to each other and to the visual elements; they also design interaction and systems for generating and manipulating sounds in real time.

With the advent of the World Wide Web, the demands for sound design have again changed. Because of the decreased amount of space and slower perceived speeds of response, sound files again need to be small or compressed in some way. Right now, sound quality suffers and much of the interactivity is reduced to sound effects. But the level of interactivity and availability to large numbers of people are and inspiring and challenging. Because the field is so closely tied to technology, it is constantly changing. In the hands of imaginative people, the future is exciting to contemplate.

See also Music Technology; Organizations, Professional Audio; Sound Installation Artist

Brenda Hutchinson

Sound Installation Artist

At the intersection of the sonic arts (music and radio art) and sculpture, a sound installation artist creates her or his work. Tracing their lineage through the Dadaists (especially Kurt Schwitters), the "found object" aesthetic of Marcel Duchamp, the music philosophy of John Cage, and the French *musique concrète* (music created from every day sounds), increasing numbers of women are turning to this mode of sonic expression to escape the formalities of concert music and its performance, and to reach different types of audiences.

Attracted by the wide range of expressions available in this venue, works created by sound artists may find kinship with conceptual art, political art, computer music and art, and electro-acoustic music. These artists often explore psychoacoustics in the creation of their works. Some sound installations are computer-based; some involve audience interaction; some involve sound sculptures playable by an audience. Many sound installation artists work collaboratively with other artists and engineers. Their art may be intended for galleries or museums (often creating "sonic environments" in the process), or they may be site specific, in which artists create works for specific locations (often outdoors). Though there are sometimes performances attached to installations, audiences generally are free to come and go during these sonic experiences. Sound installation artists shape the sonic content of their works accordingly.

Liz Phillips (b. 1951) has been making interactive sound installations for the past 30 years. She works with what she calls "responsive spaces," having initially explored theremin-like devices as a mode for audience interaction. *Sunspots* (1981) reflects this early work in its use of an archway made from coiled copper tubing and a bronze screen suspended from the ceiling. Two speakers, one near these objects and one much further away, play back a variety of sounds that change in response to subtle audience movement through the radio frequency capacitance fields generated by the sculpture. The more recent *Echo Evolution* (1999) expands audience interaction with light as well as sound in her collaboration with Ken Greenberg.

Lauren Weinger's sound installations

are site specific, use processed acoustic sounds, and are often collaborative with other artists, particularly choreographer Joanna Haigood. Weinger is interested in the ability of recorded sound to evoke memory and to "bring back" places that no longer exist. *In Steel's Shadow* (1994) was an installation/performance that transformed San Francisco's Theater Artaud back into the American Can Company's Machine Shop #108 (the original occupant of the building). Weinger's score created an aural abstraction of the actual factory activity as well as the workers' existential experiences there. In *Invisible Wings* (1998) Weinger planted audio speakers in the ground along the route of the Underground Railroad, playing back collages of narrative interviews with former slaves.

In Annea Lockwood's (b. 1939) legendary *Piano Transplants* (1968–1972) she burned, submerged and planted pianos. Her *River Archive* (1973–1980) and *A Sound Map of the Hudson River* (1983) explored river sounds and their changes from location to location. Karen Frimkiss Wolff "draws" with sound in galleries via complexes of speakers and specially designed electronic systems (*Mourning Piece*, 1976; *Resurrection*, 1981). Other American sound installation artists who have made significant contributions to this growing body of work include Maryanne Amacher (b. 1946), Ruth Anderson (b. 1928), Linda Dusman (b. 1956), Maggi Payne (b. 1945), Sarah Peebles (b. 1964), and Laetitia Sonami (b. 1957).

See also Experimental Music; Music Technology; Performance Art

For Further Reading

Chadabe, Joel. *Electric Sound: The Past and Promise of Electronic Music*. Upper Saddle River, NJ: Prentice-Hall, 1997.

Harvestworks Media Arts Center. Available: http://www.harvestworks.org

Wolff, Karen Frimkiss. "Drawing with Sound." *Leonardo* 24/1 (1991): 23–29.

Linda Dusman

Southern Arts Federation

See Organizations, Regional Arts

Spiegel, Laurie (1945–)

Laurie Spiegel is a pioneer composer and computer music programmer. With computer music software such as Music Mouse, she has reached across aesthetic boundaries, carving new territory for both composed and live electronic music. Despite somewhat limited public attention, her compositions exhibit a clear, accessible aesthetic that appeals to a wide variety of listeners.

Born in Chicago, IL, on 20 September 1945, Spiegel became involved with both music and electronics at an early age, teaching herself to play and improvise by ear on the mandolin, guitar, and banjo. As a "late bloomer" in formal musical training, she notes that in her experience age discrimination in the musical community has posed a more significant hurdle than gender bias. She received a degree in social sciences at Shimer College (1967) and participated in an exchange program at Oxford University, where she studied classical guitar with John W. Duarte, who also provided her first composition and theory lessons. Spiegel eventually moved to New York and enrolled in the Juilliard School's Extension Division; by the end of her first year she had gained admission to graduate-level courses. There she studied with composers Vincent Persichetti and Jacob Druckman.

Spiegel became interested in creating music with analog synthesizers and computers, and she began working at the

New York University Composers Workshop in 1970. From 1973 to 1979 she worked at Bell Telephone Laboratories alongside colleagues Max Mathews, Emmanuel Ghent, Ken Knowlton, and F. Richard Moore, developing compositional techniques based on the relatively new field of information theory. Her pioneering work at Bell Labs also included an expansion of Mathews's famous GROOVE system to accommodate realtime production of video as well as music, called VAMPIRE (Video And Music Program for Interactive Realtime Exploration).

Spiegel worked throughout the 1970s as a film music composer. In 1976 she wrote perhaps the first musical accompaniment to a television series composed by a woman. Working as a video artist in residence at the Experimental Television Lab at WNET in 1976, she composed soundtracks for several programs on WNET, including its weekly broadcast "VTR."

After leaving Bell Labs, Spiegel continued her work in electronic and computer music. Beginning in 1976 she consulted for the Eventide company on its digital signal processors, and she taught courses at the Electronic Music Studio at the Cooper Union for the Advancement of Science and Art (1979–1981). She also taught at New York University, founding that institution's computer music studio in 1982. From 1978 to 1981 she contributed to the alphaSyntauri computer music system, and from 1982 to 1985 she served as consultant and software director for the McLeyvier computer music system.

Spiegel began privately circulating her music and distributing her software. Music Mouse, her most famous computer program, has been used by many musicians. She describes the program as "an intelligent instrument": while informing the program with various musical details (tempo, pitch range, scale, etc.) in realtime, the user composes by moving the cursor in two dimensions along a matrix of pitches. Spiegel is featured on many recorded anthologies, including *The Virtuoso in the Computer Age III* (CDCM Series, Vol. 13), *Computer Music Journal Sound Anthology* (MIT Press, 1996), and *Women in Electronic Music* (CRI CD 728). Her solo compact disc, *Unseen Worlds* (Aesthetic Engineering, 1994), illustrates the composer's command of her electronic arsenal of instruments and her ability to weave a counterpoint of hauntingly beautiful threads into a single entity of sound. But she never lets the technological side dominate: her music, often considered to be in a postminimalist vein, has a clear voice of its own. The composer of more than 80 performed works and author of more than 45 articles, Spiegel continues to innovate and explore.

See also Experimental Music; Music Technology; Software Designer/Programmer

For Further Reading

Gagne, Cole. *Soundpieces 2*. Metuchen, NJ: Scarecrow Press, 1993.

Gann, Kyle. Liner notes to Laurie Spiegel, *Unseen Worlds*. New York: Aesthetic Engineering, 1994.

Spiegel, *Laurie. Laurie Spiegel's Retiary Ramblings*. Available: http://retiary.org/ls/

Colby Leider

Staple Singers

The Staple Singers sang blues and soul-influenced gospel music in a long, distinguished career. Their members all hailed from one family, the original line-up consisting of Roebuck "Pops" Staples and his children, son Pervis and daughters Mavis (b. 1940), Cleotha (b. 1934), and Yvonne (b. 1939). Yvonne left the act in 1955 but returned twice, once briefly during Pervis's army service in the late 1950s and again permanently when Pervis quit for good in 1970. Pervis was the lead singer until his voice changed, after which Pops and Mavis shared lead vocal duties. Mavis in particular gained widespread praise for her accomplished singing.

The Staple Singers' gospel and blues roots ran deep. Pops Staples began his career playing blues guitar at picnics and dances in Mississippi as a teenager, and he later sang and played guitar with the gospel group Golden Trumpets. Moving to Chicago in 1936, Pops joined the group Trumpet Jubilees and taught his children to sing in gospel style. He presented his performing family in public at a local church for the first time in1948.

As might be expected, their earliest releases, on the Vee Jay label, were strongly gospel oriented, leavened noticeably by Pops's prominent Delta blues–style guitar playing. Songs from the 1950s such as "Uncloudy Day" and "This May Be the Last Time" demonstrate this influence. With the album *Make You Happy* on the Columbia label (Epic EG-30635), the group began experimenting with folk and pop music protest idioms. They recorded and issued two minor singles, "Why? (Am I Treated So Bad)" and a cover of Stephen Stills's "For What It's Worth." The former illustrates the group's keen interest in the civil rights issues of the day. In 1967 the group signed with Stax Records; three years later they recorded a series of successful soul-style hits composed by the label's in-house songwriters, most notably "Heavy Makes You Happy (Sha-Na-Boom-Boom)," "Respect Yourself," "I'll Take You There," "If You're Ready (Come Go with Me)," and "Touch a Hand, Make a Friend." With Stax nearing bankruptcy, the group moved to Curtis Mayfield's Curtom label, where they released two more singles, "Let's Do It Again," and "New Orleans." They continued to record, with occasional hiatuses, into the 1990s—and although they never quite reached their heights of the early 1970s, they continued to enjoy modest success performing and recording on the rhythm and blues circuit. The group was elected to the Rock and Roll Hall of Fame in 1999.

Mavis and Pops Staples also recorded solo albums. Mavis's best releases, such as her self-titled debut (Fantasy 300) and *Only for the Lonely* (Stax SCD880122), were in a rhythm and blues style strongly overlaid with gospel influence, although later albums showed leanings toward disco and other genres (including a collaborative effort with singer Prince in 1987).

See also Gospel Music; Rock and Roll Hall of Fame

For Further Reading

Carpenter, Bil. "Staple Singers: God's Greatest Hitmakers." *Goldmine* 22/18 (30 August 1996): 19–23ff.

Himes, Geoffrey. "Staple Singers' American Roots." *Washington Post*, Weekend Section (4 July 1997): 14.

"Meet the Staple Singers." *New York Amsterdam News* (11 August 1962): 39.

David Cleary

Streisand, Barbra (1942–)

Barbra Streisand has thrived as a Broadway star, recording artist, concert performer, and actress in both television and film. Her career has spanned virtually every branch of the entertainment industry, marked by an unprecedented diversity of commercial and critical successes.

Barbra Streisand performing at the U.S. Air Arena in Washington, DC, in May 1994. *Photo © Matt Mendelsohn/CORBIS.*

In addition, she has broken new ground for women as a film director, producer, and composer, all while becoming a near-legendary benefactor to many political causes.

Born Barbara Joan Streisand on 24 April 1942 in Brooklyn, NY, she studied acting as a high school student in pursuit of her dreams to become a dramatic actress. Her early career began, and her name changed to "Barbra," however, as a nightclub singer in Greenwich Village after winning a local talent contest in 1960. Her success and following was immediate. At the end of 1961 she won a small but show-stopping role in the Broadway musical *I Can Get It for You Wholesale*, landing a Tony Award nomination in this, her first Broadway appearance. After singing in the original cast recording, she returned to the studio to record a solo album of popular songs that was released in February 1963. By March, Streisand was the highest-selling woman artist in the United States for *The Barbra Streisand Album* (Columbia CK-8807), which won Grammy Awards for woman's vocal performance and album of the year. At that time she was the youngest artist ever to win.

After a second top-selling album, Streisand solidified her status as a major star by playing the lead role in the musical *Funny Girl*, beginning in 1964 on Broadway and opening in 1966 in London. Her portrayal of the comedienne and singer Fanny Brice made *Funny Girl* a huge success, with more than 1,300 performances, and garnered her a second Tony nomination. On the strength of her recording and stage triumphs, the mid-1960s saw Streisand conquer television with a series of enormously successful specials. The first, *My Name Is Barbra*, won her two Emmy Awards in 1965.

Her movie debut returned Streisand to the role of Fanny Brice in the screen adaptation of *Funny Girl* (1968). She shared a Best Actress Academy Award with Katherine Hepburn for that, her first of a series of film musicals that included *Hello, Dolly* (1969), *On a Clear Day You Can See Forever* (1970), and *Funny Lady* (1975), the sequel to *Funny Girl*. In *A Star Is Born* (1976) she not only starred but also co-wrote the song "Evergreen" with Paul Williams, making her the first woman composer to win an Academy Award.

Her 42 gold, 26 platinum, and 13 multi-platinum albums, including *Higher Ground* (Columbia 66181), place her second behind only Elvis Presley in all-time recording sales and make her the top-selling woman recording artist of all time. In January 2000 Streisand was awarded the Cecil B. DeMille Award, the highest honor for contribution to the field of entertainment bestowed by the Hollywood Foreign Press Association. Excelling in every entertainment medium she has attempted, Barbra Streisand is the only artist ever to receive Oscar, Emmy, Grammy, Tony, Golden Globe, Cable Ace, and Peabody Awards.

See also Musical Theater; Rock and Popular Music Genres

For Further Reading

The Barbra Streisand Music Guide. Available: http://www.bjsmusic.com

Kimbrell, James. *Barbra: An Actress Who Sings*. Boston: Branden Publishing, 1992.

Pohly, Linda. *The Barbra Streisand Companion: A Guide to Her Vocal Style and Repertoire*. Westport, CT: Greenwood Publishing, 2000.

Don Byrd

String Education

The field of string education has benefited greatly from women's contributions, although this was not always the case. At the beginning of the twentieth century Albert Mitchell, who wrote the first string class method book, established in Boston the precedent of teaching of strings in class settings. Up to this point, teaching stringed instruments had happened only in private lessons, a male-dominated domain mirroring professional symphonic orchestras. The appearance of string classes in schools developed sporadically across the United States, owing to the deficit of knowledgeable teachers. Because society considered teaching an acceptable job for women, a few women began to work as professional string teachers early in the century, but women were unable to hold leadership positions until much later. It was the feminist movement of the 1960s that brought greater awareness to these inequities and opened doors.

Marjorie Murray Keller (1907–2001) was born in MacMinnville, TN, and moved in 1931 to San Antonio, TX, where she studied and taught violin. Unaware of the work begun in Boston, Keller experimented with group instruction and took a string ensemble to perform at the National Federation of Music Clubs in Minneapolis in 1933. The performance was met with great acclaim, and as a result she was offered a position at the Cincinnati Conservatory of Music teaching string methods and directing orchestras. There she not only taught many students, including outstanding twentieth-century string pedagogue Paul Rolland, but also earned her bachelor's degree in public school music and administration, and a master's degree in music. In 1946, when Paul Rolland was forming the American String Teacher Association (ASTA), she was the only woman invited to be a founding board member.

In 1944 Keller returned to Texas to be director of instrumental music in the Dallas Public Schools, and she remained there until 1974. Her string choirs performed the Andante from the *Tragic Symphony* by Franz Schubert with the Dallas Symphony in 1946 with conductor Joseph Hawthorne. During these years she developed the materials for her method book *Easy Steps to the Orchestra*, which she co-authored with Maurice Taylor. She continued to present clinics and conduct, directing the Oklahoma All State Orchestra in February 1952, an unusual achievement for a woman. In 1955 she recognized the need for a specialized high school performing group and established the Dal-Hi Chamber Players. In 1972 the Dal-Hi Chamber Players were invited to the International Music Conference in Tunisia. They disbanded in 1974 to become the Greater Dallas Youth Orchestra. In the same year Keller she moved back to San Antonio to develop a strings program at Alamo Heights. Three of her students won chairs in the 1981 Texas All-State Orchestra, the first time in 30 years that San Antonio was represented in that ensemble. Keller's contributions to the field of string education were immense.

Midway through the twentieth century women string educators were finally holding leadership positions, in the Ohio area. Elizabeth Walker from Miami University (OH) became the first president of Ohio String Teachers in 1952, followed by Helen Hannen. Walker and Hannen identified the need for quality student instruments and convinced the Scherl and Roth Company in Cleveland to produce such instruments. They also discovered Jacquelyn Dillon (b. 1933), an outstanding teacher in Oklahoma, whom they hired in 1972 to improve communication among string teachers. Dillon's accomplishments include teaching numerous clinics across the nation, editing a newsletter that advocated for quality instruments and pedagogical excellence, and writing a seminal text with Casimer Kriechbaum, *How to Design and Teach a Successful School String and Orchestra Program*. Dillon was president of the ASTA from 1994 to 1996, and she remains active as a clinician and conductor. She was teaching string pedagogy at Wichita State University (KS) at the close of the twentieth century.

An important teaching method in string education is the Suzuki approach, developed in Japan by Shinichi Suzuki. Several of the first Suzuki teachers were men, but Margery Aber (1914–2001) developed the first American Suzuki Summer Institute at Stevens Point, WI, in 1971. Summer institutes are essential for training future Suzuki teachers and young string players. Women teachers at this first institute included violin teachers Diana Tillson, Anastasia Jemplis (Eastman School of Music), Louise Behrend ([b. 1916] School for Strings in New York City), and Marilyn Kesler (b. 1941), Kalamazoo, MI, teaching cello. The founder of this institute, Aber, was born in Racine, WI, studied violin with Elmer Slaman, and majored in music at the Oberlin College Conservatory of Music. Upon graduation in 1937 she accepted a teaching position in Detroit. This makes her notable not only as a Suzuki string educator but also as one of the first public school string teachers. In 1967 Aber went to Japan to study with Suzuki, and when she returned she accepted a position at the University of Wisconsin at Stevens Point. Aber continues to inspire string educators. Kesler was the first person to win the American String Teacher School Educator Award in 1990. All other recipients of this award in the twentieth century were men.

Other women Suzuki teachers include Lorraine Fink (b. 1931), who teaches violin at Ohio University; she also edited the *Suzuki Journal* from 1977 to 1979 and published the book *Parent's Guide to String Instrument Study*. Evelyn Hermann founded a large Suzuki school in Dallas, TX, in the 1970s and wrote the book *Shinichi Suzuki: A Man and His Philosophy* (Athens, OH: Ability Development, 1981). Elizabeth Mills who organized the American Suzuki Institute of the Southwest in Pasadena, CA. Doris Preucil (b. 1932) was an important leader of the Iowa City Suzuki program. Jane Aten (b. 1935) has taught in the Southern Methodist University Preparatory Program since 1966—an outreach program for impoverished and minority children sponsored by the Dallas Symphony. Kay Slone, a leader from Lexington, KY, wrote *They're Rarely Too Young—and Never Too Old "To Twinkle"* (Ann Arbor, MI: Shar Products, 1985). Alice Joy Lewis has led a Suzuki Institute at Ottawa, KS, since 1977. Barbara Barber (b. 1954) has compiled *Solos for the Young Violinist* (Miami, FL: Summy Birchard Inc., 1997) and led the Texas Christian University Suzuki Institute from 1992 to 1998.

Another influential string educator from the Midwest was Elizabeth Green (1906–1997). She taught in the Ann Arbor public schools and at the University of Michigan. Known for her dynamic conducting workshops, Green also has written numerous books: *The Conductor and His Score*, *Modern Conductor*, *Twelve Modern Etudes for Advanced Violinists or Violists*, and *Teaching Stringed Instruments in Class*. In 1976 she was the first woman to be awarded the Distinguished Service Award by the ASTA.

Other firsts for the ASTA include Dorothy Delay (1917–2001) as the first woman to be awarded the Artist-Teacher Award. Delay was born in Medicine Lodge, KS, attended Oberlin Conservatory and Michigan State University, and received an artist diploma from the Juilliard School of Music. She was on the Juilliard faculty since 1948. Additionally, Delay taught at Meadowmount from 1949 to 1970 and at Aspen from 1971 to 1999. She was well known for producing exceptional violinists at the Juilliard School of Music.

Another college string educator who contributed to the presence of women in the string education field is Priscilla Smith (1926–2001). She trained and taught in Indiana before going on to teach at the Oberlin College Conservatory of Music. She achieved a high profile nationally as secretary of the ASTA from 1968 to 1970. Her videotape and book, *Guide to Orchestral Bowings through Musical Styles* (Madison: University of Wisconsin Press, 1984) with Marvin Rabin, is considered an invaluable source on bowing techniques for non-string players.

The first woman president of the ASTA was Phyllis Young (b. 1925), from 1978 to 1980. During her presidency membership rose from 4,125 to 5,301, broadening the base to include membership participation in nominating award winners and requests for special project funds. She redesigned the position of executive director, appointed a publications advisory board and an editorial advisory board, and increased the size of the journal. Six states reorganized or formed new chapters, and Young created new policies to strengthen state chapters. Also during Young's tenure, the Music Educator's National Conventions held more ASTA sessions than in previous years. In her work at the University of Texas at Austin, Young is noted for her String Project in which university students teach children in a supervised setting. She has also published two books to enhance string teaching, *Playing the String Game* (Austin: University of Texas Press, 1978) and *The String Play* (Austin: University of Texas Press, 1986).

Another woman of leadership in string education is Dorothy Straub (b. 1941), who was the first woman string educator to become president of the Music Educators National Conference (MENC), from 1992 to 1994. She taught in Connecticut where she built a strong string program, which she continues to supervise. During her tenure as president of MENC, the organization adopted the National Standards for the Arts as requested by the federal secretary of education to improve teaching in America. The arts were the first subject area to complete this task. This document continues to guide the music education profession into the twenty-first century.

A final event worth noting was the release of a Miramax movie featuring a woman string educator, Roberta Guaspari. Meryl Streep played the lead role in *Music of the Heart* (1999)—a film about Guaspari, who built a string program in Harlem and fought to keep it when the financial support was eliminated. The *VH1 Save the Music* cable television show, in conjunction with MENC: The National Association for Music Education, NAMM: International Music Products Association, the NARAS foundation, and the American Music Conference, spearheaded efforts to use the movie to promote string teaching, playing, and music education in general in this country.

At the end of the twentieth century there was a greater awareness of the value of string education and of the important role women played in creating that awareness. Women string educators owe a debit of gratitude to the feminists who fought for this awareness in the 1960s and opened doors to a diversity of jobs and leadership roles. Continued work toward the acceptance of women conductors of professional orchestras and an increase of women orchestral players is greatly needed.

See also Music Education; Organizations, Music Education; Performer, String

For Further Reading

American String Teacher. Quarterly publication of the American String Teachers Association with the National School Orchestra Association.

American Suzuki Journal. Quarterly publication of the Suzuki Association of the Americas.

Joanne Erwin

The Supremes

One of the most successful vocal groups of all time, the Supremes originally started as an all-girl group while the members were schoolgirls in Detroit, MI. Formed in 1960 as the Primettes (a sister group to the all-male Primes), the members included Florence Ballard (1943–1976), Diana Ross (b. 1944), and Mary Wilson (b. 1944). At times the group also included Betty Travis and Barbara Martin. After a few recordings with the Detroit-based Lupine label, Ballard, Ross, and Wilson were signed to Motown Records as a trio. Renamed the Supremes, the group released their first album, *Meet the Supremes*, in 1963 (the Primes, who also signed with Motown, were renamed the Temptations). After a number of changes that included Ross being repositioned as lead singer, and the new collaboration with songwriting team Holland-Dozier-Holland, the Supremes had their first major hit with "Where Did Our Love Go?" (Motown MOTD-5270) in 1964. This was the first of 12 number one hits the group would have, including "Baby Love," "Come See about Me," "Stop! In the Name of Love," and "Someday We'll Be Together." Poised and glamorous, they represented the trademark Motown sound and look.

In 1967 Ballard left the group and was replaced by former backup singer Cindy Birdsong (b. 1939). At that time the focus of the group almost completely shifted to Ross, and the group was renamed Diana Ross and the Supremes. Ross left the Supremes in 1970 for a solo career, and Jean Terrell (b. 1944) was brought in to fill the vacancy. Following Ross's departure, the trio continued to record songs that charted in the Top 20, such as "Stoned Love" (1970), "Nathan Jones"

(1971), and "Floy Joy" ([1972] Motown 37463-5441-2). The lineup did not remain permanent, however, and the group went through several other manifestations throughout the 1970s. Birdsong left in 1972 and was replaced by Lynda Laurence. Scherrie Payne replaced Terrell when she left in 1973. Birdsong returned, and left again, to be replaced by Susaye Greene. The 1976 album *Mary, Scherrie, and Susaye* (Motown S-873) was the Supremes' last album before disbanding. In 1988 the Supremes, with the original lineup of Ballard, Ross, and Wilson, were inducted into the Rock and Roll Hall of Fame.

See also Motown; Rock and Popular Music Genres; Rock and Roll Hall of Fame

For Further Reading

Taraborrelli, J. Randy. *Call Her Miss Ross: The Unauthorized Biography of Diana Ross*. New York: Carol Publishing Group, 1989.

Wilson, Mary, and Patricia Romanowski. *Supreme Faith: Someday We'll Be Together*. New York: HarperCollins, 1990.

Kristina Lampe Shanton

Suzuki, Pat (1930–)

Pat Suzuki was one of the first Asian American women to take a starring role in American musical theater with her role as Linda Low in the 1958 original Broadway production of Rodgers and Hammerstein's *Flower Drum Song*, the first Broadway production to feature an all-Asian cast. Despite negative attitudes toward Americans of Japanese descent in the post–World War II years, Suzuki rose to stardom through her talent and perseverance. Her career as a singer and actress has taken her from nightclubs to the recording studio, from Broadway to television. In her prime, she was compared to Judy Garland (1922–1969), Eartha Kitt (b. 1927), Ella Fitzgerald (1917–1996), Billie Holiday (1915–1959), Sarah Vaughan (1924–1990), and Ethel Merman (1909–1984).

Pat Suzuki was born Chiyoki ("a thousand times good") Suzuki in Cressy, CA, on 23 September 1930. Her parents emigrated from Toyohashi, Japan, and settled on a farm in Yamato Colony in Merced County, where she grew up. At the outbreak of World War II, when thousands of Japanese American families were gathered into internment camps, she and her family were held in Amache (Granada), CO, for four years. Suzuki studied fine arts and education and graduated from San Jose State University with a B.F.A. degree (1953). After graduating she moved to New York City, where she auditioned and was cast in a walk-on part in the national touring company of *Teahouse of the August Moon*. She left the tour in Seattle and launched her singing career at the Colony, a then-fashionable supper club, where she attracted the attention of RCA Records and talent scouts at the William Morris Agency. In 1957 Suzuki was voted Best Female Singer of the annual *Downbeat Magazine* Disc Jockey Poll. During the next three years she released four solo albums of jazz standards and Broadway show tunes with RCA Victor Records: *The Many Sides of Pat Suzuki* (VIK LX-1127), *Pat Suzuki's Broadway '59* (RCA Victor LSP-1965), and *Looking at You* (RCA Victor LSP-2186).

In 1958 Suzuki was approached by Richard Rodgers to play the role of Linda Low in his forthcoming musical *Flower Drum Song*, an adaptation of C. Y. Lee's book of the same title. The musical opened on 1 December 1958 at the St. James Theatre on Broadway, and Suzuki was catapulted to stardom as a musical theater personality. Later that month she graced the cover of *Time* magazine with her co-star, Miyoshi Umeki, and in 1959 won a Most Promising Personality award from the theater publication *Daniel Blum's Theatre World*.

In 1960 Suzuki married photographer Mark Shaw and took a one-year hiatus from performing to give birth to their son David. She soon returned to an active performing and touring schedule throughout the United States, Canada, and Europe, including an appearance at the 1970 world's fair in Osaka, Japan. She continued to perform through the mid-1970s. Suzuki is essentially retired from performing but continues to make guest appearances for special and fund-raising events.

See also Asian American Music; Musical Theater

For Further Reading

Gussow, Mel. "String Past Dragon Lady and No. 1 Son." *New York Times* (3 September 1990): Late Edition, Final Sec. (1:1).

Komai, Chris. "Miss Ponytail Returns." *Rafu Shimpo* (11 May 1994): 1.

Cynthia Wong

Svigals, Alicia (1963–)

Violinist and composer Alicia Svigals is considered one of the world's premier klezmer fiddlers. Svigals has been a prominent force not only in the revival of klezmer music but in creating a new contemporary Jewish "roots music" idiom that combines Yiddish folk traditions with a modern aesthetic. Svigals not only plays klezmer music but also has taught hundreds of students, including some of the best professional players today. She worked with Itzhak Perlman on the album *In the Fiddler's House* (Angel 55555) and also appeared nationally in that production on radio and television, including the Emmy Award–winning *Great Performances* documentary for PBS. Additionally, she collaborated with poets Allen Ginsburg and Jerome Rothenberg, as well as with dancers and choreographers Twyla Tharp, David Dorfman, and Naomi Goldberg. She wrote the score to the documentary *The Uprising of 1934* (1991).

Born on 8 January 1963 in the Bronx, NY, to Mildred Farrier and Edwin Svigals, Alicia first studied music at the Community Music School in Spring Valley, NY, with Janet and Ed Simons. After graduating from Brown University with a degree in ethnomusicology, Svigals played Greek music in and around New York. In 1986 she helped found the Klezmatics klezmer band. The new group started by studying current klezmer and vintage recordings from the YIVO archives in New York.

The Klezmatics' first album, *Shvaygn = Toyt* (Piranah 20), contained reconstructions of Yiddish folk songs and repertoire from the old 78 records. *Rhythm + Jews* (Flying Fish 591) appeared in 1990; in it Svigals played Gypsy-style fiddling in "Violin Doyna." In *Possessed* (Xenophile 4050), Svigals composed "Lomir Heybn Dem Bekher" on the basis of texts by Yiddish poets I. J. Schwartz and A. Reisen. In 1997 Svigals produced a solo album, *Fidl* (Traditional Crossrds 4286), the first klezmer fiddle recording that mixes traditional melodies and original compositions. In 1998 she and the Klezmatics collaborated with Chava Alberstein, a well-known Israeli singer, to produce *The Well*, a collection of new songs based on Yiddish poetry.

In her 1998 article "Why We Do This Anyway: Klezmer as Jewish Youth Subculture" (*Judaism* 47/1: 43–49), Svigals declares her manifesto of klezmer music in which she is against Jewish nostalgia but for promoting Jewish identity through klezmer music; for Jews to gain self-esteem through serious consideration of klezmer music; for pride in the Yiddish language; and against false definitions of "authenticity" in Jewish folk music. She believes that what musicians are creating today should be considered as authentic as music of the past.

See also Jewish Musicians; Multicultural Musics

For Further Reading

Rogovoy, Seth. *The Essential Klezmer: A Music Lover's Guide to Jewish Roots and Soul Music, from the Old World to the Jazz Age to the Downtown Avant Garde*. Chapel Hill, NC: Algonquin Books, 2000.

Slobin, Mark. *Fiddler on the Move: Exploring the Klezmer World*. New York: Oxford University Press, 2000.

Svigals, Alicia, and Ellen Markowitz. "Two Girls and a Baby." In *The Bust Guide to the New Girl Order*, eds. Marcelle Karp and Debbie Stoller. New York: Penguin Books, 1999.

Judith S. Pinnolis

Sweet Adelines

Intended for women who enjoyed singing music in the close harmony style, the Sweet Adelines singing organization was founded on 13 July 1945 in Tulsa, OK. The organization was founded to promote the barbershop style among women by teaching the members musical harmony and appreciation; the first meeting was held in the home of Edna Mae Anderson (1903–1959). By the end of 1945, the chapter had 85 members and was chartered under the name Atomaton (which came from the saying "We have an atom of an idea and a ton of energy"). Within four years it had expanded to 35 chapters in 14 states, with around 1,500 members and 60 quartets. This expansion led to the development of a national organization with bylaws, officers, and annual competitions to select the best women's barbershop quartet in the nation.

Currently the organization, known as Sweet Adelines International, has grown to around 30,000 members in the United States and 10 other countries. In addition to supporting quartets, the organization works with music educators to encourage musical excellence in vocal music programs through the Young Singers Foundation and the Young Women in Harmony program. The Young Singers Foundation provides funding to school- and community-based vocal music programs for young people, as well as scholarships for vocal music students. Young Women in Harmony provides materials, training, and opportunities for young women to learn the barbershop style.

See also Barbershop Quartet

For Further Reading

Stebbins, Robert A. *Barbershopping: Musical and Social Harmony*. London: Associated University Presses, 1993.

Sweet Adelines International. Available: http://www.sweetadelineintl.org/

Whitlock, Linda. "Get America Singing . . . Again." *Teaching Music* 3/6 (1996): 40–41.

Eric S. Strother

Swift, Katharine (Kay) (1897–1993)

The first woman to compose an entire Broadway score, Katharine (Kay) Swift was a classically trained pianist who wrote music for the stage and screen. She is best known for her 1930 show *Fine and Dandy*, as well as for her close association with composer George Gershwin.

Swift was born on 19 April 1897 in New York, the daughter of music critic Samuel Swift. She studied piano with Mrs. Bertha Fiering Tapper of the Institute of Musical Art (later the Juilliard School) and composition with Arthur

Edward Johnstone. As she earned diplomas from the Institute, she studied theory with Percy Goetschius and played with the Edith Rubel Trio.

In 1918 Swift married banker James P. Warburg, with whom she had three daughters. Warburg's employment took them to Cambridge, MA, where Katharine studied piano with Heinrich Gebhard and composition with Charles Martin Loeffler. They returned to New York in 1921, socializing with noted musical, literary, and theatrical personalities. Swift met George Gershwin in 1925, and the two developed a close professional and personal relationship. She helped him by copying music and advising him in counterpoint and orchestration. Swift, whom Gershwin nicknamed "Kay," developed an interest in Broadway and in 1927 served as rehearsal pianist for the Rodgers and Hart production *A Connecticut Yankee*. She began to write her own popular songs, with her husband providing the lyrics under the pseudonym Paul James. Several were interpolated into Broadway revues, including "Can't We Be Friends?" (1929) and "Up among the Chimney Pots" (1930). The Swift-James team wrote their only complete Broadway show in 1930, *Fine and Dandy*, which featured the title song and "Can This Be Love?" Swift became a member of the American Society of Composers, Authors and Publishers in 1931.

In 1934 Swift composed the score for *Alma Mater*, a George Balanchine ballet. After divorcing Warburg, she served as a staff composer for Radio City Music Hall, producing numbers for the Rockettes' routines. She left to become director of light music for the 1939 New York World's Fair. In 1940 Swift eloped with Faye Hubbard, a cowboy in the Fair rodeo. They settled on a ranch in Oregon, which inspired her humorous memoir *Who Could Ask for Anything More?* Her story was later made into the movie *Never a Dull Moment* (1950). Swift spent time in Hollywood helping Ira Gershwin assemble unused tunes from George Gershwin's sketchbooks to create the posthumous score for the Betty Grable movie *The Shocking Miss Pilgrim* (1946). She divorced Hubbard and was married for the third and final time in 1946 to Hunter Galloway. In 1948 they returned to New York, and Swift wrote the score for her last Broadway effort, *Paris Ninety*, a one-woman show starring Cornelia Otis Skinner. Swift completed *Reaching for the Brass Ring* (1953), a song cycle inspired by her grandchildren, and wrote *Theme and Variations for Piano and Cello* in 1960. From 1960 to 1974 she composed music for industrial shows and world's fairs. Swift continued to advise Gershwin projects for the rest of her life. She died on 28 January 1993.

See also Musical Theater; Songwriter

For Further Reading

Chernow, Ron. *The Warburgs: The Twentieth Century Odyssey of a Remarkable Jewish Family*. New York: Random House, 1993.

Ohl, Vicki. *Kay Swift, the Gershwin Liaison and "Can't We Be Friends?"* In *'S Wonderful, 'S Marvelous: A Popular Song Reader*, ed. Ann Sears. Westport, CT: Greenwood Press, forthcoming.

———. *The Machine Age on Broadway: Fine and Dandy*. In *'S Wonderful, 'S Marvelous: A Popular Song Reader*, ed. Ann Sears. Westport, CT: Greenwood Press, forthcoming.

Vicki Ohl

T

Talma, Louise Juliette (1906–1996)

Louise Juliette Talma, composer, conductor, and pedagogue, was one of Nadia Boulanger's pupils at the American Conservatory, and the only American Boulanger ever permitted to teach there (1936–1939, summers). She was the first woman to receive two Guggenheim fellowships in composition (1946 and 1947), the first woman to be awarded the Sibelius Medal (1963), and the first woman to be elected to the National Institute of Arts and Letters (1974). In 1955 Talma was awarded a Senior Fulbright Research Grant and went to Rome for 10 months to work on her opera *Alcestiad*. In 1959 the Koussevitsky Music Foundation awarded Talma a commission to write *All the Days of My Life*, a cantata for tenor, clarinet, violoncello, piano, and percussion, which she completed in 1965.

Louise Talma was born on 31 October 1906 in Arcachon, France, of American parents. In 1914 Talma was brought to New York for her formal education. From 1922 to 1930 she attended the Institute of Musical Arts (which merged with the Juilliard School, 1946). During the summers 1926–1939 she attended summer sessions at Fountainbleau, studying piano with Isadore Philipp (1926–1927) and composition with Nadia Boulanger (1928–1939). She received a B.A. from New York University (1931) and an M.A. from Columbia University (1933). Beginning in the early 1940s Talma visited the MacDowell Colony in Peterborough, NH, where she was influenced by composers Lukas Foss, Irving Fine, Arthur Berger, Claudio Spies, and Alexie Haieff. Many of Talma's works were composed while in residence at the MacDowell Colony.

Talma's compositional output comprises more than 40 works, including four orchestral pieces and a full-scale three-act opera. Talma was strongly influenced by Igor Stravinsky; like Stravinsky, she retained tonal qualities in her 12-tone works, and serialism was used as a unifying factor. After the opera *Alcestiad* (1955–1958) she combined tonal and serial elements in her works. Her compositions have been recorded on *Music of Louise Talma* (Composers Recordings Inc. 833), *Patricia Spencer—The Now and Present Flute* (Neuma 45088), and

Fabulous Femmes (Centaur 2461). Talma died on 13 August 1996 at the Yaddo Artists Colony near Saratoga Springs, NY.

See also Classical Music

For Further Reading

Ammer, Christine. *Unsung*. Revised and expanded second edition. Portland, OR: Amadeus Press, 2001.

Barkin, Elaine. "Louise Talma: The Tolling Bell." *Perspectives of New Music* 10/2 (1972): 142–52.

Louise Talma Society Website. Available: http://www.omnidisc.com/Talma.html

Amy Dunker

Tarpley, Brenda Mae

See Lee, Brenda

Tau Beta Sigma

The Tau Beta Sigma sorority was chartered in 1946, growing out of a nine-year campaign to found an organization that would serve the needs of a growing number of women band musicians throughout the United States. Like its senior counterpart, Kappa Kappa Psi, the women's honor band sorority had its headquarters at Oklahoma State University, although Wava Banes Henry began the movement itself at Texas Tech University. In 1991 both organizations moved their headquarters to the newly renovated Stillwater, OK, railway station, where they remain today.

Tau Beta Sigma operates as a student service and leadership recognition society with a primary objective of assisting band directors in developing the leadership and enthusiasm required of their bands. Of the 212 chartered chapters, over 125 are presently active with more than 2,000 members. Since 1946, over 38,000 women have pledged the sorority. Tau Beta Sigma has commissioned works from composers Fisher Tull, Francis McBeth, and Alfred Reed, among others, and joins with Kappa Kappa Psi for the biannual presentation of the National Intercollegiate Band at their national convention. Both also combine to publish the twice-yearly journal *The Podium* and the newsletter *News Notes*, as well as to maintain their Internet site.

To balance service with musicianship, Tau Beta Sigma offers a variety of awards to its members, including the Outstanding Service to Music Award, the Wava Banes Turner Award, and the Chapter Leadership Award. Through its network of chapters, Tau Beta Sigma has for over half a century realized its vision of creating "the pre-eminent organization to promote band music as an integral part of the American cultural experience . . . and to recognize deserving women and their contributions."

See also Fraternities and Sororities, Professional

For Further Reading

National HQ of Kappa Kappa Psi and Tau Beta Sigma. Available: http://www.kkytbs.org

The Podium. Kappa Kappa Psi/Tau Beta Sigma, Stillwater, OK.

Gregory Straughn

Tharpe, Sister Rosetta (1915–1973)

Singer Sister Rosetta Tharpe was one of the major innovators in the gospel music tradition. She was known not only for her musical skills but also for her influential role as a professional artist. Tharpe demonstrated her diverse talents by performing blues, jazz, gospel, and folk music. She was one of the first musicians to take gospel music into a secular setting by performing with Cab Calloway at the Cotton Club in Harlem, accompanying herself on the guitar. These appearances gave her great exposure, and in 1938 she signed a recording contract with Decca, the first gospel singer to record with a major company. By 1939 Tharpe had recorded Thomas Dorsey's "Hide Me in Thy Bosom" (recorded as "Rock Me That's All"), "My Man and I," and "Lonesome Road." On the Decca release "Rock Me," the performer was billed as "Sister Rosetta Tharpe."

Tharpe was born on 20 March 1915 in Cotton Plant, AR. Her early musical training derived from her singing in church. However, at an early age she began playing the acoustic guitar and later the amplified guitar, uncommon among women at the time. Tharpe eventually developed her guitar technique to a substantial level to accompany her performances. In 1938 Tharpe again brought gospel music into a secular setting, performing in John Hammond's "From Spirituals to Swing" concerts in Carnegie Hall. The featured singers were Tharpe, with her guitar, and the Mitchell Christian Singers. Tharpe was also one of the first gospel singers to appear at the Apollo Theater in Harlem in 1946.

As a gospel singer Tharpe was initially welcomed at churches by the black religious community, but the gospel community's enthusiasm dissipated when she and her regular pianist and singing partner, Marie Knight (b. 1925), began recording the blues. Tharpe's early hit blues recordings include "Tall Skinny Papa" (1942) and "Trouble in Mind" (1946). In 1953 she recorded blues with Leroy Kirkland's orchestra; then, in the 1960s, she toured throughout Europe singing jazz with the Chris Barber band. Her many recordings include *Live in 1960* (Southland 1007), *Sister on Tour* (Verve 3005), and *Live in Paris: 1964* (French Concerts FCD 118). On 9 October 1973 Tharpe died of a stroke at the age of 85.

See also Gospel Music

For Further Reading

Boyer, Horace Clarence. *How Sweet the Sound: The Golden Age of Gospel.* Washington, DC: Elliott and Clark Publishing, 1995.

Southern, Eileen. *The Music of Black Americans: A History*, 3rd ed. New York and London: W.W. Norton, 1997.

Clarence Bernard Henry

Thome, Diane (1942–)

Composer Diane Thome is among the first women to explore sound synthesis with the computer. After earning two undergraduate degrees from the Eastman School of Music (in piano and composition) and an M.A. degree in theory and composition from the University of Pennsylvania, Thome became the first woman to receive a Ph.D. in music from Princeton University. Her teachers have included composers Darius Milhaud, Robert Strassburg, Roy Harris, A. U. Boscovich, and Milton Babbitt. Thome's most characteristic music is subtly complex, often rich in references to music of other cultures. It frequently explores the continuum between the synthetic and the human, between machine and performer, enfolding the compositional materials into an organic whole.

Thome's composition catalog includes works for orchestra, chorus, solo instruments, chamber ensembles, and various electronic media. Her compositions have been performed throughout the United States as well as in Europe, China, Australia, Israel, and Canada. Her compositions are recorded on the Capstone, Centaur, CRI, Crystal Records, Opus One, and Tulstar labels, and they include the compact discs *Sunbursts—Solo Piano Works by 7 American Women* (Leonarda

Records 345), *America Sings!* (Capstone CPS-86130, and *Palaces of Memory* (Centaur Records CRC 2229).

Among Thome's distinctions are serving as guest of the Ecole Nationale Claude Debussy as well as composer-in-residence at the University of Sussex. She has also served as composer-in-residence at the Bennington Chamber Music Conference and the Composers Forum of the East. Additionally, she was awarded a 1998 International Computer Music Conference Commission and was named 1994 Washington Composer of the Year by the Music Teachers National Association.

See also Classical Music; Music Technology

For Further Reading

Straughn, Greg. "Composer Profile: Diane Thome." *ILWC [International League of Women Composers] Journal* (June 1993): 23.

Thome, Diane. "Reflections on Collaborative Process and Compositional Revolution." *Leonardo Music Journal: Journal of the International Society for the Arts, Sciences and Technology* 5 (1995): 29–32.

Colby Leider

Thornton, Willie Mae "Big Mama" (1926–1984)

Blues singer Willie Mae Thornton continued the legacy of such great women blues singers as Gertrude "Ma" Rainey (1886–1939), Bessie Smith (1894–1937), and others. Thornton's greatest fame came in 1953 when Johnny Otis asked composers Jerry Lieber and Mike Stoller to write a song especially for her. The song was "Hound Dog." It reached number one on the rhythm and blues chart, making Thornton a national star. A few years later "Hound Dog" was recorded by Elvis Presley.

One of seven children, Thornton was born Willie Mae Thornton, on 11 December 1926 in Montgomery, AL. Because of her size she was given the nickname "Big Mama." Her father was a minister who taught her to play harmonica and drums as a child. In her early years she sang in church choirs along with her mother. Thornton was only 14 years old when her mother died. Shortly thereafter she got her first chance to sing in public at a saloon. By 1941 she had joined Sammy Green's Hot Harlem Review of Atlanta. Then Thornton began to perform regularly on the blues circuit throughout the South. During these tours she often heard performances by some of the legendary blues singers, such as Bessie Smith, Memphis Minnie (1897–1973), and Big Maceo, who were influences on her own style.

Thornton was further exposed to great blues singers when she relocated in Houston in 1948. There she heard Junior Parker, Lightning Hopkins, Lowell Fulson, and Gatemouth Brown. In Houston Thornton also made her first recording under the name of Harlem Stars. Her next recording contract, in 1951, was with the Peacock label. Thornton eventually moved to Los Angeles to appear with bandleader Johnny Otis, where she recorded over 30 songs by the mid-1950s.

Thornton continued to perform on the blues circuit, but by 1957 the popularity of blues music had declined. However, she continued to perform, playing drums and harmonica with small local bands in San Francisco. She regained some of her fame in 1961 with the release of "Ball and Chain." A few years later Janis Joplin recorded this song to great acclaim. Thornton also recorded with Bay-Tone (1961), Sotoplay, (1963) and Kent (1964). In 1965 she toured Europe with the Folk Blues Festival troupe. She

Willie Mae "Big Mama" Thornton. *Photograph by George Pickow.*

signed a new contract with the Arhoolie label in 1964 and continued recording into the 1980s. Some of her many recordings include *Ball 'n Chain* (Arhoolie 1039), *Big Mama Thornton with Chicago Blues Band* (Arhoolie 1032), *The Original Hound Dog* (Ace 940), and *Hound Dog: The Duke-Peacock Recordings* (MCA-Duke-Peacock MCAD 10668). Thornton died of a heart attack on 25 July 1984 in Los Angeles.

See also Blues

Further Reading

Oliver, Paul. *The Story of the Blues*. Boston: Northeastern University Press, 1997.

Southern, Eileen. *The Music of Black Americans: A History*. New York and London: W.W. Norton, 1997.

Clarence Bernard Henry

Tick, Judith (1943–)

Judith Tick, professor of music at Northeastern University in Boston, is a leading authority on American music in general and the history of women in music in particular. She is co-editor of *Women Making Music: The Western Art Tradition, 1150–1950*, a pioneering work in its field, and author of *American Women Composers before 1870* as well as the highly acclaimed *Ruth Crawford Seeger: A Composer's Search for American Music*, praised by reviewers for its vibrancy, eloquence, and meticulous research. Tick also wrote the entries on "Women and Music" for *The New Grove Dictionary of American Music* and the 2001 revised edition of *The New Grove Dictionary of Music*. In addition, she has published two music editions: *The Lieder of Josephine Lang* and *Five Songs on Poems by Carl Sandburg* with music by Ruth Crawford Seeger.

Born on 4 January 1943, in Winthrop, MA, Tick earned a B.A. in music from Smith College (1964), an M.A. in music from the University of California at Berkeley (1967), and a Ph.D. in music from the City University of New York (1979). Her teaching career began at the Institute for Studies in American Music at Brooklyn College, where she became an associate professor in 1983. She also taught at Brandeis University in addition to her current position at Northeastern University, which began in 1992 and where she was appointed a Matthews Distinguished University Professor in 1999.

Other honors for Tick include the 1998 American Society of Composers, Authors and Publishers (ASCAP) Deems Taylor Award and the 1999 Society for American Music Award for best book of the year for her biography of Ruth Crawford Seeger, as well as the 1995 best article of the year award from the Sonneck Society for the Study of American Music for her essay, "Charles Ives and Gender Ideology" in *Musicology and Difference*, edited by Ruth Solie. Tick also received the ASCAP Deems Taylor Award for Women Making Music in 1987.

In addition to teaching and writing, Tick serves as an associate editor for the journal *Musical Quarterly*. Other ongoing activities include a commission from the Heckscher Museum of Art for a catalog essay on the music of Aaron Copland, whose centennial is being celebrated with an exhibit called "Copland's World, 2000." She was also invited by the Lincoln Center Chamber Music Society to present a lecture on "The American Scene" in January 2000, and she continues to serve on the National Advisory Directorate for the American Classical Music Hall of Fame.

With her record of accomplishments alone, Judith Tick constitutes a source of inspiration for younger generations of musicians. Moreover, the vivid nature of her writing makes her exemplary works of scholarship accessible to a wide readership.

See also Musicologist; Publication Awards

For Further Reading

Tick, Judith. *American Women Composers before 1870*. Ann Arbor, MI: UMI Research Press, 1983.

———. *Ruth Crawford Seeger: A Composer's Search for American Music*. New York: Oxford University Press, 1997.

Nelly Case

Tillis, Pam (1957–)

Singer Pam Tillis is one of the most versatile performers to emerge from the country music industry during the final decades of the twentieth century. Daughter of country music star Mel Tillis, she rose to success as singer, songwriter, and actress via a decidedly circuitous route. She made her singing debut on the Grand Ole Opry at age eight but consciously avoided country music during the early years of her career, trying her hand at many other genres before returning to the Nashville music scene years later.

Born in Plant City, FL, on 24 July 1957 and raised in Nashville, TN, Tillis is the eldest of five children. Because of her parents' stormy relationship, she spent many childhood hours in her bedroom singing and making up sad songs. At age 16 Tillis was involved in an automobile accident in which she was thrown through a car windshield, leaving her to face five years of painful reconstructive facial surgery. Undaunted, she enrolled in the University of Tennessee but later dropped out of college and moved to San Francisco, where she sang with the Ramsey Lewis Trio, performed with her own jazz/rock band, married Rick Mason, gave birth to son Ben, and divorced before returning to Nashville in 1979.

Even after her return to Nashville, Pam Tillis's rise to fame was gradual. During the decade preceding her eventual success, she traveled as backup singer for her father, sang as a publishing company demo singer and as a studio vocalist backing other performers, worked as a hotel lounge performer, and finally worked as a composer and vocalist for advertising jingles. Tillis starred in a local production of *Jesus Christ Superstar* and started a "Women in the Round" showcase at Nashville's famed Bluebird Cafe. Although her first recording contract for Warner Brothers Records in 1984 was largely unsuccessful, her songs fared better. Many of these were recorded by a diverse group of well-known artists, including Chaka Khan (b. 1953), Conway Twitty, the Forester Sisters, Ricky Van Shelton, and others.

Tillis began to reconnect to country music in 1987 when she produced and performed in a revue called *Twang Night* featuring classic oldies from honky-tonk and hillbilly genres. Finally, in 1990 after a string of mildly successful recordings, Tillis signed with Arista Records and began her rise to country music stardom. Since then, she has come to reside solidly at the top of her field. Her irrepressible, quirky sense of humor, songwriting talent, ability to move vocally between musical styles, and determination to avoid creating a stereotypical image for herself have made her a model for other women country artists. Her hits include the 1991 recording of "Don't Tell Me What to Do" and the 1992 songs "Maybe It Was Memphis" and "Shake the Sugartree." Among her many compact discs are *Every Time* (Arista 18861), *All of This Love* (Arista 18799), and *Sweetheart's Dance* (Arista 18758-2). Her success has resulted in prestigious honors, including the 1993 Country Music Association (CMA) award for Vocal Event of the Year, a 1994 CMA designation as Female Vocalist of the Year, a 1998 Grammy Award for Best Country Vocal Collaboration, and the 1998 CMA Founding Presidents Award.

See also Country Music; Country Music Association

For Further Reading

Bufwack, Mary A., and Robert K. Oermann. *Finding Her Voice: The Saga of Women in Country Music*. New York: Crown, 1993.

Amy Corin

Tony Awards

The Tony Awards, the highest distinction for theatrical accomplishment, were founded in 1947 by friends of Antoinette Perry (1888–1946), a pioneer who championed women and young people in the theatre. The colorful history of the Tony Award began during World War I with the development of an organization called the "Stage Women's War Relief." This organization sold liberty Bonds, organized clothing and food collection centers, and opened a canteen for servicemen on Broadway, eventually becoming one of the most successful relief organizations in the world. In 1939, the "Stage Women's War Relief" was rechristened the "American Theatre Wing War Service," and listed actress and director Antoinette Perry among its mem-

Women Winners of the Tony Award for Musicals

Year	Best Performance by a Leading Actress in a Musical	Best Performance by a Featured Actress in a Musical
1947	category eliminated	category eliminated
1948	Grace Hartman, *Angel in the Wings*	category eliminated
1949	Nanette Fabray, *Love Life*	category eliminated
1950	Mary Martin, *South Pacific*	Juanita Hall, *South Pacific*
1951	Ethel Merman, *Call Me Madam*	Isabel Bigley, *Guys and Dolls*
1952	Gertrude Lawrence, *The King and I*	Helen Gallagher, *Pal Joey*
1953	Rosalind Russell, *Wonderful Town*	Sheila Bond, *Wish You Were Here*
1954	Dolores Gray, *Carnival in Flanders*	Gwen Verdon, *Can-Can*
1955	Mary Martin, *Peter Pan*	Carol Haney, *The Pajama Game*
1956	Gwen Verdon, *Damn Yankees*	Lotte Lenya, *The Threepenny Opera*
1957	Judy Holliday, *Bells Are Ringing*	Edith Adams, *Li'l Abner*
1958	Thelma Ritter, *New Girl in Town* Gwen Verdon, *New Girl in Town*	Barbara Cook, *The Music Man*
1959	Gwen Verdon, *Redhead*	Pat Stanley, *Goldilocks*
1960	Mary Martin, *The Sound of Music*	Patricia Neway, *The Sound of Music*
1961	Elizabeth Seal, *Irma la Douce*	Tammy Grimes, *The Unsinkable Molly Brown*
1962	Anna Maria Alberghetti, *Carnival* Diahann Carroll, *No Strings*	Phyllis Newman, *Subways Are for Sleeping*
1963	Vivien Leigh, *Tovarich*	Anna Quayle, *Stop the World—I Want to Get Off*
1964	Carol Channing, *Hello, Dolly!*	Tessie O'Shea, *The Girl Who Came to Supper*
1965	Liza Minnelli, *Flora, the Red Menace*	Maria Karnilova, *Fiddler on the Roof*
1966	Angela Lansbury, *Mame*	Beatrice Arthur, *Mame*
1967	Barbara Harris, *The Apple Tree*	Peg Murray, *Cabaret*
1968	Patricia Routledge, *Darling of the Day* Leslie Uggams, *Hallelujah, Baby!*	Lillian Hayman, *Hallelujah, Baby!*
1969	Angela Lansbury, *Dear World*	Marian Mercer, *Promises, Promises*
1970	Lauren Bacall, *Applause*	Melba Moore, *Purlie*
1971	Helen Gallagher, *No, No, Nanette*	Patsy Kelly, *No, No, Nanette*
1972	Alexis Smith, *Follies*	Linda Hopkins, *Inner City*
1973	Glynis Johns, *A Little Night Music*	Patricia Elliot, *A Little Night Music*
1974	Virginia Capers, *Raisin*	Janie Sell, *Over Here!*
1975	Angela Lansbury, *Gypsy*	Dee Dee Bridgewater, *The Wiz*
1976	Donna McKechnie, *A Chorus Line*	Carole Bishop, *A Chorus Line*
1977	Dorothy Loudon, *Annie*	Delores Hall, *Your Arm's Too Short to Box with God*
1978	Liza Minnelli, *The Act*	Nell Carter, *Ain't Misbehavin'*
1979	Angela Lansbury, *Sweeney Todd*	Carlin Glynn, *The Best Little Whorehouse in Texas*
1980	Patti LuPone, *Evita*	Priscilla Lopez, *A Day in Hollywood/ A Night in the Ukraine*
1981	Lauren Bacall, *Woman of the Year*	Marilyn Cooper, *Woman of the Year*
1982	Jennifer Holliday, *Dreamgirls*	Liliane Montevecchi, *Nine*
1983	Natalia Makarova, *On Your Toes*	Betty Buckley, *Cats*
1984	Chita Rivera, *The Rink*	Lila Kedrova, *Zorba*
1985	category eliminated	Leilani Jones, *Grind*
1986	Bernadette Peters, *Song and Dance*	Bebe Neuwirth, *Sweet Charity*

Women Winners of the Tony Award for Musicals

Year	Best Performance by a Leading Actress in a Musical	Best Performance by a Featured Actress in a Musical
1987	Maryann Plunkett, *Me and My Girl*	Frances Ruffelle, *Les Misérables*
1988	Joanna Gleason, *Into the Woods*	Judy Kaye, *The Phantom of the Opera*
1989	Ruth Brown, *Black and Blue*	Debbie Shapiro, *Jerome Robbins' Broadway*
1990	Tyne Daly, *Gypsy*	Randy Graff, *City of Angels*
1991	Lea Salonga, *Miss Saigon*	Daisy Eagan, *The Secret Garden*
1992	Faith Prince, *Guys and Dolls*	Tonya Pinkins, *Jelly's Last Jam*
1993	Chita Rivera, *Kiss of the Spider Woman*	Andrea Martin, *My Favorite Year*
1994	Donna Murphy, *Passion*	Audra Ann McDonald, *Carousel*
1995	Glenn Close, *Sunset Boulevard*	Gretha Boston, *Show Boat*
1996	Donna Murphy, *The King and I*	Ann Duquesnay, *Bring in Da Noise, Bring in Da Funk*
1997	Bebe Neuwirth, *Chicago*	Lillias White, *The Life*
1998	Natasha Richardson, *Cabaret*	Audra McDonald, *Ragtime*
1999	Bernadette Peters, *Annie Get Your Gun*	Kristin Chenoweth, *You're a Good Man Charlie Brown!*
2000	Heather Headley, *Aida*	Karen Ziemba, *Contact*

bers. It was not long before Antoinette Perry was appointed chair of the board of the American Theatre Wing, which functioned as a branch of the British War Relief Society until the attack on Pearl Harbor, at which time it became an independent organization during this period. The wing continued to send performers to entertain troops and to participate in a variety of relief activities. Notable under Antoinette Perry's guidance was the creation of eight Stage Door Canteens around the country where stars of the radio, stage, and screen served coffee and doughnuts while entertaining service personnel. After the war, the Wing turned its attention to returning veterans, setting up a theatrical school offering classes in dance, music, singing, and acting that aided both up-and-coming stars and those already established.

Legend has it that shortly after Antoinette Perry's death in 1946, a Warner Brothers executive suggested that a committee be formed to preserve her ideals. The committee proposed that the American Theatre Wing institute an annual awards ceremony in Perry's name to recognize outstanding achievement in all areas of the theatre arts. It would serve as a living memorial to Perry's enthusiasm and dedication to the theatre, and it would be theatre's equivalent of Hollywood's Oscar ceremony, recognizing and rewarding distinguished service in the theatre. The early awards ceremonies were somewhat casual and the scope of the selections changed yearly, recognizing whatever was considered "outstanding" in that theatrical season. Generally, a larger proportion of these early awards were given to new talent in recognition of Antoinette Perry's lifelong devotion to encouraging young talent.

The first "Perry Awards" event was a dinner at the Waldorf Astoria on Easter Sunday, 6 April 1947, with Vera Allen (Perry's successor as chairman of the American Theatre Wing) presiding. Like every Tony Award ceremony since, it included a paying public audience and live entertainment. There were 20 winners the first year, each representing the flexibility of the award with such categories as "unfailing courtesy as treasurer, Martin Beck Theatre" and "enthusiasm as inveterate first-nighters." During the next few years, the Tony Award slowly evolved to its present form. By 1954, the eligible voting body was expanded to include theater professionals outside of the American Theatre Wing (an approximate total of 650 people), and it was not long before nominations were added to the selection procedure. Early awards consisted of a silver compact for the women or a cigarette lighter for the men presented together with a scroll. The Tony Medallion of today first appeared during the third annual award ceremony in 1949. The result of a contest sponsored by the United Scenic Artists, the Tony was designed by Herman Rosse, and depicts the masks of comedy and tragedy on one side, and the profile of Antoinette Perry on the other. From 1947 to 1965, the presentation of the Tony Awards was held in various New York City hotels and was broadcast over WOR radio and the Mutual Network. In 1967, the Tony Awards ceremony moved to the Broadway Theater setting and was televised nationally by ABC. Over the next few years, it was broadcast intermittently by ABC and NBC until it found a home with CBS in 1977. The advent of the nationally televised Tony Award allowed vast audiences to view excerpts from a variety of Broadway shows and offered previews of currently touring shows. Television exposure for nominees and their respective shows became almost as important as the award itself. The Tony Awards Ceremony became both an advertisement for Broadway, and a way of creating a less regional and more all-inclusive environment for theatrical productions. In 1997, the Tony Awards were held for the first time in Radio City Music Hall, permitting the general public and other industry members to attend.

The Tony Award today is still evolving to meet the challenges that present themselves today. With only about one-fourth as many shows open on Broadway as when the awards were first created, the Tony Award must continue to renew itself and the interests of the theater-going public yearly. Under its current format, awards are for Best Play, Best Musical, Best Book of a Musical, Best Original Score Written for the Theatre, Best Performance by a Leading Actor and Actress in a Play, Best Performance by a Leading Actor and Actress in a Musical, Best Performance by a Featured Actor and Actress in a Play, Best Performance by a Featured Actor and Actress in a Musical, Best Direction of a Play, Best Direction of a Musical, Best Scenic Design, Best Costume Design, Best Lighting Design, Best Choreography, Best Revival-Play or Musical, and Special Awards such as outstanding service to the theatre.

See also Musical Theater

For Further Reading

The American Theatre Wing's Tony Awards. Available: http://www.tonys.org

Kaufman, David. "A Night at the Tonys." *Horizons* 28/4 (May 1985): 28–32.

Lyons, Donald. "Theater: Slicing the Tony Baloney." *Wall Street Journal* (13 May 1996): Sec. A, 18.

Stevenson, Isabelle (ed.). *The Tony Award: A Complete Listing with a History of the American Theatre Wing*. New York: Crown Publishers, 1987.

Maria Purciello

Tower, Joan (1938–)

Few living composers have managed to write music that is both substantial and

Joan Tower. *Photo © Steve J. Sherman.*

capable of bringing a symphony audience to its feet, but composer Joan Tower seems to have that talent. Her characteristically bold and colorful works have been championed by major performers, who in turn commission music from her faster than she can compose it. In their enthusiasm for her music is found another reason for its success and appeal: the unusually high degree to which it makes reference to, and even rejoices in, the friendly and communal spirit of music making—a spirit in which Tower's own compositional impulses were discovered and nurtured.

Although born in New Rochelle, NY, on 6 September 1938, Tower spent almost all of her childhood living in various parts of South America, where her father was active as a mining engineer. She learned to play the piano and in 1958 entered Bennington College to study music, graduating in 1961. It was there that she first discovered an interest in composition, which she soon pursued vigorously. She went on to study at Columbia University (M.A. 1967, D.M.A. 1978), where her teachers included composers Otto Luening, Chou Wen-chung, Jack Beeson, and Charles Wuorinen. She undertook additional study with composers Darius Milhaud and Wallingford Riegger. In 1972 she began teaching at Bard College, Annadale-on-Hudson, NY, where she now occupies an endowed chair in composition.

In 1969 she founded and was pianist for the Da Capo Chamber Players, an ensemble specializing in contemporary music. It soon became a significant force, with numerous premieres, recordings, and the 1973 Naumburg Award to its credit. It was also an ideal environment for Tower's compositional development, as her daily work with friends enabled her to write music that was not only formally sound and sonically compelling but also fun to play. She remained with the group until 1983.

Tower's earliest major works (to about 1974) rely heavily on serial techniques. In works like *Breakfast Rhythms I* and *Hexachords*, tonal relations are established among the six pitches selected for the musical material, with a certain degree of balance established above and below the registral middle. Starting with works like *Breakfast Rhythms II* (1975) and *Black Topaz* (1976), her music increasingly explores Impressionist-inspired textures and sonorities. In a few cases, such as *Noon Dance* (1982), there are passages that hint deceptively at minimalism, although the sense of directed motion is ultimately the stronger force. A number of these works have titles suggesting the characteristics of materials (*Black Topaz, Platinum Spirals*) or kinds of motion. The progressive opening-up of intervals and registers in *Wings*, for instance, suggests repose, tension, and flight. All these later compositions are recorded on *Joan Tower* (Composers Recordings Inc. 582).

The first work Tower conceived for orchestra was *Sequoia* (1981), which attained instant success. She received further impetus and recognition for orchestral writing as composer-in-residence with the St. Louis Symphony Orchestra from 1985 to 1987, and she won both Friedheim and Grawemeyer Awards for *Silver Ladders* (recorded Nonesuch 79245). Works like these represent a synthesis of Tower's early serialist concern for precise control of musical materials and her increasing concern for dynamic expression. Another synthesis is at work in the concerti she has written since the mid-1980s: the combination of intimate interplay among various soloists within a brilliant orchestral context. Four of her concerti appear on the compact disc *Tower: Concertos* (D'Note Classics 1016).

See also Classical Music; Grawemeyer Award for Music Composition

For Further Reading

LePage, Jane Weiner. "Joan Tower: Composer." In *Women Composers, Conductors, and Musicians of the Twentieth Century: Selected Biographies*, vol. 3. Metuchen, NJ: Scarecrow Press, 1988, 264–280.

O'Brien, Valerie. "Joan Tower: Musician of the Month." *High Fidelity/Musical America* 32/9 (1982): 6, 8, 40.

Steve Luttmann

Tripp, Ruth (1897–1971)

Ruth Tripp was a composer, music educator, music critic, organist, and choirmaster in Rhode Island. She became the only woman to ever supervise the State WPA Symphony Orchestra and "one of the few of her sex to hold such a position in the country" (*Providence Journal*, 19 November 1940).

Tripp was born in Fall River, MA, on 26 December 1897. At the age of six she and her family moved to Central Falls, RI, where she made her home. After high school Tripp studied music at the American Conservatory at Fountainbleau near Paris, France. While at Fountainbleau she studied piano, composition, and solfeggio. Tripp studied with Isador Philipp, a famous Hungarian-French pianist. Additionally, Tripp later studied harmony, counterpoint, and composition with J. Sebastian Matthews and Stuart Mason, and she attended the Conservatory of Music in Boston for five years.

Tripp became a licentiate at Trinity College in London in 1928. After returning to the United States, she taught elementary music to grades one through five at the Gordon School in East Providence, RI. In 1940 Tripp was named WPA music leader or director. The WPA Music Project was created as part of President Roosevelt's "New Deal." Following the objectives of the Federal Music Project that was created in 1935, Tripp was dedicated to maintaining the highest level of professional standards offering free or inexpensive concerts and music lessons to adults, music for children, and training for teachers. Tripp's involvement in the Federal Music Project directly contributed to the culture of music in Rhode Island. She accomplished this by raising the level of awareness of, availability of, and appreciation for music.

In 1943 she became the principal music critic for the *Providence Journal-Bulletin*, a daily newspaper based in Providence, RI. She attended and critiqued several types of events, including oratorios, symphonic concerts, folk music, barbershop quartets, the Newport Music Festivals, and a variety of recordings. According to the *Providence Journal*, some people misunderstood her and thought that her written critiques of local events were too nice. "If that were so it was because of an enthusiasm for music and an unrelenting desire to find merit and promise in every performance" (*Providence Journal*, 20 May 1971).

Having never married and devoting her life to the appreciation and awareness of music in the state of Rhode Island, Ruth Tripp died at the age of 73 on 19 May 1971 after a brief illness. A memorial scholarship for young pianists was established in her name in June 1971; it is administered by the University of Rhode Island Department of Music.

See also Music Education

For Further Reading

The Rhode Island Composers Forum and the University of Rhode Island Department of Music, Sponsors. *New Music in Rhode Island: The Legacy of the Baroque*. A Humanistic Booklet for the Fall 1985 Rhode Island Composers Festival.

Smith, Julia Francis. *Directory of American Woman Composers*. National Federation of Music Clubs, 1970.

The World of Music: An Illustrated Encyclopedia. New York: Abradale Press, 1963.

Dawn Elizabeth Smith

Tucker, Sophie (1887–1966)

Singer and actress Sophie Tucker, the "Last of the Red Hot Mamas," had a career that spanned nearly 60 years. Although not stereotypically beautiful, she used her size and stature to her advantage, portraying a confident, sexy woman in her act and through her songs. Throughout her career she was known for singing numbers that personified

Sophie Tucker in November 1930. *Photo courtesy of Sasha/Hulton/Archive Photos.*

these qualities, like "You've Got to See Mama Ev'ry Night" and "Red Hot Mama." Tucker had a strong, full voice that was well suited to the bawdy and risqué nature of many of her songs.

She was born Sophie Abuza on 13 January 1884, the daughter of Russian-Jewish immigrants. As a child she worked in the family restaurant in Hartford, CT. It was in the restaurant that she began her singing career. She would often sing popular songs for the customers, not only boosting the restaurant's business but also earning extra tips for the family. After a brief marriage during her teens, she moved to New York to make her mark in show business. She managed to find work singing in a nightclub and also sang at amateur nights, eventually making her way into vaudeville.

She appeared on the vaudeville and burlesque circuits as well as in the second edition of the *Ziegfeld Follies* (1909). After the *Follies* she continued to perform as a headlining act in vaudeville for many years. She left vaudeville and became a regular in nightclubs and cabarets. In addition to her stage performances, she made many recordings, the earliest of which were on the Edison label. During the 1930s and 1940s she appeared in several movies. Several retrospective compact discs are available, including *Last of the Red Hot Mamas* (Memoir Classics 529) and *Some of These Days* (Pearl 7807). Tucker died on 9 February 1966.

See also Jewish Musicians; Musical Theater

For Further Reading

Antelyes, Peter. "Red Hot Mamas: Bessie Smith, Sophie Tucker, and the Ethnic Maternal Voice in American Popular Song." In *Embodied Voices: Representing Female Vocality in Western Culture*, eds. Leslie Dunn and Nancy Jones. New York: Cambridge University Press, 1994, 212–229.

Sochen, June. *From Mae to Madonna: Women Entertainers in Twentieth-Century America*. Lexington: University Press of Kentucky, 1999.

Tucker, Sophie. *Some of These Days: The Autobiography of Sophie Tucker*. New York: Doubleday, 1945.

Jay Martin

Tucker, Tanya (1958–)

Country singer Tanya Tucker began her career as a child star when at the age of 13 she recorded the tremendously popular hit song "Delta Dawn." During the following three decades she became a country music and rock-a-billy legend, often remembered more for her overtly sexy, rebellious, outlaw image, her outspoken manner, and her insistence on living "on the edge" than for her individual recordings.

Born in Seminole, TX, on 10 October 1958, Tucker was nine years old when she made the decision to pursue a singing career. She and her father visited Nashville at that time but were routinely turned away by the record companies. Tucker was 12 when her father moved the family to Henderson, NV, to further his daughter's singing career, this time hoping to secure a Las Vegas Strip singing engagement. It was in Las Vegas that songwriter and personal manager Dolores Fuller heard Tucker's demo tape. Fuller sent the tape to Tammy Wynette's producer, CBS Artists and Repertoire chief Billy Sherrill, who brought the child to Nashville to begin recording.

Tucker dropped out of school in the ninth grade to pursue her developing singing career. Beginning with her first record in 1972, the 13-year-old earned a string of consistent Top 10 hits lasting until 1978. During this period of early feminism, the teenager joined the ranks of other women country singers who portrayed an image much less demure and more overtly sexual than that with which country women singers and fans had previously been comfortable. Tucker, however, developed this image to a degree that greatly surpassed that of other women singers.

Tanya Tucker moved to Los Angeles in 1978 and continued to earn a reputation as a hard-partying vixen, as she had affairs with country music icon Merle Haggard and actor Don Johnson and carried on a publicly tempestuous relationship with 44-year-old television host and country singer Glen Campbell. Despite, or perhaps owing to, her outspoken, rough-and-tumble demeanor, Tanya Tucker is admired by an entire generation of fans who appreciate her music as much as her down-home earthy attitude and public candidness about her unconventional lifestyle.

In 1979 Tucker and her managers began a concerted attempt to market her as a rock singer, consciously crafting an image as a sex symbol. Although one album in this vein, *T.N.T.* (MCA 31152), was quite successful, in general the move proved largely unsuccessful; subsequently she moved back toward country music. In the early 1980s she again scored a number of hit records before her success slowed in the middle of the decade. Her 1986 single "One Love at a Time" (available on *Girls Like Me*, Capitol 29947) began another successful period that stretched into the early 1990s. Her 1989 hit single "Daddy and Home" (available on *Strong Enough to Bend*, Capitol 48865) was a remake of the Jimmie Rodgers country classic of 1928.

Like a number of important women country recording artists of the past few decades, including Dolly Parton (b. 1946), Reba McEntire (b. 1954), and Tammy Wynette (1942–1998), Tanya Tucker has undertaken acting roles in addition to singing. She made her acting debut co-starring with actor Don Johnson in the 1979 television movie *Amateur Night at the Dixie Bar and Grill* (Universal TV, 1979) and appeared also in the film *Hard Country* (Universal, 1981).

See also Country Music

For Further Reading

Bufwack, Mary A., and Robert K. Oermann. *Finding Her Voice: The Saga of Women in Country Music*. New York: Crown, 1993.

Dew, Joan. *Singers and Sweethearts: The Women of Country Music*. Garden City, NY: Doubleday, 1977.

Haslam, Gerald W. *Workin' Man Blues: Country Music in California*. Berkeley: University of California Press, 1999.

Amy Corin

Turner, Tina (1938–)

In the 1990s, singer and actress Tina Turner became a worldwide phenomenon with her record-breaking 1996–1997 world tour as she performed for more than three million people in 10 countries. In February 2000, at the age of 60, Tina released her best-selling album to date, *Twenty-Four Seven* (EMI 523180), which sold over 60,000 copies within its first week of circulation.

Born Annie Mae Bullock in Brownsville, TN, on 26 November 1938, Turner began her musical career in rural Brownsville, where she performed in church and talent shows until moving to St. Louis, MO, in 1956. There she met

Tina Turner in concert in London in February 1978. *Photo courtesy of Gary Merrin/Hulton/Archive Photos.*

Ike Turner, front man for the Kings of Rhythm—a rhythm and blues act that enjoyed fair notoriety throughout the area nightclub circuit. After an impromptu performance with the band, Bullock was invited to join Ike Turner's group under the name "Little Annie" and subsequently toured with the band throughout the late 1950s.

By 1960 the success of the group led them into the recording studio, where they cut "A Fool in Love" under the names Ike and Tina Turner (Ike had recommended that Annie Mae change her name, although they did not marry until 1962). The immediate success of the single prompted Ike to develop an act showcasing Tina's stage and singing talent, hiring additional musicians and several women back-up singers. With additional hits in 1961 ("It's Gonna Work Out Fine") and 1962 ("Poor Fool"), the Ike and Tina Turner Revue became one of the most popular rhythm and blues or soul acts touring the United States throughout the early to mid-1960s.

Despite the failure of "River Deep, Mountain High" in 1966, the Turners enjoyed significant chart success both in the United States and the United Kingdom following their opening for the Rolling Stones' 1969 North American tour. Commercially, the early 1970s was the most successful period for Ike and Tina Turner, with cover hits such as the Beatles' "Come Together" and their most successful remake, Credence Clearwater Revival's "Proud Mary," establishing the legacy of her signature full-throated and energetic vocal style. In 1973 they recorded their last hit single as a duo, Tina's autobiographical "Nutbush City Limits."

The debut of Turner's film career (playing the Acid Queen in the 1975 screen adaptation of the Who's *Tommy*), coupled with Ike's continuing drug abuse and violent behavior, led to the couple's separation in 1976 and divorce in 1978. In 1984, Tina Turner's first solo album, *Private Dancer* (Capitol C2-46041), sold over five million copies; it included her most successful hit to date, "What's Love Got to Do with it." In addition to earning Turner two Grammy Awards for Best Female Pop Performance and Song of the Year, "What's Love Got to Do with It" became the title of a 1993 film based on the re-release of her best-selling autobiography, *I, Tina* (1983).

See also Rock and Popular Music Genres

For Further Reading

Romanowski, Patricia, Holly George Warren, and Jon Pareles (eds.). *The New Rolling Stone Encyclopedia of Rock and Roll*. New York: Fireside Rockefeller Center, 1995.

Turner, Tina, with Kurt Loder. *I, Tina: My Life Story*. New York: Mass Media Paperbacks, 1993.

Cory Gavito

U

Ulali

Founded in 1987, the Ulali vocal trio consists of Pura Fe (Tuscarora tribe), Soni Moreno (Mayan, Apache, Yaqui tribes), and Jennifer Elizabeth Kreisberg (Tuscarora tribe). In describing the indigenous quality of their music, the group prefers the designation "First Nations" rather than "Native American" or "American Indian," taking note that the existence of the hemisphere's indigenous peoples preceded the word "America."

The group's vocal harmonies incorporate colorful dissonances and quartal and parallel interval relationships, and both gospel and Native American influences are heard in their eclectic blend of styles. Original song texts include traditional poetry, humor, and political material addressing Native concerns. Drums and rattles accompany their vocal colors as they perform music popular with audiences in concert and popular venues including rock concerts (notably with the Indigo Girls, 1997), film and video (*The Native Americans*, 1995; *Smoke Signals*, 1998), cultural centers (Smithsonian Folklife Festivals), and native events (powwows and radio shows).

The group won the American Library Association's 1997 Notable Recording Award for *Lessons from the Animal People* (Yellow Moon Press 50) with Lakota/Kiowa Apache storyteller Dovie Thomason. Other notable projects to which the group has contributed include the album *Robbie Robertson and the Red Road Ensemble* (Cema/Capitol, 1994), the collection *Heartbeat: Voices of First Nations Women* (Smithsonian Folkways, 1995) and the Aboriginal Women's Voices Project recording *Hearts of the Nations* (Sweet Grass Records, 1997).

See also Multicultural Musics; Native American Musicians

For Further Reading

Ulali Home. Available: http://www.ulali.com

Virginia Giglio

Underground

The term "underground" commonly refers to the independent punk music and the zine counterculture with a political sensibility. With its beginnings in the

1970s, punk music has always been an anti-establishment music genre that set out to rebel against the rules of the music industry and the status quo that punk's adherents often felt deserted by. As in many other realms of Western culture, the field was largely male dominated except for a few woman artists such as Patti Smith (b. 1946) and Siouxsie Sioux. Nonetheless, these women set the stage for other women to follow.

In the early 1990s young women and teens initiated what eventually came to be known as the Riot Grrrl movement, an offshoot of the punk rock scene of the 1970s and 1980s. Women wanted to break free from an onerous identity as the band members' girlfriends. They took to the stage with a desire to be punk musical artists and performers in their own right. More important, the music and the artists embodied a leftist and feminist consciousness that was primary to the music. Many artists also fought against an identity that tied them to their mothers' and second wave (the period of the women's movment from approximately 1966 to 1979) feminist ideals. In turn, their raucous style and alternative dress were designed as a rejection of second wave sensibilities. In fact, this musical current is commonly considered a trajectory of third wave feminism (the period of social change beginning in the 1980s) and clearly part of a political social movement. Included in this aesthetic were lesbian politics and an awareness that was commonly referred to as homocore or queer punk; it was expressed by such artists as Tribe 8 and the Butchies.

Olympia, WA, and Washington, DC, are commonly considered the birthplaces of the Riot Grrrl genre, with pioneers including artists such as Bikini Kill and Bratmobile. Upstart labels, out of necessity and in an effort to shun corporate rock, began to surface. Early labels included Independent K Records and Kill Rock Star Records in Olympia and Dischord in Washington, DC. This inspired other labels throughout the United States, including Simple Machines in Virginia, Thrill Jockey Records in Chicago, Candy-Ass Records in Portland, OR, and Skinnie Girl in Minneapolis—all women-fronted labels. The Riot Grrrl movement successfully combined feminism with punk. There were clear efforts to sever patriarchal patterns and strengthen young girls' and women's individual identities, sense of self, and position within society.

During the mid-1990s the Riot Grrrl movement began to disband. In 1992 many riot grrrls were unhappy about the surging amount of mainstream press coverage the movement had begun to garner, including a *Newsweek* cover. The press spotlight propelled the style into a public position of privilege and activated a mainstream profile—precisely what the young upstarts had fought against. The mainstream attention led to contract offers from major record labels. Bands such as L7 and Babes in Toyland signed on the major record label rosters, but others refused. This created ideological differences within different segments of the alterna-culture of Riot Grrrl. Since the beginning of the movement it had been apparent that the shared mantra of "corporate rock sucks" was one of solidarity and unity. The newfound media attention spawned dissolution within the movement, which broke into factions throughout the 1990s.

Simultaneous to and intertwined with the development of punk rock feminism was the development of feminist counterculture zine production. Zines are fiercely independent, leaf sheet flyers in which girls and young women—as authors and producers—express outrage and frustrations about various women-related issues, including rape, abuse, inequalities, and demeaning images of women in mainstream culture. Similar to the musical movement, these zines were an effort to dismantle patriarchy and male domination. Startup zines included *Girl Germs*, *Satan Wears a Bra*, *Quit Whining*, and *Jigsaw*. The zine movement focused on the development of community and solidarity for disenfranchised teenage girls. Teenagers found unity in the desolation, loneliness, and anger they felt living in the myth of suburbia. Similar to the musical movement, the zine movement was resistant to and refused to develop a structural organization, philosophy, or membership rules. The zine writers and publishers did not want to fall prey to an established and prescribed orthodoxy or misplaced dogma. This was exactly what they saw themselves as fighting against. Each individual was to determine her own role, her own purpose, and her own form of resistance.

The advent of the World Wide Web coincided with the birth and development of the Riot Grrrl movement and the similarly focused zines. In turn, both communities have utilized the Internet as a creative transmission tool for the same feminist political purposes. Without the backing of major record label dollars, many independent labels have ventured into the Internet to broaden their reach and promote their message-laden music.

Currently, some critics, scholars, and even the originators suggest the Riot Grrrl moniker is passé today—with so many crossing over into and attracting mainstream attention. Despite this, a feminist punk rock existence remains.

See also Garage Rock and Heavy Metal Bands; Rock and Popular Music Genres

For Further Reading

Duncombe, Stephen. *Zines: Notes from the Underground and the Politics of Alternative Culture*. London: Verso, 1997.

Ann Savage

Vaughan, Sarah (1924–1990)

Sarah Vaughan may be counted in the top echelon of women jazz singers of the twentieth century, along with Ella Fitzgerald (1917–1996) and Billie Holiday (1915–1959). Her wide range, controlled vibrato, and expressive qualities provided her with a voice that was both unique and varied. Often called bop's greatest diva, Vaughan was a great scat singer who could change a song's mood or direction by controlled delivery or enunciation, could alter timbre at any moment, and could improvise rhythmic and melodic embellishments with ease. She was a dominant performer from the late 1940s through the 1980s. Vaughan's recorded legacy is one of the largest and highest quality in modern jazz history.

Born on 27 March 1924, Vaughan was an accomplished singer and pianist by her teenage years. After winning an amateur contest at the Apollo Theatre, she was hired as a singer with the Earl Hines big band in the 1940s. When her lifelong friend Billy Eckstine broke away to form his own orchestra, Vaughan joined him to make her recording debut. Some of Eckstine's sidemen, Charlie Parker and Dizzy Gillespie, strongly influenced Vaughan during this time, and she incorporated bop phrasing into her singing.

After 1946, Vaughan spent the remainder of her career as a solo star. Her 1946–1948 selections for Musicraft added to her maturity and popularity, as she started adding bop-oriented phrasings to popular songs. She sang on the Columbia label from 1949–1953, where she recorded "Sassy." During the 1950s she recorded with Mercury and Emarcy. During the 1960s she recorded with Roulette (1960–1964) and Mercury (1963–1967). From 1971 to 1974 she sang under the Mainstream label. Vaughan's voice never lost its flexibility, range, or power as she aged; it even deepened a little. She was able to "outscat" everyone except Ella Fitzgerald, and she performed in public into the mid-1980s. Her legacy and fame continue even now. Most of her recordings are currently available on compact discs and cassettes, including *Time after Time* (Drive Archive 41021), *No Count Sarah* (Polygram 824057), and *Linger Awhile:*

Sarah Vaughan at Birdland in New York City in the 1950s. *Photo courtesy of Frank Driggs Collection.*

Live at Newport and More (Pablo 2312144).

See also Jazz

For Further Reading

Brown, Denise (ed.). *Sarah Vaughan: A Discography*. New York: Greenwood Press, 1991.

Brad Eden

Vega, Suzanne (1959–)

A folk-inspired singer-songwriter, Suzanne Vega came to international prominence in the late 1980s. "Luka," her most commercially successful single, reached number three on the *Billboard* charts. The single from Vega's second album, *Solitude Standing* (A&M 75021-5136-2), told the story of child abuse from the standpoint of the victim. Representative of many of Vega's songs, "Luka" is sung in an emotionally detached voice that often sounds half-spoken, half-sung. In the case of "Luka," her style effectively brought attention to the substance of the story. In 1987 her song "Left of Center" was included in the soundtrack of the Jon Hughes film *Pretty in Pink* (1986).

Born on 11 July 1959, Vega was raised in New York City by parents who stressed the importance of the arts. She attended the High School for the Performing Arts and Barnard College. While attending Barnard, she performed original material in folk clubs in Greenwich Village. Despite some initial reluctance, A&M signed Vega and released her self-titled debut album.

Vega's other albums include *Suzanne Vega* (A&M 75021-5072-2), which was a critically acclaimed debut, and her third album, *Days of Open Hand* (A&M 75021-5293-2). Shortly after *Days of Open Hand* was released, a group of British DJs who called themselves D.N.A. sampled Vega's vocals from the song "Tom's Diner," which was originally released on *Solitude Standing*. D.N.A. worked the sample into a dance mix that became a hit in Britain. Philip Glass incorporated her lyrics into two pieces on *Song from Liquid Days* (Columbia 39564). In her 1992 releases *99.9° F.* (A&M 314-540005-2) and *Nine Objects of Desire* (A&M 540583), Vega utilized synthesizers, which created a notable change in texture from her earlier albums.

See also Rock and Popular Music Genres; Singer-Songwriter

For Further Reading

Gaar, Gillian G. *She's a Rebel: The History of Women in Rock and Roll*. Seattle, WA: Seal Press, 1992.

O'Dair, Barbara (ed.). *Trouble Girls: The Rolling Stone Book of Women in Rock*. New York: Random House, 1997.

Garth Alper

Vincent, Rhonda (1962–)

Rhonda Vincent is one of bluegrass's most accomplished and powerful performers. In the 1980s she won the Society for the Preservation of Bluegrass Music of America's award for Female Vocalist of the Year five years in a row—and thereafter was withdrawn from the category.

Vincent was born on 13 July 1962 in Kirksville, MO. At the age of five she was already singing gospel songs in the family band, later known as the Sally Mountain Show, on their own television program, and on record. Under her father's tutelage, Vincent learned to play all the standard bluegrass instruments plus drums. Their household was filled with music and listeners nearly every evening. Before she was a teenager, she started winning a string of awards for her fiddle playing, her recordings, and her singing.

Following at least eight albums with the family band, Vincent shifted toward the country mainstream. In the late 1980s and early 1990s she pursued this goal with some success but then decided to return to bluegrass. Her albums from the early 1990s include *Timeless and True Love* (Rebel 1697), *Bound for Gloryland* (Rebel 1692), and *New Dreams and Sunshine* (Rebel 1665). Her 17th album, *Back Home Again* (Rounder 610460), contains two of her most requested songs, "Passing of the Train" and "Little Angels," a moving tribute to survivors of sexual abuse. The influence of Rhonda Vincent's clear, commanding voice and deep connection to the roots of her music are discernable in the approach of Alison Krauss (b. 1971) and many other women bluegrass artists.

See also Bluegrass

For Further Reading

Bufwack, Mary A., and Robert K. Oermann. *Finding Her Voice: The Saga of Women in Country Music*. New York: Crown Publishers, 1993.

Willis, Barry R. *America's Music—Bluegrass: A History of Bluegrass Music in the Words of Its Pioneers*. Franktown, CO: Pine Valley Music, 1998.

Craig Morrison

W

Walker, Shirley (1945–)

Composer, arranger, and film scorer Shirley Walker has been the recipient of numerous awards and is highly regarded among her peers. She has the distinction of being the first woman as sole composer for a major Hollywood studio production. Her role has been that of feature film and television score composer, and she has also served important roles in the film music industry as conductor, synthesist, orchestrator, and "score doctor." She is noted for her flexibility in creating both subtle, atmospheric backgrounds and cues that are surreptitiously intensive and riveting.

Shirley Walker, born on 10 April 1945, is a pioneer for women working in the film music industry. Although Walker began her musical career as a soloist with the San Francisco Symphony while still in high school, she began writing scores for industrial films as a result of her husband's involvement in small film production companies. Her first major motion picture assignment came as synthesist on Francis Ford Coppola's *Apocalypse Now* (1979). In the same year Walker contributed an original cue and orchestrated other cues for Carmine Coppola's score to *The Black Stallion* (1979). In the mid-1980s Walker conducted the score for *Cujo* (1983) and received co-composing credits on two low-budget horror scores with Richard Band: *Ghoulies* (1985) and *The Dungeonmaster* (1985). For these films she composed both orchestral and electronic cues.

Walker has also collaborated with two of the film industry's most important composers: Hans Zimmer and Danny Elfman. She orchestrated and conducted some of Zimmer's most important scores in the late 1980s and early 1990s, including those for *Black Rain* (1989), *Days of Thunder* (1990), and *Backdraft* (1991). Zimmer composed cues at sequencers, after which Walker transcribed the cues for orchestra from digital audiotapes and printouts of cues. On Elfman's scores, Walker's role was largely that of conductor. She conducted some of his most important scores, including those for *Batman* (1989), *Darkman* (1990), *Dick Tracy* (1990), and *Nightbreed* (1990). Additionally, she supplied some of the orchestrations for these films.

In 1993 Walker received critical acclaim for her score to the animated feature *Batman: Mask of the Phantasm* (1993). In 1995 she co-composed the score to *Escape from L.A.* (1996) with John Carpenter by creating some of the synthesized cues, followed by original orchestral cues for the film's climax. Her next solo score was for the suspense thriller *Turbulence* (1997). More recent projects include a score for NBC's highly rated television miniseries *Asteroid*, and a Disney television movie, *The Garbage Picking, Field Goal Kicking Philadelphia Phenomenon*. Walker's latest feature film is James Wong's *Final Destination* (2000), in which she supplies an eerie and menacing musical backdrop for this dark thriller.

Walker was honored with a Daytime Emmy Award as musical director for the animated *Batman* series and has received a Daytime Emmy nomination for the animated *Superman* series. She has received a Prime Time Emmy nomination for the Fox television series *Space: Above and Beyond*, and a Cable ACE nomination for the Blair Brown film *Majority Rule* (1992).

Her large palette of both electronic and acoustic sounds used in her brilliant orchestrations, coupled with her intriguing themes and dramatic sensibility, make Shirley Walker a leader in the contemporary film music world.

See also Composer; Film Composers

For Further Reading

Keaveney, Ryan, and Shirley Walker. *Phantasm: Shirley Walker*. Available: http://walker.filmmusic.com

Schelle, Michael. *The Score: Interviews with Film Composers*. Los Angeles: Silman-James Press, 1999.

Scott Locke

Warwick, Dionne (1940–)

Since her debut in 1962, Dionne Warwick has been one of the most successful pop singers, especially with her elegant and sophisticated interpretations of the songs of Burt Bacharach and Hal David during the mid-1960s. Her cool restraint and vocal polish reached the pop and soul charts time and again with continued popularity throughout the 1990s.

Dionne Warwick was born on 12 December 1940 in East Orange, NJ, and grew up in a family with a strong gospel heritage. She sang in Newark's New Hope Baptist Church choir and played piano for the Drinkard Singers, a gospel group managed by her mother. She also attended Hartt College of Music in Hartford, CT. Warwick formed the Gospelaires with her sister, Dee Dee, and aunt, Cissy Houston (b. 1932), appearing as backup singers on records by the Drifters and Garnet Mimms. In 1962 she was signed to Scepter Records, where her first collaboration with Bacharach and David, the uptown soul classic "Don't Make Me Over," reached number 21 on the pop and number five on the rhythm and blues charts.

Under the guidance of her producers and songwriters Bacharach and David, Warwick's soulful voice was gradually brought into the pop mainstream, resulting in a massively successful string of hit songs between 1963 and 1970. Songs such as "Walk on By" (1964), "You'll Never Get to Heaven" (1964), "Message to Michael" (1966), "I Say a Little Prayer" (1967), "Do You Know the Way to San Jose?" (1968), (Theme from) "Valley of the Dolls" (1968), "This Girl's in Love with You" (1969), and "I'll Never Fall in Love Again" (1970) scored on both the pop and the rhythm and blues charts.

Despite her huge commercial success in the 1960s, Warwick ended her collaboration with Bacharach and David and signed with Warner Brothers Records in 1971. This relationship resulted in only one major hit, her collaboration with the Spinners, "Then Came You" (1974). Ironically, this was Warwick's first song to reach the top of the charts.

Warwick's career was rekindled during the 1980s after her move to Arista Records, where she collaborated on many releases. In 1979 Barry Manilow produced "I'll Never Love This Way Again." In 1982 BeeGee Barry Gibb coproduced and wrote songs for *Heartbreaker* (Arista ARCD-8006). Warwick released hit singles with Johnny Mathis, "Too Much, Too Little, Too Late"; with Luther Vandross, "How Many Times Can We Say Goodbye"; and with Jeffrey Osborne, "LovePower." Her biggest hit of the 1980s was the 1985 Grammy Award–winning, "That's What Friends Are For" (Arista 12266). This single, benefiting AIDS-related causes, featured Elton John, Gladys Knight (b. 1944), and Stevie Wonder.

Warwick has received four other Grammy Awards and has five Gold albums. Her recent album, *Friends Can Be Lovers* (Arista 18682), features cameos by Sting and her cousin Whitney Houston (b. 1963). The Latin-themed *Aquarela Do Brazil* (Arista 078221877) has received generally positive reviews.

See also Rock and Popular Music Genres

For Further Reading

Gaar, Gillian G. *She's a Rebel: The History of Women in Rock and Roll*. Seattle: Seal Press, 1992.

O'Dair, Barbara (ed.). *Trouble Girls: The Rolling Stone Book of Women in Rock*. New York: Random House, 1997.

Susanna P. Garcia

Washington, Dinah (1924–1963)

Soulful singer Dinah Washington, known as the "Queen of the Blues," sang in many styles, including gospel, jazz,

Dinah Washington during a 1959 performance. *Photo © Bettmann/CORBIS*

blues, rhythm and blues, and popular standards. Her original phrasing and style drew heavily on her gospel music roots, and she was one of the most influential singers of the postwar decade. Her performances were marked by a gritty, high-pitched voice with clear and precise phrasing.

Born Ruth Lee Jones on 29 August 1924 in Tuscaloosa, AL, Washington was singing more popular music than gospel music by age 15. Her family moved from the rural and agricultural South to the North (Chicago) when she was four years old. Washington's mother, Alice Williams Jones, a pianist at Chicago's St. Luke Baptist Church, taught her to play piano. Shortly thereafter she began singing and playing piano at the church. She also became a member of the Sallie Martin Colored Ladies Quartet as an accompanist and singer. She won a contest singing "I Can't Face the Music" at the Regal Theater. From that time on, she began singing at local nightclubs. However, in an attempt to appease her disapproving mother, she continued to sing in the churches. She understood that she was not going to be able to continue this dichotomy. She also was aware that she could make more money singing in nightclubs instead of churches. While still a teenager she married John Young, who became her manager. The marriage was short (approximately three months), but her career was launched.

According to several accounts, a friend took her to hear her idol, Billie Holiday (1915–1959), at the Garrick Stage Lounge, and Dinah went back to hear her every night. When she discovered that Holiday was booked for three months, Washington convinced Joe Sherman, the owner, to book her in the upstairs room. Sherman is credited, along with Joe Glaser and Lionel Hampton, with changing her name to Dinah Washington. Sherman had invited Glaser, Lionel Hampton's manager, to his club to hear Washington. Glaser brought Hampton to hear her, and subsequently she performed with Hampton's band from 1943 to 1945.

In 1943 Washington recorded several blues songs written by jazz journalist and songwriter Leonard Feather for Keynote Records, an independent recording company. Then in 1945 she recorded with Hampton's label, Decca. Recordings from this period include *Flyin' Home (1942–1945)* (MCA 42349) and rereleases such as *Hamp: The Legendary Decca Recordings* (GRP 652) and *Lionel Hampton and His Orchestra 1945–1946* (Classics 922). Washington soon left Hampton's band, however, and embarked on an independent recording and touring career.

Washington was an astute judge of musical talent and had excellent business acumen. Her touring and recording groups included many whose talents she had personally discovered. She also had a strong impact on other musical talents who were not members of any of her ensembles. She sang at many jazz festivals, appeared on television, and performed at many concert venues in the United States and Europe. Washington was also a songwriter and top recording artist. In 1959 she received a Grammy Award for "What a Diff'rence a Day Makes" (Mercury 543300).

On 14 December 1963, in Detroit, Dinah Washington died from an apparently accidental ingestion of diet pills with alcohol.

See also Blues

For Further Reading

Gourse, Leslie. "Dinah Washington's Love Stories." *Louis' Children: American Jazz Singers*. New York: William Morrow: 1984, 224–233.

Haskins, James. *Queen of the Blues: A Biography of Dinah Washington*. New York: William Morrow, 1987.

Smith, Jessie Carney (ed.). *Notable Black American Women*. Detroit and London: Gale Research, 1992.

Monica J. Burdex

Waters, Ethel (1896–1977)

A popular singer and actress, Ethel Waters personified the rags-to-riches story prevalent among black performers early in the twentieth century. She was one of the first black singers to issue popular jazz and blues recordings and to perform on radio and television. She made several appearances on radio shows in 1922 and 1933, at the Palace Theater in New York in 1925, and on Broadway in a dramatic play in 1939. As a singer she recorded almost 50 songs that became hits. Waters's smooth, clear phrasing and exact sense of timing were coupled with a strong voice, a wide range, and a slow vibrato.

Waters was born Ethel Anderson on 31 October 1895, as the result of sexual violence. When her mother, Louise Anderson, was a teenage girl she was violently attacked and raped by a local boy named John Waters. After Ethel's birth, Anderson married a railroad worker named Norman Howard. For the first few years of her life Ethel went by the name of Howard, but eventually she finally settled for her father's name (Waters).

As a child, Ethel Waters was sent to live with her grandmother and two aunts. In her autobiography she described her childhood experience as "difficult," stating that she was never understood or accepted by her family. At an early age Waters began to work several jobs, including maid, dishwasher, and waitress. In 1917 she sang at a party in a local bar, where two vaudeville producers heard her and convinced her to join them. Waters was immediately successful, captivating her audiences with expressions of pain, happiness, and humor. Within a few years she became a musical sensation touring in musical revues.

Waters began her recording career in 1921 when Cardinal Records issued "The New York Glide" and "At the New Jump Steady Ball." Later that year she released "Down Home Blues" and *Oh Daddy* (Biograph BLP-12022) on the black-owned Black Swan label. She would eventually record over 50 songs for a variety of labels. Her appearances in stage musicals included *Hello 1919!* (1919), *Jump Steady* (1922), *Plantation Revue* (1925), *Black Bottom* (1926), *Miss Calico* (1926–1927), *Paris Bound* (1927), *Ethel Waters Broadway Revue* (1928), *Rhapsody in Black* (1930), *From Broadway to Harlem* (1932), *Stormy Weather* (1933), *As Thousands Cheer* (1934), and *Cabin in the Sky* (1940). Waters also starred in a number of films, including *On with the Show* (1929), *Stage Door Canteen* (1943), *Cabin in the Sky* (1943), and the films she is most remembered for, *Pinky* (1949) and *Member of the Wedding* (1953). She received Academy Award nominations for both of these films, along with other drama awards.

Waters wrote two autobiographies describing her life experiences of family and love relationships, racism in America, and the successes in her career: *His Eye Is on the Sparrow* (1951) and *To Me It's Wonderful* (1977). She often toured with the Billy Graham Crusades in the 1960s and 1970s. Waters died of cancer on 21 September 1977. She is remembered for her triumph over adversity and for her contributions to African American music.

See also Blues; Jazz

For Further Reading

Waters, Ethel. *His Eye Is on the Sparrow*. Westport, CT: Greenwood Press, 1951.

———. *To Me It's Wonderful*. New York: Harper and Row, 1972.

Clarence Bernard Henry

Waymon, Eunice

See Simone, Nina

Wells, Kitty (1918–)

Kitty Wells recorded a string of hit songs beginning in the 1950s and lasting well into the 1970s. As a result of these successful recordings, she became known as the "Queen of Country Music." Her signature tune, "It Wasn't God Who Made

Honky Tonk Angels," thrust her into the spotlight in 1952. The song was a response to Hank Thompson's "The Wild Side of Life," and with its pre-feminist lyrics that make reference to men cheating on their wives and leading women astray, the song paved the way for future country music feminists such as Patsy Cline (1932–1963) and Loretta Lynn (b. 1935). Wells's raw, unadorned performance was influenced by country, honky tonk, and even gospel styles.

Born Muriel Ellen Deason on 30 August 1919 in Nashville, TN, Wells began performing on the radio in 1936 with her sisters in an act called the Deason Sisters. She met and married her husband Johnnie (later Johnny) Wright of Johnnie and Jack, the following year when she was only 18 years old. Together with Wright's sister Louise, they formed Johnny Wright and the Harmony Girls; and in 1938 Jack Anglin was added to the act to form Johnny and Jack. In 1941 the group gained professional status, added a full complement of instrumentalists, and changed its name to the Tennessee Hillbillies. Muriel Deason was also renamed "Kitty Wells" after the nineteenth century ballad "Sweet Kitty Wells."

In 1952 Wells signed a contract with Decca and recorded the single "It Wasn't God Who Made Honky Tonk Angels," the first number one hit for a women country music artist, a spot she held for six weeks. Following that success Wells recorded a string of Top 10 hits over the next decade, including "Makin' Believe," "There's Poison in Your Heart/I'm in Love with You," and "I Can't Stop Loving You/She's No Angel." Her success was so great that the governor of Tennessee, Frank Clement, created a Tennessee Womanhood Award for her in 1954.

The 1960s saw the release of some of Kitty Wells's most popular songs, including "The Other Cheek" and "Heartbreak U.S.A." Throughout her long career Wells recorded numerous duets; at different times she was teamed with Red Foley, Webb Pierce, Roy Acuff, Roy Drusky, Rayburn Anthony, and her husband, Johnny Wright. Her last song that charted was in 1979 with "Thank You for the Roses," recorded on Johnny's Ruboca Records. Many of these songs may be found on recordings such as *Heartbreak U.S.A.* (Decca D1-4141), *Country All the Way* (Decca D1-4776), and *Together Again* (Decca 74906), with Red Foley. Kitty Wells was inducted into the Country Music Hall of Fame in 1976, and she won a Grammy Lifetime Achievement Award in 1991.

See also Country Music Hall of Fame

For Further Reading

Bufwack, Mary A., and Robert K. Oermann. *Finding Her Voice: The Saga of Women in Country Music*. New York: Crown, 1993.

Dew, Joan. *Singers and Sweethearts: The Women of Country Music*. Garden City, NY: Doubleday, 1977.

Kristine H. Burns

Western States Arts Federation

See Organizations, Regional Arts

Williams, Mary Lou (1910–1981)

Pianist and arranger Mary Lou Williams was one of the few major jazz figures to live through and perform in all of the jazz eras. Williams is most remembered as a pianist and composer but had an important impact as a teacher during much of her career, including a four-year tenure at Duke University. A truly versatile musician, she performed in stride, swing, post-bop, and bop styles.

Born on 8 May 1910 in Atlanta, GA, as Mary Elfrieda Scruggs, Williams grew up in Pittsburgh and began performing professionally at the age of six. In 1931 she joined the popular Kansas City band Andy Kirk and the Twelve Clouds of Joy and became known as "The Lady Who Swings the Band." Throughout the 1930s she composed hits for the Kirk band, including "Froggy Bottom," "Mary's Idea," and "Walkin, and Swingin'." She also wrote for Benny Goodman, Tommy Dorsey, Earl Hines, Louis Armstrong, Cab Calloway, Jimmie Lunceford, and Duke Ellington. Over 350 compositions have been attributed to Williams.

In the 1940s her apartment in Harlem became an informal classroom for young bebop musicians, particularly a young pianist, Thelonious Monk. Monk was profoundly influenced by Williams, as were Bud Powell, Charlie Parker, Dizzy Gillespie, Tadd Dameron, Billy Strayhorn, Sarah Vaughn (1924–1990), and many others. In 1945 Williams premiered her *Zodiac Suite* (available *Town Hall (1945): The Zodiac Suite*, Vintage Jazz Classic 1035) and orchestrated in it the following year for a Carnegie Hall performance by the New York Philharmonic.

During the 1950s Williams focused on spirituality, became involved with the Catholic Church, and devoted herself to charitable work. She founded the Bel Canto Foundation, which she funded with a thrift shop, to help impoverished and addicted musicians. Father Anthony Woods encouraged Williams to return to music as her ministry. She began teaching music theory at Seton High School in Pittsburgh, composed her first jazz mass, and enlisted her students as the performers. Williams became an innovator in sacred jazz, beginning with her first work, *Black Christ of the Andes* (Mary 32843), and culminating in *Mary Lou's Mass* (Mary M102), commissioned by the Vatican and performed by the Alvin Ailey City Center Dance Theatre in 1971.

During the 1970s Williams's focus became one of educating young people about the rich heritage of African American music and jazz. She presented lectures and concerts that featured a medley depicting the history of jazz. In 1977 Williams became artist-in-residence at Duke University, where she composed for the Duke Wind Symphony and wrote for and conducted a chorus and jazz orchestra.

Williams was devoted to education; even after being diagnosed with cancer, she continued to compose for students. Duke University awarded her its Trinity Award, and she also received honorary degrees from Boston University, Fordham University, and Loyola University. At the time of her death on 28 May 1981 she was forming the Mary Lou Williams Foundation to provide music scholarships for gifted children between the ages of six and 12. The Kennedy Center in Washington, DC, presents an annual Mary Lou Williams Festival, featuring women jazz performers and workshops for aspiring young women jazz musicians.

See also Jazz; Jazz Education

For Further Reading

Dahl, Linda. *Stormy Weather; The Music and Lives of a Century of Jazzwomen*. New York: Pantheon Books, 1984.

———. *Morning Glory, A Biography of Mary Lou Williams*. Los Angeles: University of California Press, 1999.

McPartland, Marian. *All in Good Time*. New York: Oxford University Press, 1987.

Unterbrink, Mary. *Jazz Women at the Keyboard.* Jefferson, NC: McFarland, 1983.

Kimberly McCord

Wilson, Ann (1950–) and Nancy (1954–)

As lead members of the hard rock group Heart, sisters Ann (singer/guitar) and Nancy (lead guitar) Wilson helped break down sexual barriers within the music industry in the 1970s and inspired countless young girls to write rock songs, learn guitar, or join rock bands. They themselves had few women models on which to base their careers, but they indicate that the Beatles had an enormous effect on them along with guitarists Dave Gilmour, Jimmy Page, and Jeff Beck, as well as Paul Simon and Joni Mitchell (b. 1943). The Wilsons' performances were marked by an aggressive playing style and hard-rocking attitude.

Ann, born on 19 June 1950 in San Diego, and Nancy, born on 16 March 1954 in San Francisco, grew up in Southern California and Taiwan before their father, a captain in the Marine Corps, retired to Seattle, WA. Both sisters were interested in folk and pop music as children, and although Ann never took any formal music lessons as a child, Nancy studied some guitar and flute. After attending college they returned to Seattle, with Nancy working as a folksinger and Ann joining the all-male vocal group Heart in 1970.

The group had been formed as the Army in 1963 by Steve Fossen (bass) and brothers Roger (guitar) and Mike Fisher (guitar); the name was later changed to White Heart, then simply to Heart in 1974. Upon joining, Ann became romantically involved with Mike Fisher; and when Nancy joined in 1974, she became involved with guitarist Roger. Soon after Nancy's arrival, Mike Fisher retired from the stage to become the band's sound engineer. With Howard Leese (multi-instrumentalist) as keyboardist and Michael Derosier (drummer), they recorded their debut album, *Dreamboat Annie* (Capitol C2-46491), in 1975 for Mushroom Records. After selling more than 30,000 copies in Canada, it was released in the United States and achieved Platinum status on the strength of the hit singles "Crazy on You" and "Magic Man." In 1977 Heart switched to CBS's subsidiary Portrait, resulting in a prolonged legal fight with Mushroom Records, which in 1978 released the unfinished album *Magazine* shortly after the band issued its true follow-up, *Little Queen* (Portrait RK-34799). The single "Barracuda" was a smash, and *Little Queen* sold over one million copies.

After the 1978 album *Dog and Butterfly* (Portrait RK-35555), both of the Wilsons' romances ended, and Roger Fisher left the group. In 1980 Heart issued *Bebe Le Strange*; following a lengthy U.S. tour, Fossen and Derosier left the group and were replaced by Mark Andes (bass) and Denny Carmassi (percussion). The group's commercial success waned with *Private Audition* and *Passionworks*, though Ann's duet with Mike Dean, "Almost Paradise . . . Love Theme from Footloose" rose to number seven.

In 1985 Heart joined Capitol and had a strong comeback with its issue *Heart* (Capitol C2-46157), which launched four Top 10 hits: "What about Love?" "Never," "These Dreams," and "Nothin' at All." The follow-up, *Bad Animals*, was almost as successful with "Alone," "Who Will You Run To?" and "There's the Girl." Heart's 1990 release, *Brigade*, featured the number one hit "All I Want to Do Is Make Love to You," as well as the

Top 25 hits "I Didn't Want to Need You" and "Stranded."

In the early 1990s the Wilson sisters also formed a new outfit with Sue Ennis and Frank Cox called the Lovemongers, an acoustic quartet. In 1992 they issued a four-song EP, which included a cover of Led Zeppelin's "The Battle of Evermore." While the Wilsons became involved with various solo projects, they also continued as Heart with the 1993 release of *Desire Walks On* (Capitol 99627), in which Andes and Carmassi were replaced by Fernando Saunders (bass) and Denny Fongheiser (percussion). In *The Road Home*, Heart enlisted former Led Zeppelin bassist John Paul Jones to produce a live acoustic set reprising hits like "Dreamboat Annie," "Crazy on You" and "Barracuda." In 1999 Nancy released her solo debut, *Live at McCabe's Guitar Shop* (Sony 69837), a set recorded two years earlier at the famed Santa Monica, CA, venue. On 23 January 2000 she became the parent of twin sons with her husband, writer and film director Cameron Crowe. Ann and Nancy continue to have a strong following of fans.

See also Bands, Pop Rock; Rock and Popular Music Genres; Rock Music

For Further Reading

Gaar, Gillian G. *She's a Rebel: The History of Women in Rock and Roll.* Seattle, WA: Seal Press, 1992.

Welcome to AnnAndNancy.com. Available: http://www.AnnandNancy.com

Sharon Mirchandani

Wilson, Nancy (1937–)

Jazz singer, radio host, and actress Nancy Wilson is one of the most significant recording artists of the twentieth century. Her love of the story line has carried her to fame in jazz, rhythm and blues, and popular music genres. She is a prolific recording artist, with her 60th album, *If I Had My Way* (Sony 67769), having been released in 1997. "I don't try to impress people with how high or how low my voice is, or what I can do with it melodically. I look first at the story line in the lyrics; that tells me what is going to happen for me musically" (Travis, 480).

Born on 20 February 1937 in Chillicothe, OH, Wilson began her singing career performing at local nightclubs and television stations. She toured with Rusty Bryant's Carolyn Club Band from 1956 to 1958. In 1959 she performed with Cannonball Adderly in Columbus, OH; it was he who persuaded her to move to New York and pursue a recording career. She was successful in this venture, obtaining a manager (Adderly's manager, Joe Levy) and a recording contract with Capitol Records. Her first hit song was "How Glad I Am" in 1964. Wilson is known for her active performing schedule, singing in nightclubs and jazz shows in the United States and Europe. Famous for her jazz and blues vocal stylings, Wilson has stated that her early influences included Dinah Washington (1924–1963), Billie Holiday (1915–1959), Louis Jordan, and Billy Eckstine.

Wilson has been nominated for several Grammy Awards, winning one for Best Blues Recording in 1964 for *How Glad I Am* (Capitol T-2155). She has received an honorary doctorate from the Berklee College of Music and has a star on the Hollywood Walk of Fame. At present she serves as the host of National Public Radio's *Jazz Profiles* program.

See also Jazz; Music Programmer/Host

For Further Reading

Travis, Dempsey J. *An Autobiography of Black Jazz.* Chicago: Urban Research Institute, 1983.

Kristina Lampe Shanton

Women Band Directors International

The Women Band Directors International (WBDI) was founded "to foster a spirit of friendliness, fellowship and cooperation among women band directors in the schools of America and abroad." Through its meetings the WBDI accomplishes this purpose by providing many resources for the betterment of instrumental music education and for the advancement of women in instrumental music positions. This includes confronting issues dealing with school administration, community outreach, and problems relevant to women band directors. The WBDI is also committed to creating partnerships between school bands and their communities by emphasizing the values of a sound instrumental program. Finally, the WBDI cooperates with other organizations that are dedicated to the improvement of wind bands as a "worthwhile medium of musical expression."

The Women Band Directors National Association was formed in 1969 in Chicago, IL. Because of its success, in 1997 the name was changed to the Women Band Directors International. The organization's founding president was Gladys Stone Wright, an award-winning band director from Oregon. Wright is currently the editor for *The Woman Conductor* and serves as executive secretary of the WBDI. In 1984 Wright became the first woman elected to membership in the prestigious American Bandmasters Association.

Women Band Directors International currently supports three publications. *The Woman Conductor* is the WBDI's quarterly newsletter providing news and information pertinent to WBDI. *Women of the Podium* is a historical publication containing biographical information about every member of the WBDI. *Bandworld* is the official magazine of the WBDI.

The WBDI's primary membership is made up of people who are actively engaged in, or retired from, directing bands. Student memberships are open to high school or college students interested in instrumental music education as a career. Industrial memberships are availa-

Women Presidents of the Women Band Directors International

President	Years of Service
Linda R. Moorhouse	1998–2000
Judith Grimes	1996–1998
Patricia Root	1994–1996
Catherine Heard	1992–1994
Patricia Garren	1990–1992
Noreen Linnemann	1988–1990
Marie Cotaya	1986–1988
Barbara Lovett	1984–1986
Laurie Neeb	1982–1984
Jacqueline Hunt	1980–1982
Ileane McElwee	1978–1980
Nora Arquit	1974–1978
Gladys Stone Wright	1969–1974

ble to firms or organizations interested in WBDI. An affiliate membership is available to anyone connected with music, including but not limited to private instructors, clinicians, orchestra directors, and composers.

In keeping with its mission, the WBDI strives to recognize women who have achieved at the highest levels. The International Golden Rose award honors women of national and international reputation who have demonstrated outstanding achievement in instrumental music. The Silver Baton is bestowed on WBDI members who have made outstanding contributions to the improvement of bands in America. The Scroll of Excellence honors exceptional women in instrumental music at the state, national, or international level; and the Citation of Merit honors WBDI members who have made significant contributions to the WBDI. Members who have consistently distinguished themselves in the music community both nationally and internationally are honored in the WBDI Hall of Fame.

Women Band Directors International is also committed to the future of music education. Every year, five scholarships are given to women preparing to be band directors who are enrolled in a university music education program. These awards include the Helen May Butler Memorial Scholarship, the Kathryn Siphers–Patricia Garren Scholarship, the Martha Ann Stark Memorial Scholarship, the Volkwein Memorial Scholarship, and the Gladys Stone Wright Scholarship.

See also Band Music Education; Music Education; Tau Beta Sigma

For Further Reading

The Woman Conductor. Official publication of the Women Band Directors International.

Women Band Directors International. Available: http://www.eskimo.com/~moorhous/

Christopher Anderson

Women in Music Business Association

The Women in Music Business Association (WMBA) organization began in 1993 in response to the underrepresentation of women in the music industry. Catherine Masters, an independent television producer, and Marcia Shein, an entertainment attorney, founded the WMBA, which started in Nashville and has since opened chapters in Atlanta, New York, Los Angeles, San Francisco, and New Orleans. The Association has expanded to include international membership by opening an office in London. Although each chapter holds its own seminars and workshops for specific areas of interest, the organization as a whole meets at an annual meeting—now drawing over 1,000 attendees.

Masters has stated that the primary goal of the WMBA is "to form a very solid educational, informational, and political trade association, so women who are just getting into the industry can come to the local meetings and national conferences, make contacts, and get the information they need" (*Billboard*, 8). This goal is well represented in a diverse membership comprised of talent agents, managers, lawyers, and recording executives as well as songwriters and performers, including Tammy Wynette (1942–1998), Loretta Lynn (b. 1935), and former Evangeline member Kathleen Stieffel. The networking aspect of the Association is seen in the publication of a membership directory, a newsletter, and subscription song contests.

See also Music Management; Production Manager

For Further Reading

Cosola, Mary. "Resources for Women in Music." *Electronic Musician* 13/1 (January 1997): 96–102, 159.

Gregory Straughn

Women Musicians' Alliance

The Women Musicians' Alliance (WMA) serves the central Florida region by promoting independent women creators of contemporary music and encouraging women of all ages to write and perform the music of the future. Founded in 1997, WMA has grown from a core of nine members to around 40 individuals and groups, ranging from composers and songwriters to performers and fans of women's music.

The Alliance is a forum for discussion and education about women's roles in the music industry and in creating today's music. Through bimonthly concerts such as the *Shifting Sands House Concert Series* and an annual benefit, *Not Necessarily Folk*, WMA brings together women songwriters, composers, and lyricists with performers, both men and women, thus providing a way to unite artists with a public seeking women's music. The quarterly newsletter *Echoes from the Balcony*, membership directory, and venue directory provide members a network for sharing resources, ideas, and opportunities. Recently the WMA has established a World Wide Web presence to further expand its audience and membership and will add an online resource center for updated opportunities for performers and composers. Also included on the World Wide Web site is a member profile listing the activities and works of a featured member each month. The Women Musicians' Alliance has been recognized by community organizations and newspapers for its commitment to bringing women's music to a larger audience.

See also Los Angeles Women in Music; Organizations, Regional Arts

For Further Reading

Women Musicians' Alliance (WMA). Available: http://www.womenmusicians.org

Gregory Straughn

Women-Identified Music

"Women-identified music" or, alternatively, "women's music," is the term first used in the early 1970s to denote pop and rock music created by, for, and about women. The catalyst for women-identified music was the women's liberation movement of the late 1960s. Female, mainly lesbian, musicians and audiences reacted against the sexist lyrics of pop/rock music and also against the ways in which women were shut out of the male-dominated music industry. Working collectively, these musicians created a popular music intended to express and reflect women's experiences and points of view. Women founded recording and distribution companies, women's concert production companies, women-identified music festivals, and women's music circuits whose audience is mainly women. Early albums of women-identified music were Maxine Feldman's single "Angry Atthis" and Alix Dobkin's *Lavender Jane Loves Women* (Women's Wax Works 1).

The two main components of women-identified music are feminist music and lesbian music. The overlap between these two categories or subgenres is considerable, and their differences are subtle. Feminist music has been described as highlighting political and social freedom; lesbian music, woman's personal space and freedom (Jesudason and Drew,

1992). A sampling of song titles conveys an idea of the messages in both subgenres: "A Woman's Anger," "I'm Living in an Alien Nation," "Can You Prove You're Not a Lesbian and Other Borderline Questions?" Some practitioners distinguished a "women's music" sound, characterized by accessibility, intimacy within musical groupings, musical eclecticism, and the musical integrity that comes from not trying to reach mass audiences. The collaborative nature of women's music resulted in a marked eclecticism. From the beginning most of the musicians were classically trained; others each brought to the blend music of different traditions, such as folk, pop and rock, Latin, and various black musical idioms—jazz, rhythm and blues, and gospel.

In the 1970s and 1980s, through music businesses and festivals specifically dedicated to the genre, women had opportunities that had heretofore been open only to men, such as learning to engineer and produce sound recordings. Olivia Records, the first women's record label, was founded in 1973 in Washington, DC, by Linda Tillery and Mary Watkins; more labels followed, including Redwood Records (founded by Holly Near [b. 1949]), Women's Wax Works, and Sister Sun. A network of volunteers set up the Women's Independent Labels Distributors (WILD) to distribute women-identified music labels.

Festivals of women-identified music such as the Michigan Womyn's Music Festival, Alaska Women's Music Festival, North East Women's Musical Retreat, New Hampshire Women's Music Festival, WIMINFEST, National Women's Music Festival, and Spring Fling are run entirely by women, who set up tents and performance spaces, wire stage equipment, advertise and audition, and cook for all attendees. Performances feature prominent women-identified musicians as well as up-and-coming ones, who play to capacity, all-women crowds. At the Michigan event, the largest and most prominent festival, men are not allowed admittance.

Debates have continued among practitioners of women-identified music concerning aesthetic, territorial, and monetary matters. As the number of musicians, their audiences, and the support network for women-identified music grew, so too did the commercial potential of the genre. The novelty of women's lyrics wore off, and musicians searched for distinctive musical styles. Some experimented with new musical elements, a process that others thought diluted the original intent of women-identified music. The lyrics remained radical and revolutionary, whereas the music itself "continued to employ the forms of mainstream popular music" (Petersen, 1987, p. 206).

The commercial potential of feminist music and lesbian music has attracted performers from mainstream women pop stars, even those who are not necessarily committed to the original purpose of women-identified music but aim for a wider audience. Mainstream singers have thus been accused of taking away the need, and thus the market, for women-identified music (Einhorn, 1991; Lont, 1992). Performers of women-identified music who launched their careers by gaining the support of audiences at women's music festivals, and then successfully entered the mainstream, have likewise been accused of diluting the social message in their work. Recent debate centers on the term "women-identified music" itself, with both audiences and performers contesting its meaning and its continued relevance (Hayes, 1999).

See also Lesbian Music; Womyn's Music

For Further Reading

Cash, Alice H. "Conference Report. Feminist Theory and Music: Toward a Common Language. School of Music, University of Minnesota, Minneapolis, 26–30 June 1991." *Journal of Musicology* 9/4 (1991): 521–532.

Einhorn, Jennifer. "Women's Music: Where Did It Go?" *Sojourner* 171: 34–35, 1991.

Ericson, Margaret D. "Woman-Identified Music." In *Women and Music: A Selective Annotated Bibliography on Women and Gender Issues in Music, 1987–1992*. New York: G. K. Hall, 1996, Part H.

Hayes, Eileen M. "Black Women Performers of Women-Identified Music: They Cut Off My Voice, I Grew Two Voices." Ph.D. diss., University of Washington, 1999.

Jesudason, Melba, and Sally Drew. "Feminist Music and WOMONSONG Choir of Madison, Wisconsin." *Studies in Popular Culture* 15/1 (1992): 61–74.

Petersen, Karen E. "An Investigation into Women-Identified Music in the United States." In *Women and Music in Cross-Cultural Perspective*, ed. Ellen Koskoff. Westport, CT: Greenwood Press, 1987.

Starr, Victoria. "The Changing Tune of Women's Music: A Once Powerful Movement Loses Its Identity as a New Generation Steps Out to a Different Beat." *Advocate* 604 (1992): 68–71.

Sutton, Terri. "Whatever Happened to 'Women's Music'? New Female Stars Belie Notion That There Is a Women's Music." *Utne Reader* 49 (1992): 30, 32, 34.

Roe-Min Kok

Women's Philharmonic

The Women's Philharmonic, a professional orchestra in the San Francisco area comprised entirely of women musicians, is a realization of the vision of three women: Elizabeth Min, Miriam Abrams, and Nan Washburn, who saw the importance of visibility for women who compose, conduct, or perform. They created a professional orchestra by garnishing support from the artistic, political, and activist communities. They were endorsed by the International League of Women Composers (now the International Alliance for Women in Music), San Francisco State University, women in higher education, and others. What began with a $16 donation and was followed by many more small donations from women all over the country has grown to a nationally renowned orchestra. They have received 13 American Society of Composers, Authors and Publishers (ASCAP) awards in 17 seasons, and an American Symphony League Orchestra award to the U.S. orchestra with the strongest commitment to new American music during a season. They have been featured in national media and were one of the first U.S. orchestras to be given a National Endowment for the Arts (NEA) Challenge III award, which provided funding for a two-volume anthology of works by women composers.

Originally called the Bay Area Women's Philharmonic, the orchestra presented its first concert in 1981. To date, it has performed the works of 160 women composers, including 42 commissioned works and over 129 premieres. It has released three recordings—*The Women's Philharmonic*, *Baroquen Treasures*, and *The Music of Chen Yi*, and is featured on two Koch International Classics compilations—*Women of Note* (KIC 7603) and *Uses of Music in Uttermost Parts*, which features the collaborations of Elinor Armor and Ursula K. LeGuin.

The orchestra has many ambitious goals. The $400,000 Fanfares Project is the most important and wide-reaching commission of music by women composers ever undertaken. As a way to celebrate the turn of the century and the new millennium, 10 new works, each 10 minutes long, were commissioned. The women composers' ages range from 15 to 80, and they represent diverse backgrounds. There are three outcomes for this project: (1) a consortium is created to develop a way to sustain interest in women composers; (2) 10 new works will have been written and performed; and (3) these works will be played in as many cities as the consortium can secure. The goal is that the works be played in every major city in the country.

The American Masters Series identifies and reconstructs lost compositions by women, many of which might never be otherwise heard. The project focuses on music of the nineteenth and twentieth centuries and includes research and reconstruction leading to performance. For example, three works by Florence Price (1887–1953), the first African American woman symphonist, have been reconstructed and performed by the Women's Philharmonic. Price's first symphony was performed by the Philharmonic in 1989. The NEA and other donors supported the reconstruction of two other Price works—*The Oak* and *Mississippi River*—both performed by the Philharmonic in March 2000. None of her works had been published or recorded prior to this effort. A similar reconstruction of a work by Fanny Hensel Mendelssohn has facilitated its subsequent performance by dozens of other orchestras.

Other women in the American Masterworks Series include Catherine Urner, Esther Williamson Ballou, and Ethel Leginska (1886–1970). Selected masterworks are recorded and distributed to archives, libraries, and other orchestras.

The National Women Conductors Initiative, begun in 1998, provides an avenue for women composers to hone professional skills and then advocates for them to obtain positions as conductors and music directors. A $1 million grant was given by an anonymous donor to support this project. Partnered with the Philharmonic is the American Symphony Orchestra League and OPERA America. This innovative effort gives unprecedented opportunities and support to women.

In addition to these accomplishments, the Philharmonic offers services to composers, conductors, and orchestras. For composers, a symposium called Composing a Career is held every two years to provide practical advice and opportunities for networking to composers regardless of their age or stage of development. The orchestra's new music reading sessions, Music in the Making, affords composers the opportunity to hear their works, possibly for the first time. To date, there have been 14 sessions.

For orchestras, there are program consultations, scores for rent, and online lists of selected works for orchestra and for string orchestra. When completed, the World Wide Web site will include resources for composers, a list of women conductors and resources for conductors, recommended repertoire, and a researchable database. The National Women Composers Resource Center (NWCRC), which existed separately from the Philharmonic in the early 1990s, was organized to respond to growing inquiries from orchestras and others regarding reconstructed scores and the location of existing works by women. The focus was on educating and assisting orchestras in the incorporation of these works into the standard repertoire. The NWCRC maintains a searchable database of works reconstructed and/or performed by the Philharmonic, and it offers referral services to orchestras. The NWCRC created the Lili Boulanger Award, providing mentorship to emerging women composers by commissioning and performing new orchestral works and assisting in the promotion of these works to other orchestras. Because of changes in funding and in staff, the resource center is now an integral part of the Philharmonic.

Demographically, audiences are composed of professionals, gay women, fans of new music, and supporters of progressive causes and are 25 to 30 percent male. The Philharmonic's current conductor and artistic director is Apo Hsu (b. 1956). JoAnn Falletta (b. 1954), the previous conductor, now conducts orchestras in Buffalo, NY, Norfolk, VA, and Long Beach, CA. As there are no women music directors in orchestras with a Top 25 budget, and only five from orchestras ranked 26 to 75, three of which are positions held by Falletta, the work continues. Considering that in 1998–1999, only 12 of the 1,400 works performed by American orchestras were by women, the Women's Philharmonic efforts help to balance long-term inequities. It has more than accomplished Elizabeth Min's original goal of creating an orchestra that would "dramatically change the world by setting a great example."

See also Conductor, Instrumental and Operatic; Libraries and Archives

For Further Reading

The Women's Philharmonic Home Page. Available: http://www.womensphil.org

Alicia RaMusa

Women's Sphere

The term "women's sphere" emerged from the nineteenth-century assumption, copiously affirmed in the scholarly and popular press, that society is properly divided into "separate spheres," female and male, the female sphere being private and domestic, the male sphere public. In music in the United States, observing this private/public binarism, amateur performance in the home, school, or church has been gendered female, and the wider, public aspects of music, including composing, conducting, and performing professionally, have been gendered male. A proper middle- or upper-class girl's upbringing traditionally included instruction in singing and playing the piano or other women-associated instruments such as the harp or flute. Music publishers issued an ever-growing volume of domestic music well into the twentieth century. Women music teachers, although numerous, were often less esteemed than their counterparts who were men. Women composers were at first few in number, and they composed mostly in genres for the amateur market.

Although the ideology of women's sphere is a creation of middle-class European-Americans, especially Anglo-Americans, the idea of limitations on women's musical activities extended to Americans of many other ethnic groups. Furthermore, many women of other classes and ethnicities sought to emulate these ideals as part of a general campaign of acculturation. Still, for many, living the ideals was not always practical or desirable. Hazel V. Carby (1987) has written about how Bessie Smith (1894–1937) and other African American women blues singers resisted the domestic ideal and articulated sociopolitical criticism from their experiences and environments. It should be noted, however, that such expressions were allowed for two reasons: their music ("race records") was marketed not to white audiences but to black; and perhaps more important, such expressions validated white listeners' stereotypes about black hypersexuality.

Because performing musicians, at least in the classical tradition, have often been considered the passive conduits for compositional genius, particularly male genius, recent writers such as Suzanne Cuzick (1994) suggest that performing can be understood as a "natural" mode for women. Public performers had difficulties, however, especially in the early 1900s. Public music making by a woman was considered dangerous, and that attitude persists in some circles. However highly praised, a woman musician often has to walk a tightrope between showing (off) her talent and preserving the modesty expected of the ideal woman. Opera and Broadway singers have often had to compensate for the stereotypes linking acting and prostitution by constructing artificially demure and hyperfeminine star personae, including Doris Day (b. 1924) and Olivia Newton-John early in her career. Other singers have been able to express a more extroverted sexuality, although before the 1960s they were marketed in a comic or novelty mode, such as Fanny Brice (1891–1951) and Carmen Miranda (1909–1955).

In the 1960s and 1970s, with the feminist revival, movements for civil rights and peace, and other developments, women's musical activity extending beyond the "proper sphere" intensified; women writers, poets, and musicians came into greater prominence. Overall, the twentieth century witnessed both the rearticulation of the "separate spheres" ideology and its renunciation, within and without a feminist framework. Women still find most of their success in the traditional realms of singing (in art and popular genres alike), playing, and teaching. Some feminist musicians acknowledge inherent differences between genders and use such differences to create an oppositional, feminized musical space. Some women have established composition credits alongside performing: these include Mariah Carey (b. 1970) and Sheryl Crow (b. 1962). A growing number of women are influential as composers, such as Joan Tower (b. 1938) and Ellen Taaffe Zwilich (b. 1939).

See also Separate Spheres—Sexual Aesthetics; Social Darwinism

For Further Reading

Carby, Hazel V. *Cultures in Babylon: Black Britain and African America*. London and New York: Verso, 1999.

———. " 'It Jus Be's Dat Way Sometime': The Sexual Politics of Women's Blues." *Radical America* 20 (1987): 9–22.

Cusick, Suzanne. "Gender and the Cultural Work of a Classical Music Performance." *repercussions* 3/1 (1994): 77–110.

Janeway, Elizabeth. *Man's World, Woman's Place: A Study in Social Mythology*. New York: William Morrow, 1971.

Richard Rischar

Women's Voice

The concept of "women's voice" is a feminist metaphor for women taking an active, creative role or creating a feminine narrative point of view, usually as authors, although the term is used for composers and other artists as well. However, because women are often restricted in the kinds of music-making roles they choose, the consideration of women's voice may be extended to teaching, performance, and patronage. A woman-oriented consideration of voice thereby alters the way one typically views musical creation, as it calls into question the dominance of composition, producing, and distribution. All these roles of women must be considered if women's voices are to be heard in all their breadth.

Consideration of women's voice may begin with a consideration of silence; in modern feminist discourse the silencing of women is a recurrent topic, finding a voice being equated with empowerment. Feminism itself is a contradiction of the nearly universal beliefs in the silence of a virtuous woman; if she speaks, she chatters, she gossips, she is a shrew.

Authors such as Carolyn Heilbrun (1988) and Alice Jardine (1985) argue that a chief imperative of a feminine (as opposed to biologically female) voice is the disruption of the masculine ("phallocentric") symbolic structures in Western culture. One can achieve this disruption either musically, through the creation and performance of new, enlightened works, or discursively, through deconstructing and unmasking such symbolic structures in pre-existing works. Related to this is an insistence that women see themselves collectively, not individually; some traditions of women's music follow this path.

The experience of producing music by women and principally for women can be liberating, allowing a freedom to experience a bond of sisterhood and to voice things one might not in the company of men. But for many, especially non-European-American women, such demands are too Eurocentric. The need for collectivity, for instance, tends to erase those experiences and desires of individual women that are not common within the defined collective. Further, the demand for collectivity can restrict women to the very agonistic, dominance/submission binarisms that bound them in the first place, for instance, the belief that women are more nurturing, empathetic, and intuitive than men are.

The artistic creations of most women, like women's lives, find some place between individuality and collectivity. One can bring one's gender identity to the foreground without falling into the traps of essentialism. A useful metaphor is Julia Kristeva's (1980) call for feminine art to "write the body," placing the emphasis back on the wide range of individual women's voices and experiences. What artists represent as feminine should not be limited by ideology but can include, for instance, what is peculiar to the experiences of individual women as well as what traditional masculinity represses.

Singing is the most common form of musical expression for women. However, performers such as Madonna (b. 1958) and Shania Twain (b. 1965) often send mixed messages, combining reactionary visions of courtship with empowered self-expression. Some critics simply shun those works whose texts and musical styles serve patriarchal systems. Author Suzanne Cusick (1994) argues that women run the risk of being further alienated from the musical mainstream of performance and discourse. For her, performance style itself can be a powerful tool for usurping such symbolic systems.

Women's voices continue to sing, telling the stories on which we build our lives. An awareness of the gendered aspects of singing and vocality is useful, but the story of women's voice is incomplete unless diverse musical practices are taken into account in order to battle the silence.

See also Male Gaze; Separate Spheres—Sexual Aesthetics; Women-Identified Music

For Further Reading

Cusick, Suzanne. "Gender and the Cultural Work of a Classical Music Performance." *repercussions* 3/1 (1994): 77–110.

Heilbrun, Carolyn. *Writing a Woman's Life*. New York: Norton, 1988.

Jardine, Alice. *Gynesis: Configurations of Woman and Modernity*. Ithaca: Cornell University Press, 1985.

Kristeva, Julia. *Desire in Language: A Semiotic Approach to Literature and Art*. New York: Columbia University Press, 1980.

Richard Rischar

Women Worthies

See Exceptional Woman

World Wide Web

See Internet Resources

Womyn's Music

Womyn's music was a popular genre that emerged around 1970 out of second wave feminism and was popularized by Meg Christian, Holly Near (b. 1949), Alix Dobkin, and others. "Womyn's music" was something of a euphemism for "lesbian music," as most women involved were lesbians. The spelling *womyn* was a way of omitting the letters *m-e-n* from the word *women*.

See also Lesbian Music; Women-Identified Music

For Further Reading

Brett, Philip, Elizabeth Wood, and Gary C. Thomas (eds.). *Queering the Pitch: The New Gay and Lesbian Musicology*. New York: Routledge, 1994.

Fleming, Lee (ed.). *Hot Licks: Lesbian Musicians of Note*. Charlottetown, P.E.I., Canada: gynergy books, 1996.

Martha Mockus

Wynette, Tammy (1942–1998)

Often called the "First Lady of Country Music," Tammy Wynette was one of the most popular women country performers of the 1960s, 1970s, and early 1980s. Her most memorable recording, "Stand by Your Man," written by Wynette and producer Billy Sherrill, was recorded in August 1968 during the height of the early women's liberation movement. While this song eventually became the biggest selling record ever recorded by a woman, it also became a country music anthem, earning Wynette an image of stereotyped country conservatism and female passivity that was clearly challenged by her career and personal life.

Born Virginia Wynette Pugh on 5 May 1942 in Itawamba County, MS, she was 9 months old when her father died of a brain tumor. Her mother, forced to find work in a Memphis, TN, defense plant during World War II, left Wynette to be raised by her grandparents. Wynette eventually married five times and had four children. In 1959, at age 17, she married Euple Byrd, with whom she had two daughters. In 1962, due to Euple's inability to keep steady employment, Wynette enrolled in beauty school and worked evenings as a barmaid, singing country songs for her customers. Their third daughter was born in 1965 shortly before their divorce became final. Moving to Birmingham, AL, the divorced mother of three sang on a local television show in the mornings and worked as a hairdresser by day.

Wynette moved to Nashville in 1966 and auditioned for producer Billy Sherrill, who changed her name to Tammy Wynette and signed her to Epic Records. Their first single recording, "Apartment #9," almost broke the Top 40 charts; her second, "Your Good Girl's Gonna Go Bad," reached number three on the *Billboard* charts. These early successes launched a career that eventually earned Tammy Wynette 20 number one single recordings and 11 number one albums, selling in excess of 30 million records.

While her career blossomed, Wynette's personal life was less than serene. In 1967 she married songwriter Don Chapel. That marriage ended in 1968 when Wynette left with her soon-to-be third husband, country superstar George Jones. Wynette and Jones were married in the following year and became the "King and Queen" of country performers, recording a string of duets that chronicled their relationship, telling of romance, infidelity, breakup, reconciliation, and, in 1975, divorce. Wynette's fourth marriage, to a flamboyant Nashville realtor, lasted a mere six weeks. Her fifth marriage, in 1975, to songwriting colleague George Richey, was apparently her most successful. Among her many albums are *D-I-V-O-R-C-E* (Koch International 7945), *Stand by Your Man* (Sony 66018), and *Take Me to Your World/I Don't Wanna Play House* (Koch International 7944).

Her personal life notwithstanding, Wynette's career was unparalleled in the history of women country performers. In addition to record sales, she became an accomplished actress and songwriter. She garnered three Country Music Association awards and two Grammy Awards. In the 1980s and 1990s, although her country recording success had slowed, she was honored by pop, rock, and country artists who appeared on her albums. She became a regular on the television soap opera *Capitol* and was given roles in both a movie and music video produced by Burt Reynolds. After the 1980s, Wynette suffered from many health problems, and she was hospitalized several times before her death on 6 April 1998.

See also Country Music; Country Music Association; Grammy Award

For Further Reading

Bufwack, Mary. A., and Robert K. Oermann. *Finding Her Voice: The Saga of Women in Country Music*. New York: Crown, 1993.

Dew, Joan. *Singers and Sweethearts: The Women of Country Music*. Garden City, NY: Doubleday, 1977.

Amy Corin

Young, Phyllis (1925–)

Cellist and pedagogue Phyllis Young is one of the most influential women in American string pedagogy today. She frequently publishes articles on the string education profession in journals such as the *American String Teacher* and the *Instrumentalist*, and she is the author of two best-selling string pedagogy books, *Playing the String Game* (1978) and *The String Play* (1986).

Phyllis Young was born in Milan, KS in 1925. She received her bachelor's (1949) and master's (1950) degrees in music from the University of Texas at Austin. Young studied cello with Horace Britt and Andre Navarra. She currently serves as professor of cello and string pedagogy at the University of Texas at Austin.

As an acclaimed string teacher and pedagogue, Young has presented master classes and workshops in 27 different countries and 42 American states. She has served as the national president of the American String Teachers Association, receiving a Distinguished Service Award in 1984. Young has directed the University of Texas String Project, a teacher-training program that has become a model for string programs throughout the United States and abroad, for 35 years.

See also Music Education; String Education

For Further Reading

Young, Phyllis. *Playing the String Game: Strategies for Teaching Cello and Strings*. Austin and London: University of Texas Press, 1978.

———. *The String Play: The Drama of Teaching and Playing Strings*. Austin: University of Texas Press, 1986.

Andrea Olijnek

Z

Zaimont, Judith Lang (1945–)

Judith Lang Zaimont is a distinguished and award-winning American composer, writer, teacher, and performer. Her impressive catalog of compositions includes a symphony and several other orchestral works, a chamber opera, numerous works for chorus, many piano works, chamber works, and more than 70 art songs. Reflecting as a major talent among contemporary composers, Zaimont's music is frequently performed in the United States and abroad. Her compositional style may be characterized as lyrical, expressive, dramatic, and vibrant.

Zaimont was born on 8 November 1945 in Memphis, TN, the eldest of three children of Martin Lang and music teacher Bertha Friedman. Zaimont and her sister, Doris Lang (Kosloff), began their piano study with their mother. The family moved to New York, and Zaimont received a scholarship at the Juilliard Preparatory School to study piano with Rosina Lhevinne and theory and duo-piano with Ann Hull. At age 12, she and her 11-year-old sister began what was to be a seven-year career as a two-piano team. They received national recognition performing on the Lawrence Welk and Mitch Miller television shows, and in recitals and orchestral performances. The piano duo made the first American recordings of Francis Poulenc's *Sonate*, Leland Thompson's *Two Masques*, and Robert Casadesus's *Six Pieces Pour Deux Pianos*, which were released on the Golden Crest label under the title *Concert for Two Pianos*. The sisters made their Carnegie Hall debut in 1963 and continued to perform together through 1967, when they entered graduate school.

Zaimont began composing around age 11, writing two pieces for piano. At age 17 she won first prize from the National Federation of Music Clubs for a composition for flute and piano. She received her B.A. in music from Queens College, City University of New York (1966), where she studied composition with Hugo Weisgall. She also studied twentieth-century composition privately with Leo Kraft. Zaimont holds an Artist Master's Diploma in piano (1966) from the Long Island Institute of Music and an M.A. in composition (1968) from Columbia University, where she studied composition with Jack Beeson and Otto Luening. In 1971 the Alliance Française de New York awarded the Debussy Fellowship for Study Abroad to Zaimont. The fellowship allowed her to study orchestration with Andre Jolivet in Paris.

During her long and productive career Zaimont has received many awards, including the 1995 McCollin International Composers Competition for her Symphony No. 1, which was performed by the Philadelphia Orchestra in 1996. Other awards include the International Alliance for Women in Music Recording Award (1995), Peabody Conservatory Teacher of the Year (1985), Guggenheim Foundation Fellowship (1983–1984), National Endowment for the Arts Commission Grant (1982), Gold Medal in the Gottschalk Centenary Composition (1971), MacDowell Fellowships (1971 and 1976), Woodrow Wilson National Foundation Fellowship (1966–1967), and both American Society of Composers, Authors and Publishers (ASCAP) and Broadcast Music, Inc. (BMI), awards. Additionally, Zaimont has been the recipient of numerous commissions from a variety of sources, including the Connecticut Opera, American Choral Directors Association, Baltimore Chamber Orchestra, American Guild of Organists, Gregg Smith Singers, Dale Warland Singers, and the University of Alabama.

In 1996 Zaimont delivered the address "Modern America and American Musical Women: Social, Educational and Cultural Factors" at the International Music Council, United Nations Educational, Scientific and Cultural Organization (UNESCO) in Paris. Zaimont has been the editor for three volumes of *The Musical Woman: An International Perspective* and *Contemporary Concert Music by Women Composers*. An experienced teacher, she is currently professor of composition at the University of Minnesota. Her principal publishers are Galaxy Music and Sounds Alive! Recordings of her music are available on Arabesque, Centaur, and Leonarda labels; they include *Radiance—Choral Music by Judith Lang Zaimont* (4-Tay CD), *The Vocal-Chamber Art—Music of Judith Lang Zaimont* (Leonarda CD LE 343), and *ZONES—Chamber Music of Judith Lang Zaimont* (Arabesque CD Z6686).

See also Guggenheim Award

For Further Reading

Jezic, Diane P. *Women Composers: The Lost Tradition Found*, 2d ed. New York: Feminist Press, 1994.

Judith Lang Zaimont. Available: http://www.joblink.org/jzaimont/txtbio.htm

McNeil, Linda. "The Vocal Solo Works of Judith Lang Zaimont." *NATS Journal* (May/June 1993): 5–10.

Harriett Frazey Ranney

Zines

See Underground

Zwilich, Ellen Taaffe (1939–)

Ellen Taaffe Zwilich is an important late-twentieth-century composer of orchestral and chamber music in the United States. In 1975 she became the first woman to receive a doctorate in composition from the Juilliard School. She was the first woman to win the Pulitzer Prize in music (1983), for her Symphony No. 1: Three Movements for Orchestra (1982). As the first person appointed to the Carnegie Hall Composer's Chair (1995–1999), she championed the cause of American composers by interviewing them on video, creating the "Making Music" series to highlight established colleagues and sponsoring the Zwilich Composers Workshop to encourage younger writers.

Zwilich was born in Miami, FL, on 30

Ellen Taaffe Zwilich. *Photo © Cori Wells Braun, 1989. All rights reserved.*

April 1939 to Edward Porter and Ruth (Howard) Taaffe. At an early age she learned to play piano, trumpet, and violin and was improvising piano music by age 10. After studying violin and composition at Florida State University, she moved to New York in 1964 as a freelance violinist and trained with Ivan Galamian. In 1965 she married Joseph Zwilich, a Metropolitan Opera Orchestra violinist who performed and recorded several of her works before his sudden death in 1979. She played in the American Symphony Orchestra under Leopold Stokowski (1965–1972), during which time she decided to pursue a career as a composer.

In 1972 Zwilich entered the Juilliard School, where she cultivated a powerful, atonal, and intricately structured method of composing under Elliott Carter and Roger Sessions. She received critical attention from the 1975 premieres of *Symposium* (1973), her first major orchestral work, and String Quartet 1974, an Elizabeth Sprague Coolidge Chamber Music Prize winner. She began to compose full-time around 1978. Zwilich subsequently developed a more accessible style described as more tonal, more expressive, simpler, and more direct. In this regard, Chamber Symphony for six players (1979) is a pivotal work, written shortly after her husband's death. This single-movement work evolves organically from its initial musical motives, a process that the composer has passionately nurtured with singular craft.

Zwilich has written vocal compositions, including *Passages* for soprano and instrumental ensemble (1981), with text by A. R. Ammons, but most of her creative output has been composed for orchestra or chamber ensemble. The Pulitzer Prize–winning Symphony No. 1 was commissioned by the American Composers Orchestra and premiered on 5 May 1982 at Lincoln Center's Alice Tully Hall (world premiere recording on New World Records CD 80336-2). Subsequently she began to receive several commissions. By the late 1980s she started to write concertos for solo instruments with orchestra. Additional important works include *Celebration* for orchestra (1984); Concerto Grosso 1985 for orchestra; *Symbolon* (1988), probably the first American symphonic work to be premiered in the Soviet Union; Quintet for Clarinet and String Quartet (1990); Symphony No. 3 (1992); Triple Concerto for violin, cello, piano, and orchestra (1995); *Peanuts' Gallery* for piano and orchestra (1996); and String Quartet No. 2 (1998). Symphony No. 4, "The Gardens," commissioned as a musical portrait of the environs of Michigan State University, received its premiere in February 2000. Zwilich's recordings are numerous; they but include *American Trombone Concertos* (Bis 628), *Zwilich: Symbolon, Concerto Grosso 1985, Double Quartet* (New World Records 372), and *Five American Clarinet Quintets* (Delos 3183).

Zwilich's other honors include membership in the American Academy of Arts and Letters, a Guggenheim fellowship, and designation as Musical America's 1999 Composer of the Year. Her principal publishers are Merion Music, Margun Music, and Mobart Music.

See also Guggenheim Award; Pulitzer Prize

For Further Reading

Page, Tim. "The Music of Ellen Zwilich." *New York Times Magazine*, 14 July 1985.

Schaefer, John. "Composer of the Year: Ellen Taaffe Zwilich." *Musical America International Directory of the Performing Arts* (1999): 22–28.

Victor Cardell

Bibliography

Aaron, Sabra. "Entering Pop Music's Misogynist World." *Chicago Tribune* (3 March 1990): 1, 9.

Abeles, Hal. "The Sex-Stereotyping of Musical Instruments." *Journal of Research in Music Education* 26/2 (1978): 65–75.

About Ani DiFranco: AniDiFranco.org. Available: http://www.anidifranco.org

About GALA Choruses, Inc. Available: http://www.galachoruses.org

Abramson, Joan. *The Invisible Woman: Discrimination in the Academic Profession*. San Francisco: Jossey-Bass, 1975.

Adams, Minnie. "Musical and Dramatic: Mme. Hackley Recital." *Chicago Defender* (17 May 1914): 6.

Ahlstrom, David. "Liz Phillips: Sunspots." *Computer Music Journal* 6/3 (1982): 83–85.

Albertson, Chris. *Bessie*. New York: Stein and Day, 1972.

Ali, Lorraine. "Exiled in Guyville." *Rolling Stone* (6 October 1994): 57.

Altman, Linda J. *Natalie Cole: Star Child*. St. Paul, MN: EMC Corp., 1977.

Alvarez, Barbara Jo. "Preschool Music Education and Research on the Musical Development of Preschool Children: 1900 to 1980." Ph.D. diss., University of Michigan, 1981.

American Music Center, The. Available: http://www.amc.net

Ammer, Christine. *Unsung*. Revised and expanded second edition. Portland, OR: Amadeus Press, 2001.

Anderson, E. Ruth (comp.). *Contemporary American Composers: A Biographical Dictionary*, 2d ed. Boston: G. K. Hall, 1982.

Anderson, Jamie. "Women's Music for the '90s, Interviewed by Toni Armstrong Jr." *Hot Wire* 8/3 (1992): 2–5.

Anderson, Ruth. E-mail correspondence with Linda Dusman. February 2000.

Andress, Barbara. "Toward an Integrated Developmental Theory for Early Childhood Music Education." *Bulletin of the Council for Research in Music Education* 86 (1986): 10–17.

Andress, Barbara, and Linda Miller Walker. *Readings in Early Childhood Music Education*. Reston, VA: MENC, The National Association for Music Education, 1992.

Anne LeBaron. Available: http://www.alpertawards.com/archive/lebaron.html

Anonymous 4 Website. Available: http://www.anonymous4.com

Armstrong, Edward G. "The Rhetoric of Violence in Rap and Country Music." *Sociological Inquiry* 63/1 (Winter 1993): 64–83.

Armstrong, Toni Jr. "What Is Women's Music? An Endangered Species: Women's Music By, For, and About Women." *Hot Wire* 5/3 (1989): 17–19.

Arndt, Richmond T., and David Lee Rubin (eds.). *The Fulbright Difference, 1984–1992*. New Brunswick, NJ: Transaction Publishers, 1993.

Arsis Press: Music by Women Composers. Available: http://arsispress.com

Asin, Stephanie. "Local Rapper Angers Women

Conventioneers." *Houston Chronicle* (22 July 1993): 1.

Asken, Chandra. Personal correspondence with Monique Buzzarté. Spring 2000.

Atkinson, Kim. "Profiles." *Women of Note Quarterly* 3/4 (1995): 2–6.

Bakhle, Janaki. "Criticism: A Mad Dash through the Academy." In *Critical Angles*, newsletter for the Center for Arts Criticism, St. Paul, MN, Summer 1992. Reprinted in *Sounds Australian* (Autumn 1993): 48–51.

Balfe, Judith Higgins (ed.). *Paying the Piper: Causes and Consequences of Art Patronage*. Urbana: University of Illinois Press, 1993.

Barkin, Elaine. "A Questionnaire." *Perspectives of New Music* 19/1–2 (1980–81), 460–462.

———. "In Response." *Perspectives of New Music* 20/1–2 (1981–82), 288–329.

———. "The New Music of Chen Yi." *Journal of Music in China* 1 (1999): 147–149.

Barr, Cyrilla. *Elizabeth Sprague Coolidge: American Patron of Music*. New York: Schirmer, 1998.

Barrett, Brenda Smith. A Tribute Given in Memory of Frauke Peterson Haasemann, 20 April 1991, Westminster Choir College, Princeton, NJ.

Barron, Elinor. "Are You Really Doing What You Think You're Doing?" M.A. thesis, University of California, San Diego, 1972.

Bash, Lee. "A Content Analysis of the NAJE Educator and Jazz Educators Journal, 1969–1985." *Jazz Research Papers* 6 (1986): 30–36.

———. "Reminiscences: The Founding of NAJE/IAJE." *Jazz Educators Journal* 28 (1995): 45–49.

Battersby, Christine. *Gender and Genius: Towards a Feminist Aesthetics*. London: Woman's Press, 1989.

Beam, Alix. "Berklee Gives Female Professor the Blues." *Boston Globe* (6 March 1998): D1.

Beckett, Wendy. *Peggy Glanville-Hicks*. Sydney: Angus and Robertson Imprint, 1992.

Bender, James Francis. "Three American Composers from the Young Composers Project: Style Analysis of Selected Works by Emma Lou Diemer, Donald Martin Jenni and Richard Lane." Ph.D. diss., New York University, 1988.

Bennett, Peggy D. "Sarah Glover: A Forgotten Pioneer in Music Education." *Journal of Research in Music Education* 32 (1984): 49–65.

Berger, Edward (ed.) et al. *Annual Review of Jazz Studies 6, Rutgers: State University of New Jersey. Institute of Jazz Studies*. Metuchen, NJ, and London: Scarecrow Press, 1993.

Bergethon, Bjornar, Eunice Boardman, and Janet Montgomery. *Musical Growth in the Elementary School*, 6th ed. New York: Holt, Rinehart and Winston, 1996.

Bernstein, Jane. Remarks in "Report of the Nineteenth Annual Meeting: Women's Studies in Music" by Henry Woodward. *College Music Symposium* 17/1 (1977): 180–191.

Bigelow, Barbara Carlisle (ed.) *Contemporary Black Biography, vol. 5: Profiles from the International Black Community*. Detroit and London: Gale Research, 1994.

Biggs, John. Telephone interview by Allyson Brown Applebaum. 15 January 2000.

BIMBETTA Home Page, The. Available: http://www.bimbetta.com

Birge, Edward Bailey. *History of Public School Music in the United States*. Boston: Oliver Ditson, 1928.

Birosek, Patricia Jean. *The New Age Music Guide*. New York: Collier Books, Macmillan Publishing, 1989.

Blacker, Corinne E., and Patricia Juliana Smith (eds.). *En Travesti: Women, Gender Subversion, Opera*. New York: Columbia University Press, 1995.

Blair, Karen. *The Torchbearers: Women and Their Amateur Arts Associations in America, 1890–1930*. Bloomington: Indiana University Press, 1994.

Block, Adrienne Fried. *Amy Beach, Passionate Victorian: The Life and Work of an American Composer, 1867–1944*. New York: Oxford University Press, 1998.

Block, Adrienne Fried, and Carol Neuls-Bates (eds.). *Women in American Music: A Bibliography of Music and Literature*. Westport, CT: Greenwood Press, 1979.

Boenke, Heidi M. (comp.). *Flute Music by Women Composers: An Annotated Catalog*. Music Reference Collection, no. 17. Westport CT: Greenwood Press, 1988.

Bolton, Beth Marie. "An Investigation of Same and Different as Manifested in the Developmental Music Aptitudes of Students in First, Second, and Third Grades." Ph.D. diss., Temple University, 1995.

———. *The Childsong Collection: Learning the Language of Music*. Philadelphia, PA: Bestbael Publications, 1999.

Boosey and Hawkes. *Homepage*. Available: http://www.boosey.com

Borroff, Edith. "Women Composers: Reminiscence and History." *College Music Symposium* 15 (1975): 26–33.

Boulding, Elise. *The Underside of History: A View of Women through Time*. Boulder, CO: Westview

Press, 1976. Rev. ed., Newbury Park, CA: Sage Publications, 1992.

Bowers, Jane. "Feminist Scholarship and the Field of Musicology [I, II]." *College Music Symposium* 29 (1989): 81–92; 30/1 (Spring 1990): 1–13.

———. "Recent Research on Women in Music." In *The Status of Women in College Music: Preliminary Studies*, ed., by Carol Neuls-Bates. Binghamton, NY: College Music Society, 1976.

Bowers, Jane, and Judith Tick (eds.). *Women Making Music: The Western Art Tradition, 1150–1950*. Urbana: University of Illinois Press, 1986.

Bowman, Wayne. "Contemporary Pluralist Perspectives." In *Philosophical Perspectives on Music*. New York: Oxford University Press, 1998.

Boyce-Tillman, June. "Women's Ways of Knowing." *British Journal of Music Education* 10/3 (1993): 153–161.

Boyer, Clarence Horace. *How Sweet the Sound: The Golden Age of Gospel*. Washington, DC: Elliott and Clark, 1995.

Boyer, Douglas Ralph. "The Choral Music of Libby Larsen: An Analytical Study of Style." D.M.A. diss., University of Texas, Austin, 1994.

Boyer, Horace Clarence. "The Gospel Song: A Historical and Analytical Study." M.A. thesis, University of Rochester, 1979.

Boyer-Alexander, Rene. Personal interview by Carolyn J. Bryan. 28 January 2000.

Bradley, Carol June. *American Music Librarianship: A Biographical and Historical Survey*. New York: Greenwood Press, 1990.

Brennan, Elizabeth A., and Elizabeth C. Clarage. *Who's Who of Pulitzer Prize Winners*. Phoenix, AZ: Oryx Press, 1999.

Brennan, Shawn (ed.). *Women's Information Directory: A Guide to Organizations, Agencies, Institutions, Publications, Services, and Other Resources Concerned with Women in the United States*. Detroit: Gale Research, 1993.

Brett, Philip, Elizabeth Wood, and Gary C. Thomas (eds.). *Queering the Pitch: The New Gay and Lesbian Musicology*. New York and London: Routledge, 1994.

Breunger, David. "Joining the Club." *International Trombone Association Journal* (Summer 1994): 36–39.

———. "Women at Work: Trombonists in North American Orchestras and Universities." *International Trombone Association Journal* (Spring 1992): 12–21.

Brinner, Benjamin. *Knowing Music, Making Music: Javanese Gamelan and the Theory of Musical Competence and Interaction*. Chicago: University of Chicago Press, 1995.

Briscoe, James. (ed.). *Contemporary Anthology of Music by Women*. Bloomington: Indiana University Press, 1998.

———(ed.). *Historical Anthology of Music by Women*. Bloomington: Indiana University Press, 1987.

———. "Integrating Music by Women into the Music History Sequence." *College Music Symposium* 25 (1985): 21–27.

Britton, Allen P. "Seventy-Five Years of Change." *Music Educators Journal* 68/6 (February 1982): 42–44.

Bronson, Fred. *The Billboard Book of #1 Hits*. New York: Billboard Publications, 1985.

Brooks, Tilford. *America's Black Musical Heritage*. Englewood Cliffs, NJ; Prentice-Hall, 1984.

Brower, Edith. "Is the Musical Idea Masculine?" *Atlantic Monthly* 73 (March 1894): 332–339.

Brown, Cynthia Clark. "An Interview with Emma Lou Diemer: AGO 1995 Composer of the Year." *American Organist* (November 1995): 36–44.

———. "Emma Lou Diemer: Composer, Performer, Educator, Church Musician." D.M.A. diss., Southern Baptist Theological Seminary, 1985.

Brown, Emily Freeman. "Jewish Liturgical Music by American Women since 1945." *Women of Note Quarterly* 3/1 (1995): 7–13.

Bruce, Rosemary, and Anthony Kemp. "Sex-Stereo-Typing in Children's Preferences for Musical Instruments." *British Journal of Music Education* 10/3 (1993): 213–217.

Bryant, Clora. "Riding the Basie Band Bus." *Coda Magazine* 236 (1991): 8–10.

Buckley, Gail Lumet. *The Hornes: An American Family*. New York: Knopf, 1986.

Burge, David. "Contemporary Piano: Barbara Kolb's *Solitaire* and *Appello*." *Contemporary Keyboard* 6/65 (July 1980): 65.

Burkett, Lyn. "Feminist Music Scholarship: An Informal Guide to 'Getting It'." *Indiana Theory Review* 17/1 (1996): 65–76.

Burnham, Scott. "A.B. Marx and the Gendering of Sonata Form." In *Music Theory in the Age of Romanticism*, ed., Ian Bent. Cambridge: Cambridge University Press, 1996.

———. "Theorists and 'The Music Itself'." *Journal of Musicology* 15/3 (Summer 1997); 316–329. Also in *Music Theory Online* 2/2 (March 1996).

Burnim, Mellonee V. "The Black Gospel Music

Tradition: Symbol of Ethnicity." Ph.D. diss., Indiana University, 1980.

Burr, Ramiro. "Mariachi! Mexico's Romantic Tradition." *Sing Out! The Folk Song Magazine* 37/1 (1992): 28–34.

———. "Women Helping Drive Thriving Mexican Market." *Billboard* 108/33 (1996): 1–4.

Busnar, Gene. *Superstars of Rock*, vol. 2. New York: Messner, 1984.

Campbell, Gladys B. "The Vocal Teacher of Ten Thousand." *Half-Century Magazine* 1/2 (1916): 6.

Campbell, Patricia Shehan. "Rhythmic Movement and Public School Music Education: Conservative and Progressive Views of the Formative Years." *Journal of Research in Music Education* 39 (1991): 12–22.

———. *Songs in Their Heads: Music and Its Meaning in Children's Lives*. New York: Oxford University Press, 1998.

Canadian Women's Indexing Group. *Canadian Feminist Periodicals Index, 1972–1985/ Index des periodiques feministes canadiens, 1972–1985*. Resource Series, no. 2. Toronto: Canadian Women's Indexing Group, 1991.

Cantrell, Scott. "From around the World: Omaha." *Opera News* 63/10 (April 1999): 91.

Caputo, Virginia. "Add Technology and Stir: Music, Gender, and Technology." *Quarterly Journal of Music Teaching and Learning* IV–V/4, 1 (1994): 85–90.

Cardoso Junior, Abel. *Carmen Miranda, a cantora do Brasil*. São Paulo: Cardoso Junior, 1978.

Carlos, Wendy. "Tuning: At the Crossroads." *Computer Music Journal* 11 (Spring 1987): 1, 29–43.

Carter-Schwendler, Karen L. *Mountain Born: Jean Ritchie Biography*. Available: http://www.ket.org/Programs/KET/MB/jeanritchie.html

Carton, Barbara. "Berklee to Hire Consultant on Sexism, Racism." *Boston Globe* (20 April 1992): 32.

Cartwright, Katharine. "Quotation and Reference in Jazz Performance: Ella Fitzgerald's 'St. Louis Blues,' 1957–79." Ph.D. diss., City University of New York, 1998.

Cheyenne Music. Available: http://www.globalthinking.com/cheyenne

Chicago a cappella. Available: http://members.aol.com/singwow

Chilton, John, and Buck Clayton. *Billie's Blues: Billie Holiday's Story 1933–1959*. New York: Stein and Day Publishers, 1975.

Chmaj, Betty. " 'Reality Is on Our Side': Research on Gender in American Music." *Sonneck Society for American Music Bulletin* 16/2 (Summer 1990): 53–58.

———. "Visions and Revisions: Women's Studies and the Challenge to See Anew." *Frontiers: A Journal of Women Studies* 8/3 (1986): 8–19.

Choksy, Lois. *The Kodály Context: Creating an Environment for Musical Learning*. Englewood Cliffs, NJ: Prentice-Hall, 1981.

———. *The Kodály Method 1, Comprehensive Music Education*, 3rd ed. Upper Saddle River, NJ: Prentice-Hall, 1999.

———. *The Kodály Method II, Folksong to Masterwork*. Upper Saddle River, NJ: Prentice-Hall, 1999.

Chorus America. Available: http://www.chorusamerica.org

Citron, Marcia J. "Gender and the Field of Musicology." *Current Musicology* 53 (1993): 66–75.

———. *Gender and the Musical Canon*. Cambridge: Cambridge University Press, 1993.

———. "Gender, Professionalism and the Musical Canon." *Journal of Musicology* 8/1 (1990): 102–117.

Claghorn, Charles Eugene. *Women Composers and Hymnists: A Concise Biographical Dictionary*. Metuchen, NJ: Scarecrow Press, 1984.

———. *Women Composers and Songwriters*. Metuchen, NJ: Scarecrow Press, 1996.

Clarke, Donald. (ed.). *The Penguin Encyclopedia of Popular Music*, 2d ed. Harmondsworth, Middlesex, England: Penguin Books, 1999.

———. *Wishing on the Moon: The Life and Times of Billie Holiday*. New York: Penguin Books, 1995.

Claudson, William D. "The Philosophy of Julia E. Crane and the Origin of Music Teacher Training." *Journal of Research in Music Education* 17 (Winter 1969): 399–404.

Clifford, Mike (ed.). *The Harmony Illustrated Encyclopedia of Rock*, 4th ed. New York: Harmony Books, 1983.

Coe, Judith A. *Cyberspace Music Resources*. Available: http://www.muw.edu/~jcoe/cmr

Cohen, Aaron I. *International Discography of Women Composers*. Westport, CT: Greenwood Press, 1984.

———. *International Encyclopedia of Women Composers*, 2d ed. New York: Books and Music, 1987.

Cohen, Robert. *Theatre*. 5th ed. Palo Alto, CA: Mayfield Publishing, 1999.

Cohn, Arthur. *The Literature of Chamber Music*. Chapel Hill, NC: Hinshaw Music, 1997.

———. *Recorded Classical Music: A Critical Guide to Compositions and Performances*. New York: Schirmer Books, 1981.

Coleman, Ray. *The Carpenters: The Untold Story (An Authorized Biography)*. New York: HarperCollins, 1994.

Colin, Sid. *Ella*. London: Elm Tree Books, 1987.

College Music Society Committee on the Status of Women in Music, 1984–86. *Women's Studies/Women's Status*. College Music Society Report no. 5. Boulder, CO: College Music Society, 1988.

Collins, Don. *Teaching Choral Music*. Englewood Cliffs, NJ: Prentice-Hall, 1993.

Comber, Chris, David Hargreaves, and Ann Colley. "Girls, Boys, and Technology in Music Education." *British Journal of Music Education* 10/2 (1993): 123–134.

Combs, Jo Anne. "Japanese-American Music and Dance in Los Angeles, 1930–1942." *Selected Reports in Ethnomusicology* 5 (1985): 121–151.

Comden, Betty. *Singin' in the Rain*. New York: Viking Press, 1972.

Commanday, Robert. "Singers Update Baroque in Berkeley: 'Power and Desire' and Monteverdi." *San Francisco Chronicle* (14 June 1994): E3.

Contemporary Theatre, Film, and Television, vol. 11, s. v. "Martin, Mary 1913(?)–1990." Detroit: Gale Research, 1994, 322–323.

Conway, Terry. "Heart: Traveling the Road Home." *Acoustic Musician* 2/10 (January 1996): 8–11.

Cook, Nicholas. "Music in the Academy" and "Music and Gender." In *Music: A Very Short Introduction*. London: Oxford University Press, 1998, Chapters 6, 7.

Cook, Richard, and Brian Morton. *The Penguin Guide to Jazz on CD, LP, and Cassette*. London and New York: Penguin Books, 1992.

Cook, Susan. "Women, Women's Studies, Music and Musicology: Issues of Pedagogy and Scholarship." *College Music Symposium* 29 (1989): 93–100.

Cook, Susan C., and Judy S. Tsou (eds.). *Cecilia Reclaimed: Feminist Perspectives on Gender and Music*. Urbana and Chicago: University of Illinois Press, 1994.

Cooper, Adrienne. Personal correspondence with Judith S. Pinnolis. March 2000.

Cooper, Sarah (ed.). *Girls! Girls! Girls! Essays on Women and Music*. New York: New York University Press, 1996.

Corliss, Richard. "*Viva Selena!* The Queen of Tejano Was Murdered in 1995. Now Hollywood and Her Father Present Their Version of Her Life." *Time* 49/12 (1997): 86–88.

Culbertson, D. C. "Marnie Hall: Recording Pioneer." *Signature* 2/1 (Winter 1997): 28–29, 34.

Curtis, Natalie. *The Indians' Book: An Offering by the American Indians of Indian Lore, Musical and Narrative, to Form a Record of the Songs and Legends of Their Race*. New York: Dover Publications, 1968.

Cusic, Don. *The Sound of Light: A History of Gospel Music*. Bowling Green, OH: Bowling Green State University Popular Press, 1990.

Cusick, Suzanne. "Feminist Theory, Music Theory, and the Mind/Body Problem." *Perspectives of New Music* 32/1 (1994): 8–27.

———. "Gender and the Cultural Work of a Classical Music Performance." *repercussions* 3/1 (1994): 77–110.

———. "Gender, Musicology, and Feminism." In *Rethinking Music*, eds. Nick Cook and Mark Everist. Oxford and New York: Oxford University Press, 1999.

Dahl, Linda. *Stormy Weather: The Music and Lives of a Century of Jazzwomen*. New York: Pantheon Books, 1984.

Dalby, Bruce. *Gordon Institute for Music Learning*. Available: http://www.unm.edu/~audiate/home.html

Dalheim, E. L. "Emma Lou Diemer: Four Poems by Alice Meynell for Soprano or Tenor and Chamber Ensemble." *NOTES* xxxv (1978–79): 994.

Daniel, Katinka. "Reflections and Memories of Katinka Spipiades Daniel." *Kodály Envoy* 23/1 (1996): 28–29.

Daniels, Rebecca. *Women Stage Directors Speak: Exploring the Influence of Gender on Their Work*. Jefferson, NC: McFarland, 1996.

Dargan, William Thomas. "Congregational Gospel Songs in a Black Holiness Church: A Musical and Textual Analysis." Ph.D. diss., Wesleyan University, 1982.

Darwin, Charles. *The Origin of Species*. London: J. Murray, 1859.

Davenport, Marguerite M. *Azalia: The Life of Madame E. Azalia Hackley*. Boston: Chapman and Grimes, 1947.

Davis, John H. *The Guggenheims, (1848–1988): An American Epic*. New York: Shapolsky Publishers, 1989.

Davis, Lisa E. "The Butch as Drag Artiste: Greenwich Village in the Roaring Forties." In *The Persistent Desire: A Femme-Butch Reader*, ed. Joan

Nestle. Boston: Alyson Publications, 1992, 45–53.

Davis, William A. "MTV vs. the Professor." *Boston Globe* (17 May 1991): 29.

Davis, William B. "Keeping the Dream Alive: Profiles of Three Early Twentieth Century Music Therapists." *Journal of Music Therapy* 30/1 (1993): 34–45.

"Deborah Drattell." *New York City Opera*. Available: http://www.nycopera.com/drattell.html

DeCurtis, Anthony (ed.), et al. *The Rolling Stone Illustrated History of Rock and Roll*, 3rd ed. New York: Random House, 1992.

Delzell, Judith. "Variables Affecting the Gender-Role Stereotyping of High School Band Teaching Positions." *Quarterly Journal of Music Teaching and Learning* IV–V/4, 1 (1994): 77–84.

DesMoines Symphony: Gail Williams Bio. Available: http://www.dmsymphony.org/May/gailwilliams_bio.htm

Detels, Claire. "Autonomous/Formalist Aesthetics, Music Theory, and the Feminist Paradigm of Soft Boundaries." *Journal of Aesthetics and Art Criticism* 52/1 (Winter 1994): 113–126. Special issue: "The Philosophy of Music."

———. *Soft Boundaries: Re-visioning the Arts and Aesthetics in American Education*. Westport: Greenwood Publishing, 1999.

DiamandaGalas.com. Available: http://www.diamandaGalas.com

Dickerson, James. *Women on Top: The Quiet Revolution That's Rocking the American Music Industry*. New York: Billboard Books, 1998.

Diemer, Emma Lou. "Composing for the Schools." *National Music Council Bulletin* 22 (Winter 1961–62): 12–13.

———. "My Life as a Composer." *Piano Quarterly* 129 (Spring 1985): 58–59.

———. "Writing for Mallet Percussion." *Woodwind, Brass, and Percussion* 22 (April 1983): 10–13.

Diliberto, John. "Navigating the Shifting Terrain of New Age Music: The Evolution of a Genre, from World to Folk, Classical to Space." *Billboard* 108/14 (1996): 44, 52–54.

Disch, Thomas M. "Dangerous Games." *The Nation* 249 (20 November 1989): 611–612.

Djedje, Jacqueline Cogdell. *American Black Spiritual and Gospel Songs from Southeast Georgia: A Comparative Study*, no. 7. Los Angeles: Center for Afro-American Studies, University of California, 1978.

———. "An Analytical Study of the Similarities and Differences in the American Black Spiritual and Gospel Gong from the South-East Region of Georgia." M.A. thesis, UCLA, 1972.

Dobrinski, Cynthia. Telephone interview by Allyson Brown Applebaum. 19 January 2000.

Doctorow, E. L. "Ragtime, Rhythm and Blues." *Vogue* 187 (May 1997): 314ff.

Dolloff, Lori-Anne. "Expertise in Choral Music Education: Implications for Musicianship." Ph.D. diss., University of Toronto, 1994.

Douglas, Ann. *The Feminization of American Culture*. New York: Knopf, 1977.

Drinker, Sophie. *Music and Women: The Story of Women in Their Relation to Music*. New York: Coward, McCann, 1948. Rept., New York: Feminist Press of the City University of New York, 1995, with preface by E. Wood, afterword by R. Solie.

DuBoff, Leonard. *The Performing Arts Business Encyclopedia: For Individuals and Organizations as Well as the Attorneys and Advisors Who Assist Them*. New York: Allworth Press, 1996.

Dudden, Arthur Power, and Russell R. Dynes (eds.). *The Fulbright Experience*. New Brunswick, NJ: Transaction Books, 1987.

Dudden, Faye E. *Women in the American Theatre: Actresses and Audiences (1790–1870)*. New Haven: Yale University Press, 1994.

DuPree, Mary Herron. "The Failure of American Music: The Critical View from the 1920s." *Journal of Musicology* 2 (Summer 1983): 305–315.

DuPree, Sherry Sherrod, and Herbert C. Dupree. *African-American Good News (Gospel) Music*. Washington, DC: Middle Atlantic Regional Press, 1993.

Durbin, Elizabeth. "Women and the Arts: A Survey of Recent Progress." In *'The Green Stubborn Bud': Women's Culture at the Century's Close*, eds. Kathryn F. Clarenbach and Edward L. Kamarck. Metuchen, NJ: Scarecrow Press, 1987.

Dykema, Peter W. "Musical Fraternities and the Development of Music in America." *Studies in Musical Education, History, and Aesthetics*. Oberlin, OH: Music Teachers National Association, 1933, 81–93.

Eaklor, Vicki L. "Roots of an Ambivalent Culture: Music, Education, and Music Education in Antebellum America." *Journal of Research in Music Education* 33 (1985): 87–99.

Early, Gerald. *One Nation under a Groove: Motown and American Culture*. Hopewell, NJ: Ecco Books, 1995.

Ebel, Otto. *Women Composers: A Biographical Handbook of Woman's Work in Music*. Brooklyn,

NY: F. H. Chandler, 1902. 3rd ed, New York: Chandler-Ebel, 1913.

Eddy, Sonja. Interview by author. Anderson, IN. June and July, 1995.

"Editorial: The Guy Awards." *Atlanta Constitution* (28 February 1991): A18.

Edmonds, Katharine. Telephone interview by Allyson Brown Applebaum. 12 January 2000.

Edwards, J. Michele. *Women in the Curriculum: Music Discipline Analysis*. Towson, MD: National Center for Curriculum Transformation Resources on Women, 1997.

Elazar, Daniel, and Rela Geffen Monson. "Women in the Synagogue Today." *Midstream* 4 (1981): 25–30.

Ellinwood, Leonard Webster. *The History of American Church Music*. New York: Da Capo Press, 1970.

Ellison, Cori. "Classical Music: Help Wanted: Fourth Singer, Able to Make a Singular Sound." *New York Times* (20 September 1998): Sec. 2, p. 33.

Elson, Arthur. "Famous Women in Musical History." *Musical Standard* 32 (April 1909): 89–91.

———. *Woman's Work in Music; Being an Account of Her Influence on the Art, in Ancient as well as Modern Times; a Summary of Her Musical Compositions, in the Different Countries of the Civilized World; and an Estimate of Their Rank in Comparison with Those of Men*. Boston: L. C. Page, 1903. Repr. of 1904 ed., Maine: Longwood Press, 1976; repr. of 1931 ed., Washington, DC: Zenger, 1975.

Elson, Louis Charles. "American Women in Music." Chapter 15 in *The History of American Music*. New York: Macmillan, 1904. Rev. eds., New York: Macmillan, 1915, 1925.

———. "Women Composers in America." Chapter 8 in *Woman in Music*. New York: University Society, 1918. Repr., New York: Gordon Press, 1977.

Encyclopedia of World Biography, 2d ed., s.v. "Mary Martin." Detroit: Gale Research, 1998, 292–293.

Ericson, Margaret D. *Women and Music: A Selective Annotated Bibliography on Women and Gender Issues in Music, 1987–1992*. New York: G. K. Hall, 1996.

Esposito, Tony (ed.). *The Greatest Legal Fake Book of All Time*. Seacaucus, NJ: Warner Bros. Publications, 1985.

Evenson, Laura. "Harpsichords and Combat Boots: Baroque Ensemble Bimbetta Plays Early Music with Riot Grrl Attitude." *San Francisco Chronicle* (24 February 1999): E3.

Faderman, Lillian. *Odd Girls and Twilight Lovers: A History of Lesbian Life in Twentieth-Century America*. New York: Penguin Books, 1992.

Faith, Karlene. *Madonna, Bawdy & Soul*. Toronto: University of Toronto Press, 1997.

Farber, Donald C., and Robert Viagas. *The Amazing Story of the Fantasticks*. New York: Citadel Press, 1991.

Farnsworth, Paul R. "The Effects of Role-Taking on Artistic Achievement." *Journal of Aesthetics and Art Criticism* 18/3 (March 1960): 345–349.

Farrior, Christine Bordeaux. "Body, Mind, Spirit, Voice: Helen Kemp and the Development of the Children's Choir Movement." Ed.D. diss., University of North Carolina at Greensboro, 1993.

Fausto-Sterling, Anne. *Myths of Gender: Biological Theories about Women and Men*. New York: Basic Books, 1992.

Feather, Leonard. *The Encyclopedia of Jazz*. London: Quartet Books, 1984.

———. "Flora Purim—Airto Blindfold Test." *Down Beat* 43 (11 March 1976): 31.

———. "How Jazz Education Began." *NAJE Educator* (1981): 20–21.

Feierabend, John M. *TIPS: Music Activities in Early Childhood*. Reston, VA: MENC, The National Association for Music Education, 1990.

Fernández, Raúl. Oral history interview with Celina González, La Habana, December 1998. Washington, DC: Smithsonian Institution Latino Initiative.

Ferriano, Frank. "A Study of the School Jazz Ensemble in American Music Education." *NAJE Educator* (1975): 4–6.

Fertig, Judith Pinnolis. "An Analysis of Selected Works of the American Composer Miriam Gideon (1906–) in Light of Contemporary Jewish Music Trends." Masters thesis, College-Conservatory of Music of the University of Cincinnati, 1978.

Feuer, Jane. *The Hollywood Musical*. Bloomington: Indiana University Press, 1982.

Fischel, Jack, and Sanford Pinsker (eds.). *Jewish-American History and Culture: An Encyclopedia*. New York: Garland, 1992.

Flinn, Denny Martin. *Musical! A Grand Tour: The Rise, Glory, and Fall of an American Institution*. New York: Schirmer Books, 1997.

Floyd, Samuel A. *The Power of Black Music: Interpreting Its History from Africa to the United States*. New York; Oxford University Press, 1995.

Frank, Lisa, and Paul Smith (eds.). *Madonnarama: Essays on Sex and Popular Culture*. Pittsburgh: Cleis Press, 1993.

Franklin, Marion J. "The Relationship of Black Preaching to Black Gospel Music." D.Min. thesis, Drew University, 1982.

Frazier, Jane. *Women Composers: A Discography*. Detroit Studies in Music Bibliography, no. 50. Detroit: Information Coordinators, 1983.

Freundlich, Douglas Alan. "The Development of Musical Thinking: Case Studies in Improvisation." Ed.D. diss., Harvard University, 1978.

Frisbie, Charlotte J. "Helen Heffron Roberts (1888–1985): A Tribute." *Ethnomusicology* 33/1 (1989): 97–111.

———. "Women and the Society for Ethnomusicology: Roles and Contributions from Formation through Incorporation (1952–1961)." In *Comparative Musicology and Anthropology: Essays on the History of Ethnomusicology*, eds. Bruno Nettl and Philip V. Bohlman. Chicago and London: University of Chicago Press, 1991.

Fromm, Paul. "Creative Women in Music: A Historical Perspective." In *A Life for New Music: Selected Papers of Paul Fromm*, eds. David Gable and Christoph Wolff. Cambridge, MA: Harvard University Press, 1988, 42–51.

Fry, Stephen M. "The 1993 Pauline Alderman Prize in Alaska." *ILWC [International League of Women Composers] Journal* (October 1993): 54.

———. "The Pauline Alderman Awards for New Scholarship on Women in Music." *IAWM [International Alliance for Women in Music] Journal* 2/3 (October 1996): 15.

Fuller, Sophie. *The Pandora Guide to Women Composers: Britain and the United States 1629–Present*. San Francisco, CA: Pandora, 1994.

Furman, Charles E. (ed.). *Effectiveness of Music Therapy Procedures: Documentation of Research and Clinical Practice*. Silver Spring, MD: National Music Therapy Association, 1996.

Gaar, Gillian G. *She's a Rebel: The History of Women in Rock and Roll*. Seattle: Seal Press, 1992.

Galás, Diamanda. E-mail correspondence with Kristine H. Burns. February 2000.

Gamman, Lorraine, and Margaret Marshment (eds.). *The Female Gaze: Women as Viewers of Popular Culture*. Seattle: Real Comet Press, 1989.

Gans, Eric. "Remarks on Originary Feminism." *Perspectives of New Music* 32/1 (1994): 86–89.

Ganz, Isabelle. Personal correspondence with Judith S. Pinnolis. March 2, 2000.

Gardner, Elysa. "Looking Down a New Road." *Los Angeles Times* 31 August 1997.

George, Nelson. *Where Did Our Love Go? The Rise & Fall of the Motown Sound*. New York: St. Martin's Press, 1985.

Gewertz, Daniel. "Playing Her Cards Right: Debbie Friedman Cares Enough to Write the Very Best Jewish Inspirational Songs." *Boston Herald .com* (7 April 1999). Available: http://www.bostonherald.com/bostonherald/entr/fried04071999.htm

Gideon, Miriam. Interview by Judith S. Pinnolis. 19 June 1977.

Gill, Chris. "Bonnie Raitt: A New High for the Queen of Slide." *Guitar Player* (August 1994): 42–54.

Giroux, Julie. Telephone interview by Allyson Brown Applebaum. 10 January 2000.

Glass, Beaumont. *Lotte Lehmann, a Life in Opera and Song*. Santa Barbara, CA: Capra Press, 1988.

Goehr, Lydia. *The Imaginary Museum of Musical Works*. Oxford: Clarendon Press, 1992.

Golden, Barbara. *Barbara Golden's Home Cooking*. San Francisco: Burning Books, 1984.

Golden, Kristen. "The Lion Queen." *MS.* 8 (May/June 1998): 73–74.

Goldring, Malcolm. "An Englishman's View of North American Youth and Children's Choirs." *Choral Journal* 33/3 (1992): 31–34.

Gordon, Edwin E. *A Factor Analytic Description of Tonal and Rhythm Patterns and Objective Evidence of Pattern Difficulty Level and Growth Rate*. Chicago: GIA Publications, 1978.

———. *How Children Learn When They Learn Music*. Iowa City, IA: Author, 1967.

———. *Learning Sequences in Music*. Chicago: G.I.A. Publications, Inc., 1997.

———. *Primary and Intermediate Measures of Audiation, Manual*. Chicago: G.I.A. Publications, 1992.

Gordy, Berry. *To Be Loved: The Music, the Magic, the Memories of Motown: An Autobiography*. New York: Warner Books, 1994.

Gould, Elizabeth. "Getting the Whole Picture: The View from Here." *Philosophy of Music Education Review* 2/2 (1994): 92–99.

———. "Initial Involvement and Continuity of Women Band Directors: The Presence of Gender-Specific Occupational Models." Ph.D. diss., University of Oregon, Eugene, 1996.

Gould, Elizabeth, and Carol Matthews. "Weavings: Native Women's Music, Poetry, and Performance as Resistance." *Women and Music: A Journal of Gender and Culture* 3 (1999).

Gourse, Leslie. "In the Limelight: Women Who Play Jazz." *American Visions* 4/2 (1989): 32–36.

———. *Madame Jazz : Contemporary Women*. New York: Oxford University Press, 1995.

———. *Madame Jazz: Contemporary Women Instrumentalists*. New York: Oxford University Press, 1995.

Grattan, Virginia L. *American Women Songwriters: A Biographical Dictionary*. Westport and London: Greenwood Press, 1993.

Green, Archie. "Hillbilly Music: Source and Symbol." *Journal of American Folklore* 78/309 (1965): 204–228.

Green, Elizabeth A. H. "Trends in Instrumental Music Teaching." *Music Educators Journal* 24/1 (1937): 35–36.

Green, Lucy. *Music, Gender, Education*. Cambridge: Cambridge University Press, 1997.

Green, Mildred Denby. *Black Women Composers: A Genesis*. Boston: Twayne, a division of G. K. Hall, 1983.

Greene, Ellen. *Reading Sappho: Contemporary Approaches*. University of California Press, 1996.

Gridley, Mark C. *Jazz Styles*. Englewood Cliffs, NJ: Prentice-Hall, 1978.

———. *Jazz Styles: History and Analysis*. Upper Saddle River, NJ: Prentice-Hall, 2000.

Griffith, James. "Lydia Mendoza: An Enduring Mexican-American Singer." In *Ethnic Recordings in America: A Neglected Heritage, Studies in American Folk Life*, vol. 1. Washington, DC: American Folklife Center, Library of Congress, 1982, 113, 116.

Grishman, Emily. Telephone interview by Allyson Brown Applebaum. 10 January 2000.

Groh, Jan Bell. *Evening the Score: Women in Music and the Legacy of Frédérique Petrides*. Fayetteville: University of Arkansas Press, 1991.

Guck, Marion A. "A Woman's (Theoretical) Work." *Perspectives of New Music* 32/1 (1994): 28–43.

Guo Xin. "Eastern and Western Techniques in Chen Yi's *Qi*." *Journal of Music in China* 1 (1999): 121–131.

Haasemann, Frauke Peterson. Memorial Service Program. Princeton, NJ: 20 April 1991.

Haasemann, Frauke P. and James Jordan. *Group Vocal Techniques*. Chapel Hill, NC: Hinshaw Music, 1992.

Hackley, E. Azalia. *The Foreign Scholarship*. Detroit: Author, 1909.

———. *A Guide in Voice Culture*. Philadelphia: Author, 1909.

Hafemeister, Tina. Email correspondence with Allyson Brown Applebaum. 24 January 2000.

Hager, Andrew G. *Satin Dolls: The Women of Jazz*. New York: Friedman/Fairfax Publishers, 1997.

Hall, Dennis. "New Age Music: A Voice of Liminality in Post-Modern Popular Culture." *Popular Music and Society* 18/2 (1994): 13–21.

Hall, Roberta M., and Bernice R. Sandler. *The Classroom Climate: A Chilly One for Women?* Washington, DC: Association of American Colleges, Project on the Status and Education of Women, 1982.

Hall, Russell. "From Heart . . . to the Lovemongers: The Musical Journey of Ann and Nancy Wilson." *Performing Songwriter* 5/28 (January–February 1998): 68–71.

Hall, Susan Grove. "New Age Music: An Analysis of an Ecstasy." *Popular Music and Society* 18/2 (1994): 23–33.

Halstead, Jill. *The Woman Composer*. Brookfield, VT: Ashgate Publishing, 1997.

Hamm, Charles. *Yesteryears: Popular Song in America*. New York: Norton, 1983.

Hanani, Hannah. "Portrait of a Composer." *Music Journal* 34 (1976): 25.

Handy, D. Antoinette. *Black Women in American Bands and Orchestras*, 2d ed. Lanham, MD: Scarecrow Press, 1998.

———. *The International Sweethearts of Rhythm*. Metuchen, NJ: Scarecrow Press, 1983.

Happel, Mark. "Out of Africa." *Vogue* 187 (November 1997): 220.

Harbach, Barbara. "Profile and Review—Melinda Wagner." *Women of Note Quarterly* 7/3 (August 1999): 1, 3–6.

Harding, Susan. "Introduction: Is There a Feminist Method?" In *Feminism and Musicology*, ed. S. Harding. Bloomington: Indiana University Press, 1989.

Hardy, Phil, and Dave Laing. *The Faber Companion to 20th-Century Popular Music*. London: Faber and Faber, 1990.

Haring, Judy. Telephone interview by Allyson Brown Applebaum. 10 January 2000.

Harris, Paisley Jane. "I'm as Good as Any Woman in Your Town: The Interconnections of Gender, Race, and Class in the Blues of Ma Rainey and Bessie Smith." M.A. thesis, University of Minnesota, 1994.

Harris, Sheldon. *The Blues Who's Who: A Biographical Dictionary of Blues Singers*. New York: Da Capo, 1993.

Harrison, Daphne Duval. *Black Pearls Blues Queens of the 1920s*, 3rd ed. New Brunswick, NJ: Rutgers University Press, 1993.

Haskins, James. *Lena Horne*. New York: Coward-McCann, 1983.

Haweis, Hugh Reginald. *Music and Morals*. London: Longman, Green, 1912.

Hayes, Cedric J., and Robert Laughton. *Gospel Records, 1943–1969: A Black Music Discography*. London: Record Information Services, 1993.

Hayes, Deborah. "Discovering Our History: ClarNan Editions of Early Music." *ILWC [International League of Women Composers] Journal* (February 1995): 1–3.

Hayes, Eileen M. "Black Women Performers of Women-Identified Music: They Cut Off My Voice, I Grew Two Voices." Ph.D. diss., University of Washington, 1999.

Heilbut, Anthony. *El Sound: Good News and Bad Times*, 4th ed. New York: Limelight Editions, 1992.

Heresies: A Feminist Publication on Art and Politics. Issue 10 (1980): "Women and Music," special issue.

Herfort, David A. "A History of the National Association of Jazz Educators and a Description of Its Role in American Music Education 1968–78." Doctoral diss. University of Houston, 1979.

Herndon, Marcia, and Susanne Ziegler (eds.). *Music, Gender, and Culture*. Wilhelmshaven, West Germany: Florian Noetzel Verlag, 1990.

Hicks, Wendy K. "An Investigation of the Initial Stages of Preparatory Audiation." Ph.D. diss., Temple University, 1993.

Higgins, Paula. "Women in Music, Feminist Criticism, and Guerrilla Musicology: Reflections on Recent Polemics." *19th-Century Music* 17/2 (Fall 1993): 174–192.

Hildegard Publishing Company: Home. Available: http://www.hildegard.com

Hinely, Mary Brown. "The Uphill Climb of Women in American Music." *Music Educators Journal* 70 (1983–1984), no. 8 (April 1984): 31–35 (I: Performers and Teachers) and no. 9 (May 1984): 42–45 (II: Composers and Conductors).

Hinkle-Turner, Elizabeth. "Coming Full Circle: Composing the Cathartic Experience with CD-ROM Technology." *Leonardo Journal of Art and Technology* 32/1 (1999): 49–52.

———. *Crossing the Line Volume One: Women Composers and Music Technology in the United States*. London: Ashgate Press, forthcoming.

Hinson, Glenn D. "When the Words Roll and the Fire Flows: Spirit, Style and Experience in African American Gospel Performance." Ph.D. diss., University of Pennsylvania, 1989.

Hirahara, Naomi. "Toshiko Akiyoshi Honored at Asian Women's Dinner." *Rafu Shimpo*, 21 March 1987.

Hirshey, Gerri. "The Seventies. (Women Musicians)." *Rolling Stone* 773 (1997): 64–73.

Hitchcock, H. Wiley, and Stanley Sadie (eds.). *New Grove Dictionary of American Music*. London and New York: Macmillan, Grove's Dictionary of Music, 1988.

Hixon, Don, and Don Hennessee. *Women in Music: An Encyclopedic Biobibliography*, 2d ed. Metuchen, NJ: Scarecrow Press, 1993.

Hodges, Daniel Houston. "Transcription and Analysis of Southern Cheyenne Songs." Ph.D. diss., University of Oklahoma, 1980.

Holloway, Joseph E. (ed.). *Africanisms in African Culture*. Bloomington: Indiana University Press,.

Horstmann, Sabine. Personal correspondence with Eric Johnson. May 2000.

Howard, John Tasker. *Our American Music: Three Hundred Years of It*. New York: Thomas Y. Cromwell, 1931. 4th ed. (*Our American Music: A Comprehensive History from 1620 to the Present*), New York: T.Y. Crowell, 1965.

Hubbard, Ruth. "Have Only Men Evolved?" In *Women Look at Biology Looking at Women*, eds. Ruth Hubbard, Mary Sue Henifin, and Barbara Fried. Cambridge, MA: Shenkman Publishing; 1979, 7–36.

"HUC-JR School of Music History." *Hebrew Union College—Jewish Institute of Religion*. Available: http://www.huc.edu/smhist.html

Hughes, Patricia W. "The Evolution of Orff-Schulwerk in North America (1955–1969)." *Bulletin of Historical Research in Music Education* 14 (1993): 73–91.

Hughes, Rupert. "Women Composers." *Century Magazine* 55/5 (March 1898).

———. "The Women Composers." In *Contemporary American Composers*. Boston: L. C. Page, 1900, 423–441.

Humphreys, Jere. "Sex and Geographic Representation in Two Music Education History Books." *Bulletin of the Council for Research in Music Education* 131 (1997): 67–86.

Hunt, Danica L. "Women Who Play Jazz: A Study of the Experiences of Three Los Angeles Musicians." Master's thesis, UCLA, 1994.

Hylton, John. *Comprehensive Choral Music Education*. Englewood Cliffs, NJ: Prentice-Hall, 1995.

Hyman, Paula E., and Deborah D. Moore (eds.). *Jewish Women in America: An Historical Encyclopedia*. New York: Routledge, 1997.

Idelsohn, Abraham Zebi. *Jewish Music in Its Historical Development*. New York: Schocken Books, 1967.

Index for Liz Phillips. Available: http://www.unidial.com/~sculpsound/

Indigo Girls, The. Available: http://www.epiccenter.com/EpicCenter/IndigoGirls

Isoardi, Steven L. *Central Avenue Sounds: Melba Liston. Oral History*. Los Angeles: University of California, 1996.

IWBC [International Women's Brass Conference] Home Page. Available: http://metro.turnpike.net/~iwbc/index.html

Jackson, Irene V. *Afro-American Religious Music: A Bibliography and a Catalogue of Gospel Music*. Westport, CT: Greenwood Press, 1979.

Jackson, Jerma A. "Testifying at the Cross: Thomas Andrew Dorsey, Sister Rosetta Tharpe, and the Politics of African-American Sacred and Secular Music." Ph.D. diss., Rutgers University, 1995.

Jarjisian, Catherine. Personal correspondence with Carolyn J. Bryan. 5 February 2000.

Jean Ritchie Home Page. Available: http://members.aol.com/greenhays/JRHome.html

Jefferson, Alan. *Lotte Lehmann*. London: Julia MacRae Books, 1988.

Jepson, Barbara. "Sexism in the Brass Section." *Wall Street Journal*, (7 July 1993): 10.

———. "Women in the Classical Recording Industry." In *The Musical Woman: An International Perspective III*, ed. Judith Lang Zaimont. Westport, CT: Greenwood Press, 1991, 337–352.

Jezic, Diane. *Women Composers: The Lost Tradition Found*, 2d ed. New York: Feminist Press, 1994.

Jianping, Tang. "Tradition Is Alive." *Journal of Music in China* 1 (1999): 133–146.

Johnson, Rose-Marie (comp.). *Violin Music by Women Composers: A Bio-Bibliographic Guide*. New York: Greenwood Press, 1989.

Johnson, Walter, and Francis J. Colligan. *The Fulbright Program: A History*. Chicago: University of Chicago Press, 1965.

Johnston, Nick. *Patti Smith: A Biography*. London: Omnibus Press, 1997.

Jones, John R. D. "The Choral Works of Undine Smith Moore: A Study of Her Life and Work." Ed.D. diss., New York University, 1980.

Joyner, David. "Fifty Years of Jazz Education at North Texas." *Jazz Educators Journal* 30 (1997): 53–62.

June Allyson Foundation, The. Available: http://www.augs.org/allyson/index.html

Juno, Andrea, and V. Vale. *Angry Women*. San Francisco: Re/Search Publications, 1991.

Kaminer, Wendy. *Women Volunteering: The Pleasure, Pain, and Politics of Unpaid Work from 1830 to the Present*. Garden City, NY: Anchor Press, 1984.

Kaplan, Erica. "The Lady Who Swings the Band—The Legacy of American Pianist, Composer Mary Lou Williams." *Jazz Research Papers* (1989): 129–139.

Karpf, Juanita. "The Vocal Teacher of Ten Thousand: E. Azalia Hackley as Community Music Educator, 1910–22." *Journal of Research in Music Education* 47/4 (1999): 319–30.

Katz, Ephraim et al. *The Film Encyclopedia*, 3rd ed. New York: Harperperennial Library, 1998.

Katz, S. Montana, and Veronica J. Vieland. *Get Smart: What You Should Know (But Won't Learn in Class) about Sexual Harassment and Sex Discrimination*, 2d ed. New York: Feminist Press at the City University of New York, 1993.

Keeling, Richard (ed.). *Women in North American Indian Music: Six Essays*. Bloomington, IN: Society for Ethnomusicology, 1989.

Keene, James A. *A History of Music Education in the United States*. Hanover NH: University Press of New England, 1982.

Kellogg, Jae. Interview by author. West Lafayette, IN. June and July, 1995.

Kemp, Helen. Telephone interview by Alan J. Rieck. 16 February 2000.

Kerman, Joseph. *Contemplating Music: Challenges to Musicology*. Cambridge, MA: Harvard University Press, 1985.

Kernfeld, Barry (ed.). *New Grove Dictionary of Jazz*. London and New York: Macmillan, 1988.

Kernodle, Tammy Lynn. "'Anything You Are Shows Up in Your Music': Mary Lou Williams and the Sanctification of Jazz." Ph.D. diss., Ohio State University, 1997.

Kielian-Gilbert, Marianne. "Of Poetics and Poiesis, Pleasure and Politics—Music Theory and Modes of the Feminine." *Perspectives of New Music* 32/1 (1994): 44–67.

Killam, Rosemary N. "Calamity Jane: Strength, Uncertainty, and Affirmation." *Women of Note Quarterly: The Magazine of Historical and Contemporary Women Composers* 1/3 (November 1993): 17–25.

———. "Feminist Music Theories: Process and Continua." *Music Theory Online* 1/8 (May 1994): 1–5.

———. "Women Working: An Alternative to Gans." *Perspectives of New Music* 31/2 (1993): 230–251.

King, Bruce. *Contemporary American Theatre*. New York: St. Martin's Press, 1991.

Korall, Burt. "Pop and Jazz Scene." *International Musician* 87 (1989): 10.

Koskoff, Ellen (ed.). *Women and Music in Cross-*

Cultural Perspective. Westport, CT: Greenwood Press, 1987.

Kovick, Kris. "What Is Women's Music? Whine, Women-Only and Song." *Hot Wire* 9/1 (1993): 44–45, 56.

Kowet, Don. " 'Dreamworlds' Harasses MTV for Its Sexy Videos." *Washington Times* (18 October 1991): E1.

Kozinn, Allan. "Margaret Hillis." *New York Times* (6 February 1998): Sec. D:19

Kramer, Mimi. "Secret Garden." *New Yorker* 67 (13 May 1991): 84–85.

Kurath, Gertrude P. "Memorial to Frances Densmore." *Ethnomusicology* 2/2 (1958): 70–71.

Kushner, David Z. "Margaret Hillis." In *Great Lives from History*. vol. 3, ed. Frank N. Magill. Pasadena, CA, and Englewood Cliffs, NJ: Salem Press, 1995,

Ladd, George Trumbull. "Why Women Cannot Compose Music." *Yale Review* 6/4 (July 1917): 789–806.

Laffel, J. "Betty Comden and Adolph Green, Part 1." *Films in Review* 43/3–4 (1992): 75–85.

———. "Betty Comden and Adolph Green, Part 2." *Films in Review* 43/5–6 (1992): 154–156.

Lahr, John. "Need Lyrics for Your Broadway Hit? There Is Nothing Like This Dame." *New Yorker* 73 (10 November 1997): 42ff.

Lai, Sheung-Ping. "An Asian Female Composer's Survival in the United States." *ILWC [International League of Women Composers] Journal* (February 1994): 1–4.

Lamb, Roberta. "Aria Senza Accompagnamento: A Woman behind the Theory." *Quarterly Journal of Music Teaching and Learning* IV–V/4, 1 (1994): 5–21.

———. "Feminism as Critique in Philosophy of Music Education." *Philosophy of Music Education Review* 2/2 (1994): 59–74.

———. "I Never Really Thought About It: Master/Apprentice as Pedagogy in Music." In *Equity and How to Get It*, ed. Kay Armatage. Toronto: Inanna Publications, xxxx.

Larimer, Frances. "Music Education in Russia: A Recent Perspective." *Quarterly Journal of Music Teaching and Learning* 4 (1993): 64–68.

Lather, Patti. *Getting Smart: Feminist Research and Pedagogy*. New York: Routledge, 1991.

Latta, John Arthur. "Alice Parker: Choral Composer, Arranger and Teacher." Ed.D. diss., University of Illinois at Urbana-Champaign, 1986.

Leder, Jan (comp.). *Women in Jazz: A Discography of Instrumentalists, 1913–1968*. Discographies, no. 19. Westport, CT: Greenwood Press, 1985.

Lee, William F. "Jazz Education: In Review." *Jazz Educators Journal* 28 (1995): 44.

Leech-Wilkinson, Daniel. "Love's Illusion: Music from the Montpellier Codex." *Early Music* 24/1 (1996): 176.

LeGuin, Elisabeth. "Uneasy Listening." *repercussions* 3/1 (Spring 1994): 5–19.

Lei, Vai-Meng. "Three Pieces by Contemporary Chinese Composers: Lam Bun-Ching, Chen Yi and Zhou Long." D.M.A. thesis, University of Illinois, 1990.

LePage, Jane Weiner. *Women Composers, Conductors, and Musicians of the Twentieth Century: Selected Biographies*. Metuchen, NJ: Scarecrow Press, 1980. Vol. 2, 1983. Vol. 3, 1988.

Lerner, Gerder. "Placing Women in History: Definitions and Challenges." *Feminist Studies* 3/1–2 (Fall 1975): 5–14. Repr. as "Placing Women in History: A 1975 Perspective" in *Liberating Women's History: Theoretical and Critical Essays*, 1976, ed. Berenice A. Carroll. Urbana: University of Illinois Press, 1976, 357–367.

Lessoff, Alan, and Mineke Reinders. "Public Sculpture in Corpus Christi: A Tangled Struggle to Define the Character and Shape the Agenda of One Texas City." *Journal of Urban History* 26/2 (2000): 190–193.

Levy, Emanuel. *And the Winner Is . . . The History and Politics of the Oscar Awards*. New York: Ungar, 1987.

Lewis, Ellistine Perkins. "The E. Azalia Hackley Memorial Collection of Negro Music, Dance, and Drama: A Catalogue of Selected Afro-American Materials." Ph.D. diss., University of Michigan, 1978.

Lewis, Lisa A. *Gender Politics and MTV: Voicing the Difference*. Philadelphia: Temple University Press, 1990.

Lifeblood: A Collection of Indigo Girls Information. Available: http://www.lifeblood.net

Lindeman, Carolynn A. *Women Composers of Ragtime*. Bryn Mawr, PA: Theodore Presser, 1985.

Livingston, Carolyn. "Women in Music Education in the United States: Names Mentioned in History Books." *Journal of Research in Music Education* 45 (1997): 130–144.

Lloyd, Fran (ed.). *Deconstructing Madonna*. London: Batsford, 1993.

Locke, Ralph P. "Paradoxes of the Woman Music Patron in America." *Musical Quarterly* 78 (1994): 798–825.

———. "Women in American Musical Life: Facts and Questions about Patronage." *repercussions* 3 (Fall 1994): 81–95 and 4 (Spring 1995): 102.

Locke, Ralph P., and Cyrilla Barr (eds.). *Cultivating Music in America: Women Patrons and Activists since 1860*. Berkeley: University of California Press, 1997.

Lockwood, Annea. Email correspondence with Linda Dusman, February 2000.

———. "Piano Burning and Tiger Balm." *Source* 9 (1971): 48.

Long, Janice Elaine Miller. "Alice Parker: Analytical Notes on the Cantatas, an Annotated Catalogue, a Complete Works List, and a Biography." D.M.A. diss., University of Cincinnati, 1979.

Lont, Cynthia M. "Women's Music: No Longer a Small Private Party." In *Rockin' the Boat: Mass Music and Mass Movements*, ed. Reebee Garofalo. Boston: South End Press, 1992.

Lornell, Christopher. *Happy in the Service of the Lord: Afro-American Sacred Harmony Quartets in Memphis, Tennessee*, 2d ed. Knoxville: University of Tennessee Press, 1995.

Lorraine Ali, "Exiled in Guyville." *Rolling Stone* 692 (6 October 1994): 57.

Losseff, Nicky. "The Lily and the Lamb: Chant and Polyphony from Medieval England." *Early Music* 24/1 (1996): 176.

Ludwig-Verdehr, Elsa, and Jean Raines. "Music for Clarinet by Women Composers." *Clarinet* 8, no. 2 (Winter 1981): 12–19, and no. 3 (Spring 1981): 26–36.

Lundy, Karen Saucier. "Women and Country Music." In *America's Musical Pulse: Popular Music in Twentieth-Century Society*. Westport, CT: Greenwood, 1992, 213–219.

Luty, Bryce. "Jazz Education's Struggle for Acceptance." *Music Educators Journal* (1982): 38–39.

———. "Part II Jazz Ensemble's Era of Accelerated Growth." *Music Educators Journal* (1982): 49–50.

MacAuslan, Janna (comp.). *Guitar Music by Women Composers: An Annotated Catalog*. Westport, CT: Greenwood Press, 1997.

MacCluskey, Thomas. "Youth Music Symposium." *Jazz Educators Journal* 28 (1995): 50–51.

Mairs, Nancy. *Voice Lessons*. Boston: Beacon Press, 1994.

Marco, Guy A. (ed.). *Encyclopedia of Recorded Sound in the United States*. New York: Garland Publishing, 1993.

Mark, Michael L., and Charles L. Gary. *A History of American Music Education*. New York: Schirmer Books, 1992.

Marshall, M. M. "Emma A. Hackley." In *Homespun Heroines and Other Women of Distinction*, ed. Hallie Q. Brown. Xenia, OH: Aldine, 1926; repr., New York: Oxford University Press, 1988.

Mathieu, Louise. "A Phenomenological Investigation of Improvisation in Music and Dance." D.A. thesis, New York University, 1984.

Maus, Fred. "Masculine Discourse in Music Theory." *Perspectives of New Music* 31/2 (Summer 1993): 264–293.

McCarthy, Marie. "Are Your Students Affected by Gender Associations When They Select a Musical Instrument?" *Maryland Music Educator* 41/3 (1995): 16–20.

———. "Gendered Discourse and the Construction of Identity: Toward a Liberated Pedagogy in Music Education." *Journal of Aesthetic Education* 33/4 (1999): 109–125.

McCartney, Andrea. "Inventing Images: Constructing and Contesting Gender in Thinking about Electroacoustic Music." *Leonardo Music Journal* 5 (1995): 57–66.

———. "Inventing Metaphors and Metaphors for Invention: Women Composers' Voices in the Discourse of Electroacoustic Music." In *Canadian Music: Issues of Hegemony and Identity*. Toronto: Canadian Scholars Press, 1994, 491–502.

McClary, Susan. *Feminine Endings: Music Gender, and Sexuality*. Minneapolis: University of Minnesota Press, 1991.

———. "Paradigm Dissonances: Music Theory, Cultural Studies, Feminist Criticism." *Perspectives of New Music* 32/1 (1994): 68–85.

———. "Reshaping a Discipline: Musicology and Feminism in the 1990's." *Feminist Studies* 19/2 (Summer 1993): 399–423.

McCleary, Harriett. "A Song Cycle by Libby Larsen: *ME* (Brenda Ueland)." *NATS [National Association of Teachers of Singing] Journal* 51/2 (November–December 1994): 3–8.

McCollum, Brian. "All She Wants to Do Is Hang Out, Stay Balanced and Make Music." *Detroit Free Press*, 2 May 1999.

McCord, Kimberly A. "History of Women in Jazz." *Jazz Educators Journal* 18 (1986): 15–19.

McDaniel, Mary Eileen. "The Choral Music of Emma Lou Diemer." D.M.A. diss., Arizona State University, 1987.

McDonald, Dorothy. "General Music in Education." *Design for Arts in Education* 91/5 (1990): 15–22.

McDonnel, Eveyln. "Because the Night." *Village Voice* 40/31 (1995): 21–23.

McElwee, Ileane. E-mail correspondence with Daryl W. Kinney. 21 January 2000.

McGee, Celia. "Gambling on a Garden." *New York* 24 (22 April 1991): 64–66ff.

McGinty Anne. Telephone interview by Allyson Brown Applebaum. 20 November 1999.

Meggett, Joan M. *Keyboard Music by Women Composers: A Catalogue and Bibliography*. Westport, CT: Greenwood Press, 1981.

Mellers, Wilfred Howard. *Angels of the Night: Popular Female Singers of Our Time*. Oxford and New York: Basil Blackwell, 1988.

"Memoirs of the Indiana Music Makers" (1940–1962) and "Purdue Musical Notes" (1953–1967), in the personal collection of Sonja Eddy, Anderson, IN.

Menard, Valerie. "The Making of Selena; Two Years after the Murder of the Tejano Queen, a Major Movie Hits the Screen." *Hispanic* 10/3 (1997): 30–33.

Miller, Bonny H. "Ladies Companion, Ladies' Canon? Women Composers in American Magazines from *Godey's* to the *Ladies' Home Journal*." In *Cecilia Reclaimed: Perspectives on Gender and Music*, eds. Susan C. Cook and Judy S. Tsou. Urbana and Chicago: University of Illinois Press; 1994, 156–182.

Miller, Diane Helene. *Freedom to Differ: The Shaping of the Gay and Lesbian Struggle for Civil Rights*. New York: New York University Press, 1998.

Miller, Kenneth. *Vocal Music Education*. Englewood Cliffs, NJ: Prentice-Hall, 1988.

Minnich, Elizabeth Kamarck. *Transforming Knowledge*. Philadelphia: Temple University Press, 1990.

Mitchell, James R. "The Legacy of Mary Lou Williams." *Jazz Research Papers* (1985): 105–109.

Moisala, Pirkko. "Tribute to Marcia Herndon: Pioneer in Gender Studies in Ethnomusicology." *Women and Music* 2 (1998): 123–124.

Monnar, Jennifer. "A Woman's Touch." *EQ: Professional Project Recording and Sound* 10/3 (March 1999): 75–148.

Monsour, Sally. Telephone interview by author. 14 January 2000 and 10 February 2000.

Moore, Mary Ellen. *The Linda Ronstadt Scrapbook*. New York: Grosset and Dunlap, 1978.

Mordden, Ethan. *Coming Up Roses: The Broadway Musical in the 1950s*. New York: Oxford University Press, 1998.

Morgan, Robert. *Twentieth Century Music*. New York: Norton, 1991.

Morse, Steve. "How Sheryl Crow Flies: The Pop Star Crosses the Continent—and Generation." *Boston Globe*, 18 December 1998.

Morton, Charlene. "Feminist Theory and the Displaced Music Curriculum: Beyond the Add and Stir Projects." *Philosophy of Music Education Review* 2/2 (1994): 106–122.

Mossakowska, Zofia. *Marcelina Sembrich-Kochanska. zycie i sztuka* [Marcelina Sembrich-Kochanska: Life and Art]. Kraków: PWM Edition, 1976.

Mulvey, Laura. "Visual Pleasure and Narrative Cinema." *Screen* 16 (1975): 6–18. Rep. in Mulvey, *Visual Pleasures and Narrative Cinema: Visual and Other Pleasures*. Bloomington and Indianapolis: Indiana University Press, 1989.

Mundy, Chris. "Linda Ronstadt (Interview)." *Rolling Stone* 712–13 (1995): 40–41.

Murdoch, James. "Peggy Glanville-Hicks." In *Australia's Contemporary Composers*. South Melbourne: Macmillan, 1972, 102–107.

Mursell, James, and Mabelle Glenn. *The Psychology of School Music Teaching*. New York: Silver Burdette, 1931.

Music Educators National Conference. *Prekindergarten Music Education Standards*. Reston, VA: MENC, the National Association for Music Education, 1995.

Musleah, Rahel. "The Sefardic Renaissance." *Hadassah Magazine* 81/3 (1999): 14.

Myers-Spencer, Dianthe. "Bobo and Doodles by Mary Lou Williams: A Rare Display of Contemporary Elements." *Jazz Research Papers* (1989): 166–168

Nasser, David. *A vida trepidante de Carmem Miranda*. Rio de Janeiro: Edições O Cruzeiro, 1966.

Negron-Muntaner, Frances. "Jennifer's Butt (U.S.-Born Puerto Rican Actress Jennifer Lopez in Gregory Nava's Film 'Selena')." *Aztlan—A Journal of Chicano Studies* 22/2 (1997): 181–195.

Nelson, Havelock, and Michael A. Gonzales. *Bring the Noise: A Guide to Rap Music and Hip-Hop Culture*. New York: Harmony Books, 1991.

Neuls-Bates, Carol (ed.). *The Status of Women in College Music: Preliminary Studies*. College Music Society, Report no. 1. Binghamton, NY: College Music Society, 1976.

———(ed.). *Women in Music: An Anthology of Source Readings from the Middle Ages to the Present*. New York: Harper and Row, 1982. Rev. ed., Boston: Northeastern University Press, 1996.

Nichols, Janet. *Women Music Makers: An Introduction to Women Composers*. New York: Walker, 1992.

Nochlin, Linda. *Women, Art, and Power and Other Essays*. New York: Harper and Row, 1988.

Northcutt, Rick. Telephone interview by Allyson Brown Applebaum. 14 January 2000.

O'Brien, Lucy. *She Bop: The Definitive History of Women in Rock, Pop, and Soul.* London: Penguin Books, 1995.

O'Dair, Barbara (ed.). *Trouble Girls: Rolling Stone Book of Women in Rock.* New York: Random House, 1997.

Oliveros, Pauline. "A Former UCSD Professor Speaks Up." *IAWM [International Alliance for Women in Music] Journal* 2/2 (June 1996): 28–31.

Orloff, Katherine. *Rock 'n Roll Woman.* Los Angeles: Nash, 1974.

O'Toole, Patricia. "I Sing in a Choir, But I Have No Voice!" *Quarterly Journal of Music Education* IV–V/4, 1 (1994): 65–77.

———. "A Missing Chapter from Choral Methods Books: How Choirs Neglect Girls." *Choral Journal*, 39/5 (1998): 9–32.

———. "What Have You Taught Your Female Singers Lately?" *Choral Cues* (Spring 1997): 12–14.

Outland, Joyanne Jones. "Emma Lou Diemer: Solo and Chamber Works for Piano through 1986." Ph.D. diss., Ball State University, 1986.

Palmer, Mary, and Wendy L. Sims. *Music in Prekindergarten: Planning and Teaching.* Reston, VA: MENC, the National Association for Music Education, 1993.

Palmer, Robert. *Deep Blues.* New York: Viking Press, 1981.

Palmquist, Jane E., and Barbara Payne. "The Inclusive Instrumental Library: Works by Women." *Music Educators Journal* 78/7 (1992): 52–55.

Panagapka, Jeannette, and Jerry L. Jaccard. "Lois Choksy: Outstanding Administrator." *Kodály Envoy* 22/3 (1996): 10–12.

Pareles, Jon. "In New York's Hubbub, Moody Vibes for Sheryl Crow." *New York Times*, 13 October 1998.

Parenti, Susan. "Composing the Music School: Proposals for a Feminist Composition Curriculum." *Perspectives of New Music* 34 (1996): 66–73.

Parish, James Robert, and Michael R. Pitts (eds.). *Hollywood Songsters.* Garland Reference Library of the Humanities. New York: Garland Publishing, 1991.

Parker, Alice. *Melodious Accord: Good Singing in Church.* Chicago: Liturgy Training Publications, 1991.

———. "Parker-Shaw Memories." *Choral Journal* 36/9 (April 1996): 15–18.

Payne, Barbara. "The Gender Gap: Women on Music Faculties in American Colleges and Universities." *College Music Symposium* 36 (1996): 91–102.

Payne, Maggi. E-mail correspondence with Linda Dusman. February 2000.

Peery, J. Craig, Irene W. Peery, and Thomas W. Draper. *Music and Child Development.* New York: Springer-Verlag, 1987.

Pendle, Karin (ed.). *Women and Music: A History.* Bloomington and Indianapolis: Indiana University Press, 1991.

Persellin, Diane. "Responses to Rhythm Patterns When Presented to Children through Auditory, Visual, and Kinesthetic Modalities." *Journal of Research in Music Education* 40/4 (1992): 306–315.

Peterson-Lewis, Sonja. "A Feminist Analysis of the Defenses of Obscene Rap Lyrics." *Black Sacred Music: A Journal of Theomusicology* 5/1 (Spring 1991): 68–79.

Placksin, Sally. *American Women in Jazz, 1900 to the Present: The Words, Lives, and Music.* New York: Seaview Books, 1982.

Pollock, Mary S. "The Politics of Women's Music: A Conversation with Linda Tillery and Mary Watkins." *Frontiers: A Journal of Women Studies* 10/1 (1988): 14–19.

Pool, Jeannie G. "A Critical Approach to the History of Women in Music." *Heresies* 10 (1980): 2–5.

———. "Researching Women in Music in California." In *California's Musical Wealth: Sources for the Study of Music in California*, ed. Stephen M. Fry. Los Angeles: Southern California Chapter, Music Library Association, 1988.

Porter, Lewis. "She Wiped All the Men Out." *Music Educators Journal* 71/1–2 (1994): 43–52; 42–51.

Post, Laura. *Backstage Pass: Interviews with Women in Music.* Norwich, VT: New Victoria Publishers, 1997.

Price, Deborah Evans. "They're Playing My Song." *Billboard* 111/38 (18 September 1999): 42.

Pucciani, Donna. "Sexism in Music Education: Survey of the Literature, 1972–1982." *Music Educators Journal* 70/1 (September 1983): 49–51, 68–73.

Purim, Flora. *Freedom Song: The Story of Flora Purim.* New York: Berkley Books, 1982.

Rabin, Carol Price. *Music Festivals in America:*

Classical, Opera, Jazz, Pops, Country, Old-Time Fiddlers, Folk, Bluegrass, Cajun, 4th ed. Great Barrington, MA: Berkshire House, 1990.

Randel, Don Michael (ed.). *Harvard Biographical Dictionary of Music*. Cambridge, MA: Belknap Press of Harvard University Press, 1996.

Rao, Doreen. *ACDA on Location. Vol. 1: The Children's Choir*. Lawton, OK: American Choral Directors' Association, Educational Videotape Series, 1988.

———. *Choral Music Experience: Education through Artistry*, 5 vols. New York: Boosey and Hawkes, 1987–1991.

——— (ed.). *Choral Music for Children's Chorus: An Annotated Guide*. Reston, VA: Music Educator's National Conference, 1990.

———. "Craft, Singing Craft and Musical Experience: A Philosophical Study with Implications for Vocal Music Education as Aesthetic Education." Ph.D. diss., Northwestern University, 1988.

———. *We Will Sing! A Choral Textbook for Classroom Choirs*. New York: Boosey and Hawkes, 1993.

Raspberry, William. "Foulmouthed Trash: If We Don't Respect Our Women, Why Should Anyone Else?" *Washington Post* (30 July 1993): 21.

Ray, Gordon N. *Guggenheim Fellowships: A Reprint from the Report of the President, 1978*. New York: John Simon Guggenheim Memorial Foundation, 1979.

Reich, Nancy B. "Women as Musicians: A Matter of Class." In *Musicology and Difference: Gender and Sexuality in Music Scholarship*, ed. Ruth Solie. Berkeley: University of California Press, 1993, 125–148.

Reid, Sally. "Building a Community Archive Online." *IAWM [International Alliance for Women in Music] Journal* 3/3: (Fall 1997) 9–11.

———. "Message from the Coordinating Editor." *IAWM [International Alliance for Women in Music] Journal* (February 1994): 36.

Reimer, Bennett. "Gender, Feminism, and Aesthetic Education: Discourses of Inclusion and Empowerment." *Philosophy of Music Education Review* 3/2 (1995): 107–124.

Reis, Claire Raphael. *Composers in America*. New York: Macmillan, 1947. Repr., New York: Da Capo Press, 1977.

Renton, Barbara Hampton. *The Status of Women in College Music, 1976–77: A Statistical Study*. College Music Society Report no. 2. Iowa City, IA: College Music Society.

Rhode, Deborah L. *Speaking of Sex: The Denial of Gender Inequality*. Cambridge, MA: Harvard University Press, 1997.

Rhodes, Willard. "The Years 1953–1963: Two American Views . . . A Decade of Progress." *Ethnomusicology* 7/3 (1963): 178–181.

Rich, Alan. "In Conversation with Anonymous 4." In liner notes for *Portrait*. Anonymous 4. Harmonia Mundi France. HMX2907210.

Rich, Frank. *Hot Seat: Theater Criticism for the New York Times (1980–1993)*. New York: Random House, 1998.

Ripley, Colette S. "Concert Organ Music by Women Composers from the United States." *American Organist* 31/2 (1 February 1997): 56.

Robbins, Ira A. (ed.). *The New Trouser Press Record Guide*, 3rd ed. New York: Collier Books, 1989.

Roell, Craig. *The Piano in America, 1890–1940*. Chapel Hill and London: University of North Carolina Press, 1989.

Rogal, Samuel J. (comp.). *Sing Glory and Hallelujah!* Westport, CT: Greenwood Press, 1996.

Rose, Tricia. *Black Noise: Rap Music and Black Culture in Contemporary America*. Middletown, CT: Wesleyan University Press, 1994.

Rosen, Judith, and Grace Rubin-Rabson. "Why Haven't Women Become Great Composers?"*High Fidelity Magazine* 23/2 (1973): 46–52.

Rothstein, Edward. "The Undoing of a Diva: Why Here?" *New York Times* (27 February 1994): 31H.

Runfola, Maria. "An Experimental Study of the Comparative Effectiveness of Harmonic and Melodic Accompaniments in Singing as It Relates to the Development of a Sense of Tonality." *Bulletin of the Council for Research in Music Education* 53 (1977): 23–30.

Rutkowski, Joanne. "The Effect of Restricted Song Range on Kindergarten Children's Use of Singing Voice and Developmental Music Aptitude." Ph.D. diss., State University of New York at Buffalo, 1986.

Sadie, Julie Anne, and Rhian Samuel (eds.). *The New Grove Dictionary of Women Composers*. New York: W. W. Norton, 1994.

Salvatore, Joseph A. "Jazz Improvisation: Principles and Practices Relating to Harmonic and Scalic Resources." Ph.D. diss., Florida State University, 1970.

Samuel, Rhian. "Feminist Musicology: Endings or Beginnings?" *Women: A Cultural Review* 3 (1992): 1, 65–69

Sandler, Bernice R., and Roberta M. Hall. *The Campus Climate Revisited: Chilly for Women Faculty, Administrators, and Graduate Students*.

Washington, DC: Association of American Colleges, Project on the Status and Education of Women, 1986.

———. *Women Faculty at Work in the Classroom, or, Why It Still Hurts to Be a Woman in Labor*. Washington, DC: Center for Women Policy Studies, 1991, 1993.

Sandrow, Nahma. *Vagabond Stars: A World History of Yiddish Theater*. New York: Harper and Row, 1977.

Sarkissian, Margaret. "Gender and Music." In *Ethnomusicology: An Introduction*, ed. Helen Myers. London and New York: Macmillan Press, 1992.

Saucier, Karen A. "Images of Women and Men in Country Music." In *All That Glitters: Country Music in America*. Bowling Green, OH: Bowling Green State University, Popular Press, 1993, 241–258.

Schaffer, K. "The String Quartet in the 19th Century." *Violexchange* 3/3 (1988): 38–43.

Schisler, Charles. Eulogy for Frauke Haasemann. 20 April 1991.

Schlegel, Ellen Grolman. *Emma Lou Diemer: A Bio-Bibliography*. Westport, CT: Greenwood Press, 2001.

Schloss, Myrna Frances. "Out of the Twentieth Century: Three Composers, Three Musics, One Femininity." Ph.D. diss., Wesleyan University, 1993.

Schnur, Susan. "Yay! Now We Can Sing 'Em." *Lilith* 22/4 (1997): 48.

Schruers, Fred. *Blondie*. New York: Tempo; London: Star, 1980.

Schwichtenberg, Cathy (ed.). *The Madonna Connection : Representational Politics, Subcultural Identities, and Cultural Theory*. Boulder: Westview Press, 1993.

Scott-Kassner, Carol. "Research on Music in Early Childhood." In *Handbook of Research on Music Teaching and Learning*, ed. Richard Colwell. New York: Schirmer Books, 1992.

Scrapbooks (1936–1960), Secretary's books (1938–1946), and TM "History of the Indiana Home Demonstration Chorus" by Jack Hannah (ca. 1954). Tippacanoe County Home Demonstration Chorus Collection, Tippacanoe County Historical Museum, Lafayette, IN.

Seashore, Carl E. "Why No Great Women Composers?" *Music Educators Journal* 25/5 (March 1940): 21, 88. Repr. in Carl E. Seashore, *In Search of the Beautiful in Music* (New York: Ronald Press, 1948); as "A 1940 Perspective" in *Music Educators Journal* 65/5 (Jan. 1979): 42ff; and as Section 47 in *Women in Music: An Anthology of Source Readings from the Middle Ages to the Present*, ed. by Carol Neuls-Bates (New York: Harper and Row, 1982; repr., Boston: Northeastern University Press, 1996).

Seeling, Ellen et al. "Hot Topics: How Have You Dealt with Problems of Discrimination in the Industry?" *Windplayer* 10/4 (1993):12–13ff.

Selena. Available: http://music.excite.com/artist/biography/617455

Selena—Biography. Available: http://www.neosoft.com/SELENA/biogrfy.html

Selena's Biography. Available: http://www.tejanoweb.com/selena/bio.html

Sembrich-Kochanska, Marcelina. "Poczntki mej pracy artystycznej" [Beginnings of my artistic work]. *Muzyka* 3 (1930).

Sexton, Adam. *Desperately Seeking Madonna*. New York: Dell Publishing, 1993.

Shaw, Arnold. *Honkers and Shouters: The Golden Years of Rhythm and Blues*. New York: Collier Books, 1978.

Shekerjian, Denise G. *Uncommon Genius: How Great Ideas Are Born*. New York: Viking, 1990.

Shelemay, Kay Kaufman. *Let Jasmine Rain Down: Song and Remembrance among Syrian Jews*. Chicago: University of Chicago Press, 1998.

Shortchanging Girls, Shortchanging America. New York: American Association of University Women, 1991.

Shuter-Dyson, R. "Unisex or 'Vive la différence'? Research on Sex Differences of Relevance to Musical Abilities." *Bulletin of the Council for Research in Music Education* 59 (Summer 1979): 102–106.

Sicoli, M. L. Corbin. "Women Winners: Major Popular Music Awards." *Popular Music and Society* 13/1(1989): 99–102.

Sienman, Gita (ed.). *World of Winners: A Current and Historical Perspective on Awards and Their Winners*. Detroit: Gale Research, 1989.

Signorelli, Nancy, Douglas McLeod, and Elaine Healy. "Gender Stereotypes in MTV Commercials: The Beat Goes On." *Journal of Broadcasting and Electronic Media* 38/1 (Winter 1994): 91–101.

Simon, John. "Games Better Left Unplayed." *New York* 22 (30 October 1989): 101–102.

Simone, Nina. *I Put a Spell on You*. New York: Pantheon Books, 1991.

Simpson, Helen. "Seeking the Female, through the Holistic Study of Music." *British Journal of Music Education* 10/3 (1993): 163–167.

Sinor, Jean. "The Ideas of Kodály in America." *Music Educators Journal* 72/6 (1986): 32–37.

Skowronski, JoAnn. *Women in American Music: A*

Bibliography. Metuchen, NJ, and London: Scarecrow Press, 1978.

Slobin, Mark. *Chosen Voices: The Story of the American Cantorate*. Chicago: University of Illinois Press, 1989.

———. "Klezmer: History and Culture: A Conference." *Judaism: A Quarterly Journal of Jewish Life and Thought* 47/1 (1998): 3–78.

Slonimsky, Nicholas. (ed.). *Baker's Biographical Dictionary of 20th-Century Classical Musicians*. New York: Schirmer Books, 1997.

———. *The Concise Edition of Baker's Biographical Dictionary of Musicians*, rev. 8th ed. New York: Schirmer Books, 1994.

Small, Mark. "Berkelee: Looking toward the New Millennium." *Jazz Educators Journal* 28 (1995): 20–26.

Smith, Catherine Parsons, and Cynthia S. Richardson. *Mary Carr Moore, American Composer*. Ann Arbor: University of Michigan Press, 1987.

Smith, Jessie Carney (ed.). *Notable Black American Women*. Detroit and London: Gale Research, 1992.

Smith, Julia (ed.). *Directory of American Women Composers with Selected Music for Senior and Junior Clubs*. Chicago: National Federation of Music Clubs, 1970.

Solie, Ruth. "Defining Feminism: Conundrums, Contexts, Communities." *Women and Music* 1 (1997): 1–11.

———.(ed.). *Musicology and Difference: Gender and Sexuality in Music Scholarship*. Berkeley: University of California Press, 1993.

———. "What Do Feminists Want? A Reply to Pieter van den Toorn." *Journal of Musicology* 9 (1991): 275–299.

Sounds Write—Debbie Friedman Home Page. Available: http://www.soundswrite.com/swdf.html

Sounds Write—Julie Silver Home Page. Available: http://www.soundswrite.com/swjs.html

Southern, Eileen (ed.). *Biographical Dictionary of Afro-American and African Musicians*. Westport, CT, and London: Greenwood Press, 1982.

———. *The Music of African Americans*, 3rd ed. New York: W. W. Norton, 1997.

Special Tribute to Frances Clark. Available: http://www.keyboardcompanion.com/ClarkArticle/Clark.html

Spencer, Herbert. *Social Statics: or, the Conditions Essential to Human Happiness Specified, and the First of Them Developed*. London: John Chapman, 1851.

Speziale, Marie. E-mail correspondence with Monique Buzzarté. Spring 2000.

Steblin, Rita. "The Gender Stereotyping of Musical Instruments in the Western Tradition." *Canadian University Music Review* 16/1 (1995): 128–144.

Stein Hunt, Danica L. "Women Who Play Jazz: A Study of the Experiences of Three Los Angeles Musicians." M.A. thesis, University of California at Los Angeles, 1994.

Steinberg [later Tick], Judith. "Tuning Out Women Composers." *Women: A Journal of Liberation* 3/2 (1972): 61–63.

Stern, Susan. *Women Composers: A Handbook*. Metuchen, NJ: Scarecrow Press, 1978.

Stewart, Earl. *African-American Music: An Introduction*. New York: G. Schirmer, 1998.

Stewart, Nancy L. "Julia Etta Crane." In *Women Educators in the United States, 1820–1993*, ed. Maxine Schwartz Seller. Westport, CT: Greenwood Press, 1994, 177–185.

Stewart-Green, Miriam. *Women Composers: A Checklist of Works for the Solo Voice*. Boston: G. K. Hall, 1981.

Stocking, George W., Jr. *Victorian Anthropology*. New York: Free Press, 1987.

Stubley, Eleanor. "Being in the Body, Being in the Sound: A Tale of Modulating Identities and Lost Potential." *Journal of Aesthetic Education* 32/4 (1998): 93–107.

———. "The Performer, the Score, the Work: Musical Performance and Transactional Reading." *Journal of Aesthetic Education* 29/3 (1995): 55–71.

Svigals, Alicia. Personal correspondence with Judith S. Pinnolis. 7 March 2000.

Swift, Kay. *Who Could Ask for Anything More?* New York: Simon & Schuster, 1943.

Taggart, Cynthia Crump. "An Investigation of the Hierarchical Nature of the Stages of Tonal Audiation." Ph.D. diss., Temple University, 1989.

Taggart, Cynthia Crump, et al. *Jump Right In: The Music Curriculum*, 2nd ed. Chicago: G.I.A. Publications, 2000.

Talevski, Nick. *The Unofficial Encyclopedia of the Rock and Roll Hall of Fame*. Westport, CT, and London: Greenwood Press, 1998.

Tann, Hilary. "Women in Music: Moving On." *ILWC [International League of Women Composers] Newsletter* (Spring 1988): 11.

Taylor, Timothy Dean. "The Gendered Construction of the Musical Self: The Music of Pauline Oliveros." *Musical Quarterly* 77/3 (Fall 1993): 385–396.

Taylor, Vivian. 400 pages transcribed interviews with Marga Richter. Unpublished, 1999.

Telstrom, A. Theodore. *Music in American Education, Past and Present*. New York: Holt, Rinehart and Winston, 1971.

Tera de Marez Oyens. "The Congress on Women in Music in Atlanta, Georgia." *ILWC [International League of Women Composers] Newsletter* (Spring 1986): 12–13.

Thackray, Jerry. "Sheryl Crow Meets Keith Richards." *Vox Magazine* (January 1998).

Thomas, Laurel Ann. "A Study of Libby Larsen's ME (Brenda Ueland), a Song Cycle for High Voice and Piano." D.M.A. diss., University of Texas, Austin, 1994.

Thornton, Mary. "The 1997 International Women's Brass Conference." *ITG Journal* 22/1 (1997): 41–46.

Tick, Judith. "Women in American Music: How Much Progress?" *AWC [American Women Composers] News/Forum* 6/3–4 (April–October 1986): 17–19.

To Venus and Back/Tori.com. Available: http://www.tori.com

Tong, Rosemarie Putnam. *Feminist Thought: A More Comprehensive Introduction*, 2d ed. Boulder: Westview Press, 1998.

Treitler, Leo. "Gender and Other Dualities of Music History." In *Musicology and Difference: Gender and Sexuality in Music Scholarship*. Berkeley: University of California Press, 1993, 23–45.

Trollinger, Laree M. "Sex/Gender Research in Music Education: A Review." *Quarterly Journal of Music Teaching and Learning* 4/4–5/1 (1994).

Troth, Eugene W. "The Teacher-Training Program in Music at Chautauqua Institution, 1905–1930." *Journal of Research in Music Education* 9 (Spring 1961): 37–46.

Tucker, Sherrie. "Noteworthy Women: The Politics of Impermanence—World War II and the All-Woman Bands." *Hot Wire* 9/2 (1993): 12–13ff.

———. "Telling Performances: Jazz History Remembered and Remade by the Women in the Band." *Women and Music* 1 (1997): 12–23.

Turner, Kay (ed.). *I Dream of Madonna: Women's Dreams of the Goddess of Pop*. San Francisco: Collins Publishers San Francisco, 1993.

Unterbrink, Mary. *Funny Women: American Comediennes, 1860–1985*. Jefferson, NC: McFarland, 1987.

Upton, George. *Woman and Music*. Boston: J. R. Osgood, 1880. Excerpt repr. as "A Classic Formulation of the Theory of Women's Innate Inferiority," Sec. 34 in *Women in Music: An Anthology of Source Readings from the Middle Ages to the Present*, ed. Carol Neuls-Bates. Rev. ed. Boston: Northeastern University Press, 1996.

Upton, William Treat. *Art-Song in America: A Study in the Development of American Music*. Boston: O. Ditson, 1930. New York: Johnson Reprint, 1969.

———. *A Supplement to Art Song in America, 1930–38*. Philadelphia: Oliver Ditson, 1938. Repr., New York: Johnson Reprint, 1969.

Vale, V. (ed.). *Zines*, vol. 2. San Francisco: V/Search Publications, 1997.

Valerio, Wendy H. "The Effects of Audiating a Resting Tone on the Development of Tonal Syntax among Second-Grade Children." *PMEA Bulletin of Research in Music Education* (1992).

Vaziri, Aidin. "Q & A with Sheryl Crow." *San Francisco Chronicle*, 4 April 1999.

Vehanen, Kosti. *Marian Anderson: A Portrait*. Westport, CT: Greenwood, 1970.

Vernon, Paul. *Ethnic and Vernacular Music, 1898–1960: A Resource and Guide to Recordings*. Westport, CT: Greenwood Press, 1995.

Vivace Press Home Page. Available: http://www.vivacepress.com

Voller, Debbi. *Madonna: The Style Book*. London: Omnibus Press, 1992.

Vox Femina Los Angeles. Available: http://www.voxfeminala.org

Wagner, Melinda. Telephone interview by Allyson Brown Applebaum. 10 January 2000.

Wakefield, Ralph. *A Brief History of the Crane School of Music*. St. Lawrence County Historical Association, 1986. Repr. by Potsdam College of the State University of New York.

Waldermar, Nielsen A. *The Golden Donors: A New Anatomy of the Great Foundations*. New York: E. P. Dutton, 1985.

Waleson, Heidi. "Fortune's Favorite." *Opera News* 46/15 (1982): 8–11.

Walker, Wyatt Tee. *"Somebody's Calling My Name": Black Sacred Music and Social Change*. Valley Forge, PA : Judson Press, 1979.

Walker-Hill, Helen. "Chicago's Black Women Composers: Then and Now." *Black Music Research Journal* 12/1 (Spring 1992): 1–23.

———. *Music by Black Women Composers: A Bibliography of Available Scores*. Chicago: Center for Black Music Research, Columbia College, 1995.

———. *Piano Music by Black Women Composers: A Catalog of Solo and Ensemble Works*. New York: Greenwood Press, 1992.

Walsh, Michael. "Battle Fatigue." *Time* 143/8 (1994): 61–62.

Walter, Claire. *Winners: The Blue Ribbon Encyclopedia of Awards*. New York: Facts on File, 1978.

Walters, Suzanna Danuta. *Material Girls: Making Sense of Feminist Cultural Theory*. Berkeley: University of California Press, 1995.

Ward, Ed, Geoffrey Stokes, and Ken Tucker. *Rock of Ages: The Rolling Stone History of Rock and Roll*. New York: Rolling Stone Press/Summit Books, 1986.

Warrick, Mancel, Joan R. Hillsman, and Anthony Manno. *The Progress of Gospel Music: From Spirituals to Contemporary Gospel*. New York: Vantage Press, 1977.

"Washington['s] First 'Folk-Song Festival'." Washington, DC, *Bee* (11 March 1916): 1.

Weiner, Bernard. "A Savage and Sensual Tango: Political Allegory from Argentina." *San Francisco Chronicle*, 12 August 1989.

Weintraub, Karen, and Claudia Perry. "Dozens at Black Conference Walk Out after Rapper's Sexist Comments." *Houston Post* (23 July 1993): 23.

Weisser, Albert. "An Interview with Miriam Gideon." *Dimensions in American Judaism* 4/3 (1970): 38–40.

Welter, Barbara. *Dimity Convictions: The American Woman in the Nineteenth Century*. Athens: Ohio University Press, 1976.

Wheelock, Gretchen. "*Schwarze Gredel* and the Engendered Minor Mode in Mozart's Operas." In *Musicology and Difference: Gender and Sexuality in Music Scholarship*, ed. Ruth Solie. Berkeley: University of California Press, 1993, 201–223.

Who's Who in American Music: Classical, 2d ed. New York: R. R. Bowker, 1985.

Who's Who of American Women, 11th ed., 1979–1980. Chicago: IL: Marquis Who's Who, 1981.

Wilder, Alec. *American Popular Song: The Great Innovators, 1900–1950*. London, Oxford, New York: Oxford University Press, 1972.

Wiley, Mason, and Bona, Damien. *Inside Oscar—The Unofficial History of the Academy Awards*. New York: Ballantine Books, 1987.

Williams, Ora. *American Black Women in the Arts and Social Sciences: A Bibliographic Survey*, 3rd ed. rev. and enlarged. Metuchen, NJ: Scarecrow Press, 1994.

Williamson, Judith. *Decoding Advertisements: Ideology and Meaning in Advertising*. London: Marion Boyers, 1978.

Wilson, Bruce, and Gary, Charles. "Music in Our Schools: The First 150 Years." *Music Educators Journal* 74/6 (1988): 25–101.

Womack, Virginia. "Discovery Learning and Problem Solving Skills in the 'Preparation' Phase." *Kodály Envoy* 21/3 (1995): 14–19.

Women's Philharmonic, The: Homepage. Available: http://www.womensphil.org

Wood, Elizabeth. "Review Essay: Women and Music." *Signs: Journal of Women and Culture in Society* 6/2 (1980): 283–297.

Woodbury, Mary Lazarus. "Women Brass Players in Jazz: 1860 to the Present." D.M.A. thesis, University of Cincinnati, 1996.

Woodruff, Warren L. "The Life and Performances of Diane Bish through the Joy of Music Television Series." Ph.D. diss., University of Miami School of Music, 1993.

Wright, Sandi. E-mail correspondence with Linda Pohly. 15 January 2000.

Wurm, Mary. "Woman's Struggle for Recognition in Music." *Etude* (November 1936): 687, 746.

Zaimont, Judith Lang. *Judith Lang Zaimont: Biography*. Available: http://www.joblink.org/jzaimont/txtbio.htm

———. (ed.). *The Musical Woman: An International Perspective*, 3 vols. Westport, CT: Greenwood Press, 1984, 1987, 1991.

Zaimont, Judith Lang, and Karen Famera (eds.). *Contemporary Concert Music by Women: A Directory of the Composers and Their Works*. Westport, CT: Greenwood Press, 1981.

Zasky, Jason. "Around the Globe with Sheryl Crow." *Musician Magazine* (April 1999).

Zate, Maria. "Selena Bio-Pic Hums Along. (Biographical film of slain Latin American singer Selena)." *Hispanic Business* 19/5 (1997): 48–49.

Zheng, Su de San. "Immigrant Music and Transnational Discourse: Chinese American Music Culture in New York City." Ph.D. diss., Wesleyan University, 1993.

Zhou, Jinmin. "New Wave Music in China." Ph.D. diss., University of Maryland, 1993.

Zolotow, Maurice. *No People Like Show People*. New York: Random House, 1951.

Index

Entries in **bold face type** refer to main entries.

About the Contributors

EDITOR-IN-CHIEF

KRISTINE H. BURNS, Assistant Professor of Music and Director of the Electronic Music Studios, Florida International University

ADVISORS

HARRIET HAIR, Professor of Music, University of Georgia

PAULINE OLIVEROS, President, Pauline Oliveros Foundation; Darius Milhaud Professor, Mills College

JUDITH TICK, Professor of Music, Northeastern University

ASSOCIATE EDITORS AND CONTRIBUTORS

JUDITH A. COE, Assistant Professor of Voice and Commerical Music, University of Colorado at Denver

STEPHEN FRY, Music Librarian for Reference Services and Collection Development, University of California, Los Angeles

SUZANNE L. GERTIG, Associate Professor, University of Denver

DEBORAH HAYES, Professor Emerita, University of Colorado at Boulder

CRISTINA MAGALDI, Assistant Professor, Towson University

PATRICIA O'TOOLE, Assistant Professor of Music, The Ohio State University

SALLY REID, Professor of Oboe, Theory, Composition, and Electronic Music, Abilene Christian University

CONTRIBUTING AUTHORS

GARTH ALPER, Assistant Professor, University of Lousiana at Lafayette

RICHARD AMRHEIN, University Librarian, Moellering Library, Valparaiso University

CHRISTOPHER ANDERSON, Instructor in Conducting, Abilene Christian University

ALLYSON BROWN APPLEBAUM, Assistant Chair, Fine Arts, Houston Community College—Northwest

MARK S. APPLEBAUM, Assistant Professor of Composition and Theory, Stanford University

FLORENCE AQUILINA, Lecturer, University of Cape Town, College of Music

JOHN AUGENBLICK, Associate Professor of Music, Director of Choral Studies, Florida International University

JULIE BANNERMAN, University of Lawrence, Appleton, IN

RICHARD BARNET, Professor of Recording Industry, Middle Tennessee State University

JEREMY BECK, Freelance Composer, Whittier, CA

WILLIAM G. BIDDY, Director of Theatre, Mississippi University for Women

ADRIENNE FRIED BLOCK, Music in Gotham, Graduate Center, The City University of New York

CAROL JUNE BRADLEY, Associate Director, Music Library, State University of New York, Buffalo

ANITA BRECKBILL, Associate Professor of Libraries, Head of Music Library, University of Nebraska–Lincoln

CAROLYN BREMER, Independent Composer

JEANNE BROSSART, Radio Host, WOMR Radio

DAVID L. BRUNER, Head of Bibliographic Services, Northern Arizona University

CAROLYN BRYAN, Assistant Professor of Saxophone and Music Education, Georgia Southern University

MONICA J. BURDEX, Performing Arts Librarian, California State University, Northridge

MARLA BUTKE, Ph.D. candidate in Music Education, The Ohio State University

MONIQUE BUZZARTÉ, Independent Author, Educator, and Trombonist-Composer

JEFFERY BYRD, Performance Artist, and Professor of Art, University of Northern Iowa

DON BYRD, Adjunct Instructor of Music Theory, Belmont University

VICTOR CARDELL, Music and Dance Librarian, University of Kansas

NELLY CASE, Associate Professor of Music, Crane School of Music, State University of New York, Potsdam

DELTA CAVNER, Graduate Assistant and Research Assistant, Boise State University

NAN CHILDRESS, Piano Professor, Caldwell College

KILISSA M. CISSOKO, Graduate Assistance, State University of New York, Buffalo

DAVID CLEARY, Independent Composer, Writer, and Cellist

EDWARD JOHN COFFEY III, Naumberg Fellow, Princeton University

ANDREW M. CONNELL, Ph.D. Candidate in Ethnomusicology, University of California, Los Angeles

COLLEEN CONWAY, Assistant Professor of Music Education, Michigan State University

AMY CORIN, Adjunct Professor of Music, Moorpark College

FRANCISCO CRESPO, Ph.D. Student, University of California, Los Angeles

JOHN CUCIUREAN, Assistant Professor of Music, Florida International University

MIKE DALEY, Ph.D. Candidate, York University

DIANA DANSEREAU, Graduate Student, The Pennsylvania State University

FRIEDA PATRICK DAVISON, Dean of Libraries at the University of South Carolina Spartanburg

SANTA MARIA DE LOS CONEJOS, Freelance Composer

VASANA DE MEL, Ph.D. Student, University of California, Los Angeles

DIANA DEUTSCH, Professor, University of California, San Diego

DANIEL DICENSO, Graduate Fellow, University of Pennsylvania

LISA DOLINGER, Freelance Author

LORI-ANNE DOLLOFF, Associate Professor, Music Education, University of Toronto

ROBERT B. DUNDAS, Assistant Professor of Music, Director of Opera Studies, Florida International University

AMY DUNKER, Assistant Professor of Music, Clarke College

DONNA DUPUY, Adjunct Professor of Music Theory, and Assistant Director of Operations and Coordinator of Community Music, University of North Texas

LINDA DUSMAN, Professor and Chair of Music Department, University of Maryland, Baltimore County

LAURIE EAGLESON, Undergraduate Services Librarian, University of Arizona

BRAD EDEN, Head of Cataloging, University of Nevada, Las Vegas

J. MICHELE EDWARDS, Professor, Macalaster College

PAULA ELLIOT, Head of Humanities Collection Development, Washington State University

SUSAN EPSTEIN, Assistant Professor of Music, Theory and Composition, New World School of the Arts

JOANNE ERWIN, Associate Professor of Music Education, Oberlin College Conservatory of Music

WILLIAM A. EVERETT, Assistant Professor of Music History, University of Missouri, Kansas City

AMY EVERS, B.M. student, Florida International University

INNA FALIKS, Graduate Student and Liberal Arts Assistant, Peabody Conservatory

MAXINE FAWCETT-YESKE, Assistant Professor of Music, Nebraska Wesleyan University

LEANNE FAZIO, Professor of Music Education, Mississippi State University

RAÚL FERNÁNDEZ, Professor of Social Sciences, University of California, Irvine

SUZANNE FLANDREAU, Librarian and Archivist, Center for Black Music Research

PATRICIA FLOWERS, Professor and Graduate Studies Chairperson, The Ohio State University

DIANE FOLLET, Assistant Professor of Music, Muhlenberg College

ROBERT FOLLET, Head, Music Library, Arizona State University

R.J. DAVID FREGO, Assistant Professor of Music, The Ohio State University

HILDEGARD FROEHLICH, Professor of Music Education, University of North Texas

KAREN FULLER, Director, Performing Arts Production, Florida International University

DENISE GALLO, Assistant Professor and Co-Director of Music History, The Catholic University of America

ORLANDO JACINTO GARCÍA, Professor of Music, Florida International University

SUSANNA P. GARCIA, Assistant Professor of Music, University of Louisiana at Lafayette

CORY GAVITO, Ph.D. Teaching Fellow, University of North Texas

ERIN GEE, M.M. Candidate, University of Iowa

VIRGINIA GIGLIO, President, Global Thinking, Inc.

ROBERT GJERDINGEN, Associate Professor, Northwestern University

LYNETTE MILLER GOTTLIEB, Teaching Assistant, State University of New York, Buffalo

ELIZABETH GOULD, Coordinator, Music Education, Boise State University

LAURA GAYLE GREEN, Music and Media Librarian, University of Missouri, Kansas City

ANITA HANAWALT, Senior Adjunct Professor of Music, University of La Verne

BARBARA HARBACH, Editor, *Women of Note Quarterly*

E. MICHAEL HARRINGTON, Professor of Music Business, School of Music Business at Belmont University

MARA HELMUTH, Assistant Professor in Composition, College Conservatory of Music, University of Cincinnati

CLARENCE BERNARD HENRY, Assistant Professor, Indiana State University

JEFF HERRIOTT, Graduate Student, State University of New York, Buffalo

DOROTHY E. HINDMAN, Adjunct Professor in Music Theory and Composition, Birmingham-Southern College

ELIZABETH HINKLE-TURNER, Computer Operations in Music Technology, University of North Texas

MARY ETTA HOBBS, Assistant Professor of Voice and Opera, Abilene Christian University

LESLIE HOGAN, Lecturer, The University of California–Santa Barbara

MARY HOOKEY, Associate Professor, Nipissing University

SONDRA WIELAND HOWE, Affiliate Scholar, Center for Advanced Feminist Studies, University of Minnesota

APO HSU, Artistic Director & Conductor, The Women's Philharmonic, and Music Director & Conductor, the Springfield Symphony (MO)

BRENDA HUTCHINSON, Independent Sound Artist

ERIC JOHNSON, Director of Choral Activities, Northern Illinois University, School of Music

JUANITA KARPF, Assistant Professor, Music and Women's Studies, University of Georgia

DEBORAH KAVÁSCH, Professor of Music, California State University, Stanislaus

DARYL KINNEY, Graduate Teaching Associate, The Ohio State University

AMY KNOLES, Executive Director, California E.A.R. Unit

ROE-MIN KOK, Nino Pirrotta Fellow, Harvard University

COLBY LEIDER, Naumberg Fellow in Composition, Princeton University

CAROLYN LIVINGSTON, Professor and Director of Graduate Studies in Music, University of Rhode Island

SCOTT LOCKE, Assistant Professor of Clarinet, Murray State University

RUTH LOMON, Resident Scholar, Women's Studies Program, Brandeis University

STACIE LORRAINE, Teacher, P.S. 153, New York City

STEVE LOZA, Associate Professor, University of California, Los Angeles

STEVE LUTTMANN, Music Librarian and Assistant Professor of Library Science, University of Northern Colorado

JUDITH L. MARLEY, Music/Theatre/Dance Librarian, Southern Methodist University

CHARITY MARSH, Graduate Student, York University

JAY MARTIN, Graduate Student, University of Missouri, Kansas City

GARY W. MAYHOOD, Assistant Catalog Librarian, New Mexico State University

RENÉE MCBRIDE, West European Studies Cataloger, University of California, Los Angeles

KIMBERLY MCCORD, Coordinator of Undergraduate Music Education at Illinois State University–Normal

SARAH MEYERS, Teacher, The New Jewish High School, Waltham, MA

SHARON MIRCHANDANI, Assistant Professor of Music History and Theory, Westminster Choir College of Rider University

JANICE MISURELL-MITCHELL, Lecturer, DePaul University School of Music

MARTHA MOCKUS, Lecturer in Women's Studies, State University of New York, Stony Brook

PATRICIA MOREHEAD, Professional Composer and Oboist; Assistant Professor, Roosevelt University and Lecturer, Columbia College, Chicago

CRAIG MORRISON, Independent Ethnomusicologist, Musician, Author

VICKI OHL, Professor of Piano and Theory, Heidelberg College

ANDREA OLIJNEK, Ph.D. candidate in Music Education, The Ohio State University

ROBERT PECK, Assistant Professor of Music Theory, Louisiana State University

KATHLEEN PIERSON, Adjunct Faculty in Music and Women's Studies, Theory and Composition Teacher in The Preparatory Division Towson University

JUDITH S. PINNOLIS, Reference Librarian for Publications and Training, Brandeis University

LINDA POHLY, Associate Professor of Music History, Ball State University

MARIA PURCIELLO, Ph.D Candidate and Naumberg Fellow, Princeton University

ALICIA RAMUSA, Independent Musician and Educator

HARRIETT FRAZEY RANNEY, Associate Professor and Music Librarian, University of Montana

ROXANNE REED, Visiting Lecturer, Miami University

MICHAEL REMSON, Independent Composer and Librettist

DOUGLAS REPETTO, System Administrator, Computer Music Center, Columbia University

ALAN RIECK, Assistant Professor, Choral Music and Music Education, University of Wisconsin–Eau Claire

RICHARD RISCHAR, Ph.D. Candidate in Musicology, Dickinson College

RUTH ROBERTSON, Assistant Professor of Music, Lincoln University of Missouri

KATHY M. ROBINSON, Assistant Professor of Music Education, Eastman School of Music

STEVEN L. ROSENHAUS, Composer, Lyricist, Conductor; Adjunct Assistant Professor, New York University Instructor Nassau Community College

ANNA RUBIN, Assistant Professor of Composition, Oberlin College, Conservatory of Music

VIVIAN ADELBERG RUDOW, Composer, and Director and Producer, ResMusicAmerica, Baltimore, MD

MARIA E. RUNFOLA, Associate Professor of Music Education, State University of New York, Buffalo

STEPHEN J. RUSHING, Associate Professor of Music, Southeastern Louisiana University

JOANNE RUTKOWSKI, Associate Professor of Music Education, The Pennsylvania State University

ANN SAVAGE, Assistant Professor in Telecommunication Arts, Butler University

ELLEN GROLMAN SCHLEGEL, Professor of Music, Frostburg State University

PAMELA SCHNELLER, Senior Lecturer in Choral Music, Blair School of Music, Vanderbilt University

HOLLY SCHWARTZ, Student, Abilene Christian University

JEANNE E. SHAFFER, Professor Emeritus, Huntingdon College and Producer "Eine Kleine Frauenmusik," Southeastern Public Radio

KAREN A. SHAFFER, President, The Maud Powell Society for Music and Education

KRISTINA LAMPE SHANTON, Music Librarian, Ithaca College

ALAN SHOCKLEY, Naumberg Fellow in Composition, Princeton University

MURL SICKBERT, Music Librarian, Hardin Simmons University

MARY SIMONI, Associate Professor, University of Michigan

ROSSANNA SKUPINSKY, University of California, Los Angeles

CATHERINE P. SMITH, Professor Emerita, University of Nevada, Reno

DAWN ELIZABETH SMITH, Music Educator, Westerly, Rhode Island Public Schools

SANDRA SNOW, Assistant Professor Conducting and Choral Music Education, University of Michigan

JAMES WILLIAM SOBASKIE, Lecturer, University of Wisonsin, Stevens Point

THOMAS SOVÍK, Professor of Music Theory, University of North Texas

JAYNE STANDLEY, Professor and Director of Music Therapy, Florida State University

ERIN STAPLETON-CORCORAN, Music and Dance Editor, *Encyclopedia Britannica*

GREG STEINKE, The Joseph Naumes Endowed Chair in Music at Marylhurst University (retired)

LORI STEVENS, Media Librarian, Utah Valley State College Library

LESLIE STONE, Software Design Engineer, Agilent Technologies

LESLIE STRATYNER, Associate Professor, Mississippi University for Women

GREGORY STRAUGHN, Abilene Christian University

ERIC S. STROTHER, Doctoral Student, University of Kentucky

ELEANOR STUBLEY, Associate Professor of Music, McGill University

JILL SULLIVAN, Assistant Professor, Music Education, Arizona State University

SUZANNE SUMMERVILLE, General Editor, *Arts Venture*

BARBARA TAGG, Artistic Director and Founder of the Syracuse Children's Chorus, and Affiliate Artist, Syracuse University

CHERYL TARANTO, Music Librarian, University of Nevada, Las Vegas

VIVIAN TAYLOR, Coordinator of Applied Music, Tufts University

KRISTEN STAUFFER TODD, Assistant Professor of Music History and Humanities, Oklahoma Baptist University

MAJA TROCHIMCZYK, Research Assistant Professor and Stefan and Wanda Wilk Director, Polish Music Center, Thornton School of Music, University of Southern California

NANCY USCHER, Professor of Music, Associate Dean, University of New Mexico

JUDITH VANDER, Independent Researcher, Ann Arbor, MI

KARI K. VEBLEN, Assistant Professor of Music Education, University of Western Ontario

ELIZABETH VERCOE, Independent Composer

ANNETTE VOTH, Music Librarian, Arizona State University

CHERILEE WADSWORTH WALKER, Assistant Professor of Music and Director, Vocal Jazz Ensemble, Illinois

PATRICK WARFIELD, Ph.D. Candidate, Indiana University and Lecturer, Georgetown University

MELISSA WEST, Ph.D. Candidate, York University

DAWN WILLIAMS, Independent Composer and Mezzo-Contralto

JENNY WILLIAMS, Librarian, Arizona State University Library

KENNETH WILLIAMS, Assistant Professor of Music, The Ohio State University

GAIL WOLDU, Professor of Music, Trinity College

MICHELE WOLFF, Music Librarian, Wichita, KS

CYNTHIA WONG, Graduate Student, Columbia University

DEBORAH WONG, Associate Professor of Music, University of California, Riverside

H. STEPHEN WRIGHT, Head of Branch Libraries and Associate Professor, Northern Illinois University